Essay Writing
for Canadian Students
with readings

fifth edition

Kay L. Stewart

Chris J. Bullock
Professor Emeritus, University of Alberta

Marian E. Allen
Grant MacEwan College

PEARSON

Prentice
Hall

Toronto

To our grandchildren
Caitlin and Rowan—K.S. and C.B.
Isabella—M.A.

National Library of Canada Cataloguing in Publication

Stewart, Kay L. (Kay Lanette), 1942–
   Essay writing for Canadian students : with readings / Kay L. Stewart,
Chris J. Bullock, Marian E. Allen.—5th ed.

Includes bibliographical references and index.
ISBN 0-13-120244-8

   1. Exposition (Rhetoric). 2. English language—Rhetoric.
I. Bullock, Chris, 1945– II. Allen, Marian, 1945– III. Title.

LB2369.S87 2003   808'.042   C2003-902531-4

ISBN 0-13-120244-8

Vice President, Editorial Director: Michael J. Young
Acquisitions Editor: Marianne Minaker
Sponsoring Editor: Andrew Winton
Marketing Manager: Toivo Pajo
Supervising Developmental Editor: Suzanne Schaan
Supervising Production Editor: Avivah Wargon
Copy Editor: Lesley Mann
Proofreader: Judith Turnbull
Production Manager: Wendy Moran
Page Layout: Arlene Edgar
Permissions Research: Amanda McCormick
Art Director: Julia Hall
Cover Design: Gillian Tsintziras
Cover Image: © John Still/Photonica

  4 5   08 07 06 05

Printed and bound in Canada.

Contents

Preface xvi

Acknowledgments xxi

part 1 Rhetoric 1

chapter 1 Writing Essays: An Overview 2

Essay Writing: Purposes 3
    Writing to Learn 3
    Writing to Communicate 4
Essay Writing: Product 4
    Audience 4
    Structure 5
Sample Essay: Analysis of a Film 5
Essay Writing: Process 8

EXERCISES 10

chapter 2 Clarifying Essay Topics 11

Stage 1   Clarifying Essay Topics 12
    Step 1   Defining Unfamiliar Terms 12
    Step 2   Understanding Directions 13
    Step 3   Exploring Your Subject 16
    Step 4   Deciding What Sources to Use 19

EXERCISES 21

chapter 3 Using Content Analysis to Gather Material 23

A. Thinking Analytically 24
Stage 1   Clarifying Content Analysis Topics 24
Stage 2   Gathering Material: Analyzing Your Own Experience 25

Step 1 Using Systems, Process, and Causal Analysis 25

Step 2 Categorizing Material 27

Sample Topic: From Adolescence to Adulthood 28

B. Reading Analytically 30

Stage 1 Honing Your Reading Skills 30

Stage 2 Gathering Material: Analyzing Nonfiction Sources 31

Step 1 Figuring Out the Basic Ideas 31

Step 2 Gaining a Broader Perspective 36

Step 3 Writing a Summary 38

Sample Topic: Analyzing the Content of Alison Gopnik's "Kiddy Thinks" 38

Working on Your Own Assignment 40

EXERCISES 41

chapter 4 **Writing Content Analysis Essays 1: Formulating a Thesis Statement and Drafting 42**

Stage 3 Formulating a Tentative Thesis Statement 43

Step 1 Forming an Opinion 43

Step 2 Supporting Your Opinion 44

Stage 4 Drafting 45

Step 1 Selecting Material and Making Points 45

Step 2 Organizing Your Material 46

Step 3 Making a Draft Outline 48

Step 4 Drafting Individual Paragraphs 49

Working on Your Own Assignment 49

EXERCISES 50

chapter 5 **Writing Content Analysis Essays 2: Revising Your Draft 51**

Stage 5 Revising Thesis Statement and Essay Structure 52

Step 1 Making a Revision Outline 52

Step 2   Revising Your Thesis Statement   53

Step 3   Revising Essay Structure   55

Stage 6   Revising Individual Paragraphs   57

Step 1   Revising Your Introduction   57

Step 2   Revising Middle Paragraphs   58

Step 3   Revising Your Conclusion   61

Working on Your Own Assignment   63

EXERCISES   63

chapter 6   **Using Textual Analysis to Gather Material   65**

Stage 1   Clarifying Textual Analysis Topics   66

Stage 2   Gathering Material   66

Step 1   Using Analytic Categories   67

Step 2   Connecting Textual Features to Figure Out the Work's Theme/Thesis   72

Sample Topic: Analyzing a Poem: Al Purdy's "Trees at the Arctic Circle"   73

Working on Your Own Assignment   78

EXERCISES   78

chapter 7   **Writing Textual Analysis Essays 1: Formulating a Thesis Statement and Drafting   81**

Stage 3   Formulating a Tentative Thesis Statement   82

Step 1   Forming an Opinion   82

Step 2   Supporting Your Opinion   83

Stage 4   Drafting   84

Step 1   Organizing Your Material   84

Step 2   Making a Draft Outline   86

Working on Your Own Assignment   87

EXERCISES   88

chapter 8   **Writing Textual Analysis Essays 2: Revising Your Draft   89**

Stage 5   Revising Thesis Statement and Essay Structure   90

Step 1 Making a Revision Outline   90

Step 2 Revising Your Thesis Statement   90

Step 3 Revising Essay Structure   91

Stage 6 Revising Individual Paragraphs   92

Step 1 Revising Your Introduction   92

Step 2 Revising Middle Paragraphs   94

Step 3 Revising Your Conclusion   95

Working on Your Own Assignment   97

EXERCISES   98

chapter 9 **Writing Comparison Essays   101**

Stage 1 Clarifying Comparison Topics   102

Step 1 Checking for a Basis of Comparison   103

Step 2 Looking for Similarities and Differences   103

Stage 2 Gathering Material   103

Step 1 Using Matching Categories of Analysis   103

Step 2 Clarifying the Basis of Comparison   105

Stage 3 Formulating a Comparison Thesis Statement   105

Step 1 Forming an Opinion about Each Set of Material   105

Step 2 Forming an Opinion about Overall Similarities and Differences   106

Step 3 Supporting Your Opinion about Similarities and Differences   106

Stage 4 Drafting   107

Step 1 Selecting Material   107

Step 2 Organizing Comparisons: Block and Point-by-Point Methods   108

Stage 5 Revising Thesis Statement and Essay Structure   109

Step 1 Revising Your Thesis Statement   109

Step 2 Revising Essay Structure   110

Stage 6 Revising Individual Paragraphs   111

Step 1 Revising Your Introduction   111

Step 2 Revising Middle Paragraphs   111

Step 3 Revising Your Conclusion   112
Working on Your Own Assignment   113
EXERCISES   114

chapter 10 **Evaluating Arguments and Writing Critiques   116**

Stage 1 Clarifying Evaluation Topics: Checking for the Logical Standard   117

Stage 2 Gathering Material: Arguments and Evidence   118

    Step 1 Analyzing the Writer's Reasoning and Evidence   118

    Step 2 Identifying Strengths and Weaknesses ("Fallacies") in Logic   121

    Step 3 Categorizing and Charting Strengths and Weaknesses 125

Stage 3 Formulating an Evaluative Thesis Statement   125

    Step 1 Forming an Opinion about the Relationship between Strengths and Weaknesses   126

    Step 2 Supporting Your Opinion   126

    Step 3 Indicating the Standard of Evaluation   126

Stage 4 Drafting: Sequencing Strengths and Weaknesses   127

Stage 5 Revising Thesis Statement and Essay Structure: Reasoning   128

    Step 1 Revising Your Thesis Statement: Checking for Evaluative Point   128

    Step 2 Revising Essay Structure: Argument   128

Stage 6 Revising Individual Paragraphs: *Ethos*, Argument, and Evidence   129

    Step 1 Revising Your Introduction: *Ethos*   129

    Step 2 Revising Middle Paragraphs: Arguments and Evidence   130

    Step 3 Revising Your Conclusion   131

    Sample Topic: Critiquing the Logic of Ted Byfield's Essay "Health Canada ..."   131

Working on Your Own Assignment   138

EXERCISES   139

chapter 11 **Writing Persuasive Essays   141**

Stage 1 Clarifying Evaluation Topics   142

    Step 1 Finding a Standard of Evaluation   142

    Step 2 Defining Other Key Terms   145

Stage 2 Gathering Material   146

    Step 1 Analyzing   146

    Step 2 Categorizing Strengths and
Weaknesses   147

Stage 3 Formulating an Evaluative Thesis Statement   148

Stage 4 Drafting: Working Out a Pro-Con Outline   150

Stage 5 Revising Thesis Statement and Essay
Structure   152

    Step 1 Revising Your Thesis Statement:
Checking for an Evaluative Point   152

    Step 2 Revising Essay Structure: Checking
Sequence and Pro-Con Transitions   153

Stage 6 Revising Individual Paragraphs   155

    Step 1 Revising Your Introduction: *Ethos*   155

    Step 2 Revising Middle Paragraphs: Logic and
Transitions   156

    Step 3 Revising Your Conclusion: Achieving
Balance   157

Working on Your Own Assignment   158

EXERCISES   158

chapter 12 **Gathering Material for Research
Papers   161**

Stage 1 Clarifying Research Topics   162

    Step 1 Defining Unfamiliar Terms   162

    Step 2 Understanding Directions   163

    Step 3 Choosing a Topic   163

    Step 4 Limiting Your Topic: Defining a
Research Question   163

Step 5 Choosing Material: Primary and
Secondary Sources 164

Sample Topic: The Dramatic Function of the
Graveyard Scene in *Hamlet* 164

Stage 2 Gathering Primary and Secondary Material 165

Step 1 Exploring Preliminary Sources of
Information 165

Step 2 Compiling a Working Bibliography 168

Step 3 Evaluating Secondary Sources and
Taking Notes 175

Step 4 Categorizing Material: Combining
Preliminary Analysis and Research
Material 176

Working on Your Own Assignment 177

EXERCISES 178

chapter 13 **Writing Research Papers 179**

Stage 3 Formulating a Thesis Statement: Answering
Your Research Question 180

Step 1 Forming an Opinion 180

Step 2 Supporting Your Opinion 181

Stage 4 Drafting: Making a Formal Outline 181

Stage 5 Revising: Integrating and Documenting
Research Material 182

Step 1 Integrating Research Material 183

Step 2 Documenting Research Material:
Understanding Plagiarism 184

Sample Topic (Research): The Dramatic Function
of the Graveyard Scene in *Hamlet* 187

Working on Your Own Assignment 193

EXERCISES 194

part 2 **Readings 195**

Published Writings 198

Alexander, Bruce K., and Stefa Shaler. "Addiction in Free
Markets" 198

Black, Maggie. "Wanted: The Right to Refuse" 203

Bongaarts, John. "Population: Ignoring Its Impact" 206

Byfield, Ted. "Health Canada Inadvertently Discloses Facts
Planned Parenthood Would Like to Suppress" 211

Davis, Wade. "The Ticking Bomb" 215

Edwards, Caterina. "Where They Have to Take You In" 221

Fetterley, Judith. "A Rose for 'A Rose for Emily'" 229

Forster, E. M. "My Wood" 238

Fraser, John. "Save the Last Dance" 242

Gopnik, Alison. "Kiddy Thinks" 247

Haegele, Katie. "Why I Live with My Mother" 252

Hardin, Garrett. "Lifeboat Ethics: The Case Against
Helping the Poor" 256

Hogan, Linda. "The Voyagers" 263

Iyer, Pico. "In Praise of the Humble Comma" 270

Johnston, Ann Dowsett. "A Lament for Quality" 274

Keeshig-Tobias, Lenore. "He Was a Boxer When I Was
Small" 277

Laver, Ross. "Profits by the Truckload" 282

Maté, Gabor. "Embraced by the Needle" 285

Merwin, W. S. "Unchopping a Tree" 289

Orwell, George. "Shooting an Elephant" 293

Pyper, Andrew. "The Ticking Daddy Clock" 301

Rebick, Judy. "The Poorhouse" 304

Sanders, Scott Russell. "The Men We Carry in Our
Minds" 307

Suzuki, David T. "It Always Costs" 313

Swift, Jonathan. "A Modest Proposal" 317

Wiwa, Ken. "Choosing Up Sides" 327

The English Patient Debate 331

Sample Essays 342

Ash, James. "To Peacekeep or Not to Peacekeep" 342

Jones, A. "The Complex Skill of Independent Living"
(Sample Content Analysis Essay) 344

Jones, B. "Shifts in Attitude and Form in Al Purdy's 'Trees
at the Arctic Circle'"(Sample Textual Analysis
Essay) 346

Jones, C. "Perspectives on Addictions" (Sample Comparison
Essay) 349

Jones, D. "Reflecting on Population" (Sample Critique) 352

Jones, E. "Same-Sex Marriages: Tradition and Change"
(Sample Persuasive Essay) 355

MacDonald, Joyce. "The Problem of Environmental
Costs: Suzuki vs. Merwin" 359

Smith, D. "The Making of the Tragic Hero: The Graveyard Scene in *Hamlet*" (Sample Research Paper)   362

Swanson, Karin. "Spontaneity and Enjoyment of the Natural World"   367

part 3 Handbook for Final Editing   371

Strategies for Final Editing   372

Identifying Common Problems (Chart)   373

Essay Format   375

Manuscript Conventions   375

Title Page   376

Understanding Sentence Structure   379

Recognizing Clauses and Phrases   379

EXERCISE 1   380

Recognizing Main Clauses and Subordinate Clauses   380

EXERCISE 2   381

Recognizing Simple, Compound, and Complex Sentences   382

EXERCISE 3   383

Correcting Common Errors in Sentence Structure   385

Correcting Sentence Fragments   385

EXERCISE 1   386

Correcting Comma Splices   386

EXERCISE 2   388

Correcting Fused Sentences   388

EXERCISE 3   389

REVIEW EXERCISE 1   389

Correcting Misplaced and Dangling Modifiers   389

EXERCISE 4   391

EXERCISE 5   391

REVIEW EXERCISE 2   392

Correcting Faulty Parallelism   392

EXERCISE 6   393

Correcting Faulty Coordination and Subordination   394

EXERCISE 7   395

EXERCISE 8   397

Correcting Mixed Constructions   397

EXERCISE 9   399

REVIEW EXERCISE 3   399

REVIEW EXERCISE 4   400

Improving Sentence Structure   401

Varying Sentence Lengths   402

Varying Sentence Patterns   403

EXERCISE 1   405

EXERCISE 2   405

Using Transitions to Connect Ideas   406

Continuity Within Paragraphs   406

Continuity Between Paragraphs   408

EXERCISE 1   409

EXERCISE 2   409

EXERCISE 3   409

EXERCISE 4   410

Solving Diction Problems   411

Correcting Problems with Your Level of Diction   411

EXERCISE 1   412

Correcting Problems with Word Choice: Usage   413

EXERCISE 2   418

Eliminating Wordiness   419

EXERCISE 1   421

EXERCISE 2   421

EXERCISE 3   422

Solving Verb Problems   423

Verb Forms   423

EXERCISE 1   425

Verb Tenses   425

EXERCISE 2 427

Subject–Verb Agreement 428

EXERCISE 3 429

Active and Passive Voice 429

EXERCISE 4 430

EXERCISE 5 431

REVIEW EXERCISE 1 431

REVIEW EXERCISE 2 431

Solving Pronoun Problems 432

Pronouns of Address 432

EXERCISE 1 434

Avoiding Shifts in Pronouns of Address 435

EXERCISE 2 436

Pronoun Agreement 436

EXERCISE 3 438

Pronoun Case 438

EXERCISE 4 440

Possessive Pronouns 440

EXERCISE 5 440

Pronoun Reference 441

EXERCISE 6 442

REVIEW EXERCISE 1 442

REVIEW EXERCISE 2 443

Solving Punctuation Problems 444

Apostrophe 444

EXERCISE 1 446

EXERCISE 2 446

EXERCISE 3 447

Comma 447

EXERCISE 4 449

EXERCISE 5 450

EXERCISE 6 450

Semicolon 450

EXERCISE 7 452

EXERCISE 8 453

Colon   453

EXERCISE 9   454

EXERCISE 10   454

Dash   454

EXERCISE 11   455

Parentheses   455

REVIEW EXERCISE 1   456

REVIEW EXERCISE 2   457

Quotation Marks   457

EXERCISE 12   458

Italics   458

EXERCISE 13   459

REVIEW EXERCISE 3   459

REVIEW EXERCISE 4   460

Hyphen   460

EXERCISE 14   461

Numbers, Capitalization, and Abbreviations   462

Numbers   462

Capitalization   462

Abbreviations   463

EXERCISE   465

Spelling   466

EXERCISE   467

Quotations   468

When to Quote   468

When Not to Quote   469

How to Use Quotations Effectively   469

Quotation Format   471

EXERCISE 1   474

EXERCISE 2   475

Documentation   476

What to Document   476

Systems of Reference   477

      MLA System   477

      APA System   481

part 4   Resources for Writing   485

**Common Perspectives for Content
Analysis (Chart)   486**

**General and Special Categories for Textual
Analysis (Chart)   488**

**Special Categories for Textual
Analysis   492**

Questions to Ask in Analyzing Nonfiction   492

Questions to Ask in Analyzing Fiction   495

Questions to Ask in Analyzing Poetry   499

Questions to Ask in Analyzing Drama   502

Questions to Ask in Analyzing Films and TV   505

**Annotated Survey of Reference
Sources   509**

Finding Explanations of Literary and Rhetorical Terms
and Literary Theory   509

Finding Information on Authors, Literary History, and
Genres   510

Identifying Allusions: Mythical, Religious, Symbolic, and
Other References   513

Checking Word Meanings and Usage   515

Checking Format and Documentation   518

Glossary of Rhetorical Terms   519

Index   524

Preface to the Fifth Edition

To the Student

If you are trying to figure out how to cope with essay assignments in your college or university courses, you are the student we had in mind when we wrote this book.

We present a systematic approach to writing essays. Since we believe that writing is a skill you can learn, not a talent you either have or don't have, we are convinced this method will work for most writers. Feel free to adapt it to suit your needs.

To the Instructor

If you are new to *Essay Writing for Canadian Students*, you will notice that we present the writing process as a systematic set of procedures for planning, drafting, and revising deductively organized academic essays. Like most teachers, we have found that many weaknesses in student writing stem from confused thinking about the assignment, the subject of the essay, or both. For this reason, we stress the analytical skills that help students to explore the subjects they write about more completely. We recognize that one disadvantage of this approach is that it may seem to limit creativity. The deductively organized analysis is, after all, only one kind of academic essay. Nevertheless, we believe there is value in an approach that encourages critical thinking.

Part 1, Rhetoric

This section takes students through the process of writing and revising a wide range of essays: expository essays on general topics (Chapters 3, 4, and 5); essays analyzing verbal and visual texts (Chapters 6, 7, and 8); critiques (Chapter 10); persuasive essays on general topics (Chapter 11); and research papers (Chapters 12 and 13). It also covers the skills involved in writing summaries (Chapter 3) and writing comparison essays (Chapter 9). Throughout, it emphasizes the importance of reading and thinking analytically.

This is the most extensively revised section of the book. In response to suggestions from colleagues, we have

- Added material on drafting and revising non-literary essays. To do so, we have reorganized the non-literary material in the former Chapters 5, 6, 7, and 8 into two new chapters. Chapters 3, 4, and 5 now focus on gathering material, drafting, and revising content analysis essays, with a new sample topic. In Chapters 4 and 5, our discussion of the sample topic is integrated with the discussion of general principles to keep the chapters short and avoid repetition.

- Consolidated the material on writing about literature and related forms. The former Chapter 4 is now Chapter 6, Using Textual Analysis to Gather Material. Chapters 7 and 8 focus on the features of drafting and revising specific to writing essays analyzing the formal aspects of verbal and visual texts. The new sample topic, an analysis of Al Purdy's very accessible poem "Trees at the Arctic Circle," runs through all three chapters.

- Expanded the material on evaluating the logic of an argument. In the previous edition, we introduced four standards of evaluation (logical, practical, aesthetic, and ethical) in Chapter 10, Gathering Material for Evaluation Essays, and demonstrated the use of these standards in Chapter 11, Writing Evaluation Essays. To emphasize the centrality of logical argumentation, we now devote Chapter 10 to evaluating the logic of an argument and writing a critique, a type of assignment often required of students, especially in the sciences. Chapter 11 introduces the practical, aesthetic, and ethical standards of evaluation and takes students through the process of writing a persuasive essay on a sample topic. By presenting the chapter on logical argumentation first, we lay the groundwork for students to evaluative the effectiveness of their own arguments. Both of these chapters make use of new sample topics.

In addition, we have

- Provided a new sample topic for Chapter 9, Writing Comparison Essays.
- Streamlined the presentation of writing problems and their solutions.
- Updated the information on doing electronic research in Chapters 12 and 13.

Part 2, Readings

We have selected essays published in a wide range of sources both to illustrate the types of writing we discuss in the Rhetoric section and to provide timely subjects for students to write about.

- About half the Readings are new to this edition.
- Most of the Published Writings cluster around three broad subject areas (population/environment/globalization; multiculturalism/personal identity; language/literature/other arts) in order to provide students with different points of view to compare and evaluate.
- New Sample Essays show the results of the processes of drafting and revising demonstrated in the Rhetoric section.

Part 3, Handbook for Final Editing

The Handbook gives students the tools they need to recognize and correct problems in essay format, sentence structure, grammar, punctuation, and documentation.

- New exercises have been added and others revised.
- Documentation has been updated to provide the most recent information on citing electronic sources from the *MLA Handbook, Sixth Edition,* and the *Publication Manual of the American Psychological Association*.

Throughout, we've added, deleted, and changed material to make explanations clearer, exercises more useful, and examples more interesting.

Part 4, Resources for Writing

The most useful sections have been retained and the Annotated Survey of Reference Sources updated.

How to Use This Book

For Literature and Media Courses

If you are using this text in a literature or media course, it might seem logical to skip Chapters 3–5 on content analysis. We strongly encourage you not to do so. In particular, Part B of Chapter 3, Reading Analytically, introduces concepts and skills that students can build on in analyzing verbal and visual texts. We suggest that you use this section in conjunction with selected essays from the Readings to give students practice in reading and understanding nonfiction, with which they are generally unfamiliar. Chapters 4 and 5 cover the principles involved in drafting and revising more thoroughly than the corresponding chapters on textual analysis, and so you may want to ask students to skim these chapters.

Of course you are most likely to focus on Chapters 6, 7, and 8, the ones devoted to textual analysis. The sample topic for the textual analysis chapters is a very accessible poem by Al Purdy. You may want students to write two or three essays analyzing a single subject before you ask them to tackle comparison (Chapter 9) or evaluation (Chapter 11). The varying responses to a film collected in "*The English Patient* Debate" (Readings) illustrate the many standards by which readers and viewers compare and evaluate texts. Classic essays by writers such as Swift, Forster, and Orwell provide opportunities for comparisons of style and attitude towards subjects such as poverty, consumerism, and multiculturalism in essays by contemporary authors. Chapters 12 and 13 on writing research papers use an assignment on *Hamlet* as a sample topic.

You will find valuable guides for helping students analyze a wide range of literary forms (nonfiction, fiction, poetry, drama) as well as films and television programs in Special Categories for Textual Analysis. The key features of these guides are presented in the chart General and

Special Categories for Textual Analysis. Students will find helpful aids for doing literary research in the Annotated Survey of Reference Sources. All of this material appears in Part 4, Resources for Writing.

For Writing Courses

If you are using this text in a writing course, you will find the clearer division between chapters that focus on content analysis and those that focus on textual analysis particularly helpful. Chapter 3, Part A, Thinking Analytically, lays the groundwork for students to generalize from their own experience and to write on topics of general interest. Chapters 4 and 5 will assist them in drafting and revising their essays. The chart Common Perspectives for Content Analysis (Part 4, Resources for Writing) summarizes the key questions for thinking analytically about a wide range of topics.

Chapter 3, Part B, Reading Analytically, outlines the skills students need for reading and summarizing nonfiction. You might want to follow up this section with Chapter 9, Writing Comparison Essays. The sample topic for this chapter is a comparison of two essays from the Readings. You could then introduce the more complex skills required for evaluating arguments and writing critiques covered in Chapter 10. Chapter 11 calls on students to put these skills to work in constructing their own arguments about controversial issues or in writing reviews. Students could expand their persuasive essays into research papers by following the principles set out in Chapters 12 and 13.

You will find other helpful suggestions for using this text in the Instructor's Manual. We hope you find *Essay Writing for Canadian Students* stimulating and productive.

Acknowledgments

Revising this text has been a collaborative activity, one involving not only the three of us as authors, but also many others.

First and foremost we would like to thank students past and present at the University of Alberta and Grant MacEwan College who have helped us to see what did and didn't work in previous editions and who have generously allowed us to use their writing.

Several assistants have made our work much easier. Roger Davis revised and updated the section on plagiarism. Kat Johnston revised and updated both the biographies of the authors of all the Readings and the Annotated Survey of Reference Sources. Marilyn Nikish typed all the new Readings. Ilona Ryder revised the sections on essay format and the material on quoting and documenting research materials. Judy Dunlop revised and expanded the index. We have retained some of the suggestions made by Stephen Scott in the previous edition of the Instructor's Manual. We appreciate the careful attention to detail each of them brought to these tasks.

We would also like to thank colleagues David Grant, Grant MacEwan College; Margaret Keene, Grant MacEwan College; Christine Liotta, British Columbia Institute of Technology; Paul Lumsden, Grant MacEwan College; Ranjini Mendis, Kwantlen University College; Peter Miller, Seneca College; Paul Milton, Okanagan University College; Deanna Roozendaal, Camosun College; and others who have made suggestions for improvements.

We have also benefited from the institutional support we received. Marian would like to express her appreciation for the suppport and encouragement given by Barbara North, Chair of the English Department, and Peter Mitchell, Dean of Arts and Science at Grant MacEwan College.

Many thanks as well to the staff at Pearson Education Canada for their help and timely nudges along the way: Marianne Minaker, Acquisitions Editor; Andrew Winton, Sponsoring Editor; Avivah Wargon, Production Editor; Lesley Mann, Copy Editor; and Judith Turnbull, Proofreader.

A special thanks to Developmental Editor Marta Tomins, who served also as developmental editor for the first edition. She has brought a cheering human touch to the sometimes isolating task of writing.

Professor Charles Urbanowitcz, Department of Anthropology, California State University at Chico, did his best to help us locate author Laura Bohannan so that we could secure permission to use her piece "Shakespeare in the Bush" again. Unfortunately, Professor Bohannan had died recently, and we were not able to include her essay. We hope to restore it in the next edition.

Finally, Marian would like to thank Laurie Allen for his continued support and encouragement.

Rhetoric

chapter 1   Writing Essays: An Overview

chapter 2   Clarifying Essay Topics

chapter 3   Using Content Analysis to Gather Material

chapter 4   Writing Content Analysis Essays 1:
Formulating a Thesis Statement and Drafting

chapter 5   Writing Content Analysis Essays 2:
Revising Your Draft

chapter 6   Using Textual Analysis to Gather Material

chapter 7   Writing Textual Analysis Essays 1:
Formulating a Thesis Statement and
Drafting

chapter 8   Writing Textual Analysis Essays 2:
Revising Your Draft

chapter 9   Writing Comparison Essays

chapter 10   Evaluating Arguments and Writing Critiques

chapter 11   Writing Persuasive Essays

chapter 12   Gathering Material for Research Papers

chapter 13   Writing Research Papers

part one

c h a p t e r   1

Writing Essays:
An Overview

Essay Writing: Purposes
       Writing to Learn
       Writing to Communicate

Essay Writing: Product
       Audience
       Structure
       Sample Essay: Analysis of a Film
       Discussion of the Sample Essay

Essay Writing: Process

Stage 1   Clarifying Essay Topics

Stage 2   Gathering Material

Stage 3   Formulating a Thesis

Stage 4   Drafting

Stage 5   Revising Thesis and Essay Structure

Stage 6   Revising Individual Paragraphs

Stage 7   Final Editing

This book is about essay writing. We focus on essay writing for two reasons. The first is that the thinking skills you practise in the process of writing essays are central to the work you do in college or university. The second is that the procedures you learn for writing and revising essays will help you with many other kinds of writing assignments.

Essay Writing: Purposes

Writing to Learn

How will writing essays help you to develop thinking skills? One way is by encouraging you to explore your ideas. This purpose is reflected in the French word from which the term *essay* comes: *essai*, meaning "attempt." The term was first used to refer to a particular kind of writing by the French author Michel de Montaigne, who published a book of short prose pieces entitled *Essais* in 1580. This title suggests the personal, exploratory nature of Montaigne's attempts to understand the world around him by writing on everyday subjects such as "Liars" and "The Art of Conversation." You may study informal essays of this type in composition and literature courses, and create them as well.

Since Montaigne's day, the term essay has come to include formal writing on a wide range of subjects, from the nature of love in Shakespeare's *King Lear* to theories about the origins of the universe. Writing academic essays of this kind will help you to develop systematic analytic thinking. It is this more formal type of essay writing that you will most often be asked to do in your university and college courses, and that we will focus on in this text.

Writing essays gives you the opportunity to learn what you think about a particular subject. In writing about friendship, for example, you may discover which qualities you most value in your friends. Similarly, you may not know what you really think about issues such as Canada's role as a peacekeeper or the desirability of genetic engineering until you write about them, because you have not had to define your opinion or to defend it.

Writing essays also transforms passive learning into active learning. If you were taking a painting course, you would recognize that no matter how good the instructor's lessons might be, you would learn to paint only by painting. The same holds true for writing. Through writing essays, whether formal or informal, you develop greater awareness of the language you and others use to make meaning. What may be less obvious is that you learn the theories, concepts, and procedures of academic disciplines more thoroughly by actively employing them in writing essays.

Writing to Communicate

Some of the writing you do—such as class notes, responses to reading, drafts that go nowhere—may have no other reader but yourself. Writing essays, however, is a means of sharing your understanding of a particular issue with others.

The style and organization of essays differ from discipline to discipline; so does what counts as evidence and proof. But central to most academic essays is an opinion substantiated by reasons and evidence; by setting out these reasons and evidence, you open up the possibility of dialogue with those who hold other views.

Consider, for example, an argument in which you claim that genetic research should be stopped while a friend claims it shouldn't. At this level, each statement is "just an opinion" and your discussion isn't likely to go very far. But suppose that you were to say genetic research should be stopped because lethal organisms could be released into the environment, endangering millions of lives. Given this reason, your friend might concede the possible danger. If you give reasons, your argument will be more persuasive.

In an academic essay, this combination of an opinion and the reason(s) supporting it is called a *thesis*. A thesis is like a hypothesis in a scientific experiment: it is the statement or assertion that is to be proved. Proof in an academic essay consists of the logical, orderly development of your thesis through explaining your reasons and giving evidence (such as factual information, examples, and quotations from authorities) to support them. By explaining your thesis carefully and giving evidence to support it, you are likely to persuade readers to take your opinion seriously, whether or not they agree with it.

Essay Writing: Product

Both informal essays and formal academic essays present the writer's opinion on a particular subject. But the way the writer chooses to present that opinion will depend upon the audience for whom the piece is written.

Audience

Most of the informal essays you study in composition and literature courses were originally published in magazines or newspapers where they had to compete for the reader's attention with photographs, advertising, and a host of other articles. In these circumstances, essay writers may attempt to catch the reader's eye by starting with a controversial claim they will eventually reverse, or by describing an incident from their lives. Having caught the reader's attention, popular essayists may try to maintain suspense by narrating a series of events with an unexpected outcome or by revealing their thesis at the end. You will find several essays of this type in Part 2, Readings.

Formal essays on academic subjects, in contrast, are written for specialized audiences already familiar with the subject. Readers of these essays want to know the writer's thesis from the beginning and to have the evidence supporting the thesis laid out in a logical, orderly fashion. They also appreciate essays that are well written according to the conventions of the discipline. Most of the essays you write in college and university courses will be of this second type. You will be writing for instructors and classmates who know something about the subject and want to hear your opinion about it.

Structure

You can meet your reader's needs and demonstrate your understanding of your subject most effectively by writing essays that have these main structural elements:

INTRODUCTION
The introduction establishes the context for the discussion (for example, by defining necessary terms or giving historical background) and presents the thesis of the essay.

MIDDLE PARAGRAPHS
Each middle paragraph discusses a single subpoint of the thesis. The purpose of the paragraph is defined by a topic sentence that links the paragraph to the thesis. Middle paragraphs usually contain both explanations of the point made in the topic sentence and specific details illustrating that point. Transitional words and phrases signal the movement from point to point and establish the relationship between points and the details that support them.

CONCLUSION
The conclusion ties together the points developed in the middle paragraphs and mentions the wider implications of the discussion, if any.

Sample Essay: Analysis of a Film

So that you can see what this kind of essay might look like in practice, here is an example. The essay topic asked students to choose their favourite film and explain its appeal. The main structural elements of the essay have been labelled.

WRITING SAMPLE

ROMANCE AND REALISM IN *CASABLANCA*

Introduction

Since its release in 1942, the movie *Casablanca*, directed by Michael Curtiz, has become a classic. Even people who have never seen the film recognize the theme song, "As Time Goes By," and the line "Play it again, Sam," even though this line never actually occurs in the film. Why has *Casablanca* remained so popular? The answer to this question undoubtedly lies partly in the appeal of its two stars, Humphrey Bogart and Ingrid Bergman, and talented supporting actors like Claude Rains, Sydney Greenstreet, and Peter Lorre. Its main appeal, however, is the mixture of romance and realism in its plot, setting, and characterization.

Thesis Statement

Topic sentence

The obvious romanticism of the plot tends to obscure its realistic elements. Consider the details. After a few shots of a spinning globe and Casablanca street scenes, we are introduced to Rick Blaine (Humphrey Bogart), a mysterious American expatriate who owns the Café Américain, meeting place of Casablanca's smart set, and who appears to care for nothing and nobody. Into Rick's café walk Victor Laszlo (Paul Henreid), a famous Resistance leader, and Ilsa Lund (Ingrid Bergman), his wife, in search of stolen letters of transit that would guarantee them a safe exit from Casablanca to Lisbon and America. In a flashback we learn that just before the Nazis occupied Paris, Rick and Ilsa met there and fell in love. Because of their agreement not to speak of their pasts, however, Ilsa does not tell Rick of her marriage to Laszlo, whom she believes to have died in a concentration camp. On the day that the two are to leave Paris together, Ilsa discovers Victor is still alive and, without explanation, sends Rick a note saying she still loves him but can never see him again.

Middle paragraph 1

Transition

Topic sentence

Middle paragraph 2

Rick and Ilsa's past, then, is a romantic tale of love and self-sacrifice. When they meet and fall in love again in Casablanca, they must confront more realistic problems: Rick's cynicism, a product of his sense of betrayal; Ilsa's love, respect, and admiration for Victor; Victor's own sense of honour; and the very real threat posed to them all by the Nazis' determination to prevent Victor's escape.

Topic sentence

Middle paragraph 3

The reality of this threat is emphasized by the director's use of the setting. On the one hand, Casablanca is a romantic city. In its sun-baked streets, merchants in fezzes haggle with prospective buyers; inside Rick's Café Américain, the scene of much of the action, the wealthy gamble. On the other hand, Casablanca, governed by Captain Renault (Claude Rains), a French official subservient to German "advisers," is the major point of escape for refugees from Nazi-occupied Europe. Consequently, we see the marketplace turn into a place of terror when a member of the Free French underground is shot by French police in front of the law courts bearing the motto "Liberty, Equality, Fraternity." Similarly, the glamour of Rick's café is offset by the plight of the refugees who frequent it and by the ease with which the Germans order the place closed. The setting thus emphasizes the film's mixture of romance and realism.

Transition

Topic sentence

Middle paragraph 4

What gives the film its appeal is not just the romantic hope that the good guys will eventually defeat the Nazis, however; it is the film's recognition of the struggle that goes on within characters who, while basically good, may make wrong choices. This issue arises for several of the minor characters, but is most fully explored in the relationship between Rick and Ilsa. Although Rick's past (running guns to Ethiopia, fighting in the Spanish Civil War) suggests that he is capable of idealism, his refusal to shield the man who stole the letters of credit raises the possibility that he will refuse to help Laszlo and Ilsa. Similarly, Ilsa's shift from threatening to shoot Rick for the letters of transit one minute, to planning to go away with him the next, makes us wonder whether she will again be capable of sacrificing her love for Rick to her duty to her husband. To emphasize these inner struggles, scenes between Rick and Ilsa are often shot in half-light, creating the juxtaposition between light and shadow that is one of the film's trademarks. Since most of us are faced with difficult moral choices, we identify more fully with characters who face similar struggles than we do with those who never question their own motives or behaviour.

Conclusion

In the end, it is the romantic ethic of love and self-sacrifice that triumphs, as Rick puts Ilsa and Victor on the plane for Lisbon and, with Captain Renault, strides off into the fog to join the Resistance fighters. But in its use of plot, setting, and characterization, the film reminds us that such triumphs arise out of our struggles against opposition, both without and within. It is this realistic recognition of the difficulty of living up to our best selves that gives the film its continuing appeal.

Discussion of the Sample Essay

"Romance and Realism in *Casablanca*" illustrates the effective use of the structural elements common to college and university essays. The introduction provides basic information about the film and introduces the issue of the film's popularity. It concludes with the **thesis statement**, signalled by the transitional phrase "Its main appeal, however,...." The placement of the thesis statement focuses attention on the main point: the relation between the film's popularity and the combination of romance and realism in its plot, setting, and characterization.

The thesis statement also serves as a guide to the structure of the essay as a whole. It sets out the order in which the three aspects of the film will be discussed. This order is one of **ascending interest**. That is, the writer puts the paragraph on the plot first because the point about the mixture of romance and realism in the plot is the most obvious and most easily explained. Next, the writer discusses details of the setting that illuminate the contrast between romance and realism. Then the point about characterization comes last to emphasize its importance.

In the middle paragraphs of the essay, each of these points is clearly made in a **topic sentence**. Each topic sentence identifies the aspect of the film to be discussed (such as plot) and connects that aspect to the thesis by stating how it contributes to the film's popularity. The topic sentences also provide **transitions** between one paragraph and the next.

The framework you create by establishing this kind of relationship between the thesis, topic sentences, and transitional devices will give your reader valuable assistance in following your line of thinking.

Important as this framework is, the essay would not be convincing if the middle paragraphs did not contain **details** to support the points made in the topic sentences and **explanations** to clarify what the details mean. In the first middle paragraph, for example, the point that the plot seems "romantic" would not seem very convincing without details of the plot. Details alone are not enough to define "romantic," however. And so the writer provides the explanation that the plot is romantic because it is a "tale of love and self-sacrifice."

The conclusion sums up the relationship the writer has established between the film's popularity and the mixture of romance and realism in its plot, setting, and characterization. Notice that the conclusion does not merely repeat what the writer has said in the thesis statement and topic sentences.

"Romance and Realism in *Casablanca*" thus illustrates how you can use the structure common to most college and university essays to present your opinion on a subject in a clear, straightforward way. For other ways of discussing films, see "*The English Patient* Debate" in Part 2, Readings.

Essay Writing: Process

Most people don't write an essay—or anything intended to be read by others, for that matter—by sitting down with paper and pen (or word processor) and rising an hour later with a finished product. The final draft is the last stage of a highly complex process of thinking and writing, rethinking and rewriting. If you want to produce an interesting, thoughtful essay, like the one on *Casablanca*, you have to be prepared to give time and serious attention to your subject. Without that willingness, you will not learn how to write from this book or from any other. But it is our belief that if you are willing, you can learn to write essays that have something to say and say it well.

To help you learn the skills you need, we focus on the major stages of writing academic essays:

STAGE 1:   CLARIFYING ESSAY TOPICS
Determining what your assignment requires and exploring ideas to define a topic

STAGE 2:   GATHERING MATERIAL
Using analytic categories to stimulate your thinking and to organize ideas, information, and specific details about your topic

STAGE 3:   FORMULATING A THESIS STATEMENT
Forming a main idea and points to support it from the material you have gathered

STAGE 4:   DRAFTING
Selecting and organizing material in a first draft

STAGE 5:   REVISING THESIS STATEMENT AND ESSAY STRUCTURE
Checking for possible problems with your thesis statement and essay structure and making necessary changes

STAGE 6:   REVISING INDIVIDUAL PARAGRAPHS
Checking for possible problems with your introduction, middle paragraphs, and conclusion, and making necessary changes

STAGE 7:   FINAL EDITING
Improving your sentence structure and word usage, and correcting errors in grammar, punctuation, mechanics, and format

In Part 1, Rhetoric, we demonstrate the first six stages of this process for many different kinds of essays: essays analyzing and explaining concepts, behaviour, data, and events (Chapters 3, 4, and 5); essays analyzing and explaining the formal features of verbal and visual texts, such as literary works and films (Chapters 6, 7, and 8); comparison essays (Chapter 9); essays analyzing and evaluating the logic of an argument (Chapter 10); persuasive essays (Chapter 11); and research papers (Chapters 12 and 13).

The published pieces and sample essays in Part 2, Readings, illustrate the writing strategies discussed in Part 1 and provide material for you to write about. We hope you find these readings entertaining, enlightening, informative, and thought-provoking.

In Part 3, Handbook, you will find the information you need for Stage 7: Final Editing.

Part 4, Resources, contains reference materials and a glossary of terms used in this text.

Finally, a note on the stages model we use in this text. We are not claiming that the methods we propose are the only way to write or to write effectively; we don't even claim that they reflect exactly what writers—including ourselves—do when we write. For many of us, writing is far messier than our model would suggest. This text is like a set of instructions for assembling a piece of furniture, not a videotape of one person's efforts to fashion bits of wood and glue into his or her own unique design. You may find that the order in which we present writing activities suits your method of composition perfectly; on the other hand, you may find yourself writing a draft to clarify your understanding of a topic or mentally revising the structure before a word hits the page. Try out our suggestions, adjust them to suit your needs, and fit them into a writing process that works for you.

EXERCISES

Answer each of the following questions in a sentence or two.

1. We suggest that writing essays can help you to think through your ideas and to communicate them to other people. Which of these purposes is most relevant to you as a writer? Why?

2. We briefly describe two types of essays: informal personal essays and formal academic essays. Find an example of each type in Part 2, Readings. What are the main differences you notice?

3. Consider the effects of the intended audience on the two essays you chose above. In what ways does the informal essay seek to capture and hold the interest of readers? How can you tell that the formal academic essay was written for readers familiar with the subject?

4. What is your usual approach to writing an essay? How effective do you find this approach? With which stage(s) of the process do you feel most satisfied? Least satisfied?

c h a p t e r   2

Clarifying Essay Topics

Stage 1   Clarifying Essay Topics

    Step 1   Defining Unfamiliar Terms

    Step 2   Understanding Directions
        Analysis
        Comparison
        Evaluation
        Other Terms

    Step 3   Exploring Your Subject
        Freewriting
        Brainstorming
        Tree Diagramming

    Step 4   Deciding What Sources to Use
        Primary Sources
        Secondary Sources

Stage 2   Gathering Material

Stage 3   Formulating a Thesis Statement

Stage 4   Drafting

Stage 5   Revising Thesis Statement and
    Essay Structure

Stage 6   Revising Individual Paragraphs

Stage 7   Final Editing

Stage 1 Clarifying Essay Topics

Essay assignments are designed to allow you to come to terms with the concepts you have studied, the literature you have read, or the data you have collected. But in order to write an essay that demonstrates your understanding of your subject, you first need to know what the topic requires. If you were faced with the following topics, or similar ones, would you know exactly what to do?

What is the function of the graveyard scene in *Hamlet*?

Discuss the concept of the state in Plato's *Republic*.

Compare the use of the vampire myth in the films *Dracula* and *Interview with the Vampire*.

Explain the concept of narcissism as the term is used by Freud and his followers.

Is Alice Munro's "The Red Dress" a good story? Why or why not?

Compare Chomsky's and Skinner's theories of language acquisition.

Discuss the development of Canadian abstract painting.

Evaluate Canadian and U.S. policies on pollution in the Great Lakes.

Write a 1000-word essay on some aspect of computers.

These are typical assignments for college and university courses that require essays. Although in some disciplines multiple-choice exams have replaced essay assignments and essay exams (particularly in first-year courses), you are still likely to face a wide variety of writing assignments. The first stage in writing, then, is ensuring that you understand your assignment.

Step 1 Defining Unfamiliar Terms

Make sure that you understand all the terms used in the assignment. To write on the sample essay topics listed above, you would have to know the meaning of the terms *narcissism*, *abstract painting*, *myth*, and *language acquisition*.

Learning about a subject includes learning the vocabulary that specialists in the subject use. In psychology courses, you may learn the meaning of such terms as *conditioned response*, *narcissism*, and *depression*. In literature courses, you are likely to discuss the meaning of terms such as *myth*, *point of view*, and *tragedy*.

As these examples suggest, the specialized vocabulary of each discipline is likely to include terms seldom used outside the field as well as terms used in a more restricted way than you would use them in everyday speech. When you say, "I feel depressed," for example, you may be disappointed about an exam mark, sad about a friend's moving, or temporarily in low spirits for other reasons. But you are not using the word *depressed* in the way a psychologist or psychiatrist would. Similarly, the term *tragedy*, as used in literary criticism, is not simply a disastrous event, but a certain kind of play.

You can clarify the meaning of terms by consulting your course text(s) or specialized dictionaries. Many texts, including this one, contain *glossaries* that briefly define concepts and other specialized terms. If there is no glossary, or if you are still puzzled, check the index for discussions of the term elsewhere in your text.

If your text doesn't provide all the information you need, consult a *specialized dictionary* in the appropriate field. You will find selected titles in the Annotated Survey of Reference Sources in Part 4, Resources.

Step 2   Understanding Directions

If you were doing math, you would easily recognize the symbols that tell you whether to add, subtract, multiply, or divide. But you may be less familiar with the terms that give you directions for writing essays.

Although topics for academic essays are stated in a wide variety of ways, the basic procedure is the same: *analysis*. For some topics, you may need to combine analysis with *comparison* or *evaluation*.

Analysis   The main purpose of analysis is to illuminate something, such as a concept, a text, an event, or a set of data, by examining its parts in detail. When you analyze something, you answer questions like these:

What parts can this X be divided into?

What do these parts indicate about the nature of X as a whole?

Why does X have this particular nature?

If you were analyzing the artifacts from an archaeological site, for example, you would divide them into parts according to their type (flints, trade goods, animal remains, and so forth) and according to where they were found. From your analysis of this material, you would decide what kind of site this is: a winter camp used by Assiniboines over a period of a hundred years, perhaps. To complete your analysis, you would explain why these artifacts indicate this kind of camp.

In this text we make a distinction between content analysis and textual analysis.

Content Analysis Content analysis is the examination of behaviour, data, written works, and other sources of information without regard to the form in which the information is communicated. "Explain the concept of the state in Plato's *Republic*" and "Discuss the causes of the English Civil War" are examples of topics that require content analysis. You will find step-by-step procedures for content analysis in Chapter 3, Using Content Analysis to Gather Material.

Textual Analysis Textual analysis is the examination of written works or performances (such as plays, television programs, and films) with attention both to what is being said and to how the work or performance is presented. If you were writing on William Faulkner's short story "A Rose for Emily," for example, you would discuss not only the events but also the techniques Faulkner uses in presenting the story, such as imagery and symbolism. You will find a detailed examination of textual analysis in Chapter 6, Using Textual Analysis to Gather Material, with a sample analysis of a poem. This chapter will be especially useful when you are writing essays for literature or film courses.

Comparison The main purpose of comparison is to examine the similarities and differences of two or more things in such a way as to understand both things better. The **basis of comparison** tells you which similarities and differences to focus on. You could compare apples and oranges, for example, as foods, as cash crops, or as objects to throw. Depending on which of these you chose, your comparison would illuminate not only the individual properties of apples and oranges, but also the general properties of foods, cash crops, or objects to throw.

Since comparison is based on analysis, your first step in comparing things is to divide them into parts and compare the parts. The questions you answer in making comparisons are therefore modifications of the questions for analysis:

What is the basis of comparison?

What matching parts can these things be divided into?

What is the central likeness or difference between these things?

Why are the things similar or different?

If you wanted to compare downhill and cross-country skiing, for example, you would first need to choose your basis of comparison. Would you compare them as competitive sports, forms of exercise, or recreational activities? Your basis of comparison would determine the parts you divide the two sports into, their central likeness or difference, and the reasons for that similarity or difference.

You might find comparison topics stated in these ways:

Choose two poems and show how they either attack or celebrate aspects of contemporary life.

How are the principles of solar heating systems similar to or different from the principles of geothermal systems?

Compare Chomsky's and Skinner's theories of language acquisition.

Discuss the symbolism of roses in three poems.

Compare two films.

Some of these topics state the basis of comparison ("attacks on or celebrations of contemporary life"; "principles of heating systems"; "symbolism of roses"). When the topic does not provide a basis of comparison (as in an assignment asking you to compare two theories or two films), you will have to find one. Chapter 9, Writing Comparison Essays, will show you how.

Evaluation   The main purpose of evaluation is to determine the strengths and weaknesses of something, such as government cost-cutting, a new novel by Margaret Atwood, or an argument favouring euthanasia. Like comparison, evaluation starts with analysis. To evaluate a hockey forward, for example, you would first analyze the player's skills as a skater, shooter, stick-handler, and play-maker. Your knowledge of the game and of other hockey forwards would give you a sense of what constitutes excellence in each of these categories. To evaluate a particular player, you would measure that person's strengths and weaknesses against this *standard of evaluation*.

In order to evaluate one or more things, you will need to answer questions like these:

What standard(s) of evaluation is (are) appropriate?

What parts can I divide my material into?

What are the strengths and weaknesses of each of these parts?

What is my evaluation of the overall weighting of strengths and weaknesses?

Why have I come to this evaluation?

The common *standards of evaluation* are practical, ethical, aesthetic, and logical. Since it is possible to evaluate things according to various standards, you have to define which one or ones you have chosen to use. If you chose to evaluate proposed federal policy on pollution in the Great Lakes on practical grounds, for example, you might consider the cost to participants, the technology used to control pollution, and the enforcement of government regulations. Your analysis of these areas might lead you to conclude that the proposed policy is good because it would provide cost-efficient, technologically sound, and easily enforced methods for reducing pollution. This evaluation would be based on a practical standard of evaluation. If you evaluated the proposal on ethical grounds, your conclusion might be quite different. You might decide, for example, that you found the proposal ethically unacceptable because it would infringe on Aboriginal fishing rights.

Because of the wide variety of possible viewpoints, essay topics seldom give the standard of evaluation you should use. For each of these topics, you would have to decide on an appropriate standard of evaluation:

> Is Margaret Laurence's *The Diviners* a good novel?
>
> Was the Riel Rebellion justified?
>
> Are individual rights better protected under the Canadian Charter of Rights and Freedoms or under the U.S. Constitution?

So far we have discussed evaluation as a method of arriving at your own arguments about whether something is good or bad. Chapter 10, Evaluating Arguments and Writing Critiques, will help you to weigh the reasoning and evidence that authors present in support of their arguments.

Other terms Although most essay assignments require that you analyze, compare, or evaluate, these terms may not appear in the topics, as you will have noticed from the examples. You will therefore have to think about the meaning of the terms used. For instance, the word *discuss* may seem to mean "summarize the relevant information." *It doesn't.* "Discuss" may appear in topics that require analysis, comparison, or evaluation. *Explain, examine,* and *assess* are other words whose meaning may be ambiguous. *Explain* usually means *analyze; examine* may mean *analyze* or *evaluate; assess* means *evaluate.* Some topics may ask you to *compare* things when you are actually expected to both *compare* and *evaluate* them. If you are in doubt, ask your instructor.

Step 3 Exploring Your Subject

Most essay topics set limits on what you should cover: the concept of the state in Plato's *Republic*; the use of the vampire myth in *Dracula* and *Interview with the Vampire*; Canadian and U.S. policies on pollution in the Great Lakes. Occasionally, however, you may be given an indefinite topic, such as "Write a 1000-word essay on some aspect of computers," or you may be invited to come up with a topic of your own.

Whether your topic is narrowly defined or open-ended, you can use various techniques such as freewriting, brainstorming, and tree diagramming to explore your topic and to define its limits. Limiting your topic allows you to examine your subject thoroughly enough to speak as an "expert" to less well-informed readers. If you try to write a five-page essay on a broad subject, such as computers or every aspect of the novel *Great Expectations*, your treatment is likely to be superficial. Narrowing your focus enables you to examine your subject in greater depth. It also helps you organize your information gathering and your writing.

Here are three quick ways of generating ideas about your topic.

Freewriting   Each time you come up with an idea, does another part of your brain say, "That's no good," or "You'll look silly if you say that"? Freewriting is one way of circumventing this mental editor. If you tend to agonize over a blank page, then freewriting may set your mind in motion.

Freewriting consists of writing continuously for ten minutes or longer, without stopping to organize, correct, or evaluate what you are doing. If your first freewriting does not give you a clear sense of what you might want to focus on in your essay, try variations on the freewriting process. You might, for example, look over your first freewriting material for the idea that seems most promising and then use this idea as a springboard for a second freewriting. Or, if you are trying to find an aspect of a text that interests you, you might freewrite a fantasy dialogue with the author, asking questions and recording the "replies." This dialogue may reveal possibilities that you would not have reached by more conventional means.

Brainstorming   Brainstorming is another way of circumventing your mental editor. Brainstorming consists of putting down, in point form, everything you can think of about your topic, however obvious or bizarre the ideas may seem. Begin by writing your subject in the middle of a page, and then jot down ideas as they come to you. When you finish, you will have a mixture of generalizations and details radiating from your central subject. You can then draw lines to connect related points. For example, if you wanted to explore the broad subject of fitness, you might come up with a brainstorming diagram such as the one shown in Figure 2.1 on the next page.

Much of the material in the diagram relates to the physical effects of fitness, and so you might decide to focus your essay on that subject. Or you might be intrigued by the idea of fitness as big business.

Tree Diagramming   Tree diagramming is a more systematic form of brainstorming. When you use this technique, you divide your broad subject into categories and subcategories in the form of an ever-expanding "tree." Because a tree diagram encourages you to develop equivalent

FIGURE 2.1

Sample Brainstorming Diagram

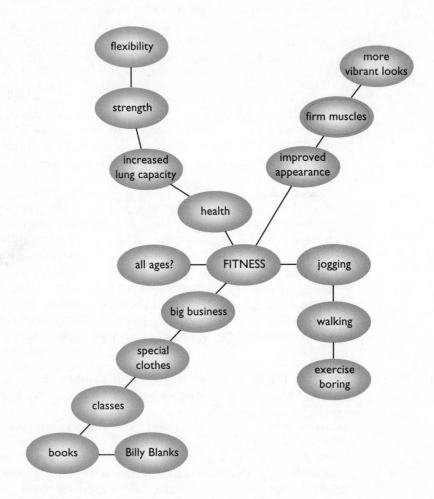

categories, it is especially useful for narrowing comparison topics and developing arguments for and against something. For example, you might construct a tree diagram as a means of exploring arguments for and against Canada's role as a peacekeeper. Figure 2.2 (p. 20) represents the type of diagram you will evolve by using this technique.

These discovery techniques are obviously useful for narrowing a broad subject such as "computers." Even when the topic is limited, you can use these techniques to prime your thinking or to discover an angle that interests you.

Step 4 Deciding What Sources to Use

Is your essay to be based solely on *primary sources*, or are you expected to consult *secondary sources* as well?

Primary sources Primary sources of information are first-hand experiences or first-hand accounts of experiences. Your own knowledge, experience, and observations would be considered primary sources of information. So would the literary works you read, the plays you see, and the questionnaires you collect for your sociology class. Official documents (for example, the British North America Act, the Canadian Charter of Rights and Freedoms), eyewitness accounts of events, letters, diaries, and contemporary newspapers are also primary sources. When you analyze, compare, or evaluate texts, your primary source of information and ideas is the texts themselves.

Secondary sources You use secondary sources of information whenever you write a *research paper*. Secondary sources consist of second-hand (or third- or fourth-hand) accounts, such as critical discussions of a novel, or books and articles about past events by modern historians. Such works are considered secondary sources because they select and present material to support a particular point of view. Only some facts are included and usually only one point of view is argued.

Assignments based on secondary sources are designed to acquaint you with the important issues in your discipline and also with its methods of research and analysis. You can also use secondary sources to supplement your analysis of primary sources. Essays that require you to use both primary and secondary sources are often difficult to write. You will find a detailed discussion of how to do this kind of research paper in Chapter 13.

Working on Your Own Assignment

Clarifying the demands of your topic is a necessary first step towards writing a good essay.

- Identify terms that need to be defined.
- Decide whether you should analyze, compare, or evaluate (or compare *and* evaluate).
- Use freewriting, brainstorming, or tree diagramming to discover an aspect of your subject that interests you.
- Decide whether to use primary sources, secondary sources, or both.

FIGURE 2.2
Sample Tree Diagram

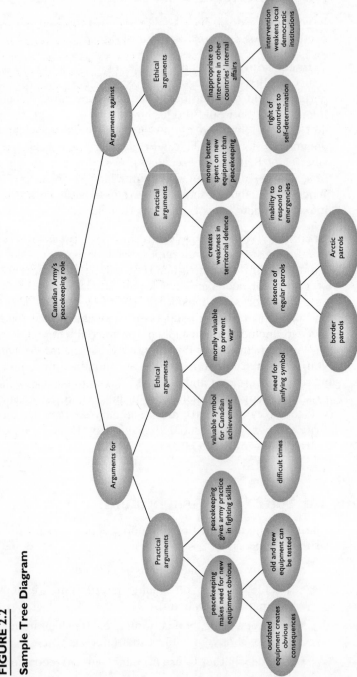

EXERCISES

A.   You are much more likely to write a successful essay, both outside of class and in an exam, if you understand exactly what the topic is asking you to do. Choose three of the topics below and practise clarifying essay topics. Define specialized terms, decide whether the topic calls for analysis, comparison, evaluation, or a combination of these procedures, and narrow down a topic that seems too general for the length of the essay required.

1. How does Swift use a persona to create irony in "A Modest Proposal"?

2. Write a 750-word essay on the concept of "sustainable growth" in the fishing industry.

3. Discuss Francis Ford Coppola's use of crosscutting in *The Godfather,* Part 1.

4. Write a 750-word essay comparing Freud's and Jung's concepts of dreams.

5. How useful is the Internet?

B.   Experiment with two of the following ways to explore your subject.

1. You have been asked to write an essay on whether or not sexually explicit material should be banned from the Internet. Freewrite for ten minutes on this topic. Then reread what you have written and summarize your ideas in one sentence.

2. You have been asked to write an essay on any aspect of the transition from adolescence to adulthood. Spend ten minutes brainstorming on this topic. Then select one or two topics that interest you and that you could discuss in an essay of 500–1000 words.

3. You have been asked to write a review of two films you have seen recently. Make a tree diagram showing the main similarities and differences and your evaluation of these aspects.

chapter 3

Using Content Analysis to Gather Material

A. THINKING ANALYTICALLY

Stage 1 Clarifying Content Analysis Topics

Stage 2 Gathering Material: Analyzing Your Own Experience

    Step 1 Using Systems, Process, and Causal Analysis

    Step 2 Categorizing Material

    Sample Topic: From Adolescence to Adulthood

B. READING ANALYTICALLY

Stage 1 Honing Your Reading Skills

Stage 2 Gathering Material: Analyzing Nonfiction Sources

    Step 1 Figuring Out the Basic Ideas

    Step 2 Gaining a Broader Perspective

    Step 3 Writing a Summary

    Sample Topic: Analyzing the Content of Alison Gopnik's "Kiddy Thinks"

Stage 3 Formulating a Thesis Statement

Stage 4 Drafting

Stage 5 Revising Thesis Statement and Essay Structure

Stage 6 Revising Individual Paragraphs

Stage 7 Final Editing

Content analysis, as we defined it in Chapter 2, is the examination of behaviour, data, events, written works, and other sources of information and ideas without regard to the aesthetic qualities of the presentation. That is, you focus on the content of your source material, not on how it is presented.

Most of the writing you do for courses other than those in literature and film studies is likely to be based on content analysis. Each academic discipline has a somewhat different way of handling this task, but the basic procedures of content analysis will work for many subjects and situations.

In this chapter we demonstrate two ways of using content analysis to gather material. The first section provides you with categories for thinking analytically about a broad range of subjects. You will find step-by-step suggestions for drafting and revising essays of this type in Chapters 4 and 5.

The second part of this chapter shows you how to analyze the kind of nonfiction writing you read in most courses (newspaper and magazine articles and essays, scholarly books and articles, and textbooks) and to summarize your reading. These skills will be useful when you write exams, critiques (see Chapter 10), and research papers (see Chapters 12 and 13).

A. THINKING ANALYTICALLY

Stage 1 Clarifying Content Analysis Topics

When you are asked to write on topics of general interest, particularly in writing courses, your material may come largely from your own knowledge and experience. Some of these assignments may be personal essays developed through narrative and description, as in Lenore Keeshig-Tobias' "He Was a Boxer When I Was Small" (Part 2, Readings). This type of essay, as we pointed out in Chapter 1, is beyond the scope of this book. You may also bring your own experience to bear in persuasive essays developed through argument and evidence, as in David Suzuki's "It Always Costs" (Part 2, Readings). You will find guidelines for writing persuasive essays in Chapter 11. Here we will focus on essay topics that ask you to use your knowledge and experience to explain such things as behaviour, concepts, data, and events without evaluating them.

Here are examples of essay topics that require you to think analytically about your experience.

- What makes a good soccer team?
- How to make an enemy into a friend.
- What causes school violence?

Stage 2   Gathering Material: Analyzing Your Own Experience

Step 1   Using Systems, Process, and Causal Analysis

To analyze, you will recall, means to divide something into parts. There are many ways of doing so. Systems, process, and causal analysis are three fundamental methods of talking about the relationships between parts and wholes. Considering your subject from each of these perspectives will give you a wealth of material to write about. (For a handy overview of these three types of analysis, see Figure 3.1.)

FIGURE 3.1

Discovery Questions for Content Analysis

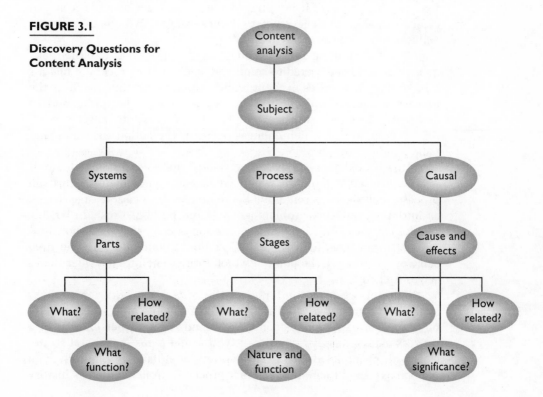

Systems analysis Is it possible to see my subject as a system that can be divided into parts? What are those parts? What is their function? How are they related?

You can think of a **system** as anything composed of parts that work together to create the whole. A car engine or a family can be analyzed as a system; so can a theory or an institution. The topic "What makes a good soccer team?" would readily lend itself to systems analysis. You would show how the parts—offensive and defensive players, goalie, coaches, fans, and sponsors—work together to create a whole: a good soccer team.

As this example suggests, your purpose when you analyze a system is not merely to describe its parts. You also want to show how the parts work together to fulfill the function of the whole. If you were analyzing the criminal justice system within a democracy, for example, you might conclude that the parts (lawmakers, courts, lawyers, juries, prisons, and so forth) are designed to balance the rights of the person charged with the rights of society. In contrast, the criminal justice system in a dictatorship would have a different function, such as maintaining the authority of those in power.

Process analysis Is it possible to see my subject as a process that can be divided into stages? What are those stages? What is their nature and function? How are they related?

Calling something a process suggests that it consists of either a sequence of actions directed to some end, such as the process of making a recording, or a series of identifiable changes over time, such as the process of aging. We think of a process as having a beginning and an end with stages in between. We divide the process into stages according to the points at which changes occur in the actions or states that make up the process.

"How to make an enemy into a friend," the second sample topic, is a general interest topic for which you could gather material through process analysis. You would divide the process into various stages such as initiating dialogue, problem-solving, and building trust. In writing your essay, you would explain the function of each stage and show how one stage prepares for the next. You would conclude with the final stage of the process: the point at which former enemies consider themselves friends.

It is important to understand the difference between process analysis and narrative. In a narrative essay, you would focus directly on your own experiences in making friends of a former enemy. In a process analysis essay, in contrast, you would focus on general strategies, with examples drawn from a variety of situations. Similarly, you may be expected to analyze abstract processes in fields such as history (for example, stages in the development of parliamentary democracy in Britain), psychology (stages of cognitive development), or sociology (stages of community development).

Causal analysis   Is it possible to analyze my subject according to its causes and/or effects? What are those causes/effects? How are those causes/effects related? What is their significance?

Causal analysis examines the **causes** that give rise to an event, a set of data, a concept, or a theory, or the **effects** that any of these produce.

An essay topic that asks "What causes school violence?" requires you to think analytically about anti-social behaviour in schools, from bullying to more extreme forms of violence. That means going beyond the immediate circumstances (such as name calling) to identify the conditions that give rise to violent behaviour (such as the influence of popular culture or some children's psychological need to dominate in order not to feel excluded).

The causes and effects you identify may be independent of each other or interconnected. For instance, you might decide that most traffic accidents are caused by road conditions, mechanical problems, and driver error. Most accidents would fall under only one category, and so in most cases these causes would be independent of each other. In specific instances, however, all three causes could be interconnected, with one cause leading to the next: rough pavement caused a blowout, which caused the driver to panic and overcompensate. Causal connections are often difficult to prove. For a discussion of potential problems in making causal arguments, see Types of Argument in Chapter 10.

Step 2   Categorizing Material

Asking discovery questions such as the ones for systems, process, and causal analysis will help you generate lots of material for your essay. These are very broad categories, however. Often you will need to develop subcategories to provide a framework for all your specific details. In the traffic accident example, for instance, the terms "road conditions," "mechanical problems," and "driver error" give you subcategories of causes that allow you to explain groups of individual accidents. Similarly, if you are writing about a process, you will need a general term to characterize each stage. If you were explaining the process of insect growth, for example, you would divide your material into the stages identified by entomologists: egg, larva, pupa, imago.

You may find it easy to think of appropriate categories when you are writing about familiar subjects, but harder when you are writing essays for academic courses. It may help to recognize that each academic discipline focuses on particular kinds of systems, processes, and causes and effects. Part of what you learn in academic courses is the analytical categories commonly used in particular disciplines. If your subject or your discipline does not suggest appropriate categories, try these common perspectives: practical/economic, political, social, and psychological. Thinking about your subject from these perspectives can help you discover different dimensions and explain them to your readers.

Sample Topic: From Adolescence to Adulthood

Stage 1 Clarifying content analysis topics To see how you might gather material for an essay explaining a subject of general interest, let's suppose that your writing instructor has asked for a short essay (500–1000 words) on any aspect of the transition from adolescence to adulthood. The essay should be suitable for publication in a magazine called *Parents and Teens*.

Through brainstorming about your own experience and that of your friends, you have narrowed the topic to this question: What do teens need to know to live independently?

Considering the needs and interests of your audience will help you to define your approach further. Since the magazine is more likely to be read by parents than teens, you may decide that your purpose should be to inform rather than to share personal experience. In order to generalize from your own knowledge and experience as a teen or parent (or both), you will have to think analytically about your subject. You will also need to define your key term: what do you mean by "live independently"?

Stage 2 Gathering material You begin by using systems, process, and causal analysis to generate material about your subject. For each type of analysis, you group your ideas into relevant subcategories.

Categorizing the Parts of a System Is it possible to see my subject as a system that can be divided into parts?

You could think of living independently as a complex system of skills and relationships, since even a person living alone is part of a social network. Choosing the most relevant of the common perspectives discussed above, you categorize your material like this:

Economic/Practical skills	Managing time
	Managing money
	Basic housekeeping
	Basic shopping/cooking
Social skills	Getting along with others at work or school
	Getting along with roommates/ landlords/neighbours

Psychological skills	Self-motivation instead of external motivation
	Knowing when and how to ask for help

This way of analyzing your subject would lead you to a thesis about the kinds of skills teens need to make a successful transition from living at home to living independently.

Categorizing the Steps in a Process Is it possible to see my subject as a process that can be divided into stages?

Another way to analyze the subject of living independently is to examine the process by which adolescents move from being part of a family to living on their own. You divide this process into three stages:

STAGE 1   PLANNING

Economic/Practical	*Social*	*Psychological*
Investigating housing market	Discussing plans with family, friends	Assessing pros and cons of independent living
Securing money for for rent/damage deposit		Deciding to give up security for greater independence
Budgeting for living expenses		

STAGE 2   MAKING ARRANGEMENTS

Economic/Practical	*Social*	*Psychological*
Finding affordable housing	Enlisting help of family, friends	Dealing with anxiety, disappointment, delays
Meeting tenancy requirements		
Acquiring household goods		
Arranging for utilities and other services		

STAGE 3   MAINTAINING A HOUSEHOLD

Economic/Practical	*Social*	*Psychological*
Paying rent and bills on time	Being responsible tenant and neighbour	Dealing with day-to-day stress
Providing necessities: food, clothing, laundry, etc.	Maintaining social relationships	Increased self-confidence

This analysis gives you a different angle on your subject, emphasizing the ongoing struggles teens experience rather than the skills they may or may not have.

Categorizing Causes and Effects   Can I divide my subject into its causes and/or effects? If so, how can I categorize them?

If you considered the subject of living independently in terms of its causes and effects, you might come up with ideas like these:

Economic/Practical causes	Need to live closer to school or work
Economic effects	Less money for discretionary spending
	Lower standard of living
	More control over finances
Social causes	Family pressure
	Media pressure
	Peer pressure
Social effects	Alienation from family
	Formation of new social relationships
Psychological causes	Need for greater autonomy
	Rebellion against parental authority
	Desire for new experiences
Psychological effects	Increased sense of competence (if transition successful)
	Loss of intimacy, feelings of failure (if not successful)

This material might lead you to a thesis about why teens want to live independently or how parents can help to ensure a successful transition.

As you can see, systems, process, and causal analysis can stimulate your thinking about your subject and allow you to develop a fresh perspective. For a short essay, you might focus on one aspect of your subject, such as the economic causes and effects of living independently. For a longer essay, you might want to include a broader range of causes and effects or to examine the subject as both a system and a process. Gathering material in this way encourages you to think analytically about your subject.

In Chapters 4 and 5 we will demonstrate how to draft and revise an essay on this topic.

B. READING ANALYTICALLY

Stage 1 Honing Your Reading Skills

Most of the material you need for writing essays in college and university will come from written sources. The reading you do will likely be much more difficult than your reading for high school. You may find the concepts new and the vocabulary unfamiliar. Or you may grasp the details but miss the overall point.

The guidelines below will help you to analyze, and therefore to understand, what you read. This ability is crucial when you are asked to explain, compare, or evaluate ideas and events you have read about (see Chapter 9, Writing Comparison Essays, and Chapter 10, Evaluating Arguments and Writing Critiques). It is an indispensable skill when you are writing research papers (see Chapter 12, Gathering Material for Research Papers). It will also aid you in explaining the relation between content and form when you are writing about literature and film (see Chapter 6, Using Textual Analysis to Gather Material). The readings in Part 2 provide many opportunities for you to practise the skills we outline below.

Stage 2 Gathering Material: Analyzing Nonfiction Sources

Step 1   Figuring Out the Basic Ideas

What is the writer's *subject*?

Check the Title For most nonfiction, you will find the answer to this question in the title or first few paragraphs. The titles of scholarly books and articles, for example, customarily state their subject: "The Effects of Television Violence on Preschoolers"; "Masculine Roles in Pat Barker's War Trilogy"; *Ukrainian Settlements in Ontario, 1870–1900*.

Not all titles, however, will identify the writer's subject so precisely. Writing intended for a general audience may have a title designed to create interest or convey the writer's attitude rather than state a subject, as in Maggie Black's "Wanted: The Right to Refuse" (Readings). Other titles may be ironic or otherwise misleading, as in W. S. Merwin's "Unchopping a Tree" (Readings).

Check the Introductory Paragraph(s) Because titles can be misleading, it's always a good idea to check the first few paragraphs to confirm or correct your sense of the writer's subject. If, for example, you relied on the title of E. M. Forster's "My Wood" (Readings), you might say that Forster's subject is a piece of property he owns. From reading the introduction, however, you would find that Forster states his subject in three ways: "What is the effect of property on the character? ... If you own things, what's their effect on you? What's the effect on me of my wood?" This introduction makes it clear that Forster is using his own experience to illustrate a broader moral question. You might say, then, that his subject is the effects of owning things on a person's character.

Check Your Sense of the Whole Sometimes identifying the subject won't be easy, either because the writer seems to discuss several subjects or because the details are so fascinating that you lose the big picture. Try to think about the work as a whole. How would you describe its particular focus, in ten words or less? Consider, for instance, Keeshig-Tobias' "He Was a Boxer When I Was Small" (Readings). On one level, of course, the subject is obvious—she is writing about her father. But lots of people write about their fathers. How would you describe her particular focus?

Reviewing your sense of the whole will help you to avoid distorting what you read by assuming the first subject the writer mentions is the actual subject, or by overemphasizing a minor point.

What is the writer's *main idea* about the subject?

Check for an Explicitly Stated Thesis Reread the piece, focusing on the main point the author is making about the subject. You may find a one- or two-sentence **thesis statement** in the introduction (as in David Suzuki's "It Always Costs"); in the conclusion (as in Forster's "My Wood"); or at another appropriate point (as in George Orwell's "Shooting an Elephant").

To make sure you understand what you have read, restate the thesis in your own words. By the time you reach the end of "My Wood," for example, you may recognize that the phrases "enormously stout, endlessly avaricious, pseudo-creative, intensely selfish" summarize Forster's thesis about the effects of owning property. But can you explain what Forster means by those terms in your own words? If so, you can be confident you understand his main idea.

Restating the thesis and main points in your own words not only ensures that you understand the material but also reduces the temptation to keep quoting sentence after sentence. Use brief quotations sparingly to give a sense of the writer's tone or to define a key term that you then explain. Make sure you include the page reference for all quotations. For further information about how to handle quotations, see Documenting Material: Understanding Plagiarism in Chapter 13, and Quotations in Part 3, Handbook for Final Editing.

If you do not understand a key term, you may miss the overall point of the piece. In the Readings, we have defined many terms for you. When you encounter unfamiliar terms in your course materials, you can look them up in your textbook or in a specialized dictionary like those listed in the Annotated Survey of Reference Sources, Part 4.

Make an Implied Thesis Explicit In pieces that are ironic, humorous, or based on personal experience, the main idea is often strongly **implied** but not stated directly. In "Unchopping a Tree," for example, the absurdity of the process Merwin describes clearly suggests an opposite meaning. But you will not find a sentence or two that spells out Merwin's point.

What do you do if there is not an explicitly stated thesis? You may have a strong enough sense of the whole to sum up its main idea from an initial reading. You will often get a more accurate sense, however, if you examine the work more closely. Jot down your initial ideas, then reconsider them after you have completed your analysis.

How does the writer *develop* this main idea?   Understanding how the writer organizes material to illustrate the main points will help you to see the relation between main points and supporting details. Pay particular attention to typographical devices such as headings, to key terms in topic sentences, and to transitions. Focus on the ideas being presented, not the details. Write a sentence or two explaining the main idea of each section in your own words.

There are six main methods writers use in developing ideas in non-fiction.

1. Telling a Story   What are the main stages in the narrative? What point does the writer make (or what point can you make) about each stage?

In nonfiction, a narrative is a (true) story told to illustrate a point. It has a beginning and an end and several incidents in between. The incidents are usually grouped into stages, marked by significant external or internal changes. Summarize the *point* made by each of the main stages: not "The first section tells about their first week kayaking up the Mackenzie" but "In their first week kayaking [stage], they had to learn to work as a team [point]."

- Key transitions

  Time words, such as *before, after, one morning, the next day*

  Example: Orwell, "Shooting an Elephant" (Readings)

2. Describing a Process   What are the main stages in the process? What point does the writer make (or what point can you make) about each stage?

A process has a beginning and an end and can be divided into stages marked by significant changes. Summarize the point made by each of the main stages: not "The next stage is denial" but "The writer explains the next stage, denial, as the mind's attempt to protect the body from feeling pain."

- Key transitions

  First, next, third, final step/stage

  Example: Alison Gopnik, "Kiddy Thinks" (analyzed below)

3. Developing a Chain of Reasoning What are the main points or stages in the argument?

A **chain of reasoning** is a series of interconnected points, each one necessary for establishing the point that follows. Here's an example: "I have to eat to live. I can't eat unless I have money. The only way to get money is to rob a bank. Therefore I am justified in robbing a bank." As you can see, to make the conclusion convincing—"I am justified in robbing a bank"—the writer would have to persuade readers to accept each step in the argument. If there are weak links in the chain—as in this example—readers will reject the conclusion.

The need to establish each step often makes works based on a chain of reasoning difficult to follow. The writer may define terms, discuss alternative possibilities, or refute opposing arguments. These sections may distract you from the main line of the argument or explanation. Use the writer's thesis as a guide to the points to watch for. Summarize each one. Pay careful attention to transitions that suggest the writer is indicating *disagreement* or *qualification*.

- Key transitions

  Words indicating cause and effect, such as *therefore, consequently, as a result*; words indicating disagreement or qualification, such as *although, while it is true that, despite*

  Example: Garrett Hardin, "Lifeboat Ethics: The Case Against Helping the Poor" (Readings)

4. Comparing and Contrasting What are the main similarities and differences the writer discusses?

Comparisons, as we explain in greater detail in Chapter 9, can be organized by the block method or the point-by-point method. Look for similar kinds of material about each subject. Make sure you note both similarities and differences.

- Key terms and transitions

  Compare, contrast, similar, different, in contrast, on the other hand, similarly, likewise

  Example: John Fraser, "Save the Last Dance" (Readings)

5. Listing a Series of Points What are the points? Writers often state in the introduction how they have divided their material: "Bodybuilding has four main effects." "There are three basic reasons for opposing medically assisted suicide." "Early settlers built two types of shelters." Summarize each section in a sentence or two.

- Key transitions

  Number words, such as *first, second, third*; other words signalling addition, such as *also, furthermore, most important*

  Example: Forster, "My Wood" (Readings)

6. Showing How the Parts of a Whole Work Together What are the main parts? What point does the writer make (or what point can you make) about each part?

As you have seen above, anything composed of parts that work together to create a whole can be considered a system. Writers often divide their subject into parts and discuss each part in a clearly identified section of their work, such as a chapter in a book or a block of paragraphs in an essay. Identify each main part and summarize the point the writer makes about it: not "Penal institutions are one aspect of the criminal justice system" but "Penal institutions, according to the writer, are the weakest link in the criminal justice system."

- Key terms and transitions

   The parts to be discussed may be identified in the introduction. Watch for the repetition of key terms and for terms such as these: *aspect, element, feature, part*

   Example: Judith Fetterley, "A Rose for 'A Rose for Emily'" (Readings)

If the work you are reading does not seem to fit one of these six patterns, don't despair. Some pieces, especially long ones, may combine different types of development. Some may simply not be well organized. Do your best to identify and summarize the main points.

What are the main types of evidence/detail the writer uses? For what purpose(s)? Each main point in a piece of nonfiction writing will be developed through **evidence** and **details** of the kinds listed below. The term *evidence* describes the specific information used to support an argument (think of the evidence offered in a murder trial). The term *details* refers specifically to particular actions in narratives and particular images in descriptions; more broadly, it refers to any material that explains or illustrates a general statement. Details may become evidence when used for a persuasive purpose (think of a prosecuting attorney reviewing the details of a murder case to decide which ones can be used as evidence of the defendant's guilt).

How much attention you pay to specific details will depend on your purpose in reading. If you are writing a research paper, specific information may be as useful to you as the writer's ideas on the subject. If you are studying for an exam, you may focus more on general principles, with a few selected facts or examples. If you are writing a summary of the piece as an assignment, you may be more interested in the *kinds* or *quality* of the evidence/details than in the specific information.

Note in a sentence or two which of these main types of evidence/detail the writer uses, and for what purpose.

- Examples

  Specific instances that illustrate a general point or principle. Taking a lost wallet to the police station could be used as an example of honesty.

- Facts and figures

  Specific information such as names of people, places, events; titles of publications and names of characters

  Precise numbers, as in measurements, statistics, dates

  Research studies and other "hard" evidence

- Quotations and other references to authorities

  Quotations from people interviewed or texts consulted

  References to recognized authorities on the subject or to authoritative texts (such as the Bible, the Koran), without direct quotation

- Narrative/descriptive details

  In telling a story or describing something, a writer may use few details (as in Caesar's "I came, I saw, I conquered") or many, as in an account of kayaking from Alaska to Tierra del Fuego. The details may seem fresh and vivid or flat and clichéd. The writer may use details for purposes such as creating suspense and conveying emotion.

- Other: definitions, analogies, allusions

  To make their explanations clearer, their arguments more persuasive, or their experiences more vivid, writers may define terms, provide analogies (the behaviour of gas molecules is like the behaviour of people in an elevator), or make passing references (allusions) to well-known historical figures and events ("My hopes sank like the *Titanic*"). For more on analogies, see Kinds of Evidence, Chapter 10; for more on allusions, see the discussion of Style, Chapter 6.

For suggestions about how to evaluate a writer's arguments and evidence, see Chapter 10, Evaluating Arguments and Writing Critiques.

Step 2 Gaining a Broader Perspective

Once you've figured out the basic ideas in a piece of nonfiction, it's time to stand back and take another look at the work as a whole. As a result of considering the work's **purpose** and **tone**, you may modify your sense of the work's subject or thesis. Thinking about the work's

context may lead you to a deeper understanding. After you've reread or thought about the whole piece, write a sentence or two answering these questions.

Purpose   Is the writer's main purpose to inform, to persuade, or to share personal experience? In "Kiddy Thinks" (Readings), for example, Gopnik's purpose is to explain the stages in children's cognitive development. In "It Always Costs" (Readings), on the other hand, Suzuki's main purpose is to persuade readers to accept his views. Keeshig-Tobias' purpose in "He Was a Boxer When I Was Small" (Readings) is to share her memories of her father and her insights into his behaviour. Consider these possibilities carefully. You may discover that works seemingly designed to explain or to share personal experience are actually making a persuasive point.

In summarizing, choose words that show you understand the author's purpose. Use the author's name every few sentences to make clear you are stating another person's ideas, not your own.

PURPOSE	WORDS THAT CONVEY PURPOSE
To inform	Explains, discusses, examines, analyzes
To persuade	Argues, claims, makes the point, criticizes
To share experience	Tells the story, reflects upon, describes

Context: Subject   What knowledge of the subject or the cultural/historical circumstances can you bring to your understanding of the work?

Take a few minutes to consider how the piece fits with other things you know about the subject. Perhaps you've seen the movie *The English Patient.* Do you agree or disagree with the opinions expressed by other viewers? (See *"The English Patient* Debate" in Readings). Or perhaps your knowledge of the ongoing "troubles" in Northern Ireland could enrich your understanding of Jonathan Swift's "A Modest Proposal" (Readings).

Context: Writer   What do you know about the writer? Does the writer mention the source of his or her knowledge about the subject? Does the writer identify herself/himself with a specific political, religious, or intellectual position? What does the work itself suggest about the writer's perspective?

Writers often give some indication of the experience or training that qualifies them to speak about their subject, as you can see in the pieces by Ken Wiwa ("Choosing Up Sides") and Suzuki ("It Always Costs," both in Readings). They may also identify the political, religious, or intellectual framework that guides their thinking, such as

Fetterley's feminist perspective on "A Rose for Emily" (Readings). The writer's perspective may be implied rather than stated. For example, Forster's biblical allusions in "My Wood" (Readings) suggest a particular religious framework. Considering these questions will help you to see the values that inform the piece of writing.

Step 3   Writing a Summary

When you finish your analysis, use your notes to write a brief summary of the piece. The summary will help you remember what you've read. You may also incorporate the summary, or parts of it, in your essay. This summary should include the following:

1. Complete bibliographical information about the piece: author, title, and other details as appropriate for the type of publication (see Documentation in Part 3, Handbook for Final Editing).
2. The writer's thesis, in your own words, near the beginning of the summary.
3. An overview of the organization of the piece and the main points in each section. State these points in your own words but include brief quotations to capture the tone of the piece. Put quotation marks around any three or more consecutive words from the piece. If the piece is longer than a page, give page numbers in parentheses after each quotation and paraphrase. Page numbers are handy in case you need to refer to specific material again. They are crucial when you are documenting research papers.
4. The main types of evidence and an explanation of their purpose.
5. Key terms and their definitions.

For an example, see the sample topic below.

Sample Topic: Analyzing the Content of Alison Gopnik's "Kiddy Thinks"

Gopnik's article "Kiddy Thinks" (first published in the *Guardian Weekly,* February 3–9, 2000) is reprinted in the Readings. You will follow this example more easily if you read Gopnik's article first.

Step 1   Figuring Out the Basic Ideas

What is the subject?   The title suggests that the article is about children and thinking. The sentences in the boxed text on page 247 tell us that the author, Alison Gopnik, is a developmental psychologist. We would therefore expect this article to be about the stages at which the thinking abilities of babies change.

What is the main idea? Gopnik states her thesis quite clearly at the end of her introduction. Here she says the traditional view that babies and young children think quite differently from adults is wrong. Babies are not passive little blank slates; instead they use the same strategies that scientists use to understand both people and their environment.

How does the writer develop this main idea? Gopnik develops her thesis through process analysis. Step by step, she sets out the stages at which babies and young children acquire specific thinking skills. As she explains each stage, Gopnik also shows how babies "observe, formulate theories, make predictions, and do experiments" (247). Like adult scientists, babies can also change their theories if they get enough evidence to contradict them.

What are the main types of evidence/detail the writer uses? For what purpose(s)? For the most part, Gopnik relies on examples taken from her experiences as a parent and from her work as a developmental psychologist. Because these examples are specific and involve familiar situations (the baby reaching for the lamp cord), they provide evidence many readers would find convincing. Gopnik also establishes her own credentials as an expert in the cognitive development of children by mentioning near the beginning of this essay that she co-authored a book titled *How Babies Think*.

Step 2   Gaining a Broader Perspective

Purpose Gopnik's main purpose is to provide readers with information on how children develop crucially important cognitive skills: the awareness that they are people with thoughts and feelings who live with other people who have both similar and different thoughts and feelings; the awareness that the predictions they make about reality may or may not be accurate.

Context Traditional assumptions about children's inability to think rationally are part of the academic context of this essay. Gopnik says that "in the past 30 years we have learned more about what young children know and how they learn than we did in the preceding 2,500 years. And this has revolutionised our view of children" (247). She ends her article with the social context. Many parents (the most likely readers of this essay) feel anxious and guilty about their ability to spend time with their children. Should parents quit their jobs? Should they take courses and buy educational toys and equipment for their children? While Gopnik is reassuring, she makes the point that more flexible work schedules and government funding for high-quality daycare would make it easier for parents to give children the attention they deserve.

Step 3   Writing a Summary

Now that you have gathered information for an analysis of a piece of nonfiction, you can clarify the connections among your points by writing a summary.

SAMPLE SUMMARY

"KIDDY THINKS"

Alison Gopnik's essay "Kiddy Thinks" (*Guardian Weekly*, February 3–9, 2000) sets out the stages at which babies and young children acquire crucial thinking skills. The major stages of this cognitive development are as follows: at birth babies know that adults are like them; at nine months babies can differentiate happiness, sadness, and anger, and they watch the adults around them for clues as to how they should respond; between fourteen months and eighteen months babies begin to understand that other people may think and feel differently than they do; two-year-olds spend much of their time testing that knowledge, but they aren't very good at hiding objects; three-year-olds understand the concept of hiding objects; four-year-olds understand that objects aren't always what they appear.

As Gopnik explains each step, she presents examples from personal experience and from her experiments as a developmental psychologist as evidence to support her thesis that even young babies use sophisticated and rational thinking skills. Gopnik suggests that babies behave like adult scientists as they "observe, formulate theories, make predictions, and do experiments" (247). Like adult scientists, babies change their theories if they get enough evidence to contradict them. Gopnik concludes her essay by urging readers to support flexible work schedules and government-funded, high-quality daycare so that parents can give these tiny scientists the attention they deserve.

Working on Your Own Assignment

The purpose of content analysis is to come to a better understanding of the nature and significance of your material by dividing it into relevant parts.

- Gain a better grasp of your subject by analyzing it as a system, a process, a series of causes and effects. Which type of analysis, or which combination, is most appropriate?

- Think about your subject from different perspectives, such as social, psychological, economic, political. Which perspective, or combination of perspectives, will give you the richest insights?

- Make more effective use of your material by analyzing its content: figure out the basic ideas; enrich your understanding by considering purpose, tone, and context; write a summary that will help you remember what you read.

EXERCISES

A.   Use systems, process, or causal analysis to generate material for a content analysis essay on one of the following topics. Consider your subject from a variety of perspectives (economic, social, political, psychological). Compare your responses with those of your classmates. Save this material for possible use in connection with Chapter 4.

- Patenting human genes
- Fast foods
- The gap between rich and poor
- Bodybuilding

B.   Write a summary of one of the following essays from Part 2, Readings. Use the sample topic above as a guide.

- Maggie Black, "Wanted: The Right to Refuse"
- Ross Laver, "Profits by the Truckload"
- David Suzuki, "It Always Costs"

C.   Write two or three sentences identifying the major strengths and weaknesses of each of the following summaries. Then revise the summaries. You will find the two essays, Ann Dowsett Johnston's "A Lament for Quality" and E. M. Forster's "My Wood," in Part 2, Readings.

1. In her essay "A Lament for Quality" Ann Dowsett Johnston is upset by the fact that her son would have to go to the United States to get a good university education. She says that government cutbacks have made it impossible for her son to get the kind of education she had. She thinks tuition should be raised so that her son will be able to attend a university with small classes like she had when she was in university.

2. "What is the effect of property on the character?" (238) E. M. Forster asks in "My Wood," and then proceeds to give us the answer. "In the first place, it makes me feel heavy" (238), he says, referring to the fact that owning things weighs people down both physically and morally. "In the second place, it makes me feel it ought to be larger" (239), he continues. "A little more, and then a little more" (239), he says, pointing to our greed for more and more possessions. Furthermore, "property makes its owner feel that he ought to do something with it" (239). He realizes, however, that his impulse to change things "spring[s] from a foolish desire to express myself and from an inability to enjoy what I have got" (239). The final effect of property is to make a person selfish. As Forster says, "I shall wall in and fence out until I really taste the sweets of property" (240). He sums it all up by saying that his property has made him "[e]normously stout, endlessly avaricious, pseudo-creative, intensely selfish" (240).

chapter 4

Writing Content Analysis Essays I: Formulating a Thesis Statement and Drafting

Stage 1   Clarifying Content Analysis Topics

Stage 2   Gathering Material

Stage 3   Formulating a Tentative Thesis
           Statement
           Step 1 Forming an Opinion
           Step 2 Supporting Your Opinion

Stage 4   Drafting
           Step 1 Selecting Material and Making
                   Points
           Step 2 Organizing Your Material
           Step 3 Making a Draft Outline
           Step 4 Drafting Individual Paragraphs

Stage 5   Revising Thesis and Essay Structure

Stage 6   Revising Individual Paragraphs

Stage 7   Final Editing

In Chapter 3 we discussed the first two stages of writing content analysis essays: Clarifying Content Analysis Topics and Gathering Material. This chapter will show you how to use your material to formulate a thesis statement and draft an essay. The principles discussed below will apply to most of the writing you do for college and university courses. In later chapters you will find suggestions for adapting these basic principles for specific types of essays: analyses of texts (Chapter 7); comparisons (Chapter 9); critiques (Chapter 10); persuasive essays (Chapter 11); and research papers (Chapter 13).

Stage 3   Formulating a Tentative Thesis Statement

At the heart of every essay, as we pointed out in Chapter 1, is the writer's thesis, the main idea that gives shape and meaning to the piece of writing. Writers of informal essays (essays based on personal experience) may not state their thesis directly, leaving readers to work out how details add up to a main idea. In formal academic writing, in contrast, readers expect to find a *thesis statement*, usually one or two sentences stating the writer's *opinion* about the subject and the main *reasons* or *support* for that opinion. We will demonstrate how to arrive at a tentative thesis statement that will serve as the starting point for drafting your essay.

Step 1   Forming an Opinion

An opinion is a belief or judgment based on your *interpretation* of events, ideas, behaviour, or other phenomena. Consider a simple example. "The temperature is 30°C" is a statement of fact; the statement can be proved to be true or false. "It's too hot for a hike" is a statement of opinion; your hiking partner might disagree, but the opinion would nevertheless be true for you. Similarly, if you were writing an essay on the First World War, you would not try to prove the point that particular battles were fought on particular days. That information is a matter of fact, not of opinion. But not everyone agrees about the main causes of the war. So your thesis might be that the main causes of the war were economic rather than political.

When you are writing about familiar subjects, you may have an opinion before you begin. When the subject is new to you, as in most academic writing, your opinion usually emerges as you perceive connections among the categories you have used for your analysis. From the material you generated by analyzing the topic of living independently as a system, as a process, and as a set of causes and effects, for instance, you might arrive at opinions like these:

- Living independently requires a wide range of skills [systems analysis].

- Learning to live independently is a complex process [process analysis].

- Moving away from home to live independently can create both difficulties and opportunities [causal analysis].

As you can see, opinions by themselves are incomplete, and therefore not very interesting. They become interesting only when they are shaped by the requirements of the essay topic and the reasons that support them.

In the excitement of generating ideas, you may have lost sight of the specific focus of your assignment. Before you go any further, check your opinion against your essay topic to make sure you are still on track. In the sample topic we have been working with (see p. 28), the instructor asked for an essay on "any aspect of the *transition* from adolescence to adulthood." Does each thesis opinion above illuminate an aspect of this transition? Yes, they do: they show that the transition involves skills, is complex, and can create both difficulties and opportunities. If you have several possibilities for a thesis opinion, and each represents a good gathering of material and is an appropriate response to the assignment, then you should choose the one that you are most interested in exploring. For the sample topic, you might decide to focus on skills because in gathering material you discovered less obvious skills that you and your readers could explore.

Step 2 Supporting Your Opinion

A good thesis statement requires not only an opinion but also one or more reasons to support it. Without the reasons that emphasize your particular interpretation of your subject, a thesis opinion merely sounds like a vague generalization, as you can tell from the examples above. If you want your reader to be interested in what you have to say and to take your opinion seriously, you have to give good reasons.

Your reasons will be a short form of the points you plan to develop in detail in the body of your essay. At this stage of the writing process, you may not have worked through your material completely enough to give precise reasons. You can often use the general categories or subcategories of your analysis to guide you as you write your draft. If you added the categories of your systems analysis to the corresponding thesis opinion above, you would come up with a tentative thesis statement like this:

- Living independently requires a wide range of skills, not only practical skills, but also social and psychological ones.

This tentative thesis statement now includes both an opinion and the main points you will cover in your essay. It still sounds quite mechanical, however, because it lacks the specific insights that would distinguish your essay on this topic from another writer's. Writing a draft often helps you to clarify and deepen your thinking about your subject. In Chapter 5 you will see how to revise your thesis statement to incorporate new insights and to make it more forceful.

Stage 4 Drafting

Write your draft well before your essay is due. It's tempting to wait until you feel inspired or until the night before the due date, but it's better to take a cue from professional writers. They cannot afford to wait for inspiration, nor do they expect to produce a perfect piece of writing the first time. Their method is almost always to write out a rough draft, let it sit for a while, and then submit it to a process of revision and fine-tuning. This is the method we recommend.

Some writers find an outline helpful at this stage. In this chapter we will show how to develop a *draft outline* to guide the process of drafting. Others prefer to freewrite a draft and then use a *revision outline* to organize their material. We will illustrate this method in Chapter 5.

Since you will eventually revise what you have written, let the writing flow, even if you find yourself departing from your outline or mental plan. You may discover new and better ideas as you write. You can revise your thesis statement, structure, and individual paragraphs when you finish drafting (see Chapter 5). Resist the temptation to polish sentences that you may discard when you revise.

Step 1   Selecting Material and Making Points

In formulating your tentative thesis statement, you focus on the categories of your analysis that provide the best support for your thesis. You may discover, however, that these categories give you too much material. It is always better to explain a few points in depth than to skim over a great many. In a short essay (500–1000 words), you can usually develop two to five main points. Thus the first step in writing a draft is to consider which topics and material to include.

- Take another look at the material generated by analyzing the subject of living independently as a system of skills (Chapter 3). If you tried to include all these ideas in a short essay, you could only do so superficially. You might decide to simplify the three topics. First you might group the *practical skills* into basic housekeeping and managing skills. The *social skills* category contains two different ideas: getting along with people of the same generation, and getting along with people outside that generation. You might decide to focus on the second, which seems the more demanding skill. The *psychological* category poses the same problem. Again you might decide to focus on one of the two issues, the issue of acquiring self-motivation.

Before you go any further you need to be sure that you can relate your topics to your thesis statement. This means you need to turn your material into point(s) about each topic, and then check that each point supports the thesis.

- From your selections you come up with the following topics and points:

MAKING POINTS ABOUT TOPICS

Topic	Point
Practical skills	Basic housekeeping and management skills are immediately required on moving away from home
Social skills	It is important to get on with people of different generations when living independently
Psychological skills	It is vital to develop self-motivation for successful independent living

Step 2 Organizing Your Material

There are three issues to consider about organizing your material:

- Whether to organize your essay deductively or inductively
- What method of development to choose
- How to present your points in an effective sequence

In each case, the audience for which you are writing will influence your choices.

Choosing deductive or inductive structure When you argue deductively, you start with a principle and then support it with reasons and evidence. When you use deductive structure in an essay, you start with your thesis and then give reasons to support it, usually through a series of points and evidence. Most academic writing follows this pattern (for an example, see Judith Fetterley's "A Rose for 'A Rose for Emily,'"

Readings). You will find deductive structure appropriate for writing essays and research papers in academic courses where your audience—your instructor and sometimes classmates—is familiar with the subject and wants to know your interpretation of it.

In contrast, when you reason inductively, you start from a specific case or cases and move towards the principles involved. To organize an essay inductively, you present events, points, or details first and withhold the thesis to be derived from them until later. Inductive structure is often used to create interest in narrative and descriptive essays (for an example, see George Orwell's "Shooting an Elephant," Readings). It is also used in persuasive essays to encourage readers to consider a viewpoint to which they might be hostile, as in Wade Davis's essay "The Ticking Bomb" (Readings).

Choosing a method of development As we discussed in the section on analyzing nonfiction writing in Chapter 3 (30–38), there are six main methods writers use in developing ideas in nonfiction:

1. Telling a story
2. Describing a process
3. Developing a chain of reasoning
4. Comparing and contrasting
5. Listing a series of points
6. Showing how parts of a whole work together

Which method you choose will depend on what your audience is, and, if you are in an academic setting, what your assignment is and what choices you yourself make. For process, causal, and systems analysis, clearly the second, third, and sixth methods are the most relevant. For a personal essay, telling the story of an incident or encounter might be very appropriate, while an informal editorial for the student newspaper might be based on listing a series of points. Comparing and contrasting are specialized methods of development which we discuss in Chapter 9.

Sequencing your draft effectively The first three of the methods of development present few problems in organizing your material. When you write a narrative essay or describe a process, you usually begin at the beginning and go through to the end. Similarly, when you develop a chain of reasoning such as a causal argument, you have to establish one point before your readers can understand the next. In each case, you are likely to end with the material you want to emphasize—the climax of the story, the final stage of the process, or the culminating point in your argument.

With the other three methods of development, the best order for presenting your material may not be so obvious. The most common arrangement for these types of essays is an **order of ascending interest**. You begin with your least important point and end with your most important. That way, you more easily keep your readers' attention and leave the strongest impression.

- In thinking about the skills for living independently, for example, you might decide that both parents and teens would acknowledge the need for practical skills, so that this is the topic you should put last in your draft. If you assume that neither teens nor parents would see psychological skills as relevant to the transition, you might decide to put this topic first.

The basic decisions about organizing material—choosing deductive or inductive structure and sequencing your points effectively—are ones you will face no matter what kind of essay you are writing. Some types of essays raise other considerations as well. You will find suggestions for organizing comparison essays in Chapter 9; for using pro-con structure to organize a persuasive essay in Chapter 11; and for organizing research papers in Chapter 13.

Step 3   Making a Draft Outline

At this point, you may find it useful to make a *draft outline* to guide you as you write your draft. Put your tentative thesis statement at the top of the page; remember to change the sequence of support if necessary in response to decisions you have made about organizing your draft. Then list your main points and subpoints in the sequence you have decided upon. You may also want to note the most important detail that supports each point, such as specific examples, references to authorities, and so forth.

- A draft outline for the essay on living independently might look like this:

DRAFT OUTLINE

Tentative thesis statement: Living independently requires a wide range of skills, psychological and social skills, and, most immediately, practical skills.

TOPIC	POINT
Psychological skills	It is vital to develop self-motivation for successful independent living
Social skills	It is important to get on with people of different generations when living independently

Practical skills	Basic housekeeping and management skills are immediately required on moving away from home

Step 4   Drafting Individual Paragraphs

Don't get stuck trying to write perfect sentences. It might help you to realize that this is the *least* important step of the drafting process. Allow time after you have revised your draft to give your essay a final edit. The chart at the beginning of Part 3, Handbook for Final Editing (373–374), suggests common problems to be aware of.

Sketching introductions   You can sketch out an introduction by writing a sentence or two on the context of your topic and then stating your thesis (if you are giving your essay a deductive structure), or asking the question your essay will answer (if you are using an inductive structure). If you can't get started without a polished introduction, consult Revising Your Introduction, Chapter 5.

Drafting middle paragraphs   Use each point in your draft outline as the basis for a topic sentence for one or more paragraphs. Paragraphs, like essays, can be organized either deductively or inductively, and so your topic sentence may appear at the beginning or end of the paragraph. When you are writing analytical essays, try not to bury your topic sentence in the middle of a paragraph where your main point may be overlooked. Explain the point fully by such methods as defining terms, referring to authorities, and providing additional information. Support each point by giving examples, citing facts and figures, and using other specific details (for a fuller discussion of how writers develop their material, see Reading Analytically, Chapter 3).

Sketching conclusions   Rather than slapping a perfunctory summary on your draft, let your thinking carry you naturally into your conclusion. Often ideas come together as you write, and a better thesis emerges—if you let it.

When you have finished your draft, let it sit for a day or two. Then revise it, using the suggestions in Chapter 5 as a guide.

Working on Your Own Assignment

- Formulate a tentative thesis statement by figuring out what main idea connects the categories you have used for your analysis.
- Decide what points to make and how to organize them.
- Make a draft outline to keep you on track as you write.
- Quickly write a draft, paying most attention to developing your middle paragraphs.

EXERCISES

A. Respond to each of the following in a sentence or two.

1. Explain the difference between a fact and an opinion, using an example of your own.

2. What is a thesis statement?

3. What are the advantages of writing a draft?

4. Explain the difference between inductive structure and deductive structure. How would you decide which one to use?

5. Define the term "order of ascending interest" and give an example.

B. Review the material you gathered in Chapter 3, Exercise 1, and formulate one or more tentative thesis statements for an essay on the topic you chose. Compare your thesis statement(s) with those written by classmates who chose the same topic. Does each tentative thesis statement express an opinion? Does it give reasons to support that opinion?

C. Work out a draft outline for an essay on the topic you have chosen. Put your thesis statement at the top of the page. List your main points in the order you plan to discuss them. Note the most important evidence you will use to support each point.

D. Write a draft of your essay, paying particular attention to developing each of your points. Keep your draft for later use.

chapter 5

Writing Content
Analysis Essays 2:
Revising Your Draft

Stage 1   Clarifying Content Analysis Topics

Stage 2   Gathering Material

Stage 3   Formulating a Tentative Thesis
           Statement

Stage 4   Drafting

Stage 5   Revising Thesis Statement and Essay
           Structure
           Step 1   Making a Revision Outline
           Step 2   Revising Your Thesis Statement
           Step 3   Revising Essay Structure

Stage 6   Revising Individual Paragraphs
           Step 1   Revising Your Introduction
           Step 2   Revising Middle Paragraphs
           Step 3   Revising Your Conclusion

Stage 7   Final Editing

Revision means literally "re-vision," seeing again. When you write a first draft, you are essentially writing it for yourself, to clarify your ideas and to try out your tentative plan for the essay. If you continue reading your work from this perspective, however, you may find it hard to see what changes are needed because you know what you mean to say. To "see again," you have to be able to adopt the perspective of your reader, to evaluate what you have written as it would appear to your intended audience.

Allow enough time before the due date to let your draft sit for a day or two after you have completed Stages 1–4. You will then be able to examine it more objectively when you revise.

The goal of revision is to improve your writing on three levels:

- The conceptual level: does this essay reflect the best thinking you are capable of doing about this topic?
- The organizational level: have you organized and presented your ideas effectively?
- The stylistic level: is your writing clear, engaging, and free from errors?

This chapter will guide you through the process of evaluating and revising your work on the conceptual and organizational levels. You will find many suggestions for improving your style in Part 3, Handbook for Final Editing.

Stage 5   Revising Thesis Statement and Essay Structure

Before you begin rewriting, read through your draft to assess its overall strengths and weaknesses in content and organization. Then examine your thesis and essay structure, as outlined below, to see if you can improve the framework of ideas in your essay.

Step 1   Making a Revision Outline

You can keep track of the changes you need to make by using a revision outline—an outline of the draft you have actually written, together with suggestions for changes. Using two columns, you note in the left column the points you make in your introduction, each of your middle paragraphs, and your conclusion. Record these points exactly as they stand in the draft, not as you intended them to be. As you go through the revision process, enter suggestions for changes in the right column. You will find an example of a revision outline for the sample topic on living independently on page 56.

Step 2   Revising Your Thesis Statement

Whether you write a draft as soon as you have gathered material or follow the suggestions for formulating a tentative thesis statement given in Chapter 4, you will likely need to revise your thesis statement because writing the draft has helped you understand your subject better.

Check both the *content* of your thesis statement and its *presentation*. Does your thesis statement give an opinion with reasons to support it? Does it suggest you have a good grasp of your subject? Does it interest readers in your interpretation of your material? If you find any of the following problems, revise as indicated.

PROBLEMS WITH THESIS STATEMENTS	EXAMPLES/SOLUTIONS	
Merely restating the argument	NOT	"I will discuss some aspects of the transition from adolescence to adulthood."
	BUT	"The practical difficulties teens encounter as they move into adulthood may reflect not only gaps in their own skills and motivation but also the realities of the local economy."
Merely stating facts	NOT	"Many adolescents move out of their parents' homes."
	BUT	"Many adolescents are ambivalent about moving out of their parents' homes because of conflicting needs for security and independence."
Failing to give reasons	NOT	"There are many reasons why teens move away from home."
	BUT	"While some teens leave home to live closer to work or school, others are driven by the desire to escape dysfunctional or abusive families."
Failing to separate your opinion from other writers' opinions	NOT	"Researchers have found that adolescents often underestimate the economic difficulties of leaving home."

	BUT	"Although current research suggests that adolescents often underestimate the economic difficulties of leaving home, many teens I interviewed had made a realistic assessment of their situation and devised workable strategies for supporting themselves."
Failing to signal essay structure	REVISE	… thesis statement or paragraph order so that points follow the order suggested by the thesis statement.
No longer fits content of essay	CHECK	… for better thesis in draft conclusion.
Too vague or mechanical	NOT	"The transition from adolescence to adulthood has practical, social, and psychological dimensions that every teen must face."
	BUT	"To move successfully from adolescence to adulthood, teens must learn to identify and solve not only the practical problems of food and rent but also the social and psychological problems of maintaining healthy relationships."

The last problem, the tentative thesis statement that is too vague or mechanical, is the most common one. Writing your draft will often provide the insights you need to make your tentative thesis statement more precise and more interesting.

- Take a look at the tentative thesis statement for the draft essay on the skills teens need to live independently, for example.

  Living independently requires a wide range of skills, psychological and social skills and, most immediately, practical skills.

In the process of drafting an essay to support this thesis statement, you might well decide that the less obvious social and psychological skills were more likely to be undervalued by both parents and teens than the more obvious practical skills. You would therefore revise your thesis statement to stress the importance of these less obvious skills:

WRITING SAMPLE

Revised thesis statement: Parents and teens may both view independent living mainly as a set of practical skills to do with managing money and maintaining a household. These skills are important for making a successful transition from adolescence to adulthood, certainly, but even more important are the less obvious skills required, the social skills of getting along with others and, most of all, the psychological skill of getting along with oneself.

Step 3   Revising Essay Structure

Each of your middle paragraphs should constitute or contribute to one specific point that supports your thesis. The paragraphs should follow the order suggested by your revised thesis statement. Use the right-hand column of your revision outline to note any of these problems and revise as suggested.

PROBLEMS WITH ESSAY STRUCTURE	SOLUTIONS
Failure to paragraph	Indicate on your revision outline where each new point begins and divide your material accordingly.
Paragraphs too long	Divide paragraphs longer than half a page and use an "umbrella" topic sentence (see below).
Paragraphs too short	Combine several short paragraphs under one topic sentence or explain your points more fully (see below).
Paragraphs don't support revised thesis statement	Delete irrelevant material.
Point(s) made in revised thesis statement lack support	Add new paragraph(s).
Paragraphs don't follow order suggested in revised thesis statement	Indicate appropriate order on draft outline.
Paragraph order not effective	Show new order on draft outline.

"Umbrella" topic sentences   Sometimes you may have more material on one aspect of your subject than you can comfortably fit into a single paragraph. If a paragraph is more than half a page, you can often divide it and then use an "umbrella" topic sentence to tie related paragraphs together, as in the following example:

"Umbrella" topic sentence	Although everyone recognizes that moving out will result in a lower standard of living for teens, neither teens nor their parents may recognize the economic benefit of their having control over their own finances.
Topic sentence for paragraph A	Having less income and more to buy clearly creates economic difficulty for newly independent teens.
Topic sentence for paragraph B	The newly independent are sometimes surprised to discover, however, that it is rewarding to have control over spending, even if the spending is less; their parents may be equally surprised by their response.

- The thinking that led you to revise the thesis statement for the sample assignment also indicates that you should change the sequence of topics in your essay. Instead of an ascending order of interest that leads from least immediate to most immediate, you now want the sequence indicated in your thesis statement: from most obvious to least obvious. You can now fill in more detail on support and transitions in the right-hand column of your revision outline.

REVISION OUTLINE

TOPIC	POINT
Practical skills	Need for household management is obvious because practical skills are immediately required on moving away from home
Social skills	Harder to see that it's important to get on with people of different generations when living independently —harder to see because of hostility necessary to separate from parents —civility needed even if sympathy not there
Psychological skills	Least obvious that it's vital to develop self-motivation for successful independent living —least obvious because of teens' defining themselves against parents and by peers —necessary for a sense of vocation and direction

To see the essay that results from this revision outline, see A. Jones, "The Complex Skill of Independent Living" in Part 2, Readings: Sample Essays.

Stage 6   Revising Individual Paragraphs

Once you have revised your thesis statement and identified ways to improve your essay structure, if necessary, you are ready to consider changes to individual paragraphs.

Step 1   Revising Your Introduction

Your introduction gives your readers a chance to prepare, emotionally and intellectually, for the essay that is to follow. In the opening sentences, check that you have identified your subject and provided a *context* for your essay and the thesis statement to follow. For instance, you might give relevant background information about historical events or define a key concept. Then check that your introduction ends with your thesis statement (for deductively organized essays) or with the question your essay will answer (for inductively organized essays).

Check your introduction for the following problems:

PROBLEMS WITH INTRODUCTION	EXAMPLES/SOLUTIONS	
Sweeping generalizations	NOT	"Throughout history youths have yearned to live free from the constraints of their elders." See Chapter 10 for this and other problems with argumentation.
Mechanical statements	NOT	"In this essay I will discuss the transition ..."; "My purpose in this paper is to analyze the process ..."
	BUT	"The transition from adolescence to adulthood...."
Too much detail		Keep your introduction to four or five sentences. Save details and examples for your middle paragraphs.
Misplaced thesis statement		Don't start your introduction with your thesis statement.

- In the draft, the only context preceding the thesis statement is a brief sentence: "It is important to recognize that skills are involved in successful independent living." In revising for context, you would ask yourself what comments are necessary to set the stage for your revised thesis statement. You might decide to include a definition of successful independent living and provide a link to the essay assignment: the transition from adolescence to adulthood. Furthermore, you could put skills in the context of other ways of looking at independent living. By adding a fuller statement of context, you might come up with a revised introduction like this one:

WRITING SAMPLE

Revised introduction: An important aspect of the transition from adolescence to adulthood is independent living: setting up a workable living arrangement outside the parental home that is self-supported, to some extent at least. There are a number of ways of looking at independent living: it could be seen as a set of behaviours, a set of relationships, or a set of attitudes. Most usefully, perhaps, independent living could be seen to involve a set of skills. Understanding exactly what skills are involved in independent living may be difficult, though. Parents and teens may both view independent living mainly as a set of practical skills to do with managing money and maintaining a household. These skills are important for making a successful transition from adolescence to adulthood, certainly, but even more important are the less obvious skills required, the social skills of getting along with others and, most of all, the psychological skill of getting along with oneself.

Step 2 Revising Middle Paragraphs

Checking topic sentences

- Does each paragraph contain a topic sentence that announces the subject and makes a *point* about the subject?
- Does that point support some aspect of your thesis statement?

When you revise, make sure that each middle paragraph has a topic sentence. The topic sentence states the main idea that other sentences in the paragraph explain and support. In this way, it functions as a mini-thesis, controlling the content of the paragraph and showing how the paragraph relates to the thesis.

Paragraphs, like essays, can be organized either deductively or inductively. If your essay is organized deductively, your reader will expect your paragraphs to be organized deductively also, with your topic sentence at or near the beginning (a transitional sentence may come first). If your essay is organized inductively, many of your paragraphs may be as well, with your topic sentence at or near the end of each paragraph.

Here are potential problems to watch for:

PROBLEMS WITH TOPIC SENTENCES	EXAMPLES/SOLUTIONS
No sentence stating subject and point	Add a sentence linking the main idea of the paragraph to the thesis statement.
Subject stated, no point made	"The second stage is making arrangements." If you use a sentence like this as a transition, make sure the next sentence states your point. Better yet, combine them: "The second stage, making arrangements, requires a lot of patience and good organizational skills."
Point not linked to thesis	"Everyone needs to know how to manage money." **REVISE** to link to independent living.
Misplaced topic sentence	Don't bury topic sentences in the middle of the paragraph. Don't end a paragraph with the topic sentence for the next paragraph.

Checking paragraph development

- Is the point you make in your topic sentence sufficiently explained and supported by specific details?

Explanations serve as a bridge between main ideas and specific details. You may explain your point by defining terms, giving reasons, or moving to a subpoint. To be convincing, each point and subpoint should be supported by specific details, including facts and figures (such as names, dates, statistics); examples (such as representative instances, case studies, hypothetical examples); and quotations from or references to authorities.

PROBLEMS WITH PARAGRAPH DEVELOPMENT	SOLUTIONS
Inadequate detail	Add examples, facts and figures, quotations, or references to authorities, as appropriate
Misleading detail	For help in identifying problems such as misleading statistics and misused authorities, see Chapter 10, pp. 123–124.
Irrelevant detail	Delete details that don't support your thesis statement.
Inadequate explanations	Add definitions, reasons, subpoints, and other material as necessary.

Note on your revision outline whether each paragraph follows this movement from general point to specific details:

REVISION OUTLINE

TOPIC SENTENCE	EXPLANATIONS	SPECIFIC DETAILS
Practical skills	Buying groceries	Buying popcorn, forgetting to buy a bowl, butter

- To see how you would identify and correct problems with topic sentences and paragraph development, consider this paragraph from the draft essay on living independently:

> Buying groceries is important for teens to learn but very hard to do. Another thing that is hard is managing money in general. Parents have probably pointed out the need to budget, but when they are not around there is no one to point this out. Teen friends will not point this out and that is the problem; teens will not stretch themselves when they are living on their own to listen to anyone but their friends. They need to deal with landlords and bosses and their attitudes make this impossible.

When you check this paragraph, you find there is no topic sentence. Your subject was intended to be practical skills, but the subpoints and details relate to social skills as well. You would note these problems on your revision outline and then use these notes as a guide to revising.

WRITING SAMPLE

Revised middle paragraph: The practical skills required for independent living are obvious because they are the ones immediately required. It often comes as a shock to teens to realize how many activities and products are required to keep a household running. When they lived with their parents and wanted butter or salt to put on their popcorn, they just reached into the kitchen cupboard. Living away from their parents, they probably remember to buy the popcorn, but how about the toppings or the bowl to put it in? Not to mention, how about the money to buy these things with? Teens who have spent most of the week's money on a film and a big meal at Earl's on Tuesday night can look forward to a diet of Mr. Noodle later in the week. It does not take long for teens to realize they need to get practical skills like budgeting under control, and if they miss seeing this need, their parents will be very ready to point it out.

Step 3   Revising Your Conclusion

Many people find conclusions as hard to write as introductions. As a result, draft conclusions tend to be skimpy and mechanical. When you revise, you can make sure that your conclusion achieves its purpose: to leave your readers with a strong sense of the importance of what you have written.

A good conclusion for an academic essay generally summarizes and expands the thesis and main points and sets them within a broader context.

Does your draft conclusion reveal any of the following problems?

PROBLEMS WITH CONCLUSIONS		EXAMPLES/SOLUTIONS
Sweeping generalizations	NOT	"No problem, as we have seen, is more important to human society than the problem of making the transition from adolescence to adulthood."
Mechanical repetition of thesis and points	NOT	"In conclusion, we have seen that making the transition to living independently requires the ability to plan, to make arrangements, and to maintain a household."
No statement of wider implications		Here are some possible solutions: a) broaden the time-frame

(for example, by moving from immediate causes and effects to more distant causes and effects) b) move from a specific case to the more general category to which it belongs (for example, by suggesting that the skills necessary for living independently are the skills necessary for living a happy adult life) c) use an image to compare your subject with something memorable (for example, by comparing the process by which adolescents turn into responsible adults with the process by which caterpillars turn into butterflies).

- Let's see what happens when you apply these principles to revising the conclusion of the draft essay on living independently.

WRITING SAMPLE

Draft conclusion: In this essay I hope I have shown that living independently requires practical, social, and psychological skills. These skills are very important to have because each generation will need them, and it will be important for them to be there at that time.

This conclusion does not connect the thesis statement with the subject of the assignment and it does not reflect the way the thesis statement has been developed in the essay. Furthermore, the statement of broader implications, while true, does not emerge out of the points made in the essay. You would revise to produce a conclusion that reflects what you have discovered in the process of your analysis and what the implications of those discoveries are.

Revised conclusion: The obvious practical skill of budgeting and managing, and the less obvious social skill of getting on with people you need rather than want, are both essential to successful independent living and a successful transition from adolescence to adulthood. These skills are not, however, the whole story. It is the gradual opening up of real desires, vocation and destiny, achieved through the psychological skill of internal motivation, that provides the push to master the often tedious disciplines of household and social management. Just as psychological motivation, in the form of a desire for freedom of expression and control of one's own circumstances, is often what propels teens towards independent living, so psychological skills are key in ensuring that independent living is successfully achieved.

After you revise your conclusion, make adjustments to your introduction, if necessary, to ensure that the two are in accord. Then give your essay a final edit. The chart at the beginning of the Handbook section will help you identify problems with sentence structure, grammar, punctuation, and format.

- The sample essay that results from revisions and final editing is A. Jones, "The Complex Skill of Independent Living" in Part 2, Readings: Sample Essays.

Working on Your Own Assignment

- Turn your draft outline into a revision outline by noting necessary changes in the right-hand column.
- Revise your thesis statement as necessary to reflect new ideas, changes in the structure of your essay or your introduction, and greater attention to diction and sentence structure.
- Check to make sure that your middle paragraphs expand upon ideas presented in your thesis statement and that they are arranged in an effective sequence.
- Check each middle paragraph for topic sentence, explanations, supporting details, and transitions.
- Keep your reader in mind as you revise introductions and conclusions. Have you provided enough context for your reader to understand the scope of your essay? Does your conclusion reflect the deeper understanding of your subject that reading your essay should provide?
- When you are satisfied with the content and organization of your essay, turn to Part 3, Handbook for Final Editing, for help in improving its style.

EXERCISES

A.   Using a revision outline, check the draft you wrote for Exercise D in Chapter 4 to see if your thesis statement and overall essay structure need revision. Write in necessary changes on your revision outline, and then write a few sentences explaining the reasons for the changes you propose. If you have written a perfect first draft, write a few sentences explaining how your first draft meets the requirements of effective thesis statement and essay structure.

B. E. M. Forster's "My Wood" and Wade Davis's "The Ticking Bomb" (both in Readings) are both inductively organized essays, with a question at the beginning and a thesis statement at the end. Choose one of these and write out a revision outline showing how you would change its inductive structure into a deductive structure. Consider whether changing the structure means changing the thesis statement. If it does, write out the new thesis statement.

C. Are the three paragraphs that follow an effective introduction, first middle paragraph and conclusion for an essay based on the causal analysis of living independently (see "From Adolescence to Adulthood," the sample topic for Chapter 3)? If they are, write a few sentences on each paragraph explaining why. If they are not, revise ineffective paragraphs with the use of a revision outline.

Draft introduction and first middle paragraph:

Independent living causes difficulties. If parents realized that living independently is a process with stages, then they would be more tolerant and not expect a satisfactory living situation to happen overnight. I will show that parents' expectations are the biggest cause of difficulties in independent living.

The first stage in a teenager moving out is planning. It looks like nothing is happening during this stage and so parents get impatient. They don't understand that rebellious behaviour is just the teen's attempt to be independent, and so they overreact to it. It is not a big deal after all if the teen does not take out the garbage the moment he or she is told to. It is unrealistic for parents to expect this.

Draft conclusion:

So I have shown that parents' expectations are the cause of difficulties for teens who are trying to live independently. Living independently is a process and the process takes time. It is a mistake for anyone to get impatient. Parents should learn to be more tolerant with their teens.

chapter 6

Using Textual Analysis to Gather Material

Stage 1   Clarifying Textual Analysis Topics

Stage 2   Gathering Material

      Step 1   Using Analytic Categories
                Subject
                Genre
                Context
                Methods of Development
                Structure
                Style
                Tone
                Point of View

      Step 2   Connecting Textual Features to Figure Out the Work's Theme/Thesis

      Sample Topic: Analyzing a Poem: Al Purdy's "Trees at the Arctic Circle"

Stage 3   Formulating a Thesis Statement

Stage 4   Drafting

Stage 5   Revising Thesis Statement and Essay Structure

Stage 6   Revising Individual Paragraphs

Stage 7   Final Editing

Every verbal and/or visual text is created from particular materials and techniques available to its creator. In creating written texts, writers use the "material" of language. Ways of using language to achieve certain effects are the "techniques." Writers learn some techniques from studying other writers, but they may also develop new ways of using language. Thus when you analyze written texts as art, you focus not only on what is said but on how it is said, on the relationship between content and form of expression. Similarly, when you analyze performances as art, as in plays, films, and television programs, you pay attention not only to the message but also to the particular ways in which the director uses the materials and techniques available.

Stage 1   Clarifying Textual Analysis Topics

In doing textual analysis you are treating a work (a poem, a movie, an essay) as a system of interrelated parts. Since one aim of textual analysis is understanding the content of the work, the parts you divide the work into overlap somewhat with the categories you use for analyzing the content of nonfiction writing (see Chapter 3). Another aim of textual analysis is appreciating the work's aesthetic qualities: the artistic choices about such matters as verse form, structure, and diction that help to shape its meaning.

There are other ways of writing about texts. Just as you can use process and causal analysis, as well as systems analysis, to analyze content, so you can use these three methods in analyzing texts. You could examine the process by which a text was composed, published, or performed, for instance. You could also look at the social, economic, or psychological causes that may have shaped a particular text or at the text's aesthetic or social effects. We focus on analyzing a text as a system because this approach gives you practice in examining a text closely. For an example of this method, see Judith Fetterley's "A Rose for 'A Rose for Emily'" (Readings).

Stage 2   Gathering Material

In this chapter we define and give examples of the general categories for analyzing a broad range of written texts and performances. If these terms are new to you, you may find it helpful to reread the definitions after you have gone through the sample topic. In Part 4, you will find a chart showing how these general categories can be adapted for specific genres of texts, as well as expanded lists of questions for each major genre (nonfiction, fiction, poetry, drama, films, and television programs). To help you better understand texts, you will also find an Annotated Survey of Reference Sources that lists such reference material as handbooks of literary and film terms; biographical dictionaries; guides to symbolism, mythology, and religion; and specialized dictionaries on word usage.

Step 1   Using Analytic Categories

These are the three basic questions for a systems analysis of a text: What are the parts of the text? What is their function within the work? How do the parts relate to each other? You can analyze a wide range of works by gathering material about these parts: subject, genre, context, methods of development, structure, style, tone, point of view. Here is a brief explanation of each of these terms.

Subject   Subject is the general issue(s) or concern(s) of the text, as you perceive it (them).

Sometimes your assignment will identify a subject for you, such as manhood in a Hemingway short story or the meaning of love in Emily Brontë's *Wuthering Heights*. But often you will have to decide what you think the subject is. Your statement about a text's subject(s) will be most useful to you if it is both tentative and precise: "This film seems to be about the meaning of heroism in war." If you keep your statement of subject tentative, you will find it easier to modify or change if necessary. And if you make it precise, you will have a better starting point from which to ask: how does the text treat this subject? Avoid both plot summary ("this film is about a soldier who ...") and vague generalizations ("this film is about man against man" or "this film is about war").

Genre   The word *genre*, which means "kind," has traditionally been used to refer to the categories into which literary works may be grouped because of similarities in form, subject, or technique. In contemporary theory, genre has been redefined as "a form of human expression loosely adhering to certain conventions that may change over time."* This definition broadens the traditional meaning to encompass a wide range of what can be considered texts: not only literary works but also other verbal and/or visual texts such as films, television programs, speeches, and paintings.

---

* Jerald Zaslove, "Bakhtin and the Image of Language: A Friendly Critique of Martin Jay's *Downcast Eyes*." Paper presented at the conference of the Canadian Association of Art History, Vancouver, 1998.

There are "major" genres and "minor" genres (subgenres). The major genres you are likely to study are nonfiction, fiction, poetry, drama, and film. Each of these has many subgenres; for example, the genre of poetry includes the subgenres of the sonnet, the ballad, and the ode, among others. Some texts cross genre boundaries. The "new journalism," for instance, is nonfiction writing that uses many techniques of fiction.

Each major and minor genre has its own conventions, "rules" that authors either adhere to or break for their own purposes. The conventions that govern fantasy, for instance, are quite different from those that govern realistic fiction. Identifying the genre and subgenre of a text makes you more conscious of the "rules" the author is working with and/or against. This knowledge will not only improve your analysis, but also help you avoid serious mistakes. Some students, for example, confuse short stories with autobiographical essays and assume that short stories are accurate accounts of the writers' own experiences. A handbook of literary or film terms will explain the conventions of many kinds of works.

Context   Context means the historical and/or cultural situation in which the text was produced, including the specific audience (if any) for which it was intended.

Texts generally reflect the outlook and concerns both of the author/director and of the era in which they are created. You may therefore find that you understand a text better if you know something about the author or director and about such factors as the historical events, social conditions, and cultural issues that enter into the work, and about the audience for which a work might have been intended. You may find this kind of information in an introduction or notes to the text itself, or you may need to look it up in one of the guides listed in the Annotated Survey of Reference Sources, Part 4. Be careful not to substitute information of this kind for a close analysis of the text. A poet may have had a drinking problem, for instance; that doesn't mean every poem he or she wrote is about alcoholism.

Methods of development   Methods of development are the specific elements, such as points, events, and descriptions, by which the author/director unfolds or elaborates the central issue or concerns of the text.

A text consists of material that develops the overall point, the theme or thesis, of the work. You can analyze this material by examining the methods of development commonly used in specific genres or subgenres. In imaginative works that tell a story (whether in poetry, fiction, drama, or film), you would pay attention to details of events, setting, and characterization. In imaginative works that do not tell a story, you might find that the theme is developed through reflections, observations, or impressions. A love poem, for example, might be developed through a list of the beloved's virtues, or a nature poem through detailed observations of the landscape. For information on characteristic methods of development in various genres, consult handbooks of literary and rhetorical terms and handbooks that focus on specific literary forms (see Annotated Survey of Reference Sources in Part 4).

Structure   The term *structure* refers to the way that units of material are organized to convey a theme or thesis.

In thinking about structure, you need to be aware both of the general principles of structure within various genres and of the particular ordering of material within the text you are analyzing. Novels, drama, and film often organize events into a rising and falling action; short stories more often, though not always, focus on a single moment of revelation; essays often, though not always, arrange a series of points into an order of ascending interest. In addition to these broad structural principles, each work will have its particular way of organizing material.

Consider the following points when you analyze the structure of specific texts:

Generic Principles of Structure   Among the conventions of various subgenres are conventions about structure. If you know that a poem is a sonnet, for instance, you can anticipate that its fourteen lines will be organized into one of two structures: an octave of eight lines setting out a problem and a sestet of six lines suggesting a solution; or three quatrains of four lines, each quatrain developing one idea, and a concluding couplet that sums up the previous lines or presents them in a new light. If you find variations on these forms, you can think about why the author violated the conventions. You can find information about the structural conventions of various genres in dictionaries of literary and rhetorical terms and in handbooks of specific literary forms.

Spatial and Chronological Principles of Structure   Space and time often function as principles in structuring material. Notice patterns of spatial structuring: contrasts between characters identified with different settings, such as city and country; events organized as a journey; changes in a character that occur as a result of moving from a familiar to an unfamiliar place.

Time is used as a structural principle in the following ways, among others: a chronological unfolding of events; movement between the present and the past; cycles of days, seasons, or years.

Typographical Devices as Indicators of Structure   Typographical devices often reinforce other kinds of structure. The most obvious are those that divide works into chapters or acts and scenes. Watch for the less obvious as well, such as the arrangement of lines on the page for some kinds of poetry.

Within the overall structure of the work, you may notice the way smaller blocks of material are organized. The overall structure of an essay, for example, might be chronological, but a paragraph of description within the essay might be organized according to a spatial arrangement of near to far. Making an outline of the text, or of its major divisions, will help you to identify its structural principles.

Style Style is the characteristic or distinctive mode of expression within a text.

In analyzing style, you examine a text at its most detailed level, the level of lines, sentences, scenes (in plays), or shots (in films). While many elements enter into the style of a work, three are most important for written texts: **diction**; **figurative language and allusions**; and the rhythm created by **sentence structure** and other methods.

Diction refers to the kinds of words the author or characters use, both in level (colloquial, informal, formal) and in origin (for example, ethnic dialect, legal jargon). What is the effect of these choices? One essayist may use the informal language of everyday speech to seem like "one of us," for instance, while another writer may use the specialized vocabulary of economics to speak as a colleague to other experts.

Figurative Language includes *images* (figures of speech such as metaphor and simile, or visual, oral, tactile, and kinaesthetic images) and *symbols* (objects or actions that stand for a more abstract idea or value, such as a pair of scales that symbolizes justice).

Allusions are references to literary, historical, mythological, or religious events and figures, such as Adam and Eve. Repeated images, symbols, or allusions that form a pattern are particularly important. For instance, the images of Emily Dickinson's poem "Because I could not stop for Death" form a pattern in which life is conceived of as a journey with death as a kindly companion.

Sentence Structure determines the rhythms of prose and, with other devices, of poetry and drama. Is there a high proportion or distinctive use of basic sentences, long or short sentences, sentence fragments, parallelism, or inversion? How do line length and sound patterns contribute to the rhythms of poetry? How does the pacing of dialogue and action contribute to the effects of drama?

In analyzing the style of film and television productions, you focus on the way the camera is used, with less attention to the language. Shooting techniques, visual images and symbols, and editing techniques together create the style.

To analyze style, you may need the help of resources such as a handbook of poetics or dictionaries of slang, symbols, or film terms.

Tone   *Tone* refers to the attitude of the author/narrator towards the self, the subject of the text, and the reader, as conveyed by style. In plays and films, this quality is referred to as the *mood* or *atmosphere* of the work.

When you read silently, you likely hear the words inside your head as though they were being spoken by the author or character. The voice may seem like that of a modest gentleman or a frightened child, a witty woman of the world or a dreamy adolescent. It is this sense of a voice speaking that we mean by the attitude towards the self created by a written work.

The tone (created through stylistic choices) establishes a particular relationship among the author or narrator, the subject of the text, and the audience. The author of an essay might, for example, adopt a playful attitude towards the subject of addiction to coffee, and treat the reader either as playmate or disapproving parent. Or the essayist might deliver a serious lecture about the dangers of caffeine and treat the reader as a peer to share ideas or as a pupil to be instructed. In plays and films, the tone or mood may be established through music, lighting, costuming, and other devices.

Terms commonly used to describe tone or mood include sentimental, businesslike, authoritative, comic, nostalgic, menacing, reflective, playful, serious. The piece is **ironic** when we understand its meaning to be different from, or the opposite of, what is expressed.

Point of view   The perspective from which the text is presented is called *point of view*.

Here are the distinctions commonly made in analyzing point of view.

Fiction: Who Is the Narrator (Storyteller)?

First-Person Narration

MAJOR PARTICIPANT: The story is told in the first person by an "I" who has a major role in the events (Naomi telling the story of her life in Joy Kogawa's novel *Obasan*).

MINOR PARTICIPANT: The story is told in the first person by an "I" who recounts events but does not have a major role in them (the unnamed narrator of William Faulkner's short story "A Rose for Emily").

Omniscient Narration   The story is told in the third person by an anonymous narrator who has access to the thoughts and feelings of more than one character (as in D. H. Lawrence's short story "The Horse-Dealer's Daughter").

Limited Omniscient Narration   The story is told in the third person by an anonymous narrator who has access to the thoughts and feelings of only one character (as in Nathaniel Hawthorne's short story "Young Goodman Brown").

Objective Narration   The story is told in the third person as though recorded by a camera, with no access to the thoughts or feelings of any character (as in Ernest Hemingway's short story "Hills Like White Elephants").

Poetry: Who Is the Speaker?   Like fiction, poems can be expressed in the first person or the third person. The most important distinction is between the first-person speaker who is a character completely separate from the poet (as in dramatic monologues such as Robert Browning's "My Last Duchess") and the first-person speaker who seems hard to distinguish from the person who wrote the poem (as in lyric poems such as Robert Frost's "Stopping by Woods on a Snowy Evening"). Although it's tempting to treat the second type as wholly autobiographical ("Frost was driving a wagon one night and ..."), this "I" too is a literary creation, one that allows poets to transform purely individual insights and experiences into ones their readers can more easily share. That's why you ordinarily refer to the "speaker" of the poem rather than to the poet. For an example of how to use this term, see Karin Swanson's "Spontaneity and Enjoyment of the Natural World," Part 2, Readings: Sample Essays.

Nonfiction: Who Is Speaking—Writer or Persona?   As you will remember from Chapter 3, nonfiction writers generally speak for themselves, in either the first or third person, or they create a **persona** to speak for them. A persona is like a character an actor might play. The writer adopts a role, usually for purposes of humour or irony. In "A Modest Proposal" (Readings), for example, Jonathan Swift creates a persona quite different from himself to comment on conditions in Ireland.

Step 2   Connecting Textual Features to Figure Out the Work's Theme/Thesis

In most texts, the features that we have just described work together to convey an overall point about the subject. The term *thesis* is generally used to refer to the more explicit point made in essays, while *theme* refers to the more indirect points made by imaginative literature.

At first glance it may seem difficult to distinguish theme/thesis from *subject*. To some extent the difference is between the general and the specific. The *subject* is the general topic of discussion in the work; the *theme* or *thesis* is the specific point the work makes about the subject. You might describe the *subject* of Alice Munro's short story "Thanks for the Ride" as the dating rituals of adolescence, and her *theme* as the necessity of recognizing the class barriers that obstruct some relationships.

A word of caution is in order here. To analyze texts effectively you will need to formulate a clear statement of thesis or theme. But remember that it is impossible to capture everything that could be said about any complex and interesting work in a brief phrase, and that this statement reflects only your current interpretation, which may change with time or reflection. There may also be discordancies, gaps, or contradictions in the text that you will need to take into account. As you write your essay, keep your mind open to other possible interpretations. Remember, too, that the thesis or theme of the text is not the same as the thesis of your essay; finding your own thesis belongs to the next stage of the writing process.

Sample Topic: Analyzing a Poem: Al Purdy's "Trees at the Arctic Circle"

We will demonstrate how to clarify essay topics and gather material for textual analysis essays by working through a sample topic, an analysis of Al Purdy's poem "Trees at the Arctic Circle." You will find it easier to follow the discussion if you first read the poem carefully.

PUBLISHED WRITING

TREES AT THE ARCTIC CIRCLE

(Salix Cordifolia—Ground Willow)

> They are 18 inches long
> or even less
> crawling under rocks
> grovelling among the lichens
> 5   bending and curling to escape
> making themselves small
> finding new ways to hide
> Coward trees
> I am angry to see them
> 10   like this
> not proud of what they are
> bowing to weather instead
> careful of themselves
> worried about the sky
> 15   afraid of exposing their limbs
> like a Victorian married couple
>
> I call to mind great Douglas firs
> I see tall maples waving green
> and oaks like gods in autumn gold
> 20   the whole horizon jungle dark
> and I crouched under that continual night

But these
even the dwarf shrubs of Ontario
mock them
25 Coward trees

And yet—and yet—
their seed pods glow
like delicate grey earrings
their leaves are veined and intricate
30 like tiny parkas
They have about three months
to make sure the species does not die
and that's how they spend their time
unbothered by any human opinion
35 just digging in here and now
sending their roots down down down
And you know it occurs to me
        about 2 feet under
those roots must touch permafrost
40 ice that remains ice forever
and they use it for their nourishment
they use death to remain alive

I see that I've been carried away
in my scorn of the dwarf trees
45 most foolish in my judgements
To take away the dignity
        of any living thing
even tho it cannot understand
        the scornful words
50 is to make life itself trivial
and yourself the Pontifex Maximus
        of nullity
I have been stupid in a poem
I will not alter the poem
55 but let the stupidity remain permanent
as the trees are
in a poem
the dwarf trees of Baffin Island

Pangnirtung

"Trees at the Arctic Circle," by Al Purdy, from
*Beyond Remembering: The Collected Poems of
Al Purdy*, Harbour Publishing, 2000.

Stage 1   Clarifying Textual Analysis Topics

Let's suppose that you are working on the following essay assignment:

> Al Purdy's poet friend Dennis Lee praised Purdy's ability to
> shift tones in his poetry. Does "Trees at the Arctic Circle" re-
> flect a shift in the speaker's attitude? If so, how does the
> poem develop this shift, and what point is made by it?

Clarifying terms   "Tone" is the one word in the assignment that you
may be uncertain of. The assignment seems to identify tone with
speaker's attitude. To be sure, you check a dictionary of literary terms
and learn that tone is the attitude a speaker/writer takes to subject,
reader, and self.

Recognizing genre and scope   Since the text you are looking at is a
poem, you will need the special version of textual analysis categories
designed for poetry. (See Special Categories for Textual Analysis:
Poetry in Part 4.) Though the first part of the assignment focuses on
tone, the comments on development and point indicate you will need
to gather material in all the categories.

Stage 2   Gathering Material

Step 1   Using analytic categories   You begin by gathering material
in the special categories for poetry.

Subject   The immediate subject is the speaker's response to the
ground willow trees that grow on Baffin Island. There seems to be a
deeper subject, though: our attitude to living things in general.

Genre   "Trees at the Arctic Circle" is a free verse lyric poem. It is a free
verse poem because the lines are different lengths, the stanzas are different lengths, and there is no set pattern of rhythm or rhyme scheme. It is a
lyric poem because it expresses the thoughts and feelings of the speaker.

Context   Al Purdy was born on December 30, 1918, in Wooler, Ontario,
and died on April 21, 2000, in Sidney, Vancouver Island, having published over forty books of poetry. "Trees at the Arctic Circle" was first
published in his poetry collection *Rooms for Rent* in 1967. In her
Foreword to *Beyond Remembering: The Collected Poems of Al Purdy*
(Madeira Park, BC: Harbour, 2000), Margaret Atwood writes:

> What interests [Purdy] can be anything at all, but above
> all the wonder that anything at all can be interesting.
> He's always turning banality inside out…. You can't see how
> it's done, but suddenly, where a second ago there was only
> a broken vase, there's a fistful of brilliant flowers. (18)

Methods of Development The *details* of this poem include many details of *setting*, which Purdy reveals in the poem's last line as Baffin Island, an enormous island in the eastern Arctic that angles north from Quebec, Ontario, and Manitoba. From your study of Canadian geography you know the landscape is harsh and rocky and the weather is very cold most of the year; nothing grows higher than one's knees. This poem seems to have been set at about the same time it was published, 1967, far enough away from the Victorian era (1837–1901) for the speaker to feel contemptuous of Victorian attitudes and behaviour.

Even more numerous are the details of *characterization* that convey the speaker's attitudes towards Baffin Island's dwarf trees (see Style below).

Poetic Structure "Trees at the Arctic Circle" is clearly divided into four stanzas. Purdy presents a **chronologically organized sequence** of the speaker's responses to the arctic willow and to himself. In stanza 1, the speaker gives us his first (negative) impressions of these little arctic trees, which he describes as insignificant and cowardly. In the second stanza, he compares the willows unfavourably to the Douglas firs, maples, and oaks of Ontario, tall trees that offer protection. In the third stanza, he takes a closer look at the arctic willow and revises his negative opinion. He now sees these trees as brave, resourceful, and even rather beautiful. In the fourth stanza, he focuses on his own attitudes, condemning his earlier criticism of the trees and punishing himself by making this record of his "stupidity" permanent in a poem.

Style Diction in the poem is closely tied to and conveys the speaker's changing attitude. The first stanza emphasizes the speaker's scorn for the arctic willow with words like *crawling, grovelling, bending, curling, small, hide, coward, not proud, bowing, careful, worried, afraid.* In the third stanza, the diction changes to indicate the speaker's dramatic shift in attitude. He now describes the arctic willow as "delicate" and "intricate" (28, 29). They are "unbothered" (34) by any human opinion. They spend their time "digging in" (35). The repetition of "down down down" (36) emphasizes the trees' strength and endurance. The diction in the fourth stanza emphasizes the speaker's contempt for his own mistaken judgments in phrases such as "most foolish" (45) and "Pontifex Maximus/of nullity" (51–52). The repetition of "stupid" (53, 55) reinforces this point.

The main strategy for **figurative language** in the poem is personification, the treatment of objects as if they were people. In the first stanza, the trees are personified as frightened little beings who make themselves as small as possible and search for new places to hide. The way the branches of the arctic willow crawl on the tundra is compared to the timidity of an overdressed Victorian couple. In the second stanza, in contrast, the great oaks of the south are "like gods" dressed in "autumn gold" (19). These trees are powerful enough to make the whole horizon as dark as a jungle. Purdy continues this personification by saying that even the dwarf shrubs of Ontario would laugh at the arctic willow.

In the third stanza, the imagery shifts to indicate the speaker's admiration for the arctic willow. He says their seed pods "glow" and compares them in a simile to "delicate grey earrings" (27, 28). He now sees how well adapted they are to their harsh environment and says in another simile that their leaves are "like tiny parkas" (30), an image of effective protection. All these images continue the personification, which climaxes in the portrayal of the trees as heroes using "death to remain alive" (42). In the third stanza, the focus shifts to the speaker, who describes himself in a single image as the "Pontifex Maximus"—the president of the Roman high priests in classical times—"of nullity" (51–52).

In the poem's **prosody**—its use of sound and rhythm—the distinctive feature is the short lines that emphasize the active movements of the personified trees—"crawling … grovelling … bending … making." They also emphasize the speaker's passionate responses ("Coward trees") and flexibility of mind: he is not fixed in his views, but rather mobile and changing.

Tone   Stanza by stanza the speaker sets out the changes in his attitude towards the arctic willow and towards himself. The stanza divisions make the shifts in tone easy to follow.

Point of View   First person. In "Trees at the Arctic Circle," the point of view seems to be that of a speaker who is both passionate and honest about his own shortcomings. This honesty makes the point of view that of a speaker we can trust.

Step 2 Connecting textual features to figure out the work's theme/thesis   The material you have gathered emphasizes the shift in attitude in the poem. Structure and the various aspects of style, in particular, all point to the need for an attitude of contempt to be replaced by one of admiration. The analysis thus confirms the theme explicitly stated in the final stanza:

> To take away the dignity
> 　　of any living thing
> even tho it cannot understand
> 　　the scornful words
> is to make life itself trivial (46–50)

The poem makes an interesting and important point. Most of us are rather limited in our capacity to respond to the natural world. We find it easier to care about baby seals than about mosquitoes. Purdy's point is that even insignificant living beings deserve respect, and the failure to give respect devalues life, creates "nullity."

Working on Your Own Assignment

Your main purpose in textual analysis is to explain the relationship between *what* the work is about (its subject and theme) and *how* the ideas and emotions are conveyed.

- Make notes on the written text or performance in the appropriate categories: subject, genre, context, methods of development, structure, style, tone, and point of view. The Questions to Ask in Analyzing Nonfiction, Fiction, Poetry, Drama, Film, and Television Programs in Part 4 will give you specific guidelines.

- For nonfiction, look for an explicitly stated thesis. Does this thesis actually explain the most significant material you've gathered? If not, what do you find to be the work's thesis?

- For imaginative works, formulate a theme that connects and explains the most significant material you have gathered.

- For examples of textual analysis, see the following essays in Part 2, Readings:
  - Judith Fetterley, "A Rose for 'A Rose for Emily'"
  - B. Jones, "Shifts in Attitude and Form in Al Purdy's 'Trees at the Arctic Circle'" (Sample Essays)
  - D. Smith, "The Making of the Tragic Hero: The Graveyard Scene in *Hamlet*" (Sample Essays)

EXERCISES

A.   Respond to each of the following questions in a sentence or two.

1. What is the main purpose of textual analysis?

2. How would a textual analysis of Pico Iyer's "In Praise of the Humble Comma" (Readings) differ from a content analysis?

3. What does the term **analytic categories** mean?

4. Write a sentence or two explaining each of the eight **general categories** of textual analysis.

B.   Analyze the figurative language in the following poem by answering the questions in the relevant section of Questions to Ask in Analyzing Poetry in Part 4 (p. 500).

PUBLISHED WRITING

LOVE LESSONS

When I said I would teach you English,
mi amante,*
I did not know
we would conjugate the verbs with our bodies.
When I promised you should write poetry again,
in another language,
mi corazon,*
I did not know
you would hold me in your arms, beating out the hexameters
absent-mindedly, on my back.
Your body, all Inca black and gold, smells of
dusky rivers, where blind white dolphins swim;
it tastes of sweet Andean woodsmoke,
blowing over the altiplano.
Your kisses glow and burn like snakes of lava
incinerating my carefully created image
as the bringer of knowledge.
When I said I would teach you English,
mi vida,*
I did not know
I would learn from you
the grammar of the heart.

Joan Seager, from *Vintage 91, Prize-Winning
Poems from the League of Canadian Poets*
(Winlaw, BC: Sono Nis Press, 1992).

C. Analyze either the structure or the tone of one of the following essays from Part 2, Readings, by answering the questions in the relevant section of Questions to Ask in Analyzing Nonfiction in Part 4 (pp. 493, 494).

- E. M. Forster's "My Wood"
- Linda Hogan's "The Voyagers"
- Andrew Pyper's "The Ticking Daddy Clock"
- George Orwell's "Shooting an Elephant"

---

* "Mi amante," "mi corazon," and "mi vida" are terms of endearment in Spanish. Literally, they mean "my lover," "my heart," and "my life."

chapter 7

Writing Textual Analysis Essays I:
Formulating a Thesis Statement and Drafting

Stage 1   Clarifying Essay Topics

Stage 2   Gathering Material

Stage 3   Formulating a Tentative Thesis Statement

    Step 1   Forming an Opinion

    Step 2   Supporting Your Opinion

Stage 4   Drafting

    Step 1   Organizing Your Material

    Step 2   Making a Draft Outline

Stage 5   Revising Thesis Statement and Essay Structure

Stage 6   Revising Individual Paragraphs

Stage 7   Final Editing

The previous chapter introduced you to Stages 1 and 2 in the process of writing textual analysis essays. You now know that when you are asked to analyze a verbal and/or visual text, you are usually expected to show the relationship between the text's content and the techniques used to create it. You also have a systematic means of gathering material in appropriate analytic categories. In this chapter we will demonstrate how to use your material effectively to draft a textual analysis essay, building on the guidelines for formulating a thesis statement and writing a draft in Chapter 4. If you need more complete information about these stages of the writing process, consult Chapter 4.

The process outlined below leads to a textual *analysis* essay. Analysis is also the first step towards evaluation, but if *evaluating* a text—determining whether or to what degree it succeeds as a work of art—is your main purpose, see the discussion of the aesthetic standard of evaluation and the procedure for writing persuasive essays in Chapter 11.

For our source of examples in this chapter, we will continue the sample topic from Chapter 6 on Al Purdy's "Trees at the Arctic Circle."

Stage 3 Formulating a Tentative Thesis Statement

Step 1 Forming an Opinion

In gathering material about a text, as we demonstrated in the last chapter, you start from an idea of the text's subject, analyze its formal elements, and connect these elements to arrive at an interpretation of the text's theme or thesis. The *opinion* part of the thesis statement in a textual analysis essay is usually a statement of this theme or thesis, shaped by the demands of the essay topic.

This does not mean, by the way, that each text has one and only one meaning that you must discover (or borrow from someone else!). It simply means that you present an interpretation of theme that you can support.

- The assignment on Al Purdy's "Trees" focuses on a shift in attitude. Combining this focus with the theme that emerged from the process of connecting textual features might give you the following thesis opinion:

> **Thesis opinion:** Al Purdy's "Trees at the Arctic Circle" suggests that, like the poem's speaker, we need to shift our attitude towards living things from contempt to admiration.

Note that an assignment may ask you for an opinion about some aspect of a text other than its theme or thesis.

- "Discuss how setting and symbol contribute to the portrayal of the speaker in Al Purdy's 'Trees at the Arctic Circle.'" This assignment indicates that the subject you are to focus on is "portrayal of the speaker." You would therefore formulate a thesis opinion based on the material you have gathered in the textual category concerned with the portrayal of characters: characterization.

Step 2 Supporting Your Opinion

In any thesis statement, the support for your opinion will come from the categories of material you used to arrive at the opinion. Most textual analysis assignments require you to go through all or most of the categories of textual analysis, each of which focuses on a formal element of the text. To indicate the *support* for the thesis opinion, you will refer to the most relevant categories or formal elements.

- To add support to your opinion on Purdy's "Trees," you would look for the categories of material that led you to that opinion. The formal elements that most reflected a change in attitude were those of structure and the various elements of style: diction, figurative language, and prosody. Adding a reference to these elements would give you a thesis statement like this:

WRITING SAMPLE

Tentative thesis statement: Structure, diction, figurative language, and prosody in Al Purdy's "Trees at the Arctic Circle" suggest that, like the poem's speaker, we need to shift our attitude towards living things from contempt to admiration.

Notice that you indicate the support for your opinion by referring to the subject of the categories, not to specific details or to the points you might make. The reason is that the thesis statement sets out a proposition that you will demonstrate in the rest of the essay.

Textual analysis assignments may occasionally demand different ways of gathering material and thus different ways of using supporting categories in your thesis statement. For example:

- "Discuss how setting and symbol contribute to the portrayal of the speaker in Al Purdy's 'Trees.'"

This assignment asks you to gather material in three categories rather than all of them. Since the assignment has already said that symbol and setting support the characterization of the speaker, you cannot simply repeat this as your thesis statement. In such cases, you will need to indicate the specific points you will develop in your essay. A tentative thesis statement for this topic might read like this:

WRITING SAMPLE

Tentative thesis statement: In Al Purdy's "Trees," the portrayal of the speaker as honest and open to change is conveyed by setting and symbolism that emphasize change and endurance.

Thesis statements in inductively organized essays (see Chapter 10) will also be more detailed statements, since they are presented in the concluding paragraphs.

- "How do some of the poems on the course illuminate the contemporary debate about our relationship to nature?"

This is not really a textual analysis assignment, since it does not ask you to examine the relationship between form and theme. You might analyze various poems to determine the range of themes about our relationship to nature, but your thesis statement would connect these themes with the contemporary debate rather than with formal elements of the poems.

Stage 4 Drafting

Step 1 Organizing Your Material

Choosing deductive or inductive structure Most textual analysis essays are organized *deductively*: that is, the thesis statement appears in the introduction and points derived from the thesis statement are developed in order in the middle paragraphs. This structure provides a framework that makes it easier for readers to grasp the significance of specific details.

It is possible to give an *inductive structure* to a textual analysis essay: you might, for example, question a widely accepted interpretation of a text, show its weaknesses one after another, and end with an alternative interpretation as your thesis. For instance, you might ask, "Is Hamlet really indecisive?" and then develop a series of points showing that he is not indecisive, that, in fact, in crucial moments he acts rashly—the thesis you develop in your conclusion. This structure works best for texts readers are very familiar with; otherwise they would find it difficult to grasp the significance of specific details.

Choosing a method of development As we pointed out in Chapter 3, writers of nonfiction use six main methods of developing ideas: telling a story, describing a process, comparing, developing a chain of reasoning, listing a series of points, and showing how the parts of a system work together. While each of these methods works for writing various kinds of nonfiction, they do not all work for writing textual analysis essays in academic situations. We will examine the appropriateness of each of these methods.

Telling a story is the worst principle for developing a textual analysis essay that you could possibly choose. Avoid the temptation to describe the unfolding of a plot, the verse-by-verse movement of a poem or the scene-by-scene development of a play or film, throwing in some commentary on the details as you go. The problem with this method is that your comments stay isolated from each other, and so when you come to the conclusion, you have nothing to say. You will be much less likely to fall into this kind of summary plus commentary if you have gathered material systematically and worked out a thesis statement to guide the writing of your draft.

Describing a process is a method of development occasionally called for by a textual analysis assignment.

- "Discuss the gradual way in which Al Purdy comes to his startling conclusion that he has 'been stupid in a poem' in 'Trees at the Arctic Circle.'"

This assignment asks you to treat the poem as a process of discovery. You would divide the process of discovery into stages and analyze each stage. In developing the essay, you would focus each paragraph on a different stage in the process; the stage would become the topic of the paragraph and the main point would be about the significance of the stage. This works well in theory and in expert hands, but often process essays on texts fall back into telling the story. Thus it is best to avoid a process structure unless your essay assignment makes it essential.

Comparing is commonly called for in textual analysis assignments. Comparison is often combined with evaluation.

- "Discuss the different ways of portraying nature in Al Purdy's 'Trees' and Margaret Atwood's 'Georgia Beach.'" (comparison assignment)
- "Does 'Trees at the Arctic Circle' or 'Georgia Beach' best persuade us to value nature?" (comparison and evaluation)

Comparison and evaluation both present special problems as methods of development. You will find suggestions for writing comparison essays in Chapter 9 and suggestions for writing evaluation essays in Chapters 10 and 11.

Developing a chain of reasoning is a common method for structuring textual analysis essays when the text is being used to make a political, social, economic, or psychological point. This kind of essay is seldom required at the undergraduate level.

- Judith Fetterley's "A Rose for 'A Rose for Emily'" (Readings) is organized around a chain of reasoning concerning the Gothic novel, feminism, and the situation of women. Fetterley uses her analysis of form and theme in a short story by William Faulkner to make the case that repressive treatment of women causes "Gothic" female behaviour.

Listing a series of points is a strategy belonging more to journalism and the informal essay, which may be organized inductively, than to academic essays, which are generally organized deductively (for an explanation of these terms, see Chapter 4, pp. 46–47). You may find that you have unintentionally used this method if you write paragraphs on formal elements such as diction, structure, and tone without showing how they relate to the work's theme or thesis. Make sure each paragraph has a topic sentence that connects it to your thesis statement.

Showing how the parts in a system work together is the structure you will most often use for textual analysis assignments, where the assumption is that a text is a system in which the formal elements work together to convey the text's theme or thesis. Your task is to organize the essay to show a particular way in which these fit together. The advantage of viewing the text as a system is that you are constantly challenged to see a connection between the parts that will illuminate the whole.

Sequencing your points effectively Once you have chosen your method of development, you can then decide how to sequence your points. Usually, as we said in Chapter 4, the best way is in order of **ascending interest**, beginning with your least important or most obvious point and ending with the most important. In a textual analysis essay, your most important point is generally about the element of the text that most clearly conveys its theme or thesis. You would therefore arrange your material to lead up to this point. This may sound easy, but, as we noted earlier, textual analysis essays always run the danger of falling into storytelling. The last part of the text is not the same thing as the most important element for conveying the theme/thesis. Be careful not to confuse the two.

Step 2 Making a Draft Outline

Using a draft outline (described in Chapter 4) will help you avoid the problem of storytelling. Make sure your outline consists of topics and points, not of plot summary and commentary. You can easily turn your draft outline into a revision outline in the next stage of the writing process by leaving space for revision notes on the right.

- In writing a draft of your essay on Purdy's "Trees," you might first try the *process* method of development because of the assignment's focus on shifts in attitude. You would no doubt find it hard to comment on structure, diction, figurative language, and prosody in each paragraph and still have a single main point. So you might decide to make a draft outline from the *system* approach, using the formal elements you refer to in your thesis statement as your paragraph topics and following the sequence you have there. Your draft outline, with space for revision notes, might look like this (MP stands for "middle paragraph," a paragraph in the middle of the essay):

DRAFT OUTLINE

TOPIC	POINT	REVISION NOTES
Introduction	Thesis: structure and style show need to change attitude	
MP 1: Structure	Based on three stages of attitude development	
MP 2: Diction	Changes from hostile terms to admiring words to words judgmental of self	
MP 3: Fig. Language	Main device is personification: trees develop from being cowards to being heroes	
MP 4: Prosody	Short lines emphasize passion, movement, mobile mind	
Conclusion	Structure and style show need to change attitude	

In writing your draft you would follow this outline as closely as possible, adding details and quotations from the poem to support your points. The next stage in the process is revision, the subject of Chapter 8.

Working on Your Own Assignment

- Begin formulating your thesis statement by presenting your *opinion* of the text's theme or thesis, unless the assignment requires your opinion on a different element of the text.
- Complete your thesis statement by adding a reference to relevant formal elements of the text as *support*.

- Decide how to organize your draft, recognizing that presenting the elements of the text as part of a *system* will usually work best.
- Make a draft outline to guide your writing. Leave spaces so that you can later insert revision suggestions.
- Quickly write a draft, paying most attention to developing middle paragraphs.

EXERCISES

A.   Respond to each of the following questions in a sentence or two.

1. If you are analyzing an essay, what is the difference between the writer's thesis and your own thesis statement?

2. Why does "telling the story" not work as a structure for a textual analysis essay?

3. What reasoning skills are particularly important for textual analysis essays?

B.   Take the material you gathered for Exercise B in Chapter 6 and formulate a thesis statement about the way figurative language helps convey the theme of "Love Lessons." Then write a paragraph on this topic, using your thesis statement as the topic sentence. Keep this material for use in Exercise B in Chapter 8.

C.   Take the material you gathered for Exercise C in Chapter 6, and formulate a thesis statement about the way structure or tone helps convey the thesis of the essay you chose. Then write a paragraph on this topic, using your thesis statement as the topic sentence.

D.   Write a paragraph summarizing the story of George Orwell's "Shooting an Elephant" (Readings). Then rewrite the paragraph as process analysis, devoting a sentence or two to each stage in the development of the main idea of the essay.

chapter 8

Writing Textual Analysis Essays 2: Revising Your Draft

Stage 1   Clarifying Essay Topics

Stage 2   Gathering Material

Stage 3   Formulating a Tentative Thesis Statement

Stage 4   Drafting

Stage 5   Revising Thesis Statement and Essay Structure
   Step 1 Making a Revision Outline
   Step 2 Revising Your Thesis Statement
   Step 3 Revising Essay Structure

Stage 6   Revising Individual Paragraphs
   Step 1 Revising Your Introduction
   Step 2 Revising Middle Paragraphs
   Step 3 Revising Your Conclusion

Stage 7   Final Editing

If you have followed the procedures for gathering material and writing a draft in Chapters 6 and 7, you might think your draft is unlikely to need much revision. Sometimes that is the case. Textual analysis essays present problems that you may need practice in identifying and solving, however. It is always a good idea to review your draft a day or two after you have written it. You will then be better able to see your work with the eyes of your audience and to make any necessary revisions.

In this chapter, we will show you how to revise thesis statements, essay structure, and individual paragraphs in textual analysis essays. You can find more general comments on these aspects of the revising process in Chapter 5.

Stage 5   Revising Thesis Statement and Essay Structure

One of the key difficulties in writing textual analysis essays is maintaining a clear boundary between the essay you are writing and the text you are writing about. We will look at different aspects of this problem and how to overcome them at each stage of revising.

Step 1   Making a Revision Outline

If you made a draft outline as described in Chapter 7, you can easily turn it into a revision outline. If you did not, you will find guidelines for making a revision outline in Chapter 5.

Step 2   Revising Your Thesis Statement

To assess the effectiveness of your thesis statement, you check

- that you have an *opinion* about the work's theme or thesis (or the aspect of the text specified in your assignment)
- that this opinion is a response to the essay assignment
- that the opinion is *supported* by reference to several aspects of the text

If you check the thesis statement for the sample topic on Al Purdy's poem "Trees at the Arctic Circle," you will find that it does not need revision at this point, for it contains opinion, response, and support:

WRITING SAMPLE

Thesis statement for sample topic: Through prosody, structure, figurative language, and diction [list of supporting topics] that all emphasize a change in attitude [focus of assignment], Purdy's "Trees" shows us we must change our attitude ... from contempt to admiration ... [writer's opinion of work's theme].

Problems with thesis statements in textual analysis essays often arise from focusing on details of the work or a critic's opinion at the expense of *your* supported opinion on these subjects. Here are some examples, with suggestions for revision.

WRITING SAMPLES

Weak thesis statements:

- "Al Purdy published 'Trees at the Arctic Circle' in 1967. This poem is written about Baffin Island up in the Arctic Circle. It is cold up there and the trees are more like shrubs. I will analyze 'Trees' to show Purdy's themes." (Revise to focus introductory details; add an opinion on Purdy's themes, a reference to the assignment, and support.)

- "Al Purdy's 'Trees' has interesting diction, good poetic structure, and a very intriguing point of view that has a lot to say about changing attitudes." (Revise to fuse disconnected evaluative comments into a supported analytical opinion.)

- "Margaret Atwood is right about Al Purdy; in 'Trees' he manipulates the elements of the poem to convey changes in attitude like a 'skillful master-conjuror.'" (A promising start, but revise to include your own opinion explicitly.)

Step 3   Revising Essay Structure

When you check your draft for essay structure, there are three main questions to consider.

- Is it your *analysis* that provides the framework for your essay, rather than details of the text?

  As we mentioned in Chapter 7, falling into a running summary of the text is one of the most common, and most serious, weaknesses of textual analysis essays. If you find that your topic sentences and paragraph divisions correspond to the sequence of the text you are examining, you will likely need to revise.

- Do your paragraphs follow the order you indicate in your thesis statement?

- Is this an effective order of ascending interest?

Use the revision column on your outline to note any problems with the analytical framework and to mark in a new order of topics and points if you need one.

- In reviewing the draft of the sample assignment, you might discover that your first middle paragraph—supposedly on structure—simply describes the development of the speaker's attitude. You would note the problem in the revision column of your draft outline (see Chapter 7, p. 87).

- In reviewing the order of points in your draft, you might reconsider your decision to end with the paragraph on prosody, since it merely shows that the speaker's mind is flexible and capable of change. Figurative language and diction most clearly demonstrate the speaker's change in attitude, and so you might decide to end with these points. Note that you would now need to revise the thesis statement to reflect this shift in order.

Stage 6 Revising Individual Paragraphs

Step 1 Revising Your Introduction

What kind of *context* do you need to provide for your thesis statement in a textual analysis essay?

If you have done research, it may be tempting to display your knowledge by presenting various critical perspectives or many details of the author's life and publications or the director's other films. This is not always inappropriate; in a research essay, for example, there are good reasons to begin with a statement of the critical debate (see Chapter 13). In a shorter textual analysis essay, however, you need to set the stage for your thesis statement rather than smother it with information.

In revising your draft introduction, then, check that

- you provide all the details necessary to identify the work(s), such as author/director and title(s)

- these details and any criticism you present are relevant to the subject identified by the assignment and to your thesis statement

- you avoid large generalizations about literature or life intended to be impressive rather than to illuminate the thesis statement

- you include any other material your readers might need to understand the thesis statement or appreciate its significance

- you make an effective transition from context material to thesis statement

- you make any changes required as a result of changes to the essay structure

Let's examine how you might revise the introduction to the essay on Al Purdy's poem.

- In the draft, the introduction begins with material about the context of the poem: the quotation from Margaret Atwood about Purdy "always turning banality inside out" (see Chapter 6, p. 75). The transition from this quotation to the thesis statement seems ineffective, however. So you might consider your readers—an instructor knowledgeable about Purdy and a group of students who have been discussing Purdy's work—and decide that a statement of the poem's immediate and deeper subjects would lead more directly to the thesis statement. Rewriting the context material and changing the order of topics, as indicated on the revision outline, might give you the following introduction:

WRITING SAMPLE

Revised introduction: In "Trees at the Arctic Circle," one of Al Purdy's subjects is, as the title of the poem suggests, the rather insignificant-looking ground willow that grows in the Canadian Arctic. His more important subject, however, is what our response to any living thing reveals about our respect for life itself. Through prosody, structure, figurative language, and diction that all emphasize a change in attitude, Purdy's "Trees" shows us we must change our attitude to even the most apparently insignificant living things from contempt to admiration, if life is to have any importance and value.

Note the problems with the following statements of context:

Weak introductory sentences:
- "Al Purdy, who was born in 1918, published over forty books of poetry. He is often seen as the greatest Canadian historical poet, since he has commented on many eras in our country's history. Now he himself is history; *Beyond Remembering*, his collected poems, was published in the fall of 2000, just after his death." (Information implies the thesis statement will be about history, not change in attitude.)

- "Throughout history, authors from every country and culture have been concerned with how to change people's attitudes. They have always known that, if minds and attitudes do not keep changing, a culture is dead, however lively it looks on the outside." (This statement of context is more relevant to the subject of the assignment, but the statement itself is large and hard to support. Has the writer really read "authors from every country and culture"?)

Step 2   Revising Middle Paragraphs

It is very common to find paragraphs in even carefully planned textual analysis essays where telling "what happens" has taken the place of making a point. This is natural. Sometimes we are carried away by a story, or the development of a metaphor, or a vivid scene in film or drama. In this stage of the revision process you will learn how to keep the vividness but use it as evidence to support your points.

Reread each middle paragraph carefully. Do you need to

- identify the (possibly hidden) topic of the paragraph?
- make a point about that topic, a point linked to the overall thesis statement?
- add examples or direct quotations?
- prune the details so that they become *evidence* for the point?

  "Telling" often replaces direct quotation, which is the best possible evidence. You may need to convert telling into quotation. For guidelines on using quotations effectively, see Quotations in Part 3, Handbook.

- explain how the evidence supports the point?

Claiming that a quotation or detail supports a point is not sufficient, since readers interpret things differently. You need to explain the connection.

Consider this draft paragraph on structure from the essay on "Trees at the Arctic Circle":

WRITING SAMPLE

Draft paragraph: In the first stanza of "Trees," the speaker gives us his first (negative) impressions of these little arctic trees, which he describes as insignificant and cowardly. In the second stanza, he compares these "Coward trees" with the great Douglas firs, maples, and oaks of Ontario. In the third stanza he takes a closer look at the arctic willow and revises his opinion. He now sees these trees as brave, resourceful, and even rather beautiful. In the final stanza, he focuses on his own values, condemning his earlier criticism of the trees and punishing himself by making this record of his "stupidity" permanent in a poem.

This summary of what happens stanza by stanza may work as *evidence*, since it seems accurate to the poem. But what is it evidence of?

To make a point about structure, you would consider how the stanzas are related. Each stanza seems to focus on a different attitude, and these attitudes follow each other chronologically. Each stanza thus represents a stage in the process by which the speaker's attitude shifts from contempt to admiration. You might therefore conclude that in the poem as a whole, structure serves the function of demonstrating that changing our attitudes is a process requiring sustained attention and reflection. You might decide to make this your overall *point* about structure. Your ideas about the functions of individual stanzas would become the *explanations* linking your overall point to your evidence.

With a transition from the preceding paragraph on prosody, your revised paragraph might look like this:

WRITING SAMPLE

Revised middle paragraph: If the prosody of the poem emphasizes movement, the structure identifies this as the movement towards change, specifically the speaker's shift in attitude. The poem is organized into four stanzas, each stanza focusing on a different attitude. In the first stanza, the speaker gives us his first (and very negative) impressions of these little arctic trees, which he describes as insignificant and cowardly. In the second stanza, he compares these "Coward trees" with the great Douglas firs, maples, and oaks of Ontario. In the third stanza, he takes a closer look at the arctic willow and revises his opinion. He now sees these trees as brave, resourceful, and even rather beautiful. In the final stanza, he focuses on his own values, condemning his earlier criticism of the trees and punishing himself by making this record of his "stupidity" permanent in a poem. By presenting these attitudes in a chronological sequence, the poet emphasizes that the speaker's shift in attitude is a process with identifiable stages.

Step 3   Revising Your Conclusion

As we pointed out in Chapter 5, your conclusion should restate and extend your thesis and suggest its broader context or implications. In drafting, however, you may have merely summarized your thesis and main points or, conversely, shifted into large generalizations about life or literature. Either of these choices will likely fail to satisfy your readers, who want to see both what greater understanding of the text your discussion has made possible, and also what the implications are for the larger issues that the assignment and the text have raised.

So in revising, ask these key questions about your draft conclusion:

- Does your conclusion expand the original thesis statement by drawing upon the more specific ideas you have developed in the body of the essay?

Focus on the *relationship* between the subject of the assignment (such as setting) and the text's form and theme/thesis, rather than merely restate thesis and points.

- Have you briefly discussed the broader implications of your essay?

   We all want to feel that what we have written is important. You can show readers that your analysis of a text has a broader significance by putting it within a larger context. That context might be such things as opinions expressed by scholarly critics or reviewers, similarities to and differences from other works by the same writer or other films of the same type, or the relevance of issues raised in the text to your readers or to the world. (In some cases, you may need to revise your introduction so that it refers to the context you will return to in your conclusion. This return to the initial context gives conclusions the sense of both extending and completing a circle.)

- Have you shown the connection between the subject of the assignment or the text you have analyzed and your statement of broader implications?

Good conclusions are both hard to write and hard to explain. Let's take a look at the concluding paragraph of the draft essay on Purdy's "Trees at the Arctic Circle."

WRITING SAMPLE

Draft conclusion: Prosody, structure, figurative language, and diction in Purdy's "Trees at the Arctic Circle" teach us the need to shift our attitude towards living things from contempt to admiration. Purdy is right. Living things need our attention. The world is a mess, and we have to take a new attitude to the living world around us, or our civilization will be doomed.

This conclusion restates the thesis, and its general comments are very much in the spirit of Purdy's poem. There is no expansion of the thesis, however, and the statement of broader implications is not connected to the analysis of subject, theme, or form. The comments on the world, as they stand now, could have been written without reading either the poem or the essay analyzing it.

To expand a thesis and draw out its implications, you have to take the time to reflect on what your analysis has led you to discover about the text and the subject of the assignment.

- In the sample topic, the text is Purdy's poem and the subject of the assignment is change of attitude. The essential discovery is that the poem presents the stages by which the speaker's attitude changes, from an initial mental flexibility and passion to, finally, a place of stillness in which everything can co-exist. If you think about how this poem relates to Purdy's work more generally, you may recall Margaret Atwood's comments about Purdy "turning banality inside out" (quoted in Chapter 6) and realize that presenting the process of change is the answer to Atwood's question about "how it's done." You could then revise the conclusion so that it begins with the quotation from Atwood and then presents your discoveries about the text and changes in attitude as the answer to her question.

This is the conclusion that might result from these changes:

WRITING SAMPLE

Revised conclusion: In her "Foreword" to *Beyond Remembering: The Collected Poems of Al Purdy*, Margaret Atwood comments that Purdy is "always turning banality inside out.... You can't see how it's done but suddenly, where a second ago there was only a broken vase, there's a fistful of brilliant flowers" (18). How ugly, insignificant trees become beings to be admired is also the magic of "Trees at the Arctic Circle." "How it's done" is through prosody, structure, figurative language, and diction. Together these teach us that shifting our attitude towards living things from contempt to admiration is a process with stages. The process involves, first, having a passionate and mobile approach to perception and judgment; second, realizing the delicacy and strength—the living quality—of living things; and third, being able to distance ourselves enough to observe and judge our own attitudes. Through this process, we can finally arrive at a place of stillness where attitude, poem, and living being can co-exist:

> I have been stupid in a poem
> I will not alter the poem
> but let the stupidity remain permanent
> as the trees are
> in a poem
> the dwarf trees of Baffin Island

Working on Your Own Assignment

- Change your draft outline into a *revision outline* by recording what you have actually done in your draft and what needs to be changed.

- Check that your thesis statement is not a description of the theme/thesis or form, but rather your supported opinion on the assignment topic.

- Check that your draft is not a running summary of the text, but rather is organized around a series of topics of ascending interest.

- Check that the *context* section of your introduction provides information that directly leads towards your thesis statement.

- Check that textual detail in middle paragraphs does not simply describe a section of the text, but rather is used as evidence to support a point.

- Check that the connection between point and detail in middle paragraphs is sufficiently *explained*, especially in the case of direct quotations.

- Check that your conclusion restates and expands the thesis and suggests broader implications appropriate to the subject of the assignment and the text.

EXERCISES

A.   Suppose that you have been asked to write an essay analyzing the theme of Robert Frost's poem "Stopping by Woods on a Snowy Evening." Here is the poem.

PUBLISHED WRITING

STOPPING BY WOODS ON A SNOWY EVENING

Whose woods these are I think I know.
His house is in the village though;
He will not see me stopping here
To watch his woods fill up with snow.

My little horse must think it queer
To stop without a farmhouse near
Between the woods and frozen lake
The darkest evening of the year.

He gives his harness bells a shake
To ask if there is some mistake.
The only other sound's the sweep
Of easy wind and downy flake.

The woods are lovely, dark and deep,
But I have promises to keep,
And miles to go before I sleep,
And miles to go before I sleep.

1. Cross out all the irrelevant statements in the following introduction to an essay analyzing the theme of this poem. You will be left with three sentences that (1) establish an appropriate context for an analysis of the poem; (2) outline the principal areas the essay will cover; (3) state the thesis of the essay. Label these three sentences. HINT: Pick out the thesis first. Then look for key words from the thesis in the sentences that lead up to it. This strategy will help you eliminate sentences that are either too general or too specific.

INTRODUCTION

Robert Frost is a very famous American poet. This poem has been quoted on many American state occasions, such as presidential inaugural addresses. People like this poem because, like all poetry, it is simultaneously auditory and visual. In many of his poems, Robert Frost wrote about the beauty of the pastoral New England landscape, but his poems are not just a simple celebration of nature. Life is often presented symbolically as a journey, just as Frost presents it in this poem. Through the imagery, rhythm, sound patterns, and structure of "Stopping by Woods on a Snowy Evening," Frost presents a human dilemma most readers can identify with. In the second stanza, Frost contrasts the speaker's desire to stop with the horse's surprise. The result is a deceptively simple pastoral lyric in which Frost presents the tension between meeting obligations and longing for a respite from them. With poems as good as this one, it's no wonder that Frost won four Pulitzer Prizes.

2. Cross out all the irrelevant statements in the following conclusion to an essay analyzing the theme of "Stopping by Woods on a Snowy Evening." You will be left with three sentences that (1) restate the thesis; (2) summarize the main points of the essay; (3) suggest the wider implications of the essay. Label these sentences.

CONCLUSION

Like all good nature poets, Frost conveys his enjoyment of the landscape he describes very powerfully. It's obvious, however, that Frost never experienced a Canadian winter, where yielding to the desire for a rest might lead to that all-too-common Canadian experience: death in the snow. As we have seen, "Stopping by Woods on a Snowy Evening" deals with that common human desire to rest both the body and the spirit before tackling responsibilities once again. Other poets we studied this term also deal with universal themes, but their poetry is much harder to understand than Frost's. Our analysis of the technical features of this poem—the hypnotically regular rhythm, the soothing sound patterns, the images of the silent, frozen landscape, and the overt clash of desires in the last stanza—confirms that Frost's apparently simple celebration of the New England landscape is really a subtle exploration of the human condition. In the last stanza, especially, we feel the pull of the darkness and the woods through the alliteration of *dark* and *deep*. "Stopping by Woods on a Snowy Evening" is thus a good example of Frost's ability to reach a wide audience through poetry that never parades its technical and moral sophistication. "Stopping by Woods on a Snowy Evening" is a great poem and I enjoyed reading it very much.

B. If you drafted a paragraph analyzing "Love Lessons" (see Exercises in Chapter 6), make a revision outline for the paragraph and then revise it. Or trade paragraphs with a classmate, make suggestions for changes, and then revise your own draft.

chapter 9

Writing Comparison Essays

Stage 1 Clarifying Comparison Topics

    Step 1 Checking for a Basis of Comparison

    Step 2 Looking for Similarities and Differences

Stage 2 Gathering Material

    Step 1 Using Matching Categories of Analysis

    Step 2 Clarifying the Basis of Comparison

Stage 3 Formulating a Comparison Thesis Statement

    Step 1 Forming an Opinion about Each Set of Material

    Step 2 Forming an Opinion about Overall Similarities and Differences

    Step 3 Supporting Your Opinion about Similarities and Differences

Stage 4 Drafting

    Step 1 Selecting Material

    Step 2 Organizing Comparisons: Block and Point-by-Point Methods

Stage 5 Revising Thesis Statement and Essay Structure

    Step 1 Revising Your Thesis Statement

    Step 2 Revising Essay Structure

Stage 6 Revising Individual Paragraphs

    Step 1 Revising Your Introduction

    Step 2 Revising Middle Paragraphs

    Step 3 Revising Your Conclusion

Stage 7 Final Editing

A special type of analysis essay you may be asked to write in many college and university courses is the comparison essay. You may be asked to compare two poems, two models of moral development, social organization in two tribal societies, or two views of a social problem. Comparison assignments help you and your reader better understand both the things you are comparing—the *objects of comparison*—and the more general subject, concept, or focus that is the *basis of comparison*.

To illustrate how basic the process of comparison is, let's consider this question: Is someone with an income of twenty thousand dollars a year a wealthy person? In comparison to most of the planet's inhabitants, the answer would be yes; in comparison to the average North American, however, the answer would be no. Without comparison, the term wealth is virtually meaningless.

Our understanding of the concept of wealth will remain fairly superficial, however, unless we take the comparison further. As we work through the similarities and differences between the situations of people with different incomes, we are forced to think not only about those specific instances, but also, and perhaps more significantly, about our own ideas of what constitutes wealth. What standard of living does each person's income provide? How many people does it support? How much of it is disposable income—that is, money that does not have to be spent on necessities such as food, clothing, and housing? Comparing the economic positions of people with different incomes would thus help us understand both the concept of wealth—the *basis of comparison*—and these different economic positions—the *objects of comparison*.

This chapter emphasizes the most problematic aspects of making comparisons: choosing a basis of comparison, arriving at a thesis, and organizing your material. You will also find general guidelines for clarifying topics, gathering material, formulating a thesis statement, and drafting and revising comparison essays. To illustrate these stages of writing, we will focus on a comparison between two essays on addiction that appear in Part 2, Readings: Gabor Maté's "Embraced by the Needle" and Bruce Alexander and Stefa Shaler's "Addiction in Free Markets." You will follow this discussion more easily if you read the essays first.

Stage 1   Clarifying Comparison Topics

Imagine you have been given the following choices for a comparison essay:

- Compare the explanations of addiction in Gabor Maté's essay "Embraced by the Needle" and Bruce Alexander and Stefa Shaler's essay "Addiction in Free Markets."
- Compare any two similar short stories from your class anthology.

Step 1   Checking for a Basis of Comparison

Comparison essay assignments will indicate, at least generally, the objects of comparison, the two (or more) things you are to compare. Assignments you can put in the form "Compare X and Y in terms of Z" also indicate the basis of comparison, the common element you are to focus on. The first topic above gives the basis of comparison:

> Compare Gabor Maté's essay "Embraced by the Needle" (X) and Bruce Alexander and Shefa Shaler's essay "Addiction in Free Markets" (Y) in terms of their explanations of addiction (Z).

This is the sample topic we will use for the rest of the chapter.

The second topic does not indicate a basis of comparison. To write successfully on this kind of topic, you will first need to choose objects that share a significant similarity. You might, for example, pick short stories with similar subjects, settings, or main characters. You could use this element as your basis of comparison, or you might discover a more interesting basis of comparison in the process of gathering material. (See Stage 2, below.)

Step 2   Looking for Similarities and Differences

Remember that "compare" always means "compare and contrast." Look for both similarities and differences in the objects of comparison.

Stage 2   Gathering Material

Step 1   Using Matching Categories of Analysis

Before you can compare two things, you need to analyze each separately. To make sure you *can* compare them, you need to use the same categories of analysis for each one. So the first step in gathering material is to find appropriate categories. If you are analyzing ideas or information, for example, you will choose relevant categories of content analysis (see Chapter 3). If you are more concerned with aesthetic qualities of form or presentation, you will find the categories of textual analysis more useful (see Chapter 6). You will perceive similarities and differences more easily if you set out your material in matching columns.

In the sample assignment, the term "explanations of addiction" indicates that you should focus on the content of the two essays, not on their literary qualities. Using the categories from Reading Analytically in Chapter 3, here is what you come up with:

CATEGORIES	MATÉ'S ESSAY	ALEXANDER AND SHALER'S ESSAY
Subject	Causes of addiction	Causes of addiction, then solutions
Main idea	Emotional pain in childhood changes brain chemistry, leading to addiction	Social dislocations in free-market societies lead to "mass addiction"; integration in real communities is the only cure
Development	Causal analysis framed by narratives	Causal analysis. Free-market societies create dislocation; dislocation creates addiction
Detail	Stories of addicts; theories of effects of stress on brain chemistry	Historical examples: present day; 16th- to 19th-century England; the history of Native Canadians
Context/ Perspective	Maté is a physician; perspective more psychological than medical	Alexander teaches in a psychology department, but the essay is more concerned with social trends than with individuals
Purpose	To gain sympathy for addicts' emotional suffering	To explore causes as a prompt to political action for change

Besides helping you focus on similarities and differences, a set of matching categories can also reveal imbalances in your material. Occasionally you may find that a category contains a lot of material on one object of comparison, but little or none on the other. In this case you must decide whether to drop the category, find more material, or explain the imbalance.

- In the matching categories for the sample assignment, there are no major imbalances of material. But let's suppose you discovered that you had much more material in the development category for Maté's essay than for Alexander and Shaler's essay. You would have three options: review Alexander and Shaler's essay and take more notes on its methods of development; drop this category as not relevant to your thesis; or find a reason for the imbalance. You might decide, for instance, that you have more notes on structure in the Maté essay because it is very loose and unsystematic, whereas Alexander and Shaler set out the problem and its solution in a straightforward manner.

Step 2   Clarifying the Basis of Comparison

Creating a set of matching categories will also help you clarify or decide upon a basis of comparison.

If your assignment has indicated a basis of comparison, this basis should be the focus of one set of matching categories. If the assignment has not indicated a basis, you can choose a key area of similarity and/or difference from your list of matching categories.

- The basis of comparison given in the sample assignment on addiction is "explanations of addiction." Under the category of subject, you note that both essays deal with the causes of addiction. You can thus make the basis of comparison more precise by identifying it as "explanations of the causes of addiction."

- If you had chosen the assignment asking you to compare two short stories, your matching categories of textual analysis would offer you a number of possibilities to try out as a basis of comparison, such as subject, characterization, setting, style, and theme. You would choose the best basis of comparison by seeing which of these connected with the pattern of material in most other categories.

  If you chose setting, for example, could you compare not only the settings themselves, but also characters' attitudes towards the setting? Figurative language used to describe the setting? The relation between setting and theme?

Stage 3   Formulating a Comparison Thesis Statement

Step 1   Forming an Opinion about Each Set of Material

You arrive at a comparison thesis opinion much as you do for other analysis essays, that is, by scanning the material in your categories to see how it is linked and what point it suggests. You begin by considering what point the material in each set of categories, considered separately, makes about the basis of comparison. (We say "considered separately," but putting the columns side by side will sharpen your sense of the qualities of each object.)

- Scanning the material on "Embraced by the Needle," you may notice that Maté's point about emotional pain in childhood causing addiction is reinforced by the narrative framework and details of individual addicts' lives. The material in several categories confirms that Maté's perspective is psychological rather than medical.

- In the Alexander and Shaler essay, the point about the social causes of addiction, the systematic causal analysis, and the historical examples all indicate a sociological perspective.

Step 2   Forming an Opinion about Overall Similarities and Differences

The next step is to consider the *relationship* between the two points you came up with in the previous step. Are the objects of comparison similar or different in relation to the basis of comparison? What generalization can you make about the similarities and/or differences? Your answer to these questions becomes the *opinion* part of your thesis statement.

- "Embraced by the Needle" and "Addiction in Free Markets" seem to embody quite different perspectives on the causes of addiction. You might write the opinion part of your thesis statement as follows:

> **Tentative thesis opinion:** In "Embraced by the Needle" Gabor Maté explains the causes of addiction from a psychological perspective, whereas Bruce Alexander and Stefa Shaler offer a sociological perspective in "Addiction in Free Markets."

Step 3   Supporting Your Opinion about Similarities and Differences

As in any analysis essay, the support for your opinion comes from the categories of material you used to arrive at the opinion. The only difference in formulating a thesis statement for a comparison essay is that you draw the support from the matching categories, not from one set alone. Problems with comparison thesis statements most often come from one-sidedness, where one of the objects of comparison receives unequal treatment either in the opinion or in the support. Take care to make the thesis statement even-handed.

- In the sample assignment, the opinion part of the thesis statement focuses on perspectives, but the perspective of each essay was confirmed by the categories of main idea, development, detail, and purpose. These categories therefore provide support for the thesis opinion.

WRITING SAMPLE

Tentative thesis statement: In "Embraced by the Needle" Gabor Maté explains the causes of addiction from a psychological perspective, whereas Bruce Alexander and Stefa Shaler offer a sociological perspective in "Addiction in Free Markets." These different perspectives are evident in the writers' points and purposes and in their handling of development and detail. *1* *2*
3

A tentative thesis statement like this gives you a starting point for exploring the similarities and differences between the things you are comparing. The process of drafting and revising often leads to deeper insights into your material.

- As you will see with the sample topic, there are important differences between a psychological and a sociological perspective. Through drafting, a better thesis emerges that explains the relationship between these two perspectives on addiction.

Stage 4 Drafting

Step 1 Selecting Material

As with other analysis essays, the categories of material you found relevant in working out your thesis will become the basis for your middle paragraphs. There are two points you need to keep in mind, however.

- Because your matching categories will give you a great deal of material, you may need to limit the number of categories you use. Drop categories where your material is skimpy, imbalanced, or not relevant to your comparison. If, for instance, you were comparing two poems, one a sonnet and one not, you would likely drop the category of structure, since there would not be much point in "proving" the obvious differences between the two.

- Make sure you include roughly equivalent amounts of material for each of the things you are comparing.

Step 2 Organizing Comparisons: Block and Point-by-Point Methods

Probably the most common problem in writing comparison essays is finding an effective method of organization. There are two basic methods of organizing comparisons: the block method and the point-by-point method.

Block method When you use the *block method*, you say everything you have to say about one subject before you discuss the other. This method can be effective for very short essays in which overall similarities and differences are more important than detailed comparisons (as you might find, for instance, in a personal essay comparing good teachers and bad teachers). The block method is also useful for in-class essays and essay exams when you are developing a few main points without extensive quotations or facts and figures as evidence.

Point-by-point method When you use the *point-by-point method*, you compare things one aspect at a time. The point-by-point method usually works better for essays over 500 words because you can explain the significance of similarities and differences as you go along. You don't risk leaving them unexplained or having to add another section to explain them.

Making a draft outline is especially valuable when you are using the point-by-point method. Note the point you intend to make about each category so you don't merely repeat that the things you are comparing are similar or different. These points will become the basis for your topic sentences.

- The sample assignment seems too long and complex for the block method, so you would choose the point-by-point method. The draft outline for your middle paragraphs (MPs) might look like this:

DRAFT OUTLINE

MP 1	Thesis and perspective	Addiction is caused by emotional pain in childhood, according to Maté's psychological perspective
		Addiction is caused by social dislocation in Alexander and Shaler's psychological perspective
MP 2	Development	Maté's causal analysis is enclosed in a narrative framework
		Alexander and Shaler's causal analysis is systematic and directly presented
MP 3	Detail	Maté emphasizes the lives of individual addicts
		Alexander and Shaler use non-individual historical examples

Stage 5 Revising Thesis Statement and Essay Structure

Step 1 Revising Your Thesis Statement

In this step you ask yourself the following questions:

- Does your thesis statement present an overall opinion about similarities and differences between two (or more) objects of comparison?

- Does this opinion reflect the relationship between similarities and differences in the material you collected in matching categories?

- Is this opinion based on, and does it indicate, a common basis of comparison?

- Does the thesis statement indicate the support that you are going to present in the body of the essay?

If the answer to any of these questions is no, your thesis statement will need revision.

- Note that the following thesis statements lack some of these components:

Weak thesis statements:
- "Maté's essay is very different from Alexander and Shaler's, as I shall show by looking at their different forms and purposes." (no basis of comparison indicated)

- "'Embraced by the Needle' is a psychological essay, while 'Addiction in Free Markets' is more systematic." (no common basis of comparison, no support)

If you answer yes to all the questions above, there is still one final question to ask:

- Does your draft suggest new ideas that will give you a better thesis?

As we suggested earlier, the tentative thesis statement for the sample assignment seems to have all the components mentioned above. Yet it focuses solely on differences and does not account for the nagging sense you might have in writing the draft that while the explanations of addiction in the two essays are different, they are not incompatible. There is a link, after all, between the emotional pain suffered by individuals and the social dislocations that give rise to emotional pain. So you might revise your thesis statement to include this idea.

WRITING SAMPLE

> **Revised thesis statement:** In "Embraced by the Needle" Gabor Maté explains the causes of addiction from a psychological perspective, whereas Bruce Alexander and Stefa Shaler offer a sociological perspective in "Addiction in Free Markets." While these differences in perspective are evident in the writers' purposes and in their handling of development and detail, the main ideas expressed in the two essays are complementary rather than contradictory, for social dislocations give rise to the emotional pain experienced by individual addicts in childhood.

Step 2   Revising Essay Structure

Use your draft outline, if you made one, or make a revision outline showing the points in each paragraph of your draft to check whether

- your choice of either block or point-by-point organization still seems appropriate. If your outline reveals each block paragraph is crammed with a variety of ideas, for example, then you should probably decide to adopt the more systematic point-by-point method. On the other hand, if your paragraphs switch back and forth like a ping-pong ball, you may need to gather your material into larger blocks.

- your discussion includes matching points about the things you are comparing. Have you inadvertently failed to cover some aspect of one object of comparison? Have you devoted much more space to one object of comparison than another? Identify problems for correction in the next stage of revision.

- your sequence of paragraphs still seems effective. In a comparison essay, your paragraphs should lead towards the point that best illustrates the most important similarity or difference. Thus if your thesis statement suggests that differences are more important than similarities, you would discuss similarities first and then differences, ending with the most significant one. If similarities are more important, you would end with the most significant similarity.

In the sample assignment, for example, the revised thesis statement requires a rethinking of the structure. It indicates you are going to move from showing differences to showing the compatibility of psychological and sociological perspectives. You would therefore start from the most obvious difference—detail—and lead towards your comparison of these perspectives. You will see the results of this reorganization in the sample essay. See C. Jones, "Perspectives on Addictions" (Readings: Sample Essays).

Stage 6 Revising Individual Paragraphs

Now that you have identified areas where your draft needs revising, it is time to tackle individual paragraphs.

Step 1 Revising Your Introduction

If you have followed our advice not to worry about your introduction until the structure of the whole essay is clear, you may find that you need to fill out the statement of context that precedes your thesis statement.

Does your statement of context

- indicate your basis of comparison and establish its importance or relevance?
- provide matching information about the objects you are comparing?

Consider the way you might have led up to your thesis statement in your draft introduction.

WRITING SAMPLE

Draft introduction: Understanding the causes of addiction is an important project and few people are better qualified for it than Dr. Gabor Maté. Dr. Maté works on Vancouver's East Side, sometimes called the drug capital of North America, and his writing shows he has on-the-ground knowledge of what he is talking about. I will compare his essay entitled "Embraced by the Needle" with an essay called "Addiction in Free Markets" by Bruce Alexander and Stefa Shaler.

This statement of context successfully indicates the basis of comparison, "understanding the causes of addiction," and provides good information about Gabor Maté. It does not explain why this is an important subject, however, or give matching information on Alexander and Shaler. For the revised version of this introduction, see the sample essay by C. Jones, "Perspectives on Addictions," Readings: Sample Essays.

Step 2 Revising Middle Paragraphs

Check to see whether

- you use topic sentences that clearly indicate your method of organization
- you use umbrella topic sentences when necessary to indicate the major divisions in your material

- you give roughly the same amount of space to developing points about each thing you are comparing

Problems in developing comparison paragraphs usually come from imbalance and one-sidedness.

- In reviewing the draft for the sample assignment, for example, you might find a paragraph like this:

WRITING SAMPLE

Draft middle paragraph: The most obvious contrast between "Embraced by the Needle" and "Addiction in Free Markets" is in the type of detail used. In "Embraced," the detail we remember is the detail of individuals: of Anna, who "wasn't wanted"; of Carl, who "had dishwashing liquid poured down his throat"; of Wayne, a tough man, who at the end of the essay "looks away and wipes tears from his eyes." No one cries in "Addiction." In that essay, the language is abstract, the kind argumentative social scientists use.

This paragraph was intended to compare the use of detail in the two essays. There are no examples to show the kinds of detail used in "Addiction," however, so the point of the comparison is not clear. In revising, you would both clarify the point and provide examples from "Addiction."

Step 3   Revising Your Conclusion

It may be tempting to conclude by simply repeating what you have said about similarities and differences. Readers expect more than this, however; they want you to step back from the specific objects you have compared and explore what your essay has revealed about your subject.

You will need to check not only that your conclusion summarizes your thesis statement and main points, but also that the development of these points leads to a deeper understanding of both the basis of comparison and the objects you have compared. If either summary or development is missing, you will need to revise.

- Consider the draft conclusion to the sample assignment:

Draft conclusion: "Embraced by the Needle" and "Addiction in Free Markets" are very different because their authors' handling of detail, development, and point are so different. Gabor Maté has a psychological perspective on the causes of addiction, while Bruce Alexander and Stefa

Shaler take a sociological point of view on the issue. These are very different perspectives on this important issue, but they may be more complementary than contradictory.

This conclusion restates the thesis but adds nothing to it. In revising, you would want to stress what you and your readers have learned from considering the causes of addiction from both a psychological and a sociological perspective.

You will find the complete revised essay in Part 2, Readings: Sample Essays (C. Jones, "Perspectives on Addictions").

Working on Your Own Assignment

Your purpose in comparing is to illuminate the similarities and differences between two (or more) **objects of comparison** in reference to a **basis of comparison**.

- Check your essay topics to make sure you know which ones ask you to compare. Are you given a basis of comparison, or will you need to work out one?

- Gather material on both objects of comparison by using the appropriate questions for content or textual analysis. Analyze the objects separately so that you don't distort them by trying to find similarities too soon.

- Arrange your material in matching categories that contain equivalent amounts of material, focusing on the categories most relevant to your topic.

- Examine your material to determine the overall relationship between similarity and difference in reference to your basis of comparison.

- Formulate a thesis statement by making a general point about this overall relationship and giving reasons to support it.

- Organize your material by the block method or the point-by-point method, depending upon the length and complexity of your essay. Your topic sentences should make clear which method you are using.

- When you revise your draft, check to see whether your paragraphs lead towards the most important similarity or difference, and whether you have given equal attention to both objects of comparison in your thesis statement, your points and detail, and your introduction and conclusion.

EXERCISES

A. Work out a basis of comparison for a short essay on each of the following subjects. Compare your responses with your classmates'.

1. The celebration of Christmas in your family and another family

2. Canadian and American television programs of a specific type (such as lawyer shows, family dramas, talk shows)

3. Different ways of looking at a local environmental or educational issue

B. Read the essays by Garrett Hardin ("Lifeboat Ethics") and Judy Rebick ("The Poorhouse") in the Readings. What would be a workable basis of comparison for these two essays? Try several possibilities. Compare your responses with your classmates'.

C. Decide whether each of the following is a good thesis statement for a comparison essay and explain your decision.

1. For an essay comparing Sigmund Freud's view of dreams with C. G. Jung's:

> In developing a theory of dreams that emphasizes their prophetic and compensatory functions, Jung departed from the view of the unconscious upon which his mentor, Freud, had built his theory of dreams.

2. For an essay comparing the principles of solar and geothermal heating systems:

> Although solar and geothermal heating systems are similar in some respects, in others they are different.

3. For an essay comparing the positions of Wade Davis and Ken Wiwa on the value of national and ethnic identity:

> Wade Davis seems utterly certain of the value of ethnic identity, while Ken Wiwa seems to find ethnic identity inevitable but partly boring.

D. Sort the following items into matching categories of advantages and disadvantages of part-time jobs for businesses and workers. Then work out a comparison thesis statement based on your categories. (This information comes from Oliver Bertin, "Part-time Work: Boon or Bust?" *The Globe and Mail*, November 6, 2002, C3.)

> Greater flexibility in scheduling
>
> Fewer benefits, if any
>
> Workers with less experience and fewer skills
>
> Less chance of advancement
>
> Lower payroll costs
>
> Easier to hire and fire as needed

More time for family

Lower wages

Ability to combine work and school

Less training

More flexible hours

Shorter shifts means less consistency

Good bridge between full-time employment and retirement

Greater turnover

Uncertain scheduling

Lower training costs

E.   Choose one of the following topics. Use the appropriate questions for textual analysis to gather material and formulate a thesis. Then make an outline showing how you would organize your middle paragraphs. Compare your work with your classmates'. All the essays mentioned are reprinted in Part 2, Readings.

1. Compare the significance of fathers and fatherhood in any two of the essays by Andrew Pyper, Lenore Keeshig-Tobias, Scott Sanders.

2. Compare the presentation of imperialism in any two of the essays by Maggie Black, George Orwell, Jonathan Swift.

3. Choose two other essays from the Readings to compare. You will need to work out your own basis of comparison.

F.   John Fraser's essay "Save the Last Dance" (Readings) is organized in a mixture of the block and point-by-point methods. Make an outline showing how you would organize this essay wholly in the point-by-point method.

chapter 10

Evaluating Arguments and Writing Critiques

Stage 1   Clarifying Evaluation Topics

Stage 2   Gathering Material

       Step 1   Analyzing the Writer's Reasoning and Evidence

       Step 2   Identifying Strengths and Weaknesses ("Fallacies") in Logic

       Step 3   Categorizing and Charting Strengths and Weaknesses

Stage 3   Formulating an Evaluative Thesis Statement

       Step 1   Forming an Opinion about the Relationship between Strengths and Weaknesses

       Step 2   Supporting Your Opinion

       Step 3   Indicating the Standard of Evaluation

Stage 4   Drafting

Stage 5   Revising Thesis Statement and Essay Structure

       Step 1   Revising Your Thesis Statement: Checking for Evaluative Point

       Step 2   Revising Essay Structure: Argument

Stage 6   Revising Individual Paragraphs

       Step 1   Revising Your Introduction: *Ethos*

       Step 2   Revising Middle Paragraphs: Arguments and Evidence

       Step 3   Revising Your Conclusion

       Sample Topic: Critiquing the Logic of Ted Byfield's "Health Canada..."

Stage 7   Final Editing

There is an important difference between *analysis*—identifying the causes of downtown parking problems, for example—and *evaluation*—judging whether arguments for a new downtown parking lot are logical or illogical, or whether the proposed lot will be beautiful or ugly. As this example suggests, analysis usually precedes evaluation. This does not mean, however, that evaluation is less significant than analysis. Whether you are arguing with a friend about a movie or campaigning for a political candidate, judging the value of things is an important human activity.

Making evaluations is equally important in academic disciplines, as you learn how to determine the worth of theories, experiments, technological innovations, or works of art. When you write evaluative essays in an academic setting, you need to be conscious of and express the criteria you use in making judgments. Although specific criteria will vary, there are four common *standards of evaluation* that provide a broad framework for making judgments. These are the *logical, aesthetic, practical*, and *ethical* standards.

In the **persuasive** essay, you use one or more of these standards to present your own position on a subject. You will find guidelines for writing this kind of essay in Chapter 11. In the **critique**, you use one or more of these standards to evaluate someone else's work, such as the methodology of a scientific experiment or the interpretation of a poem. John Bongaarts' essay "Population: Ignoring Its Impact" (Part 2, Readings) is a good example of a critique.

This chapter will show you how to write a critique evaluating the validity of reasoning and evidence in stated or implied arguments. We focus on this type of critique for two reasons: to demonstrate how to separate considerations of logic from aesthetic, practical, and ethical concerns; and to give you the tools you need to evaluate your own arguments when you write persuasive essays.

We will first outline the gathering, drafting, and revising process for this kind of essay, and then show the process at work in a sample assignment: evaluating the logic of an essay from Part 2, Readings.

Stage 1   Clarifying Evaluation Topics: Checking for the Logical Standard

The first stage in tackling any evaluation assignment is to check what standard(s) of evaluation the assignment asks you to use. You will know to use the logical standard of evaluation if

- the assignment asks you to assess reasoning, evidence, a case, arguments, methodologies, or strategies of argumentation:

    Does David Suzuki's "It Always Costs" (Readings) present
    a credible case for distrusting technological innovation?

OR

- the assignment asks whether the piece you are assessing is logical, reasonable, credible, plausible, valid, or a related term:

  Write an essay assessing Maggie Black's arguments about forced marriage in "Wanted: The Right to Refuse" (Readings).

Note that the important term *argument* may be used for the writer's overall case, for the structure of this case, and for individual points. Usually the context indicates which meaning is involved.

Stage 2 Gathering Material: Arguments and Evidence

Most of us have strong emotional responses, positive or negative, to a writer's position on a subject we care about. This emotional response can get in the way of a fair-minded assessment. The best way to avoid this problem is to analyze the reasoning and evidence first, and only then assess the strengths and weaknesses.

Step 1 Analyzing the Writer's Reasoning and Evidence

In Reading Analytically (Chapter 3) we introduced these categories for analyzing the content of nonfiction writing: subject, main idea/thesis, development, evidence/detail, purpose, and context. You use the same categories to analyze reasoning and evidence when you evaluate a piece of writing according to the standard of logic, except that you pay closer attention to types of argument (development) and kinds of evidence (detail). The discussion below will explain what to look for.

Types of argument The main types of argument are as follows.

Deductive Argument Any argument that moves from general principles to make a judgment about more particular cases could be called a deductive argument. The most rigorous kind of deductive argument is the syllogism, where a general statement (called the major premise) is linked to a specific case (called the minor premise) to produce a conclusion.

- Historians view history objectively (major premise).
- Joan is a historian (minor premise).
- Therefore Joan views history objectively (conclusion).

A deductively organized essay moves from an overall point to a series of individual points that serve to confirm and develop it.

Inductive Argument Any argument that moves from particular cases towards a general point that can be made from them could be called an inductive argument. An inductive essay is structured around the movement from individual points to a more general thesis.

- "The Ticking Bomb" (Readings) is inductively organized. In it, Wade Davis identifies key indicators of trouble in our times in order to lead to a concluding thesis: "True peace and security for the 21st century will only come about when we find a way to address the underlying issues of disparity, dislocation and dispossession that have provoked the madness of our age" (219).

Causal Argument Reasoning from cause to effect is an important form of logical reasoning. Causal reasoning becomes causal argument when a writer claims the cause and effect sequence creates something good or bad.

- Ann Dowsett Johnston uses causal argument when she claims that raising tuition fees will produce better education, and therefore tuition fees should be raised ("A Lament for Quality," Readings).

Other Types of Argument A writer may also construct an argument employing other modes of analysis.

- Process analysis: "To reduce unemployment, the government should follow these three steps."
- Systems analysis: "If Canada is to make a better showing at the Olympics, it will require dedication—and money—from athletes, coaches, sponsors, every level of government, and fans."
- Textual analysis: "Despite its star-studded cast, this movie is a failure because of its senseless plot and cliché-ridden dialogue."

Kinds of evidence Anything used to show that a statement is true or false is considered evidence. Here are the most common types.

Examples An example is a small, detailed, and specific piece of evidence intended to support a point about a larger whole. For example, a line from a poem may support a statement about the poem's theme, or an anecdote about one mugging may support a case about the causes of street crime. Examples are sometimes called "soft" evidence because they rarely prove a point; it is usually possible to find counter-examples. Nevertheless, examples can be vivid and compelling.

Facts and Figures Another kind of evidence is sometimes called "hard" evidence: statistics, research studies, scientific observation, and the like. "Hard" evidence is widely used in scientific and applied research papers, but is also frequently found in persuasive essays such as Ross Laver's "Profits by the Truckload" (Readings).

Reference to Authorities The opinion of someone who is knowledgeable about a subject is a valid kind of evidence. Within academic disciplines you are often expected to locate your ideas within a tradition of thinking about your subject. Argument by authority is thus important in academic essays, especially research essays.

- In the first letter in *"The English Patient* Debate: Round Two" (Readings, p. 333), Catherine Warren cites the feminist researcher Carol Gilligan as support for her argument that there can be a morality based on care rather than on abstract ideals.

Analogies An analogy is a comparison based on a partial similarity between the features of two unlike things. If you say that the heart is like a pump, for instance, you are using an analogy that emphasizes the similarity between the functions of the heart and the pump and ignores the differences. When you use an analogy as part of an argument, you are arguing that one situation is like another situation and will have the same outcome, good or bad.

- In "Lifeboat Ethics" (Readings) Garrett Hardin uses the analogy of the lifeboat to describe the situation of Western societies, in his view. Just as lifeboats sink when they take on too many people, he argues, so Western countries will collapse if they accept too many immigrants.
- Political arguments are often based on historical analogies: "A war in the Middle East would be another Vietnam."

Emotional Appeals Emotional appeals are comments or language designed to elicit strong feelings. An emotional appeal conveys a distinct attitude and invites the reader to share that attitude. Thus emotional appeals are often used in propaganda: written, visual, or spoken texts designed to persuade an audience to form a political or religious group, participate in particular social actions, or adopt a particular ideology. The feelings aroused by emotional appeals may be incompatible with a rational consideration of the subject. Thus emotional appeals are not really evidence in the logical sense at all. However, you need to be able to tell when a writer supports a position by emotional appeals rather than reasoned arguments.

You can most reliably identify emotional appeals by their diction and tone. The words used in emotional appeals often reflect extreme feeling: things are "unthinkable," "dreadful," "inarguable," "utterly obvious," "unquestionably valuable." The tone of these appeals may be ridiculing, satiric, or humorous.

- Professor E. J. Bond employs an emotional appeal when he describes Thomas Hurka's review of *The English Patient* as a "piece of fatuous tripe." ("*The English Patient* Debate," Round Two, Readings, p. 334)

Step 2   Identifying Strengths and Weaknesses ("Fallacies") in Logic

After you have analyzed a writer's arguments and evidence, the next step is to evaluate the material to determine its strengths and weaknesses. It is important to look for both strengths and weaknesses, however much you may agree or disagree with the writer's position, because your readers are more likely to be convinced when your critique seems fair-minded.

The following guidelines will help you determine strengths and weaknesses in reasoning and evidence. Note that problems in logic are often called logical fallacies.

Types of argument

Deductive Arguments   Deductive arguments are strong if the general principle is valid and supportable, and if the points that follow can be derived from that principle. Similarly, deductively organized essays work when the main points demonstrate the initial thesis.

Problems in deductive arguments occur when the general principle is not valid or the points do not follow from the principle. Earlier we spoke of the syllogism as the purest form of deduction. A syllogism is not valid if the major premise is untrue, the minor premise is missing, or the conclusion does not follow.

- Our example of a syllogism was this: Historians view history objectively; Joan is a historian; therefore Joan views history objectively. This syllogism would not be valid if some historians do not view history objectively; if no proof is offered that Joan is a historian; or if the argument reached the conclusion that because Joan is a historian, she would make a good politician.

You are most likely to find problems in deductive arguments when the major premise is a sweeping generalization that is either unverifiable (cannot be proved to be true or false) or untrue.

- "Throughout history humans have struggled for perfection." (unverifiable)
- "Hard work always leads to success." (untrue)

This is the fallacy of over-generalization, a fallacy also involved when you make large conclusions from limited major or minor premises:

- "Some historians are objective [limited major premise]. Joan is a historian. Therefore Joan is objective."

Another common deductive problem is the fallacy of circular reasoning, or begging the question, where a point that should be proved is assumed to begin with.

- "I will show that this dreadful practice of abortion, child murder, is morally wrong" is a thesis statement flawed by circular reasoning; it assumes that abortion involves murder. This point would have to be part of the essay's moral argument.

Inductive Arguments An inductive argument is considered strong if the particulars are connected and if they lead plausibly to some larger conclusion. Similarly, an inductive essay works if the paragraph points are connected with each other and lead towards the concluding thesis.

Problems in inductive arguments most often occur when there is a gap between the particulars and the conclusion that the essay intends to draw from them. This gap is often called the fallacy of hasty generalization.

- "My neighbours never cut their lawns and the man across the street leaves his porch light on all night; these are symptoms of the moral decay of the modern world." This is an ineffective inductive argument. The concluding point is too broad to emerge convincingly from these particulars.

Causal Argument Causal argument is effective when the effect is clearly shown to follow from the cause.

- "Many families with children have moved into the neighbourhood; therefore, enrollment in local schools is likely to rise."

Problems in causal reasoning arise when the cause-effect relationship is unconvincing. Many ineffective causal arguments suffer from what is called the *post hoc* fallacy. The full phrase in Latin is *post hoc ergo propter hoc*, meaning "after this, therefore because of this." In this fallacy, because a second event follows a first, the first is taken to be the cause of the second.

- "The team ate Mighty Bites before the game; no wonder they won."

A special version of *post hoc* is sometimes called the fallacy of single cause/single outcome, where a likely multiplicity of causes is reduced to one.

- The claim that "the increase in murders is a direct result of the suspension of the death penalty" is flawed unless further evidence is presented, since many factors are known to affect the homicide rate.

A fallacy common to several kinds of argument and evidence is the straw man fallacy, where an opponent's arguments are exaggerated or selectively presented to make them appear insubstantial. This tactic is particularly common in fallacious causal reasoning. In a straw man argument, the possible consequences of an opponent's position are misleadingly exaggerated:

- "If funding is increased for daycare centres, more children will attend them; as a result, children will cease to spend any significant time with their mothers."

Kinds of evidence

Examples   Examples are valid when they are representative of the larger point or situation they are intended to support. Examples do not prove a point, however.

Problems in handling examples arise when there is a questionable relationship between the particular example and the general point it is intended to prove. Examples can be irrelevant to the point they are supposed to support, or, more commonly, generalizations can be based on too few examples, committing what we earlier called the fallacy of hasty generalization.

- "There is a flood of books being published in North America on men's problems. I saw two new titles from Australia only last week." (irrelevant example)
- "Clearly consideration for others is disappearing in today's society; my neighbour's parties have kept me awake three nights in a row." (inadequate examples)

Facts and Figures   Facts and figures are potentially the most convincing kinds of evidence a writer can present.

Problems result from the fact that statistics and other "facts" can be manipulated. Problems in "hard" evidence arise when the sources of the evidence are not current, when the evidence does not come from a reliable and appropriate source (as when statistics about the United States are assumed to apply to Canada), or when the evidence cited is extremely selective.

Reference to Authorities   Argument by authority is used well when the writer shows a critical awareness of the orientation and expertise of the authorities cited, the authorities have real expertise in the subject, and their ideas do not overshadow the writer's own ideas.

Problems result from citing authorities not relevant to the subject. A famous chemist is a valid authority for an essay on chemistry, but not for an essay on juvenile delinquency. Other problems are vague and unsupported references ("experts claim," "research shows"), unbalanced citation of authorities (where they are all on one side of a case, for example), and general over-reliance on authorities. All these could be called the fallacy of inappropriate authority, occasionally referred to as the fallacy of the *argumentum ad verecundiam* (literally, the "argument for respect").

Analogies Analogies often have strong emotional appeal, but they are effective support for an argument only when they are used with other kinds of evidence.

Problems come from the fact that analogies are essentially metaphoric and emphasize similarities; when readers are aware of significant differences between the two objects being compared, or see the objects through the lens of a different metaphor, they will consider that the writer has committed the fallacy of false analogy.

- For example, readers who consider people as interdependent and the world as a sea in which we are all swimming will not be convinced by Garrett Hardin's claim that the lifeboat is a good analogy for Western societies ("Lifeboat Ethics," Readings).

Historical analogies are especially liable to fallacy, since historical situations are complex and often differ from one another substantially.

Emotional Appeals Emotional appeals are strong in that they touch the level where beliefs are formed; they are used well when they reinforce logical arguments.

Problems with emotional appeals come when they are used instead of logical argument, or when they are excessive. We tend to consider emotional appeals that have come unmoored from logical support as sentimental or manipulative. The common fallacy of *ad hominem* (literally "to the man") arguments—arguments directed against the arguer, not against his or her arguments—reflects a misuse of emotional appeals. So does the fallacy of *ad populem* (literally "to the populace") appeals, those designed to arouse popular unthinking sentiments.

- "In Jean-Jacques Rousseau we see the kind of confused thinking about family and education we would expect from a man who put his own children into an orphanage." (*ad hominem* argument)
- "No one who values our pioneer past can deny that the real role for women is in the home, whether that home is a cabin in Northern Quebec or a house in suburban North York." (*ad populem* argument)

This table summarizes the most common types of argument and evidence and their potential problems.

KINDS OF ARGUMENT AND EVIDENCE	FALLACIES
Deductive argument	Over-generalization, circular reasoning (begging the question)
Inductive argument	Hasty generalization
Causal argument	*Post hoc*, single cause/single outcome, straw man
Examples	Hasty generalization
Facts and figures	Outdated, inappropriate, or misleading facts and figures
Reference to authorities	Inappropriate authority (*ad verecundiam*)
Analogies	False analogy
Emotional appeals	*Ad hominem, ad populem*

Note that this is a partial list of fallacies; for a more complete list, consult a textbook on logic or persuasive writing.

Step 3 Categorizing and Charting Strengths and Weaknesses

Because of the complexity of evaluating reasoning and evidence, you may find it helpful to make an evaluation chart with one column for the analytic aspects of the writing, a second column for strengths, and a third column for weaknesses. If there is no key strength or weakness for a particular aspect, leave the space blank.

- If you were to analyze and evaluate "It Always Costs" (Readings), for example, you might decide that David Suzuki's examples (aspect column) prove his point (strength column) but are a little stereotyped (weakness column).

You will find a complete evaluation chart in the Sample Topic section of this chapter.

An evaluation chart is useful for summing up the results of gathering material; it also streamlines the process of formulating a thesis statement, as you will subsequently see.

Stage 3 Formulating an Evaluative Thesis Statement

An evaluative thesis statement for a critique essay should include an opinion about the relationship between strengths and weaknesses in the piece of writing, an indication of the main support for this opinion, and an indication of the standard(s) of evaluation you are using. Let us look at each of these components in turn.

Step 1   Forming an Opinion about the Relationship between Strengths and Weaknesses

The opinion part of the thesis statement focuses on the *overall relationship* between strengths and weaknesses. This means you must decide whether, in general, strengths outweigh weaknesses, weaknesses outweigh strengths, or strengths and weaknesses are equally balanced. An evaluative chart makes this decision easier because you can see at a glance where you have noted strengths and weaknesses and where you have left blanks. You must still decide, of course, whether each analytical category you have used is equally important to your overall assessment.

Although you may find it difficult at first, deciding on the overall relationship between strengths and weaknesses is a skill you can acquire with practice. Simply listing some strengths and some weaknesses may be easier, but it won't give you a good thesis opinion. Neither will claiming that there are only strengths or only weaknesses; you would have to work hard to overcome your readers' skepticism, since few arguments are either flawless or totally flawed. Similarly, you cannot use the judgment that strengths and weaknesses are equally balanced to avoid making up your mind. If you claim they are balanced, you will need to demonstrate the balance throughout your essay.

Step 2   Supporting Your Opinion

An evaluation chart will also reveal the most important *support* for your thesis opinion, since the fullest categories will likely become the topics you use to organize the body of your essay.

Step 3   Indicating the Standard of Evaluation

Indicating the *standard of evaluation* in the thesis statement is more important than you might realize. You know what standard of evaluation you are using, but unless you tell your readers, they may apply their own favoured standard and then be upset when your judgments differ from theirs. You may indicate the standard directly, by referring to "logic" or "logical," or indirectly, by referring to arguments or cases or by using terms like "credible" or "convincing," whichever is more suitable for your audience.

Here are examples of effective and weak thesis statements evaluating an essay according to the logical standard.

WRITING SAMPLE

Effective thesis statements evaluating logic:

- "Although some of his examples seem stereotyped [weakness], the use of appropriate evidence and a clear process structure [strengths supporting thesis opinion] makes David Suzuki's 'It Always Costs' a logically credible [standard of evaluation] essay on the costs of technology." (Putting the weakness in a dependent clause indicates that it is less important than the strengths.)

- "The strength of David Suzuki's argument in 'It Always Costs,' its clear process structure, is more than offset [overall relationship] by its weaknesses, its stereotypical examples and excessive emotional appeals."

- "Stereotypical examples and excessive emotional appeals in David Suzuki's 'It Always Costs' are balanced by logical strengths in the use of appropriate evidence and a clear process structure."

Weak thesis statements evaluating logic:

- "Maggie Black's 'Wanted: The Right to Refuse' is just the usual illogical feminist diatribe; this time it's about the evils of forced marriage." (no strengths or weaknesses)

- "Maggie Black's 'Wanted: The Right to Refuse' has some very compelling examples of brutality in forced marriages [strength], but it also has some weaknesses." (overall relationship of strengths and weaknesses not clear; weaknesses not specified; standard of evaluation not clear)

Stage 4 Drafting: Sequencing Strengths and Weaknesses

In critique essays, the relationship between strengths and weaknesses —as expressed in the thesis statement—determines the order of ascending interest. If weaknesses outweigh strengths, you begin with strengths and then move to weaknesses; if strengths outweigh weaknesses, then vice versa.

Once you have decided whether strengths or weaknesses come first, you will also need to decide on the order of points within each category. If you have written the support component of your thesis statement carefully, you should be able to use the sequence of topics it indicates. As for other essays, a draft outline is often helpful. For a critique essay, make sure the draft outline indicates strengths and weaknesses as well as topics and points. You can find a sample draft outline for a critique essay in Stage 4 of the sample topic assignment in this chapter.

Stage 5 Revising Thesis Statement and Essay Structure: Reasoning

The key principle to remember in revising is that your reader will judge your reasoning and evidence by the same standard you are using to evaluate someone else's writing. Thus you will need to review your draft to decide whether your argument as a whole is satisfactory.

Step 1 Revising Your Thesis Statement: Checking for Evaluative Point

If you are not satisfied with your argument as a whole, the problem may lie in your thesis statement.

- Does it contain an opinion about the relationship between strengths and weakness?
- Does it mention the specific strengths and weaknesses you discuss in your middle paragraphs, in the order you discuss them?
- Does it make clear that you are using the logical standard of evaluation?
- Has writing your draft given you new ideas about your argument?

You may have a good thesis statement and yet your argument may have changed during the writing of the draft. You may have come to a different understanding of the relationship between strengths and weaknesses or made changes in the specific strengths and weaknesses you discuss. If so, you will need to revise your thesis statement to reflect these changes.

Step 2 Revising Essay Structure: Argument

Problems with the overall argument may lie not in the thesis statement but in the way the argument unfolds. To check essay structure, ask yourself these questions:

- Does the sequence of topics make clear the *relationship* between strengths and weaknesses set out in the thesis statement?
- Is the topic for each paragraph an item of *support* indicated in the thesis statement?
- Does the topic sentence of each paragraph make a point about one aspect of the logical standard of evaluation, such as the weaknesses of a deductive argument or the effective use of facts and figures?

If your answer to any of these questions is no, you will need to revise accordingly. You may also discover that writing the draft has revealed flaws in the argument that you planned. If so, you will need to make a revision outline to guide you as you rewrite. For a sample revision outline, see Stage 5, Step 2 in the sample topic assignment in this chapter.

Stage 6 Revising Individual Paragraphs: *Ethos*, Argument, and Evidence

Just as you review your draft to evaluate the effectiveness of your argument as a whole, so you will need to review each paragraph to see whether you have been fair-minded, argued your points effectively, and provided good evidence to support them.

Step 1 Revising Your Introduction: *Ethos*

As we will discuss more extensively in Chapter 11, readers are likely to respond more strongly when values are an issue. Therefore, you need to consider your readers carefully when you write any kind of evaluative essay. When you are writing a critique of logic, you want to present yourself as reasonable and fair-minded. This is especially important in the introduction. If the introduction offends their values, readers may proceed no further.

To ensure that readers keep reading, check your introduction for what the ancient rhetoricians like Aristotle called *ethos*, the image of himself or herself the writer projects to the reader. If you can answer yes to the following questions, your introduction is likely to seem reasonable and fair-minded.

- Do you begin by providing a clear summary of the context, subject, and thesis of the piece you are evaluating, rather than praise or critical comments?
- Have you chosen language that is as neutral as possible, rather than language that is biased in favour of or against the piece you are evaluating?
- Is the tone of the introduction as a whole that of a fair-minded, reasonable person?

If the answer to any of these questions is no, you will need to revise. The following examples will show you how.

WRITING SAMPLE

Draft introduction: Environmentalists are *always complaining* about the technology their very lives depend on. Prominent among these environmentalist *whiners* is David Suzuki, and his essay "It Always Costs" presents the *usual* illogical mixture of *prejudice* and out-of-date science for which he is becoming *notorious*.

Revised introduction: The technology we are surrounded by—from toasters to cruise missiles—has been created both by scientists' expertise and politicians' choices. Is this technology a boon or a curse? We can perhaps help answer this question by evaluating the work of David Suzuki, a commentator on technology who is both a scientist and an environmental activist. Evaluating the logical credibility of his essay "It Always Costs" provides insights into the environmentalist view of the value of technology. [add thesis statement]

Step 2 Revising Middle Paragraphs: Arguments and Evidence

Using the list in Stage 2, Step 2 above as a guide, check each middle paragraph to see

- which type(s) of argument and kind(s) of evidence you have used
- whether you have explained your argument fully enough
- whether you have provided enough evidence
- whether you have avoided common problems and fallacies

Suppose, for example, you had written the following paragraph in an essay on David Suzuki's "It Always Costs":

Draft middle paragraph: The way David Suzuki develops his argument is particularly impressive because he demonstrates that he can change his mind. Changing one's mind really demonstrates mental flexibility because nothing is more difficult than this. Mentioning DDT, thalidomide, and DES piles up the examples of scientific errors in a very compelling way.

This paragraph comments on David Suzuki's argument, but what about your own? You may have intended to write a deductively organized paragraph meant to show how Suzuki develops his argument and to offer examples as evidence that this development is effective. The paragraph is flawed by circular reasoning, however. It asserts that Suzuki changes his mind and claims that is a good thing, but it does not explain what the change is or why it is good. The evidence is flawed by irrelevant examples, since examples concerning scientific error demonstrate nothing about change of mind. In revising the paragraph, you would present examples to show that Suzuki's essay is organized around the movement from one set of beliefs about technology to another, different set.

Step 3   Revising Your Conclusion

In the conclusion the emphasis shifts from the piece you have evaluated to your summation of strengths and weaknesses. You still need to leave readers with an image of yourself as fair-minded, however. One way you achieve this image is by mentioning both strengths and weaknesses. If the tone of some of your earlier comments has been sharp, now is the time to return to a more neutral, inclusive tone.

WRITING SAMPLE

Draft conclusion: If the environmental movement believes that the world is clogged up with paper products due to the pervasiveness of computer technology, perhaps some radically new decisions are called for. Stopping essays like "It Always Costs" from being printed could be the first step in this new direction. (no summary of strengths and weaknesses, biased tone)

Revised conclusion: David Suzuki's choice of obvious targets like DDT for his examples does encourage a stereotyped response, no question about that. However, this evidence is effective even if it is obvious, and the change-of-mind structure of the essay powerfully counteracts the effect of stereotyping, giving the essay finally a great deal of credibility.

Sample Topic: Critiquing the Logic of Ted Byfield's Essay "Health Canada ..."

In this section we will work through the process of gathering material, drafting, and revising an essay critiquing the logic of Ted Byfield's essay "Health Canada Inadvertently Discloses Facts Planned Parenthood Would Like to Suppress" (Readings). You will follow the process more easily if you read Byfield's piece first.

Stage 1   Clarifying Evaluation Topics: Checking for Logical Standard

Imagine you have been given the following assignment.

> Does Ted Byfield's essay "Health Canada ..." present a credible case about current developments in world population? Write an essay evaluating his argument.

By using the terms "credible case" and "argument," the assignment indicates that you should use the logical standard of evaluation.

To put the essay in context, you might check on its source and currency, noting that it appeared in March 2002 in the Alberta-based magazine *The Report*, of which Byfield was one of the founders.

Stage 2 Gathering Material: Arguments and Evidence

Step 1 Analyzing the writer's reasoning and evidence

Before you can evaluate the essay, you will need to understand its main ideas and strategies of argumentation. To collect material on these, you use the relevant categories of content analysis (see Chapter 3, Part B, Reading Analytically), with the categories of development and detail adapted for the analysis of logic:

Subject Your reading of the essay confirms the subject suggested by the assignment: current developments in world population.

Main Idea/Thesis Byfield's thesis seems hard to find until you realize that he presents parts of it in three different places, mostly as the opinion of various authorities. (This is a common tactic in controversial writing.) Put together, his thesis becomes

   a) Canadians are working more and having fewer children.

   b) As a consequence, there is a "serious population decline."

   c) This "decline" will have very negative economic consequences in the Western world and the world in general.

Types of Argument As this thesis indicates, the essay is organized as a causal argument, a series of causes and effects.

Kinds of Evidence Byfield brings in statistics (*facts and figures*) to support his points about work and population decline. Various countries—Canada, Italy, India, Egypt, Mexico, and Thailand—serve as examples to support these points. He also uses many *references to authorities*, both those who support his position and those he criticizes. His description of the authorities he criticizes creates *emotional appeal* through satire.

Step 2 Identifying strengths and weaknesses ("fallacies") in logic

Now that you have *analyzed* Byfield's argument and evidence, you are ready to *evaluate* this material.

Types of Argument Your analysis showed that "Health Canada" presents a *causal argument* organized into three steps. The strength of this argument is that it is systematic: one step follows another. This argument suffers, however, from the fallacy of single cause/single outcome. Byfield does not discuss or refute other explanations of the cause of declining birthrates. It does not seem credible that obsession with work is the only cause. Similarly, since Byfield does not address other arguments about the effects of current developments in population, you question whether a decline, if it were true, would have economic "havoc" as its main effect.

Kinds of Evidence

Examples How relevant are Byfield's examples? Do they support his generalizations? There is no evidence that a Canadian obsession with work is also a worldwide obsession. How representative are Byfield's other examples? You will need to look at the use of facts and figures in the essay to answer this question.

Facts and Figures The specific statistics Byfield gives as evidence for "population decline" or "absence of kids" may at first seem quite impressive. When you look more closely, however, you realize that even if Europe's birthrate is running at 1.4, this rate is more than balanced by the rates of India (3.5), Egypt (3.9), and Mexico (3). Clearly, though the birthrate is declining in some countries, the world's population is increasing.

Then you note that there are no birthrate statistics for Canada and the United States, only a casual comment implying that their birthrates are more than Thailand's (2). This means their birthrates must be above replacement. Quoting these rates would have weakened Byfield's case about "decline."

Thus the figures quoted seem to be selectively chosen and do not support the claim about "serious population decline." Furthermore, the essay contains neither examples nor facts and figures as evidence of economic "havoc," only a one-sentence assertion about "government welfare programs depend[ing] upon a steady inflow of tax money."

Reference to Authorities Although Byfield refers to authorities he agrees with and to those he disagrees with, he uses them very differently. He endorses as fact both the American Enterprise Institute's interpretation of the statistics it uses and Tom Bethell's comments about there being "too few people" in his *American Spectator* article. On the other hand, he dismisses authorities on the other side of the case—Paul Ehrlich, Planned Parenthood, the United Nations—with no summary of their actual arguments.

You decide that including authorities from both sides is a strength, but that the one-sided treatment of authorities is a weakness.

Emotional Appeals Your evaluation of the treatment of authorities is echoed in your evaluation of emotional appeals. Byfield treats authorities he agrees with objectively, whereas he describes those who perceive serious dangers in population growth in emotionally laden satiric terms as "prophets of doom," "zealous preacher[s]," and the like. This use of emotional appeals decreases the credibility of Byfield's argument.

Step 3 Categorizing and charting strengths and weaknesses
As an aid to seeing how strengths and weaknesses compare, you set them out briefly in an *evaluation chart*.

EVALUATION CHART

PART	STRENGTHS	WEAKNESSES
Argument	Systematic argument	Fallacy of single cause/ single outcome
Examples		Not representative, don't support generalization
Facts/Figures	Statistics present	Statistics flawed for Step 2, absent for Step 3, don't prove thesis
Authorities	Authorities presented	Authorities treated differently
Appeals		Satiric dismissal of authorities on other side.

Stage 3 Formulating an Evaluative Thesis Statement

Looking at this chart, you decide that the strength of the essay "Health Canada ..." is that it presents the *appearance* of a systematic causal argument supported by statistics and authorities. Its weakness is that its logic is in appearance, not in substance: its causal argument is fallacious, its treatment of authorities one-sided, and the statistics and examples do not prove its thesis. As the chart indicates, the weaknesses outweigh the strengths. To express this *relationship* between strengths and weaknesses and to mention the categories that *support* this opinion, you come up with the following thesis statement:

WRITING SAMPLE

Tentative thesis statement: "Health Canada ..." seems to have strengths: a systematic causal argument, support by statistics, and the presentation of authorities who oppose, as well as those who support, Byfield's thesis. While the statistics he quotes should make us think, they do not actually support his argument, and the essay is very one-sided in the way it deals with authorities.

Stage 4   Drafting: Sequencing Strengths and Weaknesses

Because you will argue that Byfield's essay has fewer strengths than weaknesses, you will start with strengths and move to weaknesses. Your thesis seems to suggest a workable series of paragraph topics, so you make a *draft outline* as a guide to writing.

DRAFT OUTLINE

TOPIC	POINT
Strength: Causal argument	Byfield's essay does have a 3-step causal structure
Strength: Facts and figures	Statistics presented to support two of these steps
Strength: Authorities	Most of thesis taken from authorities; essay refers to authorities on both sides of case
Weakness: Facts and figures	Figures do not support thesis
Weakness: Authorities	Authorities actually very one-sided

You then draft your essay, sketching an introduction and conclusion and developing each of these points in a middle paragraph.

Stage 5   Revising Thesis Statement and Essay Structure: Reasoning

Step 1   Revising the thesis statement: checking for evaluative point

At this point, you take a critical look at each of the three components of your tentative thesis statement.

Relationship   Writing your draft did not change your mind about the overall relationship between strengths and weaknesses, but this relationship is not stated clearly enough. You decide to insert a sentence to make the relationship explicit.

Support   You realize that you have not included the weakness in causal argument in your thesis statement. This is an important point, so you cannot omit it. This change will lead to a change in the structure of your essay.

Indication of Standard The word "logical" does not appear anywhere in your tentative thesis statement. You decide to add it to make your standard of evaluation clear.

Here is the thesis statement that results from these changes:

WRITING SAMPLE

Revised thesis statement: "Health Canada ..." seems to have logical strengths: a causal argument supported by statistics and references to authorities on both sides of the case. These strengths are more apparent than real, however. Byfield's treatment of authorities is one-sided and his statistics, while thought-provoking, do not support his point. As a result, his causal argument fails to be logically convincing.

Step 2 Revising essay structure: argument

In reviewing your draft, you note that your paragraphs move from strengths to weaknesses, but there are more strengths than weaknesses and the weaknesses do not follow an order of ascending interest. The essay also seems to need a more deliberate transition from strengths to weaknesses.

Since the logical strengths of the essay are more apparent than real, your paragraphs on these topics are skimpy. You decide to discuss all the strengths in one paragraph, add a transition paragraph, and then change the order to reflect the movement from least important to most important weakness. These changes will mean adjusting the order of support in your thesis statement. You make the following revision outline for the middle paragraphs (MPs):

REVISION OUTLINE

TOPIC	POINT
MP 1 Apparent strengths	Apparent strengths in argument and evidence
MP 2 Transition	These strengths are apparent, not real
MP 3 Weakness: Authorities	Use of authorities is one-sided
MP 4 Weakness: Evidence	Statistics don't prove point
MP 5 Weakness: Causal argument	Failure to deal with alternative causal explanations

For the middle paragraphs written from this outline, see D. Jones, "Reflecting on Population," in Part 2, Readings: Sample Essays.

Stage 6 Revising Individual Paragraphs: *Ethos,* Argument, and Evidence

Step 1 Revising your introduction: *ethos*

In writing your draft, you scribbled the following sentences to lead up to your thesis statement:

WRITING SAMPLE

> **Draft introduction:** Ted Byfield's essay "Health Canada Inadvertently Discloses Facts Planned Parenthood Would Like to Suppress" appeared in *The Report*, the Alberta-based newsmagazine that Byfield also edits, in March 2002. "Health Canada" is an essay on population that makes claims that sound incredible, and they turn out to be just that, incredible.

Considered logically, these sentences creating a context for your thesis statement have both strengths and weaknesses. The strength is that they provide details of author, title, currency, and location, as well as suggesting Byfield's subject. The main weakness is in *ethos*. The second sentence does not give the impression of fair-mindedness. You decide to replace it with a summary of Byfield's main idea.

Step 2 Revising middle paragraphs: argument and evidence

In checking individual paragraphs for effective argument and evidence, you find that your paragraph on Byfield's weakness in using authorities lacks sufficient evidence.

> **Draft middle paragraph:** For a start, it is true that "Health Canada" uses authorities from both sides of the argument about population, but the fact is that they are used very differently. Authorities who argue the dangers of population growth do not have their arguments described, but instead are dismissed in a series of satiric caricatures. The opinions of the American Enterprise Institute and of a journalist writing in *The American Spectator* are, on the other hand, directly quoted and treated as fact. This one-sided handling of authorities diminishes credibility.

Added Examples Your comment about treating opinion as fact is supported elsewhere, but your comment on satiric caricature needs examples, so you add the following sentence:

> Byfield calls Paul Ehrlich one of the "prophets of doom"; refers to Planned Parenthood as the "zealous preacher of the 'Save-the-World-with-Smaller-Families' message"; and states that the United Nations disseminates "don't-have-kids" propaganda.

Step 3 Revising your conclusion

Short of time, you wrote a one-sentence summary as your conclusion:

WRITING SAMPLE

Draft conclusion: Because of its one-sided use of authorities, failure to link evidence to point, and flawed causal argument, Ted Byfield's "Health Canada" does not achieve logical credibility.

This sentence reflects the sequence of topics you have used. It does not seem fair-minded, however, because it does not refer to the strengths of Byfield's essay. You have claimed that they are strengths of appearance, so you decide to start the conclusion by conceding that giving his essay the appearance of logic contributes to the recognition that logic is needed on this issue. You can then finish with the comment that we do, however, need the substance rather than the appearance of logic.

To read the finished version of this essay, go to D. Jones, "Reflecting on Population," in Part 2, Readings: Sample Essays.

Working on Your Own Assignment

Your main goal in a logical critique essay is to assess another writer's handling of logic, in writing that is itself logical and balanced.

- Check significant terms to make sure that your assignment requires the logical standard of evaluation.
- Analyze the piece of writing for subject, main idea, argument, and evidence.
- Evaluate the strengths and weaknesses of the argument and evidence.
- Formulate a thesis statement that states an opinion about the relationship between logical strengths and weaknesses in the writing, provides support for that opinion, and indicates, indirectly or directly, that you are using the logical standard of evaluation.
- Write a draft, sequencing the topics to reflect the relationship between strengths and weaknesses indicated in the thesis statement. Use a draft outline if possible.
- With the help of your draft outline or a revision outline, revise thesis statement and overall essay structure to ensure that your argument is logical and effective.

- Check that you begin your introduction by providing a context for the writing you will discuss rather than by immediately evaluating it, so that you convey the image of yourself as fair-minded.
- Check that your middle paragraphs make strong arguments and give effective evidence.
- Check that your conclusion presents both the strengths and weaknesses of the writing you have discussed and reflects, if possible, a development of the thesis statement.
- For examples of logical critique essays, see John Bongaarts' "Population: Ignoring Its Impact" and D. Jones's "Reflecting on Population" in Part 2, Readings.

EXERCISES

A.   Identify which of the following assignments asks you to use the logical standard of evaluation.

1. Argue for or against the position presented by James Ash in "To Peacekeep or Not to Peacekeep" (Readings: Sample Essays).

2. Is peacekeeping a reasonable activity? Evaluate the arguments that might be made for and against this activity.

3. Choose any one of the Socratic dialogues you have studied in class and assess the validity of the positions it presents.

B.   Write a sentence evaluating the following as thesis statements for logical critique essays.

1. Although there is a lunatic fringe that opposes a woman's right to abortion, this right is self-evident and I will examine some key books on the issue to show that it is rationally justified.

2. In *The Hazards of Being Male*, Herb Goldberg argues that pressures to conform to a stereotyped image of masculinity force many men to live like emotional zombies. Goldberg's thesis may be correct, but there is a problem with the arguments he uses and with his narrow range of examples.

3. Charles Taylor's *The Malaise of Modernity* is one of the most rational books I have ever come across. If you want a well-reasoned book on what's wrong with the modern world, look no further.

C.   Read Maggie Black's "Wanted: The Right to Refuse" (Part 2, Readings). Then evaluate the use of argument and evidence in the following paragraph. Identify (if you can) any common fallacies, decide on its topic and point, and then revise the paragraph so that it uses argument and evidence effectively:

> Man's brutality to man is legendary and impossible to
> change. The example of a young girl having her legs chopped

off to prevent her fleeing is a very powerful example that Maggie Black uses in "Wanted: The Right to Refuse." There is a great variety of examples. I wonder about the case of the 29-year-old man allowed to marry his pregnant 13-year-old girlfriend. Are we getting the whole picture? I also wonder about her word "dreadful" to describe things that other cultures practise. Black has written a book on early marriage so she must know a lot about these subjects. She is probably right that warlords promise security in exchange for a family giving up their daughter. She is a skilled writer giving good examples.

D. Evaluate arguments and evidence in Judy Rebick's "The Poorhouse" (Part 2, Readings). Follow the steps in this chapter for gathering material and formulating a thesis statement. Then make a draft outline, indicating the sequence in which you would treat strengths and weaknesses in order to support your thesis.

chapter 11

Writing Persuasive Essays

Stage 1   Clarifying Evaluation Topics

    Step 1   Finding a Standard of Evaluation

    Step 2   Defining Other Key Terms

Stage 2   Gathering Material

    Step 1   Analyzing

    Step 2   Categorizing Strengths and Weaknesses

Stage 3   Formulating an Evaluative Thesis Statement

Stage 4   Drafting: Working Out a Pro-Con Outline

Stage 5   Revising Thesis Statement and Essay Structure

    Step 1   Revising Your Thesis Statement: Checking for an Evaluative Point

    Step 2   Revising Essay Structure: Checking Sequence and Pro-Con Transitions

Stage 6   Revising Individual Paragraphs

    Step 1   Revising Your Introduction: *Ethos*

    Step 2   Revising Middle Paragraphs: Logic and Transitions

    Step 3   Revising Your Conclusion: Achieving Balance

Stage 7   Final Editing

In Chapter 10, you learned how to assess the strengths and weaknesses in someone else's argument in order to write a critique essay. In this chapter, you will learn how to discover and argue your own position on a subject. Essays of this type are called *persuasive* essays because their purpose is to persuade readers to agree with your position. The following are typical assignments for persuasive essays:

1. How should Canadian institutions respond to pressure to sanction same-sex marriages?
2. Should the summer holidays for schoolchildren be reduced to one month?
3. Is *Monsoon Wedding* better than *My Big Fat Greek Wedding*?

This chapter will take you through all the steps of planning, writing, and revising a persuasive essay, using the first assignment above as the sample topic, but drawing examples from the second and third topics as well.

In the planning stages, you focus on *analysis* and *evaluation*. First you analyze your subject to determine its good and bad points, its advantages and disadvantages, its strengths and weaknesses. This analysis gives you the material you need to arrive at a considered judgment: your evaluation of overall strengths and weaknesses.

In drafting and revising, you focus on *persuasion*: how to present your position so that your readers are most likely to take your arguments seriously. The strategies you use depend to some extent on your audience. You may be writing for readers who are *hostile* (unlikely to agree with your position), *neutral* (likely to have an open mind), or *friendly* (likely to agree with your position). Academic writing generally assumes a neutral reader, but we will comment briefly on techniques of persuasion for hostile and friendly readers.

Stage 1 Clarifying Evaluation Topics

Step 1 Finding a Standard of Evaluation

When you evaluate, as we pointed out in Chapter 10, you use one or more *standards of evaluation* as a basis for judging things. Your essay topic might explicitly ask you to consider the moral arguments for and against same-sex marriages, the practical advantages and disadvantages of reducing summer holidays, or the artistic merits of the films. More often, your essay topic will imply the standard(s) or expect you to figure out which ones to use. For example, if you chose the third assignment, you would need to think about what "better" might mean. More artistically satisfying? A better money-maker? Conveying a more moral view of life?

Whether you are given the standards of evaluation or have to figure them out, you will need to know how to use them. We discussed the logical standard in Chapter 10. Here is a brief discussion of the three other most useful standards of evaluation: the aesthetic, the practical, and the ethical.

Aesthetic standard   Aesthetics is literally the study of beauty. The aesthetic standard is commonly used to judge works of art or the "performance" aspect of any activity, such as a political candidate's speaking skills or a figure skater's technique. When you use an aesthetic standard, you ask one or more of these questions:

- Is it well constructed, beautiful, pleasing to the senses?
- Is it well performed?
- Is it a good example of its kind?

Behind these questions are judgments based on two key criteria for aesthetic judgments: coherence and comparison.

If something is **coherent**, then the parts work together to create a satisfying whole. For example, you might decide that *Monsoon Wedding* is a good movie because it has interesting characters, a suspenseful plot, and an exotic setting that all combine to make a valuable statement about marriage.

The judgment that something is a good example of its kind or is better than another of its kind obviously depends on **comparison** with typical features of the genre or with others of its kind. If you think that *Monsoon Wedding* is a better, more challenging film about marriage than *My Big Fat Greek Wedding*, for example, you are comparing these films not just to each other but also to an ideal model of the good film about marriage, a model that values complexity over, say, entertainment.

Your evaluation of aesthetic strengths and weaknesses will be most effective when you use both comparison and coherence as your criteria.

Practical standard   When you use the **practical** standard of evaluation, your main criteria are feasibility and usefulness. These are the key questions:

- Will this work?
- Will it be useful?
- Does it have a relevant application?

In "A Lament for Quality" (Part 2, Readings) Ann Dowsett Johnston uses a practical standard of evaluation when she argues, "But let's be realistic; at best operating grants are going to stay right where they are. Which means that if the learning environment is to improve, tuition must go up" (275).

Practical judgments connect the thing being evaluated (such as a school board, a law, a product, or a proposed action) with the social situation or context in which it will be applied or the purpose it will serve. You will produce the most effective practical evaluations by considering as many aspects of the context as possible. Ask yourself questions like these: Who benefits? In what ways? What will this help us to do? How much will it cost? How long will it take? What are the long-term and short-term effects?

- For example, if you were evaluating a plan to reduce summer holidays for schoolchildren to one month, you might note that the shortened vacation period could make it difficult for working parents to take holidays at the same time. On the other hand, the shorter holiday would decrease the amount of time teachers need to spend reviewing what students have forgotten and would use schools' physical plants more effectively. Weighing these practical advantages and disadvantages against each other could lead you to a very effective judgment.

Ethical Standard When you use the **ethical** standard, you judge an object's worth according to moral, ideological, or religious values. Ask questions like these:

- Is this right or wrong?
- Is this a position worth believing in?
- Is this a course of action worth following?

When you evaluate from a **moral** perspective, you judge whether something is right or wrong according to a set of principles about the values that should govern behaviour. Sometimes moral principles conflict. For one person, telling a lie may be good if the lie benefits more people than it hurts; for another, telling a lie is always bad because lying damages a person's integrity.

When you evaluate from an **ideological** perspective, you judge things by a set of social principles. Social principles, like moral principles, can conflict. For example, an environmentalist might argue that a proposed strip mine is bad because it would pollute the water supply and destroy wildlife habitat, whereas a business person might argue that the economic development would provide much-needed jobs in the community.

When you evaluate from a **religious** perspective, you base your judgments on the doctrines of a particular religious group. Many Roman Catholics, for example, would argue against abortion on religious grounds, just as many Jehovah's Witnesses would object to blood transfusions for religious reasons. Religious principles, like moral and social principles, may conflict over particular issues.

Values may conflict not only within each of these perspectives, but also between perspectives.

- In "Wanted: The Right to Refuse" (Part 2, Readings), Maggie Black agrees with the British Home Office statement that "Multicultural sensitivity is not an excuse for moral blindness" (205). This statement places higher value on moral judgments than on ideological judgments.

Because of the wide range of values people hold, you need to take special care when you evaluate things from an ethical perspective. Few readers are likely to accept your judgment of strengths and weaknesses simply because your system of values supports it ("Strip mining is wrong because environmentalists say so"). Try to be aware of your own system of values and make sure those values are appropriate to your subject. Your argument will be stronger if you acknowledge ethical positions that differ from your own.

Using more than one standard of evaluation Many issues invite evaluation from more than one standard of evaluation; some could be evaluated from all four. You will be able to give a more balanced assessment if you gather material using all relevant standards. Your decision about which of these to include in your final essay will depend on the assignment, the subject, your own position, and the audience. It may also depend on how confident you are about handling several standards.

- If you were evaluating a movie script for possible production, you might begin with its artistic merits (aesthetic standard), but you would also need to consider its audience appeal and the production costs (practical standard). If the content was potentially objectionable or offensive, you might also assess its moral strengths and weaknesses (ethical standard).

- The sample topic on same-sex marriage does not indicate a standard of evaluation. Logical and aesthetic standards are not relevant to the subject. You might decide to try ethical and practical standards.

Step 2 Defining Other Key Terms

Understanding the key terms of the assignment and the subject is particularly important in writing persuasive essays. You will often need to define these terms in your essay. Otherwise your readers may misunderstand or disagree because they do not understand the terms in the same way.

- For an essay on legalizing marijuana, for example, you would need to be sure your readers understood the big difference between legalizing the use of marijuana (making it available for sale under controlled circumstances, like liquor) and decriminalizing it (not prosecuting people who use it).

- For the sample topic on same-sex marriage, it would be essential for you and your readers to understand the difference between marriage as a social or religious commitment and marriage as a legal contract. Under present laws, a marriage licence can be issued only to a man and a woman. By doing a little research, you might find that at least two provinces offer a third possibility. According to a *Globe and Mail* article by justice reporter Kirk Makin, both Nova Scotia and Quebec allow same-sex couples to contract civil unions, which give them the same legal status as married partners ("Gay Marriage Options to Be Explored," *The Globe and Mail*, November 4, 2002, A4). You would need to define all these terms for your readers.

Stage 2 Gathering Material

Step 1 Analyzing

If you are clear on your standard of evaluation and think you know your position on an issue, you may be tempted to skip analysis and plunge straight into evaluation. We advise you not to. The process of analysis will lead you to examine more aspects of your subject: this will mean stronger arguments for your position and a greater awareness of the counter-arguments. It will also provide you with the details to make your arguments convincing.

To analyze, you need to find appropriate categories for dividing your subject into parts. The categories for content analysis described in Chapter 3 (systems, process, and causal analysis; economic, political, social, and psychological perspectives) will provide appropriate categories for analyzing a broad range of issues. The categories for textual analysis described in Chapter 6 (and elaborated in Part 4, Resources) will help you analyze subjects that you will evaluate by the aesthetic standard.

You can also use the standards of evaluation themselves to gather material by asking questions such as these:

- What ethical issues does this subject raise? For whom?
- What practical issues does this subject raise? For whom?
- What aesthetic issues does this subject raise? For whom?
- How valid are the arguments raised about this issue? (See Chapter 10 for detailed guidelines for evaluating arguments and evidence.)

To see how you would choose categories of analysis and put them to use, let's consider the sample topic on same-sex marriage.

- The sample topic asks, "How should Canadian institutions respond to the pressure to sanction same-sex marriages?" This question does not ask whether *you* think same-sex marriages should be legalized (though your answer will of course reflect your opinion); it asks you to consider the implications for Canadian institutions of responding to pressure to change current practices. Institutions could respond in three possible ways: by supporting legalizing same-sex marriages; by opposing legalization; or by seeking a compromise (to do nothing would have the same result as opposing legalization). As a result of defining the key terms, you would be aware that the institutions involved in questions of marriage are the federal and provincial governments (the lawmakers) and the churches. To these categories you might add the category of society, since social views often influence the actions of church and state. If you were to brainstorm about the ethical and practical issues raised for each of these groups, you might come up with the following list:

CHURCH   Opposes because of literal reading of scriptures

Supports because progressive positions draw younger people in

Supports because all churchgoers are "children of God"

Supports so as not to alienate gay and lesbian churchgoers

Opposes so as not to alienate backbone members of church and traditionalist clergy

SOCIETY   Opposition from traditionalists who value traditional two-parent family

Support from pluralists who recognize present diversity of Canadian society and/or support value of pluralism

STATE   Some support indicated by legislation in two provinces

Neutrality or opposition indicated by lack of legislation in others

Step 2 Categorizing Strengths and Weaknesses

After you have gathered material through analytic categories, you are ready to evaluate this material using the appropriate standard(s) of evaluation. You first organize the material you have gathered into appropriate evaluative categories (such as strengths and weaknesses, advantages and disadvantages, arguments for and against) and group entries within each category according to the standard of evaluation they represent.

- For the sample topic, you could categorize the points that indicate support for sanctioning same-sex marriages as *arguments for* taking that action and points that indicate opposition as *arguments against*. You would group points within each category according to the ethical and practical standards you used in brainstorming. You would come up with the following table:

CATEGORIZING ARGUMENTS	ARGUMENTS FOR	ARGUMENTS AGAINST
CHURCH	Ethical: acceptance of all as "children of God"	Ethical: condemnation through literal reading of scriptures
	Practical: value of attracting young people	Practical: value of not alienating traditionalist members and clergy
	Practical: value of not alienating gay and lesbian members	
SOCIETY	Ethical: value of pluralism	Ethical: traditionalist value of two-parent families
	Practical: accepting Canadian reality as pluralistic	
STATE	Practical: compromise of civil unions already in place in two provinces	

Stage 3 Formulating an Evaluative Thesis Statement

The general procedure in formulating a thesis is to identify the pattern created by the material in your categories, considered as a response to a specific essay assignment. As we pointed out in Chapter 10, the distinctive components of an evaluation thesis are an *opinion* about the relationship between strengths and weaknesses, an outlining of the *support* for this opinion, and an *indication* of the standard(s) of evaluation you have used.

If you are evaluating a subject about which you have an open mind, you may arrive at your opinion about the relationship between strengths and weaknesses by simply noting which category contains more points.

- Looking at the pattern of arguments for the sample topic on same-sex marriage, for instance, you might conclude that though ethical issues are fairly well balanced, the practical arguments for church and state to support same-sex marriage outweigh the practical arguments against that position. So you would write a tentative thesis statement that reflects this judgment.

WRITING SAMPLE

Tentative thesis statement (sample topic): Though there are serious reasons why voices in the state and, especially, the church resist same-sex marriages, there are better reasons to endorse not only the practical legal solution of civil unions, but also the value of church marriage for same-sex couples, a value that is social and ethical as well as practical.

As we mentioned earlier, our thinking about evaluative questions is shaped by our own values. Underlying this seemingly disinterested weighing of arguments, as you will see by reading the sample essay (E. Jones, "Same-Sex Marriages: Tradition and Change," Readings: Sample Essays), is an ideological belief in the value of pluralism. Nevertheless, this thesis statement lays the foundation for an effective persuasive essay because it takes opposing points of view into account. This is a key consideration when you are writing for a hostile audience or, as in most academic situations, a neutral audience. These readers will be more likely to consider your position if you are fair-minded in the way you present it.

The process of analysis may lead you to change your ideas about an issue by forcing you to consider positions different from your own. On the other hand, what happens if the opposing arguments seem stronger or more numerous than your deeply held beliefs about an issue? What do you do then? If you were writing for a friendly audience, one that shared your views, you might downplay or ignore other points of view. This is not an option when you write in an academic situation, where the burden of proof is on you. So you must seriously take other positions into account while putting forward the strongest possible case for your own.

- Let's consider how you might formulate an evaluative thesis statement for the sample topic if you were opposed to same-sex marriage on religious grounds. You might, for example, concede that there are strong practical arguments for sanctioning same-sex unions while arguing that ethical considerations are more important. Furthermore, you might conclude that within the ethical standard, religious arguments outweigh ideological arguments. That would leave you with two opposing religious views:

the belief that all human beings are "children of God," and therefore to be treated equally, as an argument for; and the belief that scripture condemns same-sex relationships, and therefore sanctioning same-sex unions would be morally wrong, as an argument against. In trying to balance these opposing views, you might formulate a tentative thesis statement like this:

WRITING SAMPLE

Tentative thesis statement (countering strong opposing arguments): While there are strong practical arguments for allowing same-sex marriages, practical considerations should not persuade church and government officials to sanction behaviour that is morally wrong. We may all be "children of God," but God has laid down the kind of behaviour He expects from His children in the Bible, and the Bible explicitly condemns same-sex relationships.

While this thesis statement takes other views into account, you would have great difficulty in making the argument convincing to neutral or hostile readers because many of them would not agree with the basic premise that the Bible is an appropriate guide to human behaviour.

You may also need to give special attention to formulating a thesis statement when you are both comparing and evaluating. The example below suggests how you might present the relationship between strengths and weaknesses when both things are relatively strong.

Tentative thesis statement (comparative evaluation): Although the clash between the groom's prim and repressed family and the bride's rambunctious and irrepressible family in *My Big Fat Greek Wedding* is a genuinely funny treatment of a real issue in marriage, the complex sorting out of traditional customs and contemporary values makes *Monsoon Wedding* a more deeply emotional and powerful treatment of the same issue: the ways opposites collide in a marital relationship.

Stage 4   Drafting: Working Out a Pro-Con Outline

Formulating a thesis statement completes the work of clarifying your own position on the subject you are examining. In writing your draft you shift your focus more fully to *persuasion*, finding strategies that will help to convince your readers to agree with your position. The most powerful tool for achieving this goal is known as *pro-con structure*.

Pro and *con* are the Latin words for "for" and "against." The side you have decided is stronger (whether strengths or weaknesses, arguments for or arguments against) becomes the pro argument; the weaker side becomes the con argument.

- For example, if you had formulated a thesis statement asserting that the film you were reviewing had more weaknesses than strengths, your *pro* argument would be something like "This is a bad film" and your list of weaknesses would support this position. The *con* argument would be "This film has some strengths," an opinion supported by your list of strengths.

The principle of pro-con structure is that you systematically present the arguments against your case, conceding (admitting) their validity or refuting (arguing against) them, and then present the arguments for your case. The idea is that readers hostile to your case, or predisposed against any particular argument (likely even for neutral readers), will be more persuaded by seeing their views taken seriously before you develop your own position.

Pro-con structure may be unnecessary or inadvisable when your purpose is to reinforce the values of a friendly audience rather than to discuss them, such as when you are writing articles for your own political party. Academic writing, as we said earlier, always assumes readers need to be convinced.

There are two main ways to organize a pro-con essay.

1. State all the con arguments in a paragraph or two at the beginning of your essay, deal with these arguments, and then devote the rest of the essay to the pro arguments. This method works best when strengths far outweigh weaknesses or vice versa.

   - If you were reviewing *My Big Fat Greek Wedding*, for example, you might concede that the characterization of the groom was weak and then go on to discuss the many strengths of the film.

2. Answer the arguments against your position point-by-point throughout your essay. This method is a better choice when your readers may be hostile or when there are strong arguments on both sides.

Taking con arguments into account does not mean you have to refute them all. If you concede the validity of some of the points—admit they are right or reasonable—you show more maturity and are therefore likely to be more persuasive.

You will find a draft outline invaluable for working out pro-con structure.

Follow the sequence of topics and points indicated in your thesis statement. To help you keep track of your overall argument, note whether points are pro or con and what standard of evaluation they are based on. Leave spaces to record any changes you decide to make when you revise.

- The draft outline for the sample topic would look something like this:

DRAFT OUTLINE

TOPIC	POINT	REVISION NOTES
Introduction		
MP1 SOCIETY	**Con** (ETH): Traditionalists value two-parent families	
	Pro (ETH): Value of pluralism	
MP2 STATE	**Pro** (PRAC): Civil unions provide legal protection and help society	
MP3 CHURCH	**Con** (ETH): Historical scriptures condemn same-sex relations.	
	Pro (ETH): Progressive valuation of equality also part of doctrines	
MP4 CHURCH	**Con** (PRAC): Danger of outraging gender traditionalists	
	Pro (PRAC): Danger of outraging gay and lesbian churchgoers; value of attracting younger generation and dealing with the changed world	
Conclusion		

Stage 5   Revising Thesis Statement and Essay Structure

Step 1   Revising Your Thesis Statement: Checking for an Evaluative Point

If you have followed all the steps in gathering material and formulating a thesis, your thesis statement should present, in a reasonable and fair-minded way,

- your opinion about the relationship between strengths and weaknesses
- your support for this opinion
- an indication of the standards of evaluation you have used

If your thesis statement is weak, you may have allowed strong opinions to carry you away, as in the first example below, or you may have ignored evidence contrary to your position, as in the second example.

WRITING SAMPLE

Weak thesis statements:

- "The reasons government and church officials give for resisting same-sex marriages are nonsense; if they had any sense, they would endorse not only civil unions but also church marriages for same-sex couples." (no relationship between strengths and weaknesses, no support, no standard of evaluation)

- "Though there are just as many ethical reasons to support same-sex marriages as to oppose them, the institutionalization of such marriages is simply unacceptable." (support contradicts opinion)

The tentative thesis statement for the sample topic meets all of the requirements for an effective evaluative thesis, and so there is no need to revise it at this point.

Effective thesis statement (sample topic): Though there are serious reasons why voices in the state and, especially, the church resist same-sex marriages, there are better reasons to endorse not only the practical legal solution of civil unions, but also the value of church marriage for same-sex couples, a value that is ethical as well as practical.

Step 2   Revising Essay Structure: Checking Sequence and Pro-Con Transitions

You will find it useful in revising essay structure to turn your draft outline into a revision outline by identifying the points you made, as opposed to those you intended to make, and then checking for these key elements of persuasive structure.

- Have you presented your arguments in an order of ascending interest, ending with the most important?

- If you have used a pro-con structure, have you dealt with con points first and then presented the pro points, either in the essay as a whole or paragraph by paragraph?

- Do you need to add paragraphs in order to define terms or to make transitions from one section of your argument to another?

- Are the *transitions* between strengths and weaknesses clear in the movement *between* paragraphs?
- Do individual paragraphs reveal problems with *internal transitions* or other problems that you will need to address in the next stage of revision?

Problems in persuasive structure generally come from the difficulties writers have in distinguishing strengths from weaknesses or pro arguments from con arguments. The solution lies in learning to make the multiple *transitions* a good persuasive essay requires. Let us look at this issue of transitions in more detail.

In a sense, your whole essay is in transition towards your most important argument. You end with this point so that its impact is greatest on your readers. This movement will be impeded and the impact lessened if you have not dealt with the con points you have raised—or if readers are aware of points you should have raised but have not. Check to make sure you have put con points first, and responded to them, before you present your pro points. You can usually sense when you are reading your draft whether each point is moving towards or away from the heart of your case.

The placement of points is not the only issue, however. The movement between paragraphs must be clearly marked by *transitions* so that readers know when they are moving to a paragraph beginning with a con argument, or a paragraph of definition, or a paragraph offering another aspect of the issue. (You will find additional information on this subject in Using Transitions to Connect Ideas, Part 3, Handbook.)

- In reviewing the draft for the sample assignment, you might find that the biggest problem is the lack of transition between sections of your argument. You might decide to add both a paragraph of definition and a transition paragraph to explain why legal protection for gays and lesbians in committed relationships is not sufficient. You would note these changes in the revision column of your draft outline. The abbreviated outline below illustrates the revised essay structure.

DRAFT OUTLINE TOPIC	REVISION NOTES
Introduction	
MP 1 SOCIETY	Definitions
MP 2 STATE	SOCIETY
MP 3 CHURCH	STATE
MP 4 CHURCH	Transition
MP 5	CHURCH
MP 6	CHURCH
Conclusion	

Stage 6 Revising Individual Paragraphs

Step 1 Revising Your Introduction: *Ethos*

If *ethos*—the image a writer projects of him or herself—is important in writing introductions to critique essays, as we suggested in Chapter 10, it is even more important in persuasive essays, where readers' responses are likely to be governed by deep beliefs and emotions. The goal is to present yourself as committed but fair-minded. If you present yourself as so dogmatic that you have no sympathy for or understanding of other views, then you are unlikely to convince readers who disagree with you.

In an academic situation, where open-minded critical thinking is valued, introductory sentences like those below may bias the reader against your essay.

Weak introductory sentences:

- "Things have changed. These days both marriage partners may be wearing a tuxedo. This is the new reality. Better get used to it."

- "The bureaucratic mind is known for its selfishness and stupidity, and recently it has come up with a proposal with just these qualities, the proposal to reduce school holidays to a month and force hard-working teachers to work twice as hard as before."

- "I like *My Big Fat Greek Wedding*. It has just the kind of humour that appeals to me. I know you will like it too. I have not met anyone who disliked this film."

The need to avoid obviously biased comments does not mean you should use deceit or conceal your position. It means that you should precede your thesis statement either with something likely to appeal to all readers or with something that establishes neutral ground, such as questions about the subject that you do not immediately answer.

- In the draft for the sample assignment, the thesis statement is preceded merely with a question:

WRITING SAMPLE

Draft introductory comment: How do you think Canadian governments and religious leaders should respond to increasing pressure from both gays and lesbians who want the legal protection and other less tangible benefits currently enjoyed by married couples?

This is a good question to establish neutral ground, but since there is still a good deal of prejudice against same-sex couples, hostile readers might have an immediate negative answer. So you might decide to open with a paragraph telling the story of a lesbian couple you know about where one partner lacked the legal protection that legal marriage or a formalized legal union would have given her. All readers tend to be drawn in by a story, so the device seems a good way of drawing readers into a world they might otherwise be unsympathetic to.

You can read the resulting introduction in E. Jones, "Same-Sex Marriages: Tradition and Change" (Readings: Sample Essays, p. 355).

Step 2 Revising Middle Paragraphs: Logic and Transitions

You may have identified problematic middle paragraphs in your review of essay structure. If not, this is the time to evaluate each middle paragraph and revise as necessary.

When you check middle paragraphs, make sure that

- each paragraph contains topic, point and detail that support your thesis
- you have used words, phrases, and sentences to identify pro and con arguments and create clear transitions between these arguments, and between the arguments and the detail that supports them
- your arguments and evidence are valid

Earlier we mentioned that problems in middle paragraphs arise from the difficulty of handling transitions within a pro-con structure. This is true, but often behind problems in transition are problems in logic. We have said little about the logical standard in this chapter, but of course many persuasive essays use the logical standard in combination with aesthetic, ethical, or practical standards. Whether you have used the logical standard or not, your readers will expect your own arguments and evidence to be free of errors in logic (see Stage 2, Step 2: Identifying Strengths and Weaknesses in Logic, in Chapter 10, p. 121).

- The following paragraph from the sample assignment exhibits typical problems with logic and transitions:

WRITING SAMPLE

Draft middle paragraph: There is an ethical difficulty churches face in marrying same-sex couples. Their scriptures teach love and respect though, and the spirit of inclusiveness. This is a time of sectarianism, and the spirit of inclusiveness is exactly what we need. The churches should speak out. Churches that make same-sex couples fully participating members of their own congregations send a powerful message of inclusion to society as a whole.

This paragraph meets some of the logical requirements for arguments and evidence: most church scriptures do teach love and respect, and the final argument seems reasonable. The paragraph has significant omissions, however: our era is not just a sectarian one; church scriptures teach other things besides love and respect; and the con argument announced by the topic sentence (which does not sum up the paragraph) is never developed. You could revise by first presenting the con argument about scriptures denouncing same-sex unions, then presenting a balanced statement about the literal versus the "spirit" interpretation of scripture as transition, and concluding with your pro argument about the message inclusiveness would send. The resulting paragraph is the sixth paragraph in E. Jones, "Same-Sex Marriages: Tradition and Change" (Readings: Sample Essays, p. 357).

Step 3   Revising Your Conclusion: Achieving Balance

As we pointed out in Chapter 10, you should have the same concern for *ethos* in your conclusion as in your introduction. To demonstrate your fair-mindedness in the conclusion, you include the con position as well as the pro position, though you do so in a way that reinforces rather than undermines your argument. Thus in revising your conclusion you check for

- a summary and expansion of your thesis statement that refers to both strengths and weaknesses, to the relationship between them, and to the supporting topics
- a statement of broader implications that does not dismiss the "weak" side of the case but emphasizes the implications of the "strong" side

To see how you might achieve this kind of balance, consider the draft conclusion for the sample assignment:

WRITING SAMPLE

Draft conclusion: If true leadership involves finding the best way to promote ongoing virtues in changing circumstances, then it seems valid to urge church and state to exercise leadership by recognizing the ethical and practical value of not only civil unions but also marriages for same-sex couples.

This conclusion provides a good summary of the pro argument and expands its implications into the domain of leadership. It does not refer to the "weak" side of the case, however, nor does it incorporate this weak side into a clear statement of broader implications. In looking back over your essay, you might realize that the gay and lesbian desire for an institutional recognition of love and commitment represents a continuation of a traditional value. This point, which balances your case that leadership involves the recognition of change, would make a good starting place for your conclusion. For the revised version, see the final paragraph of E. Jones, "Same-Sex Marriages: Tradition and Change," Readings: Sample Essays, p. 358.

For examples of student-written persuasive essays, see James Ash, "To Peacekeep or Not to Peacekeep," and Joyce MacDonald, "The Problem of Environmental Costs: Suzuki vs. Merwin," in Part 2, Readings: Sample Essays.

Working on Your Own Assignment

Your main goal in writing and revising a persuasive essay is to work out your position and then persuade your readers to agree with it.

- Find a standard or standards of evaluation either in the assignment or in the process of gathering material.
- Analyze your subject by choosing appropriate categories and gathering material in them.
- Identify strengths and weaknesses by applying the appropriate standard(s) of evaluation to the material in your categories.
- Formulate a thesis that states an opinion about the relationship between strengths and weaknesses, gives reasons to support your opinion, and indicates your standard(s) of evaluation.
- Construct a draft outline according to the principle of pro-con structure, and write the draft.
- Check the draft by means of a revision outline for problems in thesis statement, pro-con structure, and transitions.
- Check the introduction and conclusion for fair-mindedness; check middle paragraphs for problems in transition and logic.

EXERCISES

A. Identify the standard(s) of evaluation implied or stated in each of the following essay topics.

1. "The Catbird Seat" and "The Short Happy Life of Francis Macomber" are both stories about manhood. Which uses setting and characterization more effectively in conveying a theme about this subject?

2. Choose one of the educational theories we have discussed this term and evaluate whether or not it could be successfully used in either science or arts classes in your local high school.

3. Does Garrett Hardin's essay "Lifeboat Ethics" (Readings) convey a more fair, just, and realistic attitude to poverty than Judy Rebick's essay "The Poorhouse" (Readings)?

4. Is the term "sustainable growth" an oxymoron in the 21st century?

5. Discuss whether feminism still remains a reasonable system of beliefs for contemporary women to adopt.

B.   Write a sentence or two evaluating the following as thesis statements for evaluation essays.

1. People describe terrorism as a complex issue. What's complex about it? You have to fight terrorism by every means available; force is the only language terrorists understand.

2. It is clear that, on moral grounds, we should have the right to interfere with customs and practices of other cultures when these customs clearly degrade one or more classes of people. Other cultures have important reasons for their customs, though; these customs are often central to their religious beliefs.

3. Lenore Keeshig-Tobias' essay "He Was a Boxer When I Was Small" is really effective in conveying the complexities of a father-daughter relationship. It's nice to read something written by a Native writer.

C.   Decide what point the writer of the following paragraph is trying to prove. State that point in a topic sentence. Then reorganize the paragraph, putting the con arguments first and then the pro arguments. Compare your paragraph with your classmates'.

> Cell phones can save lives in emergencies. If your car breaks down at 3:00 a.m. on an isolated road, you can phone for help and let your family know that you will be late. Loud conversations by people using cell phones drive restaurant customers sitting in nearby tables crazy. The ringing of cell phones can destroy the climax of any movie. Cell phones are a great way to give a teenager both safety and more freedom. Drivers who talk on their cell phones while making a left turn are a menace on the roads.

D.   Choose a controversial issue and work out your own position on this issue by following the steps in this chapter for finding a standard of evaluation, gathering material, and formulating a thesis statement. Then make a draft outline indicating the sequence in which you would present the arguments for and against your position.

chapter 12

Gathering Material for Research Papers

Stage 1 Clarifying Research Topics

    Step 1 Defining Unfamiliar Terms

    Step 2 Understanding Directions

    Step 3 Choosing a Topic

    Step 4 Limiting Your Topic: Defining a Research Question

    Step 5 Choosing Material: Primary and Secondary Sources

    Sample Topic: The Dramatic Function of the Graveyard Scene in *Hamlet*

Stage 2 Gathering Primary and Secondary Material

    Step 1 Exploring Preliminary Sources of Information

    Step 2 Compiling a Working Bibliography

    Step 3 Evaluating Secondary Sources and Taking Notes

    Step 4 Categorizing Material: Combining Preliminary Analysis and Research Material

Stage 3 Formulating a Thesis Statement

Stage 4 Drafting

Stage 5 Revising Thesis Statement and Essay Structure

Stage 6 Revising Individual Paragraphs

Stage 7 Final Editing

As you take courses in a variety of academic disciplines, you will discover that methods of conducting research and writing about the results differ from field to field. The research papers you are asked to write will also differ in organization, style, and documentation. Nevertheless, research papers are basically extended versions of analysis, comparison, or evaluation essays. The special skills you need are those of finding research material and integrating it with your own ideas. Those are the skills we emphasize in this chapter. You can adapt the process of gathering material that we outline here to suit any research paper.

Research papers serve three purposes.

- To increase your understanding of a subject covered briefly in class. A sociology instructor who can spend only one class on family violence, for example, might assign research papers on various aspects of this subject.

- To acquaint you with the procedures and categories, the general ways of working, of a particular discipline. In doing a research paper in psychology, for example, you would learn how to use *Psychological Abstracts*; which journals to consult for research on a particular subject; and how experiments in psychology are conducted and reported.

- To encourage you to synthesize information and integrate it with your own ideas. A research paper is not merely a summary of other writers' work; it is an essay in which you develop your own opinion on your subject and use your research material as evidence to support that opinion.

This chapter focuses on two important steps in writing research papers: how to find secondary sources and how to combine this material with your own analysis. Our sample topic is the dramatic function of the graveyard scene in Shakespeare's *Hamlet*. In Chapter 13 we demonstrate how you would write and revise a research paper, again using this sample topic.

Stage 1 Clarifying Research Topics

Step 1 Defining Unfamiliar Terms

Since research papers are usually on specialized topics, you should be alert to the specialized use of terms. If you were writing a psychology paper on the development of the concept of narcissism, for example, you would begin by checking the definition of narcissism in your textbook and in a specialized dictionary such as the *Dictionary of Psychology* (Oxford: Oxford UP, 2001). You will find an annotated guide to such reference sources in Part 4, Resources for Writing.

Step 2   Understanding Directions

A research paper is not merely a compilation of information and opinion about your subject. In writing on a content topic, you will need to analyze, compare, and evaluate your research material. In writing on a textual topic, you will need to analyze (and perhaps compare and/or evaluate) your primary text(s) as well as consider interpretations you find in secondary sources.

Step 3   Choosing a Topic

If you haven't had much experience writing research papers, you will probably want to choose a topic that seems both interesting and relatively straightforward. Because topics are sometimes more (and sometimes less) complex than they appear, it is a good idea to spend a few minutes brainstorming about each topic when you receive the assignment. If you decide on your topic well before the due date, you give yourself more time to think about it, even when you are not actively engaged in research and writing.

Step 4   Limiting Your Topic: Defining a Research Question

One of the most important preliminary steps is turning your research topic into a research question, that is, a central question that your paper will answer. For topics that are specific in focus, you can simply put your research topic into the form of a question. "The impact of the Free Trade Agreement on Canadian auto manufacturing," for instance, would become "What has been the impact of the Free Trade Agreement on Canadian auto manufacturing?" The question form will remind you that there are many possible answers, depending upon the point of view of the writers you consult.

When you are given a broad topic, you are free to select your own focus. But the wealth of information available means that it is easy to get bogged down or sidetracked. You will find it easier to locate material, and to make decisions about its usefulness, if you begin with a well-defined research question. Use brainstorming, freewriting, or tree diagramming (see Chapter 2) to develop a wide range of questions about your subject. If you tried brainstorming about the broad topic of eating disorders, for instance, you might come up with the following research questions: What causes eating disorders? What are the physical, psychological, and/or social effects? What are the current treatments? Although you might be tempted to try to answer all of these questions, your resulting paper could be rather superficial. You would be better off to choose one of these questions and explore it fully. Keep the other possibilities in mind in case you cannot find enough material to answer your original question. If you are concerned that your research question may narrow the topic inappropriately, check with your instructor.

Step 5 Choosing Material: Primary and Secondary Sources

As we indicated in Chapter 2, research papers include both *primary* sources (such as written documents, performances, experiments, and interviews) and *secondary* sources (such as articles and books written about your subject by others). If you were writing a research paper on *Hamlet*, the play would be your primary source; works about *Hamlet* would be your secondary sources.

One of the reasons for writing research papers is to learn to evaluate and integrate different sources of information. You should therefore try to use secondary sources that represent the range of information or opinion about your subject. Be careful not to base your essay on a single author's point of view, a single experiment, or a single survey. The number of references considered adequate will depend on the discipline, the instructor, the length of the assignment, and the amount of material available on your topic. A good rule of thumb is to use at least six reference sources in the final draft of a short research essay. Your working bibliography may contain two or three times as many entries as you actually use.

Sample Topic: The Dramatic Function of the Graveyard Scene in *Hamlet*

Stage 1 Clarifying Research Topics

Let's suppose that from the list of topics for a 2000-word research paper in your first-year English course, you have chosen this one:

> Using several critical discussions of the play, explore the
> dramatic function of the graveyard scene in *Hamlet*.

This topic obviously requires textual analysis, since you are asked to focus on how a particular part of the play "works." You might need to clarify the term "dramatic function." The term suggests that you should consider why the scene comes where it does in the structure of the play, rather than focus solely on the ideas it presents. You might formulate your research question like this: What does this scene contribute to the structure and meaning of the play? The topic suggests that you should use several secondary sources to clarify and enrich your interpretation of the scene and of the play. Since 2000 words is fairly short for a research paper, six sources should be adequate. You may need to consult a dozen or more sources to find six that are relevant to your topic.

Stage 2   Gathering Primary and Secondary Material

Step 1   Exploring Preliminary Sources of Information

Getting an overview of your subject   If you are unfamiliar with your subject, you may need to do some preliminary investigation before you can plan an efficient research strategy. Here are some suggestions:

- For content analysis topics, read an overview of your subject in your textbook or an encyclopedia. For textual analysis topics, the best source may be one of the short introductory books published on most authors, genres, and literary and film topics. For both kinds of topics, reference materials such as the "Macropedia" section of the *Encyclopaedia Britannica*, or indexes like the *Index to Book Reviews* or the *Citation Index*, will help to give you a sense of the key writers on your subject. Bibliographies handed out in class and references in textbooks also often supply good starting points.

- Discuss your topic with your instructor, your classmates, or other people who know something about it. Reference librarians are an invaluable resource for helping you plan an efficient research strategy.

Analyzing your subject   You will be better able to keep your research material in perspective if, as far as possible, you produce your own analysis, comparison, or evaluation before you consult secondary sources. Here are some suggestions:

- First, jot down what you already know and think about the subject, using one of the discovery techniques discussed in Chapter 2.

- For content analysis, use the general categories of systems, process, and/or causal analysis (see Chapter 3) to organize your notes and to clarify the kinds of secondary material you need to look for. For instance, you may know something about the *kinds* of treatment available for eating disorders, but discover that you don't know anything about the actual *process* of treatment. Or if you have read an overview that suggests key issues about your subject, use these issues as categories to organize your research and note-taking.

- For textual analysis, make notes in the appropriate special categories for analyzing texts (see this section in Part 4). Or if some issues suggested by your preliminary reading or discussion seem particularly relevant to your topic, use those issues as organizing categories. For instance, from class discussion of Joy Kogawa's *Itsuka*, you might have a sense of the questions to ask when you analyze the relation between fact and fiction in a different novel.

Writing down this material will help you to keep track of which ideas are yours and which ones come from secondary sources so that you can avoid accidental plagiarism. It may also help you change or refine your research question.

Gathering material: getting an overview of *Hamlet* Before you read the critics, you need to have some idea of what *Hamlet* as a whole is about and you should work out a preliminary analysis of the graveyard scene. If you have not discussed the play in class, you might find it useful to begin by skimming an introductory book that gives a scene-by-scene explanation of the action. (If you use any ideas taken from this introductory reading, be sure to document the source. See Documenting Research Material: Understanding Plagiarism in Chapter 13.) On rereading the play, you might decide that *Hamlet* is about the prince's search for the proper action to take in a world where his high standards for determining the truth come into conflict with the corrupt Danish court.

Gathering material: analyzing *Hamlet* Your next step would be to reread the graveyard scene carefully, taking notes according to the special categories for analyzing drama (see pp. 502–505).

NOTES ON *HAMLET*

Subject and Genre: What is the scene about? Does this play belong to a particular genre (kind) of drama?

> *Subject:* death—conversation between two gravediggers about Ophelia's burial, Hamlet's jests with gravedigger about corpses and speculations about human mortality, Ophelia's funeral procession, Hamlet's quarrel with Laertes in the open grave, Claudius' decision to put his plot against Hamlet into action.

Genre: tragedy—according to my class notes, Shakespearean tragedy involves the fall of a hero of high estate as a result of both circumstances outside the hero's control and actions that stem from a flaw in his character. Because the flaw is also what makes the hero great, his death produces emotions such as sympathy, pity, fear, awe, and a sense of waste.

Dramatic Structure: What is the principle behind the selection and arrangements of events ("action")?

Structure of scene: two distinct episodes—gravediggers and confrontation with Laertes. Why does Shakespeare include the gravediggers? Why does he have Laertes and Hamlet leap into Ophelia's grave?

Relation of scene to play: Act V, scene i—only one more scene in play. Hamlet's last appearance was at the end of IV.iv., where he encounters Fortinbras' forces as he is leaving for England after killing Polonius. The intervening scenes focus on Ophelia's madness, Laertes' return to avenge his father, Claudius' plot for killing Hamlet, and the news of Ophelia's suicide. The graveyard scene thus sets the stage for the final confrontation between Hamlet and his foes.

Dramatic Setting: What is the place, time, and social environment within which the action takes place?

Place: church graveyard.

Time: day after Ophelia's death, news of Hamlet's return (see IV.vii.)

Social environment: marked contrast in social position between gravediggers and the court. The gravediggers conclude that Ophelia is to be given a Christian burial only because she is a gentlewoman; Hamlet contrasts the singing gravedigger's insensitivity with the "daintier sense" of those who don't work for a living (V.i. 65–66).

Relation of scene to play: graveyard setting connects this scene with others associated with death, such as Ghost's revelations, play within a play, murder of Polonius, Ophelia's death. The setting makes Hamlet's preoccupation with death part of the climax of the play.

Characterization: What are the characters like? How are various techniques, including dialogue and acting, used to portray them?

First Clown (gravedigger): witty, cynical, down to earth; not awed by death or by the nobility.

Hamlet: presented in the first half of the scene as philosophical about death, not morbidly obsessed as he was at the beginning of the play. Begins to rant in response to Laertes' lamentations about Ophelia, but also declares his love for her and for Laertes.

Other characters: Laertes is the other major character in the scene. What is the purpose of his excessive show of grief?

Diction, Images and Symbols, Pacing: What do I learn from usage level and word choice? What do images and symbols convey? What is the rhythm of dialogue and action?

Diction: gravediggers' speech colloquial, comic, matter of fact; language of the court mainly informal, except for Laertes', which is formal and pretentious. Hamlet's language moves between these levels, sometimes in the same sentence: the lawyer's "fine pate" is "full of fine dirt" (V.i. 100); and the "noble dust of Alexander" can be found "stopping a bunghole" (V.i. 191–192).

Images and symbols: many associated with death—skulls, grave.

Pacing: language shifts from conversational prose in gravedigger episode to blank verse in burial scene; verbal "fight" between Laertes and Hamlet is the most distinctive use of sentence structure. Action shows similar shift from slow pace in first half of scene to unexpected twist as Hamlet and Laertes fight in the grave. Doesn't this behaviour seem a bit ridiculous?

Tone: What attitude to subject or audience is evident?

The tone of the early part of the scene is playful, meditative, probing; the tone of the later part is emotional and dramatic.

Theme: What is the central idea?

The scene shows Hamlet reacting to death in two violently contrasting ways. He is playful and self-possessed, somewhat distant when he thinks of death in abstract terms; but he is much more emotional when death becomes personal (Yorick's skull, Ophelia). How does this conflict relate to his search for proper action?

These notes will help you to determine whether the critics you consult are relevant to your topic.

Step 2   Compiling a Working Bibliography

A working bibliography is a preliminary list of books and articles that, from their titles or other information available to you, seem relevant to your research question.

For each reference you will need to take down complete bibliographical details, in the form discussed below. This information will enable you to locate material in your library and to identify in your paper the sources you have used. If you record full publication data as you collect your initial references, you will save yourself the headaches involved in searching for missing information. You will also protect yourself against unintentional plagiarism: the use of ideas and information from sources that are not identified. You will find a fuller discussion of plagiarism in Chapter 13.

Recording each reference on a separate file card, on a separate page of a small research notebook, or in a computer file will enable you to add or discard items easily. You will find sample bibliography entries under Recording Bibliographical Information (pp. 173–174).

Locating references

Library Catalogues Today, most libraries provide access to the materials in their collections through online catalogues, although some retain card or microfiche catalogues. Whatever system your library uses, you can generally search for books and audio-visual materials by author, title, or subject. If you are looking for books *by* a particular author, use the author search option. If you are searching for resources *about* an author or a subject, however, you should use the subject or keyword general search option. Subject or keyword searches are often the most fruitful, but can be frustrating if you do not choose the most appropriate search terms.

To search the subject and keyword options most effectively, try several different terms and combinations of terms using the Boolean system. A keyword search on the effects of television violence on children might start like this: television AND violence AND children

Your library's online catalogue will then search for materials that deal with all three subtopics. Ask your librarian for more information about Boolean searches and for help in defining and limiting your search.

Your library may contain relevant books and other materials that do not turn up during your search of the catalogue. When you go to the stacks, take a few minutes to scan titles and check indexes of books nearby. You may discover several useful sources.

Electronic Databases and Periodical Indexes Besides books and other sources found on the main library shelves, professional, scholarly journals and popular magazines are the next largest group of resources. Whether they appear in print or are available in online databases, articles are often more up-to-date than books because these journals are published periodically—that is, weekly, monthly, bi-monthly, quarterly, semi-annually, or annually. Most areas of interest and study have one or more periodicals.

Searching for periodical articles can be time-consuming unless you know which periodicals to consult. Many periodicals are published simultaneously in print and in electronic databases. Your library may subscribe to print versions of some periodicals and electronic databases of the same or other periodicals.

- To find articles in electronic databases or CD-ROMs, be sure to check training sessions and online tutorials offered by your library.
- To find articles in the print collection, use periodical indexes; your reference librarian can help you with these.

Electronic databases offer periodical articles in a variety of different forms. Full-text articles are, of course, the most convenient because you can print, download, or send them to your own email address. In many cases, however, you may get only an abstract of the article and will have to retrieve the periodical either from your library or by electronic means.

In working with electronic databases and printed periodicals, you should also consider whether the source is peer-reviewed; that is, whether other experts in the field have deemed the article worthwhile.

Electronic sources may be the most up-to-date, but they may not include valuable historical material published before the electronic database or CD-ROM was begun. In addition, some database designers may limit access due to corporate financial decisions. Thus, if you want to make your search as complete as possible, you should always have a look at printed periodicals as well.

How to Use Electronic Databases and CD-ROM Sources A primary advantage of using electronic sources is that they are accessible through an Internet connection. Your library's main web site will provide a link to the battery of databases or CD-ROMs that your library subscribes to. An alphabetical list of general and specific databases provides access to full-text articles or abstracts in a wide variety of subject areas.

A popular general database is the *MasterFILE Premier*, a multidisciplinary database whose attributes demonstrate its versatility:

- covers virtually every subject area of general (and scholarly) interest
- provides full text for nearly 1950 general reference publications
- also includes 165 full-text reference books, nearly 100 000 biographies, 76 000 primary source documents, and an image collection of 116 000 photos, maps, and flags
- full-text articles available as far back as 1975
- updated daily via EBSCOhost

An example of a database that focuses on literary criticism is *Canadian Literary Periodicals (Reference Press)*:

- approximately 55 000 citations for most Canadian primary materials (poems, short stories, novels, plays, and literary essays) and most Canadian secondary materials (critical articles, book reviews, interviews, and bibliographies)
- indexing to 84 Canadian periodicals
- coverage 1992+

CD-ROM sources, such as the *Social Sciences Index/Full Image* disk, reproduce many articles in their original published format. This particular source indexes English-language international periodicals in a broad range of social sciences. One limitation to CD-ROMs is that they can be updated only by the addition of more CDs. Each CD would be labelled for the years it covers. CDs are, in fact, closer to printed sources.

Once you have decided which database(s) or CD-ROM to search, you will proceed in much the same way you search the online catalogue; that is, by title, author, subject, or keyword. Follow the prompts and remember to take notes or create bookmarks of promising results.

If you were writing a paper on the significance of the graveyard scene in *Hamlet*, for example, you could search the *MasterFILE Premier* database and begin with the most obvious term—Hamlet. The search takes only seconds and yields 1492 entries—far too many to sift through. Narrow your search by cross-referencing with another term. Using Hamlet AND death, the database will generate a list of 37 entries. If you expand your search to related subjects—Ophelia, for instance—a different list of articles is generated.

It is easy to assume that the computer can do your searching for you, but this is not the case. Just as your automobile cannot get you where you want to go unless you steer it, so searches with electronic databases and CD-ROM technology cannot produce the best results unless you guide them to the appropriate listings.

How to Find Printed Periodical Articles If the electronic databases that your library subscribes to do not contain the articles you need in full-text format, you may be able to find articles in print. You may also need to consult printed sources if valuable articles on your topic were published before the start date of available databases. For research on literature, the *MLA International Bibliography* has volumes going back many decades and lists sources both in Author and Subject Indexes.

It's important to remember that finding these printed articles is a two-part process. First you must consult either the electronic database or printed Periodical Indexes to find the article. The most efficient way to use a periodical index is to start with the current volume and work backwards until you have found enough entries. Copy down references exactly as they appear and then consult the key to abbreviations in the front of the volume to decipher the entries. Your goal is to find the name of the periodical in which an article was first published. Note the article's title, author, and the date (volume and number) of the periodical.

Once you have the name of the periodical, you must consult your library catalogue to locate the volume and number you need. Although periodicals are initially published separately, they later appear in bound volumes spanning various time periods. These volumes of periodicals are usually shelved in a different area of your library or even in a separate library building. They can be found by letter or by call number, depending on your library.

Other Considerations As you look for books and/or articles for your working bibliography, keep these points in mind.

1. Books are still considered by many as the most reliable and trusted sources; instructors may insist that you use at least some books in your research.

2. Articles are more specialized than books; you are therefore more likely to find articles directly related to your research question. Article titles will tell you more specifically whether they are pertinent to your topic, whereas many book titles would not—you would have to locate the book and consult the table of contents or index.

3. Current research in many fields appears in articles several years before it is available in books. Periodicals are therefore a valuable source of information in new and rapidly developing fields such as technology and science.

4. All periodical articles are not, however, created equal. Pay close attention to the organization or institution that a publication is affiliated with. The best articles will appear as *peer reviewed*, which means that other experts in the field have read and approved of the content.

5. When working with databases, you may be tempted to limit your search to full-text articles for convenience. Be aware, however, that by doing so you may miss finding the best sources which, with a bit more effort, you can retrieve or obtain in printed form.

The Internet If you have access to the Internet, you are probably aware that a simple Internet search can link you to a great deal of potentially valuable information on your topic, in the form of newsgroup postings, listserv messages, electronic journals, and files available for viewing and downloading via sites on the World Wide Web. As in the case of all online searches, choosing the most appropriate search terms will be vital to your success. You may need to experiment with several combinations to provide the best and most thorough results. Unlike library catalogues, Internet information has no common set of subject terms assigned to it, and consequently, finding valuable sources on the Internet is often hit and miss. Experimenting with different search engines is also a good idea. Some, such as Yahoo!, are organized by subject and can therefore help you weed out much of the irrelevant information that Internet searches often produce.

One problem with using the Internet as a research tool lies in the unvetted nature of much of the material you will find on it. Unlike print sources, which generally receive the scrutiny of an editor and publisher before they reach your library, only some Internet publications (primarily electronic journals) are subject to such a process of critical evaluation. Consequently, the trustworthiness and scholarly value of Internet sources are much less easy to verify. For this reason, it is usually not a good idea to rely exclusively on Internet sources in your essay.

When you discover a site or document that you believe will be useful, create a bookmark for it so that you can return to it easily. For more information on finding, evaluating, using, and documenting Internet sources, consult Andrew Harnack and Eugene Kleppinger's handbook *Online! A Reference Guide to Using Internet Sources*, 3rd edition (New York: St. Martin's, 2001) or visit their web site at <http.//www.bedfordstmartins.com/online/>.

Your own library may provide lists of recommended web sites for various fields of study or for specific subjects. Important criteria include whether a site is linked directly to a profession, created or endorsed by a reputable organization, or linked to peer-reviewed periodicals. For example, if the English Department at your college or university chooses a specific novel or author to focus on in a particular year, library staff will find and update web sites on that novel or author, and may even provide annotations or comments on each site. These *reviewed* lists are often reproduced as handouts or made available on your library's own web site.

A brief guide to documenting the most common types of Internet sources appears in Documentation in Part 3, Handbook for Final Editing.

Recording bibliographical information   For each reference you include in your working bibliography, record complete bibliographical information so that you can find the work in your library, and, if you use it in your essay, include the appropriate citation.

- Record the following information, in the order given, for each secondary source:
  a. For *books*: Complete name of author(s), last name first; title and edition or volume, if applicable; place of publication, publisher, and date of publication.

Corum, Richard. *Understanding Hamlet: A Student Casebook to Issues, Sources and Historical Documents.* Westport, CT: Greenwood Press, 1998.

b. For *printed articles*: Complete name of author(s), last name first; title of article; magazine or journal in which the article appears; day, month, and year of publication (for weekly and monthly magazines) or volume, issue number, and year (for journals); page numbers. For *electronic articles*, include the number of paragraphs.

Cohen, Michael. "'To what base uses we may return': Class and Mortality in *Hamlet* (5.1)." *Hamlet Studies* 9:1–2 (Summer–Winter 1987), 78–85.

c. For *electronic sources*: See the discussion of Internet sources above and in Documentation, Part 3, Handbook for Final Editing.

- At the bottom of the entry, note the bibliography, index, database, or catalogue in which you found the reference, in case you discover you have not recorded it accurately.

- From your library's online, microfiche, or card catalogue, copy the call number for each book or journal, and if your college or university has more than one library, note the locations of copies. If you fail to find some of your references, note "not in library" or "volume missing" on your entry.

Sample entries in your working bibliography, with a call number for the Library of Congress classification system, might look like this:

SAMPLE CITATIONS

ENTRY FOR A BOOK

Aboriginal Nurses Association of Canada. *Finding Our Way: A Sexual and Reproductive Health Sourcebook for Aboriginal Communities*. Ottawa: Author and Planned Parenthood Federation of Canada, 2000. Alberta Government Lib. Telus Plaza North Tower. E111 F56. [Source: Grant MacEwan online catalogue]

ENTRY FOR A DATABASE ARTICLE

Phiddian, Robert. "Have You Eaten Yet? The Reader in 'A Modest Proposal.'" *Studies in English Literature* 36-3 (Summer 1996) p. 603, 19 pages. [Source: *MasterFILE Premier*, full text, 8071 words, available 15/10/02]

Step 3   Evaluating Secondary Sources and Taking Notes

Evaluating secondary sources   Before you start taking notes, spend a few minutes evaluating each of your references. For books, check the table of contents and the index and skim the pages most relevant to your research question. Read the introductory and concluding paragraphs of articles.

If you decide to discard a reference because its focus seems different from your own, make a note on your file entry saying so and indicating what its focus is. References you discard at this stage may prove to be useful later on if you change the direction of your research.

Taking notes   For books, articles, and Internet sources that address relevant issues or provide useful factual information, take notes on these points:

- The issue or problem that the writer identifies.
- The main point the writer makes about the issue.
- The context of this issue. Does the writer give background information or summarize the viewpoints of other writers?
- Key points in the development of the explanation or argument and key pieces of evidence cited.
- The writer's conclusion.
- Your own reactions to and evaluation of the reference.

Summarizing   Summarize or paraphrase most material. Use point form to avoid inadvertent plagiarism and include the page reference for each point and detail. (For more complete guidelines to analyzing and summarizing what you read, see Chapter 3, Part B.)

Quoting   Use direct quotation when the precise wording may be important to your discussion, as in definitions of concepts or particularly effective ways of making a point. Try not to quote more than a sentence at a time; quote the whole sentence so that you will have the context (you can shorten quotations when you edit); copy the words *exactly* as they appear in the original (including spelling and punctuation); put quotation marks around everything you quote, however short; indicate the exact page on which each quotation occurs. If a quotation is continued from one page to another, use a slash mark to indicate the page break in case you decide to omit part of it.

Evaluating   Conclude your notes on each reference with your own evaluation of the ideas and evidence it presents, your comments on its relation to other references, and/or your notes on its place in your essay. To avoid possible confusion, put your own comments in square brackets or use some other way of identifying them.

Step 4 Categorizing Material: Combining Preliminary Analysis and Research Material

Your preliminary notes include your analysis of primary sources and your notes on secondary sources. In order to synthesize and integrate the two, you need to complete these steps:

- Choose the most relevant categories of analytic material.
- Establish appropriate categories for the secondary material.
- Put the two sets of material together so that you can see where they do and do not match.

Through this process a general point will begin to emerge that you can refine to make your thesis. To demonstrate this final step in the process of gathering material, let us see how it might apply to the sample topic.

Choosing material from your preliminary analysis All your original material may still seem relevant, or some categories may seem more relevant than others, perhaps because they form a distinct pattern, or because you now understand the assignment or the subject better.

If you review the preliminary analysis of *Hamlet* (pp. 166–168), the material in the categories of dramatic structure and characterization seems to form the most distinct pattern. In each category there is a striking contrast between elements that are down-to-earth and witty (Hamlet conversing with the gravediggers; the first gravedigger's remarks) and elements that are emotional and dramatic (Hamlet discussing Ophelia and struggling with Laertes; Laertes' distress). What dramatic function can a scene with such contrasting elements fulfill in the play as a whole?

Establishing categories for secondary material When you read literary criticism, you will often find that critics organize their material according to issues or theories rather than by the categories we suggest for textual analysis.

Nevertheless, as you will see when you combine the two sets of material, these categories of textual analysis underlie much critical commentary. Few of the critics writing about the graveyard scene have anything to say about its dramatic function; instead, they focus on what the scene shows about the development of Hamlet's attitudes towards death, an aspect of characterization. You can divide their views into three categories:

- The scene shows Hamlet developing a Christian acceptance of death (Walter King, Maynard Mack). *OR*

- It shows Hamlet developing a secular and fatalistic attitude (G. Wilson Knight, Richard Levine). *OR*
- It shows a mixture of these two attitudes (Peter Philias).

Combining material   The most effective way to bring preliminary material and research material together is to use columns that make it clear where the two sets of material match and where they do not. You might set out the *Hamlet* material in columns as follows:

PRELIMINARY ANALYSIS	SECONDARY MATERIAL
Dramatic Structure	
2 contrasting episodes: gravediggers and Hamlet Hamlet and Laertes	Scene "bring[s] into dramatic focus parts ... seemingly disparate" (Bennett, 160)
	Laertes' "ranting" creates sympathy for Hamlet (Cheadle) Bending over Ophelia creates sympathy for Hamlet (Cheadle)
Characterization	
First gravedigger: witty, cynical, down-to-earth	"ranting" (Cheadle)
Laertes: dramatic, elevated language	
Hamlet: 1st episode: witty, less metaphysical 2nd episode: feeling, dramatic	Hamlet's attitude to death: Move to Christian acceptance (King, Mack) Move to fatalism (Knight, Levine) Mixture of above (Philias)

As you can see, placing this material in columns reveals at a glance that both the preliminary analysis and the secondary material comment on the Hamlet–Laertes episode. The columns do not match, however, when it comes to the characterization of Hamlet. You can thus see more clearly what you have to contribute to the interpretation of this scene—your reasons for the shift in Hamlet's character.

Once you have brought your preliminary analysis and your research material together in a systematic way, you are ready to move on to the next stages of writing a research paper: formulating a thesis statement and writing and revising a draft. We will discuss these stages in Chapter 13.

Working on Your Own Assignment

Preliminary thinking and writing about your research paper topic will help you to plan and carry out an efficient strategy for gathering material.

- Spend a few minutes freewriting or brainstorming about each possible topic so that you understand what each one demands.
- Choose a topic that interests you and narrow your focus to one or two specific research questions.
- Use appropriate categories for content analysis (pp. 25–27) or the special categories for textual analysis (pp. 67–72) to explore and develop your approach to your topic.
- Compile a working bibliography of secondary sources by using periodical indexes and annual bibliographies (print, CD-ROM, or database versions) and catalogues of your library's holdings. You might also search the Internet for possible sources.
- For each secondary source, take down complete bibliographical information.
- Make most of your notes in point form, with short, carefully selected quotations for key ideas. Include page numbers for both quoted and paraphrased material.
- Reorganize your notes into matching columns, with your ideas on one side of the page, ideas and information from secondary sources (with references) on the other. This integration of primary and secondary material will help you with the next stage of the process, working out a thesis statement that answers the most important questions posed by your topic.

EXERCISES

A. Respond to each of the following questions in a sentence or two.

1. If you were writing an essay on Charles Dickens' novel *Great Expectations*, what would be your primary source of information? What kinds of material would be secondary sources?
2. What are the advantages of working out your own ideas about your subject before you begin to do research?
3. How would you find these four sources of information for a research paper on juvenile arthritis: a book, a scholarly article, an article in a popular magazine, a government document?
4. What is the most efficient way to take good notes on secondary sources?

B. Gather material for a mini-research paper on one of the topics below by (1) formulating a research question; (2) making notes about your own ideas on the subject; and (3) using three or four essays from Part 2, Readings, as your secondary material. Keep your notes on this material for an exercise in Chapter 13.

- Attitudes towards population growth
- Attitudes towards poverty
- Attitudes towards cultural differences
- Attitudes towards gender

chapter 13

Writing Research Papers

Stage 1 Clarifying Research Topics

Stage 2 Gathering Material for Research Papers

Stage 3 Formulating a Thesis Statement: Answering Your Research Question

    Step 1 Forming an Opinion

    Step 2 Supporting Your Opinion

Stage 4 Drafting: Making a Formal Outline

Stage 5 Revising: Integrating and Documenting Research Material

    Step 1 Integrating Research Material

    Step 2 Documenting Research Material: Understanding Plagiarism

    Sample Topic (Research): The Dramatic Function of the Graveyard Scene in *Hamlet*

Stage 6 Revising Individual Paragraphs

Stage 7 Final Editing

A research paper is the longest and most time-consuming project in most courses, and so it's especially important to plan your time carefully. This chapter will be much more useful if you have worked through all the steps in Chapter 12, Gathering Material for Research Papers, which explains the following:

- How to choose a research topic
- How to formulate a research question
- How to compile a working bibliography
- How to take notes on secondary sources and document them
- How to organize your notes to reveal the similarities and differences between your ideas and the ideas you find in other sources

In this chapter we discuss the remaining stages in writing and revising a research paper, from working out a thesis statement to revising individual paragraphs. As you will see, the most important issue is maintaining a clear relationship between your own ideas about your subject and the ideas and information in your research material.

The first part of this chapter focuses on common problems you may encounter in writing research papers. The second part takes you through the process of writing a research paper with our sample topic: the function of the graveyard scene in *Hamlet*.

Stage 3 Formulating a Thesis Statement: Answering Your Research Question

Step 1 Forming an Opinion

Because a research paper is an essay, it must have a thesis: your main point about your subject. As you look over your notes, try to find a pattern that unites your categories of material. If you have gathered material on characterization in *Macbeth*, for instance, you may find that you can connect several points by focusing on the destructive effects of gender stereotypes. Or your research into alcoholism may suggest weaknesses with the disease model that you can make central to your paper.

If you have trouble seeing connections among your categories of material, ask yourself these questions:

- What was my research question?
- What issues did I find in my research material?
- What are the connections between these issues and my research question?

The answers to these questions should lead you to an opinion about your subject. Check your opinion against your essay topic to make sure that you have not been led off-topic by your research material.

Step 2   Supporting Your Opinion

Your opinion about your subject may not differ from the views of other writers you have consulted. If you were researching Britain's entry into the First World War, for example, you might conclude, along with the historians you had consulted, that the British were initially disorganized and inefficient. You might wonder, then, how your thesis statement could be anything more than a summary of your research.

The answer is that the reasons you give to support your opinion will be your contribution to the debate. In your reading about Britain's war effort, for example, you may find one historian who blames the slow start on Prime Minister Herbert Asquith's indecisiveness; another who blames the arrogance of Field Marshall Earl Kitchener; and a third who blames the British class system and capitalist economics. In order to give reasons for your opinion, you will have to reach your own conclusions about the relevance of each of these factors. Through this process you develop the thesis statement that provides the intellectual framework for your essay, instead of depending upon the framework provided by your sources.

When you revise, check your thesis statement against the possible problems outlined in Chapter 5 and make any necessary changes.

Stage 4   Drafting: Making a Formal Outline

When you are writing short essays, you may plan your piece by jotting down your points in a draft outline (see Chapter 4). When you are writing a research paper, however, you may be asked to hand in a **formal outline** as a guide for your reader. Some writers finish the paper first and then write an outline. You can also make a formal outline before you write your draft to work out the relationship among your major points, minor points, and supporting evidence. This outline will help you maintain a balance between material you've found in your sources and your own analysis.

To make a formal outline, write your thesis statement at the top of a page. Then list your major points with Roman numerals, your subpoints under each heading with capital letters, and evidence to support each subpoint with Arabic numerals. If you need a fourth level, use lowercase letters. Your outline will look something like this:

THESIS: main idea of the whole essay

I. Major Point

   A. Minor point
      1. Evidence (writer A)
      2. Evidence (your analysis)

   B. Minor point
      1. Evidence (your analysis)
      2. Evidence (quotation from writer B)

II. Major Point

   A. Minor point
      1. Evidence (facts and figures from writer C)
      2. Evidence (your analysis)

   B. Minor point
      1. Evidence (your examples)
      2. Evidence (examples from writer D)
      3. Evidence (quotation from writer E)

Since an outline is a way of classifying information by dividing it into smaller units, you should have at least two items at each level. That means if you have an A, you must have a B; if you have a 1, you must have a 2. Difficulties in filling in your outline may indicate important gaps in your material or a need to combine small points under a broader heading.

Your formal outline will be more useful to you and your reader if you state the ideas you intend to express, not just the topic of each section or paragraph. A heading like "Hamlet and Laertes in the grave," for instance, is less useful than one like "Hamlet's grappling with Laertes in the grave foreshadows their duel and deaths." You can easily turn headings that make a point into topic sentences for your middle paragraphs. You will find an example of a formal outline in the sample topic assignment (p. 189).

Stage 5 Revising: Integrating and Documenting Research Material

As you draft your research paper, keep the same principles in mind as for other kinds of essays. When you finish, make a revision outline and check your thesis statement, essay structure, and individual paragraphs. You will find an example of this process in the sample topic that concludes this chapter. Here we will focus on the problems specific to research papers: integrating and documenting your research material.

Step 1   Integrating Research Material

When you use research material, keep the following principles in mind:

- Your main purpose in a research paper (as in any essay) is to present *your* views on a subject. Use ideas and factual information from other writers to provide additional support for your views or to provide alternative views that you will argue against.

- Write clear, focused topic sentences that guide your readers through each step of your argument or analysis.

- Make clear distinctions between your ideas and those of your sources by using appropriate transitional words and phrases (Wong's study provides further support ...; on the other hand, Friedman argues ...).

- If your subject is a work of literature, be sure to provide your own evidence from the work to explain why you agree or disagree with another writer's interpretation. Don't rely on quotations from critics to make important points for you.

- Keep quotations short and in appropriate format (see Quotations in Part 3, Handbook for Final Editing).

- Include explanations that make the significance of details apparent to your reader.

When you are trying to pull together material from a wide variety of sources, it's easy to get caught up in details and lose sight of the points those details are meant to support.

In the following paragraph, for instance, the writer draws on three sources: J. M. Bynner, *The Young Smoker* (London: Her Majesty's Stationery Office, 1969); Bernard Mausner and Ellen S. Platt, *Smoking: A Behavioral Analysis* (New York: Pergamon, 1971); and Richard Olshavsky, *No More Butts: A Psychologist's Approach to Quitting Cigarettes* (Bloomington: Indiana UP, 1977). The paragraph provides adequate *details* in a mixture of summary and quotation. It is very confusing, however, because it does not provide enough *explanation* of the relationship between the topic sentence and the various studies; indeed, one of the studies seems to contradict the others.

WRITING SAMPLE

Draft paragraph: The social causes of smoking have been established in a number of studies. According to B. Mausner and E. Platt, many smokers reported that they thought of smokers as daring and sophisticated and of non-smokers as sensible and careful (7). According to Richard Olshavsky, advertising does not seem either to inhibit or to promote cigarette smoking (98). In his study of the smoking habits of British schoolboys, J. M. Bynner discovered that "Boys who smoke thought of themselves as being fairly tough but not as tough as they would like to be. They, more than any other group, saw non-smokers as completely lacking in toughness, and thus the act of giving up smoking involved identification with a group which had a very unattractive characteristic" (93).

Notice how the revised version links the topic sentence with the research details, explains the apparent contradiction in the studies, and maintains the mixture of summary and quotation:

WRITING SAMPLE

Revised paragraph: The social causes of smoking have been established in a number of studies. Although the image of smokers conveyed by advertising may not be important, since, as Richard Olshavsky points out, advertising does not seem either to inhibit or to promote cigarette smoking (98), there is good evidence that the image smokers have of themselves is very important. In his study of the smoking habits of British schoolboys, J. M. Bynner discovered that "Boys who smoke thought of themselves as being fairly tough but not as tough as they would like to be. They, more than any other group, saw non-smokers as completely lacking in toughness, and thus the act of giving up smoking involved identification with a group which had a very unattractive characteristic" (93). Adults seem to share this kind of thinking. According to B. Mausner and E. Platt, many smokers reported that they thought of smokers as daring and sophisticated, and of non-smokers as sensible and careful (7).

Step 2 Documenting Research Material: Understanding Plagiarism

Whenever you use ideas or information from another source, you must tell your readers where the material came from, whether you quote directly or paraphrase. Failure to give credit when you use someone else's work is *plagiarism*.

Plagiarism is the act, intentional or otherwise, of copying or borrowing words or ideas without properly acknowledging the original source. Although plagiarism may be a familiar term to most students, it is often misunderstood. Many students think plagiarism is word-for-word copying of another person's text. This is one definition, yet plagiarism can take many forms. Plagiarism occurs when

- a student hands in work done wholly or in part by another person
- portions of a submitted work are taken from another source without proper reference to that source
- a student paraphrases sections of another work without acknowledging the source
- ideas in a work are borrowed, derived, or developed from another source without reference to that source (for example, "checking a few Internet sites for ideas")

Plagiarism carries serious consequences, ranging from a failing grade to expulsion, so it's important to understand that plagiarism can be unintentional (failing to state the source of ideas or information) as well as intentional (submitting a paper you did not write yourself).

The most common confusion about plagiarism is the difference between using words and using ideas. Most students understand the necessity of putting quotation marks around words they take from someone else. However, if you borrow ideas from someone else, you must also acknowledge the source of the ideas. It is a difference between quoting and paraphrasing.

When you **paraphrase**, you restate ideas and information in your own words. Although the words have changed, the ideas remain the same. For example, if you sit down to write an essay, you might check the Internet for some information on your topic. In doing so, you are looking at someone else's information and ideas. If you use this information—even if you change the wording—you must state the source. If you fail to acknowledge the source, you have committed an act of plagiarism.

The surest way to avoid plagiarism is to learn how to document research materials properly. That means giving in-text references in addition to including full bibliographical information for each source in a Works Cited or References page at the end. The following examples will demonstrate how to use your source material without plagiarizing. You will find further information on the format of in-text citations in Documentation, Part 3, Handbook for Final Editing.

Imagine writing an essay on Michael Ondaatje's novel *Coming Through Slaughter*. You might come across a published article—a hypothetical example by S. Smith—that is relevant to your essay topic.

Excerpt of published writing

Michael Ondaatje's fragmented writing in *Coming Through Slaughter* stylistically echoes the improvised, unpredictable music and actions of the main character, Buddy Bolden.

Plagiarized example 1

In *Coming Through Slaughter*, Ondaatje's **fragmented writing stylistically echoes** Buddy Bolden's music.

Clearly, the student has taken key phrases from the original without acknowledging the source. To avoid plagiarism, the student must use quotation marks to indicate that the phrases are from another source.

Revision

> S. Smith has argued that Ondaatje's "fragmented writing …
> stylistically echoes" (32) Buddy Bolden's music.

Plagiarized example 2

> Michael Ondaatje's writing echoes the music of Buddy
> Bolden.

Here, the student has taken several words from the original ("writing," "echoes," and "music") as well as the idea that compares the writing to the music. Convention dictates that three or more words in a row should be contained within quotation marks. This example does not violate that convention; however, it still constitutes plagiarism. The student has borrowed an idea as well as some words. The student must indicate the source of the idea and paraphrase the idea in original words.

Revision

> As S. Smith has noted, Ondaatje's style reflects the music of
> Buddy Bolden (32).

Plagiarized example 3

> Michael Ondaatje writes in a style similar to Buddy Bolden's
> jazz music.

In this example, the student has not quoted directly from the original, but the idea is nonetheless derived from the published writing. The student must reference that source both in the body of the essay and in the Works Cited or References page.

Revision

> Michael Ondaatje writes in a style similar to Buddy Bolden's
> jazz music (Smith 32).

As this final example demonstrates, it is easy to avoid plagiarism when paraphrasing another person's work. The only difference between the plagiarized example and the properly documented sentence is the inclusion of the parenthetical reference giving the source of the idea. If you keep track of your sources while you take notes, you can easily supply the necessary information.

With increased access to the Internet, finding information is rarely a problem. Be careful to evaluate the sources you consult, however, since not all information on the Internet is reliable, accurate, or correct. Any information you take from the Internet, like information in books and scholarly journals, must be documented properly (see Documentation, Part 3, Handbook for Final Editing, for the appropriate format). Failure to do so constitutes plagiarism. Intentional plagiarism from Internet resources, such as copying entire essays, is of course easily detectable (after all, instructors are experts in their fields and quickly recognize such instances of academic dishonesty).

Essay assignments are intended to encourage you to work through ideas and to develop your writing skills. Collecting ideas from the Internet or another source is not the same as working through and understanding those ideas. When you provide appropriate references, you demonstrate that you understand both your subject and the contributions that others have made to it.

Key questions to ask in order to avoid plagiarism:

- Have you looked at any secondary sources: books, journal articles, Internet sites?

- Have you borrowed any words or ideas from those sources?

- Are quotations clearly indicated with quotations marks, in-text author and page references, and complete bibliographical information in the Works Cited or References page?

- Have you paraphrased any material, and, if so, is the idea clearly attributed to the original source?

- Can a reader distinguish between your words and ideas and the words and ideas of other people?

Sample Topic (Research): The Dramatic Function of the Graveyard Scene in *Hamlet*

In Chapter 12 we examined the first two stages in writing a research paper on the dramatic function of the graveyard scene in *Hamlet*, clarifying the topic and gathering material. Now we will show the remaining stages in writing and revising this research paper: formulating a thesis statement, drafting, revising thesis statement and essay structure, and revising individual paragraphs.

Stage 3   Formulating a Thesis Statement

Step 1   Forming an opinion   If you review the secondary material on the graveyard scene at the end of Chapter 12, you will notice that little of it directly addresses the question of dramatic function—that is, the purpose the scene serves at this point in the play. One critic who does address this issue is B. D. Cheadle. Cheadle comments that Shakespeare uses the contrast between Hamlet and Laertes to re-establish our sympathy for Hamlet before his impending death. This comment raises the possibility that other aspects of the scene serve the same dramatic function.

Re-examining the material, you might determine that other aspects of the scene do engage our sympathy for Hamlet, forfeited by his killing of Polonius and by Ophelia's death. In the first half of the scene, the gravediggers criticize the court's using its power to ensure a Christian burial for Ophelia. Here the gravediggers provide a bridge for the audience between seeing events from the court's perspective and seeing them from Hamlet's perspective. When Hamlet enters, his first remark is on the insensitivity of the gravedigger who sings while he works. This comment makes us feel that Hamlet has finer feelings. His exchanges with the gravedigger and his speculations about the dead seem almost comic, and yet we know, as Hamlet doesn't, that the grave being dug is Ophelia's. The dramatic irony of this situation would certainly make us more sympathetic to Hamlet.

In the second half of the scene, Hamlet's declaration of love for Ophelia and for Laertes would engage our sympathy, especially since we know that Laertes has agreed to Claudius' plot to kill Hamlet. The tussle in the grave seems to foreshadow the duel between Hamlet and Laertes and its outcome. This sense of impending doom would also make us sympathetic to Hamlet.

Several aspects of the scene do seem to confirm this interpretation. Your statement of opinion, then, might be something like this:

Thesis opinion: The dramatic function of the graveyard scene is to engage the audience's sympathy for Hamlet before his death.

This opinion addresses the issue set out in the essay topic, and is therefore a suitable basis for a thesis statement.

Step 2   Supporting your opinion   To give reasons for your opinion, you would return to those aspects of the scene that support your interpretation. You could complete the thesis statement by showing how Hamlet's relations with the gravediggers, with Ophelia, and with Laertes affect the audience:

Thesis statement: The dramatic function of the graveyard scene is to engage the audience's sympathy for Hamlet before his death. The scene accomplishes this purpose in three ways: by using the gravediggers as a means to shift the audience's perspective from the court to Hamlet; by clarifying Hamlet's relationship with Ophelia; and by symbolically foreshadowing the outcome of the duel between Hamlet and Laertes.

Stage 4   Drafting

Steps 1 and 2   Selecting material and making points With research papers it is sometimes easy to focus on the criticism and lose sight of your own analysis of the text. One way you can maintain a balance is to synthesize the most relevant research in a paragraph or two at the beginning of your paper and then to develop your own analysis in detail, using references to critics to support specific points.

Step 3   Organizing material: constructing a formal outline Once you have decided what material to use and what points to make, you can organize your material by making a formal outline something like this:

THE GRAVEYARD SCENE IN *HAMLET*

Thesis statement: The dramatic function of the graveyard scene is to engage the audience's sympathy for Hamlet before his death. The scene accomplishes this purpose in three ways: by using the gravediggers as a means to shift the audience's perspective from the court to Hamlet; by clarifying Hamlet's relationship with Ophelia; and by symbolically foreshadowing the outcome of the duel between Hamlet and Laertes.

I.   Philosophical interpretations of the scene
    A. Scene shows Hamlet's Christian acceptance of death
    B. Scene shows fatalistic resignation in face of death
    C. Scene shows mixture of both these ways of viewing death
    D. Inadequacy of philosophical interpretations

II. Dramatic functions of the scene
    A. Encounter with gravediggers shifts sympathy from court to Hamlet
        1. Audience sympathizes with court in preceding scenes
        2. Hamlet presented as more sensitive than singing gravedigger
        3. Jests about death show Hamlet as neither morbidly preoccupied with death nor overly sentimental, but accepting its reality

    B. Last half of scene resolves ambiguity of Hamlet's feelings for Ophelia
        1. Earlier scenes show ambiguity in Hamlet's relations with Ophelia
        2. Hamlet regains sympathy by declaring his love for Ophelia

    C. Hamlet's grappling with Laertes in the grave foreshadows their duel and deaths

Step 4   Sketching introduction and conclusion To establish a context for the thesis about the graveyard scene, you might remind readers about its place in the action of the play as a whole. You might decide not to worry about a conclusion, since developing the body of a research paper is itself a considerable task, and merely say something about Hamlet as a tragic hero.

Step 5 Writing the draft You will find the final version of the research paper on the graveyard scene in Part 2, Readings. In the section below we will show how you would identify problems specific to research papers and make the appropriate revisions.

Stage 5 Revising Thesis Statement and Essay Structure

Step 1 Revising your thesis statement The idea of Hamlet as a tragic hero does not appear in the original thesis statement. Yet this point would help to explain *why* Shakespeare wants to engage our sympathy for Hamlet in this scene. You might therefore add this point to your thesis statement:

> **Thesis statement revision:** Without a change in character, Hamlet would not achieve the stature of a tragic hero, because his death would not arouse the pity, fear, awe, and sense of waste common to Shakespearean tragedy.

Step 2 Revising essay structure If the draft follows the order of the formal outline, the structure as a whole should be satisfactory. You might discover a problem with paragraph divisions, however, such as a middle paragraph that is far too long and contains a confusing mixture of points about Hamlet's relation to Ophelia and to Laertes. You would note the changes needed on your revision outline.

Stage 6 Revising Individual Paragraphs

Step 1 Revising your introduction In drafting your introduction, you may have provided a context for your discussion of the graveyard scene by reminding readers of previous events in the play. In revising, you may decide that this detail is excessive; furthermore, since this is a research paper, you could provide a more appropriate context by showing how your analysis relates to scholarly writing about *Hamlet*. The revised introduction makes this change and includes in the thesis statement the point about Hamlet as a tragic hero.

Step 2 Revising middle paragraphs

Checking Topic Sentences You may find that topic sentences in the draft are not very clear. The original topic sentence for the second middle paragraph, for example, does not make the point indicated on the outline: that the encounter with the gravediggers shifts the audience's sympathy from the court to Hamlet. You could revise to make this point more clearly, and link it to Hamlet's role as a tragic hero.

Draft topic sentence: But our emotional response to the scene is shaped by the fact that it opens not with the funeral procession but with the gravediggers debating the decision to give Ophelia a Christian burial.

Revised topic sentence: The graveyard scene opens not with Hamlet's entrance but with the conversation between the gravediggers. This opening allows for a gradual shift in sympathy from the court to Hamlet and humanizes the prince by making death a personal rather than a metaphysical concern.

Integrating Research Material A major task of revising research papers is clarifying the connections between your analysis and others' views. This excerpt from the draft illustrates this difficulty:

Draft middle paragraph: After trying to figure out how a coroner might have reached a verdict of drowning in "self-defence," the gravediggers conclude that only her social position has secured Ophelia burial in consecrated ground, a burial that would have been denied a social inferior. The effect of this debate, as Peter Philias points out, is to shift attention away from the religious question of salvation and damnation that had been so powerful in Hamlet's own considerations of suicide (Philias 231). The reduction of death from a metaphysical to a human concern is further emphasized by the first gravedigger's actions: he tosses skulls about and sings while he works.

Here it is not clear how Ophelia's burial or Philias' explanation relates to the point about the audience's shifting sympathies. Furthermore, the last sentence introduces a new point.

In the revised version (middle paragraph 6), the connections are spelled out:

Revised middle paragraph: But the graveyard scene does not merely shift the point of view from the court to Hamlet. It also humanizes Hamlet by making death a personal rather than a metaphysical concern. The gravediggers' debate over Ophelia's burial, as Peter Philias points out, shifts attention away from the religious questions of salvation and damnation that were so powerful when Hamlet himself was considering suicide, because the gravediggers focus on the social issues of power and status (231). The reduction of death from a metaphysical to a human concern is further emphasized by the gravedigger's actions as he tosses skulls about and sings about the human cycle of love, age, and death.

Acknowledging Sources   In writing your draft, you might attempt to synthesize views about Hamlet's character but, as in this example, fail to indicate who holds each position:

> **Draft middle paragraph:** Many critics have suggested that the episode with the gravediggers indicates a change in Hamlet's character, though they have not agreed about the meaning of that change. Some see Hamlet coming to a Christian acceptance of death; others see his attitude as that of fatalistic resignation; others argue that the scene is a mixture of both these ways of viewing death.

In revising, you would need to discuss these views in more detail and to document your sources. In the final version, this paragraph has expanded into two, the first on the Christian interpretations and the second on the other interpretations. Here is the expanded material on the Christian interpretations, with the appropriate in-text citations:

> **Revised middle paragraph:** Many critics have suggested that the episode with the gravediggers indicates a change in Hamlet's character, though they have not agreed about the meaning of that change. Maynard Mack and Walter King are representative of those who favour a Christian interpretation. According to Mack, Hamlet by the last act of the play has "learned, and accepted, the boundaries in which human action, human judgment are enclosed" and therefore no longer assumes he must single-handedly set the world to rights (521). Similarly, King argues that the graveyard scene presents "affirmation of life and love as a viable center of values in a God-created and God-centered universe," but within the context of a world in which these values "are perennially in danger of being snuffed out" (146).

Step 2   Revising your conclusion   You may have concluded your draft by saying something like, "In these ways, then, Shakespeare uses the graveyard scene to give Hamlet the qualities appropriate to his status as a tragic hero." The revised conclusion draws together the points made in the essay and again places this analysis within the context of other criticism. For the final essay, see D. Smith, "The Making of the Tragic Hero," Part 2, Readings: Sample Essays.

Once you have written a revised draft, you are ready to give your research paper a final editing. Pay particular attention to quotations that are too long, poorly introduced, or inadequately explained and to the form and adequacy of citations. Aside from quotations and documentation, you are likely to have many of the same problems with sentence structure, grammar, and punctuation in research papers as in your other essays. Check the relevant sections of Part 3, Handbook for Final Editing. Make sure you have followed the guidelines for essay format and give your paper a final proofreading.

Working on Your Own Assignment

In writing and revising a research paper, your goal is to produce a coherent essay in which you integrate your own ideas about your subject with information and ideas drawn from secondary sources.

- Formulate a thesis statement by reviewing your notes to find (a) the connections between the material you have gathered and your research question and (b) the most important similarities and differences between your ideas and the information in your secondary sources.

- Organize your material by making a formal outline that sets out the main ideas in the paper. Indicate in the outline where you want to bring in secondary material and the point you want to make about it.

- As you write your draft, keep track of your sources by putting the author and page number in parentheses after each quotation and after any paraphrased material (for APA style, include the year of publication).

- Check the thesis statement and overall structure of your draft against your formal outline. Watch for paragraphs that are too long. You may need to subdivide them, to shorten quotations, or to delete unimportant or irrelevant material. Make a note of any necessary changes.

- As you read through each middle paragraph, ask yourself two questions: What is the main point? How does this material support my thesis? If your topic sentence does not answer these questions, revise it. Put all the important points in your own words and include quotations, references, and other evidence to support them. Make clear why you agree or disagree with the opinions of other writers.

- Make it easy for readers to see which ideas are yours and which come from other sources by introducing and giving citations for both quoted and paraphrased material.

- In both your introduction and your conclusion, connect your own thinking with your research material.

EXERCISES

A. Respond in a sentence or two to each of the following questions.

1. What are the key characteristics of an effective thesis statement for a research paper?

2. What should the outline for your research paper include?

3. Define the term **plagiarism**. What are the best strategies to avoid accidental plagiarism?

4. What does it mean to **integrate** research material? What strategies can you use to integrate research material into your essay?

5. Where in this text can you find information on the format for in-text citations? Format for entries on a Works Cited page? Format for long and short quotations of poetry and prose? Guidelines for using quotations effectively? Give the appropriate page numbers.

B. Write and revise a mini-research paper on the topic you chose for Exercise B in Chapter 12.

Readings

Published Writings

"Addiction in Free Markets"
Bruce K. Alexander and Stefa Shaler   198

"Wanted: The Right to Refuse"   Maggie Black   203

"Population: Ignoring Its Impact"
John Bongaarts   206

"Health Canada Inadvertently Discloses Facts
Planned Parenthood Would Like to Suppress"
Ted Byfield   211

"The Ticking Bomb"   Wade Davis   215

"Where They Have to Take You In"
Caterina Edwards   221

"A Rose for 'A Rose for Emily'"   Judith Fetterley 229

"My Wood"   E. M. Forster   238

"Save the Last Dance"   John Fraser   242

"Kiddy Thinks"   Alison Gopnik   247

"Why I Live with My Mother"   Katie Haegele   252

"Lifeboat Ethics: The Case Against Helping
the Poor"   Garrett Hardin   256

"The Voyagers" Linda Hogan 263

"In Praise of the Humble Comma" Pico Iyer 270

"A Lament for Quality" Ann Dowsett Johnston 274

"He Was a Boxer When I Was Small"
Lenore Keeshig-Tobias 277

"Profits by the Truckload" Ross Laver 282

"Embraced by the Needle" Gabor Maté 285

"Unchopping a Tree" W. S. Merwin 289

"Shooting an Elephant" George Orwell 293

"The Ticking Daddy Clock" Andrew Pyper 301

"The Poorhouse" Judy Rebick 304

"The Men We Carry in Our Minds"
Scott Russell Sanders 307

"It Always Costs" David T. Suzuki 313

"A Modest Proposal" Jonathan Swift 317

"Choosing Up Sides" Ken Wiwa 327

The English Patient Debate 331

"The Moral Superiority of Casablanca
over The English Patient" Thomas Hurka 331

Round Two: The English Patient Rallies (Letters) 333

When Loyalty and Friendship Collide (Editorial) 336

Feminism at the Movies Margaret Wente 339

Sample Essays

"To Peacekeep or Not to Peacekeep"
James Ash   342

"The Complex Skill of Independent Living"
(Sample Content Analysis Essay)   A. Jones   344

"Shifts in Attitude and Form in Al Purdy's
'Trees at the Arctic Circle'" (Sample Textual
Analysis Essay)   B. Jones   346

"Perspectives on Addictions" (Sample
Comparison Essay)   C. Jones   349

"Reflecting on Population" (Sample Critique)
D. Jones   352

"Same-Sex Marriages: Tradition and Change"
(Sample Persuasive Essay)   E. Jones   355

"The Problem of Environmental Costs:
Suzuki vs. Merwin"   Joyce MacDonald   359

"The Making of the Tragic Hero:
The Graveyard Scene in *Hamlet*"
(Sample Research Paper)   D. Smith   362

"Spontaneity and Enjoyment of the Natural
World"   Karin Swanson   367

ADDICTION IN FREE MARKETS

by Bruce K. Alexander and Stefa Shaler

Although any person in any society can become addicted, free market societies universally dislocate their members, leading to mass addiction. This simple proposition can profoundly change the way that we deal with addictions in ourselves and others. Although often overlooked by addiction professionals, the evidence for this proposition fills our history and our everyday life.   1

In order for a "free market" to be "free," the exchange of labour, land, currency and consumer goods must be controlled by the laws of supply and demand, and must not be "distorted" by personal loyalties,   2

Bruce K. Alexander is a professor of psychology at Simon Fraser University and a research associate with the Canadian Centre for Policy Alternatives. His research interests include the causes of addiction, the effects of globalization on psychological functioning, and the history of psychology.

Stefa Shaler has run group homes for difficult-to-place wards of the British Columbia Ministry of Social Services for many years. In 1998 Shaler worked in the slums of Brazil as a volunteer for the charity Street Angels.

Reprinted by permission of University of Toronto Press. "Addiction in Free Markets" was published in Bruce Alexander's *Peaceful Measures* (University of Toronto Press, 1990). This is a shortened version, with references omitted. For the complete text, see the original publication.

village or neighbourhood responsibilities, guild or union rights, charity, family obligations, ethnic tastes and aversions, social roles, or religious values.

Disastrously, today's free market fundamentalists ignore all previously understood limits, including Adam Smith's[1] warning that national governments must resist the power of manufacturers to "become formidable to the government and ... intimidate the legislature." Smith also feared excessive profits and considered "private luxury and extravagance" to be "ruinous taxes." We've gone too far toward the free market extreme, and one of those consequences is mass dislocation and, in its train, mass addiction.   3

At the beginning of the 21st century, for rich and poor alike, jobs disappear on short notice, communities are weak and unstable, people   4 routinely change lovers, families, occupations, co-workers, technical skills, languages, nationalities, therapists, spiritual beliefs and ideologies as they navigate the shopping malls, real estate markets, and employment agencies. Prices and incomes are no more stable than social life. Even the continued viability of ecological systems is in question. For rich and poor alike, dislocation plays havoc with delicate ties between people and society that comprise psychosocial integration.

What is the relationship between dislocation and addiction? Most   5 people who cannot achieve a reasonable degree of psychosocial integration find that they must develop "substitute" lifestyles in order to endure. Substitute lifestyles entail excessive habits intended to fill the painful void of dislocation. These habits include drug use and many other activities that do not center on drug use. They also include social relationships that provide some satisfaction although they are not sufficiently close, stable or socially acceptable to comprise real psychosocial integration. People in this predicament—whether barroom drunks, internet sex surfers or needle-using junkies—cling to their substitute lifestyles with a tenacity that is properly called addiction.

Examples of forced dislocation and consequent addiction fill the   6 history of free market society. For example, by a series of increments, England moved to a full-blown free market system between the late 16th and the early 19th centuries. This was achieved in part through massive evictions of the rural poor from their farms, commons, and villages and their absorption into urban slums and a brutal, export oriented manufacturing system. Those who resisted these new realities too strenuously were further dislocated by forced apprenticeship of their children, destruction of their unions and other associations, elimination of local charity to the "undeserving poor," and by confinement in "houses of correction" where unruly behaviour was corrected with whips and branding irons.

Forced dislocation spread from England to the rest of the British   7 Isles, e.g., the "clearances" of the clan society of the Scottish Highlands, and spread to English colonies abroad, e.g., the settlement of Australia by "transportation" of convict labour. Dislocated British emigrants reproduced their own condition by dislocating aboriginal peoples wherever they landed, including Vancouver, with the support and encouragement of the imperial government.

The historical correlation between severe dislocation and addiction is strong. Although alcohol consumption and drunkenness on festive occasions was widespread in Europe during the middle ages, and although a few people became "inebriates" and "drunkards," mass alcoholism was not a problem. However, alcoholism gradually spread with the beginnings of the free markets after 1500 and eventually became a raging epidemic with the dominance of free market society after 1800.

The predictable relationship between free market society, disloca- 9
tion, and addiction is clearly visible in the history of Native Canadians.
Although murder, adultery and insanity sometimes occurred within
Canadian aboriginal culture, anthropologists have found no evidence of
large-scale addiction, despite the fact that activities were available that
have proven addictive in free market societies, such as eating, sex,
gambling, psychedelic mushrooms, etc.

Canadian aboriginal society did not have access to alcohol, but na- 10
tives in what is now called Mexico and the American southwest did. In
those societies where alcohol was readily available, it was used moder-
ately, often ceremonially, rather than addictively, prior to the destruction of native culture.

The popular explanation for rampant alcoholism among Canadian 11
natives is that they have a racial inability to control alcohol. But this is
unlikely, since addiction was not a ruinous problem among natives
until assimilation subjected them to extreme dislocation. Moreover, if
natives were handicapped by the "gene of alcoholism," the same must
be said of Europeans since those subjected to conditions of extreme
dislocation also fell into addiction almost universally. Even the Orkney
Islanders who were brought to Canada from Scotland by the Hudson's
Bay Company specifically because of their characteristic sobriety and
obedience and because they were accustomed to extreme northern
weather and life at sea, fell prey to rampant alcoholism under the
stresses of dislocation.

Members of free market societies generally still cherish the hope 12
that free markets will create universal well being. Therefore, it is only
polite to overlook connections between free markets, dislocation and
addiction. Print and electronic media help us to maintain this civil
inattention, celebrating free market achievements with blinding fireworks and deafening fanfare. They endlessly publicize new medical explanations for the puzzling epidemic of "drug" addiction and hopeful
new solutions. They continue decades of futile debate about whether
addiction is a "criminal" or a "medical" problem whereas, in fact, it is
neither. In free market society, the spread of addiction is primarily a
political and spiritual problem. If we do not find wellsprings of psychosocial integration, society, with its ever-freer markets, will manifest
even more dislocation and addiction.

The key to controlling addiction is maintaining a society in which 13
every member is included in a larger community with a sense of meaning and belonging. People need to belong within their society, not just
trade in its markets.

Changing the terms of the familiar debates on addiction is neces- 14
sary if political action is to become possible. This is a huge task since
the current manner of speaking about addiction as an individual drug-
using disease enjoys the support of free market leaders. People endure

this chronic barrage of misinformation because it complements a deeply rooted North American "temperance mentality" which makes it natural to blame social problems on drugs and alcohol, and also because it profits many institutions and professions that treat, police, prevent and 'harm reduce' the putative disease. Those who launch the misinformation campaigns prosper financially because the "War on Drugs," which has drawn its justification from them, serves vital commercial and geopolitical purposes for vested interests with very deep pockets.

Authoritative voices around the world are raising a mighty chorus of warnings against the psychological, ecological and social devastation engendered by free market extremism. Careful reflection on addiction can add a new counterpoint to this chorus, stressing the relationship between free markets, dislocation and addiction. Needless to say, a healthier society ultimately leads to a healthier economic system as well. 15

An alternative to the extreme free market orthodoxy must begin with a sense that all of us are participants in a sacred trust to nurture, protect and promote delicate and intricate bonds with every aspect of the biosphere and the invisible forces of spirit and humanitarianism. 16

NOTE

[1] Adam Smith (1723–90) was a Scottish economist whose book *The Wealth of Nations* (1776) contains the famous claim that the invisible hand of the market translates self-interest into public benefit.

VOCABULARY

biosphere—the part of the earth's crust, waters, and atmosphere where living organisms can subsist

geopolitical—based on the interrelation of geography and politics

psychosocial integration—"to be included in the larger community with a sense of meaning and belonging" (paragraph 13)

QUESTIONS

1. Alexander and Shaler take addiction to include "drug use and many other activities that do not center on drug use." What definition of addiction do you think they are using in this essay?

2. Alexander and Shaler refer extensively to three centuries of English history and to the history of native Canadians. How do they link these examples with the effects of free market society in the present? Is this argument convincing to you?

3. "Addiction in Free Markets" contains both neutral and evaluative diction. Identify 3–5 examples of each kind. How is the use of diction linked to the essay's purpose, as you understand it?

4. In this essay an explanation of the causes of addiction leads to a proposal for solutions. How effective is this problem–solution structure? To what extent would this structure be useful in your own writing?

SUGGESTION FOR WRITING

Alexander and Shaler describe the beginning of the 21st century as a time of weak communities, rapid change, and instability in work, relationships, beliefs, and places of residence. Write a short essay exploring to what extent your own experience of the beginning of the 21st century echoes this view.

WANTED: THE RIGHT TO REFUSE

Maggie Black

Take a look at Article One of the Supplementary Convention on   1
Slavery[1] and you will see as one definition: 'Any practice whereby
a woman, without the right to refuse, is given in marriage in payment
of a consideration in money or in kind ...'

Then, tell me please, why has almost no-one noticed forced mar-   2
riage as a major issue of human rights? Rape within marriage, domestic violence, yes. But about forced entry into a life sentence of a
marriage, the barest whisper of concern. Yet those are the wives most
vulnerable to rape and violence.

Marriage without consent is illegal in many countries. Yet millions   3
of girls and women still undergo this form of slavery today. Early marriage is especially common in South Asia and West Africa, where the
idea that the girl (or boy) should have any say in this family business is
laughable. In Northern Nigeria, half the women are married at age 15.

Yet in the recent past not one women's or child-rights campaigner   4
has made a loud noise about this.

Not one. Amartya Sen,[2] the renowned economist, notices '60 million   5
women missing' because of girl neglect, but he doesn't mention the practice. In India, the legal minimum age of marriage is 18 for girls. In the
state of Madhya Pradesh 16 per cent of girls are married by age 14. Are
legal cases of wrongful or forced marriage ever brought? Almost never.

At the beginning of the 21st century being a   6
child wife, even if it's illegal, puts you in limbo.
You are invisible as either child or woman, because you have been married. What a man
does to you once, if you are underage or single,
is statutory rape. What he does to you night
after night, if you are underage and married, is
fine. In rural Ethiopia, no-one goes to help a
girl of 10 when they hear her screaming out at
night. It's something she must learn to bear.
After all, she is a wife.

How about a story? Just one, about Hauwa   7
Abukar, a Nigerian girl who died at age 12. Her
family had married her to an older man to whom
they owed money. She was unhappy and kept

Maggie Black, who works for UNICEF,
specializes in international social issues
such as HIV/AIDS, maternal and child
health, and water and environmental sani-
tation. Her books include *A Cause for Our
Times* (1992), *Children First* (1996), and
The No Nonsense Guide to Development
(2002), which examines the relationship
between development and economic
growth, the impact of development on the
living conditions of the poor and on the
environment, and the future role of development within a global economy.

Reprinted with permission from *New
Internationalist*, August 2001.

running away, but because of the debt her parents were obliged to return her. Finally, her husband chopped off her legs with an axe to prevent her absconding again. She died from starvation, shock and loss of blood. No legal action was taken.

The story may not be typical. But hundreds of thousands of girls are in situations almost as dire. And even if they are not, their marriages are still technically slavery because they were married without consent in some form of exchange. In Somalia or Northern Uganda, payment by a warlord for a 12-year-old concubine may consist of assurances about family security. Among stressed populations—the extremely poor, the conflict-ridden, communities where HIV is rife—early forced unions seem to be increasing. 8

The practice is not confined to Asia and Africa. In 1998 a court in Maryland in the US gave permission for a 29-year-old man to marry his 13-year-old girlfriend because she was pregnant. So it's pregnancy that is dreadful. Not sex with a minor, not loss of freedom, not loss of education and of the chance to become an independent person able to say 'no'. Marriage is fine whatever it does to the girl or woman. Early pregnancy is not, either because it is outside wedlock and immoral, or because it's dangerous to the girl and her baby, or because—horrors!—it adds to population growth. 9

In the 1960s and 1970s, demographers pointed out that early marriage was a bad idea because it meant a woman started bearing children early. If her firstborn arrived when she was 16, she would have more children over time than if she had waited until 20 or 24. So marriage postponement was a useful contraceptive. 10

In the 1980s and 1990s, reproductive-health experts pointed out that early pregnancy was a bad idea because a girl's body is not ready. Early pregnancy is closely connected to high rates of maternal and infant death. So marriage postponement is good for public health. 11

Did anyone mention slavery or forced sex or wife purchase? No. 12

Why the silence around forced marriage? One explanation may be that the women's movement has focused its attention outside the domestic domain. And the children's movement was, for long, not concerned with gender at all. There is a difficulty about age anyway. The Supplementary Convention on Slavery says everyone under 18 is a child. But puberty comes much earlier than this. Many societies marry off their daughters soon after puberty as a means of 'girl protection' against predatory males. The assumption is that she never could or should learn to say 'no' to a man. She should be placed where the idea is superfluous. 13

So it's the 'traditional' idea of womanhood, sanctioned by customary laws, which is to blame. Societies have their customary ways of doing things and we shouldn't interfere. But 'tradition' should not be used to justify severe oppression of women—or of anyone else. 14

Recently the British Home Office issued a groundbreaking report   15
on the forced marriages of British girls of Asian origin. The Minister
stated: 'Multicultural sensitivity is not an excuse for moral blindness.'
When a UNICEF Report on Early Marriage was launched in March, the
Indian Women's Policy Officer in New Delhi was asked by the BBC
whether it wasn't a cultural intrusion for an international body to
decry such a practice. She responded in amazement. 'The practice is
illegal here, what on earth do you mean?'

Like other dreadful things that human beings do to one another in   16
the name of 'custom' and 'tradition', forced marriage is a practice
which should cease. Everyone supposes that education will in time be
the great panacea because marriage age definitely rises with school attendance. But is this really the best we can do?

NOTES

[1] Supplementary Convention on Slavery. This document added more provisions to the
Convention of 1926, which abolished slavery world wide. One of these provisions is that no
"woman, without the right to refuse, [can be] promised or given in marriage in payment of a
consideration in money or kind...."

[2] Amartya Sen, an East Indian economist who won the Nobel Prize for economics in 1998, is a
well-respected defender of tolerance and pluralism and human rights.

VOCABULARY

demographers—those who compile statistics on births, deaths, diseases in particular
population groups
panacea—cure-all

QUESTIONS

1. According to Black, what are the main reasons that forced marriages have not been
   considered an important human rights abuse?
2. List the most common reasons Black gives for girls being forced to marry.
3. Black says that we should not accept forced marriages even if they are a traditional
   custom in a particular culture. Does she present convincing evidence to support this
   assertion?

SUGGESTION FOR WRITING

Black raises some interesting questions on how we should respond to cultural practices
that violate our own concepts of human rights (the use of five- and six-year-old children
as farm or factory workers, for example). Who should decide if such practices are acceptable and who should enforce the rules? In "The Ticking Bomb" (Readings), Wade Davis
says that "we must aspire to create a new international spirit of pluralism, a true global
democracy in which unique cultures, large and small, are allowed the right to exist...."
Write a paragraph or two comparing Black's and Davis's views on cultural pluralism.

POPULATION: IGNORING ITS IMPACT

John Bongaarts

Around the world, countries are experiencing unprecedented demographic change. The best-known example is an enormous expansion in human numbers, but other important demographic trends also affect human welfare. People are living longer and healthier lives, women are bearing fewer children, increasing numbers of migrants are moving to cities, and to other countries in search of a better life, and populations are aging. Lomborg's[1] unbalanced presentation of some of these trends and their influences emphasizes the good news and neglects the bad. Environmentalists who predicted widespread famine and blamed rapid population growth for many of the world's environmental, economic and social problems overstated their cases. But Lomborg's view that "the number of people is not the problem" is simply wrong. 1

His selective use of statistics gives the reader the impression that the population problem is largely behind us. The global population growth rate has indeed declined slowly, but absolute growth remains close to the very high levels observed in recent decades, because the population base keeps expanding. World population today stands at six billion, three billion more than in 1960. According to U.N. projections, another three billion will likely be added by 2050, and population size will eventually reach about 10 billion. 2

Any discussion of global trends is misleading without taking account of the enormous contrasts among world regions. Today's poorest nations in Africa, Asia and Latin America have rapidly growing and young populations, whereas in the technologically advanced and richer nations in Europe, North America and Japan, growth is near zero (or, in some cases, even negative), and populations are aging quickly. As a consequence, nearly all future global growth will be concentrated in the developing countries, where four fifths of the world's population 3

John Bongaarts has worked with the Population Council in New York City for two decades and is currently vice president of its Policy Research Division. His research focuses on a variety of population issues, including the determinants of fertility, population-environment relationships, the demographic impact of the AIDS epidemic, and population policy options in the developing world. Bongaarts was one of four scientists invited by *Scientific American* to critique the book *The Skeptical Environmentalist* by Danish statistician Bjorn Lomborg. Bongaarts focuses on Lomborg's treatment of population; for critiques of Lomborg's methods and conclusions about global warming, energy, and biodiversity, see "Misleading Math about the Earth," *Scientific American*, January 2002.

lives. The projected rise in population in the developing world between 2000 and 2025 (from 4.87 to 6.72 billion) is actually just as large as the record-breaking increase in the past quarter of a century. The historically unprecedented population expansion in the poorest parts of the world continues largely unabated.

Past population growth has led to high population densities in 4 many countries. Lomborg dismisses concerns about this issue based on a simplistic and misleading calculation of density as the ratio of people to all land. Clearly, a more useful and accurate indicator of density would be based on the land that remains after excluding areas unsuited for human habitation or agriculture, such as deserts and inaccessible mountains. For example, according to his simple calculation, the population density of Egypt equals a manageable 68 persons per square kilometer, but if the unirrigated Egyptian deserts are excluded, density is an extraordinary 2,000 per square kilometer. It is therefore not surprising that Egypt needs to import a large proportion of its food supply. Measured properly, population densities have reached extremely high levels, particularly in large countries in Asia and the Middle East.

Why does this matter? The effect of population trends on human 5 welfare has been debated for centuries. When the modern expansion of human numbers began in the 18th century, Thomas Robert Malthus[2] argued that population growth would be limited by food shortages. Lomborg and other technological optimists correctly note that world population has expanded much more rapidly than Malthus envisioned, growing from one billion to six billion over the past two centuries. And diets have improved. Moreover, the technological optimists are probably correct in claiming that overall world food production can be increased substantially over the next few decades. Average current crop yields are still below the levels achieved in the most productive countries, and some countries still have unused potential arable land (although much of this is forested).

Agricultural expansion, however, will be costly, especially if global 6 food production has to rise twofold or even threefold to accommodate the demand for better diets from several billion more people. The land now used for agriculture is generally of better quality than unused, potentially cultivable land. Similarly, existing irrigation systems have been built on the most favorable sites. And water is increasingly in short supply in many countries as the competition for that resource among households, industry and agriculture intensifies. Consequently, each new increase in food production is becoming more expensive to obtain. This is especially true if one considers environmental costs not reflected in the price of agricultural products.

Lomborg's view that the production of more food is a nonissue 7 rests heavily on the fact that world food prices are low and have declined over time. But this evidence is flawed. Massive governmental subsidies to farmers, particularly in the developed countries, keep food prices artificially low. Although technological developments have reduced prices, without these massive subsidies, the world food prices would certainly be higher.

The environmental cost of what Paul R. and Anne H. Ehrlich[3] describe as "turning the earth into a giant human feedlot" could be severe. A large expansion of agriculture to provide growing populations with improved diets is likely to lead to further deforestation, loss of species, soil erosion, and pollution from pesticides and fertilizer runoff as farming intensifies and new land is brought into production. Reducing this environmental impact is possible but costly and would obviously be easier if population growth were slower. Lomborg does not deny this environmental impact but asks unhelpfully, "What alternative do we have, with more than 6 billion people on Earth?"

8

Lomborg correctly notes that poverty is the main cause of hunger and malnutrition, but he neglects the contribution of population growth to poverty. This effect operates through two distinct mechanisms. First, rapid population growth leads to a younger population, one in which as much as half is below the age of entry into the labour force. These young people have to be fed, housed, clothed and educated, but they are not productive, thus constraining the economy. Second, rapid population growth creates a huge demand for new jobs. A large number of applicants for a limited number of jobs exerts downward pressure on wages, contributing to poverty and inequality. Unemployment is widespread, and often workers in poor countries earn wages near the subsistence level. Both of these adverse economic effects are reversible by reducing birth rates. With lower birth rates, schools become less crowded, the ratio of dependents to workers declines as does the growth in the number of job seekers. These beneficial demographic effects contributed to the economic "miracles" of several East Asian countries. Of course, such dramatic results are by no means assured and can be realized only in countries with otherwise sound economic policies.

9

Lomborg approvingly notes the huge ongoing migration from villages to cities in the developing world. This has been considered a welcome development, because urban dwellers generally have higher standards of living than villagers. Because the flow of migrants is now so large, however, it tends to overwhelm the absorptive capacity of cities, and many migrants end up living in appalling conditions in slums. The traditional urban advantage is eroding in the poorest countries, and the health conditions in slums are often as adverse as in rural areas. This points to another burden of rapid population growth: the inability of governments to cope with large additions of new people. In many developing countries, investments in education, health services and infrastructure are not keeping up with population growth.

10

It is true that life has improved for many people in recent decades, 11 but Lomborg does not acknowledge that this favorable trend has been brought about in part by intensive efforts by governments and the international community. Investments in developing and distributing "green revolution" technology have reduced hunger, public health campaigns have cut death rates, and family planning programs have lowered birth rates. Despite this progress, some 800 million people are still malnourished, and 1.2 billion live in abject poverty. This very serious situation calls for more effective remedial action. Lomborg asks the developed nations to fulfill their U.N. pledge to donate 0.7 percent of their GNPs[4] to assist the developing world, but few countries have met this goal, and the richest nation on earth, the U.S., is one of the stingiest, giving just 0.1 percent of its GNP. The trend in overseas development assistance from the developed to the developing world is down, not up. Unfortunately, the unrelenting we-are-doing-fine tone that pervades Lomborg's book encourages complacency rather than urgency.

Population is not the main cause of the world's social, economic 12 and environmental problems, but it contributes substantially to many of them. If population had grown less rapidly in the past, we would be better off now. And if future growth can be slowed, future generations will be better off.

NOTES

[1] Bjorn Lomborg, author of *The Skeptical Environmentalist*, is a statistician and political scientist at the University of Aarthus in Denmark.

[2] Thomas Robert Malthus (1766–1834) was an English economist who argued that populations had a natural tendency to grow faster than the means to support them.

[3] In *The Population Bomb* Paul R. and Anne H. Ehrlich argued that because people usually try to live better than their parents did, the consumption of resources to support an increased population would be enormous.

[4] GNP: gross national product, the total amount of money made by a country in a year.

VOCABULARY

demographic—relevant to the vital statistics of a particular population
realized—made real

QUESTIONS

1. In this essay, Bongaarts evaluates Lomborg's arguments about population growth. Write a sentence or two expressing Bongaarts' thesis in your own words. What is his main standard of evaluation (see Chapter 10)?

2. What kinds of evidence does Bongaarts use to support his thesis and the key points in his essay?

3. Give at least three examples of how Bongaarts uses a pro-con structure to address the key points in Lomborg's argument.

4. What are the most important similarities and differences in Bongaarts' and Garrett Hardin's views on population growth? (See "Lifeboat Ethics: The Case Against Helping the Poor," Readings.)

SUGGESTION FOR WRITING

Should family size be solely a personal decision or are we morally obligated to take the global view? Make a list of the arguments for and against having a large family. Formulate a thesis statement that summarizes the main arguments and indicates which position you support. Make an outline for the essay using a pro-con structure to show how you would organize your points (see Chapter 11 for tips on how to do this).

HEALTH CANADA INADVERTENTLY DISCLOSES FACTS PLANNED PARENT-HOOD WOULD LIKE TO SUPPRESS

Ted Byfield

Canadians, says a recent study, are working too hard—too hard for   1
their health, too hard for their sanity, and above all too hard to
have children. The study, released last month at a meeting sponsored by
Calgary United Way, is the largest of its kind in Canada, involving some
31,000 workers. It found that in the struggle to balance the demands of
work and family, work continually wins. Consequently, women put off
having children and many young people opt to have none.

   The research, conducted by Professors Linda Duxbury of Carleton   2
University and Chris Higgins of the University of Western Ontario,
showed that 40% of women in professional jobs have not started a family because of work; 30% of men said they wanted no children, for the
same reason. This has profound implications, of course. If many of the
best potential parents of any society won't produce offspring, or perhaps only one child late in life, the intelligence level of the next generation will surely decline. Some achievement.

   What is most unusual about this study, however, is not so much   3
what it found as who paid for it, namely Health Canada. For by making note of our failure to have children, the
federal government has inadvertently called
attention to one of the better kept secrets of
current demographic sociology, which is this:
The much ballyhooed "population explo-
sion," which for years we were assured would
soon crowd the world with wall-to-wall people, was dead wrong. By the 1980s, predicted
Paul Ehrlich[1] back in the 1960s (he being

Ted Byfield is a Western Canadian journalist
whose articles can be seen in *The Edmonton
Sun* and other Canadian newspapers. Byfield
was one of the founders of *The Alberta
Report* magazine, now called *The Report*. He
is also connected with the creation of the
Reform Party of Canada.

one of the century's most prominent prophets of doom), 65 million Americans would die of starvation. Well, they didn't.

What actually threatens us instead is serious population decline, a 4
"birth dearth" that will wreak great havoc on the economies of much of the western world. So, at any rate, we are now told by the American Enterprise Institute[2] in Washington, which makes a point of talking about a situation most other foundations and government agencies seem reluctant to discuss.

The reason for this reticence is explained by journalist Tom 5
Bethell in a recent issue of *The American Spectator*[3] magazine. "Government officials no doubt realize," writes Mr. Bethell, "that saying there are too few people, so soon after the hue and cry about there being too many, would destroy their own credibility." Other governments are in a similar case, since pretty well everybody bought into the Ehrlich "population bomb" expectations. Indeed, even now "hardly a year goes by when Ehrlich does not receive another award or prize" for his alarming predictions. Small wonder few care to acknowledge the alarms were false.

The American Enterprise Institute does, however, and its num- 6
bers—all taken from official census and other demographic records— leave the factual case beyond doubt. To maintain zero population growth in developed countries, each woman must have an average of 2.1 children. This will replace the male and female involved, and allow for the fact that some female children will die before reaching child-bearing age. The European average 15 years ago had fallen to 1.7, and is now running at 1.4. In Italy, where about one million babies were born in 1964, only about 500,000 were born last year. This amounts to a birth rate of 1.2, an impending economic disaster.

The effects of such a decline do not appear immediately; a genera- 7
tion must grow up for them to be fully felt. But even if European fertility rates were to return to 2.1 tomorrow—a virtual impossibility—Europe's current population of 727 million would still drop by 171 million by 2050. Since government welfare programs depend upon a steady inflow of tax money, few countries will have enough people by then to support such programs.

Even more surprising, the drop is not confined to developed coun- 8
tries. India's birth rate has fallen from about 5.6 in 1960 to 3.5 and is still dropping. Egypt, whose rate in 1960 at something over 7.0 was the world's highest, is down to 3.9. Mexico has dropped from 6.8 down to 3, Thailand from 6.5 to 2, less than replacement level. Thailand's is even lower than the American and Canadian levels—whose populations are being sustained by massive immigration, most of it from the Third World.

All this, needless to say, is bad news for an organization like   9
Planned Parenthood, zealous preacher of the Save-the-World-with-
Smaller-Families message (by abortion if necessary). Will PP now turn
around and urge us to save it with bigger ones? Not very likely, when
most of its funding is predicated on the need to reduce population. At
the same time, the United Nations has been so successful in its don't-
have-kids propaganda that it is rapidly making the absence of kids the
world's No. 1 economic problem.

Meanwhile in Europe, where one government after another experi-   10
ments with costly child-bearing incentives, the universal experience is
that bribes don't work. Women must *want* to have children. So why
don't they? And why do men readily concur? Because, the Canadian
study finds, they both make their work more important. And this, we
may discover, is a very difficult mindset to change.

NOTES

[1] Paul Ehrlich is Bing Professor of Population Studies at Stanford University and author of
The Population Bomb (1968) and many other books.

[2] The American Enterprise Institute, located in Washington, D.C., is a policy research institute
which announces itself as devoted to "strengthening the foundations of freedom." Its strongest
supporter was former President Ronald Reagan.

[3] *The American Spectator* is a monthly magazine devoted to exposing the fallacies of Democratic
and left-wing policies.

VOCABULARY

demographic sociology—the branch of social science concerned with vital and
social statistics, such as births, deaths, marriages, disease rates

QUESTIONS

1. Why is it "unusual" that Health Canada would pay for the study Byfield describes?
   What assumptions about the federal government, and about governments in general, does Byfield make in this essay?

2. If it is true that Canadians prioritize work over starting a family, what do you think
   are the reasons? Do you think Byfield answers this question in the essay? If so,
   what is his answer? If not, why does he leave the question unanswered?

3. According to Byfield, American and Canadian populations "are being sustained by
   massive immigration, most of it from the Third World." Does the essay present
   such immigration as a good way of maintaining replacement levels of population?

4. What kind of audience—hostile, neutral, friendly or mixed—does Byfield seem to be
   writing for in this essay? What in the essay helps you identify its intended audience?

SUGGESTION FOR WRITING

There are likely many statements in Byfield's essay with which you strongly agree or disagree. Take any one statement and write a paragraph explaining why you agree or disagree for either practical or ethical reasons. Then rewrite the paragraph as a letter to Byfield. How does the change in audience affect the way you express your opinion? (For a discussion of standards of evaluation and their relation to audience, see Chapter 11.)

THE TICKING BOMB

Wade Davis

On Sept. 11, in the most successful act of asymmetrical warfare 1
since the Trojan horse,[1] the world came home to America. "Why
do they hate us?" asked George W. Bush. This was not a rhetorical
question. Americans really wanted to know—and still do, for their innocence had been shattered. The President suggested that the reason
was the very greatness of America, as if the liberal institutions of government had somehow provoked homicidal rage in fanatics incapable
of embracing freedom. Other, dissenting voices claimed that, to the
contrary, the problem lay in the tendency of the United States to support, notably in the Middle East, repressive regimes whose values are
antithetical to the ideals of American democracy. Both sides were
partly right, but both overlooked the deeper issue, in part because they
persisted in examining the world through American eyes.

The United States has always looked inward. A nation born in iso- 2
lation cannot be expected to be troubled by the election of a President
who has rarely been abroad, or a Congress in which 25 per cent of
members do not hold passports. Wealth too can be blinding. Each year,
Americans spend as much on lawn maintenance as the government of
India collects in federal tax revenue. The 30 million African-Americans
collectively control more wealth than the 30 million Canadians.

A country that effortlessly supports a defence budget larger than 3
the entire economy of Australia does not easily grasp the reality of a
world in which 1.3 billion people get by on less
than $1 a day. A new and original culture that
celebrates the individual at the expense of family and community—a stunning innovation in
human affairs, the sociological equivalent of
the splitting of the atom—has difficulty understanding that in most of the world the community still prevails, for the destiny of the
individual remains inextricably linked to the
fate of the collective.

Since 1945, even as the United States 4
came to dominate the geopolitical scene, the
American people resisted engagement with the
world, maintaining an almost willful ignorance
of what lay beyond their borders. Such cultural

Vancouver-born Wade Davis, who has
worked as a park ranger, forestry engineer, logger, and big game hunting guide as
well as earning degrees in biology, anthropology, and ethnobotany, is currently
Explorer-in-Residence with the National
Geographic Society. His books include *The
Serpent and the Rainbow* (1986), later made
into a motion picture; *Penan: Voice for the
Borneo Rain Forest* (1990), the subject of a
forthcoming feature film; *Shadows in the
Sun* (1992); *Nomads of the Dawn* (1995);
and *Light at the Edge of the World* (2000).

"The Ticking Bomb" was published in *The
Globe and Mail*, July 6, 2002. Copyright ©
Wade Davis.

myopia, never flattering, was rendered obsolete in an instant on the morning of Sept. 11. In the immediate wake of the tragedy, I was often asked as an anthropologist for explanations.

Condemning the attacks in the strongest possible terms, I never- 5 theless encouraged people to consider the forces that gave rise to Osama bin Laden's movement. While it would be reassuring to view al-Qaeda as an isolated phenomenon, I feared that the organization was a manifestation of a deeper and broader conflict, a clash between those who have and those who have nothing. Mr. bin Laden himself may be wealthy, but the resentment upon which al-Qaeda feeds springs most certainly from the condition of the dispossessed.

I also encouraged my American friends to turn the anthropological 6 lens upon our own culture, if only to catch a glimpse of how we might appear to people born in other lands. I shared a colleague's story from her time living among the Bedouin in Tunisia in the 1980s, just as television reached their remote villages. Entranced and shocked by episodes of the soap opera *Dallas,* the astonished farm women asked her, "Is everyone in your country as mean as J.R.?"

For much of the Middle East, in particular, the West is synony- 7 mous not only with questionable values and a flood of commercial products, but also with failure. Gamel Abdul Nasser's[2] notion of a Pan-Arabic state was based on a thoroughly Western and secular model of socialist development, an economic and political dream that collapsed in corruption and despotism. The shah of Iran[3] provoked the Iranian revolution by thrusting not the Koran but modernity (as he saw it) down the throats of his people.

The Western model of development has failed in the Middle East 8 and elsewhere in good measure because it has been based on the false promise that people who follow its prescriptive dictates will in time achieve the material prosperity enjoyed by a handful of nations of the West. Even were this possible, it is not at all clear that it would be desirable. To raise consumption of energy and materials throughout the world to Western levels, given current population projections, would require the resources of four planet Earths by the year 2100. To do so with the one world we have would imply so severely compromising the biosphere that the Earth would be unrecognizable.

In reality, development for the vast majority of the peoples of the 9 world has been a process in which the individual is torn from his past and propelled into an uncertain future only to secure a place on the bottom rung of an economic ladder that goes nowhere.

Consider the key indices of development. An increase in life ex- 10 pectancy suggests a drop in infant mortality, but reveals nothing of the quality of the lives led by those who survive childhood. Globalization is celebrated with iconic intensity. But what does it really mean? The *Washington Post* reports that in Lahore,[4] one Muhammad Saeed earns

$88 (U.S.) a month stitching shirts and jeans for a factory that supplies Gap and Eddie Bauer. He and five family members share a single bed in one room off a warren of alleys strewn with human waste and refuse. Yet, earning three times as much as at his last job, he is the poster child of globalization.

Even as fundamental a skill as literacy does not necessarily realize 11
its promise. In northern Kenya, for example, tribal youths placed by their families into parochial schools do acquire a modicum of literacy, but in the process also learn to have contempt for their ancestral way of life. They enter school as nomads; they leave as clerks, only to join an economy with a 50-per-cent unemployment rate for high-school graduates. Unable to find work, incapable of going home, they drift to the slums of Nairobi to scratch a living from the edges of a cash economy.

Without doubt, images of comfort and wealth, of technological so- 12
phistication, have a magnetic allure. Any job in the city may seem better than backbreaking labour in sun-scorched fields. Entranced by the promise of the new, people throughout the world have in many instances voluntarily turned their backs on the old.

The consequences can be profoundly disappointing. The fate of the 13
vast majority of those who sever their ties with their traditions will not be to attain the prosperity of the West, but to join the legions of urban poor, trapped in squalor, struggling to survive. As cultures wither away, individuals remain, often shadows of their former selves, caught in time, unable to return to the past, yet denied any real possibility of securing a place in the world whose values they seek to emulate and whose wealth they long to acquire.

Anthropology suggests that when people and cultures are squeezed, 14
extreme ideologies sometimes emerge, inspired by strange and unexpected beliefs. These revitalization movements may be benign, but more typically prove deadly both to their adherents and to those they engage. China's Boxer Rebellion of 1900 sought not only to end the opium trade and expel foreign legations. The Boxers arose in response to the humiliation of an ancient nation, long the centre of the known world, reduced within a generation to servitude by unknown barbarians. It was not enough to murder the missionaries. In a raw, atavistic gesture, the Boxers dismembered them and displayed their heads on pikes.

However unique its foundation, al-Qaeda is nevertheless reminis- 15
cent of such revitalization movements. Torn between worlds, Mr. bin Laden and his followers invoke a feudal past that never was in order to rationalize their own humiliation and hatred. They are a cancer within the culture of Islam, neither fully of the faith nor totally apart from it. Like any malignant growth they must be severed from the body and destroyed. We must also strive to understand the movement's roots, for the chaotic conditions of disintegration and disenfranchisement that led to al-Qaeda are found among disaffected populations throughout the world.

In Nepal, rural farmers spout rhetoric not heard since the death of   16
Stalin. In Peru, the Shining Path turned to Mao. Had they invoked instead Tupac Amaru, the 18ᵗʰ-century indigenous rebel, scion of the
Inca, and had they been able to curb their reflexive disdain for the
very indigenous people they claimed to represent, they might well have
set the nation aflame, as was their intent. Lima, a city of 400,000 in
1940 is today home to 9 million, and for the majority it is a sea of misery in a sun-scorched desert.

We live in an age of disintegration. At the beginning of the 20ᵗʰ   17
century there were 60 nation states. Today there are 190, many poor
and unstable. The real story lies in the cities. Throughout the world,
urbanization, with all its fickle and forlorn promises, has drawn people
by the millions into squalor. The populations of Mexico City and Sao
Paulo are unknown, probably immeasurable. In Asia there are cities of
10 million people that most of us in the West cannot name.

The nation state, as Harvard sociologist Daniel Bell wrote, has be-   18
come too small for the big problems of the world and too big for the little problems of the world. Outside the major industrial nations,
globalization has not brought integration and harmony, but rather a
firestorm of change that has swept away languages and cultures, ancient skills and visionary wisdom. Of the 6,000 languages spoken
today, fully half are not being taught to children. Within a single generation, we are witnessing the loss of half humanity's social, spiritual and
intellectual legacy. This is the essential backdrop of our era.

In the immediate aftermath of 9/11, I was asked at a lecture in Los   19
Angeles to name the seminal event of the 20ᵗʰ century. Without hesita-
tion I suggested the assassination of Archduke Ferdinand in 1914. Two
bullets sparked a war that destroyed all faith in progress and optimism,
the hallmarks of the Victorian age, and left in its wake the nihilism and
alienation of a century that birthed Hitler, Mao, Stalin and another
devastating global conflict that did not fully end until the collapse of
the Soviet empire in 1989.

The question then turned to 9/11, and it struck me that 100 years   20
from now that fateful date may well loom as the defining moment of
this century, the day when two worlds, long kept apart by geography
and circumstance, came together in a violent conflict. If there is one
lesson to be learned from 9/11, it is that power does not translate into
security. With an investment of $500,000, far less than the price of one
of the baggage scanners now deployed in airports across the United
States, a small band of fanatics killed some 2,800 innocent people. The
economic cost may well be incalculable. Generally, nations declare
wars on nations; Mr. Bush has declared war on a technique and there
is no exit strategy.

Global media have woven the world into a single sphere. Evidence   21
of the disproportionate affluence of the West is beamed into villages
and urban slums in every nation, in every province, 24 hours a day.
Baywatch is the most popular television show in New Guinea.
Tribesmen from the mountainous heartland of an island that embraces
2,000 distinct languages walk for days to catch the latest episode.

The voices of the poor, who deal each moment with the conse-   22
quences of environmental degradation, political corruption, overpopulation, the gross distortion in the distribution of wealth and the
consumption of resources, who share few of the material benefits of
modernity, will no longer be silent.

True peace and security for the 21st century will only come about   23
when we find a way to address the underlying issues of disparity, dislocation and dispossession that have provoked the madness of our age.
What we desperately need is a global acknowledgment of the fact that
no people and no nation can truly prosper unless the bounty of our collective ingenuity and opportunities are available and accessible to all.

We must aspire to create a new international spirit of pluralism, a   24
true global democracy in which unique cultures, large and small, are
allowed the right to exist, even as we learn and live together, enriched
by the deepest reaches of our imaginings. We need a global declaration
of interdependence. In the wake of Sept. 11, this is not idle or naïve
rhetoric, but rather a matter of survival.

NOTES

[1] The Trojan horse: Homer tells us that during the Trojan Wars, the Greeks persuaded the
Trojans to open the gates of their walled city by presenting them with the gift of a huge
wooden horse. Inside the horse were Greek soldiers who, once they were inside the city, led
an invasion that defeated Troy.

[2] Gamel Abdul Nasser (1918–1970): a political leader in Egypt who was president of the United
Arab Republic and an ardent supporter of Arab unity.

[3] Shah of Iran: leader of Iran with close ties to the United States, deposed by a Muslim
fundamentalist leadership in Iran.

[4] Lahore: city in northeastern Pakistan.

VOCABULARY

antithetical—completely opposed to

atavistic—going back to primitive roots

biosphere—the portions of the earth's land mass, waters, and atmosphere that
support living organisms

celebrated with iconic intensity—praised enthusiastically as sacred image

disenfranchisement—loss of civil rights, such as the right to vote

geopolitical—combined geographical and political factors influencing a country or region

indices of development—the ways in which development is measured

inextricably—inseparably

prescriptive dictates—rules set out with confidence and authority

secular—non-religious

QUESTIONS

1. What is "cultural myopia"? According to Wade Davis, how and why do Americans demonstrate this condition?

2. In your own words, define the term "secular modernity." According to Davis, why do some countries embrace secular modernity while other countries reject it?

3. Davis' thesis, stated in the last two paragraphs, is that we need a "new international spirit of pluralism." How would such a spirit differ from "globalization"?

4. What evidence does Davis present to support his thesis? Is this evidence convincing?

5. Which of Davis' arguments are based on practical standards of evaluation? Which are based on an ethical standard? (For a discussion of standards of evaluation, see Chapter 11.)

6. This essay was originally published in *The Globe and Mail.* Do you think Davis assumed he was writing for a friendly, hostile, or neutral audience? How can you tell? (For more information on audiences, see Chapter 11.)

SUGGESTION FOR WRITING

Write a letter to Wade Davis explaining why you agree or disagree (completely or partly) with his analysis of the causes of terrorism. Take a close look at the logic of his argument and the evidence he uses to support it. If you can, provide evidence to support your own position.

WHERE THEY HAVE TO TAKE YOU IN

Caterina Edwards

Everyone has been there, and everyone has brought back a collection of photographs.

—HENRY JAMES ON VENICE[1]

For years I had a recurring dream. I was about to arrive in Venice. 1
I could see the city shimmering before me. I was almost there. But at the moment of arrival, it vanished and I found myself instead on an empty, windswept street. I could never arrive, never return. Sometimes I had made a mistake: taken the wrong direction or miscalculated the distance. But usually there was no reason. At the moment of arrival, the city vanished. And I was suspended in a cycle of longing and loss.

To arrive was to be safe, to reach refuge, to be home. 2

As James said, everyone has been to Venice. The number of tourists 3
who visit annually is in the millions. On a summer day, they are a horde, a swarm, that invades the city, clogging the narrow streets, overloading the *vaporetti*,[2] funneling into St. Mark's Square as if it were a football stadium. Push, push, must be room for one more, though they stand practically shoulder to shoulder. They have come to see the palaces of marble, the streets of water. And too often, they find Venice reduced to a painted backdrop, assembled for their viewing. "Amazing," they say to one another. "But I wouldn't want to live here."

The city becomes a packed raft about to capsize, to sink under the 4
weight of bodies and the volume of human wastes. In the evening, the tourists retreat to the mainland, abandoning their debris: plastic bottles and bags, sandwich wrappers, papers, scattered over the ancient stones. At night the cleaners sweep up the mountains of garbage and carry it off in barges. Morning, and again, tour buses pour over the causeway, disgorging French school children, American seniors, German honeymooners, the entire first world, it seems. Most eastern Europeans arrive dazed; they have traveled a day or more on their buses to arrive in this fabled city, this wonder of the world, once beyond their reach. It seems they cannot afford even the coffee and shade of a cafe. But the sights are free, and they are free to gaze upon them and litter.

Caterina Edwards has published in a variety of genres. Her latest book is a collection of short stories, *The Island of the Nightingales*. She is currently working on a book of creative nonfiction. She lives in Edmonton with her husband and two daughters.

"Where They Have to Take You In" was published in *Wrestling with the Angel* (Calgary: Red Deer Press, 2000). Reprinted with permission of Caterina Edwards.

The last time I visited Venice, we (husband, two daughters and I) 5
avoided the tourists, renting an apartment in Castello, a working-class
neighborhood. The stone stairs to the attic apartment were cracked or
tilted alarmingly. The air was heavy with humidity and heat. We
sweated at each step. At night, since we didn't have a fan, we closed the
shutters, but not the windows. There was a *pizzeria* a few doors down,
the equivalent of a neighborhood pub. The patrons' laughter, the buzz
of their conversations, the sudden shouts of a fight, crockery smashing,
chairs splintering, kept us awake late into the night. At dawn the neighbors began hailing each other in the street, calling from window to window; the woman opposite screeched at her three-year-old son. In
Edmonton we were buffered by trees and lawns, protected by space.
Here, everything and everyone was closer, louder, brighter.

I was happy, comfortable, connected to the city by history and 6
family. Two elderly aunts, a multitude of first and second cousins lived
here: the conductor on the *vaporetto*, the girl behind the bar, the manager of a leather store, the seamstress, the fish farmer, the bank clerk,
sprinkled from one end of the lagoon to the other. I knew the city, not
as a tourist does, as a series of "sights"; I knew its daily rhythms, its
hidden life. In those labyrinthian streets, I was at home.

Yet—I am not Venetian. 7

Despite the many summers I have spent there, despite my affec- 8
tionate extended family, despite everything I know and feel about the
city, I am an outsider. Although my mother has spoken Venetian to me
since I was born, when I open my mouth to speak *Venexiane* I expose
myself as a foreigner. My words are correct, but my intonation lacks
melody. I can hear, but not reproduce, the local rhythm. Likewise, although I look stereotypically Venetian with my red hair, long face, and
heavy-lidded eyes, the way I dress and move (hesitantly, unobtrusively)
is Canadian.

At home and not at home. 9

Another year, we rented a *capanna*, a hut on the Lido beach. At 10
first, the Venetian families, who had rented their *capanne* for three
generations, ignored us, branding us tourists. But after a visit from a
cousin, our position changed. "So you're related to Michele," one
mother said, taking us up. The Venetians offered food, advice, and con-
viviality. They also observed and criticized. We were expected to dress
with a certain taste; to perform ritual courtesies, including shaking
hands on arrival and departure each day; to eat three course lunches
on proper dishes, not sandwiches cupped in napkins; to rest quietly for
two hours after lunch: in general, to follow all the unwritten rules.
"*Signora*," a voice would intrude. "Haven't your daughters been in the
sea far too long?" Or, "Shouldn't the girls change out of those wet
bathing suits?"

At home and not at home.   11

The Venetian lagoon was first settled in the fifth century by Roman   12
citizens of nearby towns seeking refuge from Attila[3] and his Huns.
With each new barbarian invasion, more refugees fled to this delta of
three rivers, this swamp of shifting sands. Searching for the safest,
most protected spot, the settlers moved from island to island. Heraclea,
Mazzorbo, and Torcello took their turns as the major center. In 810,
when Pepin[4] and his army invaded the lagoon, the inhabitants re-
treated to Rivalto, or Rialto, the core of the present city. And for a
thousand years, until Napoleon,[5] Venice was unconquerable. A thousand years of a great Republic. The series of sights the tourists come to
see exist because the city was never assailed. Venice needed no thick
walls, no fortifications; she could flaunt her splendours.

Venice remains a contradiction: a city built on water, stone that   13
floats in air. Ambiguous, Venice has long inspired its visitors to fanta-
size, rhapsodize, create bloated metaphors. Centuries pass, yet both
the Romantic poet and the latest tourist off the *vaporetto* call Venice a
ship, a haven, a museum, a backdrop, the bride of the sea. Venice is
compared to a seraglio, a freak, a fairy tale, a mausoleum. Since
Venice's decline in the eighteenth century, the city has been a symbol
of decadence, death, and dissolution. *Dust and ashes, dead and done
with*, Napoleon said as he handed the city to the Austrians. *Venice
spent what Venice earned*.

It is the strangeness, the sheer otherness, of this slippery city that   14
classifies it as a place of reversals, of transgressions. I played with the notion in my first novel.[6] The wicked carnival city, where nothing and no
one is what it seems. But with age and experience I am more skeptical of
received ideas and literary conceits. Visiting Venice is such a sensual de-
light that I wonder if her reputation for wickedness sprang from an Anglo
or Nordic puritanism. A place so dedicated to pleasure must be evil.

If Venice is sinking, her doom is recent and comes from ignoring   15
ecological rather than moral truths. Her survival is threatened by a loss
of the delicate balance between sea and city, by pollution and tourists,
and by her transformation into not the city of the dead, but the city of
the near dead, the old. The younger generation is exiled to *terra ferma*
or solid land. "Very few of my old classmates live in the city anymore,"
says Tony, a younger cousin who has managed to stay by buying a tiny
wreck of a place and, doing all the work himself, rebuilding from the
foundation up. "None of the boys I played basketball with at the parish
hall. All gone." They cannot afford the price of apartments in the city,
driven up by the international rich, who can pay an exorbitant sum for
a second home. Venice has been reduced to a holiday resort, the majority of houses (especially in the better neighborhoods) uninhabited
for most of the year.

I bemoan the trend, loudly and sincerely. But if I had the chance—   16
I would buy an apartment in a minute. On the last visit, we contacted a
real estate agent and toured various renovated flats. All four of us
found ourselves fantasizing yearly visits, then a home. Having breakfast on that terrace, setting a computer up in front of that window.
Isn't that all it takes? Cash? You buy a home, and it is yours.

You wish. Home is not simply the place where you live. Home is a   17
feeling, a haven, a cage, a heaven, a trap, a direction, an end, and the
generator of more metaphors than Venice. If I claim that I am both not
at home and at home in Venice, it is longing that keeps the contradictory states from canceling each other out.

On Via Garibaldi, where we went to buy sweet peaches and mel-   18
ons, arugula and tomatoes from an open stall, and yogurt, mineral
water, and toilet paper from what was called the supermarket but was
not much more than a hole in the wall, goods piled to the ceiling, aisles
where you had to turn sideways to pass; on Via Garibaldi, the widest
and some said the ugliest street in Venice, though the buildings were
deep red, sand, and buff and geraniums bloomed at the window; on Via
Garibaldi, where we sat out in the early evening and sipped aperitifs
and watched the parade of young and old; on Via Garibaldi, where
each time I passed the last house, the one that faced out to the lagoon,
I paused and read the plaque: *In this house lived Giovanni Caboto,*[7]
explorer and discoverer of Newfoundland; on Via Garibaldi, almost
superstitiously, I paused and felt the glimmer of that other place,
where I live and which I should call home.

Edmonton in Venice and Venice in Edmonton: in each place, I feel   19
the presence of the other. Nostalgia is always double, double presence
and double absence.

Who belongs? And where?   20

When I was growing up in Alberta, going to twelve schools in seven   21
years, when I was at university, I felt out of place. I thought I would
never belong. Like the dream, I would never arrive. With the years, my
attitude has changed, partly because most of the people in my life do
not have a specific place they call home. They are hybrids—different
in complicated and interesting ways.

My husband grew up in California and though he feels an affection   22
for dry, fierce heat and the fecundity of that inner valley land, he insists he never felt American. Or rather, he never felt *only* American. It
is entirely appropriate, he thinks, that he has three nationalities
(Italian, American, and Canadian). My adopted sister was born in
Yugoslavia, spent her childhood in a refugee camp in Genova, her adolescence in Calgary, her working girl years in New York City, and the
last twenty-five years in Puerto Rico, married to an ex-Cuban, who also
spent his early years journeying from country to country. These are
the lives we lead now—in transit, in flux.

Since the beginning, for century after century, Venice was a haven for 23
refugees: Byzantine Greeks, Sephardic Jews, Armenians, Slavs. They were
not given citizenship; they had their own neighborhoods and churches or
synagogues, but the cultures they brought influenced and altered Venice.

The aesthetic principles seem more eastern than western—gold 24
mosaics and onion domes.

To arrive was to be safe. 25

In the last few years, new migrants have come looking for refuge. In 26
the Mercerie, between Piazza San Marco and the Rialto, the Somalis
and Senegalese alight on vacant squares of pavement and spread out
their wares: fake designer bags and sunglasses. The news-paper complains of the Albanians squatting in an empty palace while I notice
more beggars planted at the feet of bridges. A gypsy woman stretches
her hand out to me. "Need," I think she says. "The war." Others have
their cardboard signs: BOSNIAN REFUGEE written in pencil. They look
wretched, hungry, desperate. Yet there is a system of refugee aid with
offices in the neighborhood police stations, jobs and housing provided
by the city council. *Extra communitari*, the Italians call them, those
from outside the community, and despite Venice's traditional role, now
the citizens debate their responsibility to these outsiders. Many of the
Venetians complain: what about us, what about that homeless family
camping in the middle of Campo Santa Margherita, what about our
sons and daughters who are forced to move away.

Venice for the Venetians. 27

(France for the French. Germany for the Germans. And so it goes.) 28

My grandfather, Renato Pagan, was born in a house on the Calle 29
delle Rasse, a narrow street that runs behind St. Mark's Basilica.
According to family lore, the Pagans, like the rest of the Venetian
upper class, had lost their fortune years before to the gaming tables.

Renato went to sea to win a new fortune or, at least, a more com- 30
fortable living. He found land and a wife in Dalmatia,[8] for centuries a
part of the Venetian empire. And he prospered, with a pretty house
and eight healthy children, he prospered until the First World War.
Although Dalmatia was a part of the Austro-Hungarian empire, he
could not imagine himself fighting on the side of the Austrians. He was
a Venetian and an Italian. Like many men in the towns of Dalmatia, he
joined the Italian navy, sailing under the command of Nazario Sauro.

The family and the historical stories divide when explaining how 31
he died. My mother claimed that he drowned in a submarine; one
cousin insisted he died of hunger, of want. "That's our history," he
says. The history book states that Sauro did command a submarine
that ran aground. The patriots were captured by the Austrians and
tried for treason. Your ethnic background makes no difference, they
were told. You live under our empire. *You owe your allegiance to us.*
They were executed.

My grandmother, Caterina Letich (a Croatian), and her children   32
were forced out of their house. Soldiers confiscated their belongings,
transported them to Fiume, and loaded them onto cattle cars. (With
other wives and other children of Sauro's troops.) *Go back to where
you came from.* Although she and all the children were born in
VeliLosinj.[9] Still, they were not sorry to be going to Italy. They thought
that in Venice, with Grandfather's family, they would be safe. Instead,
when the train reached the Italian border, the Italians declared them
foreigners. The doors of the cattle cars were closed, and they were
shunted from place to place. In the dark, without food and with little
water. They were all ill; one aunt, Antonietta, nine years old, died. They
were locked in with their body wastes and her corpse. And when finally
the doors were opened, when they were let out, my grandmother and
her children found themselves in a camp in Sicily, a camp for *enemy
aliens*. I know little of their experience there. My Aunt Maricci, who
was the oldest, told me that they were given nothing to eat. Since my
grandmother spoke Italian with an accent, it was she, Maricci, who had
to beg the guards to be allowed to take potato peels from the garbage.

Who belongs? (And where?)   33

At the end of the war, they were allowed to settle in Venice.   34
Twenty-five years later, my grandmother was dead; the seven siblings
had dispersed to jobs in the greater Veneto area. One aunt married a
fisherman and lived in Chioggia, a fishing village on the southwest end
of the lagoon. By 1944 the Veneto had become one of the focal points
of the war. A German soldier warned my aunt, *Take your children to
Venice. They'll be safe there.* And she did, leaving just before part of
her street was destroyed.

My mother, working for a bakery in Padova, was in a bomb shelter   35
when it was hit. Since she was claustrophobic, she found the crowded
shelter almost unbearable. She stayed by the entrance, and her position saved her. In the center, everyone was killed. Body parts, she told
me, shattered flesh. Nothing else, she said. My mother moved back to
Venice. She knew neither side would ever bomb that city. It meant too
much to both sides, beloved as it was of Goethe and Wagner, of Byron
and Ruskin.[10] Venice was not touched.

A safe haven.   36

My father was a royal engineer in the British army. My parents met   37
in Venice when my father's company requisitioned the house where
my mother and two aunts were living. (Which is why I am
Welsh/English/Italian and Croatian.)

Who belongs? And where?   38

My sister, the Yugoslavian/Italian/Canadian/Puerto Rican, visited   39
Venice as a child. Thirty years later, arriving again at St. Mark's
Square, she burst into tears. "I felt like I had come home," she said,

"though it didn't make sense." She reminds me that my longing for the city is commonplace rather than unique. The city is both strange and familiar to all its visitors, for its image is everywhere. As James said, "It is the easiest city to visit without going there." The world claims Venice as its own, and as its home, calling it, in the words of a UNESCO document, "a vital common asset." An international movement argues that the city is too precious for the Italians to continue to mismanage. Venice can be saved, the group argues, only if it does not remain a part of Italy but is made a world city. *It belongs to the world.*   40

This spring a group calling itself Armata Veneta Serenissima and calling for the separation of the Veneto from Italy unloaded a tank on St. Mark's Square and seized the campanile. In a survey conducted by the city's newspaper, a majority of Venetians named these separatists not terrorists but patriots. *Venice for the Venetians.*   41

Extra communitaria: one who is outside the community, yet comfortable, at home. When I wrote my first novel, I thought I would be able to exorcize my dream of Venice. But the dream repeats itself. I find myself writing this essay.   42

Venice again.   43

In explaining the origin of the name Venezia, Ruskin quotes Sansorvino, who claimed that Venezia came from the Latin VENIETIAM, come again, for no matter how often you come, you will always see new things, new beauties.   44

Return.

NOTES

[1] Henry James (1845–1916): American novelist and essayist whose works often show naïve American characters confronting worldly Europeans.

[2] *Vaporetti:* water buses

[3] Attila: king of the Huns who invaded Italy in 452; refugees from the sacked northeastern city of Aquileia founded Venice.

[4] Pepin: son of Charlemagne who laid siege to Venice for six months in 810; the successful resistance helped to form the identity of the city.

[5] Napoleon: French Emperor who invaded Venice in 1796–1797, destroying many palaces, churches, and cultural icons.

[6] "My first novel": *The Lion's Mouth,* set in Venice and Canada.

[7] Giovanni Caboto: born in Genoa; spent his youth working in the family spice shop in Venice; became a navigator; sent by Henry VII of England in search of China and the Spice Islands; landed in Newfoundland June 24, 1497; known in English as John Cabot.

[8] Dalmatia: region of present-day Croatia.

[9] Veli Losinj: town on the island of Losinj, Croatia.

[10] Johann Wolfgang von Goethe (1749–1832) was a German poet who compared Venice's emergence from the sea to the goddess Athena's emergence from the forehead of her father

Zeus. Richard Wagner (1813–1883) was a German composer who wrote many of his works in Venice and died there. George Gordon, Lord Byron (1788–1824) was an English Romantic poet who lived and wrote in Venice for several years. John Ruskin (1819–1900) was an English art critic and social commentator whose *Stones of Venice* (3 vols., 1851–1853) is a monument to his love of the city.

QUESTIONS

1. This essay's title, "Where They Have to Take You In," is an allusion to Robert Frost's poem "The Death of the Hired Man." The essay was first published in *Threshold* under the title "Where the Heart Is." The two titles suggest rather different meanings of "home." Which title do you think fits the essay better? Why?

2. In what ways is Edwards "at home and not at home" in Venice?

3. How do the popular images of Venice differ, in Edwards's view, from the reality?

4. Why does Edwards include information on the history of Venice? What light does this historical background shed on the slogan "Venice for Venetians"?

5. What is Edwards's thesis? Is it stated directly? If so, where? If not, how did you arrive at your understanding of the main idea of the essay?

6. The structure of this essay does not fit neatly into any of the methods of development described in Chapter 3. Make an outline showing the movement from section to section. How would you describe this structure? Is it effective?

SUGGESTIONS FOR WRITING

1. Both Edwards and Ken Wiwa ("Choosing Up Sides," Readings) address questions of cultural and national identity. Gather material for an essay comparing the two pieces of writing, and formulate a thesis statement that focuses on the most important similarity and/or difference in their points of view.

2. Edwards mentions a wide range of metaphors that have been used to describe Venice. Choose a metaphor for a place you know well and write a one-page essay exploring this analogy. For an example, see the analogy of university as funhouse in the sample paragraph in Solving Pronoun Problems, Exercise 2 (p. 436).

3. Write a two-page essay on what the word "home" means to you. Use specific details, as Edwards does, and include both positive and negative aspects.

A ROSE FOR
"A ROSE FOR EMILY"

Judith Fetterley

In "A Rose for Emily"[1] the grotesque reality implicit in Aylmer's idealization of Georgiana[2] becomes explicit. Justifying Faulkner's use of the grotesque[3] has been a major concern of critics who have written on the story. If, however, one approaches "A Rose for Emily" from a feminist perspective, one notices that the grotesque aspects of the story are a result of its violation of the expectations generated by the conventions of sexual politics. The ending shocks us not simply by its hint of necrophilia; more shocking is the fact that it is a woman who provides the hint. It is one thing for Poe to spend his nights in the tomb of Annabel Lee[4] and another thing for Miss Emily Grierson to deposit a strand of iron-gray hair on the pillow beside the rotted corpse of Homer Barron. Further, we do not expect to discover that a woman has murdered a man. The conventions of sexual politics have familiarized us with the image of Georgiana nobly accepting death at her husband's hand. To reverse this "natural" pattern inevitably produces the grotesque.

Faulkner, however, is not interested in invoking the kind of grotesque which is the consequence of reversing the clichés of sexism for the sake of a cheap thrill; that is left to writers like Mickey Spillane.[5] (Indeed, Spillane's ready willingness to capitalize on the shock value provided by the image of woman as killer in *I, the Jury* suggests, by contrast, how little such a sexist gambit is Faulkner's intent.) Rather, Faulkner invokes the grotesque in order to illuminate and define the true nature of the conventions on which it depends. "A Rose for Emily" is a story not of a conflict between the South and the North or between the old order and the new; it is a story of the patriarchy North and South, new and old, and of the sexual conflict within it. As Faulkner himself has implied, it is a story of a woman victimized and betrayed by the system of sexual politics, who nevertheless has discovered,

Judith Fetterley is a professor of English at the State University of New York, Albany. She has published *Provisions: A Reader from 19th-Century American Women* (1985); *Alice Cary 1820–1871: Clovernook Sketches and Other Stories* (1987); and, with Marjorie Pryse, *Writing out of Place: Regionalism, Women, and American Literary Culture* (2002). The following essay is from *The Resisting Reader* (1978). In the previous chapter Fetterley has discussed Hawthorne's "The Birthmark." She now moves on to Faulkner's "A Rose for Emily." If you have read neither story, see the first two endnotes.

The Resisting Reader: A Feminist Approach to American Fiction, by Judith Fetterley, published by Indiana University Press.

within the structures that victimize her, sources of power for herself. If "The Birthmark" is the story of how to murder your wife and get away with it, "A Rose for Emily" is the story of how to murder your gentleman caller and get away with it. Faulkner's story is an analysis of how men's attitudes toward women turn back upon themselves; it is a demonstration of the thesis that it is impossible to kill without creating the conditions for your own murder. "A Rose for Emily" is the story of a *lady* and her revenge for that grotesque identity.

"When Miss Emily Grierson died, our whole town went to her funeral." The public and communal nature of Emily's funeral, a festival that brings the town together, clarifying its social relationships and revitalizing its sense of the past, indicates her central role in Jefferson. Alive, Emily is town property and the subject of shared speculation; dead, she is town history and the subject of legend. It is her value as a symbol, however obscure and however ambivalent, for something that is of central significance to the identity of Jefferson and to the meaning of its history, that compels the narrator to assume a communal voice to tell her story. For Emily, like Georgiana, is a man-made object, a cultural artifact, and what she is reflects and defines the culture that has produced her.

The history the narrator relates to us reveals Jefferson's continuous emotional involvement with Emily. Indeed, though she shuts herself up in a house which she rarely leaves and which no one enters, her furious isolation is in direct proportion to the town's obsession with her. Like Georgiana, she is the object of incessant attention; her every act is immediately consumed by the town for gossip and seized on to justify their interference in her affairs. Her private life becomes a public document that the town folk feel free to interpret at will, and they are alternately curious, jealous, spiteful, pitying, partisan, proud, disapproving, admiring, and vindicated. Her funeral is not simply a communal ceremony; it is also the climax of their invasion of her private life and the logical extension of their voyeuristic attitude toward her. Despite the narrator's demurral, getting inside Emily's house is the all-consuming desire of the town's population, both male and female; while the men may wait a little longer, their motive is still prurient curiosity: "Already we knew that there was one room in that region above stairs which no one had seen in forty years, and which would have to be forced. They waited until Miss Emily was decently in the ground before they opened it."

In a context in which the overtones of violation and invasion are so palpable, the word "decently" has that ironic ring which gives the game away. When the men finally do break down the door, they find that Emily has satisfied their prurience with a vengeance and in doing so has created for them a mirror image of themselves. The true nature of Emily's relation to Jefferson is contained in the analogies between what those who break open that room see in it and what has brought them there to see it. The perverse, violent, and grotesque aspects of the sight of Homer Barron's rotted corpse in a room decked out for a bridal and now faded and covered in dust reflect back to them the perverseness of their own prurient interest in Emily, the violence implicit in their continued invasions of her life, and the grotesqueness of the symbolic artifact they have made of her—their monument, their idol, their lady. Thus, the figure that Jefferson places at the center of its legendary history does indeed contain the clue to the meaning of that history—a history which began long before Emily's funeral and long before Homer Barron's disappearance or appearance and long before Colonel Sartoris' fathering of edicts and remittances. It is recorded in that emblem which lies at the heart of the town's memory and at the heart of patriarchal culture: "We had long thought of them as a tableau, Miss Emily a slender figure in white in the background, her father a spraddled silhouette in the foreground, his back to her and clutching a horsewhip, the two of them framed by the back-flung front door."

The importance of Emily's father in shaping the quality of her life 6 is insistent throughout the story. Even in her death the force of his presence is felt; above her dead body sits "the crayon face of her father musing profoundly," symbolic of the degree to which he has dominated and shadowed her life, "as if that quality of her father which had thwarted her woman's life so many times had been too virulent and too furious to die." The violence of this consuming relationship is made explicit in the imagery of the tableau. Although the violence is apparently directed outward—the upraised horsewhip against the would-be suitor—the real object of it is the woman-daughter, forced into the background and dominated by the phallic figure of the spraddled father whose back is turned on her and who prevents her from getting out at the same time that he prevents them from getting in. Like Georgiana's spatial confinement in "The Birthmark," Emily's is a metaphor for her psychic confinement: her identity is determined by the constructs of her father's mind, and she can no more escape from his creation of her as "a slender figure in white" than she can escape his house.

What is true for Emily in relation to her father is equally true for 7 her in relation to Jefferson: her status as a lady is a cage from which she cannot escape. To them she is always *Miss* Emily; she is never referred to and never thought of as otherwise. In omitting her title from his, Faulkner emphasizes the point that the real violence done to Emily is in making her a "Miss"; the omission is one of his roses for her. Because she is *Miss* Emily *Grierson*, Emily's father dresses her in white, places her in the background, and drives away her suitors. Because she is *Miss* Emily *Grierson*, the town invests her with that communal significance which makes her the object of their obsession and the subject of their incessant scrutiny. And because she is a lady, the town is able to impose a particular code of behavior on her ("But there were still others, older people, who said that even grief could not cause a real lady to forget *noblesse oblige*") and to see in her failure to live up to that code an excuse for interfering in her life. As a lady, Emily is venerated, but veneration results in the more telling emotions of envy and spite: "it was another link between the gross, teeming world and the high and mighty Griersons"; "People ... believed that the Griersons held themselves a little too high for what they really were." The violence implicit in the desire to see the monument fall and reveal itself for clay suggests the violence inherent in the original impulse to venerate.

The violence behind veneration is emphasized through another 8 telling emblem in the story. Emily's position as an hereditary obligation upon the town dates from "that day in 1894 when Colonel Sartoris, the mayor—he who fathered the edict that no Negro woman should appear on the streets without an apron on—remitted her taxes, the dispensation dating from the death of her father on into perpetuity." The conjunction of these two actions in the same syntactic unit is crucial, for it insists on their essential similarity. It indicates that the impulse to exempt is analogous to the desire to restrict, and that what appears to be a kindness or an act of veneration is in fact an insult. Sartoris' remission of Emily's taxes is a public declaration of the fact that a lady is not considered to be, and hence not allowed or enabled to be, economically independent (consider, in this connection, Emily's lessons in china painting; they are a latter-day version of Sartoris' "charity" and a brilliant image of Emily's economic uselessness). His act is a public statement of the fact that a lady, if she is to survive, must have either husband or father, and that, because Emily has neither, the town must assume responsibility for her. The remission of taxes that defines Emily's status dates from the death of her father, and she is handed over from one patron to the next, the town instead of husband taking on the role of father. Indeed, the use of the word "fathered" in describing Sartoris' behavior as mayor underlines the fact that his chivalric attitude toward Emily is simply a subtler and more dishonest version of her father's horsewhip.

The narrator is the last of the patriarchs who take upon them- 9 selves the burden of defining Emily's life, and his violence toward her is the most subtle of all. His tone of incantatory reminiscence and nostalgic veneration seems free of the taint of horsewhip and edict. Yet a thoroughgoing contempt for the "ladies" who spy and pry and gossip out of their petty jealousy and curiosity is one of the clearest strands in the narrator's consciousness. Emily is exempted from the general indictment because she is a *real* lady—that is, eccentric, slightly crazy, obsolete, a "stubborn and coquettish decay," absurd but indulged; "dear, inescapable, impervious, tranquil, and perverse"; indeed, anything and everything but human.

Not only does "A Rose for Emily" expose the violence done to a woman by making her a lady; it also explores the particular form of power the victim gains from this position and can use on those who enact this violence. "A Rose for Emily" is concerned with the consequences of violence for both the violated and the violators. One of the most striking aspects of the story is the disparity between Miss Emily Grierson and the Emily to whom Faulkner gives his rose in ironic imitation of the chivalric behavior the story exposes. The form of Faulkner's title establishes a camaraderie between author and protagonist and signals that a distinction must be made between the story Faulkner is telling and the story the narrator is telling. This distinction is of major importance because it suggests, of course, that the narrator, looking through a patriarchal lens, does not see Emily at all but rather a figment of his own imagination created in conjunction with the cumulative imagination of the town. Like Ellison's invisible man,[6] nobody sees *Emily*. And because nobody sees *her*, she can literally get away with murder. Emily is characterized by her ability to understand and utilize the power that accrues to her from the fact that men do not see her but rather their concept of her: " 'I have no taxes in Jefferson. Colonel Sartoris explained it to me … Tobe! … show these gentlemen out.' " Relying on the conventional assumptions about ladies who are expected to be neither reasonable nor in touch with reality, Emily presents an impregnable front that vanquishes the men "horse and foot, just as she had vanquished their fathers thirty years before." In spite of their "modern" ideas, this new generation, when faced with Miss Emily, are as much bound by the code of gentlemanly behavior as their fathers were ("They rose when she entered"). This code gives Emily a power that renders the gentlemen unable to function in a situation in which a lady neither sits down herself nor asks them to. They are brought to a "stumbling halt" and can do nothing when confronted with her refusal to engage in rational discourse. Their only recourse in the face of such eccentricity is to engage in behavior unbecoming to gentlemen, and Emily can count on their continuing to see themselves as gentlemen and her as a lady and on their returning a verdict of helpless noninterference.

It is in relation to Emily's disposal of Homer Barron, however, that Faulkner demonstrates most clearly the power of conventional assumptions about the nature of ladies to blind the town to what is going on and to allow Emily to murder with impunity. When Emily buys the poison, it never occurs to anyone that she intends to use it on Homer,

10

11

so strong is the presumption that ladies when jilted commit suicide, not murder. And when her house begins to smell, the women blame it on the eccentricity of having a man servant rather than a woman, "as if a man—any man— could keep a kitchen properly." And then they hint that her eccentricity may have shaded over into madness, "remembering how old lady Wyatt, her great aunt, had gone completely crazy at last." The presumption of madness, that preeminently female response to bereavement, can be used to explain away much in the behavior of ladies whose activities seem a bit odd.

But even more pointed is what happens when the men try not to 12 explain but to do something about the smell: " 'Dammit, sir,' Judge Stevens said, 'will you accuse a lady to her face of smelling bad?' " But if a lady cannot be told that she smells, then the cause of the smell cannot be discovered and so her crime is "perfect." Clearly, the assumptions behind the Judge's outraged retort go beyond the myth that ladies are out of touch with reality. His outburst insists that it is the responsibility of gentlemen to make them so. Ladies must not be confronted with facts; they must be shielded from all that is unpleasant. Thus Colonel Sartoris remits Emily's taxes with a palpably absurd story, designed to protect her from an awareness of her poverty and her dependence on charity, and to protect him from having to confront her with it. And thus Judge Stevens will not confront Emily with the fact that her house stinks, though she is living in it and can hardly be unaware of the odor. Committed as they are to the myth that ladies and bad smells cannot coexist, these gentlemen insulate themselves from reality. And by defining a lady as a subhuman and hence sublegal entity, they have created a situation their laws can't touch. They have made it possible for Emily to be extra-legal: " 'Why, of course,' the druggist said, 'If that's what you want. But the law requires you to tell what you are going to use it for.' Miss Emily just stared at him, her head tilted back in order to look him eye for eye, until he looked away and went and got the arsenic and wrapped it up." And, finally, they have created a situation in which they become the criminals: "So the next night, after midnight, four men crossed Miss Emily's lawn and slunk about the house like burglars." Above them, "her upright torso motionless as that of an idol," sits Emily, observing them act out their charade of chivalry. As they leave, she confronts them with the reality they are trying to protect her from: she turns on the light so that they may see her watching them. One can only wonder at the fact, and regret, that she didn't call the sheriff and have them arrested for trespassing.

Not only is "A Rose for Emily" a supreme analysis of what men do 13 to women by making them ladies; it is also an exposure of how this act in turn defines and recoils upon men. This is the significance of the dynamic that Faulkner establishes between Emily and Jefferson. And it is equally the point of the dynamic implied between the tableau of Emily and her father and the tableau which greets the men who break down the door of that room in the region above the stairs. When the would-be "suitors" finally get into her father's house, they discover the consequences of his oppression of her, for the violence contained in the rotted corpse of Homer Barron is the mirror image of the violence represented in the tableau, the back-flung front door flung back with a vengeance. Having been consumed by her father, Emily in turn feeds off Homer Barron, becoming, after his death, suspiciously fat. Or, to put it another way, it is as if, after her father's death, she has reversed his act of incorporating her by incorporating and becoming him, metamorphosed from the slender figure in white to the obese figure in black whose hair is "a vigorous iron-gray, like the hair of an active man." She has taken into herself the violence in him which thwarted her and has reenacted it upon Homer Barron.

That final encounter, however, is not simply an image of the reciprocity of violence. Its power of definition also derives from its grotesqueness, which makes finally explicit the grotesqueness that has been latent in the description of Emily throughout the story: "Her skeleton was small and spare; perhaps that was why what would have been merely plumpness in another was obesity in her. She looked bloated, like a body long submerged in motionless water, and of that pallid hue. Her eyes, lost in the fatty ridges of her face, looked like two small pieces of coal pressed into a lump of dough." The impact of this description depends on the contrast it establishes between Emily's reality as a fat, bloated figure in black and the conventional image of a lady—expectations that are fostered in the town by its emblematic memory of Emily as a slender figure in white and in us by the narrator's tone of romantic invocation and by the passage itself. Were she not expected to look so different, were her skeleton not small and spare, Emily would not be so grotesque. Thus, the focus is on the grotesqueness that results when stereotypes are imposed upon reality. And the implication of this focus is that the real grotesque is the stereotype itself. If Emily is both lady and grotesque, then the syllogism must be completed thus: the idea of a lady is grotesque. So Emily is metaphor and mirror for the town of Jefferson; and when, at the end, the town folk finally discover who and what she is, they have in fact encountered who and what they are. 14

Despite similarities of focus and vision, "A Rose for Emily" is more implicitly feminist than "The Birthmark." For one thing, Faulkner does not have Hawthorne's compulsive ambivalence; one is not invited to misread "A Rose for Emily" as one is invited to misread "The Birthmark." Thus, the interpretation of "The Birthmark" that sees it as a story of misguided idealism, despite its massive oversights, nevertheless *works*; while the efforts to read "A Rose for Emily" as a parable of the relations between North and South, or as a conflict between an old 15 order and a new, or as a story about the human relation to Time, don't work because the attempt to make Emily representative of such concepts stumbles over the fact that woman's condition is not the "human" condition. To understand Emily's experience requires a primary awareness of the fact that she is a woman.

But, more important, Faulkner provides us with an image of retaliation. Unlike Georgiana, Emily does not simply acquiesce; she prefers to murder rather than to die. In this respect she is a welcome change from the image of woman as willing victim that fills the pages of our literature, and whose other face is the ineffective fulminations of Dame Van Winkle. Nevertheless, Emily's action is still reaction. "A Rose for Emily" exposes the poverty of a situation in which turnabout is the only possibility and in which one's acts are neither self-generated nor self-determined but are simply a response to and a reflection of forces outside oneself. Though Emily may be proud, strong, and indomitable, her murder of Homer Barron is finally an indication of the severely limited nature of the power women can wrest from the system that oppresses them. Aylmer's murder of Georgiana is an indication of men's absolute power over women; it is an act performed in the complete security of his ability to legitimize it as a noble and human pursuit. Emily's act has no such context. It is possible only because it can be kept secret; and it can be kept secret only at the cost of exploiting her image as a lady. Furthermore, Aylmer murders Georgiana in order to get rid of her; Emily murders Homer Barron in order to have him.   16

Patriarchal culture is based to a considerable extent on the argument that men and women are made for each other and on the conviction that "masculinity" and "femininity" are the natural reflection of that divinely ordained complement. Yet, if one reads "The Birthmark" and "A Rose for Emily" as analyses of the consequences of a massive differentiation of everything according to sex, one sees that in reality a sexist culture is one in which men and women are not simply incompatible but murderously so. Aylmer murders Georgiana because he must at any cost get rid of woman; Emily murders Homer Barron because she must at any cost get a man. The two stories define the disparity between cultural myth and cultural reality, and they suggest that in this disparity is the ultimate grotesque.   17

NOTES

[1] "A Rose for Emily" by William Faulkner (1897–1962) is set in the years 1865 to 1924. It is the story of Miss Emily Grierson, a remnant of the old, aristocratic, romantic South. In 1882 Emily's father, who had always kept suitors far away, dies. The following summer, Emily, now 30, meets Homer Barron, a construction foreman. He is brash and uncouth, a man of the new order. They are seen about town, causing gossip. Two female cousins arrive in Jefferson to persuade Emily to behave in keeping with her heritage. Homer leaves town to avoid the cousins and

Emily buys a suit of men's clothes and a silver toilet set, as well as rat poison. The cousins leave, and Homer returns and then disappears. The townspeople assume that Homer has left town. He is never seen again. In 1925 Miss Emily dies and a group of townspeople invade her home. Her black servant, Tobe, leaves and is never seen again, and in an upstairs bedroom, locked up, the townspeople discover the desiccated remains of Homer Barron dressed in the suit. On the pillow beside him they discover a strand of iron-grey hair, evidence that Miss Emily had lain in the bed beside him long after his death.

2 In "The Birthmark" by Nathaniel Hawthorne (American, 1804–1864), Georgiana's beauty is marred, in her scientist husband Aylmer's eyes, only by a birthmark on her cheek. In his obsessive desire to make her into a perfect object, he attempts to eradicate the birthmark. He perfects a poison that succeeds in removing the blemish but in the process kills Georgiana.

3 The grotesque in art presents an object, usually the human figure, in an exaggerated and distorted way.

4 "Annabel Lee," a lyric ballad by the nineteenth-century writer Edgar Allan Poe (1809–1849), tells of a man's loss of a beautiful and beloved woman.

5 Mickey Spillane (b. 1918) is the author of detective stories based on violence and a "tough guy" ethic rather than on mystery. His works include *I, the Jury* (1947) and *The Big Kill* (1951).

6 In Ralph W. Ellison's *The Invisible Man* (1952), the hero, an idealistic and ambitious young black man, wishes to become the new, improved Booker T. Washington. He is kept stumbling through society, being used by everyone around him, unable to realize his ambitions. Self-fulfillment becomes possible only when he realizes how people have used him for their own ends. The theme of the book is that everyone is invisible.

VOCABULARY

fulminations—bursts of lightning and thunder; angry outbursts

necrophilia—a morbid attraction to corpses

noblesse oblige—the notion that with privilege comes responsibility

prurient—given to impure, lewd thoughts

spraddled—with legs spread wide

QUESTIONS

1. Academic articles on literature often begin with a brief summary of the interpretations of other critics. Why does Fetterley make critical commentary on the "grotesque" in "A Rose for Emily" the starting point for her feminist interpretation of this story?

2. Is Fetterley's essay organized inductively, deductively, or in some other way? What is its thesis?

3. Fetterley reads "A Rose for Emily" as an "implicitly feminist" story. What, in her view, makes the story "implicitly feminist"? Are you convinced by the evidence she presents? Why or why not?

4. Defining Emily Grierson as a "lady," according to Fetterley, does "violence" to both men and women. Can you explain her use of the term "violence"? Is it justified?

MY WOOD

E. M. Forster

A few years ago I wrote a book which dealt in part with the difficulties   1
of the English in India. Feeling that they would have had no difficulties in India themselves, the Americans read the book freely. The
more they read it the better it made them feel, and a cheque to the author was the result. I bought a wood with the cheque. It is not a large
wood—it contains scarcely any trees, and it is intersected, blast it, by a
public footpath. Still, it is the first property that I have owned, so it is
right that other people should participate in my shame, and should ask
themselves, in accents that will vary in horror, this very important
question: What is the effect of property on the character? Don't let's
touch economics; the effect of private ownership upon the community
as a whole is another question—a more important question, perhaps, but
another one. Let's keep to psychology. If you own things, what's their effect on you? What's the effect on me of my wood?

In the first place, it makes me feel heavy. Property does have this   2
effect. Property produces men of weight, and it was a man of weight
who failed to get into the Kingdom of Heaven. He was not wicked, that
unfortunate millionaire in the parable, he was only stout; he stuck out
in front, not to mention behind, and as he wedged himself this way
and that in the crystalline entrance and bruised his well-fed flanks, he
saw beneath him a comparatively slim camel passing through the eye
of a needle and being woven into the robe of God. The Gospels all
through couple stoutness and slowness. They point out what is perfectly obvious, yet seldom realized: that if you
have a lot of things you cannot move about a
lot, that furniture requires dusting, dusters require servants, servants require insurance
stamps,[1] and the whole tangle of them makes
you think twice before you accept an invita-
tion to dinner or go for a bathe in the Jordan.[2]
Sometimes the Gospels proceed further and
say with Tolstoy[3] that property is sinful; they
approach the difficult ground of asceticism
here, where I cannot follow them. But as to
the immediate effects of property on people
they just show straightforward logic. It produces men of weight. Men of weight cannot, by

The opening sentence of "My Wood"
refers to the success of Edward Morgan
Forster's most famous novel, *A Passage to
India* (1924). Besides novels and short stories, Forster (1879–1970) also wrote
Aspects of the Novel (1927), a work of literary criticism; biography; travel writing; and
two collections of essays: *Abinger Harvest*
(1936), from which "My Wood" is taken,
and *Two Cheers for Democracy* (1951).

Reprinted by permission of the Provost and
Scholars of King's College, Cambridge and
The Society of Authors as the Literary
Representatives of the Estate of E. M. Forster.

definition, move like the lightning from the East unto the West, and the ascent of a fourteen-stone[4] bishop into a pulpit is thus the exact antithesis of the coming of the Son of Man. My wood makes me feel heavy.

In the second place, it makes me feel it ought to be larger.   3

The other day I heard a twig snap in it. I was annoyed at first, for I   4
thought that someone was blackberrying, and depreciating the value of the undergrowth. On coming nearer, I saw it was not a man who had trodden on the twig and snapped it, but a bird, and I felt pleased. My bird. The bird was not equally pleased. Ignoring the relation between us, it took fright as soon as it saw the shape of my face, and flew straight over the boundary hedge into a field, the property of Mrs. Henessy, where it sat down with a loud squawk. It had become Mrs. Henessy's bird. Something seemed grossly amiss here, something that would not have occurred had the wood been larger. I could not afford to buy Mrs. Henessy out, I dared not murder her, and limitations of this sort beset me on every side. Ahab[5] did not want that vineyard—he only needed it to round off his property, preparatory to plotting a new curve—and all the land around my wood has become necessary to me in order to round off the wood. A boundary protects. But—poor little thing—the boundary ought in its turn to be protected. Noises on the edge of it. Children throw stones. A little more, and then a little more, until we reach the sea. Happy Canute![6] Happier Alexander![7] And after all, why should even the world be the limit of possession? A rocket containing a Union Jack, will, it is hoped, be shortly fired at the moon. Mars. Sirius. Beyond which … But these immensities ended by saddening me. I could not suppose that my wood was the destined nucleus of universal dominion—it is so very small and contains no mineral wealth beyond the blackberries. Nor was I comforted when Mrs. Henessy's bird took alarm for the second time and flew clean away from us all, under the belief that it belonged to itself.

In the third place, property makes its owner feel that he ought to   5
do something to it. Yet he isn't sure what. A restlessness comes over him, a vague sense that he has a personality to express—the same sense which, without any vagueness, leads the artist to an act of creation. Sometimes I think I will cut down such trees as remain in the wood, at other times I want to fill up the gaps between them with new trees. Both impulses are pretentious and empty. They are not honest movements towards money-making or beauty. They spring from a foolish desire to express myself and from an inability to enjoy what I have got. Creation, property, enjoyment form a sinister trinity in the human mind. Creation and enjoyment are both very very good, yet they are often unattainable without a material basis, and at such moments property pushes itself in as a substitute, saying, 'Accept me instead— I'm good enough for all three.' It is not enough. It is, as Shakespeare

said of lust, 'The expense of spirit in a waste of shame': it is 'Before, a joy proposed; behind, a dream.'[8] Yet we don't know how to shun it. It is forced on us by our economic system as the alternative to starvation. It is also forced on us by an internal defect in the soul, by the feeling that in property may lie the germs of self-development and of exquisite or heroic deeds. Our life on earth is, and ought to be, material and carnal.[9] But we have not yet learned to manage our materialism and carnality properly; they are still entangled with the desire for ownership, where (in the words of Dante) 'Possession is one with loss.'

And this brings us to our fourth and final point: the blackberries.   6

Blackberries are not plentiful in this meagre grove, but they are   7 easily seen from the public footpath which traverses it, and all too easily gathered. Foxgloves, too—people will pull up the foxgloves, and ladies of an educational tendency even grub for toadstools to show them on the Monday in class. Other ladies, less educated, roll down the bracken in the arms of their gentlemen friends. There is paper, there are tins. Pray, does my wood belong to me or doesn't it? And, if it does, should I not own it best by allowing no one else to walk there? There is a wood near Lyme Regis,[10] also cursed by a public footpath, where the owner has not hesitated on this point. He has built high stone walls each side of the path, and has spanned it by bridges, so that the public circulate like termites while he gorges on the blackberries unseen. He really does own his wood, this able chap. Dives[11] in Hell did pretty well, but the gulf dividing him from Lazarus could be traversed by vision, and nothing traverses it here. And perhaps I shall come to this in time. I shall wall in and fence out until I really taste the sweets of property. Enormously stout, endlessly avaricious, pseudo-creative, intensely selfish, I shall weave upon my forehead the quadruple crown of possession until those nasty Bolshies[12] come and take it off again and thrust me aside into the outer darkness.

NOTES

[1] Insurance stamps: required in the U.K. to validate health and disability insurance benefits.

[2] The Jordan River flows between the Sea of Galilee and the Dead Sea.

[3] A Russian writer, author of *War and Peace* (1869) and *Anna Karenina* (1877), Leo Tolstoy (1828–1910) believed that possession of private property was an evil and practised severe asceticism.

[4] A stone equals fourteen pounds.

[5] Ahab was the seventh king of Israel from 874 to 853 B.C. His wife, Jezebel, coveting a fine vineyard adjoining the palace grounds, arranged that its owner, Naboth, be convicted of blasphemy and executed. Ahab then became legal owner of the vineyard.

[6] Canute, or C'nut, was an ambitious conqueror of the 11th century who was simultaneously King of England (1016–1035), Denmark (1018–1035), and Norway (1028–1035).

7   Alexander the Great, King of Macedonia, sought to conquer the entire world to satisfy his desire for power and glory.

8   The phrases are from Shakespeare's Sonnet 129. The single quotation marks are British usage.

9   In Forster's day the word *carnal* referred to the body as the seat of all appetites. Also, archaically, *carnal* was used as the opposite of *spiritual*.

10 Lyme Regis: a coastal town in England chartered as a royal borough in 1284 that eventually became known, in Forster's time, as a beach resort of some notoriety.

11 Dives and Lazarus figure in a biblical story. Dives, a rich man, takes no notice of Lazarus, a beggar. Dives ends up in Hades and Lazarus in heaven (Luke 16:19–31).

12 The Bolsheviks ("Bolshies") were the majority group of the Russian Social Democratic Party. They favoured revolutionary tactics to achieve socialism and seized power during the Russian Revolution to set up a workers' state.

QUESTIONS

1. In the first paragraph of "My Wood," Forster announces that his essay is concerned with the effects of owning something on a person's character. What does he mean by "character"? Does Forster confine his essay to the effects of ownership on the individual?

2. Does Forster list these effects in an order of increasing importance? In some other order? Explain.

3. Forster introduces the first three effects with similar topic sentences beginning "It [or "property"] makes me [or "its owner"] feel…." Why does he abandon this formula when he introduces the fourth effect?

4. Forster's novel *A Passage to India* (1924) is about the corrupting effects of property and imperialism on the British in India. Thus it is ironic that the proceeds of this novel allowed Forster himself to buy property. Can you find other instances of irony, or an ironic tone, in the essay? Do you think irony, rather than direct statement, makes this essay more persuasive? Explain.

5. Throughout this essay, Forster makes a number of allusions to figures in religion, history, and literature. Why does Forster include these allusions? How do they affect you as a reader?

6. "My Wood" was first published in England in 1936. Does this context illuminate any of the attitudes and concerns in this essay?

SUGGESTION FOR WRITING

Using "My Wood" as a model, write an essay explaining how owning something (a house, a car, a CD collection) corrupted your character. Organize your essay in the same way Forster does, with an introduction and three or four middle paragraphs. Deal with one effect in each paragraph. Like Forster, you can add a separate conclusion. Include allusions if you think they will strengthen your rapport with your reader.

SAVE THE LAST DANCE

John Fraser

Mikhail Baryshnikov[1] came back to dance in Toronto just a month   1
before Rudolf Nureyev[2] died in Paris on January 6. Baryshnikov was
at the O'Keefe Centre, the theatre where he orchestrated his dramatic
leap to the West in 1974 (and which he still lists as one of the worst performing houses in all of North America). Nureyev died in the city in
which he made his own leap to a new life in the West in 1961. His
memorial service was held in the ornate Paris Opera, a house he adored
and where he often left dancers in tears, so outrageous were some of his
harangues when he presided over the ballet company there in the 1980s.

Both men sported the news-wire sobriquet "Soviet defector," a spe-   2
cial category of performing artist that will soon mean very little except
as a historical footnote. Next to their obvious talent, however, it used to
mean half of their mystique, half of *everything*: exoticism, artistic distinction, aloofness, unique star quality, being set apart from all Western-
trained male dancers. Their overt sexuality on stage, differently
expressed, was the other half. Critics were rarely explicit in discussing
this, yet potency positively radiated from them during performances—
from their costumes, mannerisms, athleticism, studied stage glances,
even their curtain calls. Their artistry has formed the definition of male
dancing for the last half of the twentieth century, but it was sex appeal
that shot them both into the highest stratosphere of stardom.

Nureyev was gay and died of AIDS. Baryshnikov is straight and is   3
still fathering children; he has two with his companion, Lisa Rinehart.
(An older child is the daughter of the film ac-
tress Jessica Lange.) Nureyev was promiscu-
ous, almost to the end; Baryshnikov has
settled down, though it was not so long ago
that he led a merry chase through the ranks of
ballerinas and movie stars where the risk of
cross-sexual infection from the terrible disease is far more real than in, say, the middle-
class enclaves of north Toronto. Many
heterosexuals in North America still don't take
the risk of AIDS very seriously. Not so in the
world of the performing arts. Especially not so
in the world of ballet. Safe sex is a contradiction in terms. Baryshnikov knows that; Nureyev
laughed at it.

John Fraser (b. 1944), a prominent author
and journalist, became a Member of the
Order of Canada, Canada's second-highest
honour, in 2002. Fraser has worked for
several Canadian newspapers, including
The Globe and Mail, and served as editor of
Saturday Night for several years. His books
include *Private View: Inside Baryshnikov's
American Ballet Theatre*; *The Chinese: Portrait
of a People*; and *Eminent Canadians: Candid
Tales of Then and Now*. Currently, Fraser is
master of Massey College at the University
of Toronto.

"Save the Last Dance" was published in
Saturday Night, 1993. Used with permission
of the author.

At the outset of his career in the West, Nureyev had two noble re- 4
lationships with people older than himself that provided emotional and
perhaps sexual stability. The first was with Dame Margot Fonteyn, the
great English prima ballerina, and the other was with Erik Bruhn, the
brilliant Danish dancer who loved him deeply. In each case, Nureyev
gave generously of himself and extended his partner's performing career. In his fashion, he remained loyal to both, but his libido was rest-
less and he was notorious for seeking out anonymous, dispensable
lovers. This aroused endless pop-psychological speculation. Craig
Dodd, the author and ballet critic who knew Nureyev in the sixties, argued that this was his way of meeting people "on as nearly equal terms
as anyone famous as him is likely to do." Writing after Nureyev's death
in London's *Sunday Telegraph*, Nicholas Farrell reported that some of
the dancer's colleagues felt that "perhaps it could even have been a defiance of death—a sort of danse macabre."

What we do know is this: at the same age (their late thirties), 5
Nureyev and Baryshnikov took dramatically different paths in their personal lives. Nureyev lingered on in dangerland and Baryshnikov headed
straight for middle-class domesticity. And the impact of those personal
decisions and directions has had a profound effect on their art.

When I was a dance critic at the dawn of time, nearly a quarter- 6
century ago, I had my problems with Nureyev. I admired him enormously, of course. Only a fool wouldn't. He electrified every stage he
danced on. Kid critics nevertheless had a responsibility for making
sure the reading public didn't think we were overly awed by superstars
like Nureyev, and I took my responsibility as a *Canadian* kid critic
very seriously in those days. After paying due attention to Nureyev's
particular genius for three or four years, especially after he chose the
National Ballet of Canada to be a handsome backdrop to his own expensive productions (his *Sleeping Beauty*, which reeked of dollars
spent in the six figures, was notorious), I decided he wasn't sufficiently
appreciative of the opportunities Canada had provided him. I detected
unpleasant proof that the National Ballet was giving up too much of its
mandate just for the thrill of having a soon-forgotten summer season at
the Met in New York. I expatiated on all this, somewhat more pointedly
than I am doing here, in the pages of the Sunday *New York Times*,
where readers cared a lot more about Nureyev than about the future of
the Canadian ballet.

What a lot of fuss and bother ensued. By the time the dust and 7
chicken feathers had settled, I'd managed to add to my list of blood
enemies the legendary dancer/choreographer Martha Graham, the
New York Times dance critic Clive Barnes, all the principal dancers of
the National Ballet, and at least one American balletomane who took
the trouble to mail me faecal matter in a plastic bag. The article was

published about the same time Baryshnikov defected in Toronto, so it was a wild time in my life. Curiously, the one person I didn't make an enemy of—in the long term, anyway—was Nureyev himself. After he had whipped everyone up into a frenzy of loyalty oaths and assured himself that the kid critic spoke for no one but himself, we collaborated on a book about the Canadian dancers Karen Kain and Frank Augustyn (I did the legwork, he did the foreword). During the course of this little collaboration, we agreed that we both listened to too much idle gossip. And then we gossiped idly and amiably through an affectionately remembered dinner and past all the damage we had tried to inflict on each other.

How I loved Nureyev after that, although I never really got close to   8 him. Not close in the way I got to Baryshnikov, who walks on gold pathways as far as I am concerned, and who understands human nature, and his own, in ways Nureyev could never have begun to plumb. You could see the proof of this in the dancing they both did after they had passed their prime. Nureyev clung to all the old forms. As he went on refusing to retreat from a field fit only for young men at their peak, he became for some a sad and desperate figure, who allowed himself to be tricked out in his old costumes, half-dancing his former roles of glory. I caught one of these events in upstate New York. (He rarely took such efforts to main stages.) At first I was embarrassed for his sake and then I had a change of heart and thought the spectacle poignant and even beautiful in a weird way. For Nureyev, being on stage—any stage—was synonymous with being alive. I think it was as simple as that.

It's not all that simple for Baryshnikov. He takes the business of   9 aging very seriously. A far better technician than Nureyev, he always seemed to soar twice as high. The problem here, though, was that he lit twice as hard and the damage to his legs over the years has been considerable. Unlike Nureyev, he has never had any interest in trying to perpetuate a former self. If he was middle-aged, dammit, he would dance middle-aged. His performances with Twyla Tharp in Toronto were a triumph: witty, sophisticated, but most of all, wise. In Tharp, he has latched onto a choreographer/dancer who manages to confirm every dark, paranoid suspicion of the young Generation X feeling endlessly shafted by the hegemony of the baby boomers. Where once only youth was allowed to adorn the dance stage, Tharp and Baryshnikov announced that today's audiences don't really need the callow perspective of the under-thirty crowd. Here was a postmenopausal romp that embodied female independence, comfortable male self-acceptance, and a knowing deference to the realities and complications of relationships. Baryshnikov works around his game leg, makes a virtue of it, in fact, and, once he and Tharp established the new rules and conventions of the game, they had us all cheering.

I suppose he can go on like this for a long time and we may yet see   10
him do a dance based on *The Old Man and the Sea*. He probably
won't, though, because he is riddled through and through with common sense and a concept of decorum that is as natural to him as it was
alien to Nureyev. This is not to detract from Nureyev. He was what he
was and gave immense pleasure to millions of people. Anyone who saw
him dance, particularly when he was in top form, is marked for life; to
have known him, even fitfully, was an honour.

In private, he wasn't particularly nice about Baryshnikov—profes-   11
sional jealousy was as much a part of his personality as was generosity
to young artists—but, like dominant predators who understand their
mutual powers, they sniffed each other out early on and more or less
kept to separate territories. And Baryshnikov, for his part, always understood Nureyev's appeal. "He had the charisma and simplicity of a man of
the earth," Baryshnikov said after Nureyev's death, "and the untouch-
able arrogance of the gods." Those Russians! Those Soviet defectors!

NOTES

[1] Mikhail Baryshnikov (b. 1948) was a highly respected member of the Kirov Ballet between 1966
and 1974. After defecting to the West in 1974, he danced with the American Ballet Theatre and
the New York City Ballet. He has also starred in two films, *The Turning Point* (1977) and *White
Nights* (1985), making ballet accessible to a wider public.

[2] Rudolf Nureyev (1938–1993) trained with the Kirov dance academy in Leningrad and became a
world-renowned dancer with the Kirov Ballet. His complete disregard for Soviet ideals and
standards of behaviour got him into trouble with the government, however, so he defected
while on tour in France. He then danced with many ballet companies around the world, often
with Margot Fonteyn as his partner.

VOCABULARY

enclaves—literally, portions of a country surrounded by another country

expatiated—spoke or wrote at length

hegemony—dominance over a group or territory

sobriquet—a nickname

QUESTIONS

1. Make an outline of Fraser's comparison of Nureyev and Baryshnikov by labelling
   which paragraphs focus on Nureyev, which paragraphs focus on Baryshnikov, and
   which paragraphs refer to both dancers.

2. List the most important similarities and differences in the two men's artistic and
   personal lives.

3. Note that in addition to comparing the two dancers, Fraser also evaluates them.
   What qualities make both Baryshnikov and Nureyev great dancers? Why does

Fraser think that Baryshnikov is both a better dancer and a better person? What standard(s) of evaluation form the basis of Fraser's judgments? (See Chapter 11.)

4. Using your answers to questions 2 and 3 as a basis, state Fraser's thesis in your own words. Make sure the thesis both compares and evaluates the two dancers.

SUGGESTION FOR WRITING

List the main similarities and differences in the lives and/or careers of two actors, sports stars, or musicians. Formulate a thesis statement for an essay comparing them. Decide whether you would use a block or point-by-point method for organizing your essay. Write a paragraph explaining your reasons for this decision.

KIDDY THINKS

Alison Gopnik

When my son was a toddler his first question about a meal was always: "What's for dessert?" One day we had pineapple in kirsch. He spat it out, then looked at the adults devouring the stuff, and said: "Pineapple: it's yucky for me but it's yummy for you." For weeks afterwards, he would stop suddenly in the middle of a game and say: "Pineapple: yucky for me but yummy for you," as if he had discovered the most extraordinary fact of life. And in a sense he had: the realization that people think and feel differently is a profound one. 1

When we look around a room full of people, we don't see bags of skin and cloth draped over the furniture. We see other people, people with thoughts and emotions, desires and beliefs, sometimes like our own, sometimes not. And by the time they are 18 months old, this is what toddlers see as well. But how do such tiny children get from bags of skin to "other minds"? 2

In the past 30 years we have learned more about what young children know and how they learn than we did in the preceding 2,500 years. And this has revolutionised our view of children. For centuries, psychologists and philosophers agreed that babies were the opposite of adults. They were emotional and passive, dominated by perception and incapable of rational thought. John Locke[1] said they were "blank slates". 3

Today, scientists have only recently begun to appreciate just how much even the youngest babies know—and how much and how quickly they learn. There are three elements to this new picture. First, that children know a great deal, literally from the moment they are born. Second, that they are born with extremely powerful learning abilities. And, finally, that adults appear to be "programmed" to unconsciously teach babies and young children just the things they need to know. 4

In *How Babies Think*, my co-authors and I argue that very young children use the same strategies as scientists. They think, observe, formulate theories, make predictions, and do experiments. They also change their theories as they accumulate counter-evidence to their predictions. 5

But where scientists focus their attention on distant stars and invisible microbes, babies concentrate on everyday things: blocks, pet dogs, words and, most important: Mum and Dad 6

Alison Gopnik is a professor of developmental psychology at the University of California, Berkeley, and a researcher for the Institute of Human Development (IHD), an organized research unit at Berkeley since 1927. Gopnik's specialties in the area of psychology include cognition and language development and children's theories of mind.

© Alison Gopnik, co-author of *The Scientist in the Crib*, HarperCollins, 2000.

and Aunt Ethel. In fact understanding other people seems to be one of the most crucial items in the scientific agenda of childhood, and it's a good illustration of how early learning takes place.

To begin with, children are born knowing that people are special. 7 Newborn babies (the youngest tested was only 42 minutes old) can imitate facial expressions. There are no mirrors in the womb; newborns have never seen their own face. These tiny babies must somehow already understand the similarity between their own internal feeling (of say, sticking out their tongue) and the external face they see (a round shape from which something pink protrudes). Newborn babies not only prefer faces to things but also recognise that those faces are *like their own face*. Nature, it seems, gives human beings a jump start on the Other Minds problem.

And what a jump start. By the time they are nine months old, ba- 8 bies can tell the difference between expressions of happiness, sadness and anger, and understand something about the emotions that produce those expressions. By the time they are one, they know that they will see something by looking where other people point; they know that they should do something by watching what others do; and they know how they should feel about something by seeing how others feel.

For instance, an adult can look in two boxes. She looks into one 9 with an expression of joy and into the other with disgust. The baby will happily reach into the box that made her happy, but won't touch the box that disgusted her. The baby has discovered that its initial emotional rapport with other people extends to joint attitudes towards the world. In a simple way, one-year-olds already participate in a culture. But as babies learn that people usually have the same attitudes towards objects as they do, they are setting themselves up to learn something else, something more disturbing: they discover that sometimes people *don't* have the same attitudes.

Observe what happens when a baby reaches for a forbidden ob- 10 ject—a lamp cord, say. It must seem perverse to the one-year-old: the more clearly she indicates her desire, the more adamantly her carer keeps it away. Even though the baby and the grown-up are reacting to the same object, their attitudes toward the object seem to be different.

By the time babies are about one-and-a-half, they start to under- 11 stand the nature of these differences between people and become fascinated. If you offer a baby two bowls, one of biscuits, the other of raw broccoli, all the babies prefer the biscuits. But if the researcher indicates to the baby that she hates biscuits and loves broccoli, then hands the bowls to the baby and says: "Could you give me some?" something interesting happens. Fourteen-month-olds, with their innocent assumption that we all want the same thing, give her biscuits. But the wiser 18-month-olds give her broccoli, even though they themselves despise it. These tiny children have learned that other people's desires may conflict with their own.

This is also dramatically apparent in everyday life. Parents all 12 know, and dread, the "terrible twos". While one-year-olds seem irresistibly drawn to forbidden objects (that lamp cord again), the two-year-olds seem deliberately bloody-minded. She doesn't even look at the lamp cord. Instead, her hand goes out to touch it as she looks, steadily, gravely, at you.

This demonic behaviour is quite rational, though. Our broccoli ex- 13 periments show that children only begin to understand the differences in desires at 18 months. The terrible twos seem to involve a systematic exploration of that idea, like an experimental research programme. Toddlers are testing the extent to which their desires and those of others may conflict. The grave look is directed at you because you and your reaction, rather than the lamp cord, are the interesting thing. The terrible twos reflect a clash between children's need to understand other people and their need to live happily with them. If the child is a budding scientist, we parents are the laboratory rats.

Two-year-olds also have to learn how visual perception works. 14 Toddlers love hide and seek but aren't very good at it—a toddler will bury his head under the table with his bottom in view. In our lab, we explored when children learn how to hide things. Suppose I put a child on one side of a table and sit on the other. Then I put a screen and a toy on the table and ask the child to hide the toy from me. At 24 months, a toddler will put the toy on *my* side of the screen, so that it is actually hidden from them, but not from me. But 36-month-olds get this right. In fact, they'll often tell me they can see the toy but I can't. In the months in between, we observed many children experimenting. They would switch the toy from one side to the other, or come around to my side of the screen to make sure the toy really was hidden.

But this isn't the end of the story. Three-year-olds still have trou- 15 ble with another important fact about people. They know that we can see different things, but not that what we think about the world may be wrong.

In a classic experiment, you can give three-year-olds a shut choco- 16 late box. They open it and it turns out to have pencils inside. Then you ask them about another child in the nursery: "What will Nicky think is in the box: pencils or chocolates?" Three-year-olds report that Nicky will say there are pencils inside. They don't understand that Nicky will probably make the same mistake they made. Four-year-olds know that Nicky will be misled by the picture on the box.

Like scientists, children change their theories precisely because 17 they make the wrong predictions. In "mistaken belief" experiments, simply telling children the right answer makes no difference. Like scientists, children at first resist counter-evidence. Virginia Slaughter and I visited three-year-olds over several weeks and gave them examples of mistaken beliefs: a golf ball that turned out to be soap, a yellow duck that looked green when put behind blue plastic. Each time the child made the wrong prediction, we presented them with counter-evidence. After two weeks these three-year-olds understood a brand new "mistaken belief" task, one they had never seen before, much better than a control group.

This experiment shows that even very young children are naturally 18 able to alter their predictions in the light of new evidence. But it also shows how important other people can be: our adult behaviour had helped the children to work out the correct answer. Of course, we're developmental psychologists.

Do grown-ups naturally help children learn in their everyday lives? 19 The new research suggests they do. One of the most dramatic examples of this is the sing-song voice adults use when they talk to babies. This speech style helps children sort out the sounds of language.

Similarly, the way that parents talk about the mind seems to influ- 20 ence their children's everyday psychology. What are the consequences of this new view? The research *doesn't* mean there is some set of flashcards that will help babies be brighter. Babies are already as bright as can be. They learn through everyday play, and through the care and attention of adults around them. It also *doesn't* mean there is some "critical period" for learning in the first three years or some set of experiences children must have. Children and even adults keep learning throughout life. It definitely *doesn't* mean mothers should quit their jobs. Anyone who cares for small children and is sensitive to what interests them can teach them what they need to know.

On the other hand, the research does suggest that the every day, 21 unremunerated, unremarkable work of caring for babies and young children is extremely important. Humans have managed to learn so much because generations of adults put effort into caring for children.

Ironically, this new scientific perspective comes when young chil- 22 dren and parents are under enormous pressure. We still penalise parents for taking time off work to be with their children, instead of rewarding them. Most parents face agonising dilemmas as they balance jobs and children. If we really want babies to learn, we should ditch the videotapes and flashcards and work for paid parental leave, flexible work arrangements and publicly supported, high-quality childcare.

NOTE

[1] English philosopher John Locke (1632–1704) believed that all of our knowledge comes from our senses. He thought that children were "blank slates" (i.e., clean sheets of paper), passively acquiring knowledge through sensory impressions from the world around them.

VOCABULARY

adamantly—strongly, stubbornly

unremunerated—not paid to do

QUESTIONS

1. Gopnik begins this essay by telling a story about her own child. Is this narrative introduction effective? Why or why not?

2. Where does Gopnik first indicate her subject? Where does she present her thesis? State her thesis in your own words.

3. Gopnik uses process analysis as her main method for developing her material, but she also includes lots of specific examples. Are these examples effective in clarifying her point? How does Gopnik make an example of what one child does representative of what all children do?

4. How does Gopnik blend analysis and persuasion in this essay? Do you find the assertions she makes in the final paragraph convincing?

SUGGESTION FOR WRITING

You can use process analysis as Gopnik does in this article to explain how something happens, but you can also use process analysis to give your reader directions on how to carry out a procedure. For both kinds of writing, you need an introduction that makes the subject of your essay seem interesting and important. Choose either kind of analysis and write an introductory paragraph. Possible topics include the following: how to burn a CD, how to give a cat a bath, how diabetes can trigger mood swings, how films are made. You might consider treating your subject ironically, as W. S. Merwin does in "Unchopping a Tree" (Readings).

WHY I LIVE WITH MY MOTHER

Katie Haegele

As it turns out, you can go home again[1]

When I graduated college I was determined not to move back in
with my parents. Born in 1976, I'm a baby Gen Xer.[2] I watched
from the safety of high school as those leading the generational pack
were deposited into a jobless marketplace and went back to mom and
dad's house in droves. The culture of ironic slack[3] ensued. Like a
younger sibling, I aspired to dress and talk like Janeane Garofalo's consummate no-bullshit cool girl in *Reality Bites*. But the truth was that I
had no desire to end up like Winona Ryder, a valedictorian who was
seriously considering taking a job at the Gap.   1

I snarled with contempt when I talked about those poor kids who
"lived at home." (As in, "You're going out with the guy from the book-
store? He lives at home!" The absurdity of this expression—to say
nothing of the cruelty with which I flung it around—wouldn't dawn on
me until much later.) It was a point of pride for me: I was going to pay
rent on my own apartment with the wages from my first real job.
I wanted to decorate as offensively as I pleased, smoke cigarettes with
abandon, or have overnight male visitors if such a situation were to
present itself. (It didn't, much.)   2

I wanted my own place.   3

A few months into my job search I began to understand, deep inside, that *The New Yorker* was not going to seek me out for a staff writer
position. Much soul-searching and Smiths-
listening took place. Then I accepted a perfectly
decent staff writing position at a local university. My best friend, Kristen, and I snagged a little two-bedroom in downtown Philadelphia,
a posh neighborhood that thankfully included a
few dumpy blocks in our price range.   4

The place featured an abnormally long, narrow hallway that squashed average-sized visitors as they entered and eventually spat them
out into our living room, which we'd transformed into a pop culture shrine. We hung an   5

Katie Haegele studied linguistics at the
University of Pennsylvania. She is a regular
contributor to *Philadelphia Weekly* and has
written for *Bitch*, *Adbusters*, and *Feminista*,
the online journal of feminist construction.
Her books include *E-Advertising and E-
Marketing: Online Opportunities* and *Cool
Careers Without College for Nature Lovers*.

irony-laden Spice Girls poster in the bathroom; at 10 by 14 inches, it took up all the available wall space. The kitchen was so small we had to take turns standing in it.

Kristen and I lovingly referred to our building as "the tenement 6 slum." True to form, the other residents seemed to have hundreds of crying babies, loud music, loud, disturbing-sounding sex, and perennially overflowing garbage bags in the hall. Yeah, it was gross. But it was ours. And we decided we had the best deal on the block: The residents of the adorable colonials across the way paid astronomical rents for a view of our little squat apartment complex, while for a greatly reduced price we could imagine ourselves a part of their chic existence just by leaning out the window! For nearly a year the two of us lived it up in that apartment, raptly following stupid TV, trying half-heartedly to start a zine, stalking every boy in the building under the age of 30, and stumbling home in the wee hours from the hole-in-the-wall around the corner.

Then my dad died, and my new life came to a screeching halt. 7 Well, not so fast—he'd been ill for years, and once the end was undeniably near I started moving back home, bit by bit.

I did double duty that spring. Half the time I had to play it cool for 8 my friends and tried (and sometimes failed) to keep it together at work. The other half I spent with my parents in the house where I grew up, watching a horror story unfold. I felt guilty whenever I wasn't there. I'd start out some evenings rolling from bar to bar with Kristen but end up so overcome with anxiety that I'd catch the last train home, claiming I wanted to sleep in my old bed. Every time I got there to find my dad in his chair in front of the TV, a large black blossom of dread bloomed inside me, uncurling in my middle and spreading throughout my body with a little shiver. He didn't look right; he looked less right each time. His face had a grayish cast that was somehow also green. The chemo wasn't working and, even though nobody would say so, I knew our time with him was limited.

After learning how to fake it like an expert, it didn't take long for 9 me to feel quite alone in the world. And I certainly was alone on the train headed home every couple of days, thinking and crying in those straight-back seats while I stared out the window. Having my own place was no longer the freewheeling single gal's adventure it was supposed to be, but moving back home would be like saying what everybody had deemed unsayable: that my dad was going to die.

As is the case with many fretted-over decisions, this one was made 10 for me in the end. Dad died in June. The very next day I dragged myself to my apartment to retrieve my beloved cat and on the way back it dawned on me: I was going home. Home was home again. I couldn't believe it. Half-crazy with misery, I didn't bother bringing any clothes back with me. I just went to work every day for the next month wearing the same black T-shirt and flip-flops. In fact, I didn't fully move the rest of my things until the day before the lease was up. I was emotionally crippled, a zombie, grieving so hard my chest ached for weeks, but still it felt like another defeat to peel the posters off the walls of my first real place. Life had challenged me to a battle and tromped me.

This all happened a year and a half ago. Sometimes it seems like a 11 lifetime ago, other times like it's happening all over again. Such is the nature of grief. But I've been healing all this time, getting little bits of myself back. And there have been a few pleasant surprises along the way, too, like rediscovering home.

I sleep in my old bedroom and eat dinner at the kitchen table with 12 my mom every night. But Mom and I are different than we used to be. Plus, home isn't just the place where I live anymore. Six months ago I quit my stinking rotten day job and started working—I mean, "writing"—from home. When I first joined the ranks of the self-employed, I joked to friends that I would emerge at the end of my tenure as a freelancer like Grizzly Adams, completely desocialized and speaking my own guttural language. This hasn't quite happened. But something has changed within me, a change that didn't take place when I was living with my friends and spending all my available energy "discovering" myself. When I was 20, I needed to become myself the only way I knew how: by leaving. Now that I'm back, I think I've begun to learn what independence really means.

I am, after all, an adult now, capable of having a grown-up friend- 13 ship with my roommate—er, mom. Last weekend she and I went for Chinese. After stuffing ourselves full of fried gooey stuff we broke our fortune cookies, and here's what mine said: "There is a true and sincere friendship between you both." You both? Who ever heard of a fortune cookie that addresses more than one person? When my mom opened hers, it was empty. Sometimes something spooky has to happen to make you notice what's good in your life.

What's good is my friendship with my mother, and something 14 more. A greater good has come of the loss of my cool downtown existence. When I traded my independence for a little bit of comfort, what I got in return turned out to be worth a lot more. These days I very closely resemble the person I'm supposed to be, and that's a homecoming many people never get. Wherever I go from here, I'll be at home with myself.

NOTES

1 "You can go home again" is an allusion to an American novel by Thomas Wolfe titled *You Can't Go Home Again*.

2 Baby Gen Xer: Generation X is a term popularized by Canadian writer Douglas Coupland. In his 1991 novel of that title, characters in their mid-twenties to mid-thirties reject their consumerist society to search for something more authentic.

3 Ironic slack: "slackers" is a term used to describe Generation X. Slackers are disillusioned and refuse to take school, jobs, or anything else too seriously. "Ironic slack" involves not taking any of the above attitudes too seriously.

QUESTIONS

1. Haegele organizes her essay as a process analysis. Locate the transitions that indicate the major stages of her return home.

2. How does Haegele include and counter probable objections to her decision to move back home?

3. What is Haegele's thesis? How does she use contrast to develop her thesis?

4. What attitude does Haegele take to herself, her reader, and her subject? How does she create this tone? Do you think it is effective?

SUGGESTION FOR WRITING

Write a short essay in which you use process analysis to present a time or situation in which you changed your mind about an important issue in your life.

LIFEBOAT ETHICS: THE CASE AGAINST HELPING THE POOR

Garrett Hardin

Environmentalists use the metaphor of the earth as a "spaceship" in trying to persuade countries, industries and people to stop wasting and polluting our natural resources. Since we all share life on this planet, they argue, no single person or institution has the right to destroy, waste, or use more than a fair share of its resources.

But does everyone on earth have an equal right to an equal share of its resources? The spaceship metaphor can be dangerous when used by misguided idealists to justify suicidal policies for sharing our resources through uncontrolled immigration and foreign aid. In their enthusiastic but unrealistic generosity, they confuse the ethics of a spaceship with those of a lifeboat.

A true spaceship would have to be under the control of a captain, since no ship could possibly survive if its course were determined by committee. Spaceship Earth certainly has no captain; the United Nations is merely a toothless tiger, with little power to enforce any policy upon its bickering members.

If we divide the world crudely into rich nations and poor nations, two thirds of them are desperately poor, and only one third comparatively rich, with the United States the wealthiest of all. Metaphorically each rich nation can be seen as a lifeboat full of comparatively rich people. In the ocean outside each lifeboat swim the poor of the world, who would like to get in, or at least to share some of the wealth. What should the lifeboat passengers do?

First, we must recognize the limited capacity of any lifeboat. For example, a nation's land has a limited capacity to support a population and as the current energy crisis[1] has shown us, in some ways we have already exceeded the carrying capacity of our land. So here we sit, say 50 people in our lifeboat. To be generous, let us assume it has room for 10 more, making a total capacity of 60. Suppose the 50 of us in the lifeboat see 100 others swimming in the

Trained as an ecologist and a microbiologist at the University of Chicago and Stanford University, Garrett Hardin (b. 1915) is best known for his 1968 essay, "The Tragedy of the Commons," widely accepted as a fundamental contribution to ecology, population theory, economics, and political science. His books on population growth include *The Limits of Altruism* (1977) and *Living Within Limits: Ecology, Economics, and Population Taboos* (1993).

Reprinted with permission from *Psychology Today Magazine*, Copyright © 1974 Sussex Publications Inc.

water outside, begging for admission to our boat or for handouts. We have several options: We may be tempted to try to live by the Christian idea of being "our brother's keeper," or by the Marxist ideal of "to each according to his needs." Since the needs of all in the water are the same, and since they can all be seen as our "brothers," we could take them all into our boat, making a total of 150 in a boat designed for 60. The boat swamps; everyone drowns. Complete justice, complete catastrophe.

Since the boat has an unused excess capacity of 10 more passengers, we could admit just 10 more to it. But which 10 do we let in? How do we choose? Do we pick the best 10, the neediest 10, "first come, first served"? And what do we say to the 90 we exclude? If we do let an extra 10 into our lifeboat, we will have lost our "safety factor," an engineering principle of critical importance. For example, if we don't leave room for the excess capacity as a safety factor in our country's agriculture, a new plant disease or a bad change in the weather could have disastrous consequences. 6

Suppose we decide to preserve our small safety factor and admit no more to the lifeboat. Our survival is then possible, although we shall have to be constantly on guard against boarding parties. 7

While this last solution clearly offers the only means of survival, it is morally abhorrent to many people. Some say they feel guilty about their good luck. My reply is simple: "Get out and yield your place to others." This may solve the problem of the guilt-ridden person's conscience, but it does not change the ethics of the lifeboat. The needy person to whom the guilt-ridden person yields his place will not let himself feel guilty about his good luck. If he did, he would not climb aboard. The net result of conscience-stricken people giving up their unjustly held seats is the elimination of that sort of conscience from the lifeboat. 8

This is the basic metaphor within which we must work our solutions. Let us now enrich the image, step by step, with substantive additions from the real world, a world that must solve real and pressing problems of overpopulation and hunger. 9

The harsh ethics of the lifeboat become even harsher when we consider the reproductive differences between the rich nations and the poor nations. The people inside the lifeboats are doubling in numbers every 87 years; those swimming around outside are doubling, on the average, every 35 years, more than twice as fast as the rich. And since the world's resources are dwindling, the difference in prosperity between the rich and the poor can only increase. 10

As of 1973, the United States had a population of 210 million people, who were increasing by 0.8 percent per year. Outside our lifeboat, let us imagine another 210 million people (say the combined populations of Colombia, Ecuador, Venezuela, Morocco, Pakistan, Thailand, 11 and the Philippines), increasing at a rate of 3.3 percent per year. Put differently, the doubling time for this aggregate population was 21 years, compared to 87 years for the United States.

Now suppose the United States agreed to pool its resources with those seven countries, with everyone receiving an equal share. Initially the ratio of Americans to non-Americans in this model would be one-to-one. But consider what the ratio would be after 87 years, by which time the Americans would have doubled to a population of 420 million. By then, doubling every 21 years, the other group would have swollen to 3.54 billion. Each American would have to share the available resources with more than eight people.   12

But, one could argue, this discussion assumes that current population trends will continue, and they may not. Quite so. Most likely the rate of population increase will decline much faster in the United States than it will in the other countries, and there does not seem to be much we can do about it. In sharing with "each according to his needs," we must recognize that needs are determined by population size, which is determined by the rate of reproduction, which at present is regarded as a sovereign right of every nation, poor or not. This being so, the philanthropic load created by the sharing ethic of the spaceship can only increase.   13

The fundamental error of spaceship ethics, and the sharing it requires, is that it leads to what I call "the tragedy of the commons." Under a system of private property, people who own property recognize their responsibility to care for it, for if they don't they will eventually suffer. A farmer, for instance, will allow no more cattle in his pasture than its carrying capacity justifies. If he overloads it, erosion sets in, weeds take over, and he loses the use of the pasture.   14

If a pasture becomes a commons open to all, the right of each to use it may not be matched by a corresponding responsibility to protect it. Asking everyone to use it with discretion will hardly do, for the considerate herdsman who refrains from overloading the commons suffers more than a selfish one who says his needs are greater. If everyone would restrain himself, all would be well; but it takes only one less than everyone to ruin a system of voluntary restraint. In a crowded world of less than perfect human beings, mutual ruin is inevitable if there are no controls. This is the tragedy of the commons.   15

One of the major tasks of education today should be the creation of such an acute awareness of the dangers of the commons that people will recognize its many varieties. For example, the air and the water have become polluted because they are treated as commons. Further growth in the population or per-capita conversion of natural resources into pollutants will only make the problem worse. The same holds true for the fish of the oceans. Fishing fleets have nearly disappeared in many parts of the world; technological improvements in the art of   16 fishing are hastening the day of complete ruin. Only the replacement of the system of the commons with a responsible system of control will save the land, air, water and oceanic fisheries.

In recent years there has been a push to create a new commons called a World Food Bank, an international depository of food reserves to which nations would contribute according to their abilities and from which they would draw according to their needs. This humanitarian proposal received support from many liberal international groups, and from such prominent citizens as Margaret Mead,[2] the U.N. Secretary General, and Senator Edward Kennedy.

A world food bank appeals powerfully to our humanitarian impulses. But before we rush ahead with such a plan, let us ask if such a program would actually do more good than harm, not only momentarily but also in the long run. Those who propose a food bank usually refer to a current "emergency" or "crisis" in terms of world food supply. But what is an emergency? Although they may be infrequent and sudden, everyone knows that emergencies will occur from time to time. A well-run family, company, organization or country prepares for the likelihood of accidents and emergencies. It expects them, it budgets for them, it saves for them.

What happens if some organizations or countries budget for accidents and others do not? If each country is solely responsible for its own well-being, poorly managed ones will suffer. But they can learn from experience. They may mend their ways, and learn to budget for infrequent but certain emergencies. For example, the weather varies from year to year, and periodic crop failures are certain. A wise and competent government saves out of the production of the good years in anticipation of bad years to come. Joseph taught this policy to Pharaoh in Egypt more than 2,000 years ago. Yet the great majority of the governments in the world today do not follow such a policy. They lack either the wisdom or the competence, or both. Should those nations that do manage to put something aside be forced to come to the rescue each time an emergency occurs among the poor nations?

"But it isn't their fault!" some kind-hearted liberals argue. "How can we blame the poor people who are caught in an emergency? Why must they suffer for the sins of their governments?" The concept of blame is simply not relevant here. The real question is, what are the operational consequences of establishing a world food bank? If it is open to every country every time a need develops, slovenly rulers will not be motivated to take Joseph's advice. Someone will always come to their aid. Some countries will deposit food in the world food bank, and others will withdraw it. There will be almost no overlap. As a result of such solutions to food shortage emergencies, the poor countries will not learn to mend their ways, and will suffer progressively greater emergencies as their populations grow.

On the average, poor countries undergo a 2.5 percent increase in   21
population each year; rich countries, about 0.6 percent. Only rich countries have anything in the way of food reserves set aside, and even they
do not have as much as they should. Poor countries have none. If poor
countries received no food from the outside, the rate of their population
growth would be periodically checked by crop failures and famines. But
if they can always draw on a world food bank in time of need, their population can continue to grow unchecked, and so will their "need" for
aid. In the short run, a world food bank may diminish that need, but in
the long run it actually increases the need without limit.

Without some system of worldwide food sharing, the proportion of   22
people in the rich and poor nations might eventually stabilize. The
overpopulated poor countries would decrease in numbers while the rich
countries that had room for more people would increase. But with a
well-meaning system of sharing, such as a world food bank, the growth
differential between the rich and poor countries will not only persist, it
will increase. Because of the higher rate of population growth in the
poor countries of the world, 88 percent of today's children are born
poor, and only 12 percent rich. Year by year the ratio becomes worse as
the fast-reproducing poor outnumber the slow-reproducing rich.

A world food bank is thus a commons in disguise. People will have   23
more motivation to draw from it than to add to any common store. The
less provident and less able will multiply at the expense of the abler
and more provident, bringing eventual ruin upon all who share in the
commons. Besides, any system of "sharing" that amounts to foreign aid
from the rich nations to the poor nations will carry the taint of charity,
which will contribute little to the world peace so devoutly desired by
those who support the idea of a world food bank.

As past U.S. foreign-aid programs have amply and depressingly   24
demonstrated, international charity frequently inspires mistrust and
antagonism rather than gratitude on the part of the recipient nation.

The modern approach to foreign aid stresses the export of technol-   25
ogy and advice, rather than money and food. As an ancient Chinese
proverb goes: "Give a man a fish and he will eat for a day; teach him
how to fish and he will eat for the rest of his days." Acting on this advice, the Rockefeller and Ford Foundations have financed a number of
programs for improving agriculture in the hungry nations. Known as
the "Green Revolution," these programs have led to the development
of "miracle rice" and "miracle wheat," new strains that offer bigger
harvests and greater resistance to crop damage.

Whether or not the Green Revolution can increase food production   26
as much as its champions claim is a debatable but possibly irrelevant
point. Those who support this well-intended humanitarian effort
should first consider some of the fundamentals of human ecology.
Ironically, one man who did was the late Alan Gregg, a vice president

of the Rockefeller Foundation. Two decades ago he expressed strong doubts about the wisdom of such attempts to increase food production. He likened the growth and spread of humanity over the surface of the earth to the spread of cancer in the human body, remarking that "cancerous growths demand food, but, as far as I know, they have never been cured by getting it."

Every human born constitutes a draft on all aspects of the environment: Food, air, water, forests, beaches, wildlife, scenery and solitude. Food can, perhaps, be significantly increased to meet a growing demand. But what about clean beaches, unspoiled forests, and solitude? If we satisfy a growing population's need for food, we necessarily decrease its per capita supply of the other resources needed by people.   27

India, for example, now has a population of 600 million, which increases by 15 million each year. This population already puts a huge load on a relatively impoverished environment. The country's forests are now only a small fraction of what they were three centuries ago, and floods and erosion continually destroy the insufficient farmland that remains. Every one of the 15 million new lives added to India's population puts an additional burden on the environment, and increases the economic and social costs of crowding. However humanitarian our intent, every Indian life saved through medical or nutritional assistance from abroad diminishes the quality of life for those who remain, and for subsequent generations. If rich countries make it possible, through foreign aid, for 600 million Indians to swell to 1.2 billion in a mere 28 years, as their current growth rate threatens, will future generations of Indians thank us for hastening the destruction of their environment? Will our good intentions be sufficient excuse for the consequences of our actions?   28

Without a true world government to control reproduction and the use of available resources, the sharing ethic of the spaceship is impossible. For the foreseeable future, our survival demands that we govern our actions by the ethics of a lifeboat, harsh though they may be. Posterity will be satisfied with nothing else.   29

NOTE

[1] Hardin is referring to the energy crisis of the early 1970s (his essay was first published in 1974).

[2] Margaret Mead (1901–1978): an American anthropologist who argued that differences between men and women are created mostly by cultural influences.

VOCABULARY

commons—land belonging to the community as a whole

posterity—future generations

substantive—of considerable weight or quantity

QUESTIONS

1. Hardin sets out the premises (fundamental assumptions) of his argument in the first seven paragraphs. State these premises as clearly as you can in your own words.

2. Hardin uses both practical and ethical standards of evaluation to develop his argument. What are the main practical justifications for rich nations refusing to help poor nations? What are the main ethical justifications? (See Chapter 11 for more on these standards of evaluation.)

3. In this essay Hardin relies heavily on argument by analogy (rich nations are like lifeboats). How convincing do you find this analogy? What are the strengths and weaknesses of this method of argumentation? (For information on evaluating the logic of a piece of writing, see Chapter 10.)

4. Hardin also relies on cause and effect analysis to develop his argument. Find two or three examples of predictions of terrible consequences. How convincing are these predictions?

5. What tone does the evaluative language in the following sentence create? Is this tone effective?

   > The spaceship metaphor can be dangerous when used by
   > misguided idealists to justify suicidal policies for sharing our
   > resources through uncontrolled immigration and foreign aid.

SUGGESTIONS FOR WRITING

1. Imagine that you are either the director of your local food bank, an organization that Hardin would see as an example of the "tragedy of the commons," or an opponent of food banks. Write a letter to the editor arguing why food banks do or do not provide an important public service. (For examples of letters to the editor, see "*The English Patient* Debate," Readings.)

2. Write a short essay comparing Hardin's perspective on ownership with E. M. Forster's ("My Wood," Readings).

THE VOYAGERS

Linda Hogan

I remember one night, lying on the moist spring earth beside my 1
mother. The fire of stars stretched away from us, and the mysterious darkness traveled without limit beyond where we lay on the turning earth. I could smell the damp new grass that night, but I could not touch or hold such black immensity that lived above our world, could not contain within myself even a small corner of the universe.

There seemed to be two kinds of people: earth people and those 2
others, the sky people, who stumbled over pebbles while they walked around with their heads in clouds. Sky people loved different worlds than I loved; they looked at nests in treetops and followed the long white snake of vapor trails. But I was an earth person, and while I loved to gaze up at night and stars, I investigated the treasures at my feet, the veined wing of a dragonfly opening a delicate blue window to secrets of earth, a lusterless beetle that drank water thirstily from the tip of my finger and was transformed into sudden green and metallic brilliance. It was enough mystery for me to ponder the bones inside our human flesh, bones that through some incredible blueprint of life grow from a moment's sexual passion between a woman and a man, walk upright a short while, then walk themselves back to dust.

Years later, lost in the woods one New Year's eve, a friend found 3
the way home by following the north star, and I began to think that learning the sky might be a practical thing. But it was the image of earth from out in space that gave me upward-gazing eyes. It was the same image that gave the sky people an anchor in the world, for it returned us to our planet in a new and loving way.

To dream of the universe is to know that 4
we are small and brief as insects, born in a flash of rain and gone a moment later. We are delicate and our world is fragile. It was the transgression of Galileo[1] to tell us that we were not the center of the universe, and now, even in our own time, the news of our small being here is treacherous enough that early in the space program, the photographs of Earth were classified as secret documents by the government. It was thought, and rightfully so, that the

Linda Hogan (b. 1947), an associate professor of creative writing and Native American literature at the University of Colorado, is a Chickasaw poet, novelist, and essayist. Her recent works include the novel *Power* (1998), *The Sweet Breathing of Plants: Women and the Green World* (2000), *The Woman Who Watches over the World: A Native Memoir* (2001), and *Sightings: The Gray Whales' Mysterious Journey* (2002). "The Voyagers" comes from *Dwellings: A Spiritual History of the Living World* (1995), essays exploring Hogan's ideas about the interconnections between humans and nature.

image of our small blue Earth would forever change how we see ourselves in context with the world we inhabit.

When we saw the deep blue and swirling white turbulence of our Earth reflected back to us, says photographer Steven Meyers,[2] we also saw "the visual evidence of creative and destructive forces moving around its surface, we saw for the first time the deep blackness of that which surrounds it, we sensed directly, and probably for the first time, our incredibly profound isolation, and the special fact of our being here." It was a world whose intricately linked-together ecosystem could not survive the continuing blows of exploitation.

In 1977, when the Voyagers[3] were launched, one of these spacecraft carried the Interstellar Record, a hoped-for link between earth and space that is filled with the sounds and images of the world around us. It carries parts of our lives all the way out to the great Forever. It is destined to travel out of our vast solar system, out to the far, unexplored regions of space in hopes that somewhere, millions of years from now, someone will find it like a note sealed in a bottle carrying our history across the black ocean of space. This message is intended for the year 8,000,000.

One greeting onboard from Western India says: "Greetings from a human being of the Earth. Please contact." Another, from Eastern China, but resembling one that could have been sent by my own Chickasaw[4] people, says: "Friends of space, how are you all? Have you eaten yet? Come visit us if you have time."

There is so much hope in those greetings, such sweetness. If found, these messages will play our world to a world that's far away. They will sing out the strangely beautiful sounds of Earth, sounds that in all likelihood exist on no other planet in the universe. By the time the record is found, if ever, it is probable that the trumpeting bellows of elephants, the peaceful chirping of frogs and crickets, the wild dogs baying out from the golden needle and record, will be nothing more than a gone history of what once lived on this tiny planet in the curving tail of a spiral galaxy. The undeciphered language of whales will speak to a world not our own, to people who are not us. They will speak of what we value the most on our planet, things that in reality we are almost missing.

A small and perfect world is traveling there, with psalms journeying past Saturn's icy rings, all our treasured life flying through darkness, going its way alone back through the universe. There is the recorded snapping of fire, the song of a river traveling the continent, the living wind passing through dry grasses, all the world that burns and pulses around us, even the comforting sound of a heartbeat taking us back to the first red house of our mothers' bodies, all that, floating through the universe.

The Voyager carries music. A Peruvian wedding song is waiting to 10
be heard in the far, distant regions of space. The Navajo Night Chant[5]
travels through darkness like medicine for healing another broken
world. Blind Willie Johnson's[6] slide guitar and deep down blues are on
that record, in night's long territory.

The visual records aboard the Voyager depict a nearly perfect 11
world, showing us our place within the whole; in the image of a snow-
covered forest, trees are so large that human figures standing at their
base are almost invisible. In the corner of this image is a close-up of a
snow crystal's elegant architecture of ice and air. Long-necked geese
fly across another picture, a soaring eagle. Three dolphins, sun bright
on their silver sides, leap from a great ocean wave. Beneath them are
underwater blue reefs with a shimmering school of fish. It is an abun-
dant, peaceful world, one where a man eats from a vine heavy with
grapes, an old man walks through a field of white daisies, and children
lovingly touch a globe in a classroom. To think that the precious images of what lives on earth beside us, the lives we share with earth,
some endangered, are now tumbling through time and space, more
permanent than we are, and speaking the sacred language of life that
we ourselves have only just begun to remember.

We have sent a message that states what we most value here on 12
earth: respect for all life and ways. It is a sealed world, a seed of what
we may become. What an amazing document is flying above the
clouds, holding Utopia.[7] It is more magical and heavy with meaning
than the cave paintings of Lascaux,[8] more wise than the language of
any holy book. These are images that could sustain us through any
cold season of ice or hatred or pain.

In *Murmurs of Earth*,[9] written by members of the committee who 13
selected the images and recordings, the records themselves are described in a way that attests to their luminous quality of being: "They
glisten, golden, in the sunlight, encased in aluminum cocoons." It
sounds as though, through some magical metamorphosis, this chrysalis
of life will emerge in another part of infinity, will grow to a wholeness
of its own, and return to us alive, full-winged, red, and brilliant.

There is so much hope there that it takes us away from the dark 14
times of horror we live in, a time when the most cruel aspects of our
natures have been revealed to us in regions of earth named Auschwitz,
Hiroshima, My Lai, and Rwanda,[10] a time when televised death is the
primary amusement of our children, when our children are killing one
another on the streets.

At second glance, this vision for a new civilization, by its very pres- 15
ence, shows us what is wrong with our world. Defining Utopia, we see
what we could be now, on earth, at this time, and next to the images of
a better world, that which is absent begins to cry out. The underside of

our lives grows in proportion to what is denied. The darkness is made darker by the record of light. A screaming silence falls between the stars of space. Held inside that silence are the sounds of gunfire, the wailings of grief and hunger, the last, extinct song of a bird. The dammed river goes dry, along with its valleys. Illnesses that plague our bodies live in this crack of absence. The broken link between us and the rest of our world grows too large, and the material of nightmares grows deeper while the promises for peace and equality are empty, are merely dreams without reality.

But how we want it, how we want that half-faced, one-sided God.   16

In earlier American days, when Catholic missions were being   17 erected in Indian country, a European woman, who was one of the first white contacts for a northern tribe of people, showed sacred paintings to an Indian woman. The darker woman smiled when she saw a picture of Jesus and Mary encircled in their haloes of light. A picture of the three kings with their crowns and gifts held her interest. But when she saw a picture of the crucifixion, the Indian woman hurried away to warn others that these were dangerous people, people to fear, who did horrible things to one another. This picture is not carried by the Voyager, for fear we earth people would "look" cruel. There is no image of this man nailed to a cross, no saving violence. There are no political messages, no photographs of Hiroshima. This is to say that we know our own wrongdoings.

Nor is there a true biology of our species onboard because NASA[11]   18 officials vetoed the picture of a naked man and pregnant woman standing side by side, calling it "smut." They allowed only silhouettes to be sent, as if our own origins, the divine flux of creation that passes between a man and a woman, are unacceptable, something to hide. Even picture diagrams of the human organs, musculature, and skeletal system depict no sexual organs, and a photograph showing the birth of an infant portrays only the masked, gloved physician lifting the new life from a mass of sheets, the mother's body hidden. While we might ask if they could not have sent the carved stone gods and goddesses in acts of beautiful sexual intimacy on temple walls in India, this embarrassment about our own carriage of life and act of creative generation nevertheless reveals our feelings of physical vulnerability and discomfort with our own life force.

From an American Indian perspective, there are other problems   19 here. Even the language used in the selection process bespeaks many of the failings of an entire system of thought and education. From this record, we learn about our relationships, not only with people, but with everything on earth. For example, a small gold-eyed frog seen in a human hand might have been a photograph that bridges species, a statement of our kinship with other lives on earth, but the hand is described, almost apologetically, as having "a dirty fingernail." Even the clay of creation has ceased to be the rich element from which life grows. I recall that the Chilean poet Pablo Neruda wrote "What can I say without touching the earth with my hands?"[12] We must wonder what of value can ever be spoken from lives that are lived outside of life, without a love or respect for the land and other lives.

In *Murmurs of Earth*, one of the coauthors writes about hearing   20 dolphins from his room, "breathing, playing with one another. Somehow," he says, "one had the feeling that they weren't just some sea creatures but some very witty and intelligent beings living in the next room." This revealing choice of words places us above and beyond the rest of the world, as though we have stepped out of our natural cycles in our very existence here on earth. And isn't our world full of those rooms? We inhabit only a small space in the house of life. In another is a field of corn. In one more is the jungle world of the macaw. Down the hall, a zebra is moving. Beneath the foundation is the world of snakes and the five beating hearts of the earthworm.

In so many ways, the underside of our lives is here. Even the met-   21 als used in the record tell a story about the spoils of inner earth, the laborers in the hot mines. Their sweat is in that record, hurtling away from our own galaxy.

What are the possibilities, we wonder, that our time capsule will be   22 found? What is the possibility that there are lives other than our own in the universe? Our small galaxy, the way of the milk, the way of sustenance, is only one of billions of galaxies, but there is also the possibility that we are the only planet where life opens, blooms, is gone, and then turns over again. We hope this is not the case. We are so young we hardly know what it means to be a human being, to have natures that allow for war. We barely even know our human histories, so much having unraveled before our time, and while we know that our history creates us, we hope there is another place, another world we can fly to when ours is running out. We have come so far away from wisdom, a wisdom that is the heritage of all people, an old kind of knowing that respects a community of land, animals, plants, and other people as equal to ourselves. Where we know the meaning of relationship.

As individuals, we are not faring much better. We are young. We   23 hardly know who we are. We face the search for ourselves alone. In spite of our search through the universe, we do not know our own personal journeys. We still wonder if the soul weighs half an ounce, if it goes into the sky at the time of our death, if it also reaches out, turning, through the universe.

But still, this innocent reaching out is a form of ceremony, as if the   24 Voyager were a sacred space, a ritual enclosure that contains our dreaming the way a cathedral holds the bones of saints.

The people of earth are reaching out. We are having a collective vi-   25
sion. Like young women and men on a vision quest, we seek a way to
live out the peace of the vision we have sent to the world of stars. We
want to live as if there is no other place, as if we will always be here.
We want to live with devotion to the world of waters and the universe
of life that dwells above our thin roofs.

I remember that night with my mother, looking up at the black sky   26
with its turning stars. It was a mystery, beautiful and distant. Her body I
came from, but our common ancestor is the earth, and the ancestor of
earth is space. That night we were small, my mother and I, and we were
innocent. We were children of the universe. In the gas and dust of life, we
are voyagers. Wait. Stop here a moment. Have you eaten? Come in. Eat.

NOTES

1 Galileo (1564–1642) was an Italian physicist and astronomer who supported Copernicus's theory that the earth and planets moved around the sun. He developed the astronomical telescope, which enabled him to discover craters on the moon, and showed that the Milky Way is composed of stars.

2 Steven Meyers, photographer, is the author of *On Seeing Nature* (Golden, CO: Fulcrum, 1987).

3 Voyagers: unmanned interplanetary probes designed to send information about the outer planetary system back to earth.

4 Chickasaw: a tribe now based in Oklahoma, in the United States.

5 The Navajo are located in Arizona and New Mexico, in the United States. The Night Chant is a sacred ritual.

6 Blind Willie Johnson (c. 1902–1949) was a Texas-born religious singer-songwriter and guitarist who gave black people inspiration in difficult times.

7 Utopia, derived from the title of Thomas More's novel *Utopia* (1516), refers to an imagined ideal place or state of social or political perfection.

8 The cave paintings of Lascaux, situated in Dordogne, France, are paintings of animals believed to date from 15 000 to 13 000 B.C. They were discovered in 1940 in a cave believed to be an ancient centre for the performance of hunting and magical rites.

9 Carl Sagan et al., *Murmurs of Earth: The Voyager Interstellar Record* (New York: Random House, 1978).

10 Auschwitz was a Nazi concentration camp in Poland, operational 1940–1945, where up to four million prisoners died. Hiroshima is a city in Japan, the site of the first wartime use of the atomic bomb, in August 1945, when over 160 000 people died. My Lai refers to the massacre of civilian elderly, women, and children in a village in Vietnam by U.S. army troops in March 1968. Rwanda is a country in east-central Africa, site of the tribal massacre of half a million Tutsis in 1994.

11 NASA: National Aeronautics and Space Administration (U.S.).

12 The quotation is from "Party's End," section XIII of *Ceremonial Songs*, 1961, in Pablo Neruda, *A New Decade: Poems: 1958–1967*. Trans. Ben Belitt and Alastair Reid, New York: Grove, 1969.

VOCABULARY

ecosystem—the ecological balance of the earth's environment

metamorphosis—transformation or change of form by magic or natural development

musculature—the musular system of the body

QUESTIONS

1. How does Hogan develop her initial distinction between "earth people" and "sky people" in the course of her essay?

2. The selection of sounds and images for the Interstellar Record, as Hogan describes it, suggests both a hopeful desire to communicate with other intelligences and a desire to make ourselves look as good as possible. What, in Hogan's opinion, does the Interstellar Record suggest about what we value on our own planet?

3. What does the decision to omit some aspects of life on earth from the space capsule reveal about us?

4. How does Hogan develop a variety of possible meanings for the term *voyager*? How, for example, is the Voyager connected with the dream vision?

5. How would you describe the tone of this essay? Try to be specific about Hogan's attitude towards herself, her readers, and her subject.

6. Do you think Hogan presents a distinctively aboriginal perspective on the issues she discusses in this essay?

SUGGESTION FOR WRITING

Do you think a space capsule should present us as we wish to be seen by strangers, or should we be more honest? If you were in charge of assembling the materials for a space capsule, what aspects of human life and earth's ecosystems would you include? What would you leave out? Write a short essay on this topic.

Structure of essay

Peace
Vision Quest

— "Man" —

Innocence
Sky
Mother Earth

IN PRAISE OF THE HUMBLE COMMA

Pico Iyer

The gods, they say, give breath, and they take it away. But the same could be said—could it not?—of the humble comma. Add it to the present clause, and, of a sudden, the mind is, quite literally, given pause to think; take it out if you wish or forget it and the mind is deprived of a resting place. Yet still the comma gets no respect. It seems just a slip of a thing, a pedant's tick, a blip on the edge of our consciousness, a kind of printer's smudge almost. Small, we claim, is beautiful (especially in the age of the microchip). Yet what is so often used, and so rarely recalled, as the comma—unless it be breath itself? 1

Punctuation, one is taught, has a point: to keep up law and order. Punctuation marks are the road signs placed along the highway of our communication—to control speeds, provide directions and prevent head-on collisions. A period has the unblinking finality of a red light; the comma is a flashing yellow light that asks us only to slow down; and the semicolon is a stop sign that tells us to ease gradually to a halt, before gradually starting up again. By establishing the relations between words, punctuation establishes the relations between the people using words. That may be one reason why schoolteachers exalt it and lovers defy it ("We love each other and belong to each other let's don't ever hurt each other Nicole let's don't ever hurt each other," wrote Gary Gilmore[1] to his girlfriend). A comma, he must have known, "separates inseparables," in the clinching words of H. W. Fowler, King of English Usage.[2] 2

Punctuation, then, is a civic prop, a pillar that holds society upright. (A run-on sentence, its phrases piling up without division, is as unsightly as a sink piled high with dirty dishes.) Small wonder, then, that punctuation was one of the first proprieties of the Victorian age, the age of the corset, that the modernists threw off: the sexual revolution might be said to have begun when Joyce's[3] Molly Bloom spilled out all her private thoughts in 36 pages of unbridled, almost unperioded and officially censored prose; and another rebellion was surely marked when e. e. cummings[4] first felt free to commit "God" to the lower case. 3

Pico Iyer was born in England to Indian parents, grew up in California, and now lives in Japan. He is the author of several travel books, including *Video Night in Kathmandu* and *The Lady and the Monk*. He has recently published *The Global Soul: Jet Lag, Shopping Malls, and the Search for Home* (2000) and *Abandon* (2003). The following essay appeared in *Time*, June 13, 1988.

Punctuation thus becomes the signature of cultures. The hot-blooded Spaniard seems to be revealed in the passion and urgency of his doubled exclamation points and question marks ("*¡Caramba! ¿Quien sabe?*"), while the impassive Chinese traditionally added to his so-called inscrutability by omitting directions from his ideograms. The anarchy and commotion of the '60s were given voice in the exploding exclamation marks, riotous capital letters and Day-Glo italics of Tom Wolfe's[5] spray-paint prose; and in Communist societies, where the State is absolute, the dignity—and divinity—of capital letters is reserved for Ministries, Sub-Committees and Secretariats.   4

Yet punctuation is something more than a culture's birthmark; it scores the music in our minds, gets our thoughts moving to the rhythm of our hearts. Punctuation is the notation in the sheet music of our words, telling us when to rest, or when to raise our voices; it acknowledges that the meaning of our discourse, as of any symphonic composition, lies not in the units but in the pauses, the pacing and the phrasing. Punctuation is the way one bats one's eyes, lowers one's voice or blushes demurely. Punctuation adjusts the tone and color and volume till the feeling comes into perfect focus: not disgust exactly, but distaste; not lust, or like, but love.   5

Punctuation, in short, gives us the human voice, and all the meanings that lie between the words. "You aren't young, are you?" loses its innocence when it loses the question mark. Every child knows the menace of a dropped apostrophe (the parent's "Don't do that" shifting into the more slowly enunciated "Do not do that"), and every believer, the ignominy of having his faith reduced to "faith." Add an exclamation point to "To be or not to be ..." and the gloomy Dane has all the resolve he needs; add a comma, and the noble sobriety of "God save the Queen" becomes a cry of desperation bordering on double sacrilege.   6

Sometimes, of course, our markings may be simply a matter of aesthetics. Popping in a comma can be like slipping on the necklace that gives an outfit quiet elegance, or like catching the sound of running water that complements, as it completes, the silence of a Japanese landscape. When V. S. Naipaul,[6] in his latest novel, writes, "He was a middle-aged man, with glasses," the first comma can seem a little precious. Yet it gives the description a spin, as well as a subtlety, that it otherwise lacks, and it shows that the glasses are not part of the middle-agedness, but something else.   7

Thus all these tiny scratches give us breadth and heft and depth. A world that has only periods is a world without inflections. It is a world without shade. It has a music without sharps and flats. It is a martial music. It has a jackboot rhythm. Words cannot bend and curve. A comma, by comparison, catches the gentle drift of the mind in thought, turning in on itself and back on itself, reversing, redoubling and returning along the course of its own sweet river music; while the   8 semicolon brings clauses and thoughts together with all the silent discretion of a hostess arranging guests around her dinner table.

Punctuation, then, is a matter of care. Care for words, yes, but also, and more important, for what the words imply. Only a lover notices the small things: the way the afternoon light catches the nape of a neck, or how a strand of hair slips out from behind an ear, or the way a finger curls around a cup. And no one scans a letter so closely as a lover, searching for its small print, straining to hear its nuances, its gasps, its sighs and hesitations, poring over the secret messages that lie in every cadence. The difference between "Jane (whom I adore)" and "Jane, whom I adore—" marks all the distance between ecstasy and heartache. "No iron can pierce the heart with such force as a period put at just the right place," in Isaac Babel's[7] lovely words; a comma can let us hear a voice break, or a heart. Punctuation, in fact, is a labor of love. Which brings us back, in a way, to gods. 9

NOTE

[1] Gary Gilmore, convicted of the cold-blooded murder of a Utah gas attendant and a Utah motel owner, gained notoriety partly through his repeated demands to be executed. He is the subject of Norman Mailer's *The Executioner's Song*.

[2] H. W. Fowler (1858–1933) was the author of a number of definitive books on the use and abuse of the English language, notably *The King's English* and *A Dictionary of Modern English Usage*.

[3] James Joyce was the author of *Ulysses*, a modern novel which pioneered the description of characters in terms of the uninterrupted stream of their thoughts. *Ulysses* ends with the extended monologue by Molly Bloom, the wife of the book's central character, Leopold Bloom.

[4] e. e. cummings was an early modern poet whose typographical innovations startled his American readers in the 1920s.

[5] Tom Wolfe, contemporary American journalist and novelist, is best known for pioneering the New Journalism, a flamboyant form of nonfiction employing fictional techniques.

[6] V. S. Naipaul, prize-winning novelist, short story writer and essayist, was born in Trinidad to Indian parents, and has spent many years in England.

[7] Isaac Babel wrote short stories about Jewish life in Russia in the earlier years of the twentieth century. He was arrested in 1939, during the rule of Joseph Stalin, and died shortly afterwards.

QUESTIONS

1. List the various functions of punctuation that Pico Iyer discusses in this essay. Which of these functions does he finally see as most valuable, and why?

2. Iyer makes extensive use of similes, metaphors, and analogies in this essay. What does he compare punctuation to? How effective are these comparisons in explaining the nature and purpose of punctuation?

3. Where does Iyer's use of punctuation demonstrate his points? Is this method of explanation effective? Clear?

4. Do you agree with Iyer's statement that punctuation is the "signature of cultures"? Do his comments on the "hot-blooded Spaniard" and the "impassive Chinese" undermine the credibility of this section of the essay?

SUGGESTIONS FOR WRITING

Conventions about the use of punctuation and capitalization have changed considerably since the 18th century. Select a paragraph from Jonathan Swift's "A Modest Proposal" (Readings) and note where the punctuation is the same as it would be according to today's conventions and where it is different. Using Iyer's essay as a guide, write a paragraph explaining the purposes different types of punctuation seem to have for Swift.

OR

Select a paragraph from another essay you like in the Readings and analyze the writer's use of punctuation.

A LAMENT FOR QUALITY

Ann Dowsett Johnston

It was prom night in my neck of the woods recently, and as far as I 1
can tell, the evening unfolded pretty much according to script. The
girls were shiny and beautiful, the boys tuxed and handsome. As always, a certain handful seemed hell-bent on redefining the word fun,
and just about everyone broke curfew. But the morning after, when a
group of mothers headed off on a Sunday walk, the topic of curfews
was pretty low on the totem pole. No, the hot-button issue was the
same as it had been the week before, and the week before that as well.
Namely, where was this fresh-faced group heading in September?
Which university was the best bet? (Read: the least crowded.) One
mother was notably silent, the one whose son is headed to the States.
But for the rest, the debate was hot. If Ontario universities were going
to be filled to the rafters, what was wrong with a geographical cure?
Surely it was less crowded at UBC? McGill? Surely you could outfox
the system by heading elsewhere? Right?

Actually, wrong. It's a heck of a question, but the simple answer is 2
no. Why? Because no province in Canada has made higher education a
high priority. What we have is a series of petrie dish[1] experiments in
public policy. Some better than others, but overall, nothing to write
home about. Despite all the evidence that history has repeated itself,
with the baby boom generation producing a decent number of babies
themselves, and even though this is a knowledge economy in which
brains are the prime commodity by which we compete, the ugly truth
is this: somehow we forgot to make the proper reinvestments in higher
education. Sure, there have been some inter-
esting federal initiatives, especially those tar-
geted at research. But let's be honest: in the
battle for public dollars, health has stolen all
the thunder. As Stéphane Dion[2] once said,
"Popular pressure is on health because people
die in hospitals and they do not die in universities—except at times from boredom."

Well, sure. But doesn't the future health of 3
Canada depend on a well-educated public?
Shouldn't we have done a better job in getting

Since 1992 Ann Dowsett Johnston has
overseen the controversial *Maclean's* university rankings, a project that has won
her five gold National Magazine Awards.
A recurrent theme in Johnston's writing
on education is the need for greater ac-
countability. She is editor at large at
Maclean's and a regular columnist.

"A Lament for Quality" was published in
Maclean's, May 6, 2002. Reprinted by permission of *Maclean's* Magazine.

ready for the biggest class ever? Did it not strike anyone as odd that while the Americans boosted their investment in public universities by 30 per cent over the past 20 years, Canadians shrunk theirs by 20 per cent? Did no one notice that the Irish had followed suit? And the Koreans. And the French. And the Australians. I could go on.

When I headed to university in 1971, the student-faculty ratio was 23 to one. Today? Thirty-nine to one. And that gap will only widen. Canadian universities are expecting an additional 200,000 students over the next decade. Meanwhile, the number of faculty is 10 per cent lower than what it was a decade ago. Yikes. 4

Now, in the best of all possible worlds, the federal government and the provinces would quit their squabbling and show true leadership, working together as their counterparts did in the 1960s. In a perfect world, they would use some of that $15-billion surplus to boost operating grants, giving Canadian universities the resources they need to renew faculty. They would shift the responsibility for setting tuition to the universities themselves (as British Columbia just did). And yes, tuition would rise (as it did at B.C. institutions, when a six-year freeze was lifted in February). Finally, all universities would earmark a significant portion of the new revenue for three purposes: increased financial aid, improvement of the learning environment, and better communication with the K-12 system, to ensure that access was preserved. 5

Yes, if you dreamed in technicolour, that's what would happen. But let's be realistic: at best, operating grants are going to stay right where they are. Which means that if the learning environment is going to improve, tuition must go up. And yes, the three other conditions must apply. 6

Now, some will say that I'm letting government off the hook. But last I looked, government wasn't *on* the hook. As Canadians, we pride ourselves on university access. But isn't it time we asked: access to what? If education is one generation's debt to the next, how can we believe we are making good on that debt when course offerings are shrinking and multiple-choice exams are becoming increasingly common? Freezing tuition, or keeping it low, is not a cost-free policy for students investing upwards of four years on a mediocre experience. 7

If, as Arthur Koestler[3] once suggested, humans were equipped with necks for the sole purpose of sticking them out, isn't it time that some of us put our necks to good use? Bill Leggett, the principal of Queen's University, certainly should be commended for using his: recently, he asked Ontario to approve a proposal whereby the university would raise tuition in all regulated programs by 10 per cent in each of the next four years. By 2005, fees would amount to $5,900—less than the current tuition at Acadia. With the additional funds, the university was going to significantly boost student financial aid, upgrade the learning environment, and hire faculty and staff to reduce the student-faculty 8 ratios in Arts and Science. The government said no. Now, instead of hiring 50 faculty in Arts and Science, the university is eliminating 22 faculty positions. Quality, once again, is about to be compromised. And this mother, for one, is shaking her head.

NOTES

[1] Petrie dish: a dish used for conducting biological experiments.

[2] Stéphane Dion has been the Minister for Intergovernmental Affairs in the Canadian government since 1996.

[2] Arthur Koestler (1905–1983) was a Hungarian-born British writer, political correspondent, and scientific editor. His masterpiece is his novel *Darkness at Noon*, notable for its humanism and its portrayal of political corruption.

QUESTIONS

1. Why does Johnston use a narrative introduction to establish a context for her argument? Is it effective?

2. Johnston argues that the quality of education offered by Canadian universities is declining. What evidence can you provide to support or challenge her argument?

3. What standard(s) of evaluation does Johnston use? Identify the paragraphs where she indicates her standard(s). (See Chapters 10 and 11.)

4. Do you see any fallacies in the logic of Johnston's argument? (For information on logical fallacies, see Chapter 10.)

5. Johnston seems to be writing as a parent to other parents. Do you think her argument is effective for this audience? Would it be effective for other audiences?

SUGGESTIONS FOR WRITING

1. Write a summary of Johnston's essay (see Chapter 3).

2. Johnston's thesis is that universities should be allowed to raise tuition fees to ensure students receive an acceptable quality of education. Can you see other ways to improve the quality of post-secondary education? Draft a letter to the president of your college or university that sets out your key ideas. Then write a paragraph or two explaining why particular arguments and evidence you used in your letter will appeal to this reader.

HE WAS A BOXER WHEN I WAS SMALL

Lenore Keeshig-Tobias

His thundering rages are most vivid, his tears subtle. Watching and 1
feeling for them, but unable to bridge the gap, I learned to love,
hate him all in the same breath. No one ever knew this. They saw a kid
in love with her father.

He was a boxer when I was small. People say he was good and 2
would have made it had he started younger, but he had a wife and
growing family to provide for. Amateur boxing paid nothing, but he
loved it. I think he must have been about twenty-two then. He claims
that we were too young to have seen him fight, but I remember.

I remember the lights, the ring, my mother shouting "Kill him, 3
Don, kill him!" and my sister eating popcorn. I remember how he'd
shadow box at home, punching, dancing lightly, swinging left—left—
right, and missing because there was nothing there except air.

His prowess in the ring must have cowed my mother during his 4
drunken rages. Or maybe it was his thundering voice, or the way the
furniture went flying. Yet, with all his storming and her crying, I could-
n't help but think that there was something more, something he could-
n't articulate. When his ferocity gave way to tears of exasperation,
I would cry with him, my dad, the boxer, the young man out to beat
the world.

"It's not his fault," I would argue. "It's not all his fault, it's Mom's 5
fault too," I would tell Gramma, even if I didn't know whose fault it was.
She would disdainfully look off into the tree whenever I answered with
this. Mom had Gramma to stick up for her. Dad had no one, only me.

There were, of course, times when things were fine. Dad would 6
have a good job, Mom would be fresh with child,[1] and my sisters and brothers carefree.
We would spread a blanket in the front yard,
or gather around the kitchen table. Dad would
tell stories of Nanabush,[2] stories of long ago
when only the Indians and animals lived here.
Good ole Nanabush danced before our eyes.
We saw his courage, his generosity and love for
the animals and our people. We also saw his
anger, miserly ways, and blundering practical
jokes, but we loved him and would laugh until
we cried.

Lenore Keeshig-Tobias (b. 1950) is an
Ojibway poet, playwright, fiction writer,
editor, filmmaker, and cultural activist. She
has edited *The Ontario Indian*, *Sweetgrass*,
and *The Magazine to Re-establish the
Trickster*. Her children's book, *Bird Talk*
(1991), is a bilingual English/Ojibway story.
She recently edited *Into the Moon: Heart,
Mind, Body, Soul*, a collection of writings by
the Native Women's Writing Circle (1996).

This essay is reprinted with permission of
Lenore Keeshig-Tobias.

At other times we would play, all of us, seven, eight, nine of us   7
rolling and tumbling while Mom sat back beaming like a big fat sun.
We'd pretend box, then race, roll, and tumble again. How I wished
those times would go on and on. He would stand shoulders up to the
sky, as we climbed. He could carry all of us on his back.

One summer my sides ached with laughter. Then one day, I moved   8
to the edge of the blanket and sat back to watch my sisters and brothers giggle and climb. Dad leaned forward, then down on hands and
knees, all those laughing children on his back. That was when I noticed
grey hairs hiding in his side-burns. I went to my room, dug out his boxing pictures, and cried.

I was about ten at the time, my dad about twenty-nine, and my   9
mother twenty-eight. After that summer I never again played like that
with the others. I felt too old, and instead I stood back and watched. I
watched my sisters and brothers grow up. I watched him grow older,
fighting all the way.

When he went to school, he tells us, he spoke only Ojibway[3] and a   10
bit of French. His grandmother was French. The only English he knew
was yes and no. Indian kids, in those days, were not allowed to speak
anything but English in school. So besides being punished for speaking
Ojibway, he was also punished for giving the wrong answer which was
either yes or no.

He says he eventually learned to read, write, and do arithmetic,   11
and he laughs when he tells us how he would get on the teacher's good
side and then steal test answers for the rest of the class. She never had
to keep any of them in after class, but then she never realized how
they had cheated and helped each other. She never realized what a
bunch of stupid kids she graduated.

My dad never graduated. He learned enough to be able to go out   12
and get a job.

Once, Dad was working in Toronto as an industrial painter (Indian   13
men are noted for their surefootedness in high places). Mom, the kids,
and I sat around the supper table. We didn't expect him home until the
weekend, but there he was, standing in the doorway with his suitcase.
Later that evening, I heard him confiding to Mom his reason for coming home.

He had beat up a fellow worker, a wisecracking whiteman, who had   14
been bugging him for weeks. The ambulance was being called for when
he left. My dad was afraid, afraid because he was Indian and because
he had once been a boxer.

In between the various jobs on the reserve or high-painting and   15
ironwork off in some big city, there were bouts of drinking and bouts of
fanatical Christianity with thunderous preaching. We cowered every
weekend waiting for him to erupt.

"Damn you, goddamn you," I would curse under my breath. "Why 16
do you make our lives so miserable?"

We grew up as Christians, something I shall never forgive those 17
Catholic missionaries for, although for a time it was the most settling
thing in our lives. Dad made sure, in spite of everything else, his kids
went to church. If he couldn't be a good father to us, then God would.
But God wasn't an Indian, or a boxer, and my dad was. His visits to the
Parish priest taught him fear of the Lord. But we went faithfully to
church because of fear of our dad, and fear for our furniture.

We should all be good at sports because Indians are known for 18
that. Look at Jim Thorpe, Tom Longboat, George Armstrong.[4] We
should all get a good education and not be stupid like him. We should
all go to church every Sunday and not drink like him ... he'd preach.

I got fed up with things, eventually. I was no good at sports. School 19
was boring. I stopped going to church and even dared to argue with my
dad. Finally, Mom and Dad had the priest come talk to me, to get me to
go back to church and school.

The old man would listen when I told him that I would like to 20
pray under the trees. He laughed. We argued. He laughed again, shook
his head, and said something about excommunication. I told him off,
that I would rather go to hell and burn with the rest of my heathen
savage ancestors because there would be too few Indians in heaven
and I'd probably get lonely. The old missionary wobbled into the
house, quite shaken, and told my dad that I was "lost." Dad came out,
white-faced, and beat me. He told me to leave, that he had other kids
to worry about.

I settled into my own life, fighting bouts of my own, but continued 21
hearing of his through letters and phone calls.

Was there no end? Mom and the kids kept looking to me for an- 22
swers, as if I were the referee. I'd listen, but offer no solution. I was beginning to see what was driving him. I was beginning to understand
that he was fighting the world, and there was no way I'd turn on him
behind his back.

Afraid at first, I began to meet him blow for blow. People would say 23
that I was like my dad. I thought I was like myself. I never did learn to
box. He always laughed at the way I clenched my fists. I never was really interested in boxing. Being the eldest daughter of a boxer was
enough, quite enough. But I can, however, thunder as loud as he can.

He's mellowed somewhat. And there have been times in quiet talk 24
when he has acknowledged his weaknesses, his aspirations and exas-
perations for all of us in our effort to grow up and become educated. I
guess these talks are what comes with being the oldest of ten.

Thundering rages, subtle tears ... I have seen him cry with frustra- 25
tion, cry out in anger, and in pride, pride in his beautiful young looking

wife and her accomplishments, his kids and grandchildren. Yet, the tears that touch me the most are those that roll down his cheeks when he talks of Nanabush.

Good ole Nanabush, the paradox, the son of a mortal woman and   26
the thundering West Wind, a boy raised by his grandmother, the best loved of all Ojibway spirits. It was through his transgressions as well as his virtue that Nanabush taught his people. And they never negated or attempted to cover up his imperfections. Dad cries when he talks of Nanabush.

I dreamed of Dad. This was after he had argued and I told him why   27
I would never go to church and how I could not understand why he still went. After all, the church, like the government, had set out to break the Indian, to make him feel less than what he was. I did not hold back that time and told him everything I had ever felt or thought about concerning our people. He couldn't answer and politely admitted, "You've got me. But I can't argue with you now, I'll answer you when I'm not drinking."

This was the first time I had won an argument against him, and it   28
didn't dawn on me until days later. We had talked, sipping our beer and not shouting. Arguments in our house were usually won by whoever could shout the loudest.

In my dreams I was fighting. Someone or something evil, disguised,   29
was pushing me the wrong way, trying to make me do something I did not want to do. Thinking to expose this by disrobing it, I reached out and tugged. It turned to fend me off and guard its robe fiercely. We struggled until I stood alone with a bundle of clothes and flesh in my arms, and dread realization that I had killed another human being. Overwhelmed with guilt, I started to cry. Who would believe this act was unintentional? Then I saw him off in the distance, standing alone, his boxer's dressing-gown over his shoulders.

I could tell him. I could tell him everything. But would he listen?   30
Understand? Lowering my burden, covering and folding it carefully I cowered toward him. His head was down, his shoulders slouched. He didn't see me until I spoke.

"Dad," I sobbed, "I killed someone who was pushing me the wrong   31
way. I didn't mean to do it, Dad, help me."

He put his arms around me, tightly.   32

"I'll beat the world," he said and punched at the air.   33

NOTES

[1] Fresh with child: newly pregnant.

[2] Nanabush is a figure from Ojibway mythology; it is explained later in the story that he is "the son of a mortal woman and the thundering West Wind."

[3] Ojibway is the language of the Ojibway tribe, originally from around Lake Superior.

[4] Jim Thorpe (1887–1953), athlete of the Sauk and Fox tribes, was the winner of the gold medal for pentathlon and decathlon in the 1912 Stockholm Olympics, and also a professional baseballer from 1913 to 1919. Tom Longboat (1887–1949) was a distance runner from the Onondaga tribe. George Armstrong (b. 1930), originally from the Six Nations Reserve, was captain of the Toronto Maple Leafs when they won the Stanley Cup in 1967.

VOCABULARY

prowess—skill

QUESTIONS

1. In the opening paragraph, Keeshig-Tobias says that she "learned to love, hate [her father] all in same breath." How does she use specific details to help us understand her ambivalent response to her father?

2. How and why do her feelings about her father change as she grows older?

3. What does boxing mean to Keeshig-Tobias' father? To Keeshig-Tobias herself? Why does she begin and end the essay with boxing?

4. In what ways is her father like Nanabush? How important are these similarities?

5. What prompts Keeshig-Tobias' dream about her father? How does this dream help us to understand her feelings about him when she is an adult?

6. How closely connected are boxing and tears in Keeshig-Tobias' memories of her father?

7. What is the thesis of this essay? Do you think Keeshig-Tobias' decision to imply her thesis rather than state it directly strengthens or weakens her essay?

SUGGESTION FOR WRITING

Sometimes you can get a perspective on a person you want to write about by developing the implications of a particular activity (cooking, gardening, fixing the plumbing, playing soccer) that you associate with him or her. Choose a family member and write an essay that imitates some of the techniques you have observed in "He Was a Boxer When I Was Small." Remember that you will need to work out your thesis even though you may not state it explicitly.

PROFITS BY THE TRUCKLOAD

Ross Laver

The history of economics is full of irrational buying frenzies and other such examples of the madness of crowds. There was the notorious tulip bulb craze in 17th-century Holland, the South Sea Bubble of 1720,[1] the 1920s stock market frenzy and the speculative real estate binge of the late 1980s.

To that list, add one more: the great four-wheel-drive truck craze of the 1990s.

The evidence is on every downtown street and suburban parking lot. Where once there were cars, now there are hulking GMC Suburbans, Ford Explorers, Jeep Grand Cherokees and Land Rovers—gas-guzzling, wilderness-conquering sport utility vehicles that in the hands of most owners never venture farther off-road than the local car wash.

For the auto industry, the sport utility fad is a gold mine. In 1990, North Americans bought 700,000 SUVs. Last year, the total hit two million, and some manufacturers believe it will swell to 2.5 million in three years, representing one out of every six vehicles sold.

Not only that, but there seems to be no limit to the cost increases that image-conscious truck buyers are willing to absorb. In 1993, the sticker price on a Jeep Grand Cherokee Limited, with leather seats and other luxury appointments, was $33,555. Today it's $42,305, and buyers still can't get enough of them. In the same period, the list price of a Chevy Blazer SLE jumped from $20,898 to $30,335, while the Nissan Pathfinder SE went from $25,790 to $35,998.

To be fair, almost every sport utility on the market has been substantially upgraded in recent years, with new equipment and safety features like airbags and protective side-door beams. But even allowing for that, the price increases for SUVs have far outstripped those for cars. The Ford Explorer XLT, for example, now lists for 35 per cent more than the 1993 model, compared with the 27 per cent increase on a redesigned Ford Taurus GL sedan. "It's like everything else in this world—it's what the market will bear," says a spokesman for a rival automaker, acknowledging that his company, too, has been quick to exploit the SUV craze.

Ross Laver worked for five years as a reporter for *The Globe and Mail* before moving to *Maclean's*, where he is currently the assistant managing editor. He is co-author of *Savage Messiah* (1993), a biography of Quebec-born cult leader Roch Theriault, and author of *Random Excess: The Wild Ride of Michael Cowpland and Corel* (1998).

"Profits by the Truckload" is reprinted with permission of *Maclean's* Magazine.

But how long can it last? The manufacturers' profit on a sport util- 7
ity currently runs anywhere from $5000 to $13,000—an astonishing
margin by industry standards. Traditional four-door sedans, by comparison, have become commodity products, yielding a few hundred
dollars at best after rebates and low-interest lease deals. Many smaller
car models actually lose money and are kept in production only to satisfy U.S. government standards for average fleet fuel economy.

The optimists in the car industry predict that four-wheel-drives 8
will remain lucrative for years to come. As proof, they point to surveys
of younger car buyers. Among those born since the end of the baby
boom, well over 60 per cent select an SUV as their preferred vehicle.
(Minivans are out because their parents drove them.)

But that only takes account of the demand side of the equation. 9
Those fat profit margins ultimately depend on a shortage of supply,
which won't last forever. Last month, Chrysler announced a $1.3-billion
investment in six Detroit factories, primarily to increase truck production capacity. Chrysler is also converting a car plant in Delaware
to begin production this summer of the Dodge Durango, a new mid-
sized SUV. Meanwhile, Ford will soon launch the high-end Lincoln
Navigator—with polished walnut dashboard and acres of chrome—to
compete against Mercedes-Benz's new M-class. Chrysler, Ford and GM
are also mulling plans for compact sport-utes that could go up against
the recently launched Toyota RAV4 and Honda CR-V, as well as the
forthcoming Subaru Forester. All told, says Jim Hall, vice-president of
the market research firm AutoPacific Inc., the number of sport utility
models is forecast to grow from 34 in 1996 to 55 in the year 2005.

With profits so high, it's not surprising that everyone wants in on 10
the action. But if history teaches anything, it is that markets this hot
inevitably flame out.

NOTE

[1] These are examples, as are the two that follow, of schemes in which eager but misguided
investment frenzy was followed by market collapse.

QUESTIONS

1. In this article, Laver makes three main points about sport utility vehicles (SUVs):
   they are very popular, they are increasingly expensive, and they make lots of money
   for manufacturers. Are these points arranged in an order of increasing importance?
   Explain your answer.

2. What main kind of evidence does Laver use to support these assertions? Is this evidence convincing?

3. Does he include any evidence to support his final comment that "markets this hot
   inevitably flame out"?

4. Do you think Laver's overall purpose is to explain or to persuade?

5. Laver explains why SUVs are so popular with manufacturers, but he doesn't say much about why they are so popular with consumers. What do you think?

SUGGESTION FOR WRITING

If you had plenty of money, what kind of vehicle would enable you to express your personality and fulfill your fantasies? Write a short essay describing the vehicle (it does not have to have four wheels) of your dreams.

EMBRACED BY THE NEEDLE

Gabor Maté

Addictions always originate in unhappiness, even if hidden. They are 1
emotional anesthetics; they numb pain. The first question—always—is not "Why the addiction?" but "Why the pain?" The answer, ever the same, is scrawled with crude eloquence on the wall of my patient Anna's room at the Portland Hotel in the heart of Vancouver's Downtown Eastside: "Any place I went to, I wasn't wanted. And that bites large."

The Downtown Eastside is considered to be Canada's drug capital, 2
with an addict population of 3,000 to 5,000 individuals. I am a staff physician at the Portland, a non-profit harm-reduction facility where most of the clients are addicted to cocaine, to alcohol, to opiates like heroin, or to tranquilizers—or to any combination of these things. Many also suffer from mental illness. Like Anna, a 32-year-old poet, many are HIV positive or have full-blown AIDS. The methadone[1] I prescribe for their opiate dependence does little for the emotional anguish compressed in every heartbeat of these driven souls.

Methadone staves off the torment of opiate withdrawal, but, unlike 3
heroin, it does not create a "high" for regular users. The essence of that high was best expressed by a 27-year-old sex-trade worker. "The first time I did heroin," she said, "it felt like a warm, soft hug." In a phrase, she summed up the psychological and chemical cravings that make some people vulnerable to substance dependence.

No drug is, in itself, addictive. Only about 8 per cent to 15 per cent 4
of people who try, say alcohol or marijuana, go on to addictive use. What makes them vulnerable? Neither physiological predispositions nor individual moral failures explain drug addictions. Chemical and emotional vulnerability are the products of life experience, according to current brain research and developmental psychology.

Most human brain growth occurs following 5
birth; physical and emotional interactions determine much of our brain development. Each brain's circuitry and chemistry reflects individual life experiences as much as inherited tendencies.

Gabor Maté, who has attention deficit disorder himself, is a family physician and counsellor with a special interest in counselling adults, parents, and children with ADD. A long-time medical columnist for *The Vancouver Sun* and *The Globe and Mail*, he is also the author of *Scattered Minds: A New Look at the Origins and Healing of Attention Deficit Disorder* and *When the Body Says No: The Cost of Hidden Stress.*

"Embraced by the Needle" was published in *The Globe and Mail*, August 27, 2001.

For any drug to work in the brain, the nerve cells have to have receptors—sites where the drug can bind. We have opiate receptors because our brain has natural opiate-like substances, called endorphins, chemicals that participate in many functions, including the regulation of pain and mood. Similarly, tranquilizers of the benzodiazepine[2] class, such as Valium, exert their effect at the brain's natural benzodiazepine receptors. 6

Infant rats who get less grooming from their mothers have fewer natural benzo receptors in the part of the brain that controls anxiety. Brains of infant monkeys separated from their mothers for only a few days are measurably deficient in the key neuro-chemical, dopamine. 7

It is the same with human beings. Endorphins are released in the infant's brain when there are warm, non-stressed, calm interactions with the parenting figures. Endorphins, in turn, promote the growth of receptors and nerve cells, and the discharge of other important brain chemicals. The fewer endorphin-enhancing experiences in infancy and early childhood, the greater the need for external sources. Hence, the greater vulnerability to addictions. 8

Distinguishing skid row addicts is the extreme degree of stress they had to endure early in life. Almost all women now inhabiting Canada's addiction capital suffered sexual assaults in childhood, as did many of the males. Childhood memories of serial abandonment or severe physical and psychological abuse are common. The histories of my Portland patients tell of pain upon pain. 9

Carl, a 36-year-old native, was banished from one foster home after another, had dishwashing liquid poured down his throat for using foul language at age 5, and was tied to a chair in a dark room to control his hyperactivity. When angry at himself—as he was recently, for using cocaine—he gouges his foot with a knife as punishment. His facial expression was that of a terrorized urchin who had just broken some family law and feared draconian retribution. I reassured him I wasn't his foster parent, and that he didn't owe it to me not to screw up. 10

But what of families where there was not abuse, but love, where parents did their best to provide their children with a secure nurturing home? One also sees addictions arising in such families. The unseen factor here is the stress the parents themselves lived under even if they did not recognize it. That stress could come from relationship problems, or from outside circumstances such as economic pressure or political disruption. The most frequent source of hidden stress is the parents' own childhood histories that saddled them with emotional baggage they had never become conscious of. What we are not aware of in ourselves, we pass on to our children. 11

Stressed, anxious, or depressed parents have great difficulty initiating enough of those emotionally rewarding, endorphin-liberating interactions with their children. Later in life such children may experience 12 a hit of heroin as the "warm, soft hug" my patient described: What they didn't get enough of before, they can now inject.

Feeling alone, feeling there has never been anyone with whom to   13
share their deepest emotions, is universal among drug addicts. That is what Anna had lamented on her wall. [No matter how much love a parent has, the child does not experience being wanted unless he or she is made absolutely safe to express exactly how unhappy, or angry, or hate-filled he or she may feel at times.] The sense of unconditional love, of being fully accepted even when most ornery, is what no addict ever experienced in childhood—often not because the parents did not have it to give, simply because they did not know how to transmit it to the child.

Thesis

Addicts rarely make the connection between troubled childhood   14
experiences and self-harming habits. They blame themselves—and that is the greatest wound of all, being cut off from their natural self-compassion. "I was hit a lot," 40-year-old Wayne says, "but I asked for it. Then I made some stupid decisions." And would he hit a child, no matter how much that child "asked for it"? Would he blame that child for "stupid decisions"?

Wayne looks away. "I don't want to talk about that crap," says this   15
tough man, who has worked on oil rigs and construction sites and served 15 years in jail for robbery. He looks away and wipes tears from his eyes.

NOTES

[1] Methadone is a synthetic narcotic used in the treatment of drug addictions.

[2] Benzodiazepines (BZDs) are sedative-hypnotic agents widely used to treat conditions like anxiety and insomnia, and also to induce pre-operative relaxation.

VOCABULARY

hyperactivity—the state of being unusually or excessively active, sometimes identified as a childhood disorder

neurochemical—chemical element found in the brain

opiate—a medicine or substance containing opium

physiological—pertaining to the body

QUESTIONS

1. Maté uses several direct quotations from addicts, some in street language. Does this technique increase or decrease the credibility of his statements?

2. Maté discusses addicts' feelings, the workings of endorphins and other chemicals in the brain, and the dynamics of stressed and dysfunctional families. Can we assume that he, as a physician, has the authority to speak on these topics? Are there any places in the essay where Maté seems to lack authority for his comments?

3. How does the diction of the essay convey Maté's attitude to the drug addicts he treats? List some key words or phrases that convey his attitude.

4. The essay ends with a story about "40-year-old Wayne" rather than with a conclusion summarizing the development of the thesis. Why do you think Maté chooses to conclude in this way? Is the conclusion effective?

SUGGESTION FOR WRITING

Interview a classmate about his or her experience or views of a current social issue. Then write a one-page essay using direct quotations from the interview that support your thesis or argue against it. For guidelines on using quotations effectively, see Quotations in Part 3, Handbook for Final Editing.

UNCHOPPING A TREE

W. S. Merwin

Start with the leaves, the small twigs, and the nests that have been 1
shaken, ripped, or broken off by the fall; these must be gathered
and attached once again to their respective places. It is not arduous
work, unless major limbs have been smashed or mutilated. If the fall
was carefully and correctly planned, the chances of anything of the
kind happening will have been reduced. Again, much depends upon
the size, age, shape, and species of the tree. Still, you will be lucky if
you can get through this stage without having to use machinery. Even
in the best of circumstances it is a labor that will make you wish often
that you had won the favor of the universe of ants, the empire of mice,
or at least a local tribe of squirrels, and could enlist their labors and
their talents. But no, they leave you to it. They have learned, with
time. This is men's work. It goes without saying that if the tree was
hollow in whole or in part, and contained old nests of bird or mammal
or insect, or hoards of nuts or such structures as wasps or bees build
for their survival, the contents will have to be repaired where necessary, and reassembled, insofar as possible, in their original order, including the shells of nuts already opened. With spiders' webs you must
simply do the best you can. We do not have the spider's weaving equipment, nor any substitute for the leaf's living bond with its point of at-
tachment and nourishment. It is even harder to simulate the latter
when the leaves have once become dry—as they are bound to do, for
this is not the labor of a moment. Also it hardly needs saying that this
is the time for repairing any neighboring trees or bushes or other
growth that may have been damaged by the
fall. The same rules apply. Where neighboring
trees were of the same species it is difficult not
to waste time conveying a detached leaf back
to the wrong tree. Practice, practice. Put your
hope in that.

W. S. Merwin was born in New York in 1927
and is principally known for his poetry,
though he won the P.E.N. Translation Prize
in 1968 for his book *Selected Translations
1948–1968.* He won the Pulitzer Prize in
1970 for his book of poetry *The Carrier of
Ladders* and gave the Pulitzer Prize money
to the draft resistance. Recent titles include *The Mays of Ventadorn* and a translation of *Sir Gawain and the Green Knight*
(both 2002).

Now the tackle must be put into place or 2
the scaffolding, depending on the surroundings
and the dimensions of the tree. It is ticklish
work. Almost always it involves, in itself, further damage to the area, which will have to be
corrected later. But as you've heard, it can't be
helped. And care now is likely to save you considerable trouble later. Be careful to grind
nothing into the ground.

At last the time comes for the erecting of the trunk. By now it will 3
scarcely be necessary to remind you of the delicacy of this huge skeleton. Every motion of the tackle, every slight upward heave of the
trunk, the branches, their elaborately re-assembled panoply of leaves
(now dead) will draw from you an involuntary gasp. You will watch for
a leaf or a twig to be snapped off yet again. You will listen for the nuts
to shift in the hollow limb and you will hear whether they are indeed
falling into place or are spilling in disorder—in which case, or in the
event of anything else of the kind—operations will have to cease, of
course, while you correct the matter. The raising itself is no small enterprise, from the moment when the chains tighten around the old
bandages until the bole hangs vertical above the stump, splinter above
splinter. Now the final straightening of the splinters themselves can
take place (the preliminary work is best done while the wood is still
green and soft, but at times when the splinters are not badly twisted
most of the straightening is left until now, when the torn ends are face
to face with each other). When the splinters are perfectly complementary the appropriate fixative is applied. Again we have no duplicate of
the original substance. Ours is extremely strong, but it is rigid. It is
limited to surfaces, and there is no play in it. However the core is not
the part of the trunk that conducted life from the roots up into the
branches and back again. It was relatively inert. The fixative for this
part is not the same as the one for the outer layers and the bark, and
if either of these is involved in the splintered section they must receive applications of the appropriate adhesives. Apart from being in-
correct and probably ineffective, the core fixative would leave a scar
on the bark.

When all is ready the splintered trunk is lowered onto the splinters 4
of the stump. This, one might say, is only the skeleton of the resurrection. Now the chips must be gathered, and the sawdust, and returned
to their former positions. The fixative for the wood layers will be applied to chips and sawdust consisting only of wood. Chips and sawdust
consisting of several substances will receive applications of the correct
adhesives. It is as well, where possible, to shelter the materials from
the elements while working. Weathering makes it harder to identify
the smaller fragments. Bark sawdust in particular the earth lays claim
to very quickly. You must find your own ways of coping with this problem. There is a certain beauty, you will notice at moments, in the pattern of the chips as they are fitted back into place. You will wonder to
what extent it should be described as natural, to what extent man-
made. It will lead you on to speculations about the parentage of beauty
itself, to which you will return.

The adhesive for the chips is translucent, and not so rigid as that 5
for the splinters. That for the bark and its subcutaneous layers is trans-
parent and runs into the fibers on either side, partially dissolving them

into each other. It does not set the sap flowing again but it does pay a kind of tribute to the preoccupations of the ancient thoroughfares. You could not roll an egg over the joints but some of the mine-shafts would still be passable, no doubt. For the first exploring insect who raises its head in the tight echoless passages. The day comes when it is all restored, even to the moss (now dead) over the wound. You will sleep badly, thinking of the removal of the scaffolding that must begin the next morning. How you will hope for sun and a still day!

The removal of the scaffolding or tackle is not so dangerous, per- 6
haps, to the surroundings, as its installation, but it presents problems. It should be taken from the spot piece by piece as it is detached, and stored at a distance. You have come to accept it there, around the tree. The sky begins to look naked as the chains and struts one by one vacate their positions. Finally the moment arrives when the last sustaining piece is removed and the tree stands again on its own. It is as though its weight for a moment stood on your heart. You listen for a thud of settlement, a warning creak deep in the intricate joinery. You cannot believe it will hold. How like something dreamed it is, standing there all by itself. How long will it stand there now? The first breeze that touches its dead leaves all seems to flow into your mouth. You are afraid the motion of the clouds will be enough to push it over. What more can you do? What more can you do?

But there is nothing more you can do. 7

Others are waiting. 8

Everything is going to have to be put back. 9

QUESTIONS

1. How well does "Unchopping a Tree" satisfy the requirements for step-by-step instructions and precise, easy-to-visualize detail in the "how-to" process analysis essay?

2. At what point did you first realize that these instructions are, in fact, impossible to carry out? Is process analysis an effective way to make this point? Why?

3. Reread the first paragraph and analyze the rhythm Merwin creates through his use of sentence lengths and sentence patterns. How does this rhythm help to establish the tone of the essay?

4. Note Merwin's use of figurative language throughout this essay (for more on this, see Joyce MacDonald's essay on Merwin and Suzuki in Readings: Sample Essays). How does this language develop and strengthen Merwin's thesis?

5. Throughout the essay, Merwin adopts the persona of a teacher instructing the reader-student. Where is this persona most evident? What purposes does it serve?

6. Merwin creates irony by leaving the obvious unsaid: that it is impossible to unchop a tree. How similar is Merwin's irony to Swift's in "A Modest Proposal"? Do you think irony is an effective strategy for persuasion? Is irony ever risky?

SUGGESTION FOR WRITING

Using "Unchopping a Tree" as a model, write an essay in which the impossibility of carrying out your instructions makes a persuasive point. Remember that in an ironic essay, your real thesis is the opposite of what you seem to be saying. You will find this irony easier to create and sustain if, like Merwin, you adopt the persona of the teacher who encourages the students but who provides impossibly complex instructions. Like Merwin, you should develop your essay as a process analysis, so be sure to include transitions that help your readers to follow the steps in your procedure.

SHOOTING AN ELEPHANT

George Orwell

In Moulmein, in lower Burma,[1] I was hated by large numbers of people 1
—the only time in my life that I have been important enough for
this to happen to me. I was sub-divisional police officer of the town,
and in an aimless, petty kind of way anti-European feeling was very
bitter. No one had the guts to raise a riot, but if a European woman
went through the bazaars alone somebody would probably spit betel
juice[2] over her dress. As a police officer[3] I was an obvious target and
was baited whenever it seemed safe to do so. When a nimble Burman
tripped me up on the football field and the referee (another Burman)
looked the other way, the crowd yelled with hideous laughter. This
happened more than once. In the end the sneering yellow faces of
young men that met me everywhere, the insults hooted after me when
I was at a safe distance, got badly on my nerves. The young Buddhist
priests were the worst of all. There were several thousands of them in
the town and none of them seemed to have anything to do except
stand on street corners and jeer at Europeans.

All this was perplexing and upsetting. For at that time I had already 2
made up my mind that imperialism was an evil thing and the sooner I
chucked up my job and got out of it the better. Theoretically—and secretly, of course—I was all for the Burmese and
all against their oppressors, the British. As for
the job I was doing, I hated it more bitterly
than I can perhaps make clear. In a job like
that you see the dirty work of Empire at close
quarters. The wretched prisoners huddling in
the stinking cages of the lock-ups, the gray,
cowed faces of the long-term convicts, the
scarred buttocks of the men who had been
flogged with bamboos—all these oppressed me
with an intolerable sense of guilt. But I could
get nothing into perspective. I was young and
ill educated and I had had to think out my
problems in the utter silence that is imposed
on every Englishman in the East. I did not even
know that the British Empire is dying, still less

George Orwell (1903–1950) was born in
India as Eric Arthur Blair. Primarily a writer
and a journalist, he worked as a police officer for the Indian Imperial Police in Burma
from 1922 to 1927. His fiction includes
Animal Farm (1945) and *Nineteen Eighty-Four*
(1949). He also wrote many essays, often
exploring his ideas about democracy and
socialism; collections include *Inside the
Whale and Other Essays* (1940) and *Shooting
an Elephant and Other Essays* (1950).

"Shooting an Elephant" was first published
in the journal *New Writing* in 1936.
Copyright © Mark Hamilton as the literary
executor of the estate of the late Sonia
Brownell Orwell and Martin Secker and
Warburg Ltd.

did I know that it is a great deal better than the younger empires that are going to supplant it. All I knew was that I was stuck between my hatred of the empire I served and my rage against the evil-spirited little beasts who tried to make my job impossible. With one part of my mind I thought of the British Raj[4] as an unbreakable tyranny, as something clamped down, in *saecula saeculorum*,[5] upon the will of prostrate peoples; with another part I thought that the greatest joy in the world would be to drive a bayonet into a Buddhist priest's guts. Feelings like these are the normal by-products of imperialism; ask any Anglo-Indian official, if you can catch him off duty.

One day something happened which in a roundabout way was enlightening. It was a tiny incident in itself; but it gave me a better glimpse than I had had before of the real nature of imperialism—the real motives for which despotic governments act. Early one morning the sub-inspector at a police station the other end of the town rang me up on the 'phone and said that an elephant was ravaging the bazaar. Would I please come and do something about it? I did not know what I could do, but I wanted to see what was happening and I got on to a pony and started out. I took my rifle, an old .44 Winchester and much too small to kill an elephant, but I thought the noise might be useful *in terrorem*.[6] Various Burmans stopped me on the way and told me about the elephant's doings. It was not, of course, a wild elephant, but a tame one which had gone "must."[7] It had been chained up, as tame elephants always are when their attack of "must" is due, but on the previous night it had broken its chain and escaped. Its mahout,[8] the only person who could manage it when it was in that state, had set out in pursuit, but had taken the wrong direction and was now twelve hours' journey away, and in the morning the elephant had suddenly reappeared in the town. The Burmese population had no weapons and were quite helpless against it. It had already destroyed somebody's bamboo hut, killed a cow and raided some fruitstalls and devoured the stock; also it had met the municipal rubbish van and, when the driver jumped out and took to his heels, had turned the van over and inflicted violences upon it.

The Burmese sub-inspector and some Indian constables were waiting for me in the quarter where the elephant had been seen. It was a very poor quarter, a labyrinth of squalid bamboo huts, thatched with palm-leaf, winding all over a steep hillside. I remember that it was a cloudy, stuffy morning at the beginning of the rains.[9] We began questioning the people as to where the elephant had gone and, as usual, failed to get any definite information. That is invariably the case in the East; a story always sounds clear enough at a distance, but the nearer you get to the scene of events the vaguer it becomes. Some of the people said that the elephant had gone in one direction, some said that he had gone in another, some professed not even to have heard of any elephant.

3

4

I had almost made up my mind that the whole story was a pack of lies, when we heard yells a little distance away. There was a loud, scandalized cry of "Go away, child! Go away this instant!" and an old woman with a switch in her hand came round the corner of a hut, violently shooing away a crowd of naked children. Some more women followed, clicking their tongues and exclaiming; evidently there was something that the children ought not to have seen. I rounded the hut and saw a man's dead body sprawling in the mud. He was an Indian, a black Dravidian coolie,[10] almost naked, and he could not have been dead many minutes. The people said that the elephant had come suddenly upon him round the corner of the hut, caught him with its trunk, put its foot on his back and ground him into the earth. This was the rainy season and the ground was soft, and his face had scored a trench a foot deep and a couple of yards long. He was lying on his belly with arms crucified and head sharply twisted to one side. His face was coated with mud, the eyes wide open, the teeth bared and grinning with an expression of unendurable agony. (Never tell me, by the way, that the dead look peaceful. Most of the corpses I have seen looked devilish.) The friction of the great beast's foot had stripped the skin from his back as neatly as one skins a rabbit. As soon as I saw the dead man I sent an orderly to a friend's house nearby to borrow an elephant rifle. I had already sent back the pony, not wanting it to go mad with fright and throw me if it smelt the elephant.

The orderly came back in a few minutes with a rifle and five car- 5
tridges, and meanwhile some Burmans had arrived and told us that the elephant was in the paddy fields[11] below, only a few hundred yards away. As I started forward practically the whole population of the quarter flocked out of the houses and followed me. They had seen the rifle and were all shouting excitedly that I was going to shoot the elephant. They had not shown much interest in the elephant when he was merely ravaging their homes, but it was different now that he was going to be shot. It was a bit of fun to them, as it would be to an English crowd; besides they wanted the meat. It made me vaguely uneasy. I had no intention of shooting the elephant—I had merely sent for the rifle to defend myself if necessary—and it is always unnerving to have a crowd following you. I marched down the hill, looking and feeling a fool, with the rifle over my shoulder and an ever-growing army of people jostling at my heels. At the bottom, when you got away from the huts, there was a metalled road and beyond that a miry waste of paddy fields a thousand yards across, not yet ploughed but soggy from the first rains and dotted with coarse grass. The elephant was standing eight yards from the road, his left side toward us. He took not the slightest notice of the crowd's approach. He was tearing up bunches of grass, beating them against his knees to clean them, and stuffing them into his mouth.

I had halted on the road. As soon as I saw the elephant I knew with   6
perfect certainty that I ought not to shoot him. It is a serious matter to
shoot a working elephant—it is comparable to destroying a huge and
costly piece of machinery—and obviously one ought not to do it if it
can possibly be avoided. And at that distance, peacefully eating, the
elephant looked no more dangerous than a cow. I thought then and I
think now that his attack of "must" was already passing off; in which
case he would merely wander harmlessly about until the mahout came
back and caught him. Moreover, I did not in the least want to shoot
him. I decided that I would watch him for a little while to make sure
that he did not turn savage again, and then go home.

But at that moment I glanced round at the crowd that had followed   7
me. It was an immense crowd, two thousand at the least and growing
every minute. It blocked the road for a long distance on either side. I
looked at the sea of yellow faces above the garish clothes—faces all
happy and excited over this bit of fun, all certain that the elephant was
going to be shot. They were watching me as they would watch a con-
jurer about to perform a trick. They did not like me, but with the magical rifle in my hands I was momentarily worth watching. And suddenly
I realized that I should have to shoot the elephant after all. The people
expected it of me and I had got to do it; I could feel their two thousand
wills pressing me forward, irresistibly. And it was at this moment, as I
stood there with the rifle in my hands, that I first grasped the hollow-
ness, the futility of the white man's dominion in the East. Here was I,
the white man with his gun, standing in front of the unarmed native
crowd—seemingly the leading actor of the piece; but in reality I was
only an absurd puppet pushed to and fro by the will of those yellow
faces behind. I perceived in this moment that when the white man
turns tyrant it is his own freedom that he destroys. He becomes a sort
of hollow, posing dummy, the conventionalized figure of a sahib.[12] For
it is the condition of his rule that he shall spend his life in trying to im-
press the "natives," and so in every crisis he has got to do what the
"natives" expect of him. He wears a mask, and his face grows to fit it.
I had got to shoot the elephant. I had committed myself to doing it when
I sent for the rifle. A sahib has got to act like a sahib; he has got to appear resolute, to know his own mind and do definite things. To come
all that way, rifle in hand, with two thousand people marching at my
heels, and then to trail feebly away, having done nothing—no, that was
impossible. The crowd would laugh at me. And my whole life, every
white man's life in the East, was one long struggle not to be laughed at.

But I did not want to shoot the elephant. I watched him beating his   8
bunch of grass against his knees with that preoccupied grandmotherly
air that elephants have. It seemed to me that it would be murder to
shoot him. At that age I was not squeamish about killing animals, but I

had never shot an elephant and never wanted to. (Somehow it always seems worse to kill a *large* animal.) Besides, there was the beast's owner to be considered. Alive, the elephant was worth at least a hundred pounds; dead, he would only be worth the value of his tusks, five pounds, possibly. But I had got to act quickly. I turned to some experienced-looking Burmans who had been there when we arrived, and asked them how the elephant had been behaving. They all said the same thing: he took no notice of you if you left him alone, but he might charge if you went too close to him.

It was perfectly clear to me what I ought to do. I ought to walk up to within, say, twenty-five yards of the elephant and test his behavior. If he charged, I could shoot; if he took no notice of me, it would be safe to leave him until the mahout came back. But also I knew that I was going to do no such thing. I was a poor shot with a rifle and the ground was soft mud into which one would sink at every step. If the elephant charged and I missed him, I should have about as much chance as a toad under a steam-roller. But even then I was not thinking particularly of my own skin, only of the watchful yellow faces behind. For at that moment, with the crowd watching me, I was not afraid in the ordinary sense, as I would have been if I had been alone. A white man mustn't be frightened in front of "natives"; and so, in general, he isn't frightened. The sole thought in my mind was that if anything went wrong those two thousand Burmans would see me pursued, caught, trampled on, and reduced to a grinning corpse like that Indian up the hill. And if that happened it was quite probable that some of them would laugh. That would never do. There was only one alternative. I shoved the cartridges into the magazine and lay down on the road to get a better aim.

The crowd grew very still, and a deep, low, happy sigh, as of people who see the theater curtain go up at last, breathed from innumerable throats. They were going to have their bit of fun after all. The rifle was a beautiful German thing with cross-hair sights. I did not then know that in shooting an elephant one would shoot to cut an imaginary bar running from ear-hole to ear-hole. I ought, therefore, as the elephant was sideways on, to have aimed straight at his ear-hole; actually I aimed several inches in front of this, thinking the brain would be further forward.

When I pulled the trigger I did not hear the bang or feel the kick—one never does when a shot goes home—but I heard the devilish roar of glee that went up from the crowd. In that instant, in too short a time, one would have thought, even for the bullet to get there, a mysterious, terrible change had come over the elephant. He neither stirred, nor fell, but every line of his body had altered. He looked suddenly stricken, shrunken, immensely old, as though the frightful impact of the bullet had paralyzed him without knocking him down. At last, after what seemed a long time—it might have been five seconds, I dare say—he sagged flabbily to his knees. His mouth slobbered. An enormous senility seemed to have settled upon him. One could have imagined him thousands of years old. I fired again into the same spot. At the second shot he did not collapse but climbed with desperate slowness to his feet and stood weakly upright, with legs sagging and head drooping. I fired a third time. That was the shot that did for him. You could see the agony of it jolt his whole body and knock the last remnant of strength from his legs. But in falling he seemed for a moment to rise, for as his hind legs collapsed beneath him he seemed to tower upward like a huge rock toppling, his trunk reaching skyward like a tree. He trumpeted, for the first and only time. And then down he came, his belly toward me, with a crash that seemed to shake the ground even where I lay.

I got up. The Burmans were already racing past me across the mud. It was obvious that the elephant would never rise again, but he was not dead. He was breathing very rhythmically with long rattling gasps, his great mound of a side painfully rising and falling. His mouth was wide open—I could see far down into caverns of pale pink throat. I waited for a long time for him to die, but his breathing did not weaken. Finally I fired my two remaining shots into the spot where I thought his heart must be. The thick blood welled out of him like red velvet, but still he did not die. His body did not even jerk when the shots hit him, the tortured breathing continued without a pause. He was dying, very slowly and in great agony, but in some world remote from me where not even a bullet could damage him further. I felt that I had got to put an end to that dreadful noise. It seemed dreadful to see the great beast lying there, powerless to move and yet powerless to die, and not even to be able to finish him. I sent back for my small rifle and poured shot after shot into his heart and down his throat. They seemed to make no impression. The tortured gasps continued as steadily as the ticking of a clock. 12

In the end I could not stand it any longer and went away. I heard later that it took him half an hour to die. Burmans were bringing dahs[13] and baskets even before I left, and I was told they had stripped his body almost to the bones by the afternoon. 13

Afterward, of course, there were endless discussions about the shooting of the elephant. The owner was furious, but he was only an Indian and could do nothing. Besides, legally I had done the right thing, for a mad elephant has to be killed, like a mad dog, if its owner fails to control it. Among the Europeans opinion was divided. The older men said I was right, the younger men said it was a damn shame to shoot an elephant for killing a coolie, because an elephant was worth more than 14 any damn Coringhee coolie. And afterward I was very glad that the coolie had been killed; it put me legally in the right and it gave me a sufficient pretext for shooting the elephant. I often wondered whether any of the others grasped that I had done it solely to avoid looking a fool.

NOTES

1 Burma (Union of Myanmar) is a country in Southeast Asia, and was part of the British Empire at the time to which Orwell is referring.

2 Betel juice is produced by chewing the leaf of the betel plant wrapped around parings of the areca nut.

3 As an officer in the Indian Imperial Police, Orwell was an agent of the Empire, and thus often resented by the local population.

4 British Raj: British rule in the Indian subcontinent prior to 1947.

5 For ever and ever.

6 As a warning.

7 "Must" is a state of dangerous frenzy to which certain male animals, especially elephants and camels, are subject at infrequent intervals.

8 A *mahout* is an elephant driver.

9 The rainy season.

10 *Coolie* is a European word used to describe natives in India and elsewhere who are hired as labourers or burden carriers. Dravidia and Coringhee are both areas of India.

11 Paddy fields are fields of rice.

12 *Sahib* is a respectful term of address used by Indians and Asians to Europeans, equivalent to "Sir."

13 A *dah* is a short heavy sword, also used as a knife.

VOCABULARY

despotic—oppressive or tyrannical

imperialism—the principle, spirit, or ideology by which the existence of an empire, or the extension of territory in the name of protection of existing trading or economic interests, is justified.

QUESTIONS

1. Reread the first two paragraphs of "Shooting an Elephant." What are Orwell's attitudes towards the Burmese, the British, and his own position in Burma? How does Orwell use descriptive details and diction to establish his perspective and create the tone of this essay?

2. Note the description of the man killed by the elephant (fourth paragraph). What purposes does this description serve in the essay as a whole?

3. Make a list of Orwell's reasons for not shooting the elephant. Then make a list of the reasons he gives for shooting the elephant. Are you convinced that Orwell was justified in shooting the elephant? What would you have done if you had been in his situation?

4. Note the detailed and graphic description of the elephant's death. What purposes does this description serve? What does the elephant symbolize?

5. Where does Orwell indicate his subject? What insights into the real motives for which imperialist governments act does Orwell actually gain from his experience? What is his thesis?

6. Do you think Orwell uses narration effectively as a persuasive strategy in this essay?

SUGGESTION FOR WRITING

Like Orwell, most of us have done something we are rather ashamed of but have never forgotten because it taught us something important. Using Orwell's essay as a model, write a narrative essay in which you tell a story about a single incident. Be sure this incident has a definite beginning, middle, and end. Try to begin by establishing the context of the incident (how old you were, where it happened, why it was especially important). Include plenty of vivid, precise descriptive detail. You can imitate the structure of "Shooting an Elephant" by leading up to your thesis, which you may choose to imply rather than state explicitly.

THE TICKING DADDY CLOCK

Andrew Pyper

You're a childless guy in your 30s, minding your own business, when suddenly, at the family reunion or office picnic or some poor sucker's wedding, somebody passes you one of *them*. Aware that you're being observed by already-reproducing females, you do what's expected: make a goo-goo face, bounce her on your knee, say her name in an odd, squeaky voice, as though you've just sucked helium. The baby gurgles on cue. Spits on the shirt you just picked up at the dry cleaner. Lets rip a whoopee-cushion blast followed by a smell you wouldn't think possible coming from something so small.

But here's the twist: You don't mind. Nothing matters but these twelve-and-a-quarter pounds of brand new human wriggling in your hands. Before you can set up a patented Irony Roadblock, the thought leaps into your mind: *Maybe they're not so bad*.

And what's up with that ticking sound in your head?

We all know the female biological clock is a fact of modern life. A media cottage industry has emerged bent on cultivating baby anxiety in over-25 women. The latest cause for worry is Sylvia Ann Hewlett's book, *Creating a Life: Professional Women and the Quest for Children*. Contrary to the perception that medical advances have allowed women to wait longer than ever to safely start a family, Hewlett argues that the risks of late pregnancies persist and even the latest fertility treatments don't come with a guarantee. For Hewlett, "the biological clock is real." And after a woman's 35th birthday, time is running out.

Andrew Pyper has a B.A. and M.A. in English Literature from McGill University and a law degree from the University of Toronto. He has published a collection of stories, *Kiss Me* (1996), and two novels, *Lost Girls* and *The Trade Mission*. *Lost Girls*, a Notable Book selection of *The Globe and Mail*, *The New York Times Book Review*, and the *London Evening Standard*, also won the Arthur Ellis Award for Best First Novel. Andrew Pyper lives in Toronto.

"The Ticking Daddy Clock" was published in *Maclean's*, April 29, 2002. Reprinted with permission of the author.

Even if not all women concede the existence of literal egg timers ticking away within, men of my age agree on the issue. We can remember the day a couple of years ago when our independent, sex-for-sex's-sake female friends did a communal backflip on "life priorities"—not to mention dating strategies. What used to be candlelit dinners or flirtatious cocktails became as erotic as job interviews. Gen X's[1] mating rituals have now largely been reduced to due diligence: instead of bedroom eyes and witty banter, what crosses the table are five-year plans, mutual fund portfolios and medical histories.

A side effect of this romantic pragmatism has been that men in 6 their 30s (and even those in their suspiciously never-married 40s) who were previously considered laughable rejects enjoy the kind of feminine attention known only to firemen and the sons of ex-prime ministers. One friend recently confessed that her criteria have withered to the point that she'll now go out with any guy who is "non-violent and has his own teeth."

So the chimes of today's childless women over 30 ring louder than 7 Notre Dame's. But what of the *male* biological clock? I confess to having one. It came late, and its tolling, thankfully, has yet to reach a volume that one would consider a distraction to carrying on the head-in-the-clouds, slacker's life that men of my generation have perfected. But still, it's there. A heart leap at the sight of the neighbour's kid on his father's shoulders (watch his head on the one-way sign!). An ache whenever that wee one in the pink touque is wheeled into the Second Cup while I'm studying the sports page.

I resist the best I can. God knows, the last thing any of us needs is 8 someone else to think about besides ourselves. And if that someone can't even *talk*? We'd all be better off buying Tickle Me Elmos and spending the education savings plans on something useful, like a GameCube or those cellphones that fold out into tiny computers so you can ignore both e-mail and phone calls from anywhere in the world.

The trouble is, unlike previous generations of men who found them- 9 selves fathers before they knew what hit them, today's hypothetical daddies-to-be have played beat-the-clock for so long that once they let their guard down for a second—*wham*!—it's bring on the Jolly Jumper.

Men must consider the risks of becoming a parent at an advanced 10 age just as women do. A recent Columbia University study shows that men between 45 and 49 are twice more likely to have children with schizophrenia than those under 25, while men over 50 are three times as likely. There's also evidence that later fatherhood can contribute to conditions as diverse as prostate cancer, neurofibromatosis and dwarfism. Sure, Julio Iglesias had healthy twin girls last year at age 57—but who wants to emulate Julio Iglesias?

So do men have a biological clock? Perhaps it's best not to ask for 11 whom the bell tolls ... at least until after the playoffs.

NOTE

[1] Gen X: Generation X, a term popularized by Canadian writer Douglas Coupland. In his novel of that title, characters in their mid-twenties to mid-thirties reject the consumerist society they live in and search for something more authentic.

VOCABULARY

cottage industry—a small business

patented Irony Roadblock—a tried and true defence mechanism that enables a person to laugh off (or to pretend to be too sophisticated to notice) anything disturbing or threatening

romantic pragmatism—focusing on the practical implications of every romantic experience

QUESTIONS

1. Does Pyper use personal experience effectively to develop the central idea in this essay? Explain why or why not.
2. How does Pyper create and maintain the tone of this essay? Is this tone effective?
3. List the main similarities and differences between male and female biological clocks.

SUGGESTION FOR WRITING

Choose an issue like Pyper's in which you must balance conflicting desires and write a short personal essay. Possible topics include the following: getting married, giving up smoking, getting into shape, going back to school, becoming a step-parent.

THE POORHOUSE

Judy Rebick

Kimberly Roger's dark death,[1] while under house arrest for welfare 1
fraud in a sweltering Sudbury apartment last summer, may finally
shine a light on the increasing criminalization of poor people.

Rogers had been placed under house arrest for six months for ac- 2
cepting student loans of $14,000 while collecting welfare. Her welfare
payments were halted for three months and she had to pay back the
$13,500 she'd received over four years.

"Imagine," says Amanda Chodura, an Elizabeth Fry Society[2] case- 3
worker who visited Rogers regularly before her death, "being cooped
up in a tiny apartment with a difficult pregnancy and no money."

No doubt the coming inquest will ask why Rogers was under house 4
arrest for a first offence. Perhaps if she could have afforded a better
lawyer she would have got probation.

The Rogers case ended with a greater tragedy than most but it's 5
not unique. The National Council of Welfare has sounded the alarm:
"For the same criminal behaviour, the poor are more likely to be arrested; if arrested, they are more likely to be charged; if charged, they
are more likely to be convicted; if convicted, more likely to be sent to
prison and get longer sentences." Supporting that notion is a 1997
study by Dianne Martin, Toronto lawyer and York University professor, that found of 50 people convicted of welfare fraud, 80 percent
were sentenced to prison, the highest incar-
ceration rate for any crime except murder.

Judy Rebick writes columns for *Elm Street Magazine* and *CBC Online* and contributes regularly to the *Ottawa Citizen* and *The Globe and Mail*. Rebick is also the publisher of *rabble.ca*, an online interactive magazine. President of the National Action Committee on the Status of Women from 1990 to 1993, Rebick has been long known for her political commentary and social ac- tivism. *Imagine Democracy* (2000) is a provocative look at how Canada can deepen its democratic system by including more participation from ordinary citizens.

"The Poorhouse" originally appeared in *Elm Street Magazine* (November 2001). Reproduced with permission of the author.

With the right wing shift of governments in 6
Ontario and Alberta, Canada has moved from a
social welfare state[3] to a social control state.
Instead of income support and social services,
we offer the poor little better than alms and the
hard fist of state repression to ensure they accept the pittance. We pride ourselves on being
a humane society but that is changing.

Besides aggressive welfare fraud convictions, 7
several provinces have instituted so-called safe
street acts that make it a criminal offence to
panhandle. Reports from anti-poverty groups indicate that police harassment of poor people has

also dramatically increased as welfare rates have declined. Concern is not for the vulnerable but for the middle-class burghers who are annoyed by them.

Savage cuts in social assistance are massively reinforcing a system that already penalizes the poor. With social housing almost non-existent in most provinces, no one can live on welfare rates unless they have financial support from relatives. In Ontario, a single disabled person gets less than $1,000 per month. In other provinces, it's even worse. Rogers, who suffered from depression but was not considered disabled, put almost half of her cheque towards rent. 8

With the dramatic decline in welfare rates in most provinces over the last decade, women who may receive some extra money from family or who work under the table are treated like criminals by the government. If they report the money, it is deducted from their cheques. If they don't report, they risk being charged with fraud. 9

Welfare rates make it impossible to make ends meet. If your children were going hungry, would you risk a fraud conviction to get money to feed them? Poor women are becoming more desperate and when they get in trouble, they can't afford to defend themselves. Add reductions to legal aid to the litany of cutbacks that hit poor people the hardest. 10

The federal government talks a good game but has done little to alleviate the state of despair facing so many. Claudette Bradshaw, minister of labour and the federal coordinator on homelessness, is a lovely woman with great experience working with the poor but she has done little to solve the desperate problems of homelessness in our big cities. The child tax benefit,[4] meanwhile, does nothing for people receiving welfare since most provinces tax it back. 11

We are well on the way to creating a persecuted underclass, many of whom are single mothers with children. Poor people who barely subsist on welfare live in a world of desperation that most of us cannot even imagine. I am horrified at how little public outrage has greeted this rapid decline in our humanity to our fellow citizens. 12

NOTES

[1] According to an article published in the *National Post*, the inquest concluded that Rogers died of an overdose of prescription anti-depressants, not heat stroke ("Overdose, not heat, killed welfare recipient," August 15, 2002, A1).

[2] Elizabeth Fry Society: an organization dedicated to improving the lives of women prisoners.

[3] Social welfare state: a system of government in which the state assumes the responsibility for providing the necessities of life for all citizens.

[4] Child tax benefit: a replacement for the older system of family allowances in which income support is provided to families with children.

VOCABULARY

litany—a long list of excuses or complaints

QUESTIONS

1. Does the fact that Rogers died of an overdose of anti-depressants, not heat stroke, significantly affect your response to Rebick's article? Explain why or why not.

2. Find three to five examples of evaluative language ("savage cuts in social assistance," for example) and explain why you think they strengthen or weaken Rebick's argument.

3. How does Rebick develop her argument that the provincial and federal governments in Canada have a moral obligation to ensure an adequate standard of living for all Canadians?

SUGGESTION FOR WRITING

Rebick asks, "If your children were going hungry, would you risk a fraud conviction to get the money to feed them?" Write a 500-word essay in response to this question. Include both practical and ethical considerations and make sure your reader can see which is which.

THE MEN WE CARRY IN OUR MINDS

Scott Russell Sanders

"This must be a hard time for women," I say to my friend Anneke. 1
"They have so many paths to choose from, and so many voices
calling them."

"I think it's a lot harder for men," she replies. 2

"How do you figure that?" 3

"The women I know feel excited, innocent, like crusaders in a just 4
cause. The men I know are eaten up with guilt."

We are sitting at the kitchen table drinking sassafras tea,[1] our 5
hands wrapped around the mugs because this April morning is cool
and drizzly. "Like a Dutch morning," Anneke told me earlier. She is
Dutch herself, a writer and midwife and peacemaker, with the round
face and sad eyes of a woman in a Vermeer painting[2] who might be
waiting for the rain to stop, for a door to open. She leans over to sniff a
sprig of lilac, pale lavender, that rises from a vase of cobalt blue.

"Women feel such pressure to be everything, do everything," I say. 6
"Career, kids, art, politics. Have their babies and get back to the office
a week later. It's as if they're trying to overcome a million years' worth
of evolution in one lifetime."

"But we help one another. We don't try to lumber on alone, like so 7
many wounded grizzly bears, the way men do." Anneke sips her tea. I
gave her the mug with the owls on it, for wisdom. "And we have this
deep-down sense that we're in the *right*—we've been held back, passed
over, used—while men feel they're in the
wrong. Men are the ones who've been discred-
ited, who have to search their souls."

Scott Russell Sanders (b. 1945) is a fiction
writer, essayist, and critic, as well as a professor of English at Indiana University. His
recent publications include *Hunting for
Hope: A Father's Journeys* (1998), *The
Country of Language* (1999), and *The Force
of Spirit* (2000).

I search my soul. I discover guilty feelings 8
aplenty—towards the poor, the Vietnamese,
Native Americans, the whales, an endless list of
debts—a guilt in each case that is as bright and
unambiguous as a neon sign. But toward
women I feel something more confused, a snarl
of shame, envy, wary tenderness, and amazement. This muddle troubles me. To hide my un-
ease I say, "You're right, it's tough being a man
these days."

"Don't laugh." Anneke frowns at me, mournful-eyed, through the   9
sassafras steam. "I wouldn't be a man for anything. It's much easier
being the victim. All the victim has to do is break free. The persecutor
has to live with his past."

How deep is that past? I find myself wondering after Anneke has left.   10
How much of an inheritance do I have to throw off? Is it just the beliefs I
breathed in as a child? Do I have to scour memory back through father
and grandfather? Through St. Paul?[3] Beyond Stonehenge[4] and into the
twilit caves? I'm convinced the past we must contend with is deeper
even than speech. When I think back on my childhood, on how I learned
to see men and women, I have a sense of ancient, dizzying depths. The
back roads of Tennessee and Ohio where I grew up were probably closer,
in their sexual patterns, to the campsites of Stone Age hunters than to
the genderless cities of the future into which we are rushing.

The first men, besides my father, I remember seeing were black   11
convicts and white guards, in the cottonfield across the road from our
farm on the outskirts of Memphis. I must have been three or four. The
prisoners wore dingy gray-and-black zebra suits, heavy as canvas, sod-
den with sweat. Hatless, stooped, they chopped weeds in the fierce
heat, row after row, breathing the acrid dust of boll-weevil poison.[5]
The overseers wore dazzling white shirts and broad shadowy hats. The
oiled barrels of their shotguns flashed in the sunlight. Their faces in
memory are utterly blank. Of course those men, white and black, have
become for me an emblem of racial hatred. But they have also come to
stand for the twin poles of my early vision of manhood—the brute toil-
ing animal and the boss.

When I was a boy, the men I knew labored with their bodies. They   12
were marginal farmers, just scraping by, or welders, steel-workers, car-
penters; they swept floors, dug ditches, mined coal, or drove trucks,
their forearms ropy with muscle; they trained horses, stoked furnaces,
built tires, stood on assembly lines wrestling parts onto cars and refrig-
erators. They got up before light, worked all day long whatever the
weather, and when they came home at night they looked as though
somebody had been whipping them. In the evenings and on weekends
they worked on their own places, tilling gardens that were lumpy with
clay, fixing broken-down cars, hammering on houses that were always
too drafty, too leaky, too small.

The bodies of the men I knew were twisted and maimed in ways   13
visible and invisible. The nails of their hands were black and split, the
hands tattooed with scars. Some had lost fingers. Heavy lifting had
given many of them finicky backs and guts weak from hernias. Racing
against conveyor belts had given them ulcers. Their ankles and knees
ached from years of standing on concrete. Anyone who had worked for
long around machines was hard of hearing. They squinted, and the

skin of their faces was creased like the leather of old work gloves. There were times, studying them, when I dreaded growing up. Most of them coughed, from dust or cigarettes, and most of them drank cheap wine or whiskey, so their eyes looked bloodshot and bruised. The fathers of my friends always seemed older than the mothers. Men wore out sooner. Only women lived into old age.

As a boy I also knew another sort of men, who did not sweat and   14 break down like mules. They were soldiers, and so far as I could tell they scarcely worked at all. During my early school years we lived on a military base, an arsenal in Ohio, and every day I saw GIs in the guard-shacks, on the stoops of barracks, at the wheels of olive drab Chevrolets. The chief fact of their lives was boredom. Long after I left the Arsenal I came to recognize the sour smell the soldiers gave off as that of souls in limbo. They were all waiting—for wars, for transfers, for leaves, for promotions, for the end of their hitch—like so many braves waiting for the hunt to begin. Unlike the warriors of older tribes, however, they would have no say about when the battle would start or how it would be waged. Their waiting was broken only when they practiced for war. They fired guns at targets, drove tanks across the churned-up fields of the military reservation, set off bombs in the wrecks of old fighter planes. I knew this was all play. But I also felt certain that when the hour for killing arrived, they would kill. When the real shooting started, many of them would die. This was what soldiers were *for*, just as a hammer was for driving nails.

Warriors and toilers: those seemed, in my boyhood vision, to be   15 the chief destinies for men. They weren't the only destinies, as I learned from having a few male teachers, from reading books, and from watching television. But the men on television—the politicians, the astronauts, the generals, the savvy lawyers, the philosophical doctors, the bosses who gave orders to both soldiers and laborers—seemed as remote and unreal to me as the figures in tapestries. I could no more imagine growing up to become one of these cool, potent creatures than I could imagine becoming a prince.

A nearer and more hopeful example was that of my father, who   16 had escaped from a red-dirt farm to a tire factory, and from the assembly line to the front office. Eventually he dressed in a white shirt and tie. He carried himself as if he had been born to work with his mind. But his body, remembering the earlier years of slogging work, began to give out on him in his fifties, and it quit on him entirely before he turned sixty-five. Even such a partial escape from man's fate as he had accomplished did not seem possible for most of the boys I knew. They joined the army, stood in line for jobs in the smoky plants, helped build highways. They were bound to work as their fathers had worked, killing themselves or preparing to kill others.

A scholarship enabled me not only to attend college, a rare enough   17
feat in my circle, but even to study in a university meant for the children of the rich. Here I met for the first time young men who had assumed from birth that they would lead lives of comfort and power. And
for the first time I met women who told me that men were guilty of
having kept all the joys and privileges of the earth for themselves. I was
baffled. What privileges? What joys? I thought about the maimed, dis-
mal lives of most of the men back home. What had they stolen from
their wives and daughters? The right to go five days a week, twelve
months a year, for thirty or forty years to a steel mill or a coal mine?
The right to drop bombs and die in war? The right to feel every leak in
the roof, every gap in the fence, every cough in the engine, as a wound
they must mend? The right to feel, when the lay-off comes or the plant
shuts down, not only afraid but ashamed?

I was slow to understand the deep grievances of women. This was   18
because, as a boy, I had envied them. Before college, the only people I
had ever known who were interested in art or music or literature, the
only ones who read books, the only ones who ever seemed to enjoy a
sense of ease and grace were the mothers and daughters. Like the
menfolk, they fretted about money, they scrimped and made-do. But,
when the pay stopped coming in, they were not the ones who had
failed. Nor did they have to go to war, and that seemed to me a
blessed fact. By comparison with the narrow, ironclad days of fathers,
there was an expansiveness, I thought, in the days of mothers. They
went to see neighbors, to shop in town, to run errands at school, at
the library, at church. No doubt, had I looked harder at their lives, I
would have envied them less. It was not my fate to become a woman,
so it was easier for me to see the graces. Few of them held jobs outside the home, and those who did filled thankless roles as clerks and
waitresses. I didn't see, then, what a prison a house could be, since
houses seemed to me brighter, handsomer places than any factory. I
did not realize—because such things were never spoken of—how
often women suffered from men's bullying. I did learn about the
wretchedness of abandoned wives, single mothers, widows; but I also
learned about the wretchedness of lone men. Even then I could see
how exhausting it was for a mother to cater all day to the needs of
young children. But if I had been asked, as a boy, to choose between
tending a baby and tending a machine, I think I would have chosen
the baby. (Having now tended both, I know I would choose the baby.)

So I was baffled when the women at college accused me and my sex   19
of having cornered the world's pleasures. I think something like my baf-
flement has been felt by other boys (and by girls as well) who grew up
in dirt-poor farm country, in mining country, in black ghettos, in
Hispanic barrios,[6] in the shadows of factories, in Third World nations—

any place where the fate of men is as grim and bleak as the fate of women. Toilers and warriors. I realize now how ancient these identities are, how deep the tug they exert on men, the undertone of a thousand generations. The miseries I saw, as a boy, in the lives of nearly all men I continue to see in the lives of many—the body-breaking toil, the tedium, the call to be tough, the humiliating powerlessness, the battle for a living and for territory.

When the women I met at college thought about the joys and privi-   20
leges of men, they did not carry in their minds the sort of men I had known in my childhood. They thought of their fathers, who were bankers, physicians, architects, stockbrokers, the big wheels of the big cities. These fathers rode the train to work or drove cars that cost more than any of my childhood houses. They were attended from morning to night by female helpers, wives, and nurses and secretaries. They were never laid off, never short of cash at month's end, never lined up for welfare. These fathers made decisions that mattered. They ran the world.

The daughters of such men wanted to share in this power, this   21
glory. So did I. They yearned for a say over their future, for jobs worthy of their abilities, for the right to live at peace, unmolested, whole. Yes, I thought, yes yes. The difference between me and these daughters was that they saw me, because of my sex, as destined from birth to become like their fathers, and therefore as an enemy to their desires. But I knew better. I wasn't an enemy, in fact or in feeling. I was an ally. If I had known, then, how to tell them so, would they have believed me? Would they now?

NOTES

[1] Sassafras tea is made from the root of the sassafras tree, a small tree native to North America.

[2] Jan Vermeer (1632–1675) was a Dutch painter known in particular for his depiction of peaceful domestic scenes.

[3] St. Paul, author of one of the biblical Epistles, is known for his stern views on Christian belief and behaviour.

[4] Stonehenge is a prehistoric circle of stones on Salisbury Plain in England.

[5] The boll weevil is a beetle that attacks the seed vessels of cotton, a major crop in the American South.

[6] Spanish-speaking districts of cities or towns in the United States, especially poor neighbourhoods populated by immigrants.

VOCABULARY

arsenal—an arms repository or store

limbo—a place between heaven and hell, where the souls of the unbaptized are supposed to reside

QUESTIONS

1. How does Sanders' account of his conversation with his friend Anneke create a framework for the rest of the essay?

2. What do the men Sanders carries in his mind—convicts and guards, marginal farmers, factory workers, labourers, soldiers—have in common? How have these men shaped Sanders' attitudes towards gender issues?

3. How does Sanders use comparison as a strategy to develop and organize his ideas in this essay?

4. Do you think Sanders makes effective use of descriptive detail?

5. If you are a female reader, did Sanders' essay make you more willing to believe that men have problems? If you are a male reader, can you identify with Sanders' account of men's lives?

SUGGESTION FOR WRITING

What men or women do you carry in your mind? How have they influenced your attitudes towards whether men or women have easier lives? Write an essay in which you describe the appearance of the men or women you grew up with and the work they did. Be sure to include a range of specific sensory detail.

IT ALWAYS COSTS

David T. Suzuki

I have long believed that we have to have greater scientific literacy at all levels of society if we are to have any hope of affecting the way science and technology are impacting on our lives. That's why I went into broadcasting.

But I have only recently realized that my underlying faith in the power of greater awareness is misplaced. First of all, we must understand that there is no such thing as a problem-free technology. However beneficent, technology always has a cost.

Think, for example, of DDT[1]—it killed malaria-carrying mosquitoes in huge numbers and without question saved millions of lives in tropical countries. But geneticists could have predicted that DDT would exert incredible selective pressure for mutations that would confer resistance to DDT in the mosquitoes and that within a few years large numbers would return. They did. But once committed to a chemical approach, we had to turn to other more toxic compounds.

The ecological damage from massive use of chemical sprays has been enormous because DDT is not specific and kills all insects. Furthermore, the compound is ingested by many organisms, so that initially minute quantities become concentrated up the food chain in a process called *biomagnification*. The final result was that DDT ended up in the shell glands of birds, affecting the thickness of egg shells and eventually causing heavy bird mortality.

There are numerous examples of how technological innovations have had detrimental side effects that eventually outweighed their benefits. It has been my assumption that what we needed was some kind of vehicle, like panels of citizens representing a broad range of interests, to do a cost/benefit analysis of all new technologies. The idea was that by carefully weighing the benefits and bad side effects, we could make a more informed decision on whether to allow a new technology to be used. My belief that this would help us avoid future problems was based on faith in our predictive capabilities. Indeed, much of the testing of environmental and health impacts is made on that faith. But we can't rely on such a system.

Vancouver-born David Suzuki (b. 1936), a former university professor and researcher in genetics, is known internationally for his writings and radio and television programs on science and ecology, chief among them *The Nature of Things* and *The Sacred Balance*. He has also written *The Other Japan: Voices Beyond the Mainstream* (with Keibo Oiwa, 1999).

"It Always Costs" is taken from *Inventing the Future*, by David Suzuki. Reprinted with the permission of Stoddart Publishing Co. Limited, North York, Ontario.

For one thing, our assessments are always limited. For example, 6
suppose we do an environmental impact assessment of drilling for oil
in the high Arctic. The studies, of necessity, are carried out in a limited time within a restricted area. It is simply assumed that scaling up
the observed effects of the two drill holes by a factor of one hundred or
more gives a reasonable estimate of the impact of major exploration.

Well, there are effects called *synergistic*; several components inter- 7
act to give new or greater effects than the sum of their individual impact. Also, during an assessment, you can bet industry will be on its
best behaviour, so the results will always be on the conservative side.

It is also true that even if a study is made over ten years (which it 8
won't be) we could never anticipate all the fluctuation of conditions in
this sensitive area. I've known colleagues who have studied populations
of animals or plants over decades and find nice cycles and patterns
that are predictable until suddenly completely unexpected fluctuations
occur. They get out more publications that way, but we ought, then, to
be a lot more humble about how *little* we know.

Finally, we know that major blowouts, spills or accidents are rela- 9
tively rare. Suppose one happens an average of once every twenty
holes. By studying *two* holes and finding no effect, we are not justified
in concluding that drilling one hundred holes will also be accident free.
It would be just as invalid were an accident to happen in one of the
test holes to conclude that half of all drilling sites will have a bad
episode. The numbers are statistically meaningless.

Food additives, pesticides and drugs are extensively tested before 10
they are approved for use. But numerous cases inform us that we can't
anticipate all the effects. The DDT example is classic—at the time it
was used, we didn't even know about biomagnification, let alone its
concentration in bird shell glands.

Remember thalidomide[2] or DES?[3] Or consider the oral contracep- 11
tive. It had been extensively tested (in Puerto Rico, of course) and
shown to be efficacious without detrimental side effects. It was only
after millions of healthy, normal women had taken the pill for years
that epidemiologists could see negative effects. No amount of pretesting could have anticipated them.

So we come to a terrible conclusion. Technology has enormous 12
benefits. They are undeniable—that's why we're hooked on it. Once
technology is in place, it becomes impossible to do without it and we
can't go back to doing things the old way. But the pretesting of any new
technology is flawed because it provides only a limited assessment of
its impact. The tests are restricted in size, scope and time and are
based on what we decide a priori might be a possible effect.

But how can we test for something that we don't know will hap- 13
pen? If every technology has a cost, the more powerful the technology,

the greater its potential cost. We have to build into our judgements a large leeway for our ignorance and err on the side of extreme caution. And perhaps it's time to realize we don't have to do everything just because we can.

NOTES

[1] DDT—dichlorodiphenyltrichloroethane has been used extensively as an insecticide, particularly in combatting malarial mosquitoes. It is a persistent pesticide (it does not break down readily) and is stored in human fat almost indefinitely. Tolerance to DDT is widely variant in humans and its use has led to much controversy. It has been shown, in laboratory experiments, to be an "enzyme inducer" that breaks down estrogen, which in birds mediates calcium metabolism. It is also readily passed through the placenta into the foetus. The use of DDT is now banned in Canada and the United States, though it is still manufactured for export.

[2] Thalidomide, or alpha phthaloyl glutarimide, is a close relative of aminopteria, a drug known since 1950 to have teratogenic (causing monstrous genetic defect) properties. Thalidomide was introduced for sale in Britain in April, 1958. It was released for sale despite an almost complete lack of chemical and pharmacological testing, and of research into the scientific literature. It was touted as being perfectly safe as a sedative for pregnant women despite testing that indicated that it could completely shut down thyroid function. It caused birth defects such as shortened or absent limbs and flipper-like appendages in more than 450 births as well as nerve damage in more than 400 adults and children. Despite medical evidence of its effects, it continued to be sold until its withdrawal in November, 1961.

[3] DES or diethylstilbestrol is a chemical with many of the properties of estrogen. It was widely used as a "morning after" contraceptive as well as a treatment for menopausal symptoms, cancer of the prostate, and certain uterine disorders. DES has also been used since 1954 for fattening cattle and promoting growth in chickens. It has since been found to be related to, if not the cause of, an increase in uterine cancer in women who previously did not get such cancers, and of an increase in cancer of the testes.

VOCABULARY

a priori—*a priori* here means being knowable by reasoning from something that is considered self-evident or presupposed from general experience

epidemiologists—those who deal with the incidence, distribution, and control of diseases in large populations

QUESTIONS

1. Suzuki's title "It [technology] Always Costs" is also his thesis. How is his essay organized to support this thesis?

2. Why does Suzuki include his reassessments of the value of scientific research in his essay? How do these inclusions affect his tone? Be specific about his attitudes to himself, his readers, and his subject.

3. What does Suzuki's comment that the oral contraceptive was tested "in Puerto Rico, of course" reveal about his attitude to the scientific establishment? Do you think this comment affects Suzuki's credibility?

4. Is this essay written for the scientific industry, for specialists in environmental issues, or for the general public? Does Suzuki's style define the audience he is aiming for? (For more on Suzuki's style, see Joyce MacDonald's essay comparing Suzuki with Merwin in the Sample Essays.)

SUGGESTION FOR WRITING

Do you agree that scientific advances *always* have costs? Write a letter to Suzuki expressing your views on the costs and/or benefits of recent developments in science and technology, such as cloning, digital television screens, voice mail, web pages, cell phones.

A MODEST PROPOSAL

For preventing the Children of Poor People
from being a Burthen to
their Parents, or the Country,
and for making them
Beneficial to the Publick.

Jonathan Swift

1 It is a melancholly Object to those, who walk through this great Town,[1] or travel in the Country, when they see the *Streets*, the *Roads*, and *Cabbin-Doors*, crowded with *Beggars* of the female Sex, followed by three, four, or six Children, *all in Rags*, and importuning every Passenger for an Alms. These *Mothers* instead of being able to work for their honest Livelyhood, are forced to employ all their time in Stroling, to beg Sustenance for their *helpless Infants*, who, as they grow up, either turn *Thieves* for want of work, or leave their *dear native Country to fight for the Pretender in Spain*,[2] or sell themselves to the *Barbadoes*.[3]

2 I think it is agreed by all Parties, that this prodigious number of Children, in the Arms, or on the Backs, or at the *Heels* of their *Mothers*, and frequently of their *Fathers*, is *in the present deplorable state of the Kingdom*,[4] a very great additional grievance; and therefore whoever could find out a fair, cheap and easy method of making these Children sound and useful Members of the Commonwealth would deserve so well of the publick, as to have his Statue set up for a Preserver of the Nation.

3 But my Intention is very far from being confined to provide only for the Children of *professed Beggars*: It is of a much greater extent, and shall take in the whole number of Infants at a certain Age, who are born of Parents in effect as little able to support them, as those who demand our Charity in the Streets.

4 As to my own part, having turned my thoughts, for many Years, upon this important Subject, and maturely weighed the several *Schemes of other Projectors*, I have always found them grossly mistaken in their computation. It is true a Child, *just dropt from its Dam*, may be supported by her Milk, for a Solar year with little other Nourishment, at most not above the Value of two Shillings, which the Mother may certainly get, or the Value in *Scraps*, by her lawful Occupation of begging,

Jonathan Swift (1667–1745) is often regarded as the foremost prose satirist to write in English. Born in Ireland of English parents, he was educated at Trinity College, Dublin, and then attempted a career in writing, politics, and the church in England. Most of his best-known works, including "A Modest Proposal" (1729) and the Utopian fiction *Gulliver's Travels* (1726), were written during the thirty years from his appointment as Dean of St. Patrick's (Anglican) Cathedral in Dublin in 1714 to his death in 1745, a period in which he more and more took on the role of defender of Ireland against English absentee landlords and their Irish collaborators.

and it is exactly at one Year old that I propose to provide for them, in such a manner, as, instead of being a Charge upon their *Parents*, or the *Parish*, or *wanting Food and Raiment* for the rest of their Lives, they shall, on the Contrary, contribute to the Feeding and partly to the Cloathing of many Thousands.

There is likewise another great Advantage in my Scheme, that it will prevent those *voluntary Abortions*, and that horrid practice of *Women murdering their Bastard Children*; alas! too frequent among us; sacrificing the *poor innocent Babes*, I doubt, more to avoid the Expence, than the Shame; which would move Tears and Pity in the most Savage and inhuman breast. 5

The Number of Souls in this Kingdom being usually reckoned one Million and a half; of these I calculate there may be about two hundred thousand Couple whose Wives are Breeders; from which number I Subtract thirty Thousand Couples, who are able to maintain their own Children, although I apprehend there cannot be so many under *the present distresses of the Kingdom*; but this being granted, there will remain an Hundred and Seventy Thousand Breeders. I again Subtract fifty Thousand for those Women who miscarry, or whose Children dye by accident, or disease within the Year. There only remain an hundred and twenty thousand Children of poor Parents annually born: The question therefore is, how this number shall be reared, and provided for, which, as I have already said, under the present Situation of Affairs, is utterly impossible by all the methods hitherto proposed, for we can *neither employ them in Handicraft*, or *Agriculture*; we neither build Houses, (I mean in the Country) nor cultivate Land: They can very seldom pick up a Livelyhood *by Stealing* till they arrive at six years Old, except where they are of towardly parts, although, I confess they learn the Rudiments much earlier, during which time, they can however be properly looked upon only as *Probationers*, as I have been informed by a principal Gentleman in the County of *Cavan*,[5] who protested to me, that he never knew above one or two Instances under the Age of six, even in a part of the Kingdom *so renowned for the quickest proficiency in that Art*. 6

I am assured by our Merchants, that a Boy or Girl, before twelve Years old, is no saleable Commodity, and even when they come to this Age, they will not yield above three Pounds, or three Pounds and half a Crown at most on the Exchange, which cannot turn to Account either to the Parents or the Kingdom, the Charge of Nutriment and Rags having been at least four times that Value. 7

I shall now therefore humbly propose my own thoughts, which I hope will not be liable to the least Objection. 8

I have been assured by a very knowing *American* of my acquaintance in *London*, that a young healthy Child well Nursed is at a Year 9 old a most delicious, nourishing, and wholesome Food, whether *Stewed, Roasted, Baked, or Boiled*, and I make no doubt that it will equally serve in a *Fricasie*, or a *Ragoust*.

I do therefore humbly offer it to *publick consideration*, that of the 10 hundred and twenty thousand Children, already computed, twenty thousand may be reserved for Breed, whereof only one fourth part to be Males, which is more than we allow to *Sheep, black Cattle*, or *Swine*, and my reason is that these Children are seldom the Fruits of Marriage, *a Circumstance not much regarded by our Savages*, therefore *one Male* will be sufficient to serve *four females*. That the remaining hundred thousand may at a Year old be offered in Sale to the *persons of Quality*, and *Fortune*, through the Kingdom, always advising the Mother to let them Suck plentifully in the last Month, so as to render them Plump, and Fat for a good Table. A Child will make two Dishes at an Entertainment for Friends, and when the Family dines alone, the fore or hind Quarter will make a reasonable Dish, and seasoned with a little Pepper or Salt will be very good Boiled on the fourth Day,[6] especially in Winter.

I have reckoned upon a Medium, that a Child just born will weigh 11 12 pounds, and in a solar Year if tolerably nursed encreaseth to twenty eight Pounds.

I grant this food will be somewhat dear, and therefore very *proper* 12 *for Landlords*, who, as they have already devoured most of the Parents, seem to have the best Title to the Children.

Infant's flesh will be in Season throughout the Year, but more plen- 13 tiful in *March*, and a little before and after, for we are told by a grave Author[7] an eminent *French* Physitian, that *Fish being a prolifick Dyet*, there are more Children born in *Roman Catholick Countries* about nine Months after *Lent*, than at any other Season: Therefore reckoning a Year after *Lent*, the Markets will be more glutted than usual, because the number of *Popish Infants*, is at least three to one in this Kingdom, and therefore it will have one other Collateral advantage by lessening the Number of *Papists*[8] among us.

I have already computed the Charge of nursing a Beggars Child (in 14 which list I reckon all *Cottagers, Labourers,* and four fifths of the *Farmers*) to be about two Shillings *per Annum*, Rags included, and I believe no Gentleman would repine to give Ten Shillings for the *Carcass of a good fat Child*, which, as I have said will make four Dishes of excellent Nutritive Meat, when he hath only some particular friend, or his own Family to Dine with him. Thus the Squire will learn to be a good Landlord, and grow popular among his Tenants, the Mother will have Eight Shillings net profit, and be fit for Work till she produceth another Child.

Those who are more thrifty (*as I must confess the Times require*) 15
may flay the Carcass; the Skin of which, artificially dressed, will make
admirable *Gloves for Ladies*, and *Summer Boots for fine Gentlemen*.

As to our City of *Dublin*, Shambles may be appointed for this pur- 16
pose, in the most convenient parts of it, and Butchers we may be assured will not be wanting, although I rather recommend buying the
Children alive, and dressing them hot from the Knife, as we do *roast-
ing Pigs*.

A very worthy Person, *a true Lover of his Country*,[9] and whose 17
Virtues I highly esteem, was lately pleased, in discoursing on this mat-
ter, to offer a Refinement upon my Scheme. He said, that many
Gentlemen of this Kingdom, having of late destroyed their Deer, he
conceived that the want of Venison might be well supplied by the
Bodies of young Lads and Maidens, not exceeding fourteen Years of
Age, nor under twelve, so great a Number of both Sexes in every
Country being now ready to Starve, for want of Work and Service:
And these to be disposed of by their Parents if alive, or otherwise by
their nearest Relations. But with due deference to so excellent a
friend, and so deserving a Patriot, I cannot be altogether in his
Sentiments, for as to the Males, my *American* acquaintance assured
me from frequent Experience, that their flesh was generally Tough
and Lean, like that of our Schoolboys, by continual exercise, and their
Taste disagreeable, and to Fatten them would not answer the Charge.
Then as to the Females, it would, I think with humble Submission, *be
a loss to the Publick*, because they soon would become Breeders
themselves: And besides it is not improbable that some scrupulous
People might be apt to Censure such a Practice, (although indeed very
unjustly) as a little bordering upon Cruelty, which, I confess, hath always been with me the strongest objection against any Project, however so well intended.

But in order to justify my friend, he confessed, that this expedient 18
was put into his head by the famous *Sallmanaazor*, a Native of the
Island *Formosa*,[10] who came from thence to *London*, above twenty
Years ago, and in Conversation told my friend, that in his Country
when any young Person happened to be put to Death, the Executioner
sold the Carcass to *Persons of Quality*, as a prime Dainty, and that, in
his Time, the Body of a plump Girl of fifteen, who was crucified for an
attempt to Poison the Emperor, was sold to his Imperial *Majesty's
prime Minister of State*, and other great *Mandarins* of the Court, *in
Joints from the Gibbet*, at four hundred Crowns. Neither indeed can I
deny, that if the same use were made of several plump young Girls in
this Town, who, without one single Groat[11] to their Fortunes, cannot
stir abroad without a Chair, and appear at the *Play-House*, and
Assemblies in Foreign fineries, which they never will Pay for; the
Kingdom would not be the worse.

Some Persons of a desponding Spirit are in great Concern about   19
that vast Number of poor People, who are aged, diseased, or maimed,
and I have been desired to imploy my thoughts what Course may be
taken, to ease the Nation of so grievous an Incumbrance. But I am not
in the least pain about the matter, because it is very well known, that
they are every Day *dying*, and *rotting*, by *cold*, and *famine*, and *filth*,
and *vermin*, as fast as can be reasonably expected. And as to the
younger Labourers they are now in almost as hopeful a Condition. They
cannot get Work, and consequently pine away for want of Nourishment,
to a degree, that if at any time they are accidentally hired to common
Labour, they have not strength to perform it, and thus the Country and
themselves are happily delivered from the Evils to come.

I have too long digressed, and therefore shall return to my subject.   20
I think the advantages by the Proposal which I have made, are obvious,
and many, as well as of the highest importance.

For, *First*, as I have already observed, it would greatly lessen *the*   21
Number of Papists, with whom we are yearly over-run, being the principal Breeders of the Nation, as well as our most dangerous Enemies,
and who stay at home on purpose with a design *to deliver the Kingdom*
to the Pretender, hoping to take their Advantage by the absence *of so*
many good Protestants, who have chosen rather to leave their
Country, than stay at home, and pay Tithes against their Conscience,
to an *Episcopal Curate*.

Secondly, the poorer Tenants will have something valuable of their   22
own, which by Law may be made liable to Distress,[12] and help to pay
their Landlord's Rent, their Corn and Cattle being already seazed, and
Money a thing unknown.

Thirdly, Whereas the Maintenance of an Hundred Thousand   23
Children, from two Years old, and upwards, cannot be computed at less
than Ten Shillings a piece *per Annum*, the Nation's Stock will be
thereby encreased fifty thousand pounds *per Annum*, besides the
profit of a new Dish, introduced to the Tables of all *Gentlemen of*
Fortune in the Kingdom, who have any refinement in Taste, and the
Money will circulate among ourselves, the Goods being entirely of our
own Growth and Manufacture.

Fourthly, The constant Breeders, besides the gain of Eight Shillings   24
per Annum, by the Sale of their Children, will be rid of the Charge of
maintaining them after the first Year.

Fifthly, This food would likewise bring great *Custom to Taverns*,   25
where the Vintners will certainly be so prudent as to procure the best
receipts for dressing it to perfection, and consequently have their
Houses frequented by all the *fine Gentlemen*, who justly value themselves upon their Knowledge in good *Eating*, and a skillful Cook, who
understands how to oblige his Guests, will contrive to make it as expensive as they please.

Sixthly, This would be a great Inducement to Marriage, which all   26
wise Nations have either encouraged by Rewards, or enforced by Laws
and Penalties. It would encrease the care and tenderness of Mothers towards their Children, when they were sure of a Settlement for Life, to
the poor Babes, provided in some sort by the Publick to their annual
Profit instead of Expence. We should soon see an honest Emulation
among the married Women, *which of them could bring the fattest Child
to the Market.* Men would become as fond of their *Wives*, during the
Time of their Pregnancy, as they are now of their *Mares* in Foal, their
Cows in Calf, or *Sows* when they are ready to Farrow, nor offer to Beat
or Kick them (as it is too frequent a practice) for fear of a Miscarriage.

Many other advantages might be enumerated. For Instance, the ad-   27
dition of some thousand Carcases in our exportation of barreled Beef:
The Propagation of *Swines Flesh*, and Improvement in the Art of mak-
ing good *Bacon*, so much wanted among us by the great destruction of
Pigs, too frequent at our Tables, which are no way comparable in
Taste, or Magnificence to a well grown, fat Yearling Child, which
Roasted whole will make a considerable Figure at a *Lord Mayor's
Feast*, or any other Publick Entertainment. But this, and many others I
omit, being studious of Brevity.

Supposing that one thousand Families in this City, would be con-   28
stant Customers for Infants Flesh, besides others who might have it at
Merry-meetings, particularly *Weddings* and *Christenings*, I compute
that *Dublin* would take off annually about Twenty Thousand Carcases,
and the rest of the Kingdom (where probably they will be sold somewhat cheaper) the remaining Eighty Thousand.

I can think of no one Objection, that will possibly be raised against   29
this Proposal, unless it should be urged that the Number of People will
be thereby much lessened in the Kingdom. This I freely own, and it was
indeed one principal Design in offering it to the World. I desire the
Reader will observe, that I Calculate my Remedy *for this one individual
Kingdom of IRELAND, and for no other that ever was, is, or, I think,
ever can be upon Earth.* Therefore let no Man talk to me of other
Expedients: *Of taxing our Absentees at five Shillings a pound: Of
using neither Cloaths, nor household Furniture, except what is of our
own Growth and Manufacture: Of utterly rejecting the Materials and
Instruments that promote Foreign Luxury: Of curing the
Expensiveness of Pride, Vanity, Idleness, and Gaming in our Women:
Of introducing a Vein of Parsimony, Prudence and Temperance: Of
learning to Love our Country, wherein we differ even from LAPLAN-
DERS, and the Inhabitants of TOPINAMBOO:*[13] *Of quitting our
Animosities, and Factions, nor Act any longer like the Jews, who were
Murdering one another at the very moment their City was taken:*[14]

Of being a little Cautious not to Sell our Country and Consciences for nothing: Of teaching Landlords to have at least one degree of Mercy towards their Tenants. Lastly of putting a Spirit of Honesty, Industry and Skill into our Shopkeepers, who, if a Resolution could now be taken to Buy only our Native Goods, would immediately unite to Cheat and Exact upon us in the Price, the Measure, and the Goodness, nor could ever yet be brought to make one fair Proposal of just dealing, though often and earnestly invited to it.

Therefore I repeat, let no Man talk to me of these and the like Expedients, till he hath at least some Glimpse of Hope, that there will ever be some hearty and sincere Attempt to put them in Practice.   30

But as to my self, having been wearied out for many Years with offering vain, idle, visionary thoughts, and at length utterly despairing of Success, I fortunately fell upon this Proposal, which as it is wholly new, so it hath something Solid and Real, of no Expence and little Trouble, full in our own Power, and whereby we can incur no Danger in *disobliging* England. For this kind of Commodity will not bear Exportation, the Flesh being of too tender a Consistance, to admit a long continuance in Salt, *although perhaps I could name a Country, which would be glad to Eat up our whole Nation without it.*   31

After all, I am not so violently bent upon my own Opinion, as to reject any Offer, proposed by wise Men, which shall be found equally innocent, cheap, easy and effectual. But before something of that kind shall be advanced in Contradiction to my Scheme, and offering a better, I desire the Author, or Authors will be pleased maturely to consider two points. *First*, as things now stand, how they will be able to find Food and Raiment for an hundred thousand useless Mouths and Backs. And *Secondly*, there being a round Million of Creatures in human Figure, throughout this Kingdom, whose whole Subsistance put into a common Stock, would leave them in Debt of two Million of Pounds *Sterling*, adding those, who are Beggars by Profession, to the Bulk of Farmers, Cottagers and Labourers with their Wives and Children, who are Beggars in Effect; I desire those *Politicians*, who dislike my Overture, and may perhaps be so bold to attempt an Answer, that they will first ask the Parents of these Mortals, whether they would not at this Day think it a great Happiness to have been sold for Food at a year Old, in the manner I prescribe, and thereby have avoided such a perpetual Scene of Misfortunes, as they have since gone through, by the *Oppression of Landlords*, the Impossibility of paying Rent without Money or Trade, the want of common Sustenance, with neither House nor Cloaths to cover them from Inclemencies of Weather, and the most inevitable Prospect of intailing the like, or greater Miseries upon their Breed for ever.   32

I Profess in the sincerity of my Heart that I have not the least per- 33
sonal Interest, in endeavouring to promote this necessary Work; having
no other Motive than the *publick Good of my Country,* by *advancing
our Trade, providing for Infants, relieving the Poor, and giving some
Pleasure to the Rich.* I have no Children, by which I can propose to get
a single Penny; the youngest being nine Years old, and my Wife past
Childbearing.

NOTES

1 Dublin, Ireland

2 The Pretender is James Edward Stuart, who claimed (or "pretended" to) the throne lost by his
father, James II, in 1688. (Because of his Catholic sympathies, James II had been overthrown by
supporters of his Protestant daughter and son-in-law, Mary II and William II.) The French
upheld James Stuart's claim because of his Roman Catholicism, and, by the Limerick Treaty of
1691, Irish Roman Catholics were granted the right to bear arms in the service of France, and
thus, by affiliation, in the service of the Pretender.

3 Because of the poverty in Ireland many Irish immigrated to British colonies in America and the
West Indies, indenturing themselves to plantation owners for their passage.

4 Ireland had just suffered three successive bad harvests.

5 Soil conditions in county Cavan are particularly unsuited to tillage and require a great deal of
capital to manage. It also had a long history of high rents and exploitation.

6 Boiling was a way to render meat edible if it was beginning to turn bad.

7 François Rabelais (1494–1553) was a French humorist and satirist and anything but "grave."

8 "Papist" is a hostile name for a Roman Catholic. Swift, as an Anglican (Protestant) clergyman,
might be expected to be hostile to Catholicism, but the hostility here is, of course, ironic.

9 It is not clear whether the "true Lover of his Country" refers to an actual person or not.

10 George Psalmanazar was a Frenchman who posed as a Formosan (modern Taiwanese). His
fictitious accounts, *Historical and Geographical History of Formosa* (1704) and *A Dialogue between
a Japanese and a Formosan about some points of the religion of the time* (1707), contained passages
describing human sacrifice and cannibalism. The remainder of this paragraph is a paraphrase of
one of the stories told by Psalmanazar.

11 A groat is a small British coin worth four pence.

12 Distress or distraint is the act of distraining or legally forcing a person to give up personal
goods to be used as payment against debts.

13 The Tupinamba were a group of tribes, now extinct, that lived on the coast of Brazil from
the mouth of the Amazon to the southern part of the state of São Paulo. Swift says that even
those who live in places of extreme cold and heat love their countries better than the
Anglo-Irish.

14 In A.D. 70, the Roman Emperor Titus laid siege to, captured, and destroyed Jerusalem.
Throughout the period of siege and capture, the city was being torn apart internally by warring
religious factions.

VOCABULARY

alms—anything given freely to relieve want

artificially—with skill or artifice

burthen—burden

crown—a coin worth five shillings, a shilling being worth 1/20 of a pound or five pence. Half a crown is, therefore, a coin worth 12 1/2 pence.

dressing—preparing meat for the market, usually by bleeding and cleaning it

emulation—an attempt to equal or excel, here perhaps each other

gibbet—a gallows

importuning—pressing or urging with unreasonable requests

intailing (or usually, entailing)—settling something (e.g., land, title, obligation) on a number of persons in succession so that it cannot be bequeathed to another person

joints—a large section of meat usually including a large bone or joint

probationers—those whose fitness is being tested

repine—to complain or fret

shambles—a slaughterhouse

squire—a country gentleman, particularly the principal landowner of a district

towardly—dutiful, tractable

vintner—not only the maker but also the seller of wines

QUESTIONS

1. In this essay, Swift speaks through a persona (a mask, or second self, created by the author). Give three or four examples that show that Swift is not speaking in his own voice.

2. List the main interests and characteristics of Swift's persona.

3. How does Swift use the gap between his own feelings and opinions and those of his persona to create and sustain the irony throughout the essay? What standard(s) of evaluation does the persona employ as he presents his solution to the terrible poverty in Ireland? What standards does Swift imply?

4. Can you identify any places where Swift steps out from behind his mask?

5. For what reasons, literary or otherwise, do you think Swift chose irony, rather than direct statement, as a strategy to persuade his audience to alleviate poverty in Ireland?

6. In a satiric essay, writers achieve their purpose by undermining the apparent thesis rather than by supporting it. What is the apparent thesis of "A Modest Proposal"? How does Swift undermine it?

7. Matters like spelling, punctuation, capitalization, and the use of italics were far less standardized in Swift's day than in ours. Do these or other features of Swift's style affect your reading of this essay? If so, how?

SUGGESTION FOR WRITING

Using Swift's essay as a model, write a "modest proposal" in which you present an outrageous solution to a current social problem. Follow the structure of "A Modest Proposal" and feel free to include verbal echoes from it. Remember that you will need to adopt a persona whose attitudes and values present to your readers an exaggerated version of their own. Like Swift, you want to shock your readers into a recognition of their moral inadequacies in not responding to a social need.

CHOOSING UP SIDES

Ken Wiwa

It had to happen some time: Anyone with more than one nationality 1
knows that there are times when you have to make a choice between the places that stake a claim on your loyalty. When England
played Nigeria at the soccer World Cup this week, I found myself in
what seems to be a very 21st-century dilemma: I was caught between
two countries to which I nominally owe an allegiance.

My dilemma illustrates a growing phenomenon for many, as un- 2
precedented movements of people around the globe are reconfiguring
the map of the world. Like me, more and more people are finding
themselves in a no-man's land, where we are asked to declare either
for the country we left behind or the country we now live in. Few
events highlight this dilemma more acutely than the World Cup, an
event that arouses strong tribal passions around the planet.

The World Cup is a truly global event. Forget the Stanley Cup or 3
the "World" Series: *the Coupe du Monde* has worldwide appeal. It is a
proxy of world war, a true test of your patriotism, of individual and collective prejudice. And for those of us of mongrel heritage, the World
Cup is a cross-examination of our loyalty, of whether we have assimi-
lated and adopted the flag of our new country or whether the old country still exercises an inalienable claim on our identity.

It might seem disproportionate to invest a soccer tournament with 4
such an epic estimation but soccer is more than sport, it is a parable
that, for me, contains the germ of an interest-
ing geopolitical question: Are we really headed
for a brave new world[1] without borders where a
World Cup of national teams will soon be an
anachronism, or do old tribal loyalties still exercise the strongest pull on the individual and
collective pathology?

Although I now live in Canada, I was born 5
in Nigeria and raised in England. When you
subtract the three years I have lived in Canada,
half of my 33 years have been spent in the land
of my fathers and the other half in the land
that fathered my country. I have always
claimed to be ambivalent and even indifferent
about my nationality. I carry two passports of

Ken Wiwa is a journalist who contributes
regularly to newspapers in Canada, the
United Kingdom, South Africa, Germany,
and Holland. Born in Nigeria, he currently
lives in Canada with his family and is senior
resident writer at Massey College at the
University of Toronto. An advocate of social
justice and environmental protection, Ken
Wiwa is the son of the executed Nigerian
writer/political activist Ken Saro-Wiwa. Ken
Wiwa's book *In the Shadow of a Saint: A Son's
Journey to Understand His Father's Legacy*
(2001) explores his complicated relationship with his late father.

"Choosing Up Sides" was published in *The
Globe and Mail*, July 15, 2002.

convenience and don't care much for flag waving. At most sporting events I support whatever team tickles my passing fancy. My ambivalence usually survives intact until the World Cup comes along.

The World Cup is a paradox. The tournament is a month-long pas- 6 sion play,[2] a re-enactment of the historical triumphs, failures and ancient grudges that have defined the status-quo of nations. But it also offers a window into a new world being fashioned by today's economic trends.

This World Cup has thrown up its usual quota of games played 7 against a background flush with historical subtext. When Japan played Russia, the old rivalry between the two erupted in Moscow. Although the rioting was, as a rather sour FIFA official was quick to point out, an isolated example of soccer fever, the beautiful game has been known to kick-start wars between countries. Or even generate the emotions that a war stirs. Whenever Argentina plays England, the shadow of the 1982 Falkland Islands war is a subtext of the battle on the pitch. Argentines usually exact revenge for losing Las Malvinas, while England's bellicose soccer fans rage against the inability of their teams to reflect their military superiority.

Matches between European teams are almost always played against 8 the background of national pride and chauvinism. When Germany plays England, English fans see it as a re-enactment of the First and Second World War. Holland/Germany games have added spice due to the Nazi occupation. Even games between the usually placid Scandinavians can excite the passions. But nowhere is soccer more volatile than in South America, where Argentine antipathy to Brazil generates more pre-match tension than a Tyson fight. El Salvador and Honduras once went to war over a football match.

As much as I abhor the chauvinism that soccer sometimes in- 9 spires, the World Cup would not be the World Cup without it. You cannot isolate or fully appreciate a game between England and Argentina without the history. England's hands-to-the-pump victory against Argentina last weekend was made all the sweeter by the memory of the illegal goal Diego Maradona scored in 1986. When he suggested afterward that the "hand of God" had scored the goal, the English were incensed but probably not as angry as when he recently mused that it felt good to "pick the pocket of an Englishman."

I was actually in England when the World Cup started but left be- 10 fore the Argentina match. I had planned to be in Nigeria when the Super Eagles met the English team. When Nigeria plays England at soccer, the tribal instincts rise to the surface, puncturing my mask of neutrality to reveal that I am a Nigerian.

The fire of national chauvinism has been burning since the open- 11 ing day of the World Cup when Senegal humbled her former colonial master and world champion, France. (In these matters I wear my colonial grudges on my sleeve.) But if you looked closely at the teams, like the whole World Cup itself, you saw that behind the façade of national rivalry was the outline of a world that is busy reconfiguring the constituency of many countries, redrawing the map that assembled between 1500 and 1900.

History will not remember Papa Bouba Diop in the same breath as   12
Christopher Columbus, but in one sense the Senegalese player's goal against France was the end of a process the Italian began when he kick-started the plunder of the "new" world and Europeans divided up the globe. Since 1945, the lines of the map have been eroded by mass movements of peoples and changing political winds. So when Mr. Diop scored that winning goal, it was tempting to suggest that goal was symbolic: The Empire had struck back.

But had it? Look at the composition of the French team, for instance.   13
It was made up of Algerians, a Ghanaian, a Ukrainian, a Congolese and at least four players of Caribbean origin. The team has recently been sold as an advert for the new face of France, the multicultural antidote to the poison Le Pen[3] and the rising tide of nationalism in Europe. The far right in France may do well to dwell on the composition of the Senegalese team. Senegal had more players plying their trade in France than the multicultural, multitalented French team.

With globalization and the supposed liberalization of borders, people are, in theory, more or less free to ply their trade anywhere. The   14
creolization of the regions (clubs) is manifesting itself in the pluralism of national character (national teams). It is hardly a surprise with all this miscegenation that a supposedly inferior team like Senegal can beat the French because the movement of players between the countries has not only levelled the playing field, it has negated the aesthetic difference between Senegal and France. That the Senegalese coach, Bruno Metsu, is French merely emphasizes that when it comes to football, the only difference between the countries is the colour of the shirts on their backs. Only a few countries such as China now sport mono-cultural teams. Even the fiercely nationalist Japanese have a Brazilian in their squad.

Increasingly as money transcends old religious, political, social and   15
economic boundaries, the notion of nationalism may lose its grip on private and public consciousness. If so, it will die a long, slow and spasmodic death, as the World Cup clearly shows. Because even those of us who are suspicious of the claims of country on our identity still need to feel part of a communal love-in every now and again.

I went home to get mine. But by the time I arrived in Port Harcourt   16
on the Atlantic coastline, Nigeria had already been eliminated from the World Cup. The game against England had lost its edge, and as the two teams played pass-the-buck and settled for a soporific draw, you hoped that a world without national tension and competition would not be as dull.

NOTES

[1] Brave new world: the title of a novel by Aldous Huxley (1932) that presented a satiric vision of the future.

[2] Passion play: an enactment of the crucifixion of Christ.

[3] Le Pen: a French politician with very conservative (some would argue racist) views on immigration.

VOCABULARY

antipathy—strong dislike, hatred

chauvinism—extreme patriotism

creolization—mixing of the races

historical subtext—the historical meaning beneath the surface

inalienable—something that cannot be challenged

miscegenation—a negative term to describe marriages between people of different races

nominally—in name only, theoretically

parable—a story that teaches a lesson

paradox—a situation in which logical contradictions co-exist

pathology—disease

proxy—a substitute

soporific—something that induces sleep

volatile—violent and fiery

QUESTIONS

1. What evidence does Wiwa include to support his point that sports events re-enact rivalries and tensions between the places the teams represent? Do you find this evidence convincing? Can you provide further examples?

2. Wiwa further argues that "tribal passions" aroused by sports events are most intense when a country that had been colonized plays its former rulers (Nigeria vs. Britain or Senegal vs. France). According to Wiwa, what is at stake in these contests?

3. What are Wiwa's own feelings about nationalism, as they are shown in this essay? What position does he finally arrive at?

SUGGESTIONS FOR WRITING

1. Wiwa argues that, since most "national" teams are composed of nationals from many countries, the "notion of nationalism" may be losing its grip, in sports and in life. Write a short essay agreeing or disagreeing with this point of view.

2. Have you ever been faced with a situation that made you question your own cultural identity? Write a short personal essay exploring this situation.

THE ENGLISH PATIENT DEBATE

The film version of The English Patient, *the prize-winning novel by Canadian author Michael Ondaatje, provoked a wide range of opinion. The following pieces, published in* The Globe and Mail *between January and March 1997, illustrate different ways of evaluating both the film and other viewers' responses.*

The Moral Superiority of *Casablanca* over *The English Patient*

Thomas Hurka[1]

Both take place during the Second World War. Both are set largely in North Africa, with the desert a powerful backdrop. But one is a morally serious movie while the other is fatuous sentimentality. I'm talking about *Casablanca* and *The English Patient*.[2]   1

Casablanca's moral vision is expressed in one of the many quotable lines of Rick, Humphrey Bogart's character. Rick is deeply in love with Ingrid Bergman's Ilsa and she with him. But Ilsa is married to Victor Laszlo, a leader of the anti-Nazi resistance in his home country. It's important for the fight against Nazism that Victor escape to the United States and important to Victor's work that Ilsa go with him. Though Ilsa wants to stay with Rick, he knows she can't. As he puts her and Victor on the plane, he says, "The problems of three little people don't amount to a hill of beans in this crazy world."   2

In *Casablanca* the political can be more important than the personal. No matter how passionate one's love—and Rick and Ilsa are certainly passionate—there are situations and dangers that must take priority. The Second World War was one such situation and Nazism one such danger.   3

The English Patient is based on the novel of the same name by Canadian Michael Ondaatje. Its moral vision is expressed in a line it uses   4 twice: "Betrayals in war are childlike compared to our betrayals in peace." Or, roughly, loyalty in love is more important than loyalty in war.

The movie's central character, played by Ralph Fiennes, is Count   5
Almasy. Just before the war Almasy gave the German army crucial desert maps that enabled them to successfully attack Tobruk[3] and almost win the war in North Africa. Now, badly burned, he is dying in a villa in Italy. One character, Caravaggio, suspects Almasy's identity and wants to kill him for his betrayal. But he changes his mind and forgives Almasy when he learns what led to the betrayal.

Almasy too was deeply in love with a married woman, Katherine.   6
After a desert plane crash left her injured and unable to move, he carried her to a cave and promised to return with help. The only source of help was the German army. To get that help, and as the only way to keep his promise, he gave the Germans the maps.

In *The English Patient* the personal is more important than the po-   7
litical. Whatever the effects on the outcome of a coming war, the movie suggests, it's understandable to give priority to your personal relationships. The problems of the world, and of the millions of people threatened by Nazism, don't amount to a hill of beans beside those of two love-crazed people.

This is the immorality at the core of *The English Patient*: It exalts   8
personal emotion at the expense of everything else. In *Casablanca* Rick's love doesn't blind him to larger issues of politics. On the contrary, only after Ilsa returns that love can he care about those issues properly. But Almasy in the desert thinks only of his own small affair. And the movie presents this as making his betrayal not only forgivable but even, as the background music swells, inspiring. When, tears streaming, he emerges from the last trip to the cave, he is treated wholly sympathetically.

Questioned about his betrayal, Almasy gives Caravaggio other ex-   9
cuses. After leaving Katherine in the cave he went first to the British. Staggering into their camp without identification papers and demanding a jeep, he was instead arrested as a spy. Since they betrayed him first, Almasy says, he didn't really betray them.

But what planet was the man on? He was in contested territory on   10
the brink of war and without papers. And he expected to be given a jeep? This is again a sign of the movie's absorption in personal emotions. Almasy's blindness to the reality around him is presented not as irresponsibility but as a sign of profound and wonderful love.

In any case, the movie cheats by presenting the issue facing him as   11
just one of loyalty, of being true to your side just because they're your own. Before the war Almasy and his cosmopolitan friends are rightly scornful of this kind of parochialism. But the other side in this case is

Nazism and that should make a difference. Rick in *Casablanca* is a neutral and faces no issue of loyalty; he's an American and the U.S. isn't yet in the war. But he sees that one side is morally odious. Almasy doesn't bother to look.

In each of two movies a man deeply in love makes a choice in the   12 desert. Rick sacrifices his love for a larger political cause; Almasy sacrifices a cause because he cares only about his love. *Casablanca* is one of the most loved movies of all time. *The English Patient* is beautifully photographed, powerfully acted, and completely morally bankrupt.

NOTES

[1] Reprinted by permission of the author.

[2] *Casablanca*, directed by Michael Curtiz, came out in 1942. (See the essay on *Casablanca* in Chapter 1.) *The English Patient* (1996), directed by Anthony Minghella, is based on a 1992 book of the same name by Canadian poet and novelist Michael Ondaatje. Both films are set in North Africa.

[3] A port town in northeastern Libya that was taken alternately by the Germans and the British between 1940 and 1942.

VOCABULARY

fatuous—silly and self-congratulatory

cosmopolitan—being of the world, sophisticated, free from national and local prejudice

parochialism—the state of being narrow-minded, full of local prejudice

Round Two:

The English Patient Rallies (Letters)[4]

Re The Moral Superiority of *Casablanca* over *The English Patient* (Focus, Jan 25):

Where has Thomas Hurka been for the past 15 years? Works by   1 such people as Carol Gilligan[5] and other feminists working on the topic of morality have recognized that women, and men, too, who value relations, may speak "in a different voice" which has been undervalued, but one in which the care and response to others as a top concern has come to be seen as parallel in morality positioning to those who focus on "higher" ideals and causes.

Valuing relationships and honouring our promises to commitment   2
to others may seem "bankrupt" to Professor Hurka but many of us
have come to understand that it is allegiance to people and loving and
caring about them which gives life its fullest and finest meaning. The
two films of *Casablanca* and *The English Patient* may represent two
different morality paths but if they do, neither should be viewed as superior or inferior to the other.

Catharine E. Warren
University of Calgary

* * *

I find I must respond to the piece of fatuous tripe appearing under the   1
name of Thomas Hurka (The Moral Superiority of *Casablanca*
over *The English Patient*—Focus, Jan. 25). According to Mr. Hurka,
Casablanca is a "morally serious movie" or one of "moral vision" because it takes the political to be more important than the personal,
whereas *The English Patient* is decried on the grounds that it "exalts
personal emotion at the expense of everything else." Says Professor
Hurka: "Almasy sacrifices a cause because he cares only about his love."
Now let's look at the reality:

Almasy asks for a car from the British to save a dying woman,   2
which he has promised her he will do. The British treat him abom-
inably. Seen as a Hungarian and hence an ally of Hitler, he is shipped
off to the coast. He escapes and is forced to turn to the Germans to enable him to go back to the dying woman and try to rescue her, as he
had promised. To get the necessary fuel, he gives them expedition
maps. Assuming him to be a spy, the British shoot him down on his return flight with the body of the woman he loved. Of course he was not
a spy, but a desperate man to whom help had been refused by the
"good" side. Nor had he betrayed anyone or anything.

In point of fact, Almasy had no loyalties to any nation as such   3
(though his initial sympathies were obviously with the Allies), and like
most of his expedition comrades, believed that there were things more
important than national loyalties, such as the human values the arche-
ological expedition was devoted to, and yes, love—the deepest emotion
of which any human being is capable. He had no national "cause," only
his loves, his friendships, and his interest in the human past. (If he had
had a cause, as a "loyal" Hungarian it would have to have been Hitler's!
Otherwise he would have been a traitor!)

Yes there *are* things, human things, more important than na-   4
tional loyalties and the clash by night of ignorant armies,[6] and that is
an important part of what is being said in this novel and this film.

Casablanca is a great Bogie thriller. *The English Patient* is a deep and serious moral movie.

E. J. Bond, Professor of Philosophy
Queen's University, Kingston

* * *

Thomas Hurka's accusation that the film *The English Patient* is 1 "completely morally bankrupt" blindly equates politics, and particularly patriotism, with morality. Among the many ideas Professor Hurka chooses to ignore is the fact that the movie's so-called "absorption in personal emotions" is itself a powerful moral decision: a rejection of both war and nationalism.

"In our hearts," Graham Greene[7] once wrote, "there is a ruthless 2 dictator, ready to contemplate the misery of a thousand strangers if it will ensure the happiness of the few we love." This truth may be terrible to contemplate, but to suggest the opposite (betray the beloved and—only perhaps—save the many unknowns) is more palatable is only the moral attitude of a bean-counter.

Mr. Hurka's crude equation: selflessness in war is morally superior 3 to selflessness in love. If "morality" has no direct relation to love, leave me out of it.

Tim Conley, Montreal

* * *

The discussion in your pages over the past few days about *Casablanca* 1 and *The English Patient* has been interesting, but much has been based on a fundamental misunderstanding of the choice that Rick Blaine makes at the end of *Casablanca*.

The popular notion is that Rick chooses between a woman and a 2 cause. In fact he does not.

Rick spends most of the movie despising Ilsa, and despising the 3 memory of Paris. He is dead inside, incapable of loving Ilsa or anyone else, and doesn't believe in fighting for any cause—not even against the Nazis ("I stick my neck out for no one"). The events of the movie conspire to change Rick, to restore his love ("We'll always have Paris. We didn't have it—we'd lost it—until you came to *Casablanca*. We got it back last night.") and his ability to fight for a cause ("But I've got a job to do … it doesn't take much to see that the problems of three little people don't amount to a hill of beans in this world").

In fact Rick does not choose love or glory, he chooses both, which 4 is why the song says, "It's still the same old story, a fight for love and glory…"

If Rick had sent Victor Laszlo away without his wife, would it have   5
made much of a difference to the war effort? Probably not. But in
sending her away the audience understands that Rick's character has
grown; he understands love, not merely romance, and he has regained
his sense of justice.

Markham Cook, Toronto

NOTES

[4] Reprinted with permission from *The Globe and Mail.*

[5] Carol Gilligan is a feminist writer who compares moral development in girls and boys in her book *In a Different Voice: Psychological Theory and Women's Development* (1982).

[6] "Where ignorant armies clash by night," the final line in Matthew Arnold's poem "Dover Beach," is the Victorian poet's description of the confusions of the modern world.

[7] Graham Greene (1904–1991) wrote over thirty volumes of fiction, essays, plays, and poetry. Many of his novels deal with the conflict between differing loyalties.

When Loyalty and Friendship Collide

Editorial[8]

The practicality of philosophy has been debated at least since   1
Socrates took on the Sophists[9] and their free-market approach to
truth back in ancient Athens. Purists who believe philosophers should
confine their work to classroom lectures and abstruse articles in
learned periodicals have always been suspicious of those who go public
with their thoughts.

The result is a regrettable polarization: Many of the disciplined   2
thinkers in the universities expend their brainpower on topics of marginal usefulness to the wider world, while those who try to argue ethical issues in the media often favour rhetorical style over intellectual
substance.

Last Saturday in the Focus section of *The Globe and Mail*,   3
University of Calgary philosophy professor Thomas Hurka tried to
bridge this gap. He took it upon himself to review the popular film *The
English Patient*, based on Michael Ondaatje's prize-winning novel,
from a moral standpoint. The uproar that has resulted—see the Letters

page opposite, or listen to the arguments reverberating across the living rooms and common rooms of the nation—reveals just how engaging philosophy can be, when it chooses to.

And not just philosophy. Art too, when it is not retreating into self-regarding minimalism,[10] is still capable of making us re-examine our thinking on fundamental issues. And nothing could be more fundamental than the issue broached in *The English Patient*: On the eve of the Second World War, a man gives the Germans maps that are crucial to their campaign in North Africa. This betrayal of country, however, is for a greater good: In exchange for the maps, the man gets help for the woman he loves. Personal loyalties, to put it more crudely than Mr. Ondaatje would ever do, are more important than political loyalties.

"Fatuous sentimentality," pronounced Prof. Hurka, who contrasted this "morally bankrupt" message with the "morally serious" decision made by Rick, Humphrey Bogart's character in *Casablanca*. Choosing to send away the woman he loves and her resistance-leader husband while he stays behind in Casablanca, Rick says: "The problems of three little people don't amount to a hill of beans in this crazy world." In this case, with the Nazis at hand, politics must take priority over love.

The position Prof. Hurka staked out has proved decidedly unpopular, which may explain why so few professional philosophers dare to venture out from their academic lairs. What he calls sentimentality, others see as higher truths: Personal loyalties are paramount; emotional ambiguity in a time of conflict is a natural human response; it is war itself that is morally bankrupt.

A celebrated quote from E. M. Forster[11] was brought out to buttress this preference for the personal over the political: "If I had to choose between betraying my country and betraying my friend, I hope I should have the guts to betray my country." It is a point of view that by now is so firmly fixed in Western culture as to make Prof. Hurka look dangerously out of step. What living artist would dare to champion war over love, and expect to be treated seriously either as an artist or a thinker?

Yet take another look at that quote from Forster. If it seems familiar, that is because it was trotted out many times to defend the actions of the Cambridge traitors—Anthony Blunt, Kim Philby, Guy Burgess, Donald Maclean and John Cairncross—who gave secrets to the Soviet Union while working for British intelligence. Their physical and platonic relationships, formed in a university where friendship was the noblest ideal, took priority over loyalty to the abstract political entity of Britain. But all the same, they still compromised the lives of their fellow citizens by betraying secrets to the Soviet communism that their youthful and high-minded idealism preferred.

Not everyone who prefers the personal over the political is quite so 9
hypocritical. But it is necessary to remember that the consequences of
apolitical idealism are still political. War may well be morally bankrupt. Artists instinctively find it offensive because its intolerant values
are so clearly antiliberal.

Yet war does not go away simply because it is intellectually and 10
emotionally dissatisfying. If you betray secrets to help your loved one,
you have put war at a distance. But that help comes at a cost. Not just
your sense of betrayal, but the suffering and death of those who are affected by your betrayal.

For the ancient Greeks, such decisions were easier. They knew 11
war and hated it, but because it was so much a part of their daily life,
few citizens could ever entertain our distinction between personal and
political loyalties: The two were much the same, and to shirk war was
to consign your family and your values to the flames.

In the modern world, most of us are more remote from the decision- 12
making. Politicians, not a breed seen to be sensitive to life's moral complexities, declare war. Others do the fighting. It is far too easy in this
arrangement to feel detached from the warmaking, to feel the lure of the
human relationships that appear so much more real and personal.

But all war is ultimately personal, as even Canadians may some 13
day have to discover. Some wars must be opposed, it is true, for political loyalty is not the same as dumb and blind acceptance. But war itself can not be rejected, not as long as there is something in this crazy
world worth defending.

NOTES

8 Reprinted with permission from *The Globe and Mail.*

9 The Greek philosopher Socrates (469–399 B.C.), mentor to Plato, attacked the Sophists, a
school of professional philosophers, for focusing on the technique rather than the truth of
arguments.

10 Minimalism was a movement in abstract art and music in the 1960s that emphasized extremely
simplified composition. By extension, the term refers to trivializing simplification.

11 For more information on E. M. Forster, see the biographical note attached to his essay "My
Wood" on page 238.

VOCABULARY

abstruse—difficult, obscure

platonic relationships—close friendships of a non-sexual nature

apolitical—detached from politics

Feminism at the Movies

Margaret Wente[12]

*T*he English Patient is not only a big Oscar winner. It's turning into   1
the greatest date movie of all time. The night I saw it, the theatre
was packed with sobbing couples, bawling their eyes out over this tale
of all-consuming passion set in a world of war and loss. It's what people
used to call a three-hankie movie. Half an hour after it ended I was still
leaking into my cappuccino.

There was lots of fuss over the fact that an "independent" movie   2
swept the Academy Awards. But the triumph of *The English Patient*
was completely predictable. At its core, it's hardly more than an old-
fashioned love story in which the woman's job is to look ravishing, be
ravished, and pay the awful price for her illicit desires. She's rather
like Helen of Troy.[13] All she has to do is show up, and wreak devastation on every man in sight.

The men would have come to a much better end if Kristin/Katharine   3
had just stayed out of that darn desert. They were quite happy doing
their Egyptology[14] without her. The desert, they told her, is no place
for a woman, and they were right, although what they really meant is
that a men's club is no place for a woman. She is the snake in the garden, the worm in the apple.[15] The moment she slithers onto the scene,
you know things are definitely heading downhill.

If you are one of the six people who haven't seen the movie yet,   4
forgive me for revealing that it all ends badly. Kristin/Katharine be-
witches Count Ralph, after which her husband kills himself out of
crazed jealousy, she dies fetchingly in a cave (you should aspire to look
as good as her corpse), the Count betrays the Allied cause[16] for her
sake and then literally burns up for love. Before that happens, though,
they get to have some really hot sex, which makes it all worth while.
She looks so wonderful without her clothes that you want to run right
out and get a full-body liposuction.

In terms of women's roles, *The English Patient* is deeply, hope-   5
lessly, irrevocably reactionary. It could have been made in 1930. Its
lesson is: Women! They screw things up! (The other main woman is a
nurse—what else?—who tends the charred Ralph.)

FOR a truly fresh take on women, I advise you to rent *Fargo*, the movie   6
that did not win the best-picture Oscar even though it was far more
daring and original.

Everything about *Fargo* is an inversion of *The English Patient*.   7
Instead of desert and blistering heat, it has snow and numbing cold.
Instead of exotic Africa, with its luxurious expat clubs and people who
talk like aristocrats, you get Minnesota, with its Arby's and Hardee's and
people who talk like Bob and Doug MacKenzie. Instead of gauzy gowns
and scarves streaming in the wind, you get big ugly hats with earflaps.

And instead of Katharine you get Margie, who is the stupendously   8
pregnant police chief. Margie is the moral centre of the movie, the only
person who knows right from wrong. In *Fargo* it's the men who destroy
order and the woman who restores it.

Instead of just standing around looking stunning, Margie (played by   9
Frances McDormand, who won an Oscar even though the movie didn't)
gets to investigate the malfeasance, pursue the bad guys, and put the
world right again. Just to underline that there's no contradiction between moral authority and maternity, the scriptwriters even give her
an atypical bout of morning sickness. (Note to the Coen brothers:[17] it
generally clears up after the first trimester.)

Margie is kind, reasonable and dogged. She is not afraid of any of   10
the villains, who range from sociopathic outlaws to prosperous busi-
nessmen. (In this movie, the car dealership is America's heart of darkness.) She is not only the best person in the whole movie, she's by far
the smartest.

Margie's love interest is her husband, Norm, who doesn't bear the   11
slightest resemblance to Ralph Fiennes. Instead of making wild, sensu-
ous love in bathtubs, they put on their PJs and sweaters and go to bed
to watch nature documentaries. But it's clear their love, though domestic, is durable and deep. He gets up to fix her eggs. She stops off to find
him some night crawlers.

Anyone can love a hero. But how many women can love a pudgy,   12
bald guy whose lifetime achievement is getting his mallard on the
three-cent stamp?

In *The English Patient*, Count Ralph gets the best line in the movie   13
when he says the heart is an organ of fire. In *Fargo*, it's Margie who de-
livers the message when she ruminates on all the mayhem the men
have wrought. "And for what?" she puzzles. "For a little bit of money.
There's more to life than a little money, you know."

Margie is the woman we all try so hard to be—brave, nurturing,   14
strong, equally employed, faithful and good. Katharine is the woman
we all secretly wish we were—a love object to die for. And that's why
Fargo is only on video, and never had a hope of winning Best Picture.
Fantasy trumps feminism, every time.

NOTES

12 Reprinted with permission from *The Globe and Mail*.

13 Helen of Troy was the beautiful wife of the Greek king Menelaus. Her abduction by the Trojan prince, Paris, was the cause of the Trojan war.

14 Egyptology: studies of Egypt.

15 In the biblical story of Adam and Eve, Satan disguises himself as a snake to seduce Eve into eating, and persuading Adam to eat, the apple of knowledge.

16 The Allies were the countries allied against Germany, Italy, and Japan in the Second World War.

17 Joel and Ethan Coen wrote, directed, and produced *Fargo* and a number of other successful films, including *Raising Arizona* and *O Brother, Where Art Thou?*

QUESTIONS

1. According to Hurka, what are the main similarities between *Casablanca* and *The English Patient*? What are the main differences?

2. In your opinion, which of the letters to the editor presents the most interesting response to Hurka's article?

3. Do you think the editorial in *The Globe and Mail* presents convincing support for Hurka's attack on *The English Patient*? Explain why or why not.

4. What evidence does Wente present to support her argument that "in terms of women's roles, *The English Patient* is deeply, hopelessly, irrevocably reactionary"?

5. Hurka and Wente use different methods to organize their comparisons. Identify the method each uses and explain whether you think it is effective.

SUGGESTIONS FOR WRITING

1. If the responses of any of these participants prompt you to join *The English Patient* debate, write a letter to the editor expressing your own views. In your letter, make clear which standard of evaluation you are using: moral, aesthetic, logical.

2. Write a newspaper column in which you present your own evaluation of heroes of two films. Use Wente's column as a model.

TO PEACEKEEP OR NOT TO PEACEKEEP

James Ash

The image of a soldier in a blue beret is one that will surely charac- 1
terize the nineties. Peacekeeping is a booming business, and
Canada has established herself as the world leader in this endeavour.
There are those, however, who criticize Canada's active support of,
and enthusiastic participation in UN peacekeeping operations. They
believe that our armed forces should focus on territorial defence, and
that our defence dollar should be spent on the acquisition of new
equipment; as for peacekeeping, they believe we should leave it to bigger powers. Such critics are mistaken. Peacekeeping is the best possible role for the Canadian Armed Forces, both from the pragmatic and
the ethical point of view.

The most common objection to Canada's involvement in peacekeep- 2
ing operations is that it ties up our limited military resources abroad,
and leaves nothing for the defence of Canada. It is hard to deny the truth
of this allegation; we have so few actual soldiers in our army that it is
hard to imagine that there are any of them left in Canada, considering
our many peacekeeping commitments. But whom would these soldiers
be guarding against? Any foreign power that attacks Canada will have to
contend with the United States, and if the U.S. were to attack us, it
would be a very short war, whether our puny army was in Canada or
Yugoslavia. Either we fight alongside the U.S. or against them, and in either case the American military machine dwarfs our own so badly that
the issue of territorial defence is hardly an issue at all.

This is not to say that we do not want an army that can engage in 3
large-scale violence as efficiently as the next one, both as a point of national pride (it is nice to think that we could at least put up a fight before the Stars and Stripes flies over Parliament Hill), and as a sign that
we are willing to do our part for collective security with our allies.

However, as General Lewis Mackenzie pointed out in *Maclean's* magazine, peacekeeping is ideal training for war-making; it requires the same skills, and it provides the ideal environment for troops to practice them in, namely a real war. This same rationale can be used to answer the objection that our defence dollar would be better spent on new equipment. Yes, our armed forces do need new equipment. But they are far more likely to get this equipment if they are abroad on peacekeeping missions than if they are at home involved in tame training exercises. A few body bags being flown home because Yugoslavian small-arms fire can penetrate Canada's ancient armored personnel carriers, or because our helicopters are too decrepit to evacuate Canadian wounded, is probably the only incentive that will actually get Canada's military the tools it needs to do the job.

We have yet to even consider the merits of peacekeeping in and of itself. The first is that it allows Canada to play a legitimate, independent foreign policy role. Canada will never be a superpower, but it has the misfortune (at times) to live next to one. Peacekeeping is an opportunity for Canada to play a real role in the world beyond its border, without being an American puppet. We are not following the U.S. example with peacekeeping; we are setting one for them.

Setting an example is an idea that is central to this whole issue, because peacekeeping is becoming a symbol of Canada at a time when it desperately needs one. Peacekeeping allows Canada to be the best at something, to be famous, to earn awards. This argument may sound like an emotional one, but it is not entirely. Pragmatically, at a time when Canada is internally divided and economically exhausted, peacekeeping is a low-cost morale booster for a nation that seems to be wallowing in self-pity and cynicism.

Ultimately, though, all of these arguments for peacekeeping are window-dressing. The bottom line is that Canada should commit its defence resources to peacekeeping because it is the right thing to do. War is bad; we take this to be a self-evident truth. Consequently, the only ethical role for a peacetime army is to try and prevent war. It may not always work, it may even never work, but it is something that, morally, we should try our best at, anyhow. If it saves more lives than it costs, if it brings even temporary relief to parts of the world that have become living hells, if it serves merely as a small sign that the world will not stand by forever and let butchers and "ethnic cleansers" have their way, then peacekeeping should be supported by even the most hard-nosed pragmatist.

It seems, on balance, that there really is no good argument against Canada's involvement in UN-sponsored peacekeeping, and several good arguments for it. Maybe it is time we gave our much-maligned government a little credit for something. It seems that we have found a government expenditure where taxpayers are getting more than their money's worth.

THE COMPLEX SKILL OF INDEPENDENT LIVING*

A. Jones

outline
Main
Ideas

An important aspect of the transition from adolescence to adulthood 1
is independent living: setting up a workable living arrangement
outside the parental home that is self-supported to some extent at
least. There are a number of ways of looking at independent living: it
could be seen as a set of behaviours, a set of relationships, or a set of
attitudes. Most usefully, perhaps, independent living could be seen to
involve a set of skills. Understanding exactly what skills are involved in
independent living may be difficult, though. Parents and teens may
both view independent living mainly as a set of practical skills to do
with managing money and maintaining a household. These skills are
important for making a successful transition from adolescence to
adulthood, certainly, but even more important are the less obvious
skills required, the social skills of getting along with others and, most
of all, the psychological skill of getting along with oneself.

The practical skills required for independent living are obvious be- 2
cause they are the ones immediately required. It often comes as a
shock to teens to realize how many activities and products are required to keep a household running. When they lived with their parents and wanted butter or salt to put on their popcorn, they just
reached into the kitchen cupboard. Living away from their parents,
they probably remember to buy the popcorn, but how about the toppings or the bowl to put it in? Not to mention, how about the money to
buy these things with? Teens who have spent most of the week's
money on a film and a big meal at Earl's on Tuesday night can look forward to a diet of Mr. Noodle later in the week. It does not take long for
teens to realize they need to get practical skills like budgeting under control, and if they miss seeing this need, their parents will be very ready to
point it out.

---

* Sample content analysis essay.

Harder to understand and acquire, though, are the social skills 3
needed for independent living. If social skills just meant getting
along with your friends, teens would have no problem. Spending more
time with their friends was what a lot of them left home to do.
Getting along with classmates, workmates, bosses, landlords, and
neighbours was not, on the other hand, what they left home to do. In
fact, to leave home at all, they may have to generate a lot of hostility
towards the adults in their immediate circle. This is natural: hostility
and bad behaviour are the rocket fuels propelling teens towards independence and adulthood. However, the qualities propelling them towards independence are not the same qualities they need to live that
independence. Like it or not, to live independently with any success,
teens need to have at least civil social relations with a whole range of
people they may not feel sympathetic to. These social skills require
changing the attitudes that have got them where they are. Parents
could teach these skills, but the recently departed teens are very unlikely to listen to parental lectures on civil behaviour.

If teens are unlikely to listen to parents, they need to learn to lis- 4
ten to themselves. In many ways this is the hardest skill of all to recognize and acquire. Consider the situation. For years they have likely
defined themselves against what their parents wanted for them, and for
years they have yearned to live as part of the peer group they identify
with. Living independently, they may no longer define themselves
against their parents, but it is more than likely that they have immersed themselves in the influence of the group. What then? Will the
peer group help them get up on time for the job in the sandwich shop?
Will the peer group help them see that "borrowing" CDs and not returning them erodes friendship? Will the peer group encourage them
to discover their vocation and destiny, the real goal of independent living? Only the psychological skill of learning to shift from external to
internal motivation will do any of these things.

The obvious practical skill of budgeting and managing and the less 5
obvious social skill of getting on with people you need rather than
want are both essential to successful independent living and a successful transition from adolescence to adulthood. These skills are not,
however, the whole story. It is the gradual opening up of real desires,
vocation and destiny, achieved through the psychological skill of internal motivation, that provides the push to master the often tedious
disciplines of household and social management. Just as psychological
motivation, in the form of a desire for freedom of expression and control of one's own circumstances, is often what propels teens towards
independent living, so psychological skills are key in ensuring that independent living is successfully achieved.

SHIFTS IN ATTITUDE AND FORM IN AL PURDY'S "TREES AT THE ARCTIC CIRCLE"*

B. Jones

In "Trees at the Arctic Circle," one of Al Purdy's subjects is, as the title of the poem suggests, the rather insignificant-looking ground willow that grows in the Canadian Arctic. His more important subject, however, is what our response to any living thing reveals about our respect for life itself. Through prosody, structure, figurative language, and diction that all emphasize a change in attitude, Purdy's "Trees" shows us we must change our attitude to even the most apparently insignificant living things from contempt to admiration, if life is to have any importance and value.   1

Prosody in "Trees" is based on a constant pattern of short lines sometimes alternating with even shorter lines: lines of five, six, or seven words are set against lines having as few as two or three. Each short line focuses on an action ("crawling under rocks"), a detail ("their leaves are veined and intricate"), occasionally a reflection ("and you know it occurs to me"), often a judgment ("Coward trees"), and the poem moves between these categories freely. This pattern of prosody has two effects. First, it emphasizes passion over intellectuality: reflection is brief and specific, things are noticed, judged, felt in rapid succession. Second, the effect of free movement between categories is to emphasize movement itself, the mobility of perception and judgment.   2

If the prosody of the poem emphasizes movement, the structure identifies this as the movement towards change, specifically the speaker's shift of attitude. The poem is organized into four stanzas, each stanza focusing on a different attitude. In the first stanza, the speaker gives us his first (and very negative) impressions of these little arctic trees, which he describes as insignificant and cowardly. In the second stanza, he compares these "Coward trees" with the great Douglas firs,   3

---

* Sample textual analysis essay.

maples, and oaks of Ontario. In the third stanza, he takes a closer look at the arctic willow and revises his opinion. He now sees these trees as brave, resourceful, and even rather beautiful. In the final stanza, he focuses on his own values, condemning his earlier criticism of the trees and punishing himself by making this record of his "stupidity" permanent in a poem. By presenting these attitudes in a chronological sequence, the poem's structure emphasizes that the speaker's shift in attitude is a process with identifiable stages.

The shift in attitude from contempt to the admiration of living 4 things is most directly conveyed by the poem's figurative language and its diction. The main strategy of figurative language in "Trees" is personification. This personification develops in two stages. In the first stanza, the arctic trees are portrayed as frightened people "bending and curling to escape," covering themselves up "like a Victorian married couple," "bowing to weather," instead of ruling it, as do trees farther south. Then, in an abrupt shift, the trees are portrayed in the third stanza as attractive people with "delicate grey earrings," whose energetic involvement in survival ("digging in here and now") is even heroic, since the trees use the ice of the permafrost for nourishment, "use death to keep alive." In the final stanza, the personification disappears, to be replaced by a single image, as the speaker reflects that to "scorn" the dwarf trees is to make "yourself the Pontifex Maximus/of nullity."

Personification is a particularly appropriate device for the message 5 of "Trees at the Arctic Circle," since it helps convey the living quality of living things. The reason it disappears in the final stanza becomes clearer when we look at the poem's diction. In the first three stanzas, the diction parallels that of the poem's figurative language. In the first stanza, the speaker's scorn for the arctic willow is emphasized by a barrage of derogatory terms: *crawling, grovelling, bending, curling, small, hide, coward, not proud, bowing, careful, worried, afraid.* In the third stanza, the diction changes to indicate the speaker's dramatic shift in attitude. He now describes the arctic willow as "delicate" and "intricate"; their seed pods "glow"; they are "unbothered by any human opinion." Then in the final stanza, the diction undergoes another shift. It becomes abstract, with a focus on terms like "scorn," "dignity," "judgments," and "stupidity." These words create a more distanced perspective. Although a few of these words (like "dignity") apply to the trees, now identified with "living things[s]," most apply to the speaker himself. It seems that the diction identifies the final stage in the changing of attitudes as the process of distancing ourselves sufficiently to include our own values and attitudes as the object of observation and judgment.

In her "Foreword" to *Beyond Remembering: The Collected Poems* 6 *of Al Purdy*, Margaret Atwood comments that Purdy is "always turning banality inside out.... You can't see how it's done but suddenly, where a second ago there was only a broken vase, there's a fistful of brilliant flowers" (18). How ugly, insignificant trees become beings to be admired is also the magic of "Trees at the Arctic Circle." "How it's done" is through prosody, structure, figurative language, and diction. Together these teach us that shifting our attitude towards living things from contempt to admiration is a process with stages. The process involves, first, having a passionate and mobile approach to perception and judgment; second, realizing the delicacy and strength—the living quality—of living things; and third, being able to distance ourselves enough to observe and judge our own attitudes. Through this process, we can finally arrive at a place of stillness where attitude, poem, and living being can co-exist.

> I have been stupid in a poem
> I will not alter the poem
> but let the stupidity remain permanent
> as the trees are
> in a poem
> the dwarf trees of Baffin Island

PERSPECTIVES ON ADDICTIONS*

C. Jones

Like many Western nations, Canada has a long-standing problem with addictions. Mothers Against Drunk Driving is a group formed to fight the consequences of alcoholism; Vancouver's Downtown Eastside is one of the drug capitals of the world. Since addiction is widespread and growing, it is important to understand its causes. Two recent essays—both originating from the Vancouver area—address this issue in interesting ways. In "Embraced by the Needle," Dr. Gabor Maté, an Eastside physician, claims that addiction has its roots in emotional deprivation. In "Addiction in Free Markets," Bruce Alexander, a professor at Simon Fraser University, and Stefa Shaler, a social worker assistant for the government of British Columbia, argue that addiction rises from social dislocation. Seemingly very different in their detail, development, points, and perspectives, these essays finally seem to offer complementary rather than contradictory explanations of the causes of addiction. 1

The most obvious difference between "Embraced by the Needle" and "Addiction in Free Markets" is in the kind of detail they use. "Embraced" includes references to theories of brain chemistry and dysfunctional parenting. However, the details we remember from the essay are the stories about individuals: Anna, who "wasn't wanted"; Carl, who "had dishwashing liquid poured down his throat ... at age 5" (286); Wayne, who was "hit a lot," denies that matters and, at the end of the essay, "looks away and wipes tears from his eyes" (286). In "Addiction," in contrast, the details are general rather than specific. The authors describe the world "[a]t the beginning of the 21st century, [as one where] for rich and poor alike, jobs disappear at short notice, communities are weak and unstable, people routinely change lovers, families, occupations, co-workers, technical skills ... (198–199)." The specific examples that eventually turn up are still large-scale: "England mov[ing] to a full-blown free market system between the late 16th and the early 19th centuries" (199); "the history of Native Canadians" (200). Detail in the two essays, then, reflects a dramatic contrast between focus on the individual and focus on the general. 2

---

*Sample comparison essay.

The same contrast is reflected in the way the essays are organized. 3
Both essays present a straightforward causal sequence. According to
Maté, the lack of "warm, non-stressed, calm interactions with the parenting figures" (286) actually changes brain functioning, causing a
greater need for external calming and pleasure enhancing, a need
which, in later life, can be temporarily satisfied by drugs. In Alexander
and Shaler, the sequence can be summarized even more simply: free
market societies create social dislocation, and then social dislocation
creates addiction. If both these sequences are straightforward, the way
the essays are organized differs significantly. We remember the detail
on addicts' lives in "Embraced" because it appears at the beginning,
middle, and end of the essay, wrapping the causal sequence in a narrative framework. In "Addiction" the sequence is presented in a linear,
analytic way. The essay discusses and defines addiction and dislocation; it then gives extensive examples of the connections between the
two before finally arguing that understanding and reversing dislocation
is necessary if ever mass addiction is to be cured.

The roots of these differences between "Embraced by the Needle" 4
and "Addiction in Free Markets" lie in the different points Maté and
Alexander and Shaler are making, and the different perspectives that
lie behind these points. Maté's essay opens with his thesis: "Addictions
always originate in unhappiness, even if hidden. They are emotional
anesthetics; they numb pain" (285). "Unhappiness," "emotional,"
"numb": these terms indicate a psychological perspective on the
causes of addiction. Alexander and Shaler's thesis, similarly announced in the first sentences, is that "[a]lthough any person in any
society can become addicted, free market societies universally dislocate their members, leading to mass addiction" (198). Here terms like
"free market societies," "universally," and "mass addiction" point to
the more collective perspective of sociology.

Are these essays as different as they seem? Psychological and soci- 5
ological perspectives on the causes of addiction are different, but they
are not mutually exclusive. One significant similarity between the essays is that Maté and Alexander and Shaler have a similar sense of
whom they are arguing against. Maté insists that "[n]either physiological predispositions nor individual moral failures explain drug addictions" (285). Alexander and Shaler see their antagonists as the
addiction professionals who "continue decades of futile debate about
whether addiction is a 'criminal' or a 'medical' problem whereas, in
fact, it is neither" (200). Furthermore, Maté acknowledges that
parental stress could come "from outside circumstances such as economic pressure or political disruption" (286), whereas Alexander and
Shaler refer to the "painful void" that social dislocation creates (199).

The different ways that "Embraced by the Needle" and "Addiction 6
in Free Markets" handle detail and development, their different points
and perspectives, ensure that each essay charts a different area of
causal explanation. However, the similarity in antagonists and the acknowledgment of the other perspective reflect an important truth: while
physiological and ethical explanations of addiction are incompatible
with psychological and sociological ones, these psychological and sociological explanations of cause are not incompatible with each other.
Judging from the material in these two essays, it would be perfectly possible to show that free markets cause social dislocations and that social
dislocations, in turn, affect parental functioning and thus, via brain and
emotions, increase the likelihood of addiction in individuals. Neither
essay presents this whole causal sequence, but when compared, they
provide strong evidence that both sociological and psychological factors
are at work in causing addiction.

REFLECTING ON POPULATION*

D. Jones

Ted Byfield's essay "Health Canada Inadvertently Discloses Facts 1
Planned Parenthood Would Like to Suppress" appeared in *The Report*, the Alberta-based newsmagazine that Byfield also edits, in March 2002. Byfield begins his essay by referring to a Health Canada study that suggests Canadians are working too hard, including too hard to have children. He then goes on to argue that the real threat to the world is not population growth, but rather a "serious population decline, a 'birth dearth' that will wreak havoc on the economies of much of the western world.... making the absence of kids the world's No. 1 economic problem" (212). Population is obviously an important issue to consider these days, but is this essay a credible contribution to that consideration? "Health Canada" seems to have logical strengths: a causal argument supported by statistics and references to authorities on both sides of the case. These strengths are more apparent than real, however. Byfield's treatment of authorities is one-sided and his statistics, while thought-provoking, do not support his point. As a result, his causal argument fails to be logically convincing.

At first "Health Canada" seems to be a logical, well-supported essay 2
arguing for a startling position on world population. The essay has a clear causal argument: obsession with work leads to population decline; population decline will lead to economic chaos. This argument is supported by statistics taken from Health Canada and the American Enterprise Institute; in fact, Byfield's thesis statement appears to be a composite of opinions from these two institutions.

Byfield's position, if true, would demand a dramatic reassessment 3
of the way we see world population. Unfortunately, "Health Canada," despite the appearance of logic, fails to make this position logically credible.

It is true that Byfield refers to authorities from both sides of the ar- 4
gument about population, but these authorities are used very differently. Byfield does not give the arguments of experts who argue the dangers of population growth; instead he dismisses them in a series of satiric caricatures. Paul Ehrlich is one of the "prophets of doom" (212);

---

* Sample critique.

Planned Parenthood is the "zealous preacher of the Save-the-World-with-Smaller-Families message" (213); the United Nations runs "don't-have-kids propaganda" (213). On the other hand, he quotes the opinions from the American Enterprise Institute and Tom Bethell, a journalist writing in *The American Spectator*, and treats these opinions as fact. Such a one-sided handling of authorities diminishes the essay's credibility.

Equally lacking in credibility is Byfield's handling of evidence. At   5 first glance, the figures showing declines in the birthrate in certain Western and non-Western countries seem to support his claim for "serious population decline" (212). But further reflection, even on the examples given, suggests that even if Europe's birthrate is running at 1.4, this rate is more than balanced by the rates of India (3.5), Egypt (3.9), and Mexico (3). And what about the ones he does not quote? Oddly, given his starting place, he does not quote statistics for Canada and the United States; a chance remark about Thailand reveals that both countries have a birthrate above replacement level. Thus the statistics Byfield quotes, and those he does not quote, show that the world's population is increasing, not declining. Most damaging of all is the absence of any evidence that demonstrates current population trends are creating "the world's No. 1 economic problem" (213).

One-sided handling of authorities and selective evidence create a   6 causal argument that does not work. Its key fallacy is that of the single cause/single outcome. It is not very credible that an obsession with work demonstrated by one study in Canada should be reflected all over the world as a cause of birthrate decline, especially when there is no mention of other causes commonly and convincingly cited, such as an increase in women's access to birth control and education and increases in standards of living. And can we believe that the main effect of a slowing in the increase of population—since that is what Byfield's statistics show—is going to be economic "havoc"? It could be argued that "government welfare programs" would be endangered in a few countries particularly affected by a falling birthrate—this is Byfield's one explanation (and a surprising one, given his other views) of what he means by "havoc." However, would this effect prove more important than the massive destruction of the environment and of rural societies, and the loss of knowledge encoded in dying languages that many experts argue to be the visible and present effect of population growth? To make his argument about "economic havoc" more credible, Byfield would need to outline alternative explanations and show why they should be dismissed or minimized.

Perhaps the real contribution of Ted Byfield's "Health Canada" is   7 that, by using statistics, reference to authorities, and causal argument, the essay sends the message that we need to bring logic to discussions of issues such as population. Unfortunately, because of its one-sided use of authorities, failure to link evidence to point, and flawed causal argument, the essay itself does not achieve logical credibility. Instead, the essay makes us recognize the need for our thinking on important subjects to contain the substance of logic, and not just its appearance.

SAME-SEX MARRIAGES: TRADITION AND CHANGE[*]

E. Jones

Alice and Susan lived as a couple for ten years. During this time they worked together in the little café Alice inherited from her mother. While Alice greeted customers, served the food, and ran the cash register, Susan cooked. Together they kept the accounts and made joint decisions on changes in the menu and renovations to the café, for which both Alice and Susan felt an increasing sense of responsibility. When a pipe burst last winter and flooded the storage room, Susan sold her car to cover the cost of repairs. Last spring, Alice died in a single-vehicle traffic accident. She had never got around to making a will. Now Alice's niece wants to take over the restaurant, claiming it's hers because she is the closest blood relative. If Alice and Susan had been married, Susan would have an automatic right to half the business assets. Under current Canadian law, she has an automatic right to nothing.   1

Like many gay and lesbian Canadians who have found themselves in similar positions, Susan feels insulted, desperate, and indignant. Are her feelings justified? How do you think Canadian governments and religious leaders should respond to increasing pressure from both gays and lesbians who want the legal protection and other less tangible benefits currently enjoyed by married couples? Controversy over same-sex marriages has caused dissension in some churches and worsened relationships between some provinces and the federal government. Though there are serious reasons for resisting same-sex marriages, there are better reasons for both church and state to endorse not only the practical legal solution of civil unions, but also the value of church marriage for same-sex couples, a value that is ethical as well as practical.   2

Before we examine the main options available to the state and the church, let's define the key terms *wedding*, *marriage*, and *civil union*. A wedding is the act and ceremony of marrying. This wedding ceremony may be performed in a cathedral or a submarine. As long as it meets the church's criteria, the couple are married in the eyes of the church. They are not legally married, however, unless they meet the   3

---

[*] Sample persuasive essay.

legal requirements for getting a marriage licence. These requirements specify that the couple must be a man and a woman, so even if a same-sex couple have a church wedding, they are not married under Canadian law. A new alternative is emerging, however. A civil union, presently available to same-sex couples in Quebec and Nova Scotia, according to a recent article in *The Globe and Mail*, gives a person the same legal status as marriage. People can obtain this status by filling out the appropriate documents and registering them in a provincial registry.

The existence of civil union legislation is probably a testament to 4 changing Canadian social values. It is true that there are still traditionalists who argue that the main purpose of marriage is to create stable family stuctures in which to raise children. If the status of the family is secure, they argue, the society will be stable and prosperous. This argument has merit: children invariably prefer, and seem to thrive upon, the attention of two loving parents, and two-parent families are usually more economically stable. However, Canada is a pluralistic country. From Inuit trappers in Nunavut, to community health nurses in Newfoundland, to Sikh business people living in Vancouver, there are many ways to be Canadian. There are also many kinds of Canadian families, including single-parent families, blended families, and foster home families. Good parenting goes on in these non-traditional families, just as poor parenting goes on in some two-parent families. The existence of civil unions suggests this social acceptance of plurality is starting to extend to the institutionalization of committed relationships of non-traditional kinds.

It seems possible, then, that civil unions could become the norm 5 for same-sex couples in Canada. This development should be supported for both practical and ethical reasons. The practical advantages for same-sex couples are clear: couples who have entered into a civil union have the same legal rights as married couples, rights that include supplemental health care benefits, pension benefits, and, of course, property rights. If Susan and Alice's partnership had had the status of a civil union, Susan would have automatically had property rights. What may be less clear is that when same-sex adults form committed relationships, all of us benefit. If Tom works so that Bill can finish his medical degree and then Bill helps Tom through civil engineering training, the country has another doctor and another civil engineer. On the ethical side, there are the issues of obligation and social consensus. Because people in committed relationships make sacrifices for each other and help each other to succeed, they deserve legal protection when their relationships end. Civil unions can provide this protection without necessitating a formal redefinition of marriage itself, thus reflecting the social consensus in a way that is fair to both pluralistic and more traditional views.

However, national and provincial legislation supporting civil unions   6
is not the whole picture, for there is another institution involved in for-
malizing committed relationships, namely the church. The lack of legal
status for church weddings does not mean that they are unimportant to
same-sex couples. Gays and lesbians with strong ties to a church want
the same blessing for their commitment to each other that other members of the congregation feel entitled to. Same-sex couples also feel that
churches should provide moral leadership for the wider community. In
evaluating what churches can and should do, it is important to recognize the special difficulties they face in struggling to cope with the practical and ethical implications of marrying same-sex couples.

The ethical difficulty churches face in marrying same-sex couples   7
is that the historical precepts of most churches include injunctions
against same-sex relations. We should note, though, that these precepts also usually include injunctions concerning love, respect, faith-
fulness, and commitment. Churches insisting on a literal reading of
historical scriptures generally stick to the injunction against same-sex
relations and interpret precepts concerning love and commitment to
apply to the restricted group of "the faithful"; less fundamentalist
churches struggle over the degree to which following the "spirit" of
love and respect allows divergences from the letter of scriptural "law."
On this issue, the ethical value of leadership seems key: in an era when
either tolerance or sectarianism could win out, churches that make
same-sex couples fully participating members of their own congregations send a powerful message of inclusion to society as a whole.

If agreeing to marry same-sex couples is ethically desirable for   8
churches, the question remains: is it practically possible? As every
church is well aware, marrying same-sex couples will outrage gender
traditionalists, who may well be a congregation's most staunch supporters. What church wants to outrage its main source of volunteers
and financial support, not to mention some of its most senior and respected clergy? Although churches that perform same-sex marriages
may alienate gender traditionalists, churches that refuse to perform
such marriages will almost certainly alienate their lesbian and gay
members. Furthermore, performing same-sex marriages is likely to
arouse the sympathy and commitment of a younger generation of potential churchgoers. Progressive churches will therefore attract more
young people and ensure their own growth and vitality. The declining
attendance of young people should make the marrying of same-sex
couples a somewhat painful but still positive practical option in mainstream churches, if not in fundamentalist ones.

The issue of same-sex unions is particularly challenging to tradi-   9
tionalists, whether inside or outside the church, but they are perhaps
missing one important aspect of the growing pressure on state and

church. The pressure for not only legal protection but also for religious institutions to bless their commitment and sacrifice suggests that these traditional values are alive and well among same-sex couples. True leadership involves finding the best way to promote ongoing virtues in changing circumstances. By recognizing the ethical and practical value of both civil unions and marriages for same-sex couples, church and state would show true leadership.

THE PROBLEM OF ENVIRONMENTAL COSTS: SUZUKI VS. MERWIN

Joyce MacDonald

We live in a time of great concern for the environment. We constantly   1
need to evaluate almost everything we buy or consume in terms
of what it may be doing to our atmosphere or water supply. We have a
wide range of sometimes contradictory information at our fingertips
telling us how we can, or should, help the environmental cause. While
both David Suzuki, in his essay "It Always Costs," and W. S. Merwin, in
"Unchopping a Tree," concern themselves with the problem of environmental costs, their messages are very different. Suzuki provides a
very accessible essay using well-defined technical terms and a straightforward, academic structure. His thesis, that we must just be a little
more careful about the environment, is very practical. The entire tone
of his essay, however, is somewhat emotionally detached. Merwin, on
the other hand, provides an essay that uses complicated emotional imagery, a complex reverse-process structure, and a thesis that is totally
impractical: all forest harvesting must be stopped. What Merwin's article has that Suzuki's lacks is a tone of emotional connection to the
question of environmental costs. This sense of emotional connection is
the truly necessary feature which causes the reader to take personal
responsibility for the problems of the environment.

While Suzuki's use of well-defined technical jargon makes his essay   2
accessible to his reader, it also creates a tone of emotional distance
from the subject. He uses terms like "biomagnification" and "synergistic" followed by their definitions (313; 314). These terms may be accurate but they are hardly descriptive. When Suzuki refers to a "bad
episode" (314) on a drill site, he does not explain what the specific effects may be. Are they pollution, loss of wildlife, or loss of human life?
When he writes about the "negative effects" (314) of the pill, he does
not elaborate on how it affects a woman's mental health or how it may
increase her risks of developing cancer. By eliminating description,

Suzuki produces a tone of emotional distance from his subject. One brief description of the horror a mother would experience on the birth of a severely deformed thalidomide baby would be enough to arouse some sympathy in the reader. As it stands, the technical jargon only serves to distance the reader from the subject matter. While it explains everything clearly, it provokes no emotional response. Without emotional connection to the material, no sense of personal responsibility for the environment can be established.

Merwin, in contrast, uses elaborate imagery to evoke an emotional response in the reader, creating a tone of personal involvement. He uses the language of violation, saying that leaves, twigs, and nests have been "shaken, ripped, or broken off" and limbs "smashed or mutilated" (289). Attempts at restoration achieve "only the skeleton of the resurrection" (290). The death of the tree creates more of an emotional response than the fate of Suzuki's thalidomide babies. We are made to feel for the dead trees, whereas those deformed children are kept at a safe distance by nice technical language. The tone of personal emotional involvement created by Merwin is more conducive to creating a feeling of personal responsibility for those poor dead trees. 3

The tone created by Suzuki's academic essay structure also serves to distance the reader from the subject. The thesis, "technology always has a cost" (313), is given in the beginning. We are also handed our conclusion on a silver platter: We must "err on the side of extreme caution" (315). The reader never needs to search for any hidden meaning in this straightforward approach. The reader can remain emotionally detached from what he or she is reading. While use of the term "we" throughout may seem like an effort to involve the reader, closer examination shows this term to mean "the public in general" and not "you and I." Few of us will ever conduct "an environmental impact assessment" (314), so we can even further detach ourselves because the term seems to refer to the scientific community. The tone created is one of total emotional detachment in the reader. There are no conclusions to reason out. There is no personal stake in the state of the environment. No commitments need to be made by the reader. 4

Merwin's reverse process structure is more successful in creating a tone of personal involvement because the thesis is never stated and the conclusion is never drawn. Discovery of the point of the essay is an active process. The reader is included in the essay: "You will watch…. You will listen for the nuts to shift…. You will hear whether they are indeed falling" (290). 5

The emotions the reader is supposed to feel are carefully explained: "It is as though its weight for a moment stood on your heart…. You are afraid the motion of the clouds will be enough to push it over" (291). The sheer complexity of the process increases the reader's sense of futility: 6

> It goes without saying that if the tree was hollow in whole or
> in part, and contained old nests of bird or mammal or insect,
> or hoards of nuts or such structures as wasps or bees build
> for their survival, the contents will have to be repaired where
> necessary, and reassembled, insofar as possible, in their orig-
> inal order, including the shells of nuts already opened. (289)

Recognition of the futility of the enterprise combined with the pre-   7
scribed feelings dictated by Merwin leaves us emotionally involved. We
are responsible for coming to our own conclusions. This sense of personal responsibility is exactly what Merwin is after. Merwin wants us to
take personal responsibility for the environment. Without a sense of
personal responsibility, one does not make a commitment to a cause.

In criticism of Merwin, one might say that his proposal to stop de-   8
forestation is totally impractical, whereas Suzuki seems to have a very
reasonable approach. The problem with Suzuki is that he generalizes
wildly in his assumption that we are "hooked" on modern technology
and "can't go back to doing things the old way" (314). What about the
conservation movement that advocates returning to simpler methods
around our own homes? Suzuki ignores the ideas of composting and
recycling to reduce household wastes and using compost as an alternative to chemical fertilizers. These are certainly old ways to deal with
our modern problems. In speaking about technology on a large scale,
Suzuki misses these small individual efforts. Perhaps there are ways in
which large scale technologies can return to simpler, less destructive
techniques. Just to say that it can't be done shows a lack of faith. On
the other hand, Merwin's proposal seems totally impractical, until it is
analysed more closely. His demand for a halt to tree chopping is an
overstatement. It is almost like bartering; he asks for much more than
he ever hopes to receive. If he is lucky he will get more than he has at
present. Instead of asking for a halt to deforestation, he really is asking
for a slowdown of the devastation. Where Merwin seems to ask for too
much, Suzuki seems to show no faith, and asks for too little. Suzuki
seems to buy the technological quick fix, whereas Merwin rejects it as
not good enough.

While Suzuki seems to be all practicality and accessibility in his   9
essay, he lacks the tone of personal emotional involvement achieved by
Merwin. The future of the environment may depend much less on what
the scientific community dictates than on the contributions made by
individuals who take a personal stand on the issue and do everything in
their power to make things better. Merwin asks his reader to become involved, to accept the challenge, to change the world. If we do not aim at
something better than what we have, we will never have anything better
and we may end up with something even worse.

THE MAKING OF THE TRAGIC HERO: THE GRAVEYARD SCENE IN *HAMLET**

D. Smith

In William Shakespeare's tragedy *Hamlet, Prince of Denmark*, Act Five, Scene One, commonly known as the graveyard scene, marks Hamlet's reappearance after his interrupted voyage to England. The Hamlet we see in this scene is very different from the cruel, cynical prince of Acts III and IV. Most critics attribute this difference to a philosophical change in Hamlet's attitude towards death. In focusing on the thematic significance of this scene, however, they neglect its dramatic function: to engage the audience's sympathy for Hamlet before his death. Without a change in character, Hamlet would not achieve the stature of a tragic hero, because his death would not arouse the pity, fear, awe, and sense of waste common to Shakespearean tragedy. The graveyard scene engages our sympathy for Hamlet in three ways: by using the episode with the gravediggers as a means to shift the audience's perspective from the court to a humanized Hamlet; by clarifying Hamlet's relationship with Ophelia; and by symbolically foreshadowing the outcome of the duel between Hamlet and Laertes.

1

Most interpretations of the play fail to consider the dramatic function of the graveyard scene; instead they focus on its philosophical significance. These interpretations fall into three main groups: those that see Hamlet coming to a Christian acceptance of death; those that see his attitude as fatalistic resignation; and those that argue that the scene is a mixture of both these attitudes (Philias 226). Maynard Mack and Walter King are representative of those who favour a Christian interpretation. According to Mack, Hamlet by the last act of the play has "learned, and accepted, the boundaries in which human action, human judgment are enclosed" and therefore no longer assumes he must single-handedly set the world to rights (521). Similarly, King argues that the graveyard scene presents "affirmation of life and love as a viable

2

---

* Sample research paper.

center of values in a God-created and God-centered universe," but within the context of a world in which these values "are perennially in danger of being snuffed out" (146).

The view that Hamlet's attitude is totally, or at least partially, fatalistic is propounded by G. Wilson Knight, Richard Levine, and Peter Philias. Knight sees our sympathies as being divided between the members of the court, who for all their imperfections "assert the importance of human life," and Hamlet, whose philosophy is "inevitable, blameless, and irrefutable," but whose very existence asserts "the negation of life" (60–61). Far from admitting that there is a shift in our sympathies during the graveyard scene, he asserts that "Laertes and Hamlet struggling at Ophelia's grave are like symbols of life and death contending for the prize of love" (64). Unlike Knight, Levine sees a change in Hamlet but argues that the change is negative. In his view, Hamlet's "tragic flaw, his vacillating and faulty world view," is resolved by the prince's rejection of traditional religious belief in favour of "an attenuated stoicism" (539, 543). Peter Philias, while less negative in his assessment of Hamlet, reaches much the same conclusion. Focusing on the episode with the gravediggers, as most of the other critics do, he concludes that "the Christian framework of the play is profoundly qualified, though not replaced, by a strong fatalistic point of view" (226). 3

While these interpretations give us some insight into the philosophical issues raised by the play, they do not adequately account for the presence of the gravediggers, Hamlet's farewell to Ophelia, or the struggle in the grave. Even a critic who calls it "one of the most important scenes" because it "bring[s] into dramatic focus parts of the play which are seemingly disparate" (Bennett 160) fails to account adequately for these elements. The most useful interpretation of the scene's dramatic function is that of B.D. Cheadle. Cheadle asks Coleridge's question "What reason does it contain within itself for being as it is and no other?" (89) as a guide to understanding Hamlet's confrontation with Laertes at Ophelia's grave. Asking this question for the scene as a whole will enable us to see that these elements are explained by their role in bestowing upon Hamlet the qualities of dignity, courage, and deep feeling that make his death a waste of potential greatness. 4

The graveyard scene opens not with Hamlet's entrance but with the conversation between the gravediggers. This opening allows for a gradual shift in sympathy from the court to Hamlet and humanizes the prince by making death a personal rather than a metaphysical concern. The shift in perspective has to be gradual because we have seen little to admire in Hamlet since the early scenes of the play. In the scenes preceding his exile, as Knight points out, Hamlet "is cruel to Ophelia and his mother"; "exults in tormenting the King by the murder of Gonzago" and "takes a demoniac pleasure in the thought of preserving his life for 5 a more damning death"; "murders Polonius in error" and then makes disgusting, callous comments to Claudius about the body (55–56). Furthermore, the three scenes from which Hamlet is absent focus on Laertes' grief and anger over his father's death and on Ophelia's madness and suicide. If we are to mourn the death of a man who has caused such suffering, we need to see him in a more favourable light.

The gravediggers serve as a means of detaching our sympathies 6 from the court and transferring them to Hamlet. The dramatic goings-on and highly charged language of the court scenes seem excessive when contrasted with the matter-of-fact way in which the gravediggers go about their work. Emotional indulgence, like Christian burial for a suicide, seems a privilege accorded only to those of high social position (MacDonald 312). When Hamlet enters, however, his first comment is a criticism of the first gravedigger's singing at his work. His next is an assertion of the finer feelings of those with higher status: "The hand of little employment hath the daintier sense" (V.i.66). This exchange encourages us to forget Hamlet's earlier callousness and cynicism and to see him as a person of fine sensibility. These few lines initiate what Michael Cohen sees as "two competing subtexts in the scene, one that argues that death is the ultimate leveller of all class distinctions, another that argues, with almost equal persuasiveness, that class distinctions continue even after death" (78).

But the graveyard scene does not merely shift the point of view from 7 the court to Hamlet. It also humanizes Hamlet by making death a personal rather than a metaphysical concern. The gravediggers' debate over Ophelia's burial, as Philias points out, shifts attention away from the religious questions of salvation and damnation that were so powerful when Hamlet himself was considering suicide to the social issues of power and status (231). The reduction of death from a metaphysical to a human concern is further emphasized by the gravedigger's actions as he tosses skulls about and sings about the human cycle of love, age, and death.

Even more important in engaging our sympathy for Hamlet, how- 8 ever, is the dramatic tension created by his not knowing that the grave is for Ophelia. Although the discovery of Yorick's skull momentarily shows us Hamlet's deeper feelings and allows us to identify with the mixture of fond memory, revulsion, and jest in his response to this physical reminder of mortality, his ignorance of Ophelia's death allows him to remain witty and self-possessed. As a result, our image of Hamlet at the end of this episode is that of a person who is neither morbidly preoccupied with death (as he was at the beginning of the play) nor overly sentimental about it (as Laertes appears in the next part of the scene). Instead, he has accepted its reality. The episode with the gravediggers thus prepares us to see the burial of Ophelia from Hamlet's point of view.

The second half of the scene increases our sympathy for Hamlet by   9
revealing the depth of his feeling for Ophelia and by bringing him face
to face with the man we know will be the instrument of his death. The
simplicity of Hamlet's "I loved Ophelia" (V.i.256) dispels the mystery
surrounding their relationship. Although we hear from Ophelia of her
suitor's wild dress and melancholy behaviour when his attentions are
forbidden, we are not sure whether his actions are motivated by
"mock-madness" or, as Knight maintains, by blighted love (53). The
only two times we see Hamlet and Ophelia together—when she is acting as decoy for her father and Claudius in III.i. and when both attend
the play-within-a-play in the following scene—Hamlet treats her with
such contempt and cruelty that we question his regard for her. To establish the depth of Hamlet's love, Cheadle suggests, his leap into the
grave should be staged so that he says "This is I" (V.i. 244) as "an
avowal to the dead Ophelia that had she lived and had things been different, she would have been Queen to the Dane" (87). When a few
lines later Hamlet says "I loved Ophelia," the past tense marks not
only Hamlet's acceptance of the end of the relationship but also his acceptance of the death of love, a fact he could not accept in his mother's
remarriage. The ending of the Ophelia subplot in this manner introduces, in a way sympathetic to Hamlet, the sense of wasted lives and
lost possibilities that will become more pronounced in the final scene.

Interwoven with the burial of Ophelia is the confrontation between   10
Hamlet and Laertes. Although their behaviour seems strange and inappropriate as an expression of grief for a woman they both loved, it
makes a very powerful dramatic impact when considered as a prelude
to, and symbolic foreshadowing of, their duel and deaths. Hamlet's dignity is enhanced by his initial self-control, a deliberate contrast, as
Cheadle points out, to Laertes' "ranting" (89). Furthermore, Hamlet's
announcing himself as "Hamlet the Dane" is both "an assertion of identity and purpose" and a direct challenge to Claudius, since only the
King has the right to call himself "the Dane" (86). Claudius' plot against
Hamlet makes Laertes not only Ophelia's grief-stricken brother but also
the King's champion. The impact of the final duel would be much less,
however, if we saw Laertes only as Claudius' instrument. It is dramatically necessary for Shakespeare to bring together Hamlet and Laertes,
both of whom have vowed to avenge a father's death, so that each rec-
ognizes the justice in the other's actions and can "exchange forgive-
ness," as the dying Laertes requests in the final scene. Their struggle in
Ophelia's grave thus foreshadows the death blows they will deal each
other and the sense of wasted nobility we will feel at their deaths.

This sense of waste, and the feelings of pity, fear, and awe that ac-   11
company it, would not be so pronounced at the end of the play without
the graveyard scene to engage our sympathies. Interpretations of the

scene's philosophical significance tend to overlook the dramatic impact of the gravedigger episode, of Hamlet's farewell to Ophelia, and of the struggle between Hamlet and Laertes. These critics forget, perhaps, that our response to the play, like Hamlet's to death, is personal as well as metaphysical, and equally shaped by the dramatist's art.

WORKS CITED

Bennett, William E. "The Gravedigger's Scene: A Unifying Thread in *Hamlet.*" *Upstart Crow* 5 (Fall 1984): 160–65.

Cheadle, B. D. "Hamlet at the Graveside: A Leap into Hermeneutics." *English Studies in Africa* 22.2 (1979): 83–90.

Cohen, Michael. "'To what base uses we may return': Class and Mortality in *Hamlet* (5.1)." *Hamlet Studies* 9.1–2 (1987): 78–85.

King, Walter N. *Hamlet's Search for Meaning.* Athens, GA: U of Georgia P, 1982.

Knight, G. Wilson. "The Embassy of Death: An Essay on *Hamlet.*" *The Wheel of Fire.* 4th ed. London: Methuen, 1949. 17–46.

Levine, Richard A. "The Tragedy of Hamlet's World View." *College English* 23.7 (1962): 539–46.

MacDonald, Michael. "Ophelia's Maimèd Rites." *Shakespeare Quarterly* 37.3 (1986): 309–17.

Mack, Maynard. "The World of Hamlet." *Yale Review* 41.4 (1952): 502–23.

Philias, Peter E. "Hamlet and the Grave-Maker." *Journal of English and Germanic Philology* 63 (1964): 226–34.

Shakespeare, William. *Hamlet. The Norton Introduction to Literature.* Ed. Jerome Beaty et al. 8th ed. New York: Norton, 2002. 1670–1769.

SPONTANEITY AND ENJOYMENT OF THE NATURAL WORLD

Karin Swanson

Edward Thomas' "Adlestrop" and Robert Frost's "Stopping by Woods on a Snowy Evening" each describe a personal account of an encounter with the natural world. Frost's speaker chooses to stop and "watch [the] woods fill up with snow" (4), but is unable to enjoy the tranquillity of the forest because of his/her preoccupation with "promises" (14) and other obligations. The speaker in Thomas' poem, however, relaxes and enjoys the countryside through an express train window during an "unwonted" (4) stop at Adlestrop. Frost's speaker's premeditated attempt at enjoying nature is unsuccessful while Thomas' speaker is captivated by an unplanned encounter with the natural world. Through comparison of the setting, structure, and prosody of these two poems, it becomes clear that both poems suggest that spontaneity is the key to the genuine enjoyment of nature.

Setting, or more accurately the speakers' control over the setting, emphasizes the importance of spontaneity when visiting nature. Frost's speaker arrives in the woods with his "little horse" (5) and deliberately chooses "to stop without a farmhouse near" (6) where the owner "will not see [him] stopping" (3). The onus is on the speaker to decide when he must leave; he has control over both the location and the length of his stay in the forest. Unfortunately, this premeditated, highly controlled approach to nature conflicts with the peaceful atmosphere of the woods, described in the phrases "easy wind and downy flake" (12). This conflict ultimately impairs the speaker's ability to enjoy the natural world.

The structures of "Adlestrop" and "Stopping by Woods on a Snowy Evening" indicate shifts in the speakers' relationship regarding the natural world. At first glance, it appears that the speaker in Frost's poem is enjoying nature, only to be torn away by remembrances of obligations in the last stanza of the poem. The speaker remarks that "The woods are lovely, dark and deep / But I have promises to keep" (13–14), finally admitting to himself in the last few lines of the poem that he must leave his wooded wonderland. However, a closer examination of the organization of detail within the poem reveals that the speaker's relationship with the natural world remains static throughout the poem and that the speaker never successfully loses himself to the natural world. The speaker is constantly aware of whose property he is on (1–3) and what his horse is doing (5, 9–10). These concerns are presented before his description of the woods (11–13), which makes the actual enjoyment of the forest seem less important. These preoccupations continually interfere with his attempts to observe the loveliness of the woods, which makes the speaker's decision to leave (13–14) unsurprising.

The structure in Thomas' poem, however, indicates that the 4 speaker undergoes a shift in awareness regarding his perception of the natural world. The speaker's observations in the first two stanzas are very limited in scope. "The steam hissed" (5), "Someone cleared his throat" (5), and "No one left and no one came / On the bare platform" (6–7) are quite unremarkable descriptions of events associated with train travel. A shift in the speaker's awareness occurs in line 9 when the speaker begins a very detailed account of the countryside outside of his window. The speaker maintains this awareness throughout the remaining two stanzas. It is the express train's "unwonted" or spontaneous (4) stop which enables the speaker to lose himself in the natural world at Adlestrop.

The prosody of both poems effectively conveys the idea that an 5 unplanned approach is most conducive to the enjoyment of nature. The meter in Frost's poem is iambic, giving the poem a very even, consistent rhythm. The meter has a forward momentum to it which contrasts with the subject of the poem, *stopping* in the woods. Frost's poem also exhibits a considerable amount of rhyme. At least three out of four lines in each stanza rhyme, contributing to the precise, disciplined tone of the poem. The meticulous rhyme and rhythm in this poem is representative of the speaker's preoccupation with order and control, which is what prevents him from enjoying his stop in the woods.

The rhythm of "Adlestrop" is less militant; its rhythm is more 6 akin to ordinary conversation. There are no definite end stops; the ideas of each line flow into one another, giving the poem a serene, dreamlike quality. There is less rhyme in "Adlestrop" as well, making the tone of the poem less intense. The loose rhythm and reduced rhyme in "Adlestrop" convey the relaxed attitude of the speaker, and it is from this relaxed space that the speaker is able to experience the natural world.

Frost's poem conveys the message that the speaker's premeditated 7 and controlled approach to the woods interferes with his enjoyment of the scene. Conversely, Thomas' poem implies that the speaker is able to enjoy the countryside because his arrival at Adlestrop is unplanned.

The message is subtle, but through comparison of the setting, structure, and prosody of "Adlestrop" and "Stopping by Woods on a Snowy Evening," it becomes clear that spontaneity is required to experience true enjoyment of nature.

WORKS CITED

Frost, Robert. "Stopping by Woods on a Snowy Evening." *The Norton Anthology of Poetry*. 4th ed. Ed. Margaret Ferguson et al. New York: Norton, 1996. 1131.

Thomas, Edward. "Adlestrop." *The Norton Anthology of Poetry*. 4th ed. Ed. Margaret Ferguson et al. New York: Norton, 1996. 1147.

PUBLISHED WRITINGS

STOPPING BY WOODS ON A SNOWY EVENING

Robert Frost

1   Whose woods these are I think I know,
His house is in the village though;
He will not see me stopping here
To watch his woods fill up with snow.

5   My little horse must think it queer
To stop without a farmhouse near
Between the woods and frozen lake
The darkest evening of the year.

He gives his harness bells a shake
10   To ask if there is some mistake.
The only other sound's the sweep
Of easy wind and downy flake.

The woods are lovely, dark and deep,
But I have promises to keep,
15   And miles to go before I sleep,
And miles to go before I sleep.

1923

ADLESTROP

Edward Thomas

1   Yes, I remember Adlestrop—
The name, because one afternoon
Of heat the express-train drew up there
Unwontedly. It was late June.

5   The steam hissed. Someone cleared his throat.
No one left and no one came
On the bare platform. What I saw
Was Adlestrop—only the name

And willows, willow-herb, and grass,
10   And meadowsweet, and haycocks dry,
No whit less still and lonely fair
Than the high cloudlets in the sky.

And for that minute a blackbird sang
Close by, and round him, mistier,
15   Farther and farther, all the birds
Of Oxfordshire and Gloucestershire.

1973

From Edward Thomas, *Poems and Last Poems*, ed. Edna Longley (London: MacDonald and Evans, 1973).

Handbook for
Final Editing

Strategies for Final Editing 372

**Identifying Common Problems
(Chart)** 373

Essay Format 375

Understanding Sentence Structure 379

Correcting Common Errors in
Sentence Structure 385

Improving Sentence Structure 401

Using Transitions to Connect Ideas 406

Solving Diction Problems 411

Eliminating Wordiness 419

Solving Verb Problems 423

Solving Pronoun Problems 432

Solving Punctuation Problems 444

Numbers, Capitalization, and Abbreviations 462

Spelling 466

Quotations 468

Documentation 476

part three

Strategies for Final Editing

This is your last chance to eliminate the kinds of errors that can distract and annoy your reader. Here are some tips.

1. Wait at least a day after you have finished writing your essay. If you try to edit immediately, you will miss errors.

2. Use spelling checkers and other editing software to pick up errors. Then print out a hard copy and edit it. You will notice errors that you would miss on screen.

3. Read your essay aloud. You or your listener will notice awkward sentences, lack of transitions, and other problems that you might overlook on the page.

4. Make a list of the kinds of errors you frequently make (such as problems with pronoun agreement, apostrophes, commas) and watch particularly for them.

5. Begin editing with the last sentence in your conclusion. Read each sentence separately and work your way back to the first sentence in your introduction. This procedure will help you to see what you have actually written, not what you have memorized.

The chart on the following pages lists in alphabetical order the most common errors in sentence structure, grammar, mechanics, and format. This chart also includes common marking symbols, an example of each error, and page references to explanations and exercises in the handbook. When you get an essay back, note your errors on the chart and keep the chart handy when you edit your next essay.

Identifying Common Problems

Term	Marking Symbol	Example of Common Error (bold indicates error to be corrected)	Page Reference
abbreviation	*Abbrev*	The **pres.** of the company will visit **AB & SK** this **yr.**	463
apostrophe	*(')Apos*	We have an exciting new season in **childrens'** programs.	444
capitalization	*Caps*	My **Mother** and I lived in the **north** for seventeen years.	462
colon	*(:)∧*	The camp offered a number of activities such **as:** canoeing, swimming, and tennis.	453
comma	*(,)∧*	Bill enjoys **tennis, and** football.	447
comma splice, comma fault	*CS, CF*	Loons are an endangered **species, pollution** is destroying their habitat.	386
dangling modifier	*DM*	**After running a marathon,** exhaustion is inevitable.	391
dash	*⊖∨/*	The storm ripped and scattered all the shingles—**on the new roof.**	454
diction	*Dic*	Alison decided **to partake in** the volleyball game.	411
documentation	*Doc*	Macbeth echoes the witches' opening words when he says, "So foul and fair a day I have not seen." **(no in-text citation)**	476
essay format	*EF*	**Gender stereotypes in *Macbeth*.**	375
faulty coordination	*F Coord*	Adam was terrified **and** he burst into laughter.	394
faulty subordination	*F Subord*	**Although** Irene wanted to stop smoking, **however,** she lacked the willpower.	394
fragment	*SF, Frag*	**Which is the main reason for Allan's success.**	385
fused sentence	*FS*	The baby is **hot she** must have a fever.	388
hyphen	*⊖∨/*	The **well^prepared** athlete must be mentally and physically fit.	460
italics	*Ital.*	This summer I plan to read Tolstoy's novel **War and Peace** while I'm on holidays.	458
misplaced modifier	*MM*	I **hardly** have any money.	390
mixed construction	*Mix*	One reason he is often late **is because** his car has chronic battery problems.	397
numbers	*Num*	**15** employees refused to join **three hundred and forty seven** of their co-workers in signing a petition.	462

Term	Marking Symbol	Example of Common Error (bold indicates error to be corrected)	Page Reference
parallelism	//ism	Our servers must be hard-working, intelligent, **and they can't insult the customers**.	392
parentheses	(/)(/)	During the second period, **(the fans were holding their breath,)** our team scored the winning goal.	455
passive voice	Passive	After **the ghost was seen by Hamlet**, he hated his uncle more intensely.	429
possessive pronouns	P Poss	The jury made **it's** decision.	440
pronoun agreement	P Agr	**Every student** must check **their** bag at the door.	436
pronouns of address	P Add P Shift	By the end of the movie, **you** could see that the hero had matured.	432
pronoun case	P Case	**Her** and I have been married almost twelve years.	438
pronoun reference	P Ref	Fred doesn't know whether to get married or join the navy **which** makes him uneasy.	441
quotation format	Quot F	Hamlet's despair is clear when he says, **"O that this ... into a dew."**	471
quotation introduction	Quot	^ "The woods are lovely, dark and deep." The speaker wants to rest.	469
quotation marks	(")\"/	Following the discussion of Alice Munro's story **Boys and Girls,** the class wrote an essay.	457
semicolon	(;)/\	When the movie **ended; the** audience burst into applause.	450
sentence length and structure	S Var	**Hamlet misses his father. He is angry at his mother. He hates his uncle.**	401
spelling	Sp ◯	Elizabeth was **to** angry to speak.	466
split infinitive	Split	The rebels struggled **to strongly resist** the government forces.	390
subject–verb agreement	S/V Agr	The director's **use** of gimmicky special effects **were attacked** by the critics.	428
transitions	Trans	Peter wants to lose **weight. ^ He** refuses to diet.	406
verb forms	VF	After Sophy **had drank** the last beer, she **laid** on the couch and fell asleep.	423
verb tenses	T, Tense	Hamlet **grieves** for his father, but he **concealed** his feelings.	425
wordiness	Wordy	**Due to the fact that** the tickets sold out in the first half hour, many fans were disappointed.	419

Essay Format

Here are the most common conventions for the format of the essay and the title page. Be sure to confirm your choice of format with your instructor. For information on documenting the sources you use, see Documentation.

Manuscript Conventions

Most students use a word processor to write their papers. Familiarize yourself with the formatting functions of your word-processing program for optimum efficiency. Either your instructor or the technical support staff at your college or university can help you with special items such as page or section breaks, hanging indents for bibliographical lists, and so forth.

If you are handing in a hard copy of your paper, staple or clip the pages in the top left corner. Do not use any other method to secure the pages. If you are submitting your paper electronically, follow all manuscript conventions and give your document a concise file name that clearly identifies you and the assignment. Always keep a copy of your essay.

Manuscript Conventions for Word-Processed Essays

1. Choose a standard font and size such as Times New Roman and 12-point for all parts of your essay and title page. Make sure you have a spare black ink cartridge for your printer.

2. Use white, 8 ½ × 11-inch paper in your printer. For drafts, you can save paper by printing on both sides, but your final copy should be printed only on one side of the page.

3. Double-space all parts of your essay. Indent each paragraph with one tab and do not leave extra lines between indented paragraphs.

4. The default margins are sufficient; they are usually set at 2.5 cm or 1 inch all around a page of text.

5. Insert automatic page numbers according to the system of documentation you are using. All pages, including the first or title page and the Works Cited or Reference page, can be numbered. Using an automatic header saves space and effort.

Conventions for Handwritten Essays

1. Use blue or black ink and make sure your writing is legible.

2. Use white, 8 ½ × 11-inch ruled paper but not loose leaf, note paper, or other kinds of punched paper. Write only on one side of the page.

3. To double-space, skip every other line. Indent each paragraph one inch and do not leave extra lines between indented paragraphs.

4. Leave generous margins of at least 2.5 cm or 1 inch all around a page.

5. Number your pages consecutively, including the first or title page and the Works Cited or Reference page.

Title Page

A title page or cover sheet gives your reader a first impression and some important information, so your effort to present your work effectively is well worth it. Do not, for instance, scribble a title page at the last minute before handing in your essay.

Title

The title is important. At a minimum, it should make clear which topic you are addressing. Never simply label your paper "Essay 1." If you pay attention to the titles in essays and articles that you read, you will see that good titles are usually a short form of the thesis.

In all styles of title page format, present the title in regular font or size. Capitalize the first word and all other words except articles (*a, an, the*), coordinate conjunctions (*and, but, or, …*), short prepositions (*on, at, in, of, for*), and the *to* in infinitives. Do not underline the title of your essay or put quotation marks around it. Do not put a period after it.

FORMAT

If your title includes the name of a work you are analyzing, use either quotation marks or italics. Follow the rules for treating titles as outlined in the sections on Quotation Marks and Italics (pp. 457 and 458 in the Handbook).

For the format of your title page, follow the system of documentation you are using in your essay. Two of the most widely accepted styles of documentation are those of the Modern Language Association (MLA), used primarily in the humanities, and the American Psychological Association (APA), used in the sciences and social sciences. Some instructors, however, will want you to prepare a generic title page with the title in the middle and your name, the date, and class information in the bottom right corner.

Title page format—MLA According to the *MLA Handbook*, you do not need a separate title page. Instead, your information and title appear double-spaced on the first page of your essay. With the automatic page numbering in place (see above), put the following information in separate lines at the top left corner: your name, your instructor's name, the course number, and the date. Next comes your title, centred, immediately above the beginning of your text. Here is a scaled-down sample in the MLA style:

Swanson 1

Karin Swanson

Professor Brown

English 101 (20)

8 March 2003

Spontaneity and Enjoyment of the Natural World

Edward Thomas' "Adlestrop" and Robert Frost's

"Stopping by Woods on a Snowy Evening" each describe a personal account of an encounter with the natural world. Frost's

---

Title page format—APA The *APA Publication Manual* prescribes a separate title page with three distinct parts. First is the header with essay title (or the first few words) and the page number. Next is a line called the running head (not to exceed 50 characters) that identifies the article for publishing purposes. Finally, centred both horizontally and vertically on the page, is your title and information, all double-spaced.

Besides the title, APA format requires your name and institutional affiliation only; however, for most academic papers, you should include the instructor's name, the date, and your course number. Here is a scaled-down sample in the APA style:

The Problem of Environmental 1

Running head: THE PROBLEM OF ENVIRONMENTAL COSTS

The Problem of Environmental Costs

Joyce MacDonald

3 March 2003

Sociology 101

Professor Smith

Grant MacEwan College

Understanding Sentence Structure

If you sometimes make errors in sentence structure, then this section will help you to diagnose your problems and correct them.

Recognizing Clauses and Phrases

Knowing the difference between a clause and a phrase will help you to eliminate accidental sentence fragments, comma splices (sometimes called comma faults), and fused sentences from your writing.

A *clause* is a group of words that contains a subject and a verb.

> MAIN CLAUSE We had eaten dinner. (subject: *we*; verb: *had eaten*)
>
> SUBORDINATE CLAUSE After we had eaten dinner (subject: *we*; verb: *had eaten*)

A *phrase* is a group of words that does not contain both a subject and a verb.

> PHRASE After eating dinner (no subject, no verb)

You may think that *eating* is a verb in "After eating dinner," but words with *–ing* endings function as verbs only when they are used with auxiliaries such as *is, was, has been. Dancing*, for example, can be used as a noun (*Dancing* is good exercise) or an adjective (The *dancing* elephants delighted the crowd), as well as a verb (The elephants *are dancing*). For more information on verbs, see Solving Verb Problems.

Here are some common types of phrases:

> PREPOSITIONAL PHRASES around the corner, through the woods, of mice and men

PARTICIPIAL PHRASES while watching television, when driving on icy roads, before skiing down the slope

INFINITIVE PHRASES to come home, to breathe deeply, to save money

Clauses often include phrases:

They decided to walk home through the woods. (*to walk home* is an infinitive phrase; *through the woods* is a prepositional phrase)

Rosa, after hearing a tentative scratch on the window, peeked through the curtain. (*after hearing a tentative scratch* is a participial phrase describing Rosa; *on the window* is a prepositional phrase)

EXERCISE I

Label the following constructions P (phrase) or C (clause).

1. After we left the theatre

2. while walking and talking together

3. on the exposed wound

4. to see Paris and die happy

5. Vijay phones his mother every Sunday

Recognizing Main Clauses and Subordinate Clauses

A main clause is a group of words with a subject and a verb that can stand alone as a complete sentence.

MAIN CLAUSE We had washed the dishes.

MAIN CLAUSE We went to a movie.

A subordinate clause begins with a subordinate conjunction. It has a subject and a verb, but it cannot stand alone as a complete sentence.

SUBORDINATE CLAUSE After we had washed the dishes (*After* is a subordinate conjunction.)

If you can recognize a subordinate conjunction, then it's easy to distinguish between a main clause and a subordinate clause. Here is a list of the most common subordinate conjunctions:

SUBORDINATE CONJUNCTIONS

after	if
before	unless
when	although
while	even though
during	because
as	provided that
as long as	in order that
since	until

Relative pronouns may also serve as subordinate conjunctions:

RELATIVE PRONOUNS

who	whomever
whom	which
whoever	that*

Subordinate clauses that begin with relative pronouns describe the preceding noun or pronoun. They are often, but not always, located between the subject and verb of main clauses. The relative pronoun functions both as the subordinate conjunction and as the subject of the subordinate clause.

> The prairies, ***which*** *had been suffering through the worst drought of the century*, were deluged with rain.

> The car ***that I was telling you about*** is finally mine.

> One of the artists exhibiting at the Glenbow Museum is my youngest sister, ***who*** *lives in Cairo*.

EXERCISE 2

Put square brackets around the main clause(s) in the following sentences. Put parentheses around subordinate clauses. Underline the subject of a main or subordinate clause once; underline the complete verb (the main verb + any auxiliaries) twice.

1. While the fighting persists, the airport will remain closed.

2. The supplies that would prevent deaths from injuries and starvation have been delayed.

---

* Occasionally *that* is omitted from sentences, as in "We thought [that] we might go to a movie."

3. I am worried about my parents, who are helpless victims of the civil war.

4. Although many attempts have been made to enforce a cease-fire, the fighting has increased.

5. Hopes for an early solution are fading because neither side will compromise.

Recognizing Simple, Compound, and Complex Sentences

Being able to identify simple, compound, and complex sentences will help you to avoid common errors in sentence structure and to use commas and semicolons accurately. You will also learn to appreciate the skill with which other writers construct sentences and to introduce more variations in your own sentence structure.

The Simple Sentence

This term describes the grammatical construction of a sentence, not its content. A **simple sentence** has one main clause. It may also have a number of phrases, as in this sentence:

> I noticed a little boy, probably two or three years old,
> crouched in the doorway of the filthy shack.

In this sentence, "I noticed a little boy" is the main clause. The phrases "probably two or three years old," "crouched in the doorway," and "of the filthy shack" add more information, but they are not clauses. This is a simple sentence.

The Compound Sentence

The **compound sentence** has two or more main clauses and no subordinate clauses. These clauses may be joined with a semicolon; a comma and coordinate conjunction (*and, but, or, nor, for, yet, so*); or a semicolon and a conjunctive adverb (*therefore, thus, however, nevertheless, furthermore*).

> Civil unrest increased; people attempted to protect themselves. (main clauses joined with a semicolon)
>
> Civil unrest increased, so people attempted to protect themselves. (main clauses joined with a comma and a coordinate conjunction)
>
> Civil unrest increased; therefore, people attempted to protect themselves. (main clauses joined with a semicolon and a conjunctive adverb)

SENTENCES

The Complex Sentence

This term describes the grammatical construction of a sentence, not its content. A **complex sentence** has one main clause and one or more subordinate clauses. If the subordinate clause comes first, put a comma after it.

> Because the roads were terrible, the meeting was cancelled. (one subordinate clause at the beginning of the sentence)

> You may contact us in the evening if you are unable to control the dog. (one subordinate clause at the end of the sentence)

> Although he wanted to speak to her before the evening ended, he continued to sit in the darkest corner of the restaurant. (two subordinate clauses at the beginning of the sentence)

The Compound-Complex Sentence

The **compound-complex sentence**, as its name suggests, contains two or more main clauses and one or more subordinate clauses. Use the appropriate punctuation between clauses.

> Jack, who wasn't very well coordinated, fell down; Jill, who wasn't watching where she was going, tumbled after him. (subordinate clauses within main clauses)

> When the cat fiddled, the cow jumped over the moon and the dish ran away with the spoon. (subordinate clause introducing two main clauses)

> Little Miss Muffett was quite timid, so when a spider sat down beside her, she screamed and ran away. (subordinate clause after the coordinate conjunction introducing the second main clause)

EXERCISE 3

A. Label the following sentences simple, compound, or complex. Put square brackets around main clauses and put parentheses around subordinate clauses. Underline the subject of a main or a subordinate clause once; underline the complete verb (the main verb + any auxiliaries) twice.

1. Smoking in the hospital was prohibited, so patients huddled outside the doors in freezing temperatures.

2. *Othello* is the tragedy of a man who "loved not wisely, but too well."

3. Some people believe that tuition should be affordable enough for anyone to attend post-secondary institutions; others believe that tuition should be increased and loans made available to those who need them.

4. As the runners surged towards the finish line, the crowd cheered wildly.

5. The distraught parents searched the campground, the lakeshore, and the surrounding woods for their missing child.

6. The weather, which had remained warm for several days, suddenly turned bitterly cold.

7. In the grey dawn of a cold November morning, the hunter stood motionless at the edge of the clearing, waiting patiently, cold fingers ready to press the button on the sleek silver camera.

8. Before you take an exam, get a good night's sleep and eat a healthy meal.

B. Create two sentences of your own of each type discussed above (simple, compound, complex, compound-complex). Put square brackets around main clauses and parentheses around subordinate clauses. Underline the subject(s) of each main and subordinate clause once; underline the complete verb (the main verb + any auxiliaries) of each clause twice.

Correcting Common Errors in Sentence Structure

Correcting Sentence Fragments

As its name implies, a **sentence fragment** is an incomplete sentence. It may lack a subject, a verb, or both, or it may be a subordinate clause or a phrase punctuated as a sentence.

Occasionally a sentence fragment may be used effectively for emphasis, as in

> Another victory for our side.

If your essay contains a mixture of intentional and accidental fragments, however, you will confuse your reader. Sentence fragments may also make your writing too informal.

To correct sentence fragments, supply the missing subject, missing verb, or missing main clause, or attach the fragment to the main clause.

> FRAGMENT Given the choice of resigning or being impeached.
>
> COMPLETE SENTENCE Given the choice of resigning or being impeached, the corrupt president left the country. (main clause added)
>
> FRAGMENT Even though students had been warned that they would be expected to write an in-class essay. Many of them arrived late.
>
> COMPLETE SENTENCE Even though students had been warned that they would be expected to write an in-class essay, many of them arrived late. (subordinate clause attached to the main clause)

FRAGMENT Shakespeare's play *Richard III* deals with fundamental human problems. Such as the conflict
between good and evil.

COMPLETE SENTENCE Shakespeare's play *Richard III* deals
with fundamental human problems, such as the conflict
between good and evil. (phrase attached to main clause)

EXERCISE 1

Revise the following sentences to correct sentence fragments.

1. Many students decide not to hold part-time jobs, Because they need time to study.

2. Although the benefits of pollution regulations outweigh the costs, Every regulation has an impact on the Canadian economy.

3. Genetically modified foods, sometimes known as "Frankenfoods."

4. We are Facing A complex political decision that required a delicate balance between moral principles and self-interest.

5. Because The class system is such an important issue in nineteenth-century British novels.

6. In the last act of the play, when the hero and the villain confront each other.

7. Darwin's formulation of the theory of evolution had a profound impact on many areas of nineteenth-century thought, From history, to economics, to psychology.

8. People who want compensation for all the injustices they have endured and who will no longer accept the indifference of government bureaucracies.

9. Genetic manipulation could be useful in the treatment of some diseases, Such as diabetes.

10. In "My Last Duchess," where Browning criticizes the standards by which the Duke judges himself and other people.

Correcting Comma Splices

The **comma splice** (sometimes called the comma fault) occurs when only a comma is used to join two main clauses. There is no conjunction to show how the clauses are related. Each of the following sentences contains a comma splice.

1. The thinking behind the idea of the Divine Right of Kings is that God has invested the power of kingship in the king, whatever a king does is sanctioned by God.

2. Hamlet and Laertes have very different personalities, both are enough like us and the people we know to be believable.

3. We have high expectations of our leaders, we become cynical when they fail us.

4. He assumed the jewels were cheap fakes, therefore he believed his wife could buy them with her household money.

5. She wanted badly to win the prize, she practised hours every day.

Whenever you join two separate ideas, you need more than a comma to show how they are related. There are five ways to correct comma splices.

1. Separate main clauses with a period.

   The thinking behind the idea of the Divine Right of Kings is that God has invested the power of kingship in the king. Whatever the king does is sanctioned by God.

2. Join main clauses with a comma and a coordinate conjunction (*and, but, or, nor, for, yet, so*). Choose the conjunction that best expresses the relationship between the ideas.

   Hamlet and Laertes have very different personalities, but they are enough like us and the people we know to be believable.

3. Join main clauses with a semicolon.

   We have high expectations of our leaders; we become cynical when they fail us.

4. Join main clauses with a semicolon and a conjunctive adverb. Put a comma after the conjunctive adverb if it is more than one syllable (after *therefore*, but not after *thus*).

   Here is a partial list of conjunctive adverbs with indications of how they are used:

   • to signal that one idea is a result of another: *accordingly, consequently, therefore, thus, hence*

   • to signal that one idea is added to another: *furthermore, moreover, besides*

   • to signal a contrast in ideas: *nevertheless, however, otherwise, still*

   To choose the appropriate conjunction, consider how the ideas are related. In this sentence, the second idea is a result of the first:

   He assumed the jewels were cheap fakes; therefore, he believed his wife had bought them with her household money.

5. Change one of the main clauses into a subordinate clause. Notice that when the subordinate clause is first, it is separated from the main clause by a comma.

ERRORS

> Because she wanted badly to win the prize, she practised
> hours every day.
>
> She practised hours every day because she wanted badly to
> win the prize.

EXERCISE 2

Choose the most appropriate method to correct comma splices in the following sentences.

1. Holden wants to be like the ducks; no one seems to notice them.

2. The southern half of the province has received very little rain for the third consecutive year; poor crops are expected.

3. She was constantly late; her work was sloppy.

4. The competition in high school is intense; some students use alcohol to escape from the pressure to succeed.

5. Top government advisors have been meeting to discuss strategy; they will not reveal their position until noon tomorrow.

6. Olena has very limited vision; voice-sensitive computer software is enormously helpful to her.

7. Ultra-lite aircraft are easy to fly; however they can be very difficult to land.

8. With the new causeway, more tourists come to Prince Edward Island; they don't stay as long.

9. Marin prepared carefully for the job interview; she landed the job of her dreams.

10. Quentin studied all night for the exam; he did poorly.

Correcting Fused Sentences

Fused sentences (sometimes called run-on sentences) contain two or more main clauses, but there is no punctuation to show how the clauses are related.

> Television networks make money by selling advertising time
> therefore programs must appeal to people who can afford the
> products advertised.
>
> Jeans are a status symbol in Russia they sell for hundreds of
> dollars on the black market.

Fused sentences can be corrected in the same way as comma splices. Be sure not to create a comma splice by merely putting a comma between main clauses.

EXERCISE 3

Revise the following fused sentences by adding conjunctions and adjusting punctuation as necessary.

1. It is easy to make this delicious dessert just follow these instructions.

2. Some adolescents are sullen, rebellious, and lazy others work to support themselves and to help their families.

3. Einstein abhorred the practical use of his theories by the military in the future we may find more humanitarian uses for his concepts.

4. Some leaders brutally impose their policies they get sullen compliance at best.

5. The window display stopped passersby in their tracks it featured a mannequin wrapped in a bloody sheet with a boot on its neck.

REVIEW EXERCISE 1

1. Correct all the fragments, comma splices, and fused sentences in the paragraph below.

For most of my life, I have used and appreciated good knives. This comes from growing up on a farm, Where I often needed a good knife. I quickly learned to distinguish a good quality knife from one of poor quality. *However* Finding a good knife was often difficult. ~~Because~~ The knives being sold now are made by companies that care more about profit than about quality. Consequently, I always kept an eye out for knives made in the early part of the century, knives constructed then are usually made from better quality materials. I faithfully attended auctions and garage sales, in the hope of finding these early knives. I had to be content with whatever style I found, there were not many styles available.

Correcting Misplaced and Dangling Modifiers

A **modifier** is a word, a phrase, or a clause that supplies further information about another word in the sentence. Modifiers can act as adjectives to describe nouns or pronouns or as adverbs to describe verbs, adjectives, or other adverbs.

The dog barked loudly. (*loudly* is an adverb describing "barked")

When the stranger entered the yard, the dog barked loudly. (*When the stranger entered the yard* is a subordinate clause functioning as an adverb to describe "barked")

The dog, barking loudly, attacked the stranger. (*barking loudly* is an adjective phrase describing "dog")

The dog, who had been barking for hours, went to sleep. (*who had been barking for hours* is a subordinate clause functioning as an adjective to describe "dog")

For clarity, a modifier must be as close as possible to the word it modifies, and there must be a word in the sentence for it to describe. If these conditions are not met, the modifier is either **misplaced** or **dangling**.

Correcting Misplaced Modifiers

Misplaced modifiers Misplaced modifiers are single words (*especially, almost, even, hardly, just, merely, nearly, only, scarcely*), phrases, or clauses that are too far away from the word they describe to be clear.

This film *only* runs fifty-eight minutes. (Is this the only film that runs fifty-eight minutes, or does it run only fifty-eight minutes?)

She told him *on Friday* she was quitting. (Did she tell him on Friday, or is she quitting on Friday?)

He *just* said he would be a few minutes late. (Did he say this very recently, did he say that he would be only a few minutes late, or did he say only this?)

You can easily correct a misplaced modifier by moving it as close as possible to the word it describes.

Only this film runs fifty-eight minutes. **OR** This film runs only fifty-eight minutes.

On Friday she told him she was quitting. **OR** She told him she was quitting on Friday.

He said he would be just a few minutes late.

A special type of misplaced modifier is a **split infinitive**. An infinitive is *to* + a verb: *to walk, to think, to breathe*. An infinitive is split when a modifier (usually an adverb) is placed between *to* and the verb: *to seriously think*. Try to avoid splitting an infinitive when the resulting construction is awkward.

SPLIT INFINITIVE Alex tried to carefully prepare for the exam.

REVISED Alex tried to prepare carefully for the exam.

EXERCISE 4

Revise the following sentences to eliminate misplaced modifiers.

1. The Wongs were amazed to see a bear on the main street while vacationing in Jasper.

Split infinitive

2. Selina needed time to mentally prepare for the lawyer's questions.

3. Antonio stared at the attractive young women across the aisle over his glasses.

4. Marissa had nearly driven all the way home when she stopped to pick up a hitch-hiker.

5. Beena was just trying to rapidly read through the whole chapter before class.

Correcting Dangling Modifiers

Dangling modifiers A dangling modifier is a phrase, often at the beginning of the sentence, which has no logical connection with the rest of the sentence. The phrase dangles because there is no word in the sentence for it to modify.

> Bitterly regretting his misspent youth, his days in jail seemed endless.

> When empty, return them to the store.

You can't eliminate a dangling modifier by moving it to another position in the sentence; instead, you need to revise the structure of the sentence itself. You can do this in two ways:

1. Expand the dangling modifier into a subordinate clause.

   > Because he regretted his misspent youth, his days in jail seemed endless.

   > When the bottles are empty, return them to the store.

2. Revise the main clause so that it contains a word for the introductory phrase to modify.

   > Bitterly regretting his misspent youth, the prisoner found his days in jail endless.

   > When empty, the bottles should be returned to the store.

EXERCISE 5

Revise the following sentences to eliminate all dangling modifiers.

Sara was   thus

1. Determined to finish her essay, all interruptions were ignored.

2. After hearing the manager's plans to reorganize the office, it was difficult for the workers to remain calm.

3. A lover of movies since childhood, his plan was to become an actor.

4. When recovering from major surgery, strenuous exercise should be avoided.

5. Just before starting school, Domingo's parents moved to Halifax.

✳ REVIEW EXERCISE 2

Revise the following sentences to eliminate misplaced and dangling modifiers.

1. He scarcely knew anyone at the party.

After 2. ~~the~~ *the student studied* ~~Even after studying~~ all night, many of the exam questions seemed unfamiliar.

3. After a hot, strenuous day of sightseeing, the hotel pool looked inviting.

4. By blaming the poor for their problems, responsibility to create a more just society can be avoided by politicians.

5. After experiencing the natural consequences of misbehaviour, the relationship between the parent and child will improve.

6. When underage, Louis XIV's ministers had charge of the government.

7. By regulating the disposal of hazardous wastes, the environment will be preserved.

8. To successfully jump from this height, you'll need a special parachute.

9. One terrible night, while showing off my new car to my friends, the engine exploded.

10. In writing stories for popular magazines, the readers always want a happy ending.

Correcting Faulty Parallelism

Parallelism When sentence elements (words, phrases, clauses) are parallel, they have the same grammatical construction.

> She was *lucky, intelligent,* and *brave.* (parallel adjectives)
>
> *Slowly* and *painfully,* the lone survivor crawled towards the camp. (parallel adverbs)
>
> The riders made their way *over the mountain, through the valley,* and *into the town.* (parallel phrases)
>
> *What we say, what we think,* and *what we do* are often at odds. (parallel clauses)

Parallel sentence structure is especially important whenever you have a list (of steps in a procedure, for example) and when you join parts of a sentence with coordinate conjunctions (*and, but, or, nor, for, yet, so*) or correlative conjunctions (*neither ... nor, either ... or, not only ... but also*).

Before you leave, close the windows, turn off the lights, and lock the doors. (parallel steps)

The cowardly fail because of their fear, but the courageous succeed in spite of their fear. (parallel main clauses joined with a coordinate conjunction)

Your choice in this situation is either to finish the project or to fail the course. (parallel phrases joined with correlative conjunctions)

Faulty parallelism As its name suggests, faulty parallelism occurs whenever sentence elements are not parallel. You can correct faulty parallelism by balancing words with words, phrases with phrases, and clauses with clauses.

NOT PARALLEL To write an effective conclusion, restate your thesis, summarize your main points, and the broader context of your subject should be suggested.

PARALLEL To write an effective conclusion, restate your thesis, summarize your main points, and suggest the broader context of your subject.

NOT PARALLEL As a winner you will achieve success, and respect will also come your way.

PARALLEL As a winner, you will achieve both success and respect.

EXERCISE 6

A. Revise the following sentences to correct faulty parallelism.

1. Many children do poorly in school because of inadequate diet, poor instruction, and they are not very interested.

2. To prevent shock, cover the victim with a blanket, speaking reassuringly.

3. To clean this oven, I need either atomic weapons or perhaps a miracle will happen.

4. You could end your speech with a quotation, by asking a question, or suggest the broader implications of your subject.

5. The successful candidate for this position must be self-motivated, have an ability to learn quickly, and reliability is very important. *reliable*

B. Write five sentences of your own containing parallel elements. Include parallel words, parallel phrases, and parallel clauses. Use correlative conjunctions in at least one sentence. Underline the parallel elements.

Correcting Faulty Coordination and Subordination

Coordination and subordination help you to use the structure of the sentence to emphasize your main point. Use **coordination** to join points of equal importance. To create coordination, join words, phrases, and clauses with coordinate or correlative conjunctions.

Your analysis of this problem is both *thorough and creative*.

This will be a step *out of the frying pan and into the fire*.

Only those *who have a diploma in Early Childhood Education or who have equivalent work experience* need apply for this position.

Use **subordination** to join points of unequal importance. To create subordination, put your main point in the main clause and your less important point in a subordinate clause or phrase.

Although everyone was aware of the problem, no one knew what to do about it.

Marta had her car serviced before she set out on her journey.

The clause or phrase at the end of the sentence always gets more emphasis. Thus, for maximum emphasis, put your main idea in a main clause and put that clause at the end of the sentence. Notice the difference in the emphasis given to the main clause in these two sentences.

Although the meeting was well publicized, it attracted little interest. (Putting the main clause last gives it maximum emphasis.)

The meeting attracted little interest even though it was well publicized. (Putting the subordinate clause last evens the emphasis given to both clauses.)

Faulty coordination Faulty coordination can occur when the elements you join are not grammatically parallel. (For an explanation of parallelism, see above.)

NOT PARALLEL On the camping trip, Lewis learned to despise canned food, to loathe outdoor toilets, and he was afraid of bears.

REVISED On the camping trip, Lewis learned to despise canned food, to loathe outdoor toilets, and to fear bears.

Faulty coordination can also occur if you join ideas that are unrelated or not of equal importance.

ERRORS

UNRELATED IDEAS The movie was boring and pretentious and hundreds of people lined up for hours to see it.

REVISED Although the movie was boring and pretentious, hundreds of people lined up for hours to see it.

UNEQUAL IDEAS Hamlet is Prince of Denmark and he is disillusioned by his mother's hasty remarriage.

REVISED Hamlet, Prince of Denmark, is disillusioned by his mother's hasty remarriage.

Don't use *and* as an all-purpose conjunction. Although *and* can sometimes be a weak signal of causal connection (I was late and I missed the bus), it's best to use *and* only when you want to signal that what follows is a coordinate fact or idea.

NOT   Dan was chronically tired and he had anemia.

BUT   Dan was chronically tired because he had anemia.

EXERCISE 7

Revise the following sentences to correct errors in coordination.

1. Angus is an ardent outdoorsman and conservationist and he lives in rural New Brunswick.

2. In the summer, Andrea enjoys working in the garden, taking long walks, and she likes to read romances.

3. Marco forgot to pay a speeding ticket and he received a summons to appear in court.

4. To function effectively as a social worker, you need to be both knowledgeable and compassion is important.

5. As far as I can tell, Ingrid has no interest either in getting a job and school doesn't interest her.

Faulty subordination Faulty subordination occurs when subordinate conjunctions are used inappropriately. Here are the most common causes of this error.

1. Attaching the subordinate conjunction to the wrong clause.

FAULTY Although they missed the plane, they left in plenty of time to reach the airport.

REVISED They missed the plane although they left in plenty of time to reach the airport.

2. Using an imprecise subordinate conjunction (especially *since* and *as*). *Since* can mean "because," but *since* can also mean "from the time that." If these two meanings might be confused, use *because* to indicate a causal connection.

CONFUSING Since she broke her ankle, she has been housebound.

CLEAR Because she broke her ankle, she has been housebound.

CLEAR From the time she broke her ankle, she has been
housebound.

As can be used to mean *because*, but it's best to use *as* to mean "while."

CLEAR As Felicity struggled to listen to the lecture, her mind
began to wander.

CONFUSING As Raul is the manager, he thinks he should
make all the decisions.

CLEAR Raul thinks he should make all the decisions because
he is the manager.

3. Using two conjunctions that mean the same thing.

MIXED Because he did not want to pay a late penalty for his
income tax, therefore he rushed to the post office just
before midnight.

REVISED Because he did not want to pay a late penalty for
his income tax, he rushed to the post office just before
midnight.

OR He did not want to pay a late penalty for his income tax;
therefore, he rushed to the post office just before midnight.

Excessive subordination This error occurs when you try to subordinate too many clauses in a sentence. Avoid beginning and ending a
sentence with similar subordinate clauses.

EXCESSIVE SUBORDINATION Because she was afraid of a hail
storm, she covered all the windows because the force
of the hail might break them.

REVISED Fearing a hail storm, she covered all the windows to
protect them.

Excessive subordination can also occur if you put too many
clauses beginning with *that*, *which*, and *who* into one sentence.

EXCESSIVE SUBORDINATION The novelist who wins this contest which is sponsored by a major publisher will be taken on a cross-country tour that begins July 1.

REVISED The novelist who wins this contest, sponsored by a major publisher, will be taken on a cross-country tour beginning July 1.

EXERCISE 8

Revise the following sentences to eliminate faulty or excessive subordination. Write C beside a correct sentence.

1. When Jing-Mei learned about the fashion opportunities in Montreal when she was living in Lethbridge, she packed her bags and bought an airline ticket.

2. Since Karl had a seizure caused by an allergic reaction, he has been cautious about all medications.

3. Because the assistant manager is autocratic and arrogant, therefore no one wants to work with her.

4. As the main character ties his sense of masculinity to clan traditions, he feels threatened when these structures begin to crumble.

5. Although Amin desperately needed a job, he was determined never again to work for his father.

Correcting Mixed Constructions

A **mixed construction** will occur if you begin a sentence with one grammatical construction and complete it with one that is different and incompatible. Any of the errors listed below will produce an awkward sentence.

Putting a subordinate clause before or after a linking verb
Readers expect linking verbs, such as *is* and *was*, to be followed by a noun or noun clause, not by a subordinate clause that modifies the verb. Formulations like *an example of this is when* or *the reason for this is because* are typical of this sort of mixed construction.

MIXED *An example* of his hostility *is when* he turns his homicidal bull loose on the mushroom pickers.

MIXED *One reason* she dropped out of school *is because* she was in constant conflict with authority.

You can revise these sentences by supplying the missing noun or noun clause.

ERRORS

REVISED An example of his hostility is his decision to turn his homicidal bull loose on the mushroom pickers.

REVISED One reason she dropped out of school is her constant conflicts with authority.

Another way to revise these sentences is to replace the linking verb.

REVISED He shows his hostility when he turns his homicidal bull loose on the mushroom pickers.

REVISED She dropped out of school because she was in constant conflict with authority.

Omitting the subject Leaving out the subject typically produces sentences like this:

MIXED In this documentary makes the point that gorillas are a seriously endangered species.

This sentence is confusing because the prepositional phrase *In this documentary*, which normally introduces a grammatically complete sentence, seems to be the subject of the sentence. You could revise by omitting the preposition.

REVISED This documentary makes the point that gorillas are a seriously endangered species.

Or you could keep the prepositional phrase and add a subject to the main clause.

REVISED In this documentary, the filmmaker shows that gorillas are a seriously endangered species.

Leaving out part of a comparison Sentences that begin with phrases such as *the more, the less, the worse, the further* suggest a comparison. You will confuse your reader if you fail to complete the comparison.

MIXED The less time I have, I have a lot to do.

You could revise this sentence by pairing *less* with *more*.

REVISED The less time I have, the more I have to do.

Mixing a question and a statement

MIXED The little boy plaintively asked his mother when will she finish writing her essay?

You could revise this sentence by rephrasing the question as direct speech.

REVISED The little boy plaintively asked his mother, "When will you finish writing your essay?"

You could also make the question a statement.

REVISED The little boy plaintively asked his mother when she would finish writing her essay.

EXERCISE 9

Revise the following sentences to eliminate mixed constructions.

1. In *A Man for All Seasons*, it shows that the reason Sir Thomas More becomes a martyr is because he is willing to die for his beliefs.
2. An example of her cunning is when she persuades her client not to consult another lawyer.
3. By denying that the government intended to raise taxes increased the credibility gap between the Minister of Finance and the public.
4. The more Yvette loathed her family, she did not want to live with them.
5. The frustrated mother asked her daughter when will she ever grow up?

REVIEW EXERCISE 3

Revise the following sentences to eliminate faulty parallelism, faulty coordination and subordination, and mixed constructions.

1. To complete this degree, you could take three more courses or a thesis could be written.
2. Although he loved her, he didn't want to marry her although she was rich.
3. The more the accused man protested his innocence, the jury didn't believe him.
4. The frustrated customer demanded to know when could she speak to the manager?
5. Julia has travelled extensively in the Far East and she teaches dance.
6. Because the roads through the mountains were hazardous, he decided to fly home because he didn't want to drive.
7. They vowed to remain married for better and worse, for richer and poorer, and whether or not they were both healthy.
8. As Timothy was the last to be hired, he was also the first to be fired.
9. He had forgotten about the test until the class started, although he did well on it.
10. Charles Dickens is an important nineteenth-century novelist who experienced poverty as a child and who is very sympathetic to poor children in his novels.

REVIEW EXERCISE 4

Rewrite the following paragraph to eliminate sentence fragments, comma splices, fused sentences, dangling and misplaced modifiers, faulty parallelism, and mixed constructions. Do not omit any of the ideas in the paragraph.

From January to mid-June is when the bay is covered with ice. Then twice-weekly air transportation replaces the three-hour ferry trip to the mainland. On a clear, windless day the twenty minutes in the air can be heavenly. A sightseer's bliss. Moose and caribou can be spotted and you can follow snowmobile trails as they wend their way over and around ponds, brooks, hills and dales. The snow gleaming and glistening like a fairy-tale scene. But this is no Boeing 747 this only is a four-seater Cessna. Commonly referred to as a matchbox with wings, you squeeze and squirm into a bearable position. Positioning yourself over bags of mail, boxes of freight, and the luggage you brought. Your knees bump against your chin, you clench your teeth in preparation for take-off. Hoping and praying that the weather remains good, if it doesn't you are in for the most unpleasant twenty minutes of your life.

Improving Sentence Structure

When all your sentences are about the same length and have the same structure, it is difficult for a reader to distinguish main points from supporting details. Consider this paragraph analyzing symbolism in Margaret Atwood's novel *Cat's Eye*:

> The most important symbol in Margaret Atwood's novel is the cat's eye. *Cat's Eye* is the title. *The Dictionary of Symbols and Imagery* by Ad de Vries gives several meanings of both cats and eyes. Cats have several symbolic interpretations, both good and evil. The eye also has both good and evil interpretations. Cats are beautiful and cuddly on the outside. They are highly independent. They are thought to be the most cunning and untrustworthy of all animals. The duality of their nature is most apparent in their "inverted playfulness" (de Vries 86). Cats turn the act of killing a mouse into a game. The eye can be either evil or protecting. De Vries says that "the divinity can be malevolent: the evil eye, one that scorches" (171). The eye can also be a charm against evil. The Eye of Horus in folklore protects against the Evil Eye of envy, malice, and the like (de Vries 172). The main character of the novel is Elaine. As a child Elaine carries her cat's eye marble everywhere. It is a charm that she hopes will protect her from the cruelty of the girls at school. She finally realizes that she has become like the glass marble. Glass eyes are unmoving and unfeeling.

This paragraph is hard to understand for two main reasons.

1. All the sentences have the same basic structure and are about the same length. As a result, it's hard to distinguish the ideas from the examples that support them.

2. There are no transitions: no words, phrases, or clauses that establish relationships between sentences. As a result, it is hard to tell whether the writer intended a particular statement to reinforce, qualify, or contradict another statement or to suggest a cause and effect relationship.

By varying sentence structure and length and providing transitions, you can help your reader to understand the connections among your ideas. If you compare the paragraph above with the revised version, you can see just how big a difference these simple changes make.

> The most important symbol in Margaret Atwood's novel is the image of the cat's eye that gives the book its title. According to Ad de Vries in the *Dictionary of Symbols and Imagery*, both the cat and the eye have several symbolic meanings, good and evil. Cats have a dual nature: beautiful and cuddly on the outside, they are nevertheless highly independent and thought to be the most cunning and untrustworthy of all animals. The duality of their nature is most apparent in their "inverted playfulness" (de Vries 86): they turn the act of killing a mouse into a game. Similarly, the eye can be either an Evil Eye, "one that scorches" (de Vries 171) or a protecting presence, like the Eye of Horus that serves as a charm against the Evil Eye of envy and malice (de Vries 172). As a child Elaine, the main character of the novel, uses her cat's eye marble as a charm to protect herself against the cruelty of the girls at her school. By the end of the novel Elaine realizes that she has become like the glass marble, unmoving and unfeeling.

Varying Sentence Lengths

Your main points will be clearer and more emphatic if you express them in short sentences. Use longer sentences to gather details, reasons, and examples that support and develop your main points.

> In constructing the Imperial Hotel in Tokyo, Frank Lloyd Wright had to solve several architectural problems (main point: 16 words). He had to deal with difficulties created by earthquake tremors, correct the weak soil base of the hotel site, and keep the building from cracking (series of explanations: 25 words).

VARIETY

Varying Sentence Patterns

The basic sentence pattern in English is subject + verb + object (Jennifer hit the ball). If all of your sentences follow this pattern, however, your writing will soon become as monotonous as a grade-one reader. You will also make it more difficult for your reader to distinguish major and minor points.

Common Sentence Patterns

Here are the most common sentence patterns:

The loose sentence: subject + verb + modifier

> The team lost money, despite better players and an improved stadium.

This is the most common sentence pattern and is thus the easiest for most readers to understand. The modifier gains emphasis because it is placed at the end of the sentence. Readers would expect the sentence that follows it to focus on the improvement in players and the stadium.

The periodic sentence: modifier + subject + verb

> Despite better players and an improved stadium, the team lost money.

Because we have to wait for the subject and the verb, this sentence pattern creates suspense and interest. It puts maximum interest on the fact that the team lost money, so readers would expect the next sentence to deal with this issue.

The embedded sentence: subject + modifier + verb

> The team, despite better players and an improved stadium, lost money.

This sentence pattern slows the reader down because the subject and the verb are separated by a lengthy modifier. It is useful if you want to imitate the process of thinking through a problem. It also leads readers to expect that the sentence that follows it will begin to explore the real reasons for the team's inability to make a profit.

The balanced construction The balanced construction creates a compound sentence in which two closely related main clauses with the same structure are joined with a semicolon, a comma and a coordinate conjunction, or a semicolon and a conjunctive adverb. It is especially useful when you want to suggest a choice between two equal possibilities.

> Perhaps Dmitri will treat his relationship with Anna as one
> more casual affair, or perhaps he will fall genuinely in love
> for the first time.

Sentences with parallel elements Sentences containing a series of parallel words, phrases, or clauses arranged in an order of increasing importance are useful when you want to sum up a number of factors or details.

> By the end of *The Mayor of Casterbridge*, Henchard has lost
> his family, his home, his standing in the community, and his
> hopes for the future.

Effective Sentence Variety

Varying the structure of your sentences will help you to avoid monotony and to clarify the relationships among ideas, explanations, and details. On the other hand, if every sentence follows a different pattern, your reader will find your paragraph confusing. Here are some guidelines for varying sentence structure effectively.

1. Keep the structure of topic sentences fairly simple. When you are making major points, you don't want to lose your reader in elaborate sentence patterns.
2. Change your sentence structure when you introduce an explanation. If your explanation takes more than one sentence, keep the sentences in similar patterns.
3. When you shift from explanation to details, change your sentence pattern.
4. Keep similar sentence patterns for all your details.

The simplest and most obvious way to change the structure of your sentences is to experiment with different ways to begin a sentence. Here are some possibilities to consider.

Ways to Begin Sentences

1. With the subject: *John A. Macdonald* was a colourful prime minister.
2. With a prepositional phrase: *Before Confederation* he had proved his skill as a politician.
3. With single-word adjectives: *Bold, shrewd, and stubborn*, he had clung to power for over thirty years.
4. With a participial phrase: *Drinking heavily*, he nevertheless maintained a firm grip on his party and the country.

5. With a subordinate clause: *Because he helped to bring about the birth of the nation and presided over it in its infancy*, he is known as the Father of Confederation.

6. With an appositive: *A man with great historical importance as well as undeniable personal weaknesses*, Macdonald continues to fascinate historians and biographers.

As these examples demonstrate, you can create emphasis by paying careful attention to the length and structure of your sentences. Avoid using italics (underlining) or capitalization to create emphasis.

NOT   Hamlet is in deep despair. He feels totally *isolated*.

BUT   Feeling totally isolated, Hamlet sinks into despair.

EXERCISE I

Rewrite the following paragraph to make the relationship among points, explanations, and details clearer by varying sentence structure and length.

> The most dangerous and most hated group of Oldboys at boarding school were the very few who, while not physically powerful, were able to control the larger, dumber ones. Kravic was one of the controllers. He was small and physically immature for his age. He smiled constantly, and his laugh was a forced malicious chatter, never spontaneous. He had the dark glittery stare of an insane child. Simpson was one of the larger, dumber ones. Kravic controlled him. Simpson was fifteen. He had one eyebrow, a full beard, and the build of a man of thirty. He was extremely slow and easily led. He was also as bad tempered as a grizzly. Kravic, Simpson, and a few other Oldboys would come into a Newboy dorm. They would corner a Newboy and antagonize him. Kravic would slap his face, steal things from his locker, or destroy his personal possessions. The Newboy would watch helplessly. Kravic would try to bait larger Newboys into hitting him. If the Newboy fell for the trap, Simpson and the other Oldboys would beat him up. They would justify the beating by saying they were "defending" the smaller Kravic.

EXERCISE 2

Find a paragraph of your own writing that could be improved by varying sentence structure and length. Revise the paragraph and bring both versions to class for discussion.

VARIETY

Using Transitions to Connect Ideas

Transitional words and phrases are important for two reasons. They increase your reader's understanding of how your ideas are related. They also create a sense of continuity, both within and between paragraphs, because one idea leads smoothly to the next.

Continuity Within Paragraphs

Sentence Hooks

Sentence hooks are words and phrases used to create continuity between sentences. You can hook sentences together with pronouns, demonstrative pronouns, synonyms, and repeated words and phrases.

Pronouns After the first reference by name, use pronouns and possessive pronouns to indicate a continuity of subject. Make sure that the reference is clear (see Solving Pronoun Problems).

> Margaret Atwood has written several novels. *Her* most recent
> is ... *She* has also written ...

Demonstrative pronouns To avoid repeating your last point, refer to it with a demonstrative pronoun (*this, that, these, those*) and a noun that identifies the subject to which you are referring.

> During the Depression, prairie farmers suffered because of
> the severe drought. *This problem* ...

> Macbeth murders Duncan and is responsible for the murder
> of Banquo and several others. *These acts* of violence ...

Synonyms and repeated words and phrases Keep your reader's attention on your subject by repeating key words and phrases or by using synonyms. Notice the continuity created by the repetition of "race" and "racism" in the following paragraph.

> So what is racism? Racism is the idea, whether in the back of your mind or deep in your heart, that there are large groupings within humanity that can be distinguished as separate *races*, and that the race you belong to is superior to other races in mind, body, and character. The problem with this concept, outside of the monstrous behaviour that such a belief justifies, is that the very notion of *race* has no scientific value. It is true that there are differences as to how people from different parts of the planet look. That much is obvious. But most of us are unaware that we differ in only 5% of our bodily features. This hardly seems like enough to classify us as separate "races." And even though some of these differences are dramatic, we also note that there is as much variation *within* a so-called race as *between* the so-called races. And how do we deal with people of mixed-"race" parentage? How do we describe them? And what about those sub-"race" nationalities that look significantly like other peoples of other "races," like the African Kalahari desert dwellers who appear to be Asians, or the Australian and Dravidian aborigines who appear to be straight-haired Africans?

Transitional Words and Phrases

Transitional words and phrases are means of indicating relationships in time, space, and logic.

RELATIONSHIP		SAMPLE TRANSITIONAL WORDS AND PHRASES
time		before, after, meanwhile, as soon as, during, until, then
space		on the right, near, farther away
logic	1. addition	and, another, a second, also, too, furthermore, moreover, not only ... but also, first, second, etc.
	2. contrast	but, in contrast, yet, however, on the other hand, nevertheless, otherwise

TRANSITIONS

3. similarity	just as, like, likewise, similarly, in the same way
4. examples	for example, for instance, to be specific, in particular, to illustrate
5. cause and effect	therefore, thus, so, for, hence, because, consequently, as a result, accordingly
6. concession and qualification	although, despite, while it is true that ...
7. emphasis	most important, a crucial point, significantly, of overwhelming importance

TRANSITIONS

Continuity Between Paragraphs

Paragraph Hooks

Paragraph hooks are words and phrases that recall key ideas to create continuity between paragraphs.

1. Repeat single words or phrases or use synonyms to link the last sentence of one paragraph to the first sentence of the next.

   LAST SENTENCE OF PARAGRAPH 1 His pride thus leads him to reject his friends' offers of help.

   FIRST SENTENCE OF PARAGRAPH 2 His pride also prevents him from helping himself.

2. Use phrases, clauses, or occasionally whole sentences that briefly recall the ideas of one paragraph at the beginning of the next.

   FIRST TOPIC SENTENCE Mackenzie King, Diefenbaker, and Pearson ...

   SECOND TOPIC SENTENCE These three Prime Ministers were not the only ones to favour such a policy ....

Transitional Words and Phrases

Transitional words and phrases also indicate relationships in time, space, and logic between paragraphs.

Sample topic sentences with transitions

TOPIC SENTENCE, PARAGRAPH 1 Opponents of rapid transit are quick to point out that the present city bus system loses money each year.

TOPIC SENTENCE, PARAGRAPH 2 It is true that any rapid transit is extremely expensive to build; thus for a few years our taxes will go up.

TOPIC SENTENCE, PARAGRAPH 3 If we invest sufficient funds to create a convenient, efficient rapid transit system, it will actually generate a profit.

EXERCISE 1

Underline the transitional words and phrases in the following paragraph analyzing Dee Brown's account of a U.S. cavalry attack on a Northern Cheyenne village in 1876.

Brown's account, on the other hand, begins by disputing the cavalry's rationale for the attack on the Northern Cheyenne village. He says that "most of these Cheyenne had not been in the Little Bighorn battle" where General Custer's troops were slaughtered. He also points out that these Cheyenne had left the reservation because the army had "stopped their rations." By suggesting that the villagers were innocent victims, Brown emphasizes the cowardice and brutality of the cavalry attack. According to his account, many of the Cheyenne warriors were killed "as they came awake." He describes other Indians struggling to protect the women and children. His description implies that the soldiers and their Indian mercenaries were cowardly enough to attack these helpless members of the tribe. This image of a cowardly attack upon the helpless is repeated in the final detail of the account: the cavalry's destruction of the trapped Indian ponies. This image reinforces both the cowardliness and the injustice of the attack from the Indians' point of view.

EXERCISE 2

Identify transitions in two paragraphs from one of the following essays (Part 2, Readings). Then write a paragraph discussing the kinds of transitions the author uses and their effectiveness.

1. Linda Hogan's "The Voyagers"
2. George Orwell's "Shooting an Elephant"
3. John Fraser's "Save the Last Dance"

EXERCISE 3

Use transitional words and phrases to clarify the relationships among ideas, explanations, and details in the following paragraph on the limitations of "ethical vegetarianism."

We do need to be more respectful of other living beings—
not just animals, but all living beings. We should stop force-
feeding growth hormones and other toxic substances to
animals. We should stop suffocating plants with chemical
fertilizers and deadly pesticides. We should be more conscious of the wastefulness inherent in eating meat. Any self-
respecting vegetarian can tell you that only two thirds of an
animal's body is used as food. The rest is discarded. We
should consider the waste of plants that occurs in kitchens
every day. Most restaurant meals are served with a sprig of
parsley on top. Who ever eats that? Unattractive plates are
covered with attractive beds of lettuce. Who eats the lettuce? We should ask waiters not to bother with plants that
will be wasted.

EXERCISE 4

Underline the transitional devices in a paragraph of your own writing. Then, if necessary, rewrite the paragraph to improve the transitions. Bring the paragraph(s) to class
for discussion.

Solving Diction Problems

Diction refers to the individual words you use to express your ideas. These choices can make your writing sound breezy or bureaucratic, superficial or supercilious, confident or cantankerous. At one end of the scale is the very informal language characteristic of conversations among friends; at the other end is the highly formal language characteristic of specialists writing to other specialists (in legal documents, for example). Your diction should suggest that you are a friendly, serious, reasonable person writing to equally friendly, serious, and reasonable readers who might be less well informed or who might have different opinions about your subject. If your diction creates a different impression of your relation to your subject and readers, you can make the following revisions.

Correcting Problems with Your Level of Diction

1. Eliminate very informal language and slang; they suggest you do not take your subject seriously.

   NOT   Hamlet was cheesed off by his mom's hasty marriage to his uncle.

   BUT   Hamlet was infuriated by his mother's hasty marriage to his uncle.

2. While the presence of some contractions (*don't, can't*) will give your writing a friendlier tone, too many contractions will make your writing seem too casual for a formal essay.

   NOT   Hamlet decides he'll feign madness while he's gathering proof that the ghost's telling the truth.

BUT   Hamlet decides he will feign madness while he is gathering proof that the ghost is telling the truth.

3. Eliminate or define specialized vocabulary that may be unfamiliar to your reader.

NOT   Self-worth is affirmed when one's self-image is validated by one's significant others.

BUT   People like themselves better when their ideas and feelings about themselves are confirmed by those they care about.

4. Rewrite sentences that are too abstract or too grandiose.

NOT   The interpersonal interaction between volunteer counsellors and clients can provide the opportunity for both parties to gain a sense of self-worth and significance in the midst of our institutionalized society. (too abstract)

BUT   Meetings between volunteer counsellors and clients can help both to feel more worthwhile.

NOT   Throughout history man has struggled to understand his place in the ever-changing world in which he was only one infinitesimal link in the infinite chain of being. (too grandiose and sexist)

BUT   Men and women often struggle to understand their place in the world.

5. Eliminate expressions that are too apologetic or argumentative.

NOT   I hope I will be able to show that some doctors over-prescribe medications because they want to meet their patients' expectations. (too apologetic)

BUT   Some doctors over-prescribe medications because they want to meet their patients' expectations.

NOT   Any fool can see that the emission of greenhouse gases is a worldwide problem.

BUT   The emission of greenhouse gases is a worldwide problem.

EXERCISE I

Rewrite the following paragraph so that its tone is appropriate for a university essay. You may need to check your dictionary to find replacements for some words.

How does my generation, the unfortunate souls forever trapped between the "Boomers" and the "Xers," cope with our amorphous identity? As I hope to show, mostly we fake it.

DICTION

We gather up our backpacks, Lennon sunglasses, and similar paraphernalia and head to the nearest café. There we simulate the behaviour and attitudes of another generation, "Boomer" or "Xer." We sit on high stools, listen to folksy, then thrashy, then classical music. We puff long-filtered ciggies and drink cappa-mocha-ccino-lattes in tiny cups or tall ones. We pontificate about politics and world hunger and the rain forest, and we'll play a game of Scrabble just to prove that we weren't bozos in university. We ask why they have so few smoking sections now and why they're taking away all the cool traffic circles and shouldn't they really be fixing the potholes instead? We agonize over the penury that renders Birkenstocks prohibitive, but realize that we can purchase "fake Birks" for twenty bucks at another shopping emporium, and that we should dig out the far-out fringe vests and neato purple socks our aunts and uncles gave us in 1968 because we could sell them. We pretend that we're not only "Boomer"-worthy but "Xer"-worthy as well. You'd have to be an idiot not to see we're faking it.

Correcting Problems with Word Choice: Usage

Some diction errors are spelling mistakes (*there* instead of *their*), while others occur when one meaning of a word is confused with another (*realize* meaning "to make real" for *realize* meaning "to understand"). The term *usage* refers to the customary use of words, phrases, and expressions in English. Here is a list of the most common problems:

1. *A lot* is always spelled as two words. *Alot* is never correct. *A lot*, however, is quite informal. When possible, choose a more formal expression (such as *much, a great deal of, great, many*).

   Hyperactive children have a lot of trouble concentrating.

   Hyperactive children have great difficulty concentrating.

2. *Affect* and *Effect*

   a. *Affect* is usually a verb.

   The early frost affected the tomatoes.

   b. *Effect* is usually a noun.

   The effect of the early frost on the tomatoes was obvious.

3. *All right* is always spelled as two words. *Alright* is never correct.

   "All right," the bank manager said with a smile, "your loan has been approved."

4. *Allude* and *Elude*

   a. Use *allude* when you mean to refer to, as in an allusion to the Bible or the Koran.

     Forster frequently alludes to the Bible in his essay "My Wood."

   b. Use *elude* when you mean to avoid or escape.

     The clever thief eluded the police for seven years.

5. *Allusion* and *Illusion*

   a. An *allusion* is a reference to a piece of literature, a historical event or figure, or a popular movie or television show.

     The speaker's frequent allusions to characters in popular television shows entertained the audience.

   b. An *illusion* is something that deceives by creating a false impression. An *illusion* can also refer to the state of mind in the person who is deceived.

     The use of perspective in the painting created the illusion of depth.

     Alison clung to the illusion that Juan would never forget her.

6. *Among* and *Between*

   a. Use *among* when you refer to more than two things.

     Divide the candy canes evenly among all the Christmas hampers.

   b. Use *between* when you refer to two things.

     Divide the prize money between the two winners.

7. *Amount* and *Number* (See also *Less* and *Fewer*)

   a. Use *amount* to refer to things considered as a mass.

     Melt a small amount of butter in a pan.

   b. Use *number* to refer to things that can be counted as individual units.

     A small number of delegates attended the convention.

8. *Compare with* and *Compare to*

   a. Use *compare with* when you examine the similarities and differences in things.

     A comparison of the American Senate with the Canadian Senate strengthens the argument for electing senators.

   b. Use *compare to* when you want to point out the similarities in two things.

     I would compare her eating habits to those of a pig.

9. *Differ from* and *Differ with*

   a. Use *differ from* to indicate that two things are unalike.

      The stage version of the play differs enormously from the film version.

   b. Use *differ with* to express disagreement with a person.

      I wish to differ with your assessment of the mayor's voting record.

10. *Different from* (not *different than*)

    The effects of an expectorant cough syrup are different from the effects of a cough suppressant.

11. *Elusive* and *Illusory*

    a. Use *elusive* when you want to describe something that is good at escaping or difficult to define or express.

       The elusive mouse disappeared through a crack in the wall.

       The specific implications of the new immigration policy remained elusive.

    b. Use *illusory* when you want to describe something that is false or unreal.

       The benefits of the proposed tax reduction are illusory.

12. *Eminent* and *Imminent*

    a. Use *eminent* when you mean "prominent" or "notable."

       He married into an eminent Quebec family.

    b. Use *imminent* to refer to a danger or threat near at hand.

       Flooding was imminent after the heavy rains.

13. *Flaunt* and *Flout*

    a. Use *flaunt* to refer to a conspicuous display of a person's attributes or possessions.

       Only the newly rich flaunt their wealth.

    b. Use *flout* to mean "to treat with scorn or contempt."

       Rebellious teens often flout authority.

14. *Good* and *Well*

    a. *Good* is usually an adjective.

       a good book, a good cookie

    b. *Well* is usually an adverb.

       to drive well, to sing well

15. *Hopefully.* Some guides to usage accept *hopefully* as a sentence modifier meaning "I hope" or "perhaps."

    Hopefully, I can leave work early.

Some readers, however, find this usage confusing and insist that *hopefully* should be used only as an adverb meaning "full of hope."

> Dressed in Halloween costumes, the children shouted hope-fully at the door.

Discuss this issue in class and see whether you can come to some agreement.

16. *Imply* and *Infer*

    a. Use *imply* to mean "hint."

    > His lack of response to her entreaties implied his refusal to grant her wish.

    b. Use *infer* to mean "make an educated guess" or "draw a conclusion."

    > The detective inferred from the blood on the sheets that the victim had been murdered in his sleep.

17. *It's* and *Its*

    a. *It's* means "it is."

    > It's raining for the third day in a row.

    b. *Its* is a possessive pronoun.

    > The horse broke its leg.

18. *Less* and *Fewer*

    a. Use *less* to refer to things considered as a mass.

    > Although I am earning more, I seem to have less spending money.

    b. Use *fewer* to refer to things that can be counted.

    > Fewer students than expected signed up for this course.

19. *Lie* and *Lay*

    a. The principal parts of the verb *to lie* (to recline) are *lie*, *lay*, *lying*, and *lain*.

    > She has been lying in the sun all afternoon.

    b. The principal parts of the verb *to lay* (to place) are *lay*, *laid*, *laying*, and *laid*.

    > The soldiers are laying down their weapons.

20. *Like* and *As*

    a. Use *like* when you are not introducing a clause.

    > He looks like his father.

    b. Use *as* to introduce a clause.

    > That night she dressed as she did when she was a girl.

21. *Loose* and *Lose*

    a. *Loose* is usually an adjective (loose talk), but it can be used as a verb meaning "to let loose."

    Loose the dogs of war.

    b. *Lose* is a verb.

    She is afraid she will lose her job.

22. *Partake of* and *Take part in*

    a. Use *partake of* when you mean to have a share of something (usually a meal).

    The guests were invited to partake of the enormous turkey.

    b. Use *take part in* when you mean to join or participate.

    Will you take part in our volleyball game?

23. *Principle* and *Principal*

    a. *Principle* means a fundamental belief.

    Most Canadians accept the principle of universal medical coverage.

    b. *Principal* means most important, first in rank.

    My principal objection is that cuts in services will inflict the most damage on the most vulnerable members of the community.

    He is the principal dancer with the Royal Winnipeg Ballet Company.

24. *Realize*

    a. *Realize* can mean "to make real," as in "to realize a profit."

    b. *Realize* can also mean "to understand fully," as in "to realize that he was wrong."

    You can avoid confusing these two meanings of *realize* if you use "realize that" when you mean "understand fully."

    NOT   He realized his mother's unhappiness.

    BUT   He realized that his mother was unhappy.

25. *Simple* and *Simplistic*

    a. Use *simple* when you mean "plain, easy to understand."

    Follow these simple directions.

    b. Use *simplistic* when you want to indicate something has been oversimplified. *Simplistic* always conveys a negative judgment.

    The premier offered only simplistic solutions to complex problems.

DICTION

26. *There* and *Their*

    a. Use *there* as an adverb or as a dummy subject.

        Put the piano there.

        There were many problems.

    b. *Their* is a possessive pronoun.

        their problem, their tough luck

27. *Uninterested* and *Disinterested*

    a. Use *uninterested* to mean "not interested in."

        I am uninterested in politics.

    b. Use *disinterested* to mean impartial.

        We need a disinterested third person to settle our dispute.

28. *You're* and *Your*

    a. *You're* means "you are."

        You're going to pay for this.

    b. *Your* is a possessive pronoun.

        Your car is in my parking space.

EXERCISE 2

Revise the following sentences to correct errors in usage. Most sentences contain more than one error.

1. From the noise in the lecture theatre, its reasonable to imply that a large amount of people were quite disinterested in the topic.

2. By now, it should hopefully be obvious that acid rain has alot of affects on all of us.

3. Engineers must realize there responsibility to protect the environment.

4. Even on formal occasions, Ted dresses like he is going to a hockey game.

5. Cindy refused to partake in any of the celebrations connected with her mother's wedding.

6. Fred immersed himself in the illusion that his status as an outsider made him an uninterested party in the family dispute.

7. The principle difference in my two jobs is that I now work less hours and make more money.

8. The next command you're going to learn is how to make your dog lay down on command.

9. "Alright," the driving instructor said, "this time you did good enough to pass."

10. The results of the medical tests were different than what the doctor had predicted.

Eliminating Wordiness

When you write a draft, you may find yourself repeating ideas, making false starts on sentences, and using inexact, wordy language because you are still working out your ideas. Sometimes the whole essay may be wordy because you have circled around ideas instead of including evidence to support them.

You can see both problems in the following draft paragraph from an essay comparing homeless people and nomads.

> There is a difference between being a homeless person and being a nomad. Being homeless is a state of mind; being a nomad is a way of life. Homeless people have no place to live. Many of them do not want to stay in one place. When they are placed in shelters or housing, they leave because they do not want ties with family or society. They do not want a home. Homeless people have few possessions, and because they have no permanent place to stay, they tend to carry their few possessions around with them. Nomads, on the other hand, are defined as people who move from place to place, usually seasonally. They have no fixed residence, but they tend to stay within a certain territory, where they stay in different spots. Traditional nomads live in family groups or small communities, and the whole group moves together. Modern nomads don't have a permanent residence. They may travel to different family members. They may stay with different family members for a few months at a time. When they travel, they store most of their belongings. They take only the most essential things with them when they move. In these ways nomads are different from homeless people.

Don't pad your essay with unnecessary words, phrases, sentences, and paragraphs just to reach the word limit. This strategy will only irritate your reader and weaken the force of your ideas. When you revise, try to be more concise. Here are some suggestions:

1. Choose exact nouns, verbs, and modifiers.

   NOT We walked slowly and quietly in the direction of the run-down little house. (13 words)

   BUT We crept toward the hovel. (5 words)

2. Replace vague words, such as *very*, *somewhat*, *really*, and *rather* with a more exact word.

   NOT They were really frightened by the ghost.

   BUT They were terrified by the ghost.

3. Avoid carelessly repeating words and ideas.

   NOT Entries to this competition are restricted to students only; no one else need apply. (14 words)

   BUT Only students may enter this competition. (6 words)

4. Condense prepositional phrases to single words.

   NOT She was dressed in a fashionable manner.

   BUT She was dressed fashionably.

5. Don't overuse *there is/are* and *it is ... that* to introduce sentences.

   NOT There are a number of factors that we should consider before we make this decision.

   BUT We should consider several factors before we make this decision.

   NOT It is Hagar's pride that causes many of her problems.

   BUT Hagar's pride causes many of her problems.

6. Combine several short sentences into one longer sentence by reducing sentences to clauses, clauses to phrases, and phrases to single words.

   NOT Television cameras filmed the demolition of the Regency Theatre. The Regency Theatre was one of the most ornate movie-houses in western Canada.

   BUT Television cameras filmed the demolition of the Regency Theatre, one of the most ornate movie-houses in western Canada.

WORDINESS

A study done on smokes revealed that

EXERCISE I

Revise the following groups of sentences to make them more concise.

1. A study has been done on smokers. This study revealed that much smoking is an automatic response to certain activities. These activities might be driving, typing, reading, or drinking alcohol and coffee.

2. The book *A Circle of Children* and its successor, *Lovey,* are stories about a teacher of children who are emotionally disturbed. Mary MacCracken wrote an account of her experiences working with children with emotional problems and described her growth as a teacher. She began as a teacher's aide and gradually became a teacher who was fully qualified to work with emotionally disturbed children. The books show her development as a teacher.

3. Being a video game player, I find it my duty to give a good name to video games because I find them challenging. I would like to change people's attitudes towards video games by giving some information in the hope that many people will discard their belief that these are mindless games and learn that these games require many years of practice.

4. A society that maintained a balance between the needs of the society and the preservation of the environment would be the best kind of society. I would like to live in it.

5. He drove his car down the highway. He drove his car very fast. He was travelling about 150 km an hour. Suddenly he hit a very icy section of the road. The car went out of control and slid quite quickly in the direction of the ditch.

EXERCISE 2

Rewrite the following paragraph to make it more concise. Add specific examples to illustrate major points.

Both daytime and prime time soap operas always contain a certain amount of violence. In the soaps someone is always working on a scheme to get more money or to destroy one person or another. The violence often comes to a head with maimings and killings as several characters try to stop the scheme or stop one person from destroying another person. Here of course we find the age-old tradition of good vs. bad. The good guys want to protect the innocent people, while the bad guys will stop at nothing to increase their power, destroying all who dare to cross their path. In the process many people are killed or wounded. Some are warned verbally or physically to stop trying to figure out what is going on. No one who is a real hero listens to such advice; instead, the hero struggles even more against the forces of evil. Of course, all this violence doesn't seem like a relaxing time for the viewers, but mystery and adventure add excitement to their usually ordinary lives.

EXERCISE 3

Revise a paragraph of your own writing to make it more concise. Bring both versions to class for discussion.

Solving Verb Problems

Verb Forms

A **verb** is a word or group of words that expresses action, existence, possession, or sensation.

> He **plays** hockey. She **has been playing** hockey. (action)
>
> I **am** here. I **have been** here. (existence)
>
> You **have** the measles. Soon we **will have** the measles. (possession)
>
> The bread **smells** mouldy. Your hands **feel** cold. (sensation)

Main Verbs and Auxiliary Verbs

A verb phrase is formed by joining one or more auxiliary verbs to the main verb: **have been waiting, might be stolen**. The last word in the verb phrase is the main verb; the other words are auxiliaries. Here is a list of the most common auxiliary verbs:

1. forms of *to be*: *am, is, are, was, were, be, been, being*
2. forms of *to have*: *have, has, had, having*
3. forms of *to do*: *do, does, did, done*
4. others: *can, could, may, might, must, shall, will, should, would, ought to, have to, supposed to, used to*

Principal Parts of Verbs

Principal parts of regular verbs Regular verbs, as their name suggests, form their principal parts in a regular, predictable way. The four main parts of a verb are the present tense, the past tense (formed by adding *ed* to the present tense), the present participle (formed by adding *ing* to the present tense), and the past participle (formed by adding *has* or *have* to the past tense).

The present tense usually expresses habitual action (Every day I *walk* to school), whereas the present participle is used with an auxiliary to express ongoing action (I *am walking* to school now). The past participle is used to express action that began in the past and continues to the present (I *have lived* in Canada for twenty years) or to express action that began and ended in the past (I *had lived* in Germany for twelve years before I came to Canada).

To name a verb, give its infinitive form: *to walk, to fill.*

PRESENT	PAST	PRESENT PARTICIPLE	PAST PARTICIPLE
walk	walked	walking	walked
fill	filled	filling	filled

Principal parts of irregular verbs Irregular verbs form their principal parts in various unpredictable ways. Here are three different patterns of irregular verbs.

PRESENT	PAST	PRESENT PARTICIPLE	PAST PARTICIPLE
drink	drank	drinking	drunk
burst	burst	bursting	burst
steal	stole	stealing	stolen

The present participle of irregular verbs is always formed by adding *ing* to the present tense. It's the past tense and the past participle that may cause problems. You need either to memorize these forms or to check your dictionary. Here are some of the most troublesome irregular verbs to watch for in your writing.

Principal parts of troublesome verbs

INFINITIVE	PAST TENSE	PAST PARTICIPLE
to be	was	been
to break	broke	broken
to choose	chose	chosen
to come	came	come
to cost	cost	cost
to go	went	gone
to lay (place)	laid	laid

VERBS

to lie (recline)	lay	lain
to hang (a person)	hanged	hanged
to hang (a picture)	hung	hung
to lead	led	led
to rise	rose	risen

Note 1: Don't confuse *lose* and *loose*.

NOT   She is afraid that she will loose her mind.

BUT   She is afraid that she will lose her mind.

Note 2: Be sure to add the past tense ending to *use* and *suppose* when they are followed by an infinitive.

NOT   Rosa use to play soccer.

BUT   Rosa used to play soccer.

NOT   Alix is suppose to make dinner.

BUT   Alix is supposed to make dinner.

Note 3: In speech, the contractions for "would have" (*would've*) and "should have" (*should've*) sound like "would of" and "should of." These forms are never correct.

NOT   You should of seen *The Lord of the Rings*.

BUT   You should have seen *The Lord of the Rings*.

EXERCISE I

Correct any errors in verb usage in the following sentences. Put C beside a correct sentence.

1. Because he had laid in the sun all afternoon, he was horribly sunburnt.
2. I'll put my money in a safe place so I won't loose it.
3. After three months in her new job, she still wasn't sure what she was suppose to do.
4. When the soldiers surrendered, they laid down their weapons in the sand.
5. The car loan costed more than he had anticipated.
6. I need to borrow your vacuum cleaner because mine is broke.
7. The clues have lead the detective straight to the murder suspect.
8. I have a headache, so I think I'll lay down for an hour.
9. Their bubble of happiness finally burst.
10. After she had drank all of the magic potion, she suddenly felt very tall.

Verb Tenses

Verb tenses indicate the time of existence, action, possession, or sensation. The basic tenses in English are the present, past, and future.

VERBS

The tenses used in a sentence or series of sentences must accurately indicate the time relationships involved.

> She walks to the door. She opens her umbrella. She leaves.
> (all verbs in the present tense)
>
> She walked to the door. She opened her umbrella. She left.
> (all verbs in the past tense)
>
> When she finishes her meal (present tense), she will walk to the door, open her umbrella, and leave. (future tense)
> (change in tense necessary to indicate time relationships)

Identifying Unnecessary Shifts in Tense

Unnecessary shifts in tense occur when the verb forms do not correspond to the time relationships. In the following sentence, the tense shifts are confusing.

> When she finished her meal, she walks to the door, opens her umbrella, and will leave.

Correcting Unnecessary Shifts in Tense

If you are caught up in the ideas you are trying to convey, you may switch from present to past or vice versa without noticing. These suggestions will help you keep your tenses consistent.

1. When you are writing about literary works, keep your analysis and your account of events in the present tense:

   NOT   The small-town setting of "A Rose for Emily" *explains* the attitude of the townspeople towards Emily because people in small communities traditionally *rejected* and *excluded* those who *were* different from them. Faulkner's description of the setting *emphasizes* Emily's isolation. Most of the action *took* place in and around the house where Emily *lived* all her life. This old, lonely house *was* "all that was left to her" (1608) after her father *died*. Not only *was* Emily alone inside of the house, but the house itself *is* isolated in its environment. At the time of her death, "only Miss Emily's house was left" of what had once been the town's "most select street" (1605).

   BUT   The small-town setting of "A Rose for Emily" *explains* the attitude of the townspeople towards Emily because people in small communities *have* traditionally *rejected* and *excluded* those who *are* different. Faulkner's description of the setting *emphasizes* Emily's isolation. Most of the action *takes* place in and around the house where Emily *has lived* all her life. This old, lonely house is "all that was left to her" (1608) after her father *dies*. Not only *is* Emily alone inside of the house, but the house itself is isolated in its environment. At the time of her death, "only Miss Emily's house was left" of what had once been the town's "most select street" (1605).

2. Use the simple present or past tense in preference to *–ing* verbs.

   NOT   Freud *is discussing* the relationships among the id, ego, and superego.

   BUT   Freud *discusses* the relationships among the id, ego, and superego.

3. If you sometimes omit verb endings, writing "he learn" instead of "he learns" or "he learned," check each verb.

4. If you know you have a problem with verb tenses, proofread your final draft a paragraph at a time, checking all verbs to make sure that (a) they are in the same tense and (b) changes in tense are justified by the time relationships.

EXERCISE 2

Underline all the verbs in the following paragraph. Then correct unnecessary tense shifts. Do not make any other changes.

I was walking around the pet store, trying to decide what kind of pet I could keep in my new apartment, when I remember Hammy, the curious brown hamster. I saw him in Zellers when I first moved to Canada. For very little money my parents buy Hammy for me, a black hamster for my brother Paul, a whole complex of compartments and tubes of hamster housing, a running wheel, a ten kilogram bag of food, and sawdust to cover the bottom of the cages. When we were setting it all up in my bedroom, my uncle comes in and forbids us to keep our pets upstairs—they would have to live in the basement with the dogs. We live in his house; therefore we have to live by his rules. But later that week I go away to summer camp and forget about poor Hammy. While I learned about canoeing, painting, and weaving, and while I went hiking, exploring, and swimming, Hammy's food bowl was getting emptier and emptier. I come back to find him lying on his side, thin, quiet, and cold.

Subject–Verb Agreement

Verbs must agree with their subjects in number: if the subject of the sentence is singular, the verb must be singular; if the subject is plural, the verb must be plural.

> The engine is hot. (singular subject, singular verb)

> The engines are hot. (plural subject, plural verb)

By the time you reach college or university, you probably won't make subject–verb errors very often. When you do, you may have lost track of the subject, as in the following cases.

1. Prepositional phrase between the subject and the verb. Remember that the noun in the prepositional phrase (of the *children*, between the *hedges*, beneath the *sheets*) is never the subject of the sentence.

   NOT   The reaction to these incidents were quick and angry.

   BUT   The <u>reaction</u> to these incidents <u>was</u> quick and angry.

2. Phrases that imply a plural subject when the actual subject is singular: *as well as, in addition to, along with, including*.

   NOT   The cost, including parts and labour, were far more than the estimate.

   BUT   The <u>cost</u>, including parts and labour, <u>was</u> far more than the estimate.

3. Indefinite pronouns that may seem plural but take a singular verb:

anybody	anyone	anything	each (of)
everybody	everyone	everything	either (of)
nobody	no one	nothing	neither (of)
somebody	someone	something	

   NOT   Each of the passengers have a headphone.

   BUT   <u>Each</u> of the passengers <u>has</u> a headphone.

   NOT   Neither of the soldiers were wounded.

   BUT   <u>Neither</u> [one] of the soldiers <u>was</u> wounded.

4. *There is/are* constructions. In these constructions, the subject comes after the verb. *There* is never the subject of the sentence.

   NOT   There is three important issues to consider.

   BUT   There <u>are</u> three important <u>issues</u> (subject) to consider.

5. Singular subjects joined with *or*.

   NOT   John or Carol are meeting you at the airport.

   BUT   <u>John</u> or <u>Carol</u> <u>is meeting</u> you at the airport.

6. A combination of singular and plural subjects joined with *either ... or, neither ... nor, not only ... but also*. With these constructions, the verb agrees with the subject closer to it.

   NOT   Neither the students nor the teacher were satisfied with the test results.

   BUT   Neither the students nor the <u>teacher</u> <u>was</u> satisfied with the test results.

   Note: In these constructions, it is best to put the plural subject second.

   Neither the teacher nor <u>the students</u> <u>were</u> satisfied with the test results.

EXERCISE 3

Underline the subject of the sentence. Then circle the correct verb form.

1. There (doesn't/don't) seem to be any books or articles on this subject.
2. Banff National Park, with its breathtaking scenery, its nature programs, and its plentiful campsites, (attracts/attract) millions of visitors every year.
3. Neither of the women (was/were) willing to vote for the candidate.
4. Not only the athletes but also the coach (is/are) tired at the end of the game.
5. The demand for luxury products (is/are) decreasing.

Active and Passive Voice

Verbs have two voices: active and passive. In the **active voice**, the subject of the sentence performs the action. In the **passive voice**, the subject is acted upon.

   ACTIVE Jasmine drove the car.

   PASSIVE The car was driven by Jasmine.

Uses of the Passive Voice

Usually the active voice is preferable because it is more direct and concise. Sometimes, however, the passive voice is necessary, as in the following instances.

VERBS

1. When the agent of the action is understood, unimportant, or unknown:

   I was born in Saskatoon.

   The roads were sanded regularly.

2. When you want to focus attention on the procedure and the results rather than on the agent.

   Ten milligrams of sodium chloride were placed in a beaker.

Passive constructions are often used in scientific writing to suggest that the steps and outcome will be the same no matter who performs the experiment. Researchers who place more emphasis on their own role in the experiments use the active voice more often.

Misuses of the Passive Voice

1. Avoid the passive voice when the active voice would be more concise, more direct, or more emphatic.

   NOT   It was reported to the president by the vice-president that an agreement was reached between the workers and the management.

   BUT   The vice-president reported to the president that the workers and the management had reached an agreement.

2. Avoid mixing the active and passive voices in the same sentence.

   NOT   Psychologists have found that more realistic estimates of control over future events are made by mildly depressed people.

   BUT   Psychologists have found that mildly depressed people make more realistic estimates of their control over future events.

EXERCISE 4

Identify the verbs in the following sentences as active or passive. Revise sentences in which the passive voice is inappropriate or ineffective.

1. The desire by Swift in "A Modest Proposal" for better food, clothing, and housing for the Irish is expressed.

2. Their house was bombed during the war.

3. Skilled helicopter pilots lifted terrified flood victims from their rooftops.

4. The autopsy on the famous race horse was performed this morning.

5. The demand for better employment opportunities was forcefully expressed by the Métis in Alberta and Saskatchewan.

EXERCISE 5

Write a paragraph in which all of the verbs are in the active voice. Then rewrite the paragraph so that all of the verbs are in the passive voice. Bring both paragraphs to class for discussion. What are the strengths and weaknesses of each? Does a mixture work best?

REVIEW EXERCISE 1

Correct all problems with subject–verb agreement, tense shifts, troublesome verbs, and inappropriate use of the passive voice in the following paragraphs.

> As the bus passed under the bridge of wrought-iron elephants and giraffes, I am reminded of childhood visits to the zoo. Once a week my friend and I rushed in to see the polar bears balancing on their bright blue world. We never seen them play. In all my life I never seen anything but that balanced pacing, always waiting for winter. Having heard rumours that they did in fact play, my fingers, arms, legs, and eyes were crossed, desperately wishing for them to toss the plastic barrels in a game of catch, or perhaps to dazzle us with an elaborate juggling act. No small sign of contentment was ever displayed. I knew they had more potential than to loll on their fake ice drifts, as their haunches were lapped by the luke-cold water. I knew they were missing home, but want them somehow to find a way to be happy in this strange world of ours.
>
> On the rare occasions when I am visiting the zoo now, a magnetic force still drew me to the polar bear habitat first. I am always struck by the bears' forlorn, slightly crazed eyes. They are trapped; they are separated from home. Professional polar bears now, they pretended to live their lives normally for the watching crowd. Once they would of died to get out of our world and back into theirs, if only they could of dived deep enough into the painted pool-bottom and surface somewhere in the Arctic Ocean. But what happens when the real home is less promising than the imitation home? If they could of got out, the place that use to be their home would no longer be accepting them. They would of been expelled like foreign bodies.

REVIEW EXERCISE 2

Check your own writing for problems with subject–verb agreement, tense shifts, troublesome verbs, and inappropriate use of the passive voice. Bring examples to class for discussion.

VERBS

Solving Pronoun Problems

Pronouns of Address

Using First-Person Pronouns: "I"

When you are writing about personal experiences, you naturally use first-person pronouns (*I, me, mine, we, us, ours*). In most college and university essays, however, you will want your reader to focus on your subject rather than your responses to your subject. To keep the focus on your subject, use first-person pronouns sparingly. When you do want to refer to yourself, follow these guidelines.

1. To express agreement or disagreement with another viewpoint, use a phrase such as "I think" or "I believe." Make such phrases inconspicuous by putting them inside the sentence.

   NOT   I think Jones is right when she calls *The Merchant of Venice* a flawed play.

   BUT   Jones is right, I think, when she calls *The Merchant of Venice* a flawed play.

2. When you use a personal example to support a point, use "I" instead of awkward expressions such as "this writer."

3. Avoid using "I" when you intend your opinions to have a more general application.

   NOT   I had a hard time figuring out what these two lines mean. (implies it's your fault)

   BUT   The meaning of these two lines is hard to grasp. (implies that others would have the same difficulty)

4. Avoid such "I" expressions as "this is only my opinion" and "I hope I will be able to show." These statements sound uncertain and apologetic and weaken your statement.

Using First-Person Pronouns: "We" and "One"

1. Use "we" sparingly to include readers in your discussion. Make "we" references unobtrusive or revise the sentence to omit "we."

   NOT   We have seen that oil is a major factor in the politics of the Middle East.

   BUT   Oil, as we have seen, is a major factor in the politics of the Middle East.

   OR   Oil is thus a major factor in the politics of the Middle East.

2. Use "we" sparingly to refer to people in general. Be careful not to overgeneralize.

   NOT   We all remember our high school principals with affection.

   BUT   Many of us remember our high school principals with affection.

3. "One" is sometimes used in formal speech and writing to mean "people in general, including the writer," as in "One might wish for better weather." Because "one" sounds stilted when used extensively, try to eliminate it, either by using "I" (if that is what you mean) or by using a noun.

   NOT   When one watches television, one is dismayed by the scarcity of good programs.

   BUT   When I watch television, I am dismayed by the scarcity of good programs.

   OR   Many television viewers are dismayed by the scarcity of good programs.

Using Second-Person Pronouns: "You"

Second-person pronouns are appropriate when you want to speak directly to your reader, for example when you give instructions.

You will need to wear gloves when you give your cat a bath.

Avoid using "you" to refer to people in general.

PRONOUNS

> NOT By the end of the play, you can see that Macbeth is desperate.
>
> BUT By the end of the play, Macbeth's desperation is obvious.

Using Third-Person Pronouns: "He," "She," "They"

Most often in college and university essays, you will use third-person pronouns to keep your reader's attention focused on your subject. When you use these pronouns, be careful to avoid sexist language and pronoun agreement errors.

Although *he* and other masculine singular pronouns have traditionally been used to refer to both men and women, as in the example, "The driver is responsible for the safety of all passengers in *his* vehicle," many people feel that this usage contributes to gender stereotyping. To avoid alienating your reader, try to use more inclusive language, but be careful not to introduce errors in pronoun agreement, as in "The driver is responsible for the safety of all passengers in *their* vehicle." Here are some suggestions for avoiding both sexist language and pronoun agreement errors. For more on the latter, see Pronoun Agreement.

1. Reword the sentence to eliminate unnecessary gender pronouns.

   > NOT The average commuter drives his car fifty kilometres a day.
   >
   > BUT The average commuter drives fifty kilometres a day.

2. Make the noun and pronouns plural.

   > NOT The enterprising executive sends his managers to study foreign business practices.
   >
   > BUT Enterprising executives send their managers to study foreign business practices.

3. Alternate references to boys and girls, men and women in examples.

   > NOT Teachers sometimes complain about their students: "He never does his homework," "He constantly disrupts the class," "He never listens."
   >
   > BUT Teachers sometimes complain about their students: "She never does her homework," "He constantly disrupts the class," "She never listens."

EXERCISE I

Revise each of the following sentences to eliminate errors in the use of pronouns of address. Put C beside a correct sentence.

1. In this essay I hope to show that poison imagery pervades *Hamlet*.

2. We all remember junior high school dances with warm nostalgia.

3. To train a dog effectively, you should avoid games that involve pitting the dog's strength and agility against yours.

4. By the end of the novel, you can see that the protagonist is doomed.

5. The average student finds that working ten hours a week is about all he can handle in addition to his school work.

Avoiding Shifts in Pronouns of Address

Once you have decided on first-, second-, or third-person pronouns as your basic mode, be consistent in using them. If you shift pronouns without good reason, you will confuse or jar your reader.

In the example below, the writer begins with a third-person reference ("a person"), shifts to "you" in the second sentence, and ends with the formal "one" in the last sentence.

> In addition to confronting crises, a person with chronic fatigue syndrome also has to come to grips with everyday worries. You worry over whether you can negotiate a curb, tolerate flowers without wheezing, make it to a bathroom quickly enough, eat breakfast without vomiting, keep the level of back pain low enough to get through the workday, and sleep through the night. One needs perseverance to get through each day.

Depending on your audience and purpose, you could correct these unnecessary pronoun shifts by using either second- or third-person pronouns consistently.

> If you have chronic fatigue syndrome, you not only have to confront crises, you also have to come to grips with everyday worries. You worry over whether you can negotiate a curb, tolerate flowers without wheezing, make it to a bathroom quickly enough, eat breakfast without vomiting, keep the level of back pain low enough to get through the workday, and sleep through the night. You need perseverance to get through each day. (second person)

> In addition to confronting crises, people with chronic fatigue syndrome also have to come to grips with everyday worries. They worry over whether they can negotiate a curb, tolerate flowers without wheezing, make it to a bathroom quickly enough, eat breakfast without vomiting, keep the level of back pain low enough to get through the workday, and sleep through the night. They need perseverance to get through each day. (third person)

PRONOUNS

A more common problem is the inappropriate use of first- or second-person pronouns in a piece of writing that is primarily in the third person, as in the following example:

> The student board governing the residence hall recently approved the installation of a security system designed to curb theft and vandalism by outsiders. With this system, you have locked doors, identification cards, security guards, and an obligatory sign-in procedure for visitors. Unfortunately, the system is ineffective because most of the damage is done by students who live in the residence.

You could eliminate the inappropriate shift to "you" in this paragraph by beginning the second sentence with "this system includes."

EXERCISE 2

Revise the following paragraph to eliminate all pronoun shifts.

> Attending university is like spending four years in some maniacal funhouse controlled by an evil sprite. When I bought my ticket, the place seemed innocuous enough, but then the package arrives that will be the student's map through the bizarre maze of course descriptions, scheduling conflicts, and rules of conduct. Without it, you may wander away from the path of degree requirements, forever lost, or students may be found in violation of some obscure infraction and unceremoniously ejected. Then they enter a long hall of mirrors, each distorting the image before them into a vague shadow of the person. The first-year glass deflates your ego. The second-year mirror presents the person realistically. The third projects a cocky image. The final mirror is bizarre, reflecting an image of a person ugly, stupid, and too weak to support herself. You emerge after four years looking a bit like each.

Pronoun Agreement

A singular noun must be matched with a singular pronoun, a plural noun with a plural pronoun. Most pronoun agreement errors occur in these contexts:

1. When the noun refers to a type of person: the patient, the student, the player. You can correct this error by making the subject plural.

   NOT   The first-year student may have problems adjusting to their new freedom.

BUT First-year students may have problems adjusting to their new freedom.

2. When a singular noun is followed by a prepositional phrase ending with a plural noun (*of the workers, of the children*).

NOT One of the children left their lunch on the kitchen table.

BUT One of the children left his lunch on the kitchen table.

OR One of the children left her lunch on the kitchen table.

3. When the writer is trying to avoid gender bias. If you don't want to imply that a singular subject (the single parent, the nurse, the engineer) is always male or female, you may make errors in pronoun agreement.

Every doctor these days complains that paper work encroaches on the time *they* can spend with their patients.

Although this error in pronoun agreement is gradually becoming more acceptable, you may want to avoid it with these strategies.

a. Make the subject plural (single parents, nurses, engineers).

b. Use *him or her, he or she* (never *he/she* or *s/he*) to refer to a singular subject.

Typically, a two-year-old will insist that he or she be the focus of all attention.

This strategy works well in a single sentence but becomes cumbersome in a longer piece of writing.

c. Rewrite the sentence to avoid pronouns.

Typically, a two-year-old insists on being the focus of all attention.

d. Refer to the subject with masculine pronouns in one paragraph and feminine pronouns in the next.

4. When the subject is an indefinite pronoun. In formal writing, use singular pronouns to refer to *each* and to words that end with *–body*, *–one*, and *–thing*: *anybody, everybody, nobody; anyone, everyone, no one; anything, everything, nothing.*

INFORMAL SPOKEN Everyone wanted to have their picture taken.

FORMAL WRITTEN Everyone at the convention wanted his or her vote on this issue recorded.

5. When the subject is a collective noun and the sentence indicates unanimous action. Some of the common collective nouns are *family, school, community, band, group, committee, flock, herd.*

PRONOUNS

The committee circulated the minutes of its [not *their*] last meeting.

The band has made its [not *their*] last public appearance.

EXERCISE 3

Correct all the errors in pronoun agreement in the following sentences.

1. When a firm meets government pollution emission standards, their expenses increase.

2. The steel worker wants to have some control over their working conditions.

3. A cancer patient may be misled by quack cures that seem to promise them miraculous results.

4. The House of Commons said that they will enforce new security measures. Everyone entering the building will be searched to determine whether they are carrying firearms.

5. Because it loses less energy than copper wire, fibres are used to transmit thousands of signals simultaneously in enormous bandwidths.

Pronoun Case

Subject and Object Pronouns

Subject pronouns, as their name implies, are most commonly used in the subject position in the sentence: *He* and *I* went to a movie. Object pronouns are used as the object of a verb or preposition: Gabriella and Simon met *him* and *me* at the concession.

SUBJECT PRONOUNS		OBJECT PRONOUNS	
Singular	*Plural*	*Singular*	*Plural*
I	we	me	us
you	you	you	you
he/she/it	they	him/her/it	them
who	who	whom	whom

If you use a subject pronoun where you should use an object pronoun, or vice versa, you have made an error in pronoun case.

Use subject pronouns

1. In the subject position in the sentence. Be sure to use a subject pronoun when there are two subjects in the sentence.

NOT   My brother and me bought a car together.

BUT   My brother and I bought a car together.

2. When the subject pronoun is followed by an explanatory noun.

   NOT   Us students were enraged by the exam.

   BUT   We students were enraged by the exam.

3. After comparisons using *than* and *as*.

   NOT   The other team is weaker than us.

   BUT   The other team is weaker than we [are].

4. As the subject of a subordinate clause beginning with *that*.

   NOT   Mr. Ramsay said that him and his sister had rented
         the house on the corner.

   BUT   Mr. Ramsay said that he and his sister had rented the
         house on the corner.

Use object pronouns

1. As the object of a verb.

   NOT   The coach told Rajiv and he to come early.

   BUT   The coach told Rajiv and him to come early.

2. After a preposition.

   NOT   The manager left a message for my roommate and I.

   BUT   The manager left a message for my roommate and me.

Notes: (1) *Me* is not an informal form of *I. Me* is a perfectly acceptable object pronoun. (2) Don't substitute *myself* for *me* when you need an object pronoun.

   NOT   Please contact either the supervisor or myself if you
         have problems.

   BUT   Please contact either the supervisor or me if you have
         problems.

Who and *whom*

1. *Who* is a subject pronoun. Use *who* to refer to a subject noun.

   Dr. Wong is the distinguished biologist. She will give the
   opening address.

   Dr. Wong is the distinguished biologist who will give the
   opening address.

2. *Whom* is an object pronoun. Use *whom* after prepositions and
   to refer to an object noun.

   Claudius is a smooth politician. Hamlet distrusts him.

   Claudius is a smooth politician whom Hamlet distrusts.

EXERCISE 4

Revise the following sentences to correct all errors in pronoun case. Put C beside a correct sentence.

1. For now, let's keep this plan a secret between you and I.
2. Caterina said that her and Bill might get married this summer.
3. Give the money to whoever you like.
4. Us residents strongly oppose the increase in property taxes.
5. Luis has consistently put more effort into this project than she.
6. Direct all complaints to the caretaker or myself.

Possessive Pronouns

When you want to show ownership, use these possessive pronouns: *my/mine, his, her/hers, their/theirs, your/yours, whose*. Remember that possessive pronouns do not take apostrophes.

1. Don't confuse the possessive pronoun *its* with the contraction *it's* (it is).

   POSSESSIVE The board has made its ruling.

   CONTRACTION It's obvious that no one was listening.

2. Don't confuse the possessive pronoun *whose* with the contraction *who's* (who is).

   POSSESSIVE We must decide whose responsibility this is.

   CONTRACTION Who's responsible for this?

3. Don't confuse the possessive pronoun *their* with the dummy subject *there*.

   POSSESSIVE The Inuit in the region are close to settling their land claim.

   DUMMY SUBJECT There are still a few issues to be resolved.

4. Don't confuse the possessive pronoun *your* with the contraction *you're*.

   POSSESSIVE Don't forget to put your signature on the expense claim.

   CONTRACTION If you don't hurry, you're going to be late.

EXERCISE 5

Revise the following sentences to eliminate all errors in the use of possessive pronouns.

1. The company management has stated it's final position on the union's proposal.
2. If your satisfied with this offer, then we will accept it.

3. We still don't know whose going to teach this class.

4. Luigi and Caterina devoted all of there attention to running the pet store.

5. That beautiful cottage on the shore of the lake is their's.

Pronoun Reference

Errors in pronoun reference occur whenever a pronoun does not clearly refer to a specific noun. Here are some ways to correct ambiguous pronouns.

1. Keep the pronoun close to the noun to which it refers.

   NOT   Luigi told George that he was a terrible baseball player. He was furious.

   BUT   George was furious because Luigi called him a terrible baseball player.

   OR   Because Luigi was furious, he called George a terrible baseball player.

2. Use pronouns to refer only to nouns or pronouns, not to possessive adjectives such as *his*, *her*, *Shakespeare's*.

   James snapped the guitar's neck that belonged to his mother.

   In this sentence, *that* refers to the guitar's neck, an error suggesting that only the guitar's neck belonged to James's mother. You could make clear that the whole guitar belonged to James's mother like this:

   James snapped the neck of his mother's guitar.

3. Make sure *that*, *this*, and *which* refer to a specific noun or pronoun, not to the idea in the preceding sentence or clause. Clarify vague pronoun references by rewriting the sentence or supplying the missing noun or pronoun.

   NOT   He did not know whether she would leave or wait for him. This made him anxious.

   BUT   He did not know whether she would leave or wait for him. This uncertainty made him anxious.

   OR   He was anxious because he did not know whether she would leave or wait for him.

4. Do not use *they* to refer to people in general or to the author of a text.

   NOT   They said hurricanes are affected by the rain cycles in Africa.

   BUT   Meteorologists say hurricanes are affected by the rain cycles in Africa.

PRONOUNS

NOT   They say in Shaw's play *Major Barbara* that the only crime is poverty.

BUT   In Shaw's play *Major Barbara,* Undershaft says that the only crime is poverty.

5. Do not use *it* or *they* to refer to an implied subject. Supply the missing noun or rewrite the sentence.

NOT   I spent two weeks studying for the exam, but it didn't improve my grade.

BUT   I spent two weeks studying for the exam, but this effort did not improve my grade.

OR   Two weeks of studying for the exam did not improve my grade.

NOT   I wrote to Canada Customs and Revenue Agency about my income tax assessment, but they have not yet replied.

BUT   I wrote to Canada Customs and Revenue Agency about my income tax assessment, but the taxation officials have not yet replied.

OR   I have not yet received a reply to my letter to Canada Customs and Revenue Agency about my income tax assessment.

EXERCISE 6

Revise the following sentences to eliminate ambiguous pronoun references.

1. An important part of being a successful goalie is building up a determination to defend the net. It must occupy his or her complete attention.

2. Many people who renovate to make their houses more energy efficient are unaware that it will increase their property value and are surprised when they assess their property for increased taxes.

3. Gradually the public began to accept the theory of evolution, which forced the clergy into less vocal opposition.

4. She left flowers in the teacher's office who had been such a help to her.

5. The two children hid their margarine sandwiches from their classmates because they were ashamed to let them see how poor they were.

REVIEW EXERCISE I

Revise this paragraph to eliminate errors in pronoun agreement and ambiguous pronoun references.

PRONOUNS

There are serious problems with the way the province administers health care to their citizens. Both consumers and providers are frustrated with the way it is run. They agree that waiting lists are too long and that life-saving treatment is being rationed based on a person's medical history and their future usefulness to society. Doctors and other health care professionals have fled to the U.S., which is more lucrative and less stressful. A patient with enough money may also seek treatment for their medical problems in the U.S. The provincial government has imposed stringent cost-cutting measures for several years, and now they promise it will improve again. Given these problems, it is easy to see why they are proposing throwing out the old system and implementing a new one, which is what some people in the medical, political, and general communities want.

REVIEW EXERCISE 2

Check your own writing for problems with pronoun agreement, pronoun case, and pronoun reference. Bring examples to class for discussion.

Solving Punctuation Problems

Apostrophe

The **apostrophe** is used to indicate missing letters in *contractions* and to show *possession*.

Recognizing Plurals, Contractions, and Possessives

Plurals, contractions, and possessives are often confused because they sound the same.

> PLURAL Three bikes have been stolen in the last week.
>
> CONTRACTION This bike's for sale. (*bike's* = bike is)
>
> POSSESSIVE The bike's front wheel is warped. (front wheel belonging to the bike)

In order to use apostrophes correctly, you need to be able to distinguish among these three forms. The following points will help you.

1. Only nouns and indefinite pronouns (such as *everybody, someone, anything*) take an apostrophe to show possession.

2. Be careful, especially with proper nouns, not to add an apostrophe when you want to indicate a plural.

> PLURAL All the Lees [plural of *Lee*] want to invite you to their reunion.
>
> POSSESSIVE The Lees' garage burned down last year. (The apostrophe shows that the garage belongs to the Lees.)

3. Do not use an apostrophe with possessive pronouns (*yours*, *hers*, *its*, *ours*, *theirs*).

NOT   This problem is your's to solve.

BUT   This problem is yours to solve.

NOT   The dog pressed it's nose against the window.

BUT   The dog pressed its nose against the window.

Using Apostrophes to Show Possession

How to make indefinite pronouns and singular nouns possessive

1. To make an indefinite pronoun possessive, add *'s*.

   Everybody's salary will be affected by the budget cutbacks.

2. To make a singular noun that does not end with *s* possessive, add *'s*.

   This little boy's epilepsy is getting worse.

3. To make a singular noun that ends with *s* or *ss* possessive, add *'s* if the word is one syllable. Add only an apostrophe if the word is more than one syllable.

   Charles's car is in the shop again.

   The albatross' death haunted the Ancient Mariner.

How to make plural nouns possessive

1. If the plural noun ends in *s*, add only an apostrophe.

   Both boys' bathing suits were lost.

   All the students' marks were excellent.

2. If the plural noun does not end in *s*, add *'s*.

   All children's toys, men's coats, and women's shoes are on sale.

Joint possession and separate possession

1. Joint possession: To indicate that two or more people possess something together, add *'s* to the last name.

   Tom and Brenda's house is for sale.

2. Separate possession: To indicate that two or more people possess things separately, add *'s* to each name.

   Tom's and Brenda's cars are for sale.

EXERCISE I

Add an apostrophe or 's where necessary in the following sentences.

1. Sonya and Edwards bicycles were found as a result of their parents determined efforts.
2. Our boss main interest is in creating stronger international business connections.
3. The childrens destructive behaviour alarmed the staff.
4. This problem is nobodys fault but yours.
5. The Huis trailer was broken into.

Other Uses of the Apostrophe

1. Expressions of time can be used as possessives. Be sure that the placement of the apostrophe indicates whether the noun naming the time period is singular or plural.

   I'll contact you in a month's time. (one month)

   We wasted two weeks' work.

2. To make letters plural, italicize the letter and add *'s.*

   Have you dotted your *i*'s and crossed your *t*'s?

3. To put a word referred to as a word in the plural, italicize the word and add 's.

   There are too many *however*'s in this sentence.

4. To make an abbreviation plural, you can add either *s* or *'s.*

   All the SPCAs in this province are running out of money.

5. To make a date plural, add *s* or *'s.*

   Throughout most of the 1980s Canada faced a constitutional crisis.

Note that forming plurals without the apostrophe is becoming the preferred usage for both abbreviations and dates.

EXERCISE 2

Correct missing or misused apostrophes as necessary in the following sentences.

1. Throughout most of the 1930s prairie farmers watched in dismay as their crops shrivelled in the sun.
2. Katia took a years leave of absence to do research in Womens Studies.
3. Nadeem would be a more effective public speaker if he used fewer *know-what-I-means* in his opening comments.

4. Drug testing at international sports competitions has made many athletes uneasy about nutritional supplements actual contents.

5. Its no surprise the SPCAs kennels are crowded.

EXERCISE 3

Make a list of words with missing or misused apostrophes in signs, advertisements, and similar material. Bring your list to class for discussion.

Comma

Main Clauses

Use a **comma** to separate main clauses joined by a coordinate conjunction (*and, but, or, nor, for, yet, so*).

> Inflation is under control, but unemployment is still a problem.

> No one has succeeded in proving the existence of UFOs, yet many have tried.

✱ Subordinate Clauses

Use a comma to set off a subordinate clause at the beginning of a sentence.

After
when ,
meanwhile

> When economic conditions are poor, the incidence of family violence increases.

> Because the highways were icy, we postponed our trip.

Introductory Phrases

Use a comma to set off long (more than five words) or potentially confusing phrases at the beginning of a sentence.

> In his search for the meaning of life, he examined many religions. (long phrase)

> In winter, darkness comes early. (could be misread)

Items in a Series

Use a comma to separate more than two items joined by *and* or *or*. Include a comma before the conjunction so that the last two items are not read as a unit.

> We watched the children slide, swing, and climb.

COMMA

The horses galloped over the field, across the stream, and down the road.

He ordered toast, eggs, coffee, and milk for breakfast.
(comma indicates that four items were ordered)

Non-Restrictive Modifiers

Use a pair of commas to enclose non-restrictive modifiers (words, phrases, and clauses that add information but are not necessary to identify the noun they describe).

    a. Adjectives and participial phrases following nouns.

        The play, witty and well acted, delighted the audience.

        The actors, after removing their greasepaint, celebrated their success.

    b. Appositives (nouns or noun phrases that rename the preceding noun).

        The Beatles, the most popular rock group of the sixties, sold millions of records.

Note: Do *not* set off an appositive that is necessary to identify the noun it describes (restrictive).

        The film *The Compleat Beatles* is a history of the group's rise and fall. (restrictive)

    c. Non-restrictive clauses beginning with *which, who, whom,* or *whose*.

        The development of fibre optics, which revolutionized communications, also had a great impact on medicine.

        Orthopaedic surgeons, who often treat athletic injuries, use fibre optic instruments to assess knee damage.

Note: Do *not* set off restrictive clauses. Clauses beginning with *that* are almost always restrictive.

        Tom Smith, whose knees were badly injured in a skiing accident, is slowly recovering. (non-restrictive clause)

        Athletes who injure their knees often recover slowly. (restrictive clause)

        The hand that rocks the cradle rules the world. (restrictive clause)

Parenthetical Expressions

Use commas to set off transitional words and phrases and other expressions that break the flow of the sentence.

Developing countries, in contrast, may be resource-rich but capital-poor.

This situation, I believe, leads to economic instability.

Well, I'd better be going.

There were, amazingly enough, thirty thousand people at the demonstration.

Dates and Place Names

Use a comma with dates and place names when more than one item of information is given.

The centre of the Canadian automobile industry is Windsor, Ontario.

Canada officially entered the Second World War on September 10, 1939.

Quotations

Use a comma to set off brief quotations from introductory material.

One minister said, "This policy should never have been adopted."

"This policy," said one minister, "should never have been adopted."

Never separate subject from verb.

EXERCISE 4

Use a pair of commas to set off non-restrictive modifiers in the following sentences. Do not enclose restrictive modifiers with commas.

1. Children who are emotionally neglected by their parents will seek attention from other adults.

2. My car, which had not been plugged in for three days in -30°C weather, miraculously started.

3. David Adams Richards, a respected Maritime writer will read tonight from his novel *Mercy Among the Children*.

4. The actress starring in tonight's miniseries made her debut in the soaps.

5. The book that I lent you is now three weeks overdue at the library.

6. Both of the companies now facing bankruptcy once employed more than a thousand workers.

7. *Hearts of Darkness*, a film about the making of *Apocalypse Now*, provides fascinating insights into the difficulties faced by a film director.

8. An employee who suggests possible improvements in working conditions should be rewarded.

9. The Canadian champions, elated after winning the gold medal for ice-dancing were surrounded by adoring fans.

10. The Acadians, descendants of early French settlers in the Maritimes, were pawns in the struggle between the French and the British for control of North America.

EXERCISE 5

Add commas, where appropriate, to the following sentences.

1. Because, he could find no way to avoid the task, he got to work.

2. In the morning, light shone through the cracks in the roof.

3. Marvin on the other hand, is steady, hard-working, and rather unimaginative.

4. Indeed, some of these arguments deserve closer attention.

5. The negotiators were tired and hungry, so they made little progress.

6. According to William Blake, "Imagination has nothing to do with Memory."

7. In 1842, the Webster–Ashburton Treaty between Canada and Great Britain defined the Canadian frontier.

8. The United States and Britain declared war on Japan on December 8, 1941, the day after the bombing of Pearl Harbor, Hawaii.

9. Returning home after a strenuous workout, Julia showered, reached for a cold drink, and collapsed on the sofa.

10. First Night festivities offer participants musical performances, street theatre, plays, readings, and a spectacular finale complete with fireworks.

EXERCISE 6

If you have problems with commas, decide which three uses of the comma you most need to focus on to increase the clarity and effectiveness of your writing. Make a list with examples of each of the three types of comma problems and bring your list to class for discussion.

Semicolon

The **semicolon** is used in two ways: to join main clauses and to join a series of phrases or clauses that is too complicated for commas alone to clarify.

When to Use a Semicolon

1. Use a semicolon to join main clauses.

   a. When the ideas are closely related and there is no coordinate conjunction (*and, but, or, nor, for, so, yet*) to join the clauses.

   Mary was an idealist; Martha was a pragmatist.

b. With a coordinate conjunction when the clauses are long or contain commas.

> The hard-boiled detective, as we have seen in the works of Dashiell Hammett, Raymond Chandler, and Ross MacDonald, is a distinctively American creation; but the amateur sleuth, popularized by British writers such as Dorothy Sayers, Agatha Christie, and Michael Innis, also appears in American fiction.

c. When the second clause begins with a conjunctive adverb (*accordingly, consequently, therefore, thus, hence, furthermore, moreover, besides, likewise, nevertheless, however, otherwise, still*). Put a comma after a conjunctive adverb of more than one syllable. (See Note below.)

> Byron's poetry soon eclipsed Scott's; therefore, Scott turned to writing novels.

> Few members of the legislature thought an election was necessary; nevertheless, the premier called one.

2. Use a semicolon to separate items within a series that contains commas.

> The defence attorney called three witnesses: her client's brother, who testified that his sister was with him the night of the crime; the brother's caretaker, who testified that he saw the defendant arrive at 10:15 p.m.; and the brother's neighbour, who glimpsed the sister as she left at 11:30 p.m.

When Not to Use a Semicolon

1. Do not use a semicolon to join a main clause and a subordinate clause.

NOT The restaurant switched to Fair Trade coffee; because the manager knew that customers would support the change.

BUT The restaurant switched to Fair Trade coffee because the manager knew that customers would support the change.

OR The restaurant switched to Fair Trade coffee; the manager knew that customers would support the change.

Note: Some writers misuse semicolons because they confuse subordinate conjunctions and conjunctive adverbs. Here is an easy way to remember the difference: conjunctive adverbs can be moved to different positions in a clause, whereas subordinate conjunctions cannot.

> The premier called an election; however [conjunctive adverb], few members of the party thought an election was necessary.

> The premier called an election; few members of the party thought an election was necessary, however.

> The premier called an election even though [subordinate conjunction] few members of the party thought an election was necessary.

2. Do not overuse semicolons. Too many semicolons will make your writing seem stuffy, as in the following passage.

NOT   A good opera for beginners is *Carmen*. It is always a hit; it is packed full of recognizable tunes. The lead mezzo soprano has to ooze with sex and burn with a fiery bitchiness; she has to be the consummate gypsy. In this story love is not the conqueror or sustainer; it is a colourful bird, rebellious and inconsistent. No one knows where it will perch; worse, no one knows when it will fly away. The key to *Carmen* is not heart-breaking emotion; it is passionate drama. If done well *Carmen* becomes absolutely thrilling; if done poorly the music is still great.

Notice how the passage is improved when some ideas are joined through subordination rather than coordination.

BUT   A good opera for beginners is *Carmen*. Packed full of recognizable tunes, it is always a hit. The lead mezzo soprano has to be the consummate gypsy, oozing with sex and burning with a fiery bitchiness. In this story love is not the conqueror or sustainer but a colourful bird, rebellious and inconsistent. No one knows where it will perch; worse, no one knows when it will fly away. Passionate drama, not heartbreaking emotion, is the key to *Carmen*. Done well, the opera is absolutely thrilling; done poorly, the music is still great.

EXERCISE 7

Homework for Nov 2

Add semicolons where appropriate to the following sentences.

1. Early in the play, Macbeth seems to recognize the futility of his ambition to remain king; nevertheless he pursues his bloody ambitions.

2. Lady Macbeth has been described as fiendish; however, some critics argue that she is the ideal wife.

3. Macbeth believes the witches' prophecy that he will be killed by no man born of a woman he therefore feels invincible.

4. After the murder, Lady Macbeth, partly because she lacks Macbeth's vivid imagination, focuses on the immediate need to hide incriminating evidence but this strategy, which ignores Macbeth's susceptibility to supernatural fears, sets in motion the chain of events that dooms them both.

5. When Macbeth is terrified by his imagination, he arouses sympathy when he acts, he arouses contempt and hatred.

EXERCISE 8

What does Pico Iyer ("In Praise of the Humble Comma," Part 2, Readings) have to say about semicolons? Which uses of the semicolon does he illustrate in his essay?

Colon

Usually the **colon** indicates that what follows is an expansion of what has already been said. Use a colon for the following purposes:

1. To introduce a list that follows a complete clause. The items following the colon should be grammatically parallel.

   Car manufacturers have introduced several improvements: better restraint systems, better pollution control devices, and better rust-proofing.

Note: Do not use a colon when the list begins with *such as* or *for example*.

   Car manufacturers have introduced several improvements, such as better restraint systems, better pollution control devices, and better rust-proofing.

2. To introduce a phrase or clause that explains the preceding statement.

   He wanted only one thing out of life: to make money. (explanatory phrase)

   My new car is a real lemon: it has broken down for the third time this month. (explanatory clause)

3. To introduce a quotation. Both the quotation and the sentence that introduces it must be grammatically complete.

   Goldberg dismissed the arguments against changes in the Fisheries Act: "Contrary to the opinions expressed by packers and the fisheries unions, the proposed changes are not designed to increase federal control over the fishing industry."

Note: Do not use a colon when the sentence introducing the quotation ends with *that*.

> In her essay "The Poorhouse" (Readings), Judy Rebick cites reports indicating that "police harassment of poor people has ... dramatically increased as welfare rates have declined" (304–305).

EXERCISE 9

Add colons, where appropriate, in the following sentences. Put C beside any sentence that is correctly punctuated.

1. The setting was perfect for a horror movie: a foggy night, an isolated house, shrieks and groans coming from unseen sources.

2. When Marc finished high school, he wanted only one thing: never to set foot in a classroom again.

C 3. When you are preparing for a long winter drive, be sure to bring some emergency equipment such as a sleeping bag, a candle, and several chocolate bars.

C 4. Macbeth clings to the witches' prophecies, saying that "I will not be afraid of death and bane, / Till Birnam forest come to Dunsinane."

5. Alexander and Shaler argue that there is a direct relationship between addiction and dislocation: "Most people who cannot achieve a reasonable degree of psychosocial integration find that they must develop 'substitute' lifestyles in order to endure" ("Addiction in Free Markets," Readings).

EXERCISE 10

Write a paragraph in which you use colons in each of the three ways described above. Then replace the colons with dashes or other types of punctuation. Discuss with your classmates how these changes affect the tone of the paragraph.

Dash

A **dash** (or pair of dashes) indicates an interruption in a train of thought or in the structure of the sentence. It creates an air of informality and so should be used sparingly in formal writing. Use the dash for the following purposes:

1. To set off abrupt shifts in thought.

   > My Aunt Sadie—you remember her, don't you?—lived to be a hundred.

2. To set off a list when it comes in the middle of a sentence.

   > She had established her goals in life—to travel, to have an interesting career, to develop close relationships—before she was sixteen.

Note: When the list comes at the end of the sentence, use a colon unless you want to indicate special emphasis.

> COLON Before she was sixteen, she had established her goals in life: to travel, to have an interesting career, to develop close relationships.

> DASH At fourteen, Beth had only one ambition—to win a place on the Junior Olympic Wrestling Team.

EXERCISE 11

Write a paragraph using dashes for the purposes described. Then replace the dashes with colons or other punctuation. Discuss with your classmates how the punctuation affects the tone.

Parentheses

Use **parentheses** in these ways:

1. To enclose bibliographical information in the body of your essay.

   Alice Harwood's *The End of the Game* (Toronto: Dominion Press, 1984) is a study of the decline of amateur sports.

2. To enclose explanatory material, such as brief definitions and historical information.

   British drivers open the bonnet (hood), put luggage in the boot (trunk), and fill their tank with petrol (gas).

   Mozart (1756–1791) was an accomplished musician by the time he was six.

3. To indicate that explanatory material is relatively unimportant.

   The mayor (who was re-elected by a slim majority) promised to improve transportation in the city.

If you want to emphasize explanatory material, set it off with dashes. If you don't want either to emphasize or to minimize its importance, set if off with commas.

Note: Don't use parentheses to enclose essential information.

> NOT At a council meeting this morning, the mayor (who holds stock in several land development companies) disqualified herself from voting on the proposal to annex areas north and west of the city.

> BUT At a council meeting this morning, the mayor—who holds stock in several land development companies— disqualified herself from voting on the proposal to annex areas north and west of the city.

Punctuating Material in Parentheses

1. If a complete sentence in parentheses is contained within another sentence, do not begin the parenthetical sentence with a capital letter or end it with a period.

   When spring finally arrived (winter had seemed endless), children suddenly appeared on the street.

2. If the phrase, clause, or sentence within parentheses requires a question mark or an exclamation mark, put the appropriate punctuation mark inside the closing parenthesis.

   Although credit cards sometimes lead people disastrously into debt (and who hasn't been appalled by a monthly statement?), they are essential for many business transactions.

REVIEW EXERCISE I

Insert commas, semicolons, colons, dashes, and parentheses where appropriate in the following sentences.

1. Let's divide our supplies into two categories inexpensive items in constant use expensive items used only occasionally.

2. *Spider-Man* which attracted large audiences in 2002 spawned plenty of spin-off accessories.

3. There are two types of crimes in which the perpetrator deliberately chooses to break the law crimes of desperation and crimes of defiance.

4. A woman with a limited income perhaps a single parent might steal food for example to feed her family.

5. Dickens vividly portrays the monotonous mechanical lives of factory workers in his description of Coketown "It contained several large streets all very like one another ..." p. 213.

 6. The goal of modern correctional institutions should not be punishment or revenge it should be the rehabilitation of the whole person.

7. *The Stone Angel* (Macmillan) 1964, established Margaret Laurence as an important Canadian novelist.

8. The Pope needed only to show Galileo, the instruments of torture, Galileo's medical knowledge of what those instruments would do accomplished the rest.

9. When I returned home, most unexpectedly I might add, I was astounded at the changes that had occurred during my absence.

10. Ancient Chinese and Hindu societies had much in common: both were unified through stable religious and cultural patterns, both had little curiosity about foreign lands, both were exploited by the West.

REVIEW EXERCISE 2

Find sentences in your own writing where you could use semicolons, colons, dashes, and parentheses more effectively. Bring these examples to class for discussion.

Quotation Marks

This section covers the appropriate use of quotation marks as punctuation. For information on the format of quotations, the use of ellipses, and the integration of quotations into your writing, see Quotations.

Use **quotation marks** to indicate direct speech, quotations from other writers, and titles of short works.

1. Put quotation marks around direct speech.

   DIRECT SPEECH Marie said, "I should get more exercise."

   INDIRECT SPEECH Marie said that she should get more
   exercise.

2. Put quotation marks around three or more consecutive words from any printed material.

   In her comments on Faulkner's "A Rose for Emily," Judith
   Fetterley says that "the grotesque aspects of the story are a
   result of its violation of the expectations generated by the
   conventions of sexual politics" (229).

3. Use single quotation marks for quotations within quotations.

   In her interpretation of *Macbeth*, Carlyle argues that "the audience's sense of the futility of Macbeth's actions is confirmed in the 'She should have died hereafter' speech."

4. Use quotation marks to enclose titles of brief works (essays, magazine and newspaper articles, poems, short stories, songs, single
   episodes of a television series) that are part of larger works.

   In his article "The Influence of Popular Culture on the
   Poetry of John Doak," Martin Sommers points out that
   Doak's poem "Coming on Down" contains echoes of the
   Rolling Stones' song "Jumping Jack Flash."

5. You can put quotation marks around words referred to as
   words, but it's often clearer to italicize them. (See below,
   Italics.)

   You use "because" three times in this sentence.

   Do not put quotation marks around slightly informal expressions.

   NOT   Michaela needs to learn to "stand up" for herself.

ITALICS

Using Other Punctuation with Quotation Marks

1. Place commas and periods inside quotation marks.

   "Many plant species," he said, "are in danger of extinction."

2. Place colons and semicolons outside quoted material.

   Fetterley argues that Emily's "status as a lady is a cage from which she cannot escape" (231); to the ever-curious towns-people, she is Miss Emily and "she is never referred to and never thought of as otherwise."

3. a. Place other punctuation marks (question marks, exclamation marks, dashes) inside the quotation marks if they punctuate only the quoted words.

      The first lines of Keats's poem "La Belle Dame sans Merci" are "O, what can ail thee, knight-at-arms, / Alone and palely loitering?"

   b. Place these punctuation marks outside the quotation marks if they punctuate the sentence containing the quotation.

      Do you agree with Keats's statement that "Beauty is truth, truth beauty"?

EXERCISE 12

Write a dialogue in which you incorporate as many different ways of using quotation marks as possible. Remember to use single quotation marks for quotations inside quotations.

Italics

Slanted writing indicates italics in typeset and word-processed material. In typed and handwritten work, indicate by underlining. Use **italics** in the following ways.

1. For the titles of works published separately (books, plays, magazines, newspapers, record albums, films, television series). Titles of works that have been published separately are italicized even when these works are included in anthologies.

   The book *False Economies* consists of a series of articles first published in *The Journal of Economic Analysis*.

   The students referred to *Hamlet* in their copies of *The Norton Introduction to Literature*.

2. For the names of ships and airplanes, works of art, and long musical compositions.

   The choir practiced three months for the performance of Handel's *Messiah*.

3. For words and letters referred to as words or letters.

The word *truly* does not contain an *e*.

4. For foreign words and phrases that have not been incorporated into English.

The setting epitomized what the Germans would call *Gemütlichkeit*.

5. For emphasis.

Library materials *must* be returned by the end of term.

Be careful not to overuse italics for emphasis, especially in formal academic writing.

EXERCISE 13

Insert quotation marks or underline to indicate italics as necessary in the following sentences. Together these sentences form a paragraph on setting in James Joyce's collection of short stories, *Dubliners*.

1. In Dubliners Joyce describes the city of Dublin as if to describe the characters living in it.

2. In A Painful Case, for example, Joyce describes the aloof Mr. Duffy as having a face that was of the brown tint of Dublin streets (119).

3. The story Araby also contains striking images that link the city with its inhabitants.

4. The houses are described as detached … on blind streets; they gaze at one another with brown imperturbable faces (39).

5. Through images such as these, characters in Dubliners are identified with the setting.

REVIEW EXERCISE 3

Insert commas, parentheses, dashes, quotation marks, and italics as necessary in the paragraph below. Do not make any other changes. The paragraph is from an essay on *Dubliners*, a collection of short stories by James Joyce.

underline Book title

The final story of Dubliners returns to the subject of the first story mortality. Joyce divides The Dead into two separate scenes the Christmas gathering of family and friends and the hotel room where the main character Gabriel and his wife Gretta spend the night. Gabriel who is named for the archangel of good news Luke 1:26 believes he is the master of his surroundings. During the Christmas gathering he certainly seems to be in control. He is responsible for drunk Freddy he carves the turkey and he gives the speech. In the second scene Gabriel comes to the realization that he is not in control. When he and Gretta arrive at their hotel room Gabriel is consumed by passion and wants to dominate his wife. As he says he wants to be "master of her strange mood" (p. 235) Gretta however, is overwhelmed by long-buried grief for the young man who died for love of her. When Gretta tells her husband about Michael Furey, Gabriel is forced to realize that it is death that controls people's lives. Many characters in Dubliners long to escape from their city and their lives most obviously Eveline in the story of that name and Chandler in A Little Cloud. Only Gabriel realizes there is no escape except through death.

REVIEW EXERCISE 4

Bring to class an advertisement that uses a variety of punctuation. What is the effect of the punctuation? What tone does it create?

Hyphen

Use a **hyphen** in these ways:

1. With some compound words: *brother-in-law*, *major-general*, *buy-in*.

Note: Other compound words are written as a single word (*textbook*, *stepmother*, *railway*) or as two words (*income tax*, *down payment*, *gallows humour*). There is no set pattern for forming compound words, so check your dictionary.

2. With two-word numbers (from twenty-one to ninety-nine) and with fractions used as adjectives. Do *not* hyphenate when the fraction functions as a noun.

   The gas tank was one-third full. (*one-third* as adjective)

   One third of the students withdrew from the course. (*one third* as noun)

3. To join two words that function as a single adjective and convey a single idea. If this construction comes after the noun, do *not* hyphenate unless the construction is conventionally spelled with a hyphen. Do *not* hyphenate if the construction contains an *ly* adjective.

   a well-organized essay

   The essay is well organized.

   a poorly organized essay

4. With the prefixes *self* (*self-sufficient*), *ex* (*ex-wife*); with prefixes that come before proper nouns (*anti-Catholic*); with the suffix *elect* (*president-elect*).

5. To prevent confusion: re-mark (mark again), ten-year-old children/ten year-old children.

6. To show that two or more prefixes share a common root.

   The results of both the pre- and the post-test were excellent.

How to Hyphenate Words at the End of a Line

Avoid dividing a word at the end of a line whenever possible.

Do not hyphenate

1. One-syllable words. (*Dragged*, for example, should not be hyphenated.)

2. Words of six or fewer letters even if they contain two or more syllables. (Do not hyphenate *diet*, *beauty*, *elegy*)

3. Words in more than two consecutive lines in a paragraph, the last word in a paragraph, or the last word on a page.

To hyphenate a word

If you occasionally need to hyphenate a word, follow these rules:

1. Try to divide it into two approximately equal parts that convey the sense of the whole word.

2. Divide the word between syllables, making sure that the first part of the word contains at least three letters: *com-fort*, *impor-tance*.

3. If a double consonant appears at the end of a word because you have added a suffix (*running*, *committed*), divide the word between the double consonants (*run-ning*, *commit-ted*). If the double consonant is part of the root word, divide between the root word and the suffix (*drill-ing*).

4. Include a one-letter syllable with the first part of the word (*tabu-late* not *tab-ulate*).

EXERCISE 14

Hyphenate each of the following words as if it appeared at the end of a line. Put C beside a word that should not be hyphenated.

1. conferred
2. usable
3. heroes
4. recommend
5. stipulate
6. butterfly
7. begged
8. spilling
9. definitely
10. language

Numbers, Capitalization, and Abbreviations

Numbers

Use numerals (1, 2, 3,...):

1. To express numbers in scientific and technical writing.
2. For a series of numbers.
3. For numbers that cannot be expressed in two words.
4. For dates.
5. For page, verse, act, scene, and line numbers.

Use words:

1. For numbers that can be expressed in one or two words.
2. When you begin a sentence with a number.

Capitalization

All proper nouns are capitalized. A proper noun names a specific person, place, or thing.

> We'll meet this afternoon for a picnic in the **park**. (common noun)

> We'll meet this afternoon for a picnic in **Central Park**. (proper noun)

Use capitalization in the following ways.

1. Capitalize titles of family members when the title substitutes for a name.

   I asked Mother for a ride downtown.

   Do *not* capitalize titles of family members if they are preceded by a possessive pronoun: my father, your aunt, their brother.

2. Capitalize the names of languages, nationalities, and religions: English, Canadian, Buddhism.

3. Do *not* capitalize the name of an academic discipline unless it's the name of a language: chemistry, psychology, French.

4. Capitalize the names of specific courses: Chemistry 101, Psychology 260.

5. Capitalize the names of faculties: the Arts Faculty, the Faculty of Education.

6. Capitalize the words *college* and *university* if they are part of the name of an institution (Camrose Lutheran College) or used as a short form of the name: "Today the College announced a $500 000 budget deficit."

7. Capitalize the days of the week and the months, but not the seasons: Tuesday, January, spring.

8. Capitalize Native and First Nations when referring to Aboriginal peoples. Do not capitalize colour words used to refer to ethnic groups: black, white.

9. Do *not* capitalize the names of directions unless they are used as place names.

   Turn north after you cross the bridge.
   The old priest had lived in the North for twenty years.

10. Do *not* capitalize to create emphasis.

Abbreviations

1. Use abbreviations sparingly in most essays. If it's desirable to abbreviate a term you repeat frequently, give the term in full the first time; then give the abbreviation.

   Sudden infant death syndrome (SIDS) is not fully understood. It seems, however, that SIDS occurs more frequently in the winter months.

2. Do *not* abbreviate days of the week or months of the year.

ABBREVIATIONS

3. Put B.C. ("before Christ") after the year to refer to dates before the birth of Christ.

Socrates committed suicide in 399 B.C.

Use A.D. ("in the year of our Lord") before the year to refer to dates after the birth of Christ up to A.D. 500.

Venice was founded by refugees from Attila's Huns in A.D. 452.

Some writers prefer to use BCE ("before the common era") and CE ("common era"). Both these abbreviations appear after the year.

4. Do *not* abbreviate *and* with an ampersand (&). Use the ampersand only when you are copying the name of an organization, such as a publisher for a bibliographical entry: McClelland & Stewart.

5. Avoid abbreviations for Latin terms, such as e.g. (*exempli gratia*) or i.e. (*id est*). Instead, write out their English equivalents.

NOT   From then on he was considered a coward; e.g., no one forgot that he had saved himself first when the hotel caught fire.

BUT   From then on he was considered a coward; for example, no one forgot that he had saved himself first when the hotel caught fire.

NOT   Susan gradually came to understand the erosion of self-esteem caused by racism: i.e., the assumption that a person's worth could be reliably assessed by the colour of his or her skin.

BUT   Susan gradually came to understand the erosion of self-esteem caused by racism: that is, the assumption that a person's worth could be reliably assessed by the colour of his or her skin.

6. Avoid using *etc.* Use a phrase such as "and so on," "and similar items" at the end of the list, or use "such as" or "for example" at the beginning of the list.

NOT   Unemployment in this region has increased because of plant closures, the decline in tourism, the decreased demand for agricultural produce, etc.

BUT   Unemployment in this region has increased because of factors such as plant closures, the decline in tourism, and the decreased demand for agricultural produce.

EXERCISE

Correct all errors in the use of numbers, capitalization, and abbreviations in the sentences below.

1. On October thirtieth, the V.P. announced that the Northern end of the railway line had finally been completed.

2. My Brother & I like to go camping for 2 weeks every Summer.

3. The native friendship centre in our area hosts an annual barbecue to which everyone in the neighbourhood is invited. 151 people attended last year.

4. On our trip to the middle east last december, we noticed considerable tension between fundamentalist christians and muslims.

5. When Susan and her husband were robbed in an outdoor café in Rome, they lost most of their valuables: their passports, wallets, traveller's cheques, cameras, etc.

Spelling

Here are some tips that will help you to proofread for spelling errors more efficiently.

1. Check the spelling of the subjects you are writing about, including titles, authors' names, place names, technical terms, and so on. If you put your instructor's name on your title page, check the spelling of that too.

2. Use the spelling checker on your word processor. If you are a weak speller and your word processor lacks this feature, consider buying one. You might also consider buying a hand-held spelling checker/thesaurus. Spelling checkers will pick up most typos and commonly misspelled words. They will not, however, pick up homonyms: *to/too, there/their/they're, your/you're, it's/its, compliment/complement*. Nor will they pick up typos that would be legitimate words in a different context, such as insurance "clams" (for "claims").

3. Spelling checkers may show Canadian spellings (*labour/defence/centre*) as errors. If you find this irritating, you can add Canadian spellings to the spelling checker or select Canadian English from the language options of your word-processing software.

4. Be consistent in your use of either Canadian or American spellings. Don't write *theatre* in one sentence and *theater* in the next.

5. Don't rely on spelling checkers to find all your spelling errors. Print out a hard copy and read it carefully, sentence by sentence. Make a list of the words you often misspell and check your work for them. Headliners on the list of commonly misspelled words include the following. It's worthwhile to memorize them:

a lot, acquire, among, argument, conscience, conscious, definitely, dependent, develop, embarrass, environment, even though, existence, interest, occurred, occurrence, prejudiced, privilege, rhyme, rhythm, separate, similar, subtly, tragedy, unnecessary, weird

6. Some instructors regard errors in the use of apostrophes as spelling mistakes, whereas others see them as punctuation errors. Either way, apostrophe errors can significantly undermine the quality and the credibility of your writing. If you are not sure how to use apostrophes, check the section on apostrophes and try to memorize the rules.

7. If you are not sure how to spell a word, don't guess. Consult a dictionary.

EXERCISE

Correct all the spelling errors in the following sentences. Most sentences contain more than one error. Correct any errors in the use of apostrophes.

1. Tanis intrest in school has increased noticably since she seperated from her husband.

2. At the begining of the term, Tanis draged herself to all her class, but her heart was definately not in her studys.

3. Like most people, Tanis was embarassed by her marriage problems and rather lonly as well, but now she is enjoying her independance.

4. She is also acheiving better grades, especially in her childrens' literature and micro computer managment courses.

5. Eventhough Tanis worrys that people might be prejudice against a women who has decided to abandon the priviledges of the affluent middle class, she has decided to devote her summer to an enviromental protection project on Bafin Island.

Quotations

When you are analyzing texts or writing research papers, you will often need to include direct quotations. Used effectively, quotations can provide convincing evidence to support and illustrate your points. Used awkwardly or excessively, quotations can detract from the clear, orderly presentation of your ideas.

When to Quote

1. When the precise wording of a short passage of prose, such as the definition of a key term, is the starting point for your analysis or evaluation of a concept, theory, proposal, or text.

2. When you can use a particularly well-expressed opinion by an authority on your topic to support your position, such as a statement by a respected scientist on the depletion of the ozone layer, or a literary critic's interpretation of an image in a poem.

3. When you need to illustrate a point you are making about a text. Include at least one quotation to support every major interpretative point. If you were analyzing the tone of Andrew Pyper's essay "The Ticking Daddy Clock" (Readings), for example, you would use a quotation like the one below to illustrate your point.

   In discussing men's biological urgings toward parenthood, Pyper initially adopts a comic tone that masks any real feelings: "You're a childless guy in your 30s, minding your own business, when suddenly, at the family reunion or office picnic or some poor sucker's wedding, somebody passes you one of *them*" (301).

When Not to Quote

1. When you can paraphrase someone's words or ideas without loss of meaning or impact.

Note: When you paraphrase, you must still document the source of your information. For more on this, see Chapter 13, Writing Research Papers, and Handbook, Documentation.

2. When you are summarizing factual information.

3. When the quotation merely repeats your point.

4. When you have used the quotation elsewhere in your essay. Find another passage to illustrate your point.

How to Use Quotations Effectively

1. Make all the major points in your own words and use quotations to support them. Don't rely on the quotation to make the point for you.

   NOT   Hamlet says, "I am but mad north-northwest: when the wind is southerly, I know a hawk from a handsaw" (II.ii. 387–388).

   BUT   In a conversation with his school friends Rosencrantz and Guildenstern, Hamlet reveals that he is merely feigning madness when he confides, "I am but mad north-northwest: when the wind is southerly, I know a hawk from a handsaw" (II.ii. 387–388).

2. When you are using a quotation to support a point, make the point first, then give the quotation. In this way, you let your reader know what to look for in the quotation.

   NOT   "I was annoyed at first, for I thought that someone was blackberrying, and depreciating the value of the undergrowth" (239). Here Forster ironically comments that owning something arouses the selfish desire to keep everyone else away from it ("My Wood," Readings).

   BUT   By ironically commenting on his own desire to defend even his blackberries, Forster makes the point that owning something arouses the selfish desire to keep everyone else from using it: "I was annoyed at first, for

I thought that someone was blackberrying, and depreciating the value of the undergrowth" ("My Wood," Readings, 239).

3. Make the context of the quotation clear to your reader by identifying the speaker and the circumstances of the quotation.

NOT   Even in countries where it is illegal to force young people to marry, many girls still experience this form of slavery, especially in South Asia and West Africa. "Yet in the recent past not one women's or child-rights campaigner has made a loud noise about this" (203).

BUT   In "Wanted: The Right to Refuse" (Readings), Maggie Black points out that even in countries where it is illegal to force young people to marry, many girls still experience this form of slavery, especially in South Asia and West Africa. "Yet in the recent past," Black claims, "not one women's or child-rights campaigner has made a loud noise about this" (203).

4. Keep your quotations short. You can often quote only part of the sentence or line of poetry and paraphrase the rest, as in these examples.

PROSE
"A Modest Proposal" concludes with the narrator's earnest assertions that his sole motive is "the *publick Good*" and that he himself would receive not even the profit of "a single Penny" (324).

POETRY
The speaker in Robert Frost's "Stopping by Woods on a Snowy Evening" resists the lure of the dark woods by reminding himself that he has "promises to keep" (14).

5. Do not string quotations together to make a series of points. Separate quotations with paraphrased material and explanations.

NOT   In "Shooting an Elephant" (Readings), George Orwell says that, as a "sub-divisional police officer of the town, I was hated by large numbers of people" (293). "I was an obvious target and was baited whenever it seemed safe to do so" (293). After he shot the elephant, Orwell "often wondered whether any of [them] grasped that I had done it solely to avoid looking a fool" (299).

BUT   In "Shooting an Elephant," George Orwell explains
that as a police officer in Burma, he was hated "by
large numbers of people" (293). He was often the target of deliberate schemes to discredit him. In the final
analysis, Orwell wonders whether anyone understood
that he had killed the elephant "solely to avoid looking
a fool" (299) in the eyes of these people.

6. Do not take quotations out of context and use them in a way
that is misleading, as in the following example.

The Bible says, "Cain rose up and slew his brother Abel." In
another place it says, "Go thou and do likewise." Therefore
we should kill our brothers.

7. Make sure the quotation fits grammatically with the sentence
or phrase that introduces it.

NOT   The speaker in Robert Frost's poem "Stopping by
Woods on a Snowy Evening" says he knows

Whose woods these are I think I know.
His house is in the village though;
He will not see me stopping here (1–3)

BUT   The speaker in Robert Frost's poem "Stopping by
Woods on a Snowy Evening" seems to consider himself almost a trespasser:

Whose woods these are I think I know.
His house is in the village though;
He will not see me stopping here (1–3)

QUOTATIONS

Quotation Format

Indicating Changes in Quotations

1. **Deletions:** Use an ellipsis (…) to indicate that you have left out
part of a quotation. Be sure that what remains is grammatically
complete.

NOT   According to Forster, property gives the owner
"a vague sense … leads the artist to an act of creation"
("My Wood," Readings, 239).

BUT   According to Forster, property gives the owner
"a vague sense that he has a personality to express—
the same sense which … leads the artist to an act of
creation" (239).

Note: Do not use an ellipsis before or after a quotation that is obviously incomplete.

> NOT Polonius tells his daughter that Hamlet's protestations of love are mere "… springes to catch woodcocks" (I.iii. 115).

> BUT Polonius tells his daughter that Hamlet's protestations of love are mere "springes to catch woodcocks" (I. iii. 115).

2. **Insertions:** Put brackets around words added to clarify something in the quotation or to make the quotation fit into the grammatical structure of your sentence.

> INSERTION "Unlike the warriors of older tribes, however," Sanders points out, "they [the soldiers of his youth] would have no say about when the battle would start or how it would be waged" ("The Men We Carry in Our Minds," Readings, 309).

> CHANGE Sanders points out that modern soldiers "have no say about when the battle [will] start or how it [will] be waged" (309).

3. **Error in the text:** Put [*sic*] (Latin for "so," "thus") after the error to indicate typographical errors, deviant spellings, grammatical mistakes, or confused wording in the original.

> According to one study, "Each of the provinces are [*sic*] contributing to the problem of acid rain."

Quoting Prose

Short quotations

1. Prose quotations shorter than four lines may be indented for emphasis, but they are usually included in quotation marks within the body of your essay. Put the page reference in parentheses after the final quotation mark. Put a period **after the page reference**, not inside the quotation marks.

> Suzuki points out that for decades people believed that "by carefully weighing the benefits and bad side effects, we could make a more informed decision on whether to allow a new technology to be used" ("It Always Costs," Readings, 313).

2. Use single quotation marks to indicate a quotation within a quotation. Do not use single quotation marks elsewhere in your essay.

Iyer demonstrates that a comma in the wrong place can result in a totally different meaning. "Add a comma," he says, "and the noble sobriety of 'God save the Queen' becomes a cry of desperation bordering on double sacrilege" ("In Praise of the Humble Comma," Readings, 271).

Long quotations If you are quoting more than four lines of prose, set off the quotation from the body of your essay. Triple-space before and after the quotation. Double-space the quotation. Indent ten spaces from the left-hand margin. Do not indent a paragraph within the quotation unless you quote more than one. If you need to indicate a new paragraph, indent three additional spaces. Do not put quotation marks around the passage unless they appear in the original to indicate direct speech. Remember to introduce the quotation. Put the page reference, in parentheses, *after* the final punctuation.

> In "The Ticking Bomb" (Readings), Wade Davis argues that we in the industrialized nations must listen to the voices of the poor who suffer because of our excesses:
>
>> True peace and security for the 21st century will only come about when we find a way to address the underlying issues of disparity, dislocation and dispossession that have provoked the madness of our age. What we desperately need is a global acknowledgment of the fact that no people and no nation can truly prosper unless the bounty of our collective ingenuity and opportunities are available and accessible to all. (219)

Quoting Poetry

Short quotations If you are quoting no more than three lines of poetry, include the quotation in the body of your essay. Use a slash, with a space before and after it, to indicate divisions between lines. Retain the capitalization and punctuation in the original. Put the line reference in parentheses after the quotation, followed by a period.

> In the first stanza of "Trees at the Arctic Circle," the ground willows are portrayed as frightened people "afraid of exposing their limbs / like a Victorian married couple" (15–16).

Long quotations If you are quoting more than three lines of poetry, set them off as you would a long quotation of prose. Be sure to give the lines exactly as they are in the original, followed by the line reference.

> Purdy's poem finally arrives at a place of stillness where the speaker's judgments, the poem, and the willows can co-exist:

> I have been stupid in a poem
> I will not alter the poem
> but let the stupidity remain permanent
> as the trees are
> in a poem
> the dwarf trees of Baffin Island (52–57)

Quoting Plays

Depending on the play, you may be quoting prose or poetry. Follow the guidelines above as appropriate. For verse plays divided into acts and scenes, give the act, scene, and line numbers in parentheses after the quotation, rather than the page number. If the play is not divided into acts, scenes, and lines, give the page number on which the quotation appears in parentheses after the quotation.

EXERCISE I

This exercise is designed to give you practice in integrating quotations. Introduce the quotation appropriately, quote only the most relevant material, and punctuate correctly.

1. "Even though this is a knowledge economy in which brains are the prime commodity by which we compete, the ugly truth is this: somehow we forgot to make the proper reinvestments in higher education." (274) In this quotation Ann Dowsett Johnston (Readings) identifies the reason for the decline in quality of higher education.

2. Thomas Hurka makes the following point about *Casablanca*: "In *Casablanca* the political can be more important than the personal. No matter how passionate one's love—and Rick and Ilsa are certainly passionate—there are situations and dangers that must take priority. The Second World War was one such situation and Nazism one such danger" ("*The English Patient* Debate," Readings, 331).

3. The idea that blindness is a mental rather than a physical condition is clear when Gloucester perceives in Act Four, Scene Two, lines 21–26 of *King Lear* that he:

> I stumbled when I saw. Full oft 'tis seen,
> Our means secure us, and our mere defects
> Prove our commodities. O dear son Edgar
> The food of thy abused father's wrath!
> Might I but live to see thee in my touch
> I'd say I had eyes again!

4. An added benefit, Swift's narrator notes, is that this proposal will decrease the number of Roman Catholics in Ireland.

> For, *First*, as I have already observed, it would greatly lessen
> *the Number of Papists*, with whom we are yearly over-run,

being the principal Breeders of the Nation, as well as our most dangerous Enemies, and who stay at home on purpose with a design *to deliver the Kingdom to the Pretender*, hoping to take their Advantage by the absence *of so many good Protestants*, who have chosen rather to leave their Country, than stay at home, and pay Tithes against their Conscience, to an *Episcopal Curate*. (321)

5. Ken Wiwa believes that the globalization of sports, most evident in the World Cup, has not only made teams like France and Senegal more nearly equal but also blurred distinctions in their styles of play. On page 329 in "Choosing Up Sides" (Readings), he writes that "when it comes to football, the only difference between the countries is the colour of the shirts on their backs."

EXERCISE 2

Find examples from your own writing of passages in which you could have used quotations more effectively (or ones in which you used quotations particularly well). Bring examples to class for discussion.

Documentation

Whenever you write a research paper, you need to acknowledge the sources of ideas and information you use. To present an idea without acknowledgment implies that it is your own. If it is not, you have committed plagiarism. Since even inadvertent plagiarism may result in severe penalties, you must protect yourself by making sure that your citations are both accurate and complete.

There are more positive reasons for documenting your sources. Using references is a vital part of learning to write like a specialist in your field. Citing the work of experts lends weight and depth to your paper and allows readers to follow up interesting ideas.

Various disciplines have their own standard format for references. We will discuss two of the most widely accepted: the in-text citation system of the Modern Languages Association (MLA), used primarily in the humanities; and the author-date system of the American Psychological Association (APA), used in the sciences and social sciences. (For more details, see Checking Format and Documentation in Annotated Survey of Reference Sources, Part 4.)

What to Document

1. All quotations of three consecutive words or more from primary or secondary sources. You will find examples below for both the MLA and APA systems of documentation. You do not need to document familiar quotations unless they are part of the subject of your essay. For example, if you used the line "yon Cassius has a lean and hungry look" as an allusion, you would not document the quotation; however, if you were writing an essay on *Julius Caesar*, you would.

2. Ideas and opinions you have paraphrased from any source.

3. Factual information that is not readily verifiable or that may differ according to the source you consult. You would cite the source of unemployment figures, for example, since those figures not only change over time but also vary according to the criteria used to compile them. You do not need to document factual information that is considered "common knowledge" (the kind of information you might find in an encyclopedia).

Most of your material is likely to come from published or electronic sources; you should also credit information and ideas that come from other sources, such as films and interviews. You will find detailed guidelines below.

Systems of Reference

MLA System

When you are writing essays and research papers for courses in literature and film, you will likely be asked to use the MLA system of documentation. The MLA system consists of in-text citations accompanied by a list of Works Cited at the end of the paper. In-text citations give only enough information to identify the source of material you have quoted or paraphrased. Complete bibliographical information for each of these sources appears in the list of Works Cited.

In-text citations Whenever you quote or paraphrase, give the author's name and the page number(s) where you found the material. For electronic sources, give the paragraph number if used in the source (see p. 480). When you cite more than one work by the same author, such as several plays by Shakespeare, include the title or a short form of it. Some or all of this information is put in parentheses.

The following examples illustrate different ways to set up in-text citations to ensure that all necessary information is included.

Quotation from Primary Text (author not identified within your introduction)

> Contrary to popular opinion as spread by the media, "Men must consider the risk of becoming a parent at an advanced age just as women do" (Pyper 302).

Quotation from Primary Text (author identified as part of your introduction)

> Swift's final remark reconfirms that his proposal is not to be taken literally: "I have no Children, by which I can propose to get a single Penny; the youngest being nine Years old, and my Wife past Childbearing" (324).

Short Titles to Identify Works (more than one work by same author, Shakespeare)

> In loving someone above her station, Ophelia is similar to Helena, who laments her ambition: "The hind that would be mated by the lion / Must die for love" (*All's Well* I.i.103).

Quotation from Research Material

> As Michael MacDonald points out, "It would be hard to think of a case better suited to illuminating the problems that identifying suicides and burying their bodies presented than the passive drowning of a madwoman of high birth" (316).

Paraphrased Research Material

> The death and burial of Ophelia reveal all the ambiguities surrounding cases of suicide (MacDonald 316).

Works cited On a separate page entitled Works Cited (centred, without any punctuation), list all the sources from which you have quoted or from which you have taken information or ideas. Every source that you refer to in your essay should appear in the Works Cited, including your primary text(s); no work should appear in the Works Cited that you do not refer to in your essay. Remember to include films, videos, interviews, and electronic sources as well as printed materials.

Format Each entry begins at the left margin; subsequent lines in the same entry are indented one-half inch (one tab). HINT: Make use of your word processor functions by applying hanging-indent to the entire list of entries. Double space the entire Works Cited page; do not leave extra spaces between entries. Do not number them. For punctuation, see the examples below.

Order of entries List sources alphabetically by author's surname. If an entry has no author (an encyclopedia entry, for example), include it alphabetically by its title. HINT: Make use of your word processor functions by applying SORT to the entire list of entries (each is considered a paragraph of text). Give names exactly as they appear in the source. If an author's full name is given—for instance, Judy Rebick—do not abbreviate it in your entry to Rebick, J. For works with more than one author, give the names in the order they appear on the title page of the work; do not rearrange them.

Information Required

Books After the author's name, put the title of the work or the part of the work you have used. The title is followed by the name of the editor or translator, the edition, and number of volumes, if pertinent. Next comes the following publication information: the city where the work was published, the name of the publisher, and the year of publication, in that order. (If the city is not well known or could be confused with another place, include the province, state, or country, as appropriate.)

1. Book with a single author

> Gray, Charlotte. *Flint & Feather: The Life and Times of E. Pauline Johnson, Tekahionwake*. Toronto: HarperFlamingoCanada, 2002.

2. Subsequent works by the same author. Arrange titles alphabetically. Instead of repeating the author's name, type three hyphens followed by a period. Leave one space and type the title and other information.

> Forster, E. M. (Edward Morgan). *A Passage to India*. New York: Harcourt, 1924.
>
> ---. *Where Angels Fear to Tread*. London: E. Arnold, 1975.

3. Book with two or more authors or editors. Invert the first name only.

> Greenberg, Robert A., and William B. Piper. *The Writings of Jonathan Swift*. New York: Norton, 1973.

4. Part of a book

> Mairs, Nancy. "On Being a Cripple." *Plaintext: Essays by Nancy Mairs*. Tuscon: U of Arizona P, 1986. 9–20.

5. Work in an anthology

> Faulkner, William. "A Rose for Emily." *The Norton Introduction to Literature*. 8th ed. Eds. Jerome Beaty et al. New York: Norton, 2001. 531–38.

Articles The author's name is followed by the title of the article, the title of the periodical, the volume, number, and year of publication, and the page numbers.

1. Article in a scholarly journal

> Rutter, Carol Chillington. "Snatched Bodies: Ophelia in the Grave." *Shakespeare Quarterly* 49.3 (1998): 299–320.

2. Article in a magazine. No volume or number is necessary for weekly or monthly magazines, just the date and page numbers.

> Smith, Matthew. "Citizenship or Consumerism." *Alberta Views* Sept./Oct. 2000: 44–45.

3. Article in an encyclopedia. Page references are not necessary for encyclopedia entries or for other works arranged alphabetically.

If the entry is signed, put the author's name first in the note. If it is unsigned, start with the title of the entry. You do not need to give full publication data, just the year of the edition.

"David Suzuki." *The Canadian Encyclopedia.* 2000 ed.

Electronic Sources The basic elements and format of Works Cited entries for electronic sources are similar to those for print sources, but some additional information must be provided to allow a reader to locate a source.

- Provide your means of accessing the source—the database, CD-ROM and its vendor, or the network address (World Wide Web site). For punctuation, see the samples.

- Include the date of retrieval. Electronic sources come and go. If you are concerned that your source may no longer be available, have a hard copy ready to hand in to your instructor.

- Indicate the number of paragraphs in the article if they are numbered. When you quote from an electronic source, you refer to paragraphs rather than page numbers in your in-text citation.

Here are samples of the most common types of electronic sources. Provide as much of the information as is available. Be aware, however, that many sources do not supply all desired information because standards governing electronic publication are still evolving. When in doubt, ask your librarian.

1. Database article

    Suzuki, David. "Expanding the Health Care Debate."
    Canadian Medical Association Journal 166.13 (2000):
    14 pars. MasterFile Premier. 16 Oct. 2002
    <http://www.lrc.gmcc.ab.ca/research/databases/>

2. CD-ROM article

    Goldstein, Lauren. "Headaches with a Family History."
    Psychology Today 31.1 (1998): 14. *Social Sciences Index*.
    CD-ROM. UMI-ProQuest. Vers. 4.41.

3. Internet World Wide Web site

    Amdur, Reuel S. "Harris' Double Welfare Standard."
    Straightgoods 20 Aug. 2002. 16 Oct. 2002
    <http://www.straightgoods.ca/ViewFeature.cmf?REF=102>.

Other Types of Material

1. Film. Give the title of the film, the director, principal actors, distributor, and date.

    The Dead. Dir. John Huston. Perf. Anjelica Huston and Donal
    McCann. Vestron, 1987.

Note: If, instead of the film itself, you are citing the work of the director, an actor, or a screenwriter, you would begin the entry with that person's name. Add any other information pertinent to your discussion, such as the name of the choreographer of a musical, before the distributor and date.

2. Interview. Give the name of the person interviewed, his or her position (if not mentioned in the essay), the type of interview (personal interview, e-mail interview), and the date.

> Edwards, Caterina. Personal interview. 3 Feb. 1998.

You will find an example of MLA in-text citations and a list of works cited with the sample research paper "The Making of the Tragic Hero: The Graveyard Scene in *Hamlet*" in Part 2, Readings. For further information, refer to Joseph Gibaldi, ed., *MLA Handbook for Writers of Research Papers*, 6th ed. (New York: Modern Languages Association, 2003). A particularly helpful source for documenting Internet sources is Andrew Harnack and Eugene Kleppinger's *Online!: A Reference Guide to Using Internet Sources*, 3rd ed. (New York: St. Martin's, 2001). Harnack and Kleppinger also provide through their web site the latest information on documenting Internet materials. The web site can be visited at <http.www.bedfordstmartins.com/online/>.

APA System

The American Psychological Association employs a system of documentation similar to the MLA system of in-text citations. The chief difference is that sources are cited by name, date, and page number rather than name and page number alone. Like the MLA system, it employs a list of works cited to document sources. This list, however, is called "References." Full bibliographical information is included in the list of references. The format for entries differs from the MLA format, especially in punctuation. The APA system is widely accepted as the standard for papers in the sciences and social sciences.

In-text citations Within the text of your essay, place parenthetical citations immediately after a quotation or reference. Unless you are quoting, give only the author's surname and the year of publication. If you are quoting directly, include the page number after the year (the paragraph number if you are citing an electronic source). If you are not quoting directly but wish to direct the reader to a part of a source, such as a page number, chart, table, or appendix, include the appropriate reference. Omit the author's name if it appears in your text.

> In his analysis, Suzuki (1989) concludes that empirical testing of new technology simply cannot guarantee knowledge of its final environmental impact.

> In attempting to fit into an unfamiliar environment, people
> may develop new coping strategies that can eventually be-
> come addictions (Alexander & Shaler, 2001).
>
> In many affluent households, cars have been replaced by
> "gas-guzzling, wilderness-conquering sport utility vehicles
> that in the hands of most owners never venture farther
> off-road than the local car wash" (Laver, 1997, p. 282).

For sources that have two or more authors, give both (or all) sur-
names, in the order in which they appear in the source, and the year
of publication.

> (Hunt, Kyoto, & Kellogg, 1991)

Thereafter, use only the first surname and et al., with the year.

> (Hunt et al., 1991)

Where no author is given, use the first two or three words of the
title as it appears in the list of references.

References Include full bibliographical information about your
sources in an appended list entitled References. The purpose of the reference list is to identify your sources in such a way that your reader
can find them quickly. Include *only* the sources you cite in your paper,
and include *all* the sources you cite.

The entries in the list of references appear in alphabetical order
arranged by surname. A source reference with two or more authors includes all the names in the order in which they appear in the source. If
there are six or more authors, only the first three are listed, followed
by "et al." The final two authors' names are joined with a comma followed by an ampersand (&). When you have used more than one
source by an author, arrange them by year of publication, starting with
the earliest. Two or more works by the same author in the same year
are arranged alphabetically by the title of the work.

Each element of a bibliographical entry is followed with a period.
The titles of articles in journals or periodicals are not placed in quotation marks and only the first word of the title is capitalized. Any other
material necessary to identify the piece (such as editor, translator) is
placed in brackets after the title.

As in the MLA system, all entries are double spaced with the second and subsequent lines indented. Remember to use your word
processor functions by applying hanging indent to the entire list.

Articles The author's name, surname first, as it appears in the article,
followed by a period. The date of the publication, in parentheses, followed by a period. The title of the article, without quotation marks, only
the first word and any proper names capitalized, followed by a period.

The name of the journal/periodical and volume number in italics, followed by an issue number in parentheses, if necessary, a comma, and the inclusive page numbers of the article, followed by a period. Do not use p. or pp. for the page numbers of journal articles, but do use them for magazine and newspaper articles.

> Salonius, P. (1999). Population growth in the United States and Canada: A role for scientists. *Conservation Biology 13*(6), 1519–1529.

Books After the author, date, and title, put the place of publication and the publisher.

> Dowd, N. E. (2000). *Redefining Fatherhood.* New York: New York University Press.

If you need to include other information, put it where it will best clarify any misunderstanding that might arise. For example, to indicate that the name beginning an entry is that of the editor, place Ed(s). in parentheses immediately after the name(s). If a book is published in a city not generally known, include the state, province, or country, usually in an abbreviated form. If a work is a translation or a revised edition or one of a multivolume set, such additional information would be noted after the title, in parentheses.

Electronic Sources The basic elements and format of Reference page entries for electronic sources are similar to those for print sources, but as in the MLA system, additional information will help your reader locate an electronic source.

- Means of accessing the source, including the name of database, CD-ROM, or the electronic address of the source
- Date of retrieval

Here are the same samples used in the section on electronic sources in the MLA style, but converted to the APA style. Note the treatment of authors' names, placement of publication date, capitalization in titles, words added, and general punctuation.

1. Database article

> Suzuki, D. (2000). Expanding the health care debate. *Canadian Medical Association Journal 166*(13). Retrieved October 16, 2002, from MasterFILE database.

2. CD-ROM article

> Goldstein, L. (1998). Headaches with a family history. *Psychology Today 31*(1). From *Social Sciences Index*. CD-ROM, version 4.41, UMI-ProQuest.

3. Internet World Wide Web site

> Amdur, R.S. (2002). Harris' double welfare standard.
> *Straightgoods*. Retrieved October 16, 2002 from
> http://www.straightgoods/ca/ViewFeature.cmf?REF=102

Government Documents Always cite a government department from the most general to the most specific (Department/Agency/ Committee/ Subcommittee). A committee chairperson is not considered an author, so cite the department that issued the report as author. When the author and publisher are the same, simply write the word "Author" after the place of publication. If there is a catalogue or report number, cite it in parentheses after the title only.

> Alberta Bureau of Statistics. (1991). *Alberta population
> growth: 1986, 1ˢᵗ quarter–1991, 4ᵗʰ quarter*. Edmonton:
> Author.

For further information, see the *Publication Manual of the American Psychological Association*, 5ᵗʰ ed. (Washington, D.C.: American Psychological Association, 2001). For help with documenting Internet sources, see Harnack and Kleppinger's *Online!*, cited above.

Resources
for Writing

Common Perspectives for
Content Analysis (Chart)   486

General and Special Categories for
Textual Analysis (Chart)   488

Special Categories for Textual Analysis (Chart)   492

Annotated Survey of Reference Sources   509

Glossary of Rhetorical Terms   519

part four

Common Perspectives for Content Analysis

TYPE OF ANALYSIS	COMMON PERSPECTIVES
	Economic Perspective: Focuses on events, sets of data, phenomena, concepts, or theories as they relate to the production, circulation, or distribution of wealth, goods, or services
Systems Analysis What are the main parts of this event, set of data, phenomenon, concept, or theory? What is the nature and function of the parts? How are the parts related?	**Economic system:** **Example** *Data*: statistics on unemployment *Parts*: total labour force, number of people employed, number actively seeking work, number of "discouraged" job seekers, number of unemployed
Process Analysis What are the main stages in the evolution of this event, set of data, phenomenon, concept, or theory? What is the nature and function of these stages? How are these stages related?	**Economic process:** **Example** *Data*: statistics on unemployment *Stages*: in the rise and fall of employment; in the way unemployment figures are calculated
Causal Analysis What factors have brought about, or might have brought about, this event, set of data, phenomenon, concept, or theory? What changes have occurred, or might occur, as a result? How are these causes/effects related?	**Economic causes/effects:** **Example** *Data*: statistics showing high unemployment *Causes*: high interest rates; decrease in exports; loss of manufacturing *Effects*: rollbacks in wages and benefits; government incentives to create jobs; fewer part-time and summer jobs for students

FOR CONTENT ANALYSIS

Social Perspective: Focuses on events, sets of data, phenomena, concepts, or theories as they relate to a society, community or group	Political Perspective: Focuses on events, sets of data, phenomena, concepts, or theories as they relate to government, power, or authority	Psychological Perspective: Focuses on events, sets of data, phenomena, concepts, or theories as they relate to the needs, drives, or behaviour of individuals
Social system: **Example** *Phenomenon*: the family *Parts*: parent(s), child(ren), other relatives, other members of a household	**Political system:** **Example** *Event*: parliamentary elections *Parts*: political parties, candidates, voters, media	**Psychological system:** **Example** *Theory*: Freud's theory of the unconscious *Parts*: concepts of the id, the ego, the superego
Social process: **Example** *Phenomenon*: the family *Stages*: in the formation of a family, such as courtship, marriage, childbirth; in the evolution of the family in Western society, such as the tribe, the extended family, the nuclear family	**Political process:** **Example** *Event*: parliamentary elections *Stages*: in the evolution of parliamentary elections; in a particular election	**Psychological process:** **Example** *Theory*: Freud's theory of the unconscious *Stages*: in Freud's process of developing the theory; in the theory of psycho-sexual development
Social causes/effects: **Example** *Phenomenon*: contemporary family *Causes*: high rates of divorce and remarriage; increased recognition of gay and lesbian families; increasing number of consensual households *Effects*: less peer disapproval of children in non-nuclear families	**Political causes/effects:** **Example** *Event*: parliamentary election *Causes*: desire to capitalize on party's popularity; defeat of major legislation; vote of non-confidence *Effects*: shifts in regional power; minority government; increased representation of women and minorities	**Psychological causes/effects:** **Example** *Theory*: Freud's theory of the unconscious *Causes*: in Freud (self-analysis, influences of others) *Effects*: on others (therapeutic transformation)

General and Special Categories for Textual Analysis

GENERAL CATEGORIES	SPECIAL CATEGORIES	
	NONFICTION	**FICTION**
Subject What is the work about?	What issue, idea, event, or person is this work about?	What is the novel or short story about?
Subgenre Does it belong to a special *kind* of text?	Is it a particular kind of non-fiction?	Is it a particular kind of fiction?
Context For what audience and in what situation was it produced?	For what audience and in what situation was it written?	For what audience and in what situation was it written?
Methods of Development What are the particular details that give the work substance?	A. **Evidence** What kind of evidence does the author give to support the argument?	A. **Setting** What is the place, time, and social environment within which events take place?
	B. **Detail** What kind of detail to develop explanatory, narrative, or descriptive writing?	B. **Characterization** What are the characters like? What techniques are used to portray them?
Structure How is the work put together?	**Structure** How is the argument, explanation, narrative, and/or description selected and arranged?	**Narrative Structure** What is the principle behind the selection and arrangement of events ("plot")?

POETRY	DRAMA	FILM AND TV
What is the poem or sequence of poems about?	What is this play about?	What is the film or program about?
Does it belong to a particular kind of poetry?	Does it belong to a particular kind of drama?	Is it a particular kind of film or TV program?
For what audience and in what situation was it written?	For what audience and in what situation was it written/produced?	For what audience and in what situation was it written/produced?
A. Setting What is the place, time, and social environment within which the development of the poem takes place? **B. Characterization** How is (are) the speaker and/or other character(s) portrayed?	**A. Setting** What is the place, time, and social environment within which the action takes place? What do costuming, music, lighting, sets, etc., indicate about the setting? **B. Characterization** What are the characters like? How are various techniques, including dialogue and acting, used to portray them?	**A. Setting** What is the place, time, and social environment established by the locations, by music, etc.? **B. Characterization** What are the characters like? How are various techniques, including dialogue and acting, used to portray them?
Poetic Structure What is the principle behind the selection and arrangement of details in the poem?	**Dramatic Structure** What is the principle behind the selection and arrangement of events ("action")?	**Structure** What is the principle behind the selection and arrangement of events ("action")?

General and Special Categories
for Textual Analysis (continued)

GENERAL CATEGORIES	SPECIAL CATEGORIES	
	NONFICTION	**FICTION**
Style How does the author/director use the "language" of the medium?	**A. Diction** What do usage level and word choice convey?	**A. Diction** What do usage level and word choice convey?
	B. Figurative Language and Allusions Are images, symbols, and/or allusions used to comment on the subject? How?	**B. Figurative Language and Allusions** Do images, symbols, and/or allusions create patterns of meaning? How?
	C. Sentence Structure What do sentence patterns indicate?	**C. Sentence Structure** What do sentence patterns indicate?
Tone What is the author's/director's attitude towards self, subject, and audience, as conveyed by the work?	**Tone** What is the author's attitude to subject and reader, as conveyed by the work?	**A. Tone** What attitude does the narrator (and/or author) adopt towards the story and the reader?
		B. Point of View Who is the narrator? How does this affect the way the story is told?
Theme or Thesis What is the central idea of the work?	**Thesis** What is the central idea of the work?	**Theme** What is the central idea of the novel or short story?

POETRY	DRAMA	FILM AND TV
A. Diction What do usage level and word choice tell me?	**A. Diction** What do usage level and word choice in individual characters and in the play as a whole tell me?	**A. Shooting Techniques** What do camera angles, shot length, etc., convey about setting or characters?
B. Figurative Language Do images, symbols, and allusions create patterns of meaning? How?	**B. Figurative Language** Do images, symbols, and allusions create patterns of meaning? How?	**B. Images, Symbols, Allusions** Do these create patterns of meaning? How?
C. Prosody How are sound, rhythm, and other techniques of line and verse construction used in the poem?	**C. Pacing** What is the rhythm of dialogue and action?	**C. Editing Techniques** What movement of action does the editing create?
A. Tone What is the tone and how does it reflect the speaker's attitude?	**Tone** (a) Playwright: What attitude to subject and audience is evident? (b) Director: What attitude to subject and audience is evident?	**Tone** What is the director's attitude to the subject and audience, as conveyed by the film or program?
B. Point of View Who is the speaker in the poem? Is the speaker a created character or an aspect of the poet? How does this affect the way the poem is written?		
Theme What is the central idea of the poem?	**Theme** What is the central idea of the play?	**Theme or Thesis** What is the central idea of the film or program?

Special Categories for Textual Analysis

Questions to Ask in Analyzing Nonfiction

A. Identifying Textual Features

Subject, subgenre, context

1. What issue, idea, event, or person is this work about?

2. Does this work belong to a particular subgenre (kind) of nonfiction writing (e.g., autobiography, argumentative essay, historical writing, scientific article)? What are the main characteristics of this subgenre?

3. Can you identify the likely audience for this work (e.g., academic, popular, special interest)? Is information about the social, historical, and/or cultural situation in which the work was produced relevant to understanding the work?

Evidence and detail The material used to support evaluative or analytic points, or to give substance to explanation, narration, or description.

1. What material does the author use to support evaluative or analytic points? Examples? Facts? Statistics? References to, or quotations from, authorities on the subject? Imaginary situations? Predictions? (See Chapter 10 for kinds of evaluative arguments and detail.)

2. Does the author give substance to narration by extended accounts of a small number of events or by brief accounts of many events? Is description panoramic (using selected details to summarize a wide range of experience), or dramatic (using lots of details to convey a particular experience)?

Structure The selection and arrangement of points, narrative incidents, and/or descriptive detail.

1. Does the work use the structure appropriate to a particular sub-genre (e.g., inductive structure in personal writing)?

2. Does the work use the structure appropriate to a particular mode of discourse? For example:

   a. Is the main purpose of the work to present an evaluation (another commonly used term is *argument*)? If so, what principle determines the order in which points are presented (e.g., pro–con structure)?

   b. Is the main purpose of the work to present an analysis (another commonly used term is *exposition*)? If so, what principle determines the order in which points are presented (e.g., order of ascending interest)?

   c. Is the main purpose of the work to present a narrative or a description? If so, what principle governs the order (e.g., past to present, near to far)?

   d. If the work mixes evaluation and/or analysis with narration and/or description, what is the organizing principle?

3. Do typographic devices help to indicate structure?

Diction The author's general level of usage and particular word choices.

1. Is the general level of usage in the work that of formal, educated speech; informal, everyday speech; the colloquial speech associated with a particular dialect or subculture; or a mixture of these levels? Are there significant shifts between levels of usage?

2. Is a specialized vocabulary (e.g., the vocabulary of the biologist or the banker) important to this work?

3. Are there significant patterns of word choices (e.g., euphemisms designed to hide unpleasant facts)?

Figurative language and allusions Images are figures of speech and, more generally, descriptions of sensations; symbols are objects, actions, gestures, or patterns of images used to express a more abstract idea; allusions are references to literary, historical, mythological, or religious figures, events, places, or ideas.

1. Does the author use any significant figures of speech (metaphor, simile, personification) or descriptions of sensations (sight, hearing, touch, smell, taste, body movement) in discussing issues, ideas, events, or persons (e.g., the metaphor of rich nations as lifeboats in Garrett Hardin's essay "Lifeboat Ethics" [Readings])?

2. Are there any objects, actions, gestures, or images that have or take on a symbolic meaning (e.g., shooting an elephant in George Orwell's essay of that title)?

3. Are there references to literary or other figures (e.g., biblical allusions in E. M. Forster's "My Wood")? Are any references repeated? Do these references form a pattern?

Sentence structure Sentence length and type.

1. What are the characteristic features of the author's sentences? Long or short? Simple or complex? Is there a distinctive use of parallelism or of other rhetorical devices? (See Improving Sentence Structure in Part 3, Handbook.)

2. Are there significant exceptions to, or changes in, the author's habitual sentence structure?

Tone The attitude towards self, subject, and readers, as conveyed in the work: the counterpart of "tone of voice" in speech.

1. Is there a narrator who is distinctly different from the author (a persona)? If so, how would you characterize the narrator's attitude towards the subject and/or the reader? Contemptuous? Confiding? Reasonable, as Swift's narrator seems in "A Modest Proposal"?

2. How would you characterize the author's attitude towards his or her subject (and narrator)? Serious? Humorous? Detached? Impassioned?

3. How would you characterize the author's attitude towards his or her readers? Friendly? Pompous? Critical? Condescending?

4. Are there significant shifts in tone? If so, where and to what purpose?

5. How apparent, and how important to the work, is the personality of the author?

B. Connecting Textual Features to Figure Out the Work's Thesis

1. If the work belongs to a distinct genre (kind), in what ways does it conform to and depart from the conventions of the genre?

2. How does the title relate to the work as a whole?

3. What is the relationship between structure and evidence/detail? Is one part of the evaluation or analysis supplied with more evidence or detail than another, for example?

4. How do elements of style (diction, figurative language and allusion, sentence structure) relate to structure and evidence/detail? Does the style seem appropriate to the purpose of the work?

5. What is your interpretation of the author's thesis, based on your analysis of the work and your sense of how its elements are related?

6. Does the author state a thesis directly?

7. Is there a difference between your interpretation of the thesis and the thesis stated in the work? If so, what accounts for this difference?

Questions to Ask in Analyzing Fiction

A. Identifying Textual Features

Subject, subgenre, context

1. What is the novel, novella, or short story about?

2. Does this work belong to a particular subgenre (kind) of fiction or fictional tradition (e.g., romance, Gothic novel, science fiction)? What are the main characteristics of this subgenre?

3. Is knowledge of the intended audience and/or the social, historical, or cultural situation in which the work was produced relevant to understanding the work?

Setting The place, time, and social environment within which the action takes place.

1. What are the most important locations in the work? Are they interior locations (inside houses, prisons, caves) or exterior ones? How extensively are they described?

2. During what historical period is the work set? What period of time does it encompass?

3. Does the work create a particular social environment through the portrayal of manners, customs, and moral values?

Characterization Techniques used in portraying the characters.

1. Is the main character a hero(ine), a villain, or an anti-hero (a character presented as decidedly unheroic)? Are the characters round (with complex or contradictory aspects) or flat (type characters, stereotypes)? Is there a broad or narrow range of characters?

2. What physical, psychological, and moral traits are associated with particular characters, and how are these traits revealed?

Through dialogue? Through description of physical appearance or mental process? Through distinctive behaviour? Through the perceptions or comments of other characters? In some other way?

3. Do these traits change in the course of the novel or short story? If so, how and to what purpose?

4. What do the characters think about each other? Are there significant differences in characters' conceptions of each other?

Narrative structure The selection and arrangement of events ("plot").

1. Does the narrative structure follow the conventions of a particular subgenre (e.g., the three tasks of many fairy tales)?

2. How does the narrative use spatial and chronological principles of structure? For example:

   a. Are events presented in chronological order? If not, in what order are they presented? Are flashbacks used?

   b. To what extent are events presented as a series of dramatic scenes? To what extent are events summarized (e.g., "five years had passed, five hard years in which the cow had died, the barn had burned, and Jane had married Tom")?

   c. What is the principle by which events are linked? Cause-and-effect (e.g., the consequences of wife-selling in Thomas Hardy's *The Mayor of Casterbridge*)? The development of the main character (e.g., Alice Munro's *Lives of Girls and Women*)? A physical, mental, or spiritual quest (e.g., *The Lord of the Rings*)? A seemingly random association?

   d. Is the work divided into parts? Do these parts correspond to stages in the development of the action?

   e. Does the action lead towards a climax or turning point? Is there a resolution of conflicts or a revelation? If there is no climax and resolution, how does the action develop?

   f. Why does the work end as it does?

3. Do typographic devices (e.g., chapter headings) indicate structure?

Diction The general level of usage (formal, informal, colloquial) within the narrative, as well as the speech styles and word choices of particular characters.

1. Is the general level of usage in the narrative that of formal, educated speech; informal, everyday speech; the colloquial speech associated with a particular dialect or subculture; or a mixture of these levels?

2. What is the general level of usage of specific characters? Are there characters who shift among these levels of usage? If so, in what situations? Why?

3. Do any characters use a distinctive vocabulary (e.g., the Jungian psychoanalyst in Robertson Davies' *The Manticore*)?

Figurative language and allusions Images are figures of speech and, more generally, descriptions of sensations; symbols are objects, actions, gestures, or patterns of images used to express a more abstract idea; allusions are references to literary, historical, mythological, and religious figures, events, places, or ideas.

1. Are there figures of speech (metaphors, similes, personification) employed in the narrative or by the characters that seem significant because of repetition or placement (e.g., Hagar's statement that she "turned to stone" the night her son John died in Margaret Laurence's *The Stone Angel*)?

2. Are there descriptions of sensations (e.g., heat, cold, light, dark, colours, smells, sounds) that seem significant because of repetition or placement (e.g., engulfing vegetation in Ken Kesey's *Sometimes a Great Notion*).

3. Are there any objects, actions, gestures, or images that have or take on a symbolic meaning? Are there any conventional symbols (as a bishop's mitre symbolizes religious power)? Are there any universal symbols (as still water symbolizes the unknown in Janet Frame's story "The Reservoir")? Are there any contextual symbols (as the rocking horse symbolizes relentless ambition in D. H. Lawrence's story "The Rocking-Horse Winner")?

4. Do images and symbols combine to form significant patterns of meaning in the novel or story (e.g., food and eating in Margaret Atwood's novel *The Edible Woman*)?

5. Are there allusions (e.g., references to Noah in Timothy Findley's *Not Wanted on the Voyage*)?

Sentence structure Sentence length and type.

1. What are the characteristic features of the sentences of the narrator and/or main characters? Are the sentences long or short, simple or complex? Is there a pronounced use of parallelism or of other rhetorical devices?

2. Are there significant exceptions to or changes in characteristic sentence structure? If so, where? What is their purpose?

Tone Attitude to subject and audience.

1. How would you describe the tone of the novel, novella, or short story? Serious? Playful? Ironic? Detached?

2. Is there a difference in tone between the narrator's attitude towards the story and the narrator's attitude towards the reader (e.g., Jane Austen presents the dilemmas of her main characters seriously and sympathetically, but the narrative voice also invites readers to maintain some degree of ironic detachment)?

3. Does the tone change at any point? If so, where and to what purpose?

Point of view   Vantage point from which the action is presented.

1. What is the point of view from which the story is told? First person ("I"); third-person limited (restricted to one character's thoughts and feelings) or omniscient (moving in and out of characters' minds at will); "camera eye" (objective narration)?

2. Is the narrator also a major or minor character in the action? Is his or her part in the action likely to affect his or her reliability as narrator?

3. Does the novel or short story draw your attention to the process of narration by addressing the reader directly, by discussing the difficulty of telling the story, or by other means?

B. Connecting Textual Features to Figure Out a Theme in the Work

1. If the novel or story belongs to a particular subgenre (kind) of fiction, in what ways does it conform to and depart from the conventions of the subgenre?

2. How does the title relate to the work as a whole?

3. How does the narrative structure of the novel or story help to reveal character?

4. How does setting contribute to characterization and narrative structure? Are particular events or particular characters associated with particular places (e.g., in Emily Brontë's *Wuthering Heights*, Wuthering Heights is associated with Heathcliff and the Earnshaws, while Thrushcross Grange is associated with the Lintons)?

5. How do the elements of style (diction, figurative language and allusions, and sentence structure) help to portray action, setting, and character?

6. How do action, setting, characterization, style, point of view, and tone combine to convey a theme?

7. What is this theme?

Questions to Ask in Analyzing Poetry

A. Identifying Textual Features

Subject, subgenre, context

1. What is this poem about?

2. Does this poem belong to a distinct subgenre (kind) of poetry or poetic tradition (e.g., lyric, elegy, ballad, dramatic monologue)? What are the main characteristics of this subgenre?

3. Is knowledge of the intended audience and/or social, historical, or cultural situation relevant to understanding the work?

Setting   The place, time, and social environment within which the development of the poem takes place.

1. What are the most important locations in the poem?

2. Is the poem set during a specific historical period? What period of time does the poem itself encompass?

3. Is a particular social environment portrayed or suggested?

Characterization   The techniques used in portraying details of speaker or characters.

1. Does the poem present various characters, only a speaker, or both speaker and characters?

2. Is the speaker distinctly different from the poet (as in dramatic monologues)? Or does the speaker appear to speak for the poet? What are the important perceptions, observations, or judgments associated with the speaker?

3. What physical, psychological, and moral traits are associated with the character(s) of the poem? How are they portrayed? Do these traits change in the course of the poem?

4. Do we, as readers, see characters differently from the way they are perceived by the speaker or by other characters?

Poetic structure   The selection and arrangement of events, ideas, sensations and feelings, as well as the arrangement of lines.

1. Does the poetic structure follow the conventions of a particular subgenre (e.g., Petrarchan sonnet)?

2. How does the poem use the principles of spatial and chronological or logical structure? For example:

   a. What is the organizing principle of the poem? A sequence of events? A train of thought? The movement of sensations or feelings? A mixture of these?

    b. Why does the poem begin and end as it does? What are the main stages in its development? Is there a turning point?

3. Do typographic devices indicate structure (e.g., by marking off stanzas)?

Diction The general level of usage, as well as particular word choices, in the poem.

1. Is the general level of usage in the poem that of formal, educated speech; informal, everyday speech; the colloquial speech associated with a particular dialect or subculture; or a mixture of these levels?

2. Can you identify any distinctive word choices in the poem (e.g., use of archaisms, deliberate alteration of expressions normal in prose)?

Figurative language and allusions Images are figures of speech and, more generally, descriptions of sensations; symbols are objects, actions, gestures, or patterns of images used to express a more abstract idea; allusions are references to literary, historical, mythological, or religious figures, events, places, or ideas.

1. Are there any figures of speech (e.g., metaphors, similes, personification) that seem significant because of repetition or placement (e.g., Burns's "My Luv's like a red, red rose")?

2. Are there descriptions of sensations (sight, hearing, touch, smell, taste, body movement) that seem significant because of repetition or placement (e.g., references to sleep in Frost's "Stopping by Woods on a Snowy Evening")?

3. Do images in the poem group into significant patterns (e.g., controlling metaphor or metaphysical conceit, as, for example, the compasses in John Donne's "A Valediction: Forbidding Mourning")?

4. Are there any objects, actions, gestures, or images that have or take on a symbolic meaning? Are there any conventional symbols (as the moon symbolizes the feminine in Sylvia Plath's "The Moon and the Yew Tree")? Are there any universal symbols (as spring represents a time of rebirth in Shelley's "Ode to the West Wind")? Are there any contextual symbols (as a loaded gun is a symbol of life in Emily Dickinson's "My Life had stood—a Loaded Gun")?

5. Are the symbols in the poem part of a larger symbolic pattern in the poet's work as a whole (e.g., roses in Blake's poems, gyres in Yeats's poems)?

6. Are there any allusions in the poem (e.g., to the Icarus story in Auden's "Musée des Beaux Arts")?

Prosody The use of sound and rhythm in poetry.

1. What is the rhythm of individual lines in the poem? Do they have a regular metre (e.g., iambic, trochaic)? Or no regular metre (e.g., free verse, prose poems)?

2. Is the line length regular (e.g., tetrameter, pentameter) or irregular (free verse)? Does the poem combine metre and line length in a special form (e.g., blank verse—unrhymed iambic pentameter)?

3. Do lines correspond to units of meaning? How are pauses used (e.g., end-stopping, caesura)?

4. Does the poem use rhyme? If so, is it regular end rhyme or a special form of rhyme (e.g., internal rhyme, slant rhyme, eye rhyme)?

5. Does the poem use sound in other ways (e.g., alliteration, assonance, consonance, onomatopoeia)?

Tone Attitude to self, subject, and/or audience.

1. How would you describe the tone of the poem? Melancholy? Playful? Sarcastic? Conversational?

2. Does the tone change at any point in the poem? If so, where, how, and to what purpose?

3. Is the tone of the poem determined by the attitudes to subject and audience of the poet speaking, or by those of a speaker distinct from the poet? If the attitudes are those of a distinct speaker, are there indications of the poet's attitudes as well?

Point of view The vantage point from which the development of the poem is presented.

1. From which point of view is the poem presented? First person? Third-person limited? Omniscient? Camera eye?

2. Is the speaker of the poem closely involved in the events, ideas, sensations, or feelings developed in the poem? Is the speaker's account to be trusted?

B. Connecting Textual Features to Figure Out a Theme in the Work

1. If the poem belongs to a particular subgenre (kind), in what ways does it conform to and depart from the conventions of the subgenre?

2. How does the title relate to the work as a whole?

3. How is the structure of the poem linked to characterization and setting?

4. How do elements of style (diction, figurative language and allusions, and prosody) contribute to structure, characterization, and setting?

5. How do poetic structure, setting, characterization, diction, images and symbols, prosody, and tone combine to convey a theme of the poem?
6. What is this theme?

Questions to Ask in Analyzing Drama

A. Identifying Textual Features

Subject, subgenre, context

1. What is this play about?
2. Does this play belong to a particular subgenre (kind) of drama (e.g., comedy, tragedy)? What are the main characteristics of this subgenre?
3. Is knowledge of the intended audience and/or the social, historical, or cultural situation relevant to the understanding of the play?

Setting   The place, time, and social environment within which the action takes place.

1. In what particular location(s) is the play set (e.g., park, city apartment, classroom)? Is a larger geographical location indicated (e.g., a particular city, region, country)?
2. Is the play set during a specific historical period? What period of time does the play itself encompass?
3. Is a particular social environment conveyed through the portrayal of manners, customs, and moral values?
4. How is the setting created? Through characters' comments (e.g., "Here we are in Rome")? Through stage directions? Through costumes, lighting, make-up, music, props?
5. Does the kind of stage on which the play is represented (Renaissance, proscenium arch, thrust, theatre-in-the-round) contribute to the setting?

Characterization   Techniques for portraying characters.

1. Which are the major and which are the minor characters? Is there a distinct protagonist (hero or heroine) and antagonist (villain)? Are there one or more characters who serve as foils for another character by exaggerating his/her qualities? Are there any type characters (confidante, revenger)? Are there any stock (stereotyped) characters (nosy neighbour, faithful servant, tyrannical boss)?

2. What physical, psychological, and moral traits are associated with particular characters, and how are these traits revealed? Through what the character says, or what is said about the character, in dialogue, monologue, soliloquy, or asides? Through the character's (or actor's) actions or gestures? Through physical appearance (including costuming and make-up)?

3. Do these traits change in the course of the play? If so, where, how, and to what purpose?

4. What do the characters think about each other? Are there significant differences in characters' conceptions of each other? Are there significant differences between the characters' conceptions and the audience's (e.g., to Othello, Iago is "honest Iago"; to the audience, Iago is a villain)?

Dramatic structure The selection and arrangement of events ("action").

1. Does the dramatic structure follow the conventions of a particular subgenre (e.g., revenge tragedy, romantic comedy)?

2. How does the play use the principles of spatial and chronological structure? For example:

   a. Does the action begin with the gradual unfolding of the plot (as *King Lear* begins with Lear's testing of his daughters), or does it begin after the occurrence of some significant event revealed early in the play (as *Hamlet* begins after the murder of Hamlet's father)?

   b. Does the action lead towards a climax (rising action) and a resolution of conflicts (falling action)? If not, how does the action develop?

   c. Why does the play end as it does?

3. Do typographic devices indicate structure? For example, if the play is divided into acts (and scenes), what is the principle that governs these divisions?

Diction The general level of usage (formal, informal, colloquial) within the play as a whole, as well as the speech styles and word choices of particular characters.

1. Is the general level of usage of a particular character that of formal, educated speech; informal, everyday speech; the colloquial speech of a particular dialect or subculture; or a mixture of these levels? What is the general level of the play as a whole?

2. Are there characters who shift among these levels of usage? If so, in what situations? Why?

3. Do any characters use a distinctive vocabulary (e.g., the vocabulary of salesmanship in *Death of a Salesman*)?

Figurative language and allusions Images are figures of speech and, more generally, descriptions of sensations; symbols are objects, actions, gestures, or patterns of images used to express a more abstract idea; allusions are references to literary, historical, mythological, or religious figures, events, places, or ideas.

1. Are there any figures of speech (metaphors, similes, personification) that seem significant because of repetition or placement (e.g., metaphors of disease in *Hamlet*)?

2. Are there descriptions of sensations (sight, hearing, touch, smell, taste, body movement) that seem significant because of repetition or placement (e.g., images of sight and blindness in *King Lear*)?

3. Are there any objects, actions, gestures, or images that have or take on a symbolic meaning? Are there any conventional symbols (as a flag symbolizes patriotism, or a certain posture symbolizes despair)? Are there any universal symbols (light, dark, water, fire, etc.)? Are there any contextual symbols (as the action of washing clothes becomes symbolic in Marsha Norman's *Third and Oak: The Laundromat*)?

4. Do images and symbols combine to form significant patterns of meaning in the play?

5. Do costumes, lighting, make-up, sets, music, or props have any symbolic value?

6. Are there allusions in the play (as in the title of Edward Albee's *Who's Afraid of Virginia Woolf?*)? Is there a pattern to these allusions?

Pacing The rhythm of dialogue and action.

1. Does the rhythm of language in the play have a specific form (e.g., blank verse), or can it be described more impressionistically (e.g., deliberate, philosophical, light, staccato, fast-paced)?

2. Are there distinctive features of sentence structure in characters' speech? Does a particular character speak in monosyllables or in long, complex sentences? Is there a pronounced use of parallelism or other rhetorical devices?

3. What is the pace of the action? Is it fast-paced or slow-paced? Does it proceed with deliberation or with unexpected turns and twists?

Tone Attitude to subject and/or audience.

1. How would you describe the tone of the play as a whole? Of particular acts? Of particular scenes? Serious? Romantic? Nostalgic? Ironic?

2. Are there significant shifts in tone? If so, where and why?

3. For performances: How do elements under the director's control (acting, sets, make-up, sound, music, lighting) contribute to the tone?

B. Connecting Textual Features to Figure Out a Theme in the Work

1. If the play belongs to a distinct subgenre (kind), in what ways does it conform to and depart from the conventions of this subgenre?

2. How does the title relate to the work as a whole?

3. How does the dramatic action reveal character?

4. How does setting affect plot and characterization?

5. Are particular images or symbols associated with particular events, places, characters? If so, what is the purpose of this association?

6. How do diction and pacing help to create tone?

7. How do setting, characterization, structure, style, and tone help to convey theme?

8. What is this theme?

Questions to Ask in Analyzing Films and TV*

A. Identifying Textual Features

Subject, subgenre, context

1. What is this film or program about?

2. Does it belong to a particular subgenre (kind) of film (e.g., *film noir*) or television production (e.g., soap opera)? What are the main characteristics of this subgenre?

3. Is knowledge of the intended audience and/or the social, historical, or cultural situation relevant to understanding the film or program? Is a knowledge of specific conditions of production relevant?

Setting The place, time, and social environment within which the action takes place.

---

* To analyze documentaries, newscasts, and similar programs, use Special Categories for Analyzing Nonfiction in conjunction with the questions on shooting and editing techniques given here.

1. What are the important locations in this film or program? Are they interior, exterior, or both?

2. During what historical period is the film or program set?

3. What picture do you get of the society in which the action takes place? What features of the setting convey the society's manners, customs, and moral values (e.g., expensive houses, cars, and clothes might suggest a society that values material possessions)?

4. What special techniques (lighting, music, shot length, angle, etc.) are used to portray setting? What do these techniques convey?

Characterization Techniques for portraying characters.

1. What physical, psychological, or moral traits are associated with particular characters, and how are these traits revealed? Through what the character says, or what is said about the character? Through the character's (and actor's) actions and gestures? Through physical appearance (including costuming and make-up)?

2. Do these traits change in the development of the action? If so, where, how, and to what purpose?

3. Are there significant differences in characters' conceptions of each other? Are there significant differences between the characters' conceptions and the audience's?

Structure The selection and arrangement of events ("action").

1. Does the structure follow the conventions of a particular sub-genre (e.g., the climactic shoot-out in the Western)?

2. How does the film or program use the principles of spatial or chronological structure?

3. Do events lead to a climax (turning point) and resolution of conflicts? If so, where does the climax occur and how are conflicts resolved? If not, what happens?

4. Why does the film or television program end as it does? What is conveyed by the closing scene, closing shots, closing titles?

Shooting techniques Ways of photographing with a motion picture or television camera.

1. Is there a distinctive use of camera placement (close-up, medium shot, long shot) or camera movement (panning, tracking, craning, zoom shots) in the film or program? If so, what is its purpose (e.g., close-up = intensity; long shot = detachment)?

2. Is there a distinctive use of camera angle (e.g., high angle, low angle, oblique angle, tilt shots) in the film or program? If so, what is its purpose?

3. Is there a distinctive use of composition (e.g., symmetry, asymmetry) in the shots? If so, what is its purpose?

4. Is there a distinctive use of camera speeds (e.g., slow motion, time lapse, speed-up) or lenses (wide angle, telephoto)? If so, what is its purpose?

5. Is there a distinctive use of colour, texture (e.g., graining), or lighting (high key, low key)? If so, what is the purpose?

Images, symbols, allusions Images are figures of speech and, more generally, descriptions of sensations; symbols are objects, actions, gestures, or patterns of images used to express a more abstract idea; allusions are references to literary, historical, mythological, or religious figures, events, places, or ideas.

1. Are there images that seem important because of repetition or placement (e.g., the hand imagery in *The Color Purple* that conveys many of the film's main issues: silencing, isolation, connection, reconciliation)?

2. Are there objects, actions, gestures, or images in the film or program that have or take on a symbolic meaning (e.g., the feather in *The Joy Luck Club* that symbolizes the hopes and good intentions that bind generations of mothers and daughters)?

3. Do images and symbols combine to form significant patterns of meaning in the film or program (e.g., fishing as a symbol of art, self-discipline, brotherhood, and redemption in *A River Runs Through It*)?

4. Are there allusions in the film or program? Are they established verbally or visually? Do they form a pattern?

Editing techniques Methods governing the sequence and combination of individual shots.

1. Does the film or program make any distinctive use of cuts (cross cuts, jump cuts, flash cuts) and fades (fade-out, fade-in, dissolves) within scenes? If so, to what purpose?

2. How are episodes put together to convey the passage of time (cuts, fades, dissolves)? Are there flashbacks or other special techniques used in between-scenes editing?

3. How are sound effects, including music, used?

Tone   The director's attitude to subject and/or audience, as conveyed by the film or program.

1. How would you describe the tone of the film or program as a whole? Menacing? Comic? Romantic? Nostalgic? Are there shifts in tone? If so, where and why?

2. What techniques (e.g., shooting, editing, music, lighting) are used to help establish the tone of the film or program?

B. Connecting Textual Features to Figure Out a Theme or Thesis in the Work

1. If the film or program belongs to a distinct subgenre, in what ways does it conform to and depart from the conventions of the subgenre?

2. How does the title relate to the work as a whole?

3. How does the structure of the film or program contribute to characterization?

4. How does setting affect plot and characterization? For example, are particular places associated with certain characters or significant events?

5. Are particular images or symbols associated with particular events, places, characters? If so, what does this association convey?

6. How are shooting or editing techniques used to convey action, setting, character?

7. How are action, setting, and characterization linked to the tone?

8. How do the elements of the film or program combine to convey a theme or thesis?

9. What is the theme or thesis?

Annotated Survey of Reference Sources[*]

This brief survey provides background material for your reading and writing, especially for textual analysis. Use this survey as a starting place to explore the resources of your own library.

Finding Explanations of Literary and Rhetorical Terms and Literary Theory

Although their coverage varies, most dictionaries of literary and rhetorical terms will include, in alphabetical order, brief discussions of items such as these: (1) the major periods of literary history, such as the Renaissance, and literary movements or groups, such as Imagists; (2) literary genres, from broad forms, such as drama, to specific forms, such as the revenge tragedy, dream allegory, and comedy of intrigue; (3) terms commonly used in literary and rhetorical criticism, such as point of view, irony, metaphysical conceit; and (4) historical events, philosophical terms, and similar material seen as especially relevant to the study of literature. Works that explain terms from cultural criticism and literary theory will help you understand what is meant by *feminist criticism* and *postmodernist theory*, for example.

Abrams, M. H. *A Glossary of Literary Terms*. 7th ed. Fort Worth: Harcourt, 1999.

Childers, Joseph, and Gary Hentzi. *The Columbia Dictionary of Modern Literary and Cultural Criticism*. New York: Columbia UP, 1995.

---

[*] Compiled by Kevin Crandlemire; revised by Len Falkenstein (1993); revised by Kat Johnston (2002).

Cuddon, J. A. *A Dictionary of Literary Terms and Literary Theory*. Revised by C.E. Preston. 4th ed. Oxford: Blackwell, 1998.

Raman, Selden, Peter Widdowson, and Peter Brooker. *A Reader's Guide to Contemporary Literary Theory*. 4th ed. New York: Prentice, 1997.

Finding Information on Authors, Literary History, and Genres

General Guides to Literature in English

Evans, Denise, and Mary L. Onorato, eds. *Nineteenth-Century Literary Criticism*. Detroit: Gale. This series of annual volumes, first published in 1981, collects excerpts from the year's work in 19th-century criticism.

Hawkins-Dady, Mark. *Reader's Guide to Literature in English*. Chicago: Fitzroy, 1996.

Narms, Brigham, and Deborah Stanley, eds. *Contemporary Literary Criticism*. Detroit: Gale. This series of annual volumes, begun in 1973, collects excerpts from the year's work in criticism of contemporary writing.

Parker, Peter. *A Reader's Guide to Twentieth-Century Writers*. New York: Oxford UP, 1996.

Stringer, Jenny. *The Oxford Companion to Twentieth-Century Literature in English*. New York: Oxford UP, 1996.

Specialized Guides to Literature

Literature by women

Blain, Virginia, Patricia Clements, and Isobel Grundy. *The Feminist Companion to Literature in English: Women Writers from the Middle Ages to the Present*. New Haven: Yale U, 1990.

Shattock, Joanne. *The Oxford Guide to British Women Writers*. New York: Oxford UP, 1993.

National literature

Benson, Eugene, and L. W. Conolly. *Encyclopedia of Post-Colonial Literatures in English*. New York: Routledge, 1994.

Benson, Eugene, and William Toye, eds. *The Oxford Companion to Canadian Literature*. 2nd ed. Toronto: Oxford UP, 1997.

Bercovitch, Sacvan. *The Cambridge History of American Literature*. Cambridge: Cambridge UP, 1994.

Drabble, Margaret, ed. *The Oxford Companion to English Literature*. 6th ed. New York: Oxford UP, 2000.

Howatson, M. C., ed. *The Oxford Companion to Classical Literature*. 2nd ed. Oxford: Oxford UP, 1989.

New, William H., ed. *Encyclopedia of Literature in Canada*. Toronto: U of Toronto P, 2002.

Welch, Robert. *The Oxford Companion to Irish Literature*. Oxford: Clarendon, 1996.

Wilde, W. H., Joy Hooton, and Barry Andrews. *The Oxford Companion to Australian Literature*. 2nd ed. New York: Oxford UP, 1994.

Zell, Hans M. et al., eds. *A New Reader's Guide to African Literature*. 2nd, completely rev. and expanded ed. New York: Africana, 1983.

Children's literature

Carpenter, Humphrey, and Mari Prichard. *The Oxford Companion to Children's Literature*. New York: Oxford UP, 1999.

Drama

Though coverage will vary, most theatre handbooks will offer, in alphabetical order, information on topics such as these: (1) forms of theatre, such as Noh, puppet theatre, masque, and Kathakali; (2) important figures, including playwrights, characters, actors, directors, producers, patrons, and theatre owners; (3) technical terminology like *rake*, *grave trap*, and *cellar*; (4) famous theatres, such as the Strand, Imperial, and Phoenix; (5) histories of the theatre in various countries and the theatres and companies of those countries; and (6) the plays themselves.

Benson, Eugene, and L. W. Conolly, eds. *The Oxford Companion to Canadian Theatre*. Toronto: Oxford UP, 1990.

Berney, K. A. *Contemporary American Dramatists*. London: St. James, 1994.

———. *Contemporary British Dramatists*. London: St. James, 1994.

———. *Contemporary Women Dramatists*. London: St. James, 1994.

Bordman, Gerald Martin. *The Oxford Companion to American Theatre*. 2nd ed. New York: Oxford UP, 1992.

Hawkins-Dady, Mark. *The International Dictionary of Theatre*. Chicago: St. James, 1992.

Film

Dictionaries of film will cover a wide range of topics, including discussions of (1) principal figures, such as actors, directors, critics, producers, and writers; (2) film genres, such as abstract film, *film noir*, and gangster film; (3) film techniques and processes like deep focus, diffusion, and VistaVision; (4) analytic terms used in film criticism (e.g., *mise-en-scène*); (5) organizations, such as DEFA, SFTA, and the British Film Institute; and (6) other aspects of film production, manufacture, and distribution.

Bordwell, David, and Kristin Thompson. *Film Art: An Introduction*. 6th ed. New York: McGraw, 2001.

Kuhn, Annette, and Susannah Radstone. *The Women's Companion to International Film*. Berkeley: U of California P, 1994.

Pendergast, Tom, and Sara Pendergast, eds. *International Dictionary of Films and Filmmakers*. 4th ed. Detroit: St. James, 2000.

Penney, Edmund F. *The Facts on File Dictionary of Film and Broadcasting*. New York: Facts on File, 1991.

Thomson, David. *The New Biographical Dictionary of Film*. New York: Knopf, 2002.

Poetry

Most handbooks of poetry will discuss (1) technical devices, such as rhyme and rhythm; (2) forms, such as the sonnet and haiku; (3) philosophies or schools, such as Imagist poetry and concrete poetry; and (4) the history and tradition of poetry.

Hamilton, Ian. *The Oxford Companion to Twentieth-Century Poetry in English*. New York: Oxford UP, 1994.

Packard, William. *The Poet's Dictionary: A Handbook of Prosody and Poetic Devices*. 1st ed. New York: Harper, 1994. Apt, clever, and effective examples of techniques, forms, and principles.

Short stories

Haerens, Margaret, and Drew Kalasky, eds. *Short Story Criticism*. Detroit: Gale. A series of annual volumes, first published in 1988, containing criticism on selected short stories.

Biographical Dictionaries and Bibliographies

Most biographical dictionaries contain not only information about authors' lives but also bibliographies of their work and bibliographies of works written about them.

Brown, Susan W., ed. *Contemporary Novelists*. 7th ed. New York: St. James, 2000.

Dictionary of Literary Biography. Detroit: Gale. A multivolume series covering various literary periods.

Kirkpatrick, D. L., ed. *Contemporary Poets*. 4th ed. New York: St. Martin's, 1985.

Magnusson, Magnus, ed. *Cambridge Biographical Dictionary*. New York: Cambridge UP, 1990. Over 19 000 entries ranging from the classical to the current, from Socrates to Madonna. This is not a literary reference work; its range fills in the gaps left by works more closely focused on literature.

Rooney, Terry M., and Jennifer Gariepy, eds. *Contemporary Authors*. Detroit: Gale. This series of annual volumes, first published in 1967, collects short pieces of literary biography on selected writers.

Sutherland, John. *The Stanford Companion to Victorian Fiction*. Stanford: Stanford UP, 1989.

Identifying Allusions: Mythical, Religious, Symbolic, and Other References

Allusions are references to well-known figures, places, events, or sayings from mythology, religion, or literature. Often allusions work by describing a figure, event, or place in terms of a counterpart from the past. The decline of common knowledge of the Bible, of classical mythology, and of some standard texts like Shakespeare's means that the modern reader is likely to miss many allusions. These dictionaries and guides are thus invaluable resources.

Allusions—General

Cole, Sylvia, and Abraham H. Lass. *The Facts on File Dictionary of Modern Allusions*. New York: Checkmark, 2001.

Lass, Abraham. *Dictionary of Allusions*. London: Sphere, 1989. Short but invaluable guide that includes not only figures and events from mythology, literature, and the Bible but also well-known sayings, like "Inherit the wind."

Webber, Elizabeth, and Mike Feinsilber. *Merriam-Webster's Dictionary of Allusions*. Springfield, MA: Merriam-Webster, 1999.

Mythology, Religion, and Folklore

Dictionaries and encyclopedias of mythology, religion, and folklore will normally contain, in alphabetical order, discussions of (1) principal figures, both historical and mythical, including their origins, attributes, feats, symbologies, and relationships to the cultures with which they are associated; (2) important events, such as the biblical flood; (3) significant artifacts, such as the Golden Fleece of Greek mythology or the Ark of the Covenant of the Old Testament; (4) cities, temples, rivers, mountains, and other important places; and (5) significant philosophical principles, religious doctrines, superstitions, songs, and other aspects of a particular mythology or religion. Most works are copiously illustrated and many include maps and genealogies.

Achtemeier, Paul J., ed. *Harper's Bible Dictionary*. San Francisco: Harper, 1985.

Brunvald, Jan Harold. *American Folklore: An Encyclopedia*. New York: Garland, 1996.

Bulfinch, Thomas. *Complete Mythology*. London: Spring, 1989.

Hammond, N. G. L., and H. H. Scullard. *The Oxford Classical Dictionary*. 3rd ed. London: Oxford UP, 1996.

Hinnells, John R., ed. *A New Dictionary of Religions*. Oxford: Penguin, 1995. Includes entries on African, Amerindian, Arctic, and other religions as well as the major world religions.

Jeffrey, David L., ed. *A Dictionary of Biblical Tradition in English Literature*. Grand Rapids, MI: Eerdmans, 1992.

Jones, Alison. *Larousse Dictionary of World Folklore*. Edinburgh: Larousse, 1995.

Larrington, Carolyne, ed. *The Woman's Companion to Mythology*. London: Pandora, 1997, © 1992. [Previous title: *The Feminist Companion to Mythology*]

Dictionaries of Symbols

Many things have traditional as well as personal symbolic significance: objects, whether natural or manufactured; properties, such as colour and taste; processes, such as journey and growth; and abstracts, such as dreams and emotions. A dictionary of symbols explains both the more common symbolic meaning of a word and the less obvious meaning that an individual writer or culture may attach to it.

Carr-Gomm, Sarah. *Dictionary of Symbols in Art: The Illustrated Key to Western Painting and Sculpture*. London: Duncan Baird, 2000.

Chevalier, Jean. *A Dictionary of Symbols*. Oxford: Blackwell, 1994.

Cirlot, Juan Eduardo. *A Dictionary of Symbols*. Trans. by Jack Sage. Mineola, NY: Dover, 2002.

Dictionaries of Quotations

Dictionaries of quotations are designed to help you discover the source of a familiar quotation and its significance in its original context.

Andrews, Robert. *Columbia Dictionary of Quotations*. New York: Columbia UP, 1993.

Bartlett, John G. *Familiar Quotations*. 15th ed. Boston: Little, 1980.

The Concise Oxford Dictionary of Proverbs. [Comp. by] John Simpson and Jennifer Speake. 3rd ed. New York: Oxford UP, 1998.

Colombo, John Robert. *The Dictionary of Canadian Quotations*. Toronto: Stoddart, 1991.

Knowles, Elizabeth. *The Oxford Dictionary of Quotations*. 5th ed. New York: Oxford UP, 1999.

The New Beacon Book of Quotations by Women. [Comp. by] Rosalie Maggio. Boston: Beacon, 1996.

The New Penguin Dictionary of Modern Quotations. [Comp. by] Robert Andrews, with the assistance of Kate Hughes. London: Penguin, 2000.

Dictionaries of Names

Dictionaries of names are generally arranged alphabetically and include the symbolic meanings of names, their origins, and their historical and/or literary significance.

Davis, J. Madison, and A. Daniel Frankforter. *The Shakespeare Name Dictionary*. New York: Garland, 1995.

Goring, Rosemary. *The Larousse Dictionary of Literary Characters*. Edinburgh: Larousse, 1993.

Rintoul, M. C. *A Dictionary of Real People and Places in Fiction*. London: Routledge, 1993.

Room, Adrian. *Cassell Dictionary of Proper Names*. New York: Cassell, 1994, © 1992. [Previous title: *Brewer's Dictionary of Names*]

Checking Word Meanings and Usage

Dictionaries of Specialized Terms

The specialized diction of art, music, theatre, medicine, law, and other fields is necessary for essays on these topics; this diction is also, of course, found throughout literature.

The Book of Jargon. [Comp. by] Don Ethan Miller. New York: Macmillan, 1981. Divided into sections and subsections, such as Business–Advertising. Within these subsections the book is organized alphabetically and is quite comprehensive.

Colman, Andrew M. *A Dictionary of Psychology.* New York: Oxford UP, 2001.

Dictionary of Anthropology. Ed. Charlotte Seymour-Smith. New York: Macmillan, 1987.

Dictionary of Ecology and Environmental Science. Ed. Henry W. Art. New York: Holt, 1995.

Dictionary of Economics. [Comp. by] Frank Livesey. UK: Pitman, 1993.

Dictionary of New Information Technology: A Guide for Industry, Business, Education and the Home. [Comp. by] A. J. Meadows. London: Chapman, 1987.

Dictionary of Philosophy and Religion. [Comp. by] William L. Reese. Atlantic Highlands, NJ: Humanities, 1996.

Downing, Douglas, et al. *Dictionary of Computer and Internet Terms.* 7th ed. Hauppauge, NY: Barron's, 2000.

The New Harvard Dictionary of Music. [Comp. by] Don Michael Randel. Cambridge, MA: Belknap-Harvard UP, 1986. Broad scope, including non-Western music, popular music, and musical instruments of all cultures.

The Penguin Dictionary of Science. [Comp. by] E. B. Uvarov et al. 7th ed. New York: Penguin, 1993.

Pfaffenberger, Bryan. *Webster's New World Computer Dictionary.* 9th ed. New York: Hungry Minds, 2001.

The Prestel Dictionary of Art and Artists of the 20th Century. New York: Prestel, 2000.

The Random House Dictionary of Art and Artists. [Comp. by] David Piper. New York: Random, 1988.

Sadie, Stanley, and John Tyrrell, eds. *The New Grove Dictionary of Music and Musicians.* 2nd ed. New York: Grove, 2001.

Dictionaries of Catch Phrases, Idioms, and Slang

Dictionaries of catch phrases, clichés, idioms, and slang contain terms that may not find entry into even the best unabridged dictionaries.

Aylo, John. *The Oxford Dictionary of Modern Slang.* New York: Oxford UP, 1992.

Brandreth, Gyles. *Everyman's Modern Phrase and Fable*. London: Dent, 1990. Traces origins and explains British, Australian, and American usage.

Le Mot Juste: A Dictionary of Classical & Foreign Words & Phrases. New York: Random, 1991.

Partridge, Eric. *A Dictionary of Catch Phrases, American and British, from the Sixteenth Century to the Present Day*. Rev. and updated ed. Ed. Paul Beale. New York: Stein, 1992.

Random House Historical Dictionary of African-American Slang. New York: Penguin, 1994.

Room, Adrian. *Brewer's Dictionary of Phrase and Fable*. 16th ed. New York: HarperResource, 1999.

Rubinstein, Frankie. *A Dictionary of Shakespeare's Sexual Puns and Their Significance*. 2nd ed. New York: St. Martin's, 1995.

Schur, Norman W. *British English, A to Zed*. Rev. and updated ed. New York: Facts on File, 2001. Focuses on British usages that differ from American English, and gives American equivalents of English idioms, colloquialisms, and slang.

Dictionaries: Unabridged, Historical, and Etymological

An unabridged dictionary attempts to present a complete description of modern language usage. A historical dictionary traces the changing forms and meanings of a word through time. An etymological dictionary usually traces only the origins of a word.

Avis, Walter S., et al. *Gage Canadian Dictionary*. Rev. and expanded ed. Toronto: Gage, 1997.

Barber, Katherine, ed. *The Canadian Oxford Dictionary*. Toronto: Oxford UP, 1998.

Canadian Dictionary of the English Language. Toronto: Nelson, 1997.

Pearsall, Judy. *The Concise Oxford Dictionary*. 10th ed., rev. New York: Oxford UP, 2001. An abridged version of the *Oxford English Dictionary* (below), it is nonetheless a very useful historical dictionary.

Simpson, J. A., and Edmund S. C. Weiner. *Oxford English Dictionary*. 2nd ed. in 20 vols. Oxford: Oxford UP, 1989. The most complete historical and etymological dictionary with over 2 400 000 quotations.

Thesauruses

Thesauruses are usually simple compilations of synonyms of everyday words. Unfortunately for the person who relies on a thesaurus, there are no exact synonyms in the English language. Any word has nuances and shades of meaning that make it distinct from any other word, and using a word without knowing those nuances is liable to undermine the effectiveness of your work. Have a dictionary at hand when you use a thesaurus.

Kipfer, Barbara Ann, ed. *Roget's International Thesaurus*. 6th ed. New York: HarperResource, 2001.

Checking Format and Documentation

Editor's Association of Canada / Association canadienne des rédacteurs-réviseurs. *Editing Canadian English*. 2nd ed. Toronto: Macfarlane, 2000.

Gibaldi, Joseph, ed. *MLA Handbook for Writers of Research Papers*. 6th ed. New York: Modern Language Association, 2003.

Harnack, Andrew, and Eugene Kleppinger. *Online!: A Reference Guide to Using Internet Sources*. 3rd ed. New York: St. Martin's, 2001. Updates: <http.www.bedfordstmartins.com/online/>

Publication Manual of the American Psychological Association, 5th ed. Washington, D.C.: American Psychological Association, 2001.

Glossary of Rhetorical Terms[*]

Analyze To divide something into parts in order to understand both the parts and the whole. This can be done by systems analysis (where the object is divided into its interconnected parts), process analysis (where the object is divided into stages of development), and causal analysis (where the object is divided into the reasons that brought it into being, or into its consequences). The main purpose of analysis is to explain something, such as a concept, a text, an event, or a set of data, by examining its parts in detail. *See also* Content analysis; Textual analysis; Textual analysis, general categories for; Textual analysis, special categories for.

Causal analysis *See* Analyze.

Compare To show the similarities and differences between two things, or among more than two things, in order to reveal the qualities of each more clearly.

Comparison, basis of The common element in terms of which two or more things are compared. Topics that can be put in the form "Compare X and Y in terms of Z" specify the basis of comparison, Z. The basis of comparison tells you which features of the things you are comparing are relevant and thus gives you a focus for gathering information and writing your essay.

Comparison, methods of organizing The block method consists of organizing your middle paragraphs* so that you finish everything you have to say about one of the things you are comparing before taking up another. The point-by-point method consists of organizing your middle paragraphs so that in each paragraph or series of paragraphs you discuss only one aspect of each of the things you are comparing.

---

* Asterisks indicate terms defined elsewhere in the glossary.

Conclusion The concluding paragraph in your essay provides the chance for both you and your reader to step back from the essay and survey the development of your thesis.* The conclusion should restate the thesis, tie together the points developed in the middle paragraphs,* and mention the wider implications of the discussion, if any.

Content analysis The analysis of behaviour, data, written works, and other sources of information without regard to the form in which the information is communicated.

Context The social, historical, and/or cultural situation in which a text is written or produced.

Deductive and inductive structure These terms provide the most common way of making a distinction between essays that begin with the thesis (deductive structure) and essays that lead up to a thesis at or towards the end of the essay (inductive structure).

Development, methods of The uses of evidence and detail to give substance to a point.

Diction A writer's level of word usage (formal, informal, colloquial) and particular word choices. An aspect of style* that also contributes to tone.*

Discuss An ambiguous term frequently used in essay topics. It does not mean "summarize the relevant information." Check the essay topic carefully to determine whether you are expected

to analyze,* compare,* or evaluate* a body of information. "Discuss the significance of X in Y" means to analyze the relationship between X and Y; "discuss X and Y" means to compare X and Y; "discuss the validity of X" means to evaluate X.

Evaluate To determine the strengths or weaknesses of something—a plan, a performance, a work of art, or a theory, for example. Content evaluation usually asks you to evaluate an idea, position, argument, or viewpoint. Textual evaluation usually asks you to determine how effective the presentation of a theme* or thesis* is.

Evaluation, standard of A set of criteria based on accumulated judgments of things of the same kind that you can use as a standard against which to measure the material you are evaluating. The most common standards of evaluation are aesthetic (how effective is the relationship between form and content in the work?), logical (how convincing is the reasoning?), practical (will it work and is it useful?), and ethical (is it morally right or wrong?).

Evidence The factual information, examples, and references to and quotations from authorities that you use to support your thesis.

Genre and subgenre We use the term *genre* to refer to the broad kinds of text (e.g., novel, play, film). We use *subgenre* to refer to more specific types within the form (e.g., Gothic novel, Greek tragedy, *film noir*).

Inductive structure *See* Deductive structure.

Introduction The introductory paragraph prepares your reader both intellectually and emotionally for the essay to follow. It establishes the context by defining necessary terms, giving historical background, and so forth, and indicates the structure of the essay by mentioning, in order, the main points you plan to cover. The introduction usually ends with your thesis.*

Middle paragraphs Paragraphs between the introduction and conclusion that explain and illustrate subpoints of the thesis.* The purpose of each paragraph is defined by a topic sentence* that links the paragraph to the thesis. Middle paragraphs usually contain both explanations of the point made in the topic sentence and specific details illustrating that point. Transitional words and phrases show how points, explanations, and details are related.

Middle paragraphs, order of There are four common ways of organizing a sequence of middle paragraphs.

1. Chronological order: The arrangement of material according to units of time. The simplest chronological order starts with events furthest away in time and ends with events closest in time.

2. Spatial order: The arrangement of material according to locations in space. Spatial order may move from near to far, top to bottom, right to left, etc.

3. Logical order: The arrangement of material according to a chain of reasoning. The order in which material is presented is determined by the need to establish one point so that it will serve as the basis for the next.

4. Order of ascending interest: The arrangement of material to lead up to the most important or most interesting point. An order of ascending interest may also accommodate a chronological, spatial, or logical order. *See also* Comparison, Methods of organizing.

Persona The mask or second self created by the author, especially in poetry and in ironic essays where the stated thesis and the implied thesis are completely different. In "A Modest Proposal," for example, Swift creates a persona who argues that eating the poor is the best way to solve the problems created by the poor. Swift's real thesis is that his readers need to see the Irish poor as human beings and find a humane solution to their problems.

Primary source Any first-hand source of information, such as the literary work you are analyzing, a performance you have seen, your own observations and experience, the raw data from a scientific experiment, or the historical documents on which historians base their interpretations of events.

Process analysis *See* Analyze.

Research paper An extended analysis, comparison, or evaluation essay that includes information from secondary sources* as well as from primary sources.* A research paper is not merely a summary of other writers' ideas; it is an essay in which you develop your own opinion on your subject and use your research material as part of your evidence to support that opinion.

Secondary source Material that provides information about, or criticism and analysis of, a primary source. A historian, for example, may write a book (secondary source) interpreting the meaning of historical documents (primary sources). An anthropologist may collect data (primary sources) about various cultures and write an article comparing those cultures (secondary source). A literary critic may write a review (secondary source) of a new novel (primary source). In secondary sources, material is selected and presented to support a particular point of view.

Structure The selection and ordering of parts in a written work or performance. *See also* Middle paragraphs, order of.

Style The distinctive way of writing that belongs to a particular writer. For analytic purposes, it is helpful to see style as consisting of a writer's use of diction,* image and symbol, figurative language and allusions, and sentence structure.

Subgenre *See* Genre and subgenre.

Subject The text, issue, theory, proposal, and so on that a writer writes about. If your essay topic is "Assess the role of the peasants in the French Revolution," the subject of your essay is the role of the peasants in the French Revolution.

Systems analysis *See* Analyze.

Textual analysis The analysis of written works or performances (such as plays, television programs, and films) with attention both to what is being said and to how the work or performance is presented. Your purpose in analyzing a text is to determine the relation between the work's form (its manner of presentation) and its content.

Textual analysis, general categories for The parts into which you can divide the text you are analyzing if you are not familiar with the special categories appropriate to that particular kind of text (e.g., play, film, poem). The general categories of textual analysis are subject,* structure,* development,* tone,* and theme* or thesis.*

Textual analysis, special categories for The categories commonly used in literary criticism and related fields to analyze written works and performances.

Theme The main statement made about a subject in fiction, drama, poetry, film, and imaginative literature generally. A theme is usually implied, whereas a thesis* is usually stated directly.

Thesis The main statement made about a subject in nonfiction. The purpose of the essay is to develop and confirm the thesis. In your essay, the thesis statement will consist of an opinion with one or more reasons to support it. Like the hypothesis in a scientific experiment, the thesis is the statement or assertion you are proving.

Tone The attitude a writer takes to a subject and to a reader, the equivalent of "tone of voice" in conversation. The tone of a work can be described as serious or light, witty or ponderous, condescending or apologetic, and in many other similar ways. In your own essays, tone can be thought of as a product of diction* and pronouns of address.

Topic sentence The sentence in a middle paragraph,* usually at the beginning, that states the main idea of the paragraph and shows how the material in the paragraph supports the thesis* of the whole essay. Topic sentences are thus the bridge between the generalization you make in your thesis statement and the specific details you give in your middle paragraphs. An "umbrella" topic sentence covers points made in more than one paragraph.

Index

abbreviations
  apostrophe, 446
  marking symbol, 373
  use of, 463–64
  exercises: abbreviations, 465
Aboriginal, capitalization, 463
academic disciplines, capitalization,
  463
academic essays
  audience for, 4–5, 148–51,
    155–56
  basic structure, 5
  deductive structure, 46–47, 84
  purposes, 3–4, 36
  stages of writing, 9–10
  sample: film analysis, 5–8
  exercises: writing essays, 10
active voice
  active or passive voice, 429–30
  exercises: active or passive voice,
    430, 431
A.D. and *B.C.*, 464
"Addiction in Free Markets." *see*
  Alexander, Bruce K.
ad hominem argument, 124, 125
adjectives
  beginning sentences with, 404
  hyphens with two words used as
    one, 460
  parallel adjectives, 392
"Adlestrop" by Edward Thomas,
  370
  textual analysis, 367–69
ad populem argument, 124, 125
adverbs
  conjunctive adverbs, 382, 387,
    451
  parallel adverbs, 392–93
ad verecundiam argument, 124,
  125
aesthetic standard of evaluation,
  15–16, 143, 145–46
affect and *effect,* 413
airplane names, italics use, 458
Alexander, Bruce K., and Stefa
  Shaler, "Addiction in Free
  Markets," 198–201
  discussion: comparison essay,
    102–13
  exercises: reading and writing,
    201–2
all right, 413
allude and *elude,* 414
allusion and *illusion,* 414
allusions. *see also* figurative language and allusions

about, 70, 513
  in drama, 491, 504
  in fiction, 70, 490, 497
  in film and television, 491, 507
  in nonfiction, 36, 490
  in poetry, 491, 500
  reference sources about allu-
    sions, 513–15
  as style element, 70
  exercises: on readings, 241
a lot, 413
American and Canadian spelling,
  466
American literature, reference
  sources, 511
American Psychological Association
  (APA) documentation. *see*
  APA documentation
among and *between,* 414
amount and *number,* 414
ampersand (&), 464
analogy
  arguments by, 120, 124
  in nonfiction, 36
  exercises: on readings, 228, 262
analysis. *see also* causal analysis;
    content analysis; process
    analysis; systems analysis;
    textual analysis
  about, 13–14
  analysis, definition, 13, 519
  first step in evaluation, 15–16
  exercises: clarifying essay topics,
    21
and usage, 395
anthologies (books). *see* APA documentation; MLA documentation
APA documentation (American
    Psychological Association),
    481–84
  articles, 482–83
  books, 483
  electronic sources (database, CD-
    ROM, Internet), 483–84
  government documents, 484
  in-text citations, 481–82
  references about APA documen-
    tation, 484
  References (full bibliographical
    information), 481–84
  References format, 482
  title page format, 377–78
apologetic expressions in essays,
  412
apostrophe, 444–47

abbreviations, 446
contractions, 440, 444, 445
dates, 446
indefinite pronouns, 444, 445
marking symbol, 373
plural and singular nouns, 444,
  445
plural letters (*x's* and *y's*), 446
not with possessive pronouns,
  440, 445
with possessives, 444–46
time expressions, 446
words referred to as words, 446
exercises: apostrophe, 446–47,
  467
exercises: possessive pronouns,
  440–41
appositives
  beginning sentences with, 405
  commas with, 448
argumentation in critiques, 117–40.
    see also fallacies; persuasive
    essays
  analogies, 120, 124
  authorities, 120, 123–24, 125,
    133–34, 137
  causal argument, 119, 122–23,
    125, 132–34
  deductive argument, 118,
    121–22, 125
  emotional appeals, 120–21, 124,
    125, 133–34
  evidence, 119–21, 123–26,
    132–34
  examples as evidence, 123, 125
  inductive argument, 119, 122,
    125
  sample topic: critique of Byfield's
    "Health Canada," 131–38
  exercises: argument and evi-
    dence, 139–40
  exercises: evaluation by logical
    standard, 118–21
  exercises: on readings, 276
articles. *see also* APA documenta-
    tion ; MLA documentation
  APA documentation, 483–84
  evaluation of research articles,
    169–70, 172, 175–76,
    186–87
  how to find, 169–73
  MLA documentation, 480
  working bibliographies, 173–74
  sample: working bibliography,
    174
art works, italics, 458

as, using subject pronouns after, 439

as and *like,* 416

as and *since,* 396

ascending interest order. *see* order, ascending interest

Ash, James, "To Peacekeep or Not to Peacekeep" (sample essay), 342–43

sample: tree diagram, 20

exercises: logical standard of evaluation, 139

assess, definition, 16

atmosphere. *see* tone

audience

academic essays, 4–5, 148–50, 155–56

as context, 68, 488–89, 492

ethos and, 129–30, 137, 155–56, 157

informal essays, 4–5

persuasive essays, 143, 145, 148–50

tone as establishing relationship to, 71

exercises: audience, 10

exercises: on readings, 213, 214, 220, 269, 276, 312, 316

authorities

arguments from, 120, 123–24, 125

evaluating use, 133–34, 137

authors, reference sources, 510–13

auxiliary verbs. *see* verbs

balanced construction sentence patterns, 403

B.C. and *A.D.,* 464

between and *among,* 414

bias in persuasive essays, 155–56

Bible, reference sources, 513–14

bibliographies. *see* APA documentation; MLA documentation; working bibliographies

biographical dictionaries and bibliographies, 512–13

Black, Maggie, "Wanted: The Right to Refuse," 203–5

discussion: ethical standard of evaluation, 145

discussion: thesis statements, 127

exercises: argument and evidence, 139–40

exercises: comparison, 115

exercises: writing summaries, 41

exercises: reading and writing, 205

block method of organization

comparison essays, 108, 110, 519

persuasive essays, 151, 153–54

exercises: organization (block and point-by-point), 115

Bond, E.J., "*The English Patient* Rallies (Letters)," 334–35

discussion: emotional appeals, 121

exercises: reading and writing, 341

Bongaarts, John, "Population: Ignoring Its Impact," 206–9

exercises: reading and writing, 209–10

books. *see also* APA documentation; MLA documentation

APA documentation, 483–84

evaluation for research papers, 169–70, 172, 175–76

how to find, 169–73

MLA documentation, 478–79

working bibliographies, 173–74

sample: working bibliography, 174

Boolean searches of online resources, 169, 171

brackets in quotations for insertions, 472

brainstorming

for ideas, 16–18

research topics, 163–64

sample: brainstorming diagram, 18

exercises: brainstorming, 21

Byfield, Ted, "Health Canada Inadvertently Discloses Facts Planned Parenthood Would Like to Suppress," 211–13

discussion: critique, 131–38

exercises: reading and writing, 213–14

Canadian Literary Periodicals (Reference Press) database, 171

Canadian literature, reference sources, 510–11

Canadian or American spelling, 466

capitalization of words, 462–63

capitalization uses, 462–63

marking symbol, 373

not for emphasis, 405

proper nouns, 462

exercises: capitalization, 465

causal analysis

definition, 519

about, 25–27

argument, 119, 122–23

basic questions to ask, 25–27, 67

categorizing causes and effects (general topic), 30

categorizing parts (general topic), 27–28

diagram of discovery questions, 25

perspectives (social, psychological, economic, political), 28–30, 486–87

persuasive essays, 146–47

sample: analysis of Byfield's "Health Canada," 132–34

sample: categorizing causes and effects (general topic), 30

exercises: gathering material, 41

exercises: on readings, 262

causal argument, 119, 122–23, 125, 132–34

CD-ROM articles. *see also* working bibliographies

APA documentation, 483

evaluation of resources for research, 169–70, 172, 175–76

finding references in electronic sources, 169–71

how to find, 169–73

MLA documentation, 480

sample: working bibliography, 174

chain of reasoning

defined, 34

textual analysis essays, 85–86

characterization

drama, 167–68, 177, 488–89, 502–3

fiction, 488, 495–96

film and television, 488–89, 506

poetry, 76, 488–89, 499

textual analysis categories (development method), 488–89

sample topic: textual analysis (poetry), 76

children's literature, reference sources, 511

"Choosing Up Sides." *see* Wiwa, Ken

chronological order, 69–70, 76, 521

circular reasoning, 122, 125

clarifying essay topics (stage 1), 11–21

about, 12–16

checklist for your assignments, 19–20

comparison essays, 14–15, 102–3, 105

content analysis (general topic), 24–25, 28

evaluation standards, 15–16, 117–18, 131–32, 144–45

persuasive essays, 142–46

research papers, 162–65

specialized terms in topics, 16, 75

stages model of writing (stage 1), 9–10

textual analysis, 66, 75

sample topic: content analysis (independent living), 28

sample topic: research papers (*Hamlet*), 164–65

sample topic: textual analysis (poetry), 75

exercises: clarifying essay topics, 21

exercises: identifying standards, 158–59

clauses

about, 379–80

colons with clauses, 453

comma splice correction, 387–88

commas with clauses, 447, 448

identifying, 379–80

main clauses, 380–81, 447

mixed constructions, 397–98

non-restrictive and restrictive clauses, 448

parallel clauses, 392–93, 404

semicolons with clauses, 450–52

subordinate clauses, 380–81, 397–98, 405, 439, 447

verbs in clauses, 379–80
exercises: identifying clauses, 380
exercises: identifying main and subordinate clauses, 381–82
exercises: mixed constructions, 399, 400
exercises: parallel clauses, 393
coherence as aesthetic standard, 143
college words, capitalization, 463
colons, 453–54
explanatory clauses and phrases, 453
marking symbol, 373
quotation marks, 458
quotations, 453
series and lists, 453
exercises: colons, 454, 456–57
colour words for racial/ethnic groups, not to capitalize, 463
comma fault. *see* comma splices
commas, 447–49
appositives, 448
clauses, 447, 448
conjunctive adverbs, 387
dates, 449
explanatory material, 455
marking symbol, 373
non-restrictive modifiers, 448
parenthetical expressions, 448–49
phrases, 447
place names, 449
quotation marks, 458
quotations, 449
series and lists, 447–48
exercises: commas, 450, 456, 459–60
exercises: modifiers, 449–50
comma splices
how to correct, 386–88
marking symbol, 373
exercises: comma splices, 388, 389, 400
compare with and *compare to,* 414
comparison and comparison essays, 101–15
definition, 14, 102, 519
aesthetic standards, 143, 145–46
block organization, 108, 110, 519
checklist for your assignments, 113
clarifying essay topics, 14–15, 34, 85, 102–5
comparison basis, 14–15, 102–5, 113, 519
comparison objects, 102–3, 113
drafting, 107–8
gathering and categorizing material, 103–5
matching categories of textual analysis, 103–7
outlines, 108
point-by-point organization, 108, 110, 519
revising, 110–13
similarities and differences, 103, 106, 109
thesis statements, 105–7, 109–10

sample essay: "Perspectives on Addictions," 349–51
sample topic: comparison (addiction explanations), 102–13
exercises: clarifying essay topics, 21
exercises: comparison basis, 114–15
exercises: organization (block or point-by-point), 115
exercises: thesis statements, 114–15
exercises: on readings, 205, 210, 228, 245, 262, 272, 291, 300, 303, 312, 341
comparisons in sentences
mixed constructions with incomplete comparisons, 398
exercises: mixed constructions, 399, 400
complex sentences. *see* sentences
"The Complex Skill of Independent Living." *see* Jones, A.
compound-complex sentences. *see* sentences
compound sentences. *see* sentences
compound words and hyphens, 460
computer programs
spelling checkers, 372, 466
word processing, 375–76, 478
conciseness
how to be concise, 419–20
passive voice, 429–30
exercises: active or passive voice, 430, 431
exercises: conciseness, 421–22
conclusions
definition, 520
about, 61–63
checklist for your assignments, 95–96
comparison essays, 112–13
content analysis essays, 61–63
context (statement of broader context), 61–63, 95–97
critiques, 131, 138
persuasive essays, 157–58
problems and solutions, 61–62
purposes, 5
research essays, 189, 192
sketching conclusions, 49
textual analysis essays, 95–97
sample: comparison (addiction explanations), 112–13
sample: content analysis (independent living), 62–63
sample: critique, 131
sample: film analysis, 7–8
sample: persuasive essay, 156–58, 157
sample: textual analysis (poetry), 96–97
exercises: content analysis (independent living), 64
exercises: textual analysis (poetry), 99–100
exercises: on readings, 288
conjunctions, coordinate
and use, 395
comma splice corrections, 387

compound sentences, 382, 447
coordinate constructions, 394
examples, 382, 395
parallel constructions, 392–93
semicolon use, 450–51
exercises: faulty coordination, 395
exercises: parallel constructions, 393
conjunctions, correlative
coordinate constructions, 394
parallel constructions, 392–93
exercises: parallel constructions, 393
conjunctions, subordinate
examples, 381
faulty subordination, 395–96
exercises: faulty subordination, 397, 399
conjunctive adverbs
comma splice correction, 387
compound sentences, 382
examples, 382
semicolons, 451
Conley, Tim, "*The English Patient* Rallies (Letters)," 335
exercises: reading and writing, 341
content analysis, 24–41. *see also* content analysis of general subject; content analysis of nonfiction
definition, 14, 24, 520
about, 13–14, 25–28
categorizing parts (general topic), 27–28
checklists for your assignments, 49, 63
diagram of discovery questions, 25
perspectives (social, psychological, economic, political), 28–30, 486–87
exercises: gathering material, 41
content analysis of general subject, 24–30
about, 24
clarifying essay topics, 24–25
diagram of discovery questions, 25
drafting, 45–49
formulating thesis statement, 43–45
gathering material, 25–28
sample topic: content analysis (independent living), 28–30, 43–49, 52–63
sample topic essay: "Complex Skill of Independent Living," 344–45
content analysis of nonfiction, 30–40
about, 30–31
checklists for your assignments, 40–41
detail and evidence, 35–36, 488, 492
development methods, 33–35, 47
gathering material, 31–38
how to identify main ideas, 32–33

how to identify subjects, 31–32, 72–73
summaries of content, 38
sample topic: "Kiddy Thinks," 38–40
content analysis of secondary sources
research papers, 163, 166
context in essays
conclusions include broader context, 61–63, 95–97
introductions include context, 92–93, 111
quotations include context, 470, 471
context in textual analysis
about, 37–38, 68, 520
audience and, 68, 488–89, 492
drama, 489, 502
fiction, 68, 488, 495
film and television, 68, 489, 505
nonfiction, 37–38, 488, 492
poetry, 489, 499
of subject of essay, 37, 68
textual analysis general category, 68, 488–89
of writer of essay, 37–38, 68
sample topic: textual analysis (poetry), 75
exercises: on readings, 241, 276
continuity devices. see transitions
contractions
avoid in academic essays, 411–12
not to use of for have (would've or would have, not would of), 425
possessive pronoun confusions, 440, 444, 445
Cook, Markham, "The English Patient Rallies (Letters)," 335–36
exercises: reading and writing, 341
coordinate conjunctions. see conjunctions, coordinate
coordinate constructions
faulty coordination, 394–95
marking symbol, 373
exercises: faulty coordination, 395, 399
correlative conjunctions. see conjunctions, correlative
critiques. see evaluation essays and critiques

dangling modifiers. see modifiers
dashes, 454–55
marking symbol, 373
quotation marks, 458
uses of dash or pair of dashes, 454–55
exercises: colons or dashes, 454, 455
exercises: dashes, 456–57, 459–60
database articles
APA documentation, 483
evaluation of articles for research, 169–70, 172, 175–76
how to find, 169–73

MLA documentation, 480
sample: working bibliography, 174
dates
apostrophe, 446
B.C. and A.D., 464
comma use, 449
Davis, Wade, "The Ticking Bomb," 215–19
discussion: inductive argument, 119
exercises: comparison, 114
exercises: structure (inductive or deductive), 64
exercises: reading and writing, 220
days of week, 463
deductive argument, 118, 121–22, 125
deductive structure
definition, 46, 84, 520
in paragraphs, 59, 130
statement in draft introduction, 46–47
textual analysis essays, 84, 86
thesis in deductive essays, 84, 520
exercises: revising structure (inductive or deductive), 64
defining terms. see also clarifying essay topics (stage 1)
essay topics, 12–13
persuasive essays, 145–47
reference sources for defining terms, 509–10, 515–16
research papers, 162–63
sample topic: textual analysis (poetry), 76
demonstrative pronouns for continuity, 406
detail and evidence
about, 35–36, 520
arguments from, 119–21, 123–26, 132–34
authorities (quotations and references), 36
evaluation by logical standard, 118–21, 130
examples as evidence, 36, 133–34
facts and figures, 36, 119–20, 123, 125, 133–34
introductions not to include, 57
kinds of evidence, 119–21
narrative details, 36
nonfiction, 35–36, 488, 492
problems and solutions (paragraph development), 59–60
textual analysis special category, 488–89
sample topic: analysis of Byfield's "Health Canada," 132–34
sample topic: film analysis, 8
sample topic: nonfiction ("Kiddy Thinks"), 39
sample topic: textual analysis (poetry), 76
exercises: logical standards, 139
exercises: on readings (details), 228, 281, 299, 300, 312

exercises: on readings (evidence), 205, 209, 213, 220, 276, 283, 287, 288, 330, 341
development methods
definition, 68, 520
about, 33–35, 68–69
detail and evidence, 35–36
textual analysis, 68–69, 84–86, 488–89
textual analysis (nonfiction), 33–35, 47
sample topic: nonfiction ("Kiddy Thinks"), 39
sample topic: textual analysis (poetry), 76
dictionaries, 513–17
allusions, 513–15
biographical, 512–13
etymological, historical, and unabridged, 517
names, 515
phrases, idioms, and slang, 516–17
quotations, 515
specialized terms, 13, 515
symbols, 514
diction as style element
definition, 70, 520
in drama, 168, 491, 503
emotional appeals, 120–21, 124, 125, 133–34
in fiction, 70, 490, 496–97
in nonfiction, 490, 493
in poetry, 76, 491, 500
textual analysis special category, 70, 490–91
sample topic: textual analysis (poetry), 76
exercises: on readings, 201, 288, 299
diction in academic essays, 411–22
definition, 411
how to be concise, 419–20
marking symbol, 373
problems and solutions, 411–12
usage problems, 413–18
exercises: conciseness, 419–20
exercises: level of diction, 412–13
exercises: usage, 418
different from, 415
differ from and differ with, 415
directions, capitalization, 463
direct speech and quotation marks, 457
discovery techniques. see brainstorming; freewriting; tree diagramming
discuss, definition, 16, 520
disinterested and uninterested, 418
dividing words at line end with hyphens, 461
documentation, 476–84. see also APA documentation; MLA documentation; quotations
factual information, 477
final editing of research papers, 192
marking symbol, 373
paraphrased material, 476, 478

reference resources for documentation, 481, 484, 518
reference resources for documenting electronic sources, 173, 481
what to document, 476–77
drafts and drafting (stage 4)
about, 45–49
checklist for your assignments, 87–88
comparison essays, 107–8
content analysis essays (nonfiction), 45–49
critiques, 127, 134
draft outlines, 45–49, 86–87
outlines, 45–49, 86–87, 108, 150–52, 154
persuasive essays, 150–52, 154
research papers, 181–82, 189–90
sketches of introduction and conclusion, 49
stages model of writing (stage 4), 9–10
textual analysis essays, 84–87, 86–87
sample: draft outline (comparison essay), 108
sample: draft outline (independent living), 48–49
sample: draft outline (persuasive essay), 152, 154
sample: draft outline (textual analysis), 87
sample topic: content analysis (independent living), 45–49
exercises: draft outlines, 50, 115, 140
drama (textual analysis)
characterization, 167–68, 177, 488–89, 502–3
chart of general and special categories, 488–91
context, 68, 488–89, 502
development methods, 68–69
diction, 70, 168, 491, 503
figurative language and allusions, 70, 168, 491, 504
pacing, 168, 491, 504
quotations format, 474
reference sources on drama, 511
setting, 167, 488–89, 502
structure, 69–70, 167, 177, 488–89, 503
style, 491
subgenre, 68, 167, 488–89, 502
subject, 72–73, 166, 488–89, 502
textual analysis questions, 502–5
theme, 168, 491
theme identification by connecting textual features, 72–73, 505
tone, 71, 168, 491, 504–5
sample topic: combining resource material (Hamlet), 177
sample topic: gathering material for textual analysis (Hamlet), 166–68
sample topic: research papers (Hamlet), 164–68

sample research essay: "The Making of the Tragic Hero: The Graveyard Scene in *Hamlet*," 362–66

economic perspective content analysis, 28–30, 486–87
sample topic: categorizing (general topic), 28–30
editing techniques for film and television, 70, 491, 507
Edwards, Caterina, "Where They Have to Take You In," 221–28
exercises: reading and writing, 228
effect and *affect*, 413
e.g., use of, 464
either ... or and subject–verb agreement, 429
electronic sources documentation (database, CD-ROM, Internet). *see also* APA documentation; MLA documentation
evaluation of resources for research, 169–70, 170, 172, 175–76, 186–87
how to find, 169–73
References (APA), 483–84
Works Cited (MLA), 480
ellipsis in quotations, 471–72
elude and *allude,* 414
elusive and *illusory,* 415
embedded sentence patterns, 403
"Embraced by the Needle." *see* Maté, Gabor
eminent and *imminent,* 415
emotional appeals
definition, 120
argumentation using emotional appeals, 120–21, 124–25, 133–34
emphasis
active or passive voice, 429–30
capitalization, not to use, 405, 463
italics, not to use, 405
italics, use, 459
sentence coordination and subordination, 394–95
sentence structure, 402–4
transitional words and phrases, 407–8
exercises: active or passive voice, 430, 431
exercises: faulty coordination and subordination, 399
encyclopedia articles, documentation. *see* articles
encyclopedias for research subject overview, 165
English literature, reference sources, 511
"*The English Patient* Debate," 331–38
"*The English Patient* Rallies (Letters)," 333–36
discussion: reference to authorities, 120
exercises: reading and writing, 341

essay format
handwritten essays, 376, 458
marking symbol, 373
title page, 376–78
word-processed essays, 375–76
essays. *see* academic essays
essay structure. *see* organization and structure
essay topics. *see also* clarifying essay topics (stage 1); gathering material (stage 2)
brainstorming for ideas, 16–18
defining unfamiliar terms, 12–13, 162–63
directions on essay topics, 13–16, 163
freewriting for ideas, 16–17
limiting, 16–17
limiting research topics, 163–64
limiting with basis of comparison, 107
tree diagramming for ideas, 16–18, 20
when to use primary or secondary sources, 19, 164–66
sample topic: content analysis (general topic), 28–30
exercises: clarifying essay topics, 21
exercises: freewriting, brainstorming, tree diagramming, 21
etc., use of, 464
ethical standard of evaluation
about, 117
categorizing pro-con arguments, 146–48
clarifying essay topics, 15–16, 144–45
sample: pro-con categories chart, 148
ethos in evaluation and persuasive essays, 129–30, 137, 155–56, 157
evaluation essays and critiques, 116–40. *see also* argumentation in critiques; persuasive essays
definition, 15, 520
about, 15–16, 117
checklist for your assignments, 138–39
clarifying essay topics, 15–16, 117–18, 131–32
conclusions, 131, 138
drafting, 127, 135
ethos, 129–30, 137, 155–56, 157
evaluation chart, 125, 126, 134
gathering material for, 118–25
introductions, 129–30, 137
middle paragraphs, 127–29, 130, 136, 137
revising, 128–31
standards of evaluation (logical, aesthetic, practical, ethical), 15–16, 117, 126, 142–45, 146–48
strengths and weaknesses, 125–27, 134, 136
structure, 127, 128–29, 136

thesis statement, 125–28, 134, 135–36
sample: conclusion, 131
sample: draft outline, 135
sample: evaluation chart, 134
sample: introduction, 129–30
sample: middle paragraphs, 130
sample: thesis statements, 127, 134, 136
sample essay: Jones, D., "Reflecting on Population," 352–54
sample topic: critique of Byfield's "Health Canada," 131–38
exercises: clarifying essay topics, 21
exercises: critique draft, 140
exercises: evaluation by logical standard, 139
exercises: thesis statements, 139, 159
evaluation of resources for research, 170, 172, 175–76, 186–87
evaluation standards
    definition, 15, 520
    aesthetic, 15–16, 143, 145–46
    basic questions, 15
    categorizing arguments, 146–48
    clarifying essay topics, 15–16, 131–32
    ethical, 15–16, 117, 144–47
    gathering material using, 146–48
    logical, 117–18
    practical standard, 15–16, 117, 143–44, 146–48
    thesis statement includes, 126, 134, 135–36
    using several standards, 145
    sample: pro-con categories chart, 148
    exercises: identifying standards, 158–59
    exercises: on readings, 209, 214, 220, 262, 276, 306, 325, 341
evidence and detail. *see* detail and evidence
examine, definition, 16
examples as argument, 123, 125, 137
exclamation marks
    within parentheses, 456
    with quotation marks, 458
explain, definition, 16
explanatory material
    colon use, 453
    parentheses use, 455–56

facts and figures as argument, 119–20, 123, 125, 133–34. *see also* detail and evidence
fallacies, 122–25. *see also* argumentation in critiques
    ad hominem argument, 124, 125
    ad populem argument, 124, 125
    ad verecundiam (argument for respect), 124, 125
    post hoc (single cause/single outcome), 122–23, 125
    straw man fallacy, 123, 125
    sample: analysis of Byfield's "Health Canada," 132–34

exercises: argument and evidence, 139–40
exercises: on readings, 276
family names and titles, capitalization, 463
faulty parallelism. *see* parallelism
female authors, reference sources, 510
"Feminism at the Movies." *see* Wente, Margaret
Fetterley, Judith, "A Rose for 'A Rose for Emily,'" 229–37
exercises: reading and writing, 237
fewer and *less,* 416
fiction (textual analysis)
    characterization, 488, 495–96
    chart of general and special categories, 488, 490
    context, 68, 488, 495
    development methods, 68–69
    diction, 70, 490, 496–97
    figurative language and allusions, 70, 490, 497
    narrative structure (plot), 69–70, 488, 496
    point of view, 71–72, 490, 498
    sentence structure, 70, 490, 497
    setting, 488, 495
    subgenre, 68, 488, 495
    subject, 67, 72–73, 488, 495
    textual analysis questions, 495–98
    textual analysis special category, 490
    theme, 490
    theme identification by connecting textual features, 72–73, 498
    tone, 71, 490, 497–98
figurative language and allusions
    drama, 491, 504
    fiction, 70, 490, 497
    film and television, 70, 491, 507
    nonfiction, 490, 493–94
    poetry, 76–77, 491, 500
    as style element, 70, 76–77
    textual analysis special category, 70, 490–91
    exercises: poetry analysis ("Love Lessons"), 78–79, 88
    exercises: on readings, 228, 272, 291
film and television (textual analysis)
    characterization, 488–89, 506
    chart of general and special categories, 488–91
    context, 68, 488–89, 505
    development methods, 68–69
    differences from written texts, 70
    editing techniques, 70, 491, 507
    figurative language and allusions, 70, 491, 507
    references documentation (MLA), 480–81
    reference sources on films, 512
    setting, 488–89, 505–6
    shooting techniques, 70, 491, 506–7
    structure (action), 69–70, 488–89, 506

style, 70, 490–91
subgenre, 67–68, 488–89, 505
subject, 72–73, 488–89, 505
    as text, 67
    textual analysis questions, 505–8
    theme or thesis, 491
    theme or thesis identification by connecting textual features, 72–73, 508
    tone, 71, 491, 508
    sample: film analysis, 6–8
final editing (stage 7)
    chart of common problems, 373–74
    checklist for final editing, 372
    research papers, 192
    stages model of writing (stage 7), 9–10
First Nations, capitalization, 463
first-person narration, 71–72
first-person pronouns (*I, we, one*) in academic essays, 432–33
flaunt and *flout,* 415
folklore, reference sources, 513–14
foreign words and phrases, italics, 459
formal outlines for research papers, 180–81, 189
format. *see* documentation; essay format; quotations
format, reference sources, 518
Forster, E. M., "My Wood," 238–41
    exercises: reading and writing, 241
    exercises: revising structure (inductive or deductive), 64
    exercises: textual analysis of structure or tone, 79, 88
    exercises: writing summaries, 41
Fraser, John, "Save the Last Dance," 242–45
    exercises: organization (block and point-by-point), 115
    exercises: paragraph transitions, 409
    exercises: reading and writing, 245–46
freewriting
    for ideas, 16–17
    research topics, 163
    exercises: freewriting, 21
Frost, Robert, "Stopping by Woods on a Snowy Evening"
    poem, 98–99, 369
    exercises: textual analysis, 98–100, 367–69
fused sentences
    how to correct, 388
    marking symbol, 373
    exercises: fused sentences, 389, 400

gathering material (stage 2)
    analysis for gathering material, 24
    categorizing parts (general topic), 28–30
    causal analysis, 30
    comparison essays, 103–5
    content analysis (general topic), 25–28

content analysis (nonfiction), 31–38
critiques, 118–21, 132–34
evaluation of resources for research, 169–70, 172, 175–76, 186–87
persuasive essays, 146–48
research papers, 165–78
stages model of writing (stage 2), 9–10
textual analysis, 66–73, 75–77
sample: comparison essays, 103–5
sample: content analysis, nonfiction, 38–40
sample topic: categorizing parts (general topic), 28–30
sample topic: research paper (*Hamlet*), 166–77
sample topic: textual analysis (poetry), 75–78
exercises: critiques, 140
exercises: research papers, 178
gender pronouns, 434, 437
general categories, content analysis
about, 28–30
chart of common perspectives, 486–87
sample topic: categorizing (general topic), 28–30
general categories, textual analysis
about, 67–72
chart, 488–91
context, 68, 488–89
development methods, 68–69, 84–86, 488–89
genre/subgenre, 67–68, 488–89
structure, 69–70, 488–89
style, 70, 490–91
subject, 67, 72–73, 488–89
theme or thesis, 82–84, 490–91
tone, 71, 490–91
exercises: general categories, 78
generalizations
argumentation problems, 121–22, 125
conclusion of essay, 61
introduction of essay, 57
genres. *see also* subgenres
definition, 67, 520–21
aesthetic standard of evaluation, 143
conventions, 68
reference sources, 510–13
textual analysis, general category, 67–68
sample topic: textual analysis (poetry), 75
glossary
to define specialized terms, 13
in this text, 519–23
good and *well*, 415
Gopnik, Alison, "Kiddy Thinks," 247–50
discussion: content analysis, 38–40
sample: summary of essay, 40
exercises: reading and writing, 251
government documents, APA documentation, 484

Haegele, Katie, "Why I Live with My Mother," 252–55
exercises: reading and writing, 255
Hamlet, by William Shakespeare. *see* research and research papers
handwritten essays, 376, 458
Hardin, Garrett, "Lifeboat Ethics: The Case Against Helping the Poor," 256–61
discussion: analogies, 120, 124
exercises: comparison basis, 114
exercises: identifying evaluation standards, 159
exercises: reading and writing, 262
"Health Canada Inadvertently Discloses Facts Planned Parenthood Would Like to Suppress." *see* Byfield, Ted
"He Was a Boxer When I Was Small." *see* Keeshig-Tobias, Lenore
Hogan, Linda, "The Voyagers," 263–68
exercises: paragraph transitions, 409
exercises: reading and writing, 269
exercises: textual analysis of structure or tone, 79, 88
hopefully, 415–16
Hurka, Thomas, "The Moral Superiority of *Casablanca* over *The English Patient,*" 331–33
exercises: reading and writing, 341
hyphens, 460–61
marking symbol, 373
exercises: hyphens, 461

ideological perspective as ethical standard, 144–45
idioms, reference sources, 516–17
i.e., use of, 464
illusion and *allusion,* 414
illusory and *elusive,* 415
images, definition, 70. *see also* figurative language
imminent and *eminent,* 415
imply and *infer,* 416
inclusive language and pronoun agreement errors, 434, 437
indefinite pronouns
apostrophe, 444, 445
verb agreement, 428, 437
index use for research, 175, 194
inductive argument, 119, 122, 125
inductive structure
definition, 47, 84, 521
draft introduction statement, 47
in paragraphs, 59
textual analysis essays, 84, 86
thesis statement in inductive essay, 84
exercises: revising structure (inductive or deductive), 64
infer and *imply,* 416

infinitives
infinitive phrases, 380
marking symbol, 374
split infinitives, 390
troublesome verbs, 424–25
informal essays
audience, 4–5
exercises: writing essays, 10
"In Praise of the Humble Comma." *see* Iyer, Pico
Internet research. *see also* working bibliographies
APA documentation, 483–84
avoiding plagiarism, 169, 184–87
evaluation of resources, 169–70, 172, 175–76, 186–87
how to find resources, 169–73
MLA documentation, 480
interviews as resources
MLA documentation, 481
in-text citations
APA system, 481–82
MLA system, 477–78
parentheses use, 455
sample: *Hamlet* research paper (MLA), 362–66
introduction of essay
definition, 5, 521
analysis essays, 57–58
checklist for your assignments, 92
comparison essays, 111
context statement, 92–93, 111
critiques, 129, 137
defining subject and context, 92–93, 111
drafts and sketches, 49
generalizations, 57, 121–22, 125
persuasive essays, 155–56
problems and solutions, 57
purposes, 5
research papers, 189, 190
textual analysis essays, 92–93
thesis statement, 57
sample: comparison, 111
sample: content analysis (independent living), 58
sample: critique, 129–30, 137
sample: persuasive, 155
sample: research paper (*Hamlet*), 190
sample: textual analysis (film), 6–7
sample: textual analysis (poetry), 93
exercises: revising introductions (independent living), 64
exercises: revising introductions (poetry), 98–99
exercises: on readings, 237, 241, 251, 276
irony
definition, 71
persona, defined, 72, 521
tone, 71
exercises: on readings, 241, 291, 292, 325
italics, 458–59
marking symbol, 373
not for emphasis, 405

uses of italics, 458–59
exercises: italics, 459–60
"It Always Costs." *see* Suzuki,
    David T.
It is . . . that, overuse, 420
it's and *its,* 416, 440
Iyer, Pico, "In Praise of the Humble
    Comma," 270–72
    exercises: reading and writing,
        272–73
    exercises: semicolon use, 453
    exercises: textual or content
        analysis, 78

Johnston, Ann Dowsett, "A Lament
    for Quality," 274–76
    discussion: causal argument, 119
    discussion: practical standard of
        evaluation, 143
    exercises: reading and writing, 276
    exercises: writing summaries, 41
Jones, A., "The Complex Skill of
    Independent Living" (sample
    content analysis essay)
    discussion: content analysis,
        28–30, 43–49, 52–63
    essay, 344–45
Jones, B., "Shifts in Attitude and
    Form in Al Purdy's 'Trees at
    the Arctic Circle'" (sample
    textual analysis essay)
    discussion: textual analysis,
        73–78, 82–87, 91–97
    essay, 346–48
    poem, 73–74
Jones, C., "Perspectives on
    Addictions" (sample compari-
    son essay)
    discussion: comparison essay,
        102–13
    essay, 349–51
Jones, D., "Reflecting on
    Population" (sample critique)
    discussion: logical critiques,
        116–40
    essay, 352–54
Jones, E., "Same-Sex Marriages:
    Tradition and Change" (sam-
    ple persuasive essay)
    discussion: persuasive essay,
        146–58
    essay, 355–58
journal articles. *see* articles

Keeshig-Tobias, Lenore, "He Was a
    Boxer When I Was Small,"
    277–81
    exercises: comparison, 115
    exercises: reading and writing,
        281
key terms, defining in essay,
    145–46, 147
keyword searches of resources, 169,
    171
"Kiddy Thinks." *see* Gopnik, Alison

"A Lament for Quality." *see*
    Johnston, Ann Dowsett
languages, capitalization, 463
Latin abbreviations, 464

Laver, Ross, "Profits by the
    Truckload," 282–83
    exercises: reading and writing,
        283–84
    exercises: writing summaries, 41
lay and *lie,* 416
less and *fewer,* 416
lie and *lay,* 416
"Lifeboat Ethics: The Case Against
    Helping the Poor." *see* Hardin,
    Garrett
like and *as,* 416
limited omniscient narration, 71–72
lists. *see* series and lists, develop-
    ment method; series and lists,
    punctuation
literature, reference sources, 509–13
    biographical dictionaries and bib-
        liographies, 512–13
    children's literature, 511
    English literature, 510–13
    general guides, 171, 510
    for identifying allusions, 513–15
    literary history, 509–13
    literary terms and theory,
        509–10
    literature by women, 510
    national literature, 510–11
logical standard of evaluation
    arguments and evidence, 118–21,
        130, 132–34
    clarifying essay topics, 15–16,
        117–18, 131–32
    logical order, defined, 521
    thesis statement includes, 126,
        128, 134, 135–36
    exercises: evaluation by logical
        standard, 139
loose and *lose,* 417, 425
loose sentence patterns, 403
lose and *loose,* 417, 425
"Love Lessons" (poem) by Joan
    Seager, 79
    exercises: figurative language, 78,
        88
    exercises: revision, 100
    exercises: thesis statement, 88

MacDonald, Joyce, "The Problem of
    Environmental Costs: Suzuki
    vs. Merwin," 359–61
magazine articles. *see* articles
main clauses. *see also* clauses
    comma and coordinate conjunc-
        tions to separate, 382, 447
    compound sentences, 382
    semicolon to separate, 450–52
main verb. *see* verbs
"The Making of the Tragic Hero:
    The Graveyard Scene in
    Hamlet." *see* Smith, D.
marking symbols, 373–74
MasterFILE Premier database, 170,
    171
Maté, Gabor, "Embraced by the
    Needle," 285–87
    discussion: comparison essay,
        102–13
    exercises: reading and writing,
        287–88

me, myself, and *I,* 439
"The Men We Carry in our Minds."
    see Sanders, Scott Russell
Merwin, W. S., "Unchopping a
    Tree," 289–91
    exercises: reading and writing,
        291–92
methods of development. *see* devel-
    opment methods
middle paragraphs (MP) (stages 4
    and 5)
    definition, 521
    ascending interest order, 7–8, 48,
        86, 127, 136, 521
    checklist for revising your own
        assignments, 94
    chronological order, 69–70, 76
    comparison essays, 107–8,
        111–12
    critiques, 128–29, 130, 135–37
    development, problems and solu-
        tions, 59–61
    drafts, 49
    inductive or deductive order, 59,
        130
    length, 55
    persuasive essays, 156–57
    problems and solutions, 55
    purposes, 5
    research papers, 189, 190–92
    revising, 55–61, 94–95, 111–12
    spatial order, 69–70, 521
    textual analysis, 84–87, 94–95
    topic sentences, 58–59
    transitions, 153–54, 156–57
    transitions between paragraphs,
        153–54, 156–57, 408–9
    transitions within paragraphs,
        406–8
    sample: comparison essay, 112
    sample: critique, 130
    sample: film analysis, ascending
        order, 7–8
    sample: persuasive essay, 156
    sample topic: research *(Hamlet),*
        191–92
    sample topic: revising middle
        paragraphs (independent liv-
        ing), 60–61
    sample topic: textual analysis
        (poetry), 94–95
    exercises: paragraph transitions,
        409–10
    exercises: revising middle para-
        graphs (independent living),
        64
minor genres. *see* subgenres
misplaced modifiers. *see* modifiers
mixed constructions
    how to correct, 397–99
    marking symbol, 373
    exercises: mixed constructions,
        399, 400
MLA documentation (Modern
    Languages Association),
    477–81
    articles, 479–80
    books, 478–79
    electronic sources (database, CD-
        ROM, Internet), 480

films, 480–81
interviews, 481
in-text citations, 477–78
paraphrased material, 478
quotation from primary text, 477
quotation from research material, 478
title page format, 377
Works Cited (full bibliographical information), 477–78
Works Cited format, 478
sample: Works Cited *(Hamlet),* 366
MLA documentation reference sources, 481
MLA International Bibliography, 171
"A Modest Proposal." *see* Swift, Jonathan
modifiers
definition, 389
commas, 448
dangling, 390, 391
marking symbols, 373
misplaced, 390
non-restrictive and restrictive modifiers, 448
in sentence patterns, 403
exercises: dangling modifiers, 391–92, 400
exercises: misplaced modifiers, 391, 392, 400
exercises: non-restrictive modifiers and commas, 449–50
months, 463
mood. *see* tone
moral perspective as ethical standard, 144–45
"The Moral Superiority of *Casablanca* over *The English Patient.*" *see* Hurka, Thomas
MP (middle paragraph). *see* middle paragraphs (MP)
musical compositions, italics, 458
mythology, reference sources, 513–14
"My Wood." *see* Forster, E.M.

names, reference sources, 515
narrative structure (plot). *see* fiction (textual analysis)
narrative (telling a story). *see also* point of view
as development method, 33, 36, 68–69
textual analysis essays, not to use in, 85, 86
nationalities, capitalization, 463
national literature, reference sources, 510–11
Native, capitalization, 463
neither ... nor, subject-verb agreement, 429
nonfiction (textual analysis). *see also* content analysis of nonfiction
chain of reasoning, 85–86
chart of general and special categories, 488, 490
context, 68, 488, 492
detail and evidence, 119–21,

132–34, 488, 492
development methods, 47, 58–61
diction, 70, 490, 493
figurative language and allusions, 70, 490, 493–94
persona, 72, 521
point of view (writer or persona), 72, 521
questions for textual analysis, 492–95
sentence structure, 70, 490, 494
structure, 69–70, 488, 493
subgenre, 68, 488, 492
subject, 72–73, 488, 492
telling a story (narrative), 68–69, 84–85
thesis, 490
thesis identification by connecting textual features, 72–73, 494–95
tone, 71, 490, 494
exercises: textual analysis of structure or tone, 79, 88
note-taking for research papers, 175–76
not only ... but also and subject-verb agreement, 429
nouns
apostrophes with, 444, 445
capitalization, 462–63
plural and possessive, 444
pronoun agreement, 436–38
proper nouns, 462
number and *amount,* 414
numbers
hyphens and two-word numbers, 460
marking symbol, 373
numerals or spelling out, 462
exercises: numbers, 465

objective narration, 72
object pronouns, 438–40
omniscient narration, 71–72
opinions in essays
first-person pronouns (*I, we, one),* 432–33
values and opinions, 148–50, 151
opinions in thesis statements
comparison essays, 103–5, 109
content analysis (nonfiction), 43–45
critiques, 125–28, 134, 135–36
opinion included, 43–45, 53, 82–83, 90–91, 180–81
opinion support included, 44–45, 83–84, 90–91, 106–7, 126, 135–36, 181
persuasive essays, 148–50, 152–53
research paper, 180–81
textual analysis, 82–84, 90–91
sample: thesis statements (comparison), 106–7, 109–10
sample: thesis statements (nonfiction), 43–45
sample: thesis statements (persuasive), 149, 150, 153
sample: thesis statements (poetry), 83–84

exercises: thesis statements with opinions, 50
or, subject-verb agreement, 429
order, ascending interest
definition, 48, 521
critiques, 127, 136
development method, 48, 86
sample: film analysis, 7–8
order (chronological, logical, spatial)
definitions, 521
sample topic: poetry analysis (chronological), 76
organization and structure (stages 4 and 5)
definition, 69, 522
analysis essays, 46–48
chronological order, 69–70, 76
comparison essays (block or point-by-point), 108, 110, 519
critiques, 125, 127–31, 134–38
deductive structure, 46–47, 84, 520
drama, 489, 503
fiction (plot), 69–70, 488, 496
film and television, 69–70, 488–89, 506
general principles, 69–70
inductive structure, 46–47, 84, 521
nonfiction, 489, 493
persuasive essays (block or point-by-point), 150–52, 153–54
poetry, 76, 489, 499
problems and solutions, 55
pro-con structure in persuasive essays, 150–52, 153–54, 156–57
purposes, 5
research papers, 176–77, 181–84, 187–92
revising essay structure, 55–57, 91–92, 110, 128–29
sample: point-by-point in comparison, 108
spatial principles, 69–70, 521
stages model of writing (stages 4 and 5), 9–10
textual analysis, 69–70, 91–92, 488–89
typographical devices, 69–70
sample: pro-con categories chart, 148
sample topic: textual analysis (poetry), 76
exercises: pro-con paragraph structure, 159
exercises: revising structure (content analysis), 63–64
exercises: structure (comparison), 115
exercises: structure (critiques), 140
exercises: on readings, 202, 210, 237, 241, 246, 300, 312, 315, 316, 341
Orwell, George, "Shooting an Elephant," 293–99
exercises: comparison, 115

exercises: paragraph transitions, 409
exercises: process analysis, 88
exercises: reading and writing, 299–300
exercises: textual analysis of structure or tone, 79, 88
outlines
comparison essays, 107–8
content analysis, 48, 52, 56–57, 60
draft outlines, 45, 48–49, 86–87, 108, 150–52
formal outlines for research papers, 181–82, 189
persuasive essays (pro-con outline), 150–52, 153–54
revision outlines, 45, 52, 56–57, 60, 136
textual analysis, 86–87
sample: draft outline (comparison), 108
sample: draft outline (critique), 135
sample: draft outline (independent living), 48–49
sample: draft outline (persuasive), 152
sample: draft outline (poetry analysis), 87
sample: formal outline (research paper), 189
sample: revision outline (critique), 136
sample: revision outline (independent living), 56, 60
exercises: draft outlines, 50, 115, 140
exercises: on readings, 228, 245, 283

pacing in drama, 491, 504
paragraph hooks for continuity, 408
paragraphs. *see* middle paragraphs (MP)
parallelism
definition, 392
coordinate constructions, 394–95
faulty parallelism, 392–93
marking symbol, 374
summary sentences, 404
exercises: faulty parallelism, 393, 399, 400
paraphrasing to avoid plagiarism, 185–87
parentheses
marking symbol, 374
uses, 455–56
exercises: parentheses, 456–57, 459–60
parenthetical expressions and commas, 448–49
partake and *take part in,* 417
participial phrases
beginning sentences with, 404
commas with phrases following nouns, 448
recognizing phrases, 379–80
passive voice
active or passive voice, 429–30

marking symbol, 374
exercises: active or passive voice, 430, 431
periodical indexes for locating resources, 169–70
periodic sentence pattern, 403
periods
comma splice correction, 387
with quotation marks, 458
persona, 72, 521
personal essays. *see* content analysis of general subject; informal essays
personification, 76–77
perspectives for content analysis (social, psychological, economic, political)
chart, 486–87
gathering material, 28–30
persuasive essays, 146–47
sample topic: categorizing (general topic), 28–30
exercises: gathering material, 41
"Perspectives on Addictions." *see* Jones, C.
persuasive essays, 141–59
definition, 142
audience, 142, 145, 148–50, 155–56
bias, 155–56
categorizing pro-con arguments, 146–48
checklist for your assignments, 158
clarifying evaluation topics, 142–46
conclusions, 157–58
defining key terms, 145–46
drafting, 150–52
emotional appeals, 120–21, 124, 125, 133–34
ethos, 155–56, 157
final editing, 372
gathering material, 146–48
introductions, 155–56
middle paragraphs, 156–57
organization (block or point-by-point), 150–52, 153–54
outlines, 150–52, 153–54
pro-con categories, 146–48
pro-con outlines, 150–52, 153–54
standards of evaluation, 15–16, 117, 142–46
strengths and weaknesses, 147–48, 150
thesis statements, 148–50, 152–54
sample: draft middle paragraph, 156–57
sample: pro-con categories chart, 148
sample: thesis statements, 149, 150, 153
sample topic: same-sex marriages, 146–58
sample essay: Jones, E., "Same-Sex Marriages: Tradition and Change," 355–58
exercises: pro-con paragraph structure, 159

exercises: thesis statements, 159
exercises: on readings, 201, 210, 300
phrases
about, 379–80
beginning sentences with, 404
colon use with, 453
commas with phrases, 447, 448
dangling modifiers, 390, 391
how to be concise, 420
infinitive phrases, 380
mixed constructions with prepositional phrases, 398
parallel phrases, 392–93, 404
participial phrases, 380
prepositional phrases in subject-verb agreement errors, 428
verbs in phrases, 379–80
exercises: conciseness, 421–22
exercises: identifying phrases, 380
exercises: mixed constructions, 399, 400
exercises: parallel phrases, 393
phrases and words, reference sources, 516–17
place names, comma use, 449
plagiarism
avoiding plagiarism, 169, 184–87
checklist for your assignments, 187
note-taking, 175
sample: revising plagiarized text, 185–86
plays. *see* drama (textual analysis)
plot (narrative structure). *see* fiction (textual analysis)
plural letters *(x's and y's)* with apostrophe, 446
poetry (textual analysis)
characterization, 488–89, 499
chart of general and special categories, 488–91
context, 68, 75, 488–89
development methods, 68–69, 76
diction, 70, 76, 491, 500
figurative language and allusions, 70, 76–77, 491, 500
persona, defined, 72, 521
point of view (speaker), 71–72, 77, 491, 501
prosody, 77, 491, 501
quotations format, 473–74
reference sources for poetry, 512
setting, 488–89, 499
speaker, 72
structure, 69–70, 75, 488–89, 499
style, 76–77
subgenre, 68, 75, 488–89, 499
subject, 72–73, 75, 488–89, 499
textual analysis questions, 499–502
theme, 491
theme identification by connecting textual features, 72–73, 77–78, 501–2
tone, 71, 77, 491, 501
typographical devices, 69

sample topic: analyzing a poem (Purdy's "Trees at the Arctic Circle"), 73–78, 82–87, 90–97
sample essays: analyzing poetry, 346–48, 369–70
exercises: textual analysis ("Love Lessons"), 78–79, 88, 100
exercises: textual analysis ("Stopping by Woods on a Snowy Evening"), 98–100
point-by-point method of organization
  comparison essays, 108, 110, 519
  persuasive essays, 151–52, 153–54
  exercises: block and point-by-point, 115
point of view
  definition, 71
  fiction, 71–72, 490, 498
  poetry (speaker), 71–72, 77, 491, 501
  textual analysis, special category, 71–72, 490–91
  sample topic: textual analysis (poetry), 77
political perspective content analysis, 28–30, 486–87
"The Poorhouse." see Rebick, Judy
"Population: Ignoring Its Impact." see Bongaarts, John
possession, apostrophe use, 444–46
post hoc fallacy, 122–23, 125
practical standard of evaluation
  about, 117, 143–44
  clarifying essay topics, 15–16
  sample: pro-con categories chart, 148
prefixes with hyphens, 460–61
prepositions and prepositional phrases
  beginning sentences with, 404
  examples, 379
  how to be concise, 420
  mixed constructions with prepositional phrases, 398
  pronoun agreement errors, 437
  pronouns as object of preposition, 438–40
  subject-verb agreement problems, 428
  exercises: conciseness, 421–22
primary sources for research papers
  about, 19
  definition, 521–22
  combining primary and secondary material, 176–77
  when to use primary sources, 19, 164–66
  sample: chart, combining primary and secondary material, 177
principle and *principal*, 417
"The Problem of Environmental Costs: Suzuki *vs*. Merwin." see MacDonald, Joyce
process analysis
  about, 25–27
  basic questions to ask, 25–27, 67

categorizing parts (general topic), 27–28
categorizing stages (general topic), 29–30
categorizing stages (nonfiction), 33–34
diagram of discovery questions, 25
perspectives (social, psychological, economic, political), 28–30, 486–87
persuasive essays, 146–47
textual analysis, 85
type of argument, 119
sample: categorizing stages (general topic), 29–30
sample topic: nonfiction ("Kiddy Thinks"), 38–40
exercises: gathering material, 41
exercises: process analysis (nonfiction), 88
exercises: on readings, 251, 255, 291, 292
pro-con arguments
  categorizing pro-con arguments, 146–48
  pro and *con*, 151
  pro-con categories, 146–48
  pro-con outlines, 150–52, 153–54
  transitions between paragraphs, 153–54, 156–57
  sample: pro-con categories chart, 148
  exercises: pro-con paragraph structure, 159
  exercises: on readings, 210
"Profits by the Truckload." see Laver, Ross
pronouns, 432–43
  agreement, 436–38
  apostrophes with, 444, 445
  gender pronouns, 434, 437
  indefinite pronouns, apostrophe, 444, 445
  indefinite pronouns, verb agreement, 428, 437
  marking symbol, 374
  first-person pronouns (*I, we, one*), 432–33, 435–36
  second-person pronouns (*you*), 433–34, 435–36
  third-person pronouns (*he, she, they*), 434, 435–36
  object pronouns (case), 438–40
  possessive pronouns, 440, 444, 445
  pronoun references, 441–42
  pronouns of address, 432–36
  relative pronouns in subordinate clauses, 381
  sentence hooks for continuity, 406
  subject pronouns (case), 438–40
  that, this, which, it and *they*, vague use of, 441–42
  exercises: possessive pronouns, 440–41
  exercises: pronoun agreement and pronoun references, 438, 442–43

exercises: pronoun shifts, 436
exercises: pronouns of address, 434–35, 436
exercises: subject and object pronouns, 440, 443
proofreading
  checklist for your assignments, 466–67
  marking symbols, 373–74
  spelling, 372, 466–67
proper nouns, 462
prosody in poetry, 77, 491, 501
psychological perspective
  content analysis, 28–30, 486–87
  sample topic: categorizing (general topic), 28–30
Purdy, Al, "Trees at the Arctic Circle," 73–74
  discussion: textual analysis, 73–78, 82–87, 91–97
  poem, 73–74
  textual analysis essay, 346–48
Pyper, Andrew, "The Ticking Daddy Clock," 301–2
  exercises: comparison, 115
  exercises: reading and writing, 303
  exercises: textual analysis of structure or tone, 79, 88

questions
  mixed constructions with questions, 398–99
  exercises: mixed constructions, 399, 400
question marks
  within parentheses, 456
  with quotation marks, 458
quotations, 468–75. see also APA documentation; MLA documentation
  block indentation of long quotations, 473
  colons to introduce quotations, 453–54
  comma use, 449
  context included, 470, 471
  deleting and inserting words, 471–72
  evidence and detail, 36
  final editing, 192
  format, 471–74
  grammatical fit, 471
  guidelines for use, 468–71
  marking symbols, 374
  plays, 474
  poetry, 473–74
  prose, 472–73
  quotation marks, 457–58, 472–73
  reference sources on quotations, 515
  research papers, 175
  when to quote or not to quote, 468–69
  exercises: quotation marks, 458, 459–60
  exercises: quotations, 474–75
  exercises: on readings, 288

realize, 417
reasons in argumentation. *see* argumentation in critiques
reasons in thesis statement. *see* thesis and thesis statements
Rebick, Judy, "The Poorhouse," 304–5
  exercises: comparison basis, 114
  exercises: identifying evaluation standards, 159
  exercises: argumentation and evidence, 140
  exercises: reading and writing, 306
References (full bibliographical information). *see* APA documentation
reference sources, annotated survey, 509–18
"Reflecting on Population." *see* Jones, D.
religions, capitalization, 463
religions, reference sources, 513–14
religious perspective as ethical standard, 144–45
repetition
  as continuity device, 407, 408
  unnecessary repetition, 420
  exercises: conciseness, 421–22
research and research papers, 161–94. *see also* APA documentation; MLA documentation
  about, 162, 522
  acknowledging sources, 192
  analyzing your subject, 165–68
  checklist for your assignments, 177–78, 193
  clarifying and limiting essay topics, 162–65
  combining primary and secondary material, 176–77
  conclusions, 189, 192
  defining unfamiliar terms, 162–63
  directions on essay topics, 163
  documenting research material, 184–87
  drafting, 181–82
  evaluation of resources, 169–70, 172, 175–76, 186–87
  as extended essay (analysis, comparison, or evaluation), 162
  final editing, 192, 372
  formal outlines, 181–82, 189
  gathering material, 165–78
  integrating research material, 182–84, 191–92
  introductions, 189, 190
  notes on secondary sources, 175–76
  organization and structure, 176–77, 181–84, 187–92
  overview of essay topic, 165, 166
  plagiarism, 169, 175, 184–87
  preliminary analysis of essay subject, 165–68
  primary sources, 19, 164–66
  purposes, 162
  secondary sources, 19, 164, 175–76

thesis statements, 180–81, 187–88, 190
working bibliography, 168–74
sample: chart, combining primary and secondary material, 177
sample: plagiarism, 185–86
sample: thesis statements, 188, 190
sample: working bibliography, 174
sample essay: "The Making of the Tragic Hero: The Graveyard Scene in *Hamlet,*" 362–66
sample topic: gathering material *(Hamlet),* 166–68
sample topic: integrating research *(Hamlet),* 183–84, 191–92
sample topic: overview of essay topic *(Hamlet),* 166
sample topic: research papers *(Hamlet),* 164–68
sample topic: revising research material *(Hamlet),* 187–90
exercises: gathering material, 178
exercises: writing mini-research papers, 178, 194
revising (stages 5 and 6)
  about, 52
  checklists for your assignments, 63, 97–98, 129
  comparison essays, 109–13
  conclusions, 61–63, 95–97, 112–13, 131, 157–58
  critiques, 128–31, 135–36
  how to be concise, 419–20
  introductions, 57–58, 92–93, 92–97, 111
  middle paragraphs, 55–61, 94–95, 111–12, 129–30
  persuasive essays, 152–58
  research papers, 182–87, 190–92
  revision outlines, 52, 56–57, 60, 136
  stages model of writing (stages 5 and 6), 9–10
  structure, 52–57, 91–92, 110, 128–29
  thesis statement, 52–55, 90–91, 109–10, 128
  sample: integrating research material (research paper), 183–84
  sample: revision outline (evaluation essay), 136
  sample: revision outline (independent living), 56, 60
  sample: revision outline (persuasive essay), 154
  exercises: avoiding wordiness, 421–22
  exercises: revision outlines, 100
  exercises: revision outlines (content analysis), 63–64
rhetorical terms, reference sources, 509–10

"A Rose for 'A Rose for Emily'". *see* Fetterley, Judith
run-on sentences. *see* fused sentences

"Same-Sex Marriages: Tradition and Change." *see* Jones, E
Sanders, Scott Russell, "The Men We Carry in Our Minds," 307–11
  exercises: comparison, 115
  exercises: reading and writing, 312
"Save the Last Dance." *see* Fraser, John
seasons, not to capitalize, 463
secondary sources for research papers. *see also* quotations
  about, 19, 522
  avoiding plagiarism, 169, 175, 184–87
  combining primary and secondary material, 176–77
  evaluation of resources, 169–70, 172, 175–76, 186–87
  how many to use, 164, 165
  how to evaluate, 175–76
  how to take notes, 175–76
  when to use secondary sources, 19, 164
  sample: chart, combining primary and secondary material, 177
second-person pronouns *(you)* in academic essays, 433–34, 435–36
semicolon, 450–52
  clauses and phrases, 450–52
  comma splice corrections, 387
  marking symbol, 374
  quotation marks, 458
  series of items, 451
  when not to use, 451–52
  exercises: semicolon, 452–53, 456–57
sentences, 379–405. *see also* sentence structure; sentence structure as style
  combining sentences to be concise, 420
  complex sentences, 383
  compound-complex sentences, 383
  compound sentences, 382
  marking symbols, 373
  within parentheses, 456
  sentence fragments, 385–86
  sentence hooks for continuity, 406–7
  sentence patterns, 403–4
  simple sentences, 382
  exercises: conciseness, 421–22
  exercises: sentence fragments, 386, 389, 400
  exercises: simple, compound, or complex sentences, 383–84
sentence structure, 401–5. *see also* sentence structure as style
  how to be concise, 420
  how to begin sentences, 404–5

parallelism, 392–93, 404
sentence patterns, 403–4
varying lengths, 401–2
varying patterns, 403–5
exercises: conciseness, 421–22
exercises: varying patterns and
    length, 405
sentence structure as style. see also
    sentence structure
fiction, 70, 490, 497
nonfiction, 490, 494
textual analysis special category,
    70, 490
exercises: on readings, 291
sequencing. see order
series and lists, development
    method
series of points, 34–35, 86
transition terms, 34–35
series and lists, punctuation
colons with, 453, 455
commas with, 447–48
dash with, 454–55
lists with such as or for example,
    453
semicolons with, 451
setting
drama, 502
fiction, 488, 495
film and television, 488–89,
    505–6
poetry, 499
textual analysis categories, 489
sample topic: textual analysis
    (poetry), 76
sexist language and pronoun agree-
    ment errors, 434, 437
Shaler, Stefa. see Alexander, Bruce
    K., and Stefa Shaler
"Shifts in Attitude and Form in Al
    Purdy's 'Trees at the Arctic
    Circle.'" see Jones, B.
ships, italics, 458
"Shooting an Elephant." see Orwell,
    George
shooting techniques (film and tele-
    vision) as style, 70, 506–7
short stories, reference sources,
    512
sic to indicate errors, 472
similarities and differences. see
    comparison and comparison
    essays
simple and simplistic, 417
simple sentences. see sentences
since and as, 396
single quotation marks, 457, 472
slang, reference sources, 516–17
slang in academic essays, 411
Smith, D., "The Making of the
    Tragic Hero: The Graveyard
    Scene in Hamlet" (sample
    research paper)
discussion: research paper,
    164–68, 176–77, 187–92
essay, 362–66
social perspective content analysis,
    28–30, 486–87
sample topic: categorizing
    (general topic), 28–30

spatial order, 69–70, 521
special categories
chart of general and special cate-
    gories (textual analysis),
    488–91
chart of perspectives (content
    analysis), 486–87
specialized terms
academic essays, 412
clarifying essay topics, 12–13, 75
reference sources, 515–16
research papers, 162–63
exercises: clarifying essay topics,
    21
spelling
checklist for your assignments,
    466–67
marking symbol, 374
plurals, 444–45
spelling checkers, 372, 466
usage problems, 413–18
exercises: spelling, 467
split infinitive, 390
"Spontaneity and Enjoyment of the
    Natural World." see Swanson,
    Karin
standards of evaluation. see evalua-
    tion standards
"Stopping by Woods on a Snowy
    Evening." see Frost, Robert
storytelling. see narrative (telling a
    story)
straw man fallacy, 123, 125
structure (stages 4 and 5). see orga-
    nization and structure (stages
    4 and 5)
style. see also diction as style ele-
    ment; sentence structure as
    style
definition, 70, 522
analysis of, 70, 490–91
drama, 491
fiction, 490
figurative language, 70, 490–91
film and television, 70, 491
nonfiction, 490
poetry, 76–77, 491
textual analysis, general cate-
    gory, 70, 490–91
tone, 71, 490–91
exercises: on readings, 273, 315,
    325
subgenres. see also genres
definition, 68, 520–21
conventions, 68, 143
drama, 502
fiction, 68, 488, 495
film and television, 67–68,
    488–89, 505
nonfiction, 492
poetry, 499
reference sources for subgenres,
    510–13
textual analysis general category,
    68, 488–89
subject pronouns, 438–40
subjects in content analysis
definition, 67, 522
context in nonfiction, 37–38
how to identify, 31–32

sample topic: nonfiction ("Kiddy
    Thinks"), 38
subjects in textual analysis
definition, 67, 72, 522
about, 72–73
drama, 72–73, 166, 488–89, 502
fiction, 67, 72–73, 488, 495
film and television, 72–73,
    488–89, 505
general category, 72–73, 488–89
nonfiction, 31–32, 72–73, 488,
    492
poetry, 72–73, 75, 488–89, 499
sample topic: textual analysis
    (poetry), 75
subjects of sentences
beginning sentences with sub-
    jects, 404
marking symbol, 374
mixed constructions with miss-
    ing subjects, 398
in sentence patterns, 403
subject-verb agreement, 428–29
indefinite pronouns, 428, 437
plural and singular subject
    phrases, 428, 429
prepositional phrases, 428
there is and there are, 428
exercises: mixed constructions,
    399, 400
exercises: subject-verb agree-
    ment, 429, 431
subordinate clauses. see also
    clauses
beginning sentences with, 405
comma after introductory, 447
subject pronouns in, 439
subordinate conjunctions. see con-
    junctions
subordination, 395–97
excessive subordination, 396–97
faulty subordination, 395–96
marking symbol, 373
exercises: faulty or excessive
    subordination, 397, 399
suffixes and hyphens, 460
summaries
what to include, 38, 40
sample topic: nonfiction ("Kiddy
    Thinks"), 40
exercises: writing summaries, 41
exercises: on readings, 276
supposed to, 425
Suzuki, David T., "It Always Costs,"
    313–15
discussion: revising critiques,
    129–31
discussion: thesis statements,
    127
exercises: writing summaries, 41
exercises: reading and writing,
    315–16
Swanson, Karin, "Spontaneity and
    Enjoyment of the Natural
    World," 367–70
Swift, Jonathan, "A Modest
    Proposal," 317–24
exercises: clarifying essay topics,
    21
exercises: comparison, 115

exercises: reading and writing, 325–26

syllogism in deductive argument, 118, 121–22, 125

symbols. *see also* figurative language
 about, 70
 reference sources on symbols, 514
 as style, 490–91

synonyms for continuity, 407, 408

systems analysis
 about, 25–26
 basic questions to ask, 25–27, 67
 categorizing parts (general topic), 27–29
 categorizing parts (nonfiction), 35
 diagram of discovery questions, 25
 perspectives (social, psychological, economic, political), 28–30, 486–87
 persuasive essays, 146–47
 textual analysis, 86
 type of argument, 119
 sample: categorizing parts (general topic), 28–29
 exercises: gathering material, 41

take part in and *partake,* 417

television. *see* film and television (textual analysis)

tenses, verb. *see* verbs

text, defined, 67–68

textual analysis
 sample: matching categories (comparison), 104

textual analysis and textual analysis essays, 65–100. *see also* comparison and comparison essays; textual analysis, general categories; textual analysis, special categories
 definition, 14, 522
 about, 13–14
 checklists for your assignments, 78, 87–88, 97–98
 clarifying essay topics, 66, 75
 conclusions, 95–97
 drafting, 84–87
 evaluation includes analysis, 15–16
 gathering material, 66–73
 introductions, 92–93
 middle paragraphs, 94–95
 organization and structure, 84–87, 90–92
 questions to ask (basic), 25–27, 67
 reference sources useful for textual analysis, 509–18
 research papers, 163, 166
 revising, 90–97
 as systems analysis, 86
 thesis statements, 54–55, 82–84, 90–93
 type of argument, 119
 sample topic: clarifying research topic *(Hamlet),* 164–65

sample topic: research papers *(Hamlet),* 164–68, 177, 183–84, 187–92

sample topic: analyzing a poem (Purdy's "Trees at the Arctic Circle"), 73–78, 82–87, 90–97, 346–48

exercises: textual analysis of structure or tone (nonfiction), 79, 88

exercises: textual analysis ("Stopping by Woods on a Snowy Evening"), 98–100

textual analysis, general categories
 definition, 522
 chart of general and special categories, 488–91
 context, 68, 488–89
 development methods, 33–35, 68–69, 84–86, 488–89
 genre, 67–68, 488–89
 point of view, 71–72, 77, 490–91
 questions to ask, 488–91
 structure, 69–70, 488–89
 style, 70, 490–91
 subject, 72–73, 488–89
 tone, 71, 490–91, 508

textual analysis, special categories
 definition, 522–23
 chart of general and special categories, 488–91
 questions to ask, 492–508

than and *that,* using subject pronouns after, 439

theatre. *see* drama (textual analysis)

their and *there,* 418, 440

theme. *see also* thesis and thesis statement (stages 3 and 5)
 definition, 72, 523
 connecting textual features to identify, 72–73
 drama, 491
 fiction, 490
 film and television, 491, 508
 poetry, 491
 textual analysis, general category, 490–91
 theme or thesis, distinguishing, 72
 sample topic: textual analysis (poetry), 77–78, 98–100

there and *their,* 418, 440

there is and *there are*
 overuse, 420
 subject-verb agreement, 428

thesauruses, reference sources, 518

thesis and thesis statement (stages 3 and 5). *see also* opinions in thesis statements
 definitions, thesis and thesis statement, 4, 43, 72, 523
 checklist for your assignments, 87–88
 comparison essays, 103–7, 109–10
 conclusion includes thesis restatement, 61–63
 content analysis (nonfiction), 43–45

critiques, 125–27, 134, 135–36

deductive essays, 84, 520

draft thesis statement, 45–49

evaluative thesis statement, 125–27, 134, 135–36

explicit or implied thesis, 32–33

film and television, 491

identifying by connecting textual features, 72–73, 494–95

identifying by connecting textual features (poetry), 77–78, 494–95

importance in academic essays, 4

inductive essays, 84

introduction placement, 57

missing reasons, 53

nonfiction, 32–33, 490

opinion included, 43–45, 82–83, 187–88

opinion supported, 44–45, 83–84, 106–7, 188

persuasive essays, 148–50, 152–53

placement in academic essays, 57

problems and solutions, 53–54, 91

reasons in thesis statement, 190

research papers, 180–81, 187–88, 190

revising thesis statements, 52–57, 91–92, 109–10

stages model of writing (stages 3 and 5), 9–10

tentative thesis statement, 54–55, 82–84

textual analysis, general category, 490–91

theme or thesis, distinguishing, 72

sample: comparison, 106–7, 109–10

sample: critique, 127, 134, 136

sample: film analysis, 6–8

sample: persuasive, 149, 150, 153

sample: research paper, 188, 190

sample: textual analysis (poetry), 83–84, 90–91

sample topic: content analysis (nonfiction), 55

sample topic: nonfiction ("Kiddy Thinks"), 39

sample topic: textual analysis (poetry), 77–78

exercises: persuasive and evaluation essays, 159

exercises: thesis statements (comparison), 114–15

exercises: thesis statements (critiques), 139, 140

exercises: thesis statements (poetry), 88, 99

exercises: thesis statements with opinions, 50

exercises: on readings, 220, 237, 245, 246, 251, 255, 281, 291, 300, 315, 325, 326, 341

"The Ticking Bomb." *see* Davis, Wade
"The Ticking Daddy Clock." *see* Pyper, Andrew
"The Voyagers." *see* Hogan, Linda
third-person narration, 71–72
third-person pronouns *(he, she, they)* in academic essays, 434, 435–36
Thomas, Edward, "Adlestrop," 370
    discussion: textual analysis, 367–69
time expressions with apostrophe, 446
title page format, 376–78
titles of works
    italics, 458
    quotation marks, 457
tone. *see also* diction as style element; diction in academic essays
    definition, 71, 523
    drama, 491, 504–5
    emotional appeals, 120–21, 124, 125, 133–34
    fiction, 71, 490, 497–98
    film and television, 71, 491, 508
    nonfiction, 36–37, 490, 494
    poetry, 75, 77, 491, 501
    textual analysis, general category (style), 71, 490–91
    sample topic: textual analysis (poetry), 77
    exercises: on readings, 255, 262, 300, 303, 306, 315
"To Peacekeep or Not to Peacekeep." *see* Ash, James
topic sentences
    definition, 523
    comparison essays, 111–12
    critiques, 130
    inductive or deductive sequence, 59
    problems and solutions, 59
    revising topic sentences, 58–61
    sentence patterns preferred, 404
    umbrella topic sentences, 55–56
    sample: content analysis (independent living), 60–61
    sample: film analysis, 6–8
transitions, 406–10
    chain of reasoning, 34
    comparing and contrasting, 34
    marking symbol, 374
    between paragraphs, 408–9
    between paragraphs in persuasive essays, 153–54, 156–57
    within paragraphs, 407–9
    parenthetical expressions, 448–49
    sentence and paragraph hooks, 406–8
    series and lists, 34–35
    words and phrases, 407–8

sample: film analysis, 7–8
exercises: paragraph transitions, 409–10
exercises: words and phrases, 409
exercises: on readings, 255
tree diagramming
    for ideas, 16–18
    research topics, 163
    sample: tree diagram, 20
    exercises: tree diagramming, 21
"Trees at the Arctic Circle." *see* Purdy, Al

umbrella topic sentences, 55–56
"Unchopping a Tree." *see* Merwin, W. S.
underlining for italics, 458
uninterested and *disinterested,* 418
university words, capitalization, 463
usage
    definition, 413
    problems, 413–18
    exercises: usage, 418
used to, 425

values in ethical standards of evaluation, 144–45, 148–50
verbs, 423–31
    definition, verbs, 423
    definition, verb tenses, 425
    active or passive voice, 429–30
    auxiliary verbs, 379, 423
    in clauses, 379–80
    irregular and troublesome verbs, 424–25
    main verbs, 423
    marking symbol (verb tenses and verb forms), 374
    mixed constructions with linking verbs, 397–98
    participles, 424–25
    phrases, 379–80
    pronouns as objects of, 439
    regular verbs, 424
    in sentence patterns, 403
    split infinitive, 390
    subject-verb agreement, 428–29
    verb tenses, 424–25
    verb tenses, unnecessary shifts, 426–27
    exercises: active or passive voice, 430, 431
    exercises: mixed constructions, 399, 400
    exercises: subject-verb agreement, 429, 431
    exercises: troublesome verbs, 431
    exercises: unnecessary tense shifts, 427, 431
    exercises: verb usage, 425

"Wanted: The Right to Refuse." *see* Black, Maggie
Warren, Catherine, "*The English Patient* Rallies (Letters)," 333–34
    discussion: reference to authorities, 120
    exercises: reading and writing, 341
well and *good,* 415
Wente, Margaret, "Feminism at the Movies," 339–40
    exercises: reading and writing, 341
"When Loyalty and Friendship Collide," 336–38
"Where They Have to Take You In." *see* Edwards, Caterina
who and *whom,* 439
whose and *who's,* 440
"Why I Live with My Mother." *see* Haegele, Katie
Wiwa, Ken, "Choosing Up Sides," 327–30
    exercises: comparison, 114
    exercises: reading and writing, 330
women, references sources for literature by, 510
word choice. *see* diction as style element; diction in academic essays
wordiness, 419–22
    how to be concise, 419–20
    marking symbol, 374
    exercises: avoiding wordiness, 421–22
word processing of essays, 375–76, 478
words and phrases, reference sources, 516–18
words referred to as words
    apostrophe, 446
    italics for, 457, 459
    quotation marks, 457
working bibliographies, 168–74
    definition, 168
    avoiding plagiarism, 169, 184–87
    evaluation of resources, 169–70, 172, 175–76, 186–87
    finding references, 169–73
    what to record, 173–74
    where to record information, 169
    sample: working bibliography, 174
Works Cited. *see* MLA documentation
world wide web site. *see* Internet research
writing process
    stages model, 8–10
    exercises: writing process, 10

you're and *your,* 418, 440